UML-Based Software Product Line Engineering with SMarty

Edson OliveiraJr
Editor

UML-Based Software Product Line Engineering with SMarty

 Springer

Editor
Edson OliveiraJr
Informatics Department
State University of Maringá
Maringá, Paraná, Brazil

This work was supported by CAPES, CNPq, Araucária Foundation of Paraná, and UEM

ISBN 978-3-031-18558-8   ISBN 978-3-031-18556-4   (eBook)
https://doi.org/10.1007/978-3-031-18556-4

This Springer imprint is published by the registered company Springer Nature Switzerland AG
The registered company address is: Gewerbestrasse 11, 6330 Cham, Switzerland

*To my **little bear Beatriz.***

Foreword

Introduction

I was pleased to be asked to write a foreword for this book on software product lines. Software product lines and product line engineering emerged from the software reuse and generative programming movements of the 1970s. Fast forward to today, product lines are ubiquitous. We can think of them as a highly developed, high-payoff, and industry-relevant way to build variability-intensive (or *configurable*) systems. In today's competitive and fast-paced markets where users expect software to adapt to their specific needs, most modern software-intensive products and services implement ideas and concepts that were first enabled through product line engineering. Several chapters in this book cover the fundamental principles of the field. However, deciding what a "highly configurable" system should do, architecting and designing it, modeling it for different stakeholders, building and deploying it, and evolving it over time are still challenging activities. The chapters of this book also address these challenges in various ways. In this foreword, I want to take the opportunity to briefly explore some of the *non-technical* challenges that arise when developing and maintaining such systems. I also want to briefly contrast product line research and practice.

Product Lines and "Value"

The first challenge I want to discuss is *value*. While product lines promise "value" (e.g., less painful development and maintenance of software products and services that share commonalities), it may be worth reflecting on what "value" (and, for the sake of completeness, "waste") means for different types of stakeholders. In general, product lines promise a reduction in development and maintenance cost, hence providing "value" to developers in the sense that they can complete their tasks in shorter time and at lower costs. This on the other hand also provides "value" to end users and customers who potentially get software products and services faster and cheaper. Regarding "waste" in software development, Sedano and colleagues[1] identified nine types of waste: building the wrong feature or product, mismanaging the backlog, rework, unnecessarily complex solutions, extraneous cognitive load, psychological distress, waiting/multitasking, knowledge loss, and ineffective communication. Product lines help reduce some of these types of waste. For example, they reduce building the wrong product since product lines reuse proven features across different product instances. On the other hand, product lines may introduce complexity and increase cognitive load, in particular for less experienced developers who join a new project. Proper modeling tools and techniques and languages like the Unified Modeling Language (UML) can help developers represent and reason about variability and product line design to reduce this type of waste. This book includes some chapters that present approaches that aim at reducing waste and increasing value during product line engineering.

We can also look at "value" from a broader perspective and think beyond business, economic, and technical value. Value can then also include broader human values, such as compassion, social responsibility, and justice.[2] The question then becomes how a software-intensive system built for different products or services within a market segment or technology domain can satisfy the values of stakeholders of those different products and services. Or should we assume that all stakeholders within a market or domain agree on broader values their software should comply with?

Modern Product Lines with Data-Driven Capabilities

The second challenge I want to discuss is somewhat related to the previous one. Modern software systems (including product lines) are often "data-intensive" and rely on artificial intelligence (AI) capabilities and related technologies, such as machine learning. For these systems, ethical considerations become first-class citizens. In fact, from a software engineering point of view, ethical considerations could be considered "non-functional" requirements. Think of Tesla's models Model S, Model X, Model 3, and Model Y which could all be considered software-intensive systems that process huge amounts of data. Tesla vehicles' software is regularly updated via wireless Internet connections when new software versions become available. Tesla also offers the option to unlock features after purchase (e.g., basic "Autopilot," "Full Self-Driving"). The software deployed across models could be

---

[1] T. Sedano, P. Ralph, C. Péraire, Software development waste, in: Proc. International Conference on Software Engineering, ICSE, 2017, pp. 130–140.

[2] H. Perera, W. Hussain, J. Whittle, A. Nurwidyantoro, D. Mougouei, R.A. Shams, G. Oliver, A study on the prevalence of human values in software engineering publications, 2015–2018, in: Proc. International Conference on Software Engineering, ICSE, 2020, pp.409–420.

considered a product line. Also, the software used in such cars handles tremendous amounts of data, and inappropriate access can compromise an individual's safety and privacy. Therefore, questions related to data governance are important, and developers need to consider many non-technical architectural decisions during the design of the product line related to a larger data (retention) life cycle management process, and how and where the data will be collected, processed, preserved, archived, versioned, or deleted. Therefore, any product line in emerging and data-intensive domains needs to ensure that product instances support transparency (i.e., understanding the data and how algorithms change the data).

Product Line Research Versus Product Line Practice

The last challenge I would like to touch on is about the relevance of product lines and product line research. Industry-academia collaboration in software engineering and the relevance of software engineering research in general have been discussed over many years. This is not different for the field of software product lines. Product line engineering as a discipline started from joint initiatives of applied research in academia, industry research, and software engineering practice (see, for example, early industry initiatives driven by Carnegie Mellon's Software Engineering Institute (SEI) and industry-driven research projects in Europe in the early days of product line engineering).[3] Interestingly, investigations into what product line researchers and practitioners find interesting found that topics that practitioners think are relevant and emerging have often already been well researched.[4] This means, we as a community of academics and researchers need to do a better job presenting and communicating our work to practitioner audiences. Furthermore, when we look at actual product line research published by practitioners and researchers, it seems that practitioners (unlike academic researchers) are more interested in architecting and architecture-related issues of product lines.[5] Therefore, it is great to see that this book features chapters on modeling that also include practical examples to illustrate the real-world use of proposed concepts and ideas.

---

[3] K. Schmid, R. Rabiser, M. Becker, G. Botterweck, M. Galster, I. Groher, D. Weyns, Bridging the gap: voices from industry and research on industrial relevance of SPLC, in: Proc. 25th ACM International Systems and Software Product Line Conference, SPLC, 2021, 184–189.

[4] R. Rabiser, K. Schmid, M. Becker, G. Botterweck, M. Galster, I. Groher, D. Weyns, Industrial and Academic Software Product Line Research at SPLC: Perceptions of the Community, in: Proc. 23rd International Systems and Software Product Line Conference, SPLC, 2019, 189–194.

[5] R. Rabiser, K. Schmid, M. Becker, G. Botterweck, M. Galster, I. Groher, D. Weyns, A study and comparison of industrial vs. academic software product line research published at SPLC, in: Proc. 22nd International Systems and Software Product Line Conference, SPLC, 2018, 14–24.

Concluding Remarks

This book contains many interesting chapters on the design, implementation, and maintenance of software product lines. It focuses on how *Stereotype-based Management of Variability* (SMarty) can be useful to design, develop, and maintain software product lines. SMarty offers a UML profile and process to manage variability and to represent a software product line.

I do hope that you find the chapters helpful in your own practice and research to understand and develop next-generation software-intensive systems. Although great progress has been made, we still struggle with building high-quality software systems "for the real world" that provide true value to users while remaining maintainable over their lifetime.

University of Canterbury, Christchurch, New Zealand   Matthias Galster
February 2022

Preface

What Is This Book About?

The software product line (SPL) subject has been in the software engineering spotlights in the last decades as a systematic, prescriptive, and non-opportunistic way to reuse software assets, developed for a given domain, to provide mass customization at deriving new specific products. Therefore, this way of developing software intends to speed up the production of new software, thus reducing time-to-market and increasing return on investment.

This book is mainly about SPLs designed and developed taking UML diagrams as the primary basis, modeled according to a rigorous approach composed of an UML profile and a systematic process for variability management activities, named Stereotype-based Management of Variability (SMarty).

While SPL is the main subject dealt with in all of the chapters of this book, it is also about several distinct but related topics, which serve as a complement to the SPL life cycle activities. Among such topics are variability management activities; component-based and ISO/IEC metric-based design, evaluation, and optimization of SPL architectures (PLA); inspection and testing; feature interaction reduction; and experimentation in SPL. Nevertheless, the reader will see a specific part for related work developed by different research groups, which adopted the SMarty approach basis treated in this book to provide particular solutions in the SPL domain.

Who Should Read This Book?

The target audience of this book is **newcomers and experienced** students, lecturers, and practitioners.

Students might benefit from this book in several ways by: learning about the SPL engineering process, mass customization, SPL configuration activities, and variability management in software-intensive systems; learning and designing

UML-based diagrams, creating and managing UML profiles, applying profiles to diagrams, and creating and maintaining variant rich use case diagrams, class diagrams, component diagrams, sequence diagrams, and activity diagrams; practicing checklist and perspective UML-based inspections; performing model-based tests; quali-quantitatively evaluating PLA using ISO/IEC-based metrics; optimizing a PLA using different algorithms; preventing feature interactions during SPL development; and learning how to plan and conduct proper document-controlled experiments with many examples in the SPL context.

In the perspective of **lecturers**, they might use this book for both undergraduate and graduate levels: as a start guide to teach SPL fundamentals and life cycle activities; as a textbook on teaching how to create UML profiles and apply it to diagrams with several examples; as a reference to create and inter-operate new SPL tools with the SMartyModeling and other existing tools; for demonstrating how experiments might be carried out and well documented based on many examples in the SPL domain; for introducing verification and validation activities with many examples; for introducing students how to perform qualitative and quantitative evaluations for PLA.

For **practitioners**, this book might be of useful for: planning a transitioning from single-product development to an SPL-based process with several SPL development activities illustrated; sketching a PLA version from existing similar products developed based on refactoring techniques; learning how to document inherent variability from a given domain; training on fundamentals of the advanced use of the UML profiling mechanism to support variability; analyzing potential feature interactions in the company's products modeled with SMarty; planning PLA quality evaluations based on ISO/IEC metrics; and learning how controlled experimentation is applied, thus adapting it to a company's quality and development strategy.

How Is This Book Structured?

This book consists of five parts. **Part I** provides overall and essential concepts on SPL in terms of the first development methodologies; proactive, extractive, and reactive approaches; the core assets role; and exemplary UML-based SPLs. Variability is also presented and exemplified. SPL architectures are also discussed, thus finishing with the SMarty approach. **Chapter 1** presents fundamentals of SPLs, first- and second-generation methodologies, and development approaches. **Chapter 2** is dedicated to present and discuss SPL variability, its definition and general management aspects, as well as UML-based variability management approaches. **Chapter 3** discusses the main concepts of software architectures and SPL architectures (PLA), as well as PLA design and description. **Chapter 4** is dedicated to the SMarty approach fundamentals, including its history, UML-supported diagrams, its SPL engineering process support, and an application example.

Part II is focused on the design, verification, and validation of SMarty SPLs, composed of four chapters. **Chapter 5** provides a tutorial on how to design SPLs with SMarty based on all of its supported diagrams, as well as to perform traceability, configuration, and exporting activities. **Chapter 6** focuses on designing component-based PLAs using the SMartyComponents approach. **Chapter 7** is dedicated to SPL inspections using two techniques: SMartyCheck, for checklist-based inspections, and SMartyPerspective, for perspective-based ones. **Chapter 8** presents how to perform model-based testing on SPLs based on two techniques: SPLiT-MBt and SMartyTesting.

Part III focuses on the SPL architecture evolution based on ISO/IEC metrics, the SystEM-PLA method, optimization with the MOA4PLA method, and feature interaction prevention. **Chapter 9** provides a set of ISO/IEC 25010 Maintainability metrics for PLA evaluation. **Chapter 10** presents the SystEM-PLA method for PLA evaluation. **Chapter 11** focuses on the optimization of PLA using the MOA4PLA approach. **Chapter 12** details how to prevent feature interaction using optimization algorithms.

Part IV brings out important works developed taking into account SMarty as a basis, such as the M-SPLearning SPL for mobile learning applications, the PLeTs SPL for testing tools, the PlugSPL plugin environment for supporting the SPL life cycle, the SyMPLES approach for designing embedded systems with SysML, the SMartySPEM process for software process lines (SPrLs), and re-engineering of class diagrams into an SPL. **Chapter 13** presents an SPL for mobile learning applications. **Chapter 14** provides an SPL for creating testing tools. **Chapter 15** relies on an environment to support the SPL life cycle. **Chapter 16** presents an approach for designing embedded systems with SMarty and SysML. **Chapter 17** is dedicated to a software process line (SPrL) approach for variability representation in software processes. **Chapter 18** demonstrates how to re-engineer UML class diagram variants into an SPL.

Part V promotes controlled experimentation in UML-based SPLs, presenting essential concepts on how to plan and conduct experiments, as well as showing several experiments carried out with SMarty. **Chapter 19** presents how to support performing controlled experimentation in the SPL domain. **Chapter 20** presents a series of controlled experiments for evaluating SMarty, comparing it to other UML-based variability management approaches.

How Did This Book Start?

Software product lines (SPLs) have been in my life since I was a freshman in 1998 at the State University of Maringá (UEM). I was enrolled in a bachelor's course in informatics, attending to several challenging courses, such as calculus, statistics, and discrete mathematics. However, an interesting course appeared: Introduction to Software Engineering. In this course, I began learning about the motivation to improve software development and its life cycle, as well as its important practices. Such a course made me decide to become a software analyst for my entire life.

Such a decision prompted me to take up advanced-level software engineering courses as a sophomore. However, all of a sudden, I was presented an opportunity to be part of a software engineering research group. So, I started investigating how software processes and products might be improved based on software reuse. During this time, SPL research came into my life as a way to provide customization throughout SPL architecture reuse based on variability. Then, I investigated how SPLs could take advantage of UML to identify and represent variabilities for deriving specific products configuration. I did it for the rest of my undergraduate tenure, which I finished with a final project on providing an SPL architecture for workflow systems with explicit variabilities.

During my master's course in computer science (2003–2005) at UEM, I decided to systematize a process to identify and represent variability in UML-based SPLs, named *Stereotype-based Management of Variability* (**SMarty**). Such process counts on guidelines to aid the users and an UML 2 profile with stereotypes, tagged-values, and constraints to correctly provide syntactic and semantic value. SMarty was empirically evaluated in different SPL UML models, which makes it to improve, including support to use case, class, component, activity, and sequence diagrams.

In my PhD in computer science (2006–2010) at the Institute of Mathematics and Computer Sciences (ICMC), University of São Paulo (USP), I worked on a systematic method (SystEM-PLA) to evaluate UML-based SPL architectures by means of metrics definition, empirical validation, and controlled experiments. Although SystEM-PLA takes as a basis SMarty, it may be easily used with other UML-based variability representation approaches, by customizing the available metrics.

In August 2011, I started my tenure at UEM as Assistant Professor of Software Engineering. I thus supervised many undergraduate students in their scientific initiation projects and final projects. I also supervised more than 20 master's students. Such supervisions have as results several works published regarding UML-based SPLs techniques, process, metrics, ontologies, controlled experiments, qualitative studies, and systematic reviews and mappings.

With such results, I decided to organize this book gathering all research on UML-based SPLs experience since my undergraduate period, including the supervised students of my **Research Group on Systematic Software Reuse and Continuous Experimentation (GReater)**.

Working with UML models, especially for high-configurable systems, is a challenging task. With this book, I intend to demonstrate how to deal with most non-trivial tasks for SPL development, by taking advantage of a standardized notation as UML.

I really hope this book might contribute to your academic and professional development as a software product line engineer.

Maringá, Paraná, Brazil   Edson OliveiraJr
June 2022

Acknowledgments

I would like to start by thanking the State University of Maringá (UEM), in its greatness, value, and inclusive character, for having me as a computer science undergraduate (1998–2002) and graduate student (2003–2005), and as a tenure-based lecturer in software engineering (since 2011) in the Informatics Department (DIN). I would also like to enormously thank the University of São Paulo (ICM-C/USP) which embraced me during my PhD in computer science (2006–2010) and the University of Waterloo, Canada (2009), during my sandwich period. This recognition is straightforward important as UEM and ICMC/USP strongly contributed to my education, and thus, consequently, to this book.

I would also like to enormously thank all students I supervised, who contributed directly or indirectly to the results in this book. I also include here all students and researchers from UEM and other institutions who developed any research related to this book. **They are the foundation of this book! None of this would be possible without your beliefs and efforts!**

The chapter authors and I would like to thank the invited researchers for providing professional and outstanding comments and feedback after reviewing each chapter. They are named as follows in alphabetical order:

- **Prof. Dr. Aline M. M. M. Amaral** – State University of Maringá (UEM)
- **Prof. Dr. André T. Endo** – Federal University of São Carlos (UFSCar)
- **Prof. Dr. Avelino Francisco Zorzo** – Pontifical Catholic University of Rio Grande do Sul (PUC-RS)
- **Prof. Dr. Crescêncio Rodrigues Lima Neto** – Federal Institute of Bahia (IFBA)
- **Prof. Dr. Elder Rodrigues** – Federal University of Pampa (Unipampa)
- **Prof. Dr. Igor Steinmacher** – Northern Arizona University (NAU)
- **Prof. Dr. Ivan Machado** – Federal University of Bahia (UFBA)
- **Prof. Dr. Juliana Alves Pereira** – Pontifical Catholic University of Rio de Janeiro (PUC-Rio)
- **Prof. Dr. Lilian Scatalon** – State University of Maringá (UEM)
- **Prof. Dr. Marcelo Morandini** – University of São Paulo (USP Leste)

- **Prof. Dr. Ricardo T. Geraldi** – Federal Technology University of Paraná (UTFPR-AP)
- **Prof. Dr. Rodrigo Pereira dos Santos** – Federal University of the State of Rio de Janeiro (UNIRIO)
- **Prof. Dr. Rosana Braga** – University of São Paulo (ICMC/USP)

Last but not least, I would like to thank CAPES/Brazil, CNPq/Brazil, Araucária Foundation of Paraná/Brazil, and UEM for funding most of the research carried out in this book over the years.

Maringá, Paraná, Brazil   Edson OliveiraJr
June 2022

Contents

Part V   Software Product Line Experimentation

Contributors

Fellipe Araújo Aleixo Federal Institute of Rio Grande do Norte, Academic Department of Administration and Information Technology, Natal, Rio Grande do Norte, Brazil

Ana Paula Allian Department of Computer Systems, University of São Paulo, São Carlos, Brazil

Wesley Klewerton Guez Assunção ISSE, Johannes Kepler University Linz, Linz, Austria
OPUS, Pontifical Catholic University of Rio de Janeiro, Rio de Janeiro, Brazil

Luciane Nicolodi Baldo State University of Maringá, Informatics Department, Maringá, Paraná, Brazil

Ellen F. Barbosa University of São Paulo, Department of Computer Systems, São Carlos, São Paulo, Brazil

David Benavides University of Seville, Escuela Tecnica Superior de Ingeniería Informática, Dpto. de Lenguajes y Sistemas Informáticos, Sevilla, Spain

Márcio H. G. Bera State University of Maringá, Informatics Department, Maringá, Paraná, Brazil

Giovanna Bettin State University of Maringá, Informatics Department, Maringá, Paraná, Brazil

Thelma Elita Colanzi State University of Maringá, Informatics Department, Maringá, Paraná, Brazil

André Felipe Ribeiro Cordeiro State University of Maringá, Informatics Department, Maringá, Paraná, Brazil

Leandro Teodoro Costa Unisinos, São Leopoldo, Rio Grande do Sul, Brazil

Rogério F. da Silva Federal University of Paraná, Jandaia do Sul, Paraná, Brazil

Jaime Dias State University of Maringá, Informatics Department, Maringá, Paraná, Brazil

Rodrigo Pereira dos Santos Federal University of the State of Rio de Janeiro, Department of Applied Informatics, Rio de Janeiro, Rio de Janeiro, Brazil

Nemésio F. Duarte Filho Federal Institute of Education, Science and Technology of São Paulo, Informatics Department, Sertãozinho, São Paulo, Brazil

Venilton FalvoJr University of São Paulo, Department of Computer Systems, São Carlos, São Paulo, Brazil

Willian Marques Freire State University of Maringá, Informatics Department, Maringá, Paraná, Brazil

Viviane R. Furtado State University of Maringá, Informatics Department, Maringá, Paraná, Brazil

Matthias Galster University of Canterbury, Christchurch, New Zealand

Ricardo Theis Geraldi State University of Maringá, Informatics Department, Maringá, Paraná, Brazil

Itana M. S. Gimenes State University of Maringá, Informatics Department, Maringá, Paraná, Brazil

Alexandre A. Giron Federal Technology University of Paraná, Toledo, Paraná, Brazil

Marcos Kalinowski Pontifical Catholic University of Rio de Janeiro, Informatics Department, Rio de Janeiro, Rio de Janeiro, Brazil

Uirá Kulesza Federal University of Rio Grande do Norte, Informatics and Applied Mathematics Department, Natal, Rio Grande do Norte, Brazil

Crescencio Lima Federal Institute of Bahia, Vitória da Conquista, Bahia, Brazil

Roberto E. Lopez-Herrejon LOGTI, ETS, University of Quebec, Montreal, QC, Canada

Carlos D. Luz State University of Maringá, Informatics Department, Maringá, Paraná, Brazil

Ivan Machado Federal University of Bahia, Salvador, Bahia, Brazil

José C. Maldonado University of São Paulo, Department of Computer Systems, São Carlos, São Paulo, Brazil

Luciano Marchezan Federal University of Pampa, Department of Computer Systems, Alegrete, Rio Grande do Sul, Brazil

Anderson S. Marcolino Engineering and Exact Science Department, Federal University of Paraná, Palotina, PR, Brazil

Jabier Martinez Tecnalia, Basque Research and Technology Alliance, Derio, Spain

Mamoru Massago State University of Maringá, Informatics Department, Maringá, Paraná, Brazil

Aline M. M. Miotto Amaral State University of Maringá, Informatics Department, Maringá, Paraná, Brazil

Elisa Yumi Nakagawa Department of Computer Systems, University of São Paulo, São Carlos, Brazil

Thaís S. Nepomuceno State University of Maringá, Informatics Department, Maringá, Paraná, Brazil

Edson OliveiraJr State University of Maringá, Informatics Department, Maringá, Paraná, Brazil

Maicon Pazin State University of Maringá, Informatics Department, Maringá, Paraná, Brazil

Kleber Lopes Petry State University of Maringá, Informatics Department, Maringá, Paraná, Brazil

Elder M. Rodrigues Federal University of Pampa, Department of Computer Systems, Alegrete, Rio Grande do Sul, Brazil

Lilian P. Scatalon State University of Maringá, Informatics Department, Maringá, Paraná, Brazil

Leandro F. Silva State University of Maringá, Informatics Department, Maringá, Paraná, Brazil

Igor F. Steinmacher Northern Arizona University, Flagstaff, AZ, USA

Eldânae Nogueira Teixeira Federal University of Rio de Janeiro, Rio de Janeiro, Rio de Janeiro, Brazil

Nelson Tenório UniCesumar, Informatics Department, Maringá, Paraná, Brazil

Silvia Regina Vergilio Federal University of Paraná, Informatics Department, Curitiba, Paraná, Brazil

Henrique Vignando State University of Maringá, Informatics Department, Maringá, Paraná, Brazil

Aline Zanin Pontifical Catholic University of Rio Grande do Sul, Porto Alegre, Rio Grande do Sul, Brazil

Avelino Francisco Zorzo Pontifical Catholic University of Rio Grande do Sul, Porto Alegre, Rio Grande do Sul, Brazil

Part I
Fundamentals of Software Product Lines and the SMarty Approach

Chapter 1
Principles of Software Product Lines

Edson OliveiraJr and David Benavides

Abstract Software product lines (SPL) has been consolidated in the last decades as a de facto and non-opportunistic way of mass customization and reuse of software artifacts to produce specific products. Over the years, SPLs and their construction processes have evolved based on several seminal works and technologies. In this chapter, we characterize an SPL, present its terminology, chronologically present its first construction methodologies and second-generation ones, and describe SPL development approaches. We conclude the chapter with final remarks and considerations for the next chapters.

1.1 Characterizing Software Product Lines

The first Industrial Revolution began in Great Britain in the mid-eighteenth century (1760 to 1820–1840), which was a transition from handmade products manufacturing to a machine-based production. At that time, new inventions were made possible due to increasing iron and chemical processes, such as water and steam power. Therefore, textile industry led employment and mass production [21, 38].

Due to these advancements in production, Henry Ford defined the first assembly line manufacturing process in which semi-built parts are assembled together moving from one workstation to another. Thus, an assembled product is built faster than usual hand-based single product production [47]. Then, in 1913, Ford launched the assembly line of a car, named Ford Model T (Fig. 1.1).

Since then, Ford assembly lines concept has impacted the overall industry in the manufacturing process by mass production, which might be defined as the

E. OliveiraJr (✉)
State University of Maringá, Informatics Department, Maringá, Paraná, Brazil
e-mail: edson@din.uem.br

D. Benavides
University of Seville, Escuela Tecnica Superior de Ingeniería Informática, Dpto. de Lenguajes y Sistemas Informáticos, Sevilla, Spain
e-mail: benavides@us.es

© Springer Nature Switzerland AG 2023
E. OliveiraJr (ed), *UML-Based Software Product Line Engineering with SMarty*,
https://doi.org/10.1007/978-3-031-18556-4_1

Fig. 1.1 Ford assembly line [47]

production of a large amount of standardized products using standardized processes that allow producing a big amount of the same product in a reduced time to market. However, mass production was starting to be not enough in a highly competitive and segmented market [31], and mass customization became a must for market success. Therefore, mass customization can be defined as "producing goods and services to meet individual customer's needs with near mass production efficiency" [31]. Mass customization drastically reduced costs and increasing production. Nowadays, this concept has been successfully applied to the software manufacture industry under the concept of a software product line (SPL) [11, 36, 41].

One of widely adopted definition for software product line is *"a set of software-intensive systems that share a common, managed set of features satisfying the specific needs of a particular market segment or mission and that are developed from a common set of core assets in a prescribed way"* [11]. Such definition is in accordance with the IEEE software engineering definition, which is *"the application of a systematic, disciplined, quantifiable approach to the development, operation and maintenance of software; that is, the application of engineering to software"* [23].

The concept of SPL takes into account consolidated software engineering practices as domain engineering [15, 37]. Domain engineering aims at engineering an understanding the applications domain using development principles, techniques, and tools for static and dynamic attributes, support technology, management and organization, rules and regulations, and human behavior [8]. Figure 1.2 depicts main activities of domain engineering and application engineering.

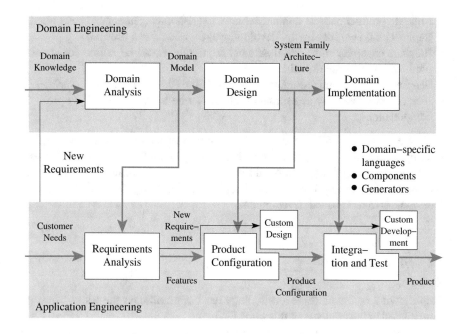

Fig. 1.2 Domain and application engineering [14]

Domain engineering begins with the domain analysis phase, in which knowledge of the domain form the basis for the abstraction of the domain model. Then, domain design is performed taking as input the domain model, which guides the implementation of an infrastructure to support the system family architecture. Based on such architecture, the **application engineering** produces single products by its first phase: requirement analysis. New requirements and features might be added, and then a single product is configured for a custom designing. Once designed, a product is integrated and tested under the customer requirements.

These two cycles mainly compose the foundations of modern SPLs. They provide capability for an SPL to derive several different specific products based on a common architecture and similar/variable features. For further comprehension, Chap. 2 exploits the concept of features and variability in software product lines, whereas Chap. 3 provides basics on product line architectures (PLA).

SPL provides several benefits, such as [11, 36, 44–46]:

- Lower time to market by accelerating the production of similar products with non-opportunistic reuse techniques.
- Enhance product quality as reusable core assets are previously verified and validated.
- Increase productivity as a set of core assets is previously built based on common domain characteristics.
- Decrease production costs by reusing de facto self and COTS components.

- Mitigate product risks as domain engineering risk management can be applied.
- Support market agility by not developing each product at a time.
- Enhance customer satisfaction as most requirements can be reused for specific products of the same domain.
- Support mass customization by mainly using the concept of software variability.
- Increase predictability as estimation effort can be mitigated based on pre-built components.

On the other hand, SPL development might experience some difficulties as SPL training as technical management activities, a considerable amount of investment (financial, time, and people) to obtain return on investment, and SPL architecture integration and testing issues, especially when transiting from single-product development to SPL-based development.

1.2   SPL Terminology

The following non-exhaustive terminology has been built over the years. They are more related to the contents of this book [24].

Core asset: is any output of the domain engineering process. It can be reused at producing products during application engineering. They include, for instance, features, models, requirements specifications, domain architecture, domain components, and test cases.

SPL architecture (PLA): is the architecture, which includes structure and texture (e.g., common rules and constraints), that constrains all member products within an SPL. It usually provides variability represented in its components.

Variability: represents characteristics that may differ among products (members) of an SPL. Such differences are captured from multiple viewpoints such as functionality, quality attributes, and environments.

Variation point: representation corresponding to given variable characteristics of products, core asset, and application assets in the context of an SPL. Variation points show what of the SPL varies. Each variation point should have at least one variant.

Variant: is an alternative to realize a particular variation point. Selection and binding of variants for a specific product delimit the characteristics of the particular variability for the product. Very often, a variant refers to a concrete configuration of an SPL.

Binding: it represents the time when variants are bound to resolve a variation point or an specific variability.

Commonality: it refers to functional and nonfunctional characteristics shared to all members in an SPL.

Feature: is a high-level characteristics of a system functionality that can be communicable with customers and relevant stakeholders.

Variability management: it consists of tasks for overseeing variability in the level of the entire SPL, creating and maintaining variability models, ensuring consistencies between variability models, managing all variability and constraint dependencies across the SPL, and managing the traceability links between a variability model and associated domain and application assets (e.g., requirements models, design models).

SPL configuration: refers to resolving all variabilities enabling the derivation of a specific SPL product.

1.3   SPL Engineering Methodologies and Reference Model

In this section we present consolidated SPL methodologies and reference models. They are used to design, implement, and derive specific SPL products in a systematic and prescriptive way.

1.3.1   First-Generation Methodologies

SPL research and practice are nowadays divided into first- and second-generation methodologies. The first ones are those which aided SPL research and practice to deal with several issues, such as variability modeling, feature composition and modeling, resolution of variabilities and derivation of specific SPL products, and maintenance of SPLs.

1.3.1.1   FODA: Feature-Oriented Domain Analysis (1990)

Feature-oriented domain analysis (FODA) [28] is a method for performing domain analysis. FODA emphasizes the identification of features the user commonly expects in an application of a given domain.

Figure 1.3 depicts the processes and products of FODA, which are: **context analysis** to produce a structure diagram and a context diagram; **domain modeling** to produce an E-R model, a feature model, a functional model, and a domain terminology dictionary; and **architecture modeling** to produce a Process interaction model and a module structure chart.

Figure 1.4 depicts **products of domain analysis** and roles involved to tailoring a **new system development**.

The tailoring process starts with products from the domain analysis. The domain analyst and the requirements analyst add, modify, or delete features from the context and scope domain to form a new system context with the participation of the user. The same occurs for the domain model to tailor a new system software specification. To the domain architecture, the domain analyst, the requirements analyst, and

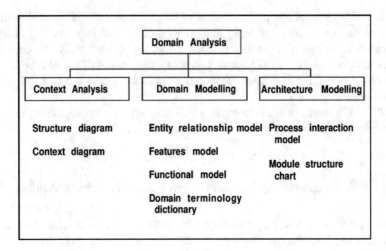

Fig. 1.3 Feature-oriented domain analysis process and products [28]

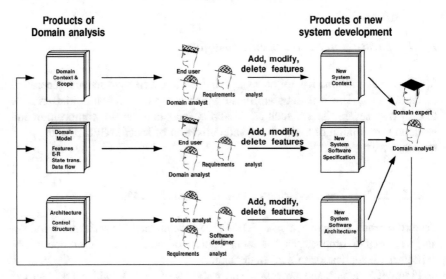

Fig. 1.4 Feature-oriented domain analysis tailoring products [28]

the software engineer work on the domain architecture to produce a new system software architecture. These three tailored artifacts are then verified by the domain expert and the domain analyst to produce a new product.

1.3.1.2 RSEB: Reuse-Driven Software Engineering Business (1997)

The Reuse-Driven Software Engineering Business (RSEB) [25] is a use case-driven systematic reuse process. It was created in 1997 as a single-system develop and reuse process.

In 1998, Griss et al. [19] integrated the feature modeling technique from FODA to RSEB to provide a high-level view of the domain architecture and reusable assets. Therefore, users are provided with a more concise and expressive picture of the way to build systems in the application family (SPL).

Different sources are used to build a feature model, such as system exemplars, early domain models, and requirements. These sources aid at establishing domain scoping and context modeling, and the expected feature model.

1.3.1.3 FORM: Feature-Oriented Reuse Method for Product Line Software Engineering (1998)

The Feature-Oriented Reuse Method (FORM) [29] is a systematic method focused on identifying commonalities and differences of several applications from a given domain in terms of features to develop domain architectures and components.

Commonalities and differences are identified in a "feature model" to support both engineering of reusable domain artifacts and development of applications using the domain artifacts. As a domain is described in terms of common and different units of computation, they are used to build different configurations of reusable architectures.

Figure 1.5 depicts the FORM engineering processes [29].

FORM is composed of two engineering processes: **domain engineering** and **application engineering**. Domain engineering consists of activities for analyzing systems and creating architectures and reusable components. The architectures and reusable accommodate the differences and commonalities of the systems in the domain. Application engineering consists of activities for developing applications using the artifacts. For typical applications in a given domain, such process should be trivial compared to the traditional application development approach as it provides built pieces implemented and tested, ready to be reused.

As one can see, FORM is based on the principles of the FODA method to deliver software stakeholders an organized set of processes to develop and reuse domain analysis artifacts into a single-software tailored by means of the application engineering process.

1.3.1.4 FAST: Family-Oriented Abstraction, Specification, and Translation (1999)

Family-Oriented Abstraction, Specification, and Translation (FAST) [48] is a development process for producing software in a family-oriented flavor. It separates

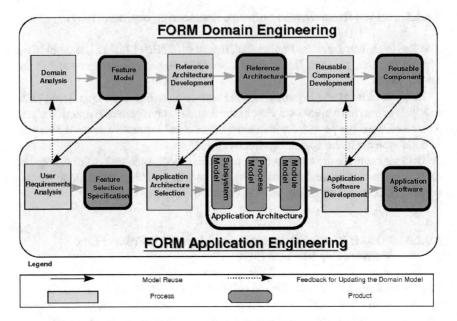

Fig. 1.5 FORM engineering processes [29]

software product line engineering process into one step to provide the core and another one to produce different software products from such a family.

FAST adopts software product line architecture principles into a software engineering process. A common platform is specified to a family of software products.

Such a platform is established with similarities between several products as a basis. Variabilities among product family members are implemented with different variation techniques such as parameterization or conditional compilation.

The domain engineering step creates abstractions in the family-oriented perspective, which are used to create the design of the family to define standard libraries for prospective implementations. The abstractions are the basis for modeling specific applications, which are materialized by the composition of common implementations from the domain engineering and tailored components to such specific family members.

1.3.1.5 PuLSE: Fraunhofer Product Line Software Engineering (1999)

The Product Line Software Engineering (PuLSE) [7] methodology aims at conceiving and deploying software product lines in a large variety of enterprise contexts, which is allowed via a straightforward product-centric focus throughout the phases of PuLSE. Such phase aims at customization of components, incremental capability, and maturity scaling for evolution.

The deployment phases describe the activities performed to set up and use a given product line, which are [7] initialization, baselines, and customized PuLSE as a result; infrastructure construction to scope, model, and architect the product line infrastructure; infrastructure usage to create product line members; and evolution and management to evolve the infrastructure over time.

The technical components are [7]: customizing to perform the initialization phase, scoping to effectively scope the infrastructure to define products, modeling to specify the product characteristics, architecting to develop the reference architecture and maintain the traceability to the model, instantiating to perform the usage phase, and evolving and managing to deal with configuration management issues as products accrue over time.

The support components are [7] project entry points to customized PuLSE to major project types, maturity scale to provide integration and evolution to enterprises using PuLSE, and organization issues to provide guidelines to set up and maintain the right organization structure for developing and managing product lines.

1.3.1.6   KobrA: Komponenten basierte Anwendungsentwicklung (2000)

The KobrA method [4, 5] gathers up different software engineering processes, including software product line development, component-based software development, frameworks, architecture-centric inspections, quality modeling, and process modeling. Thus, KobrA's goal is to provide a systematic approach to the development of high-quality, component-based application frameworks in a prescriptive way mainly based on UML.

In the perspective of product lines, KobrA is an object-oriented customization of the PuLSE method by taking advantages of the UML notation. The infrastructure construction phase of PuLSE corresponds to KobrA's framework engineering activity, the infrastructure usage phase of PuLSE corresponds to KobrA's application engineering activity, and the product line evolution phase of PuLSE corresponds to the maintenance of the frameworks and applications.

Figure 1.6 depicts the overall KobrA activities

1.3.1.7   SEI Framework for Software Product Line Practice (2002)

The framework for software product line practice (PLP) [46] was created by the Software Engineering Institute (SEI) in 2002[1] to describe essential activities and practices (technical and organizational) to benefit from fielding a product line of software or software-intensive systems.

---

[1] First version of the framework https://resources.sei.cmu.edu/library/asset-view.cfm?assetid=495357.

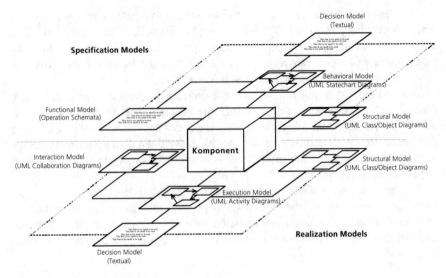

Fig. 1.6 KobrA overview [4]

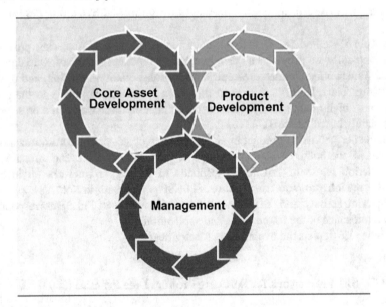

Fig. 1.7 The SEI's framework for software product line practice [46]

Its main objective is identifying fundamental concepts and activities underlying SPLs and defining example practices in each practice area by providing guidance on how to move to an SPL approach. Figure 1.7 depicts the PLP essential activities.

Core asset development is mainly responsible for defining the main artifacts with respective variabilities, which will be reused in the next activity. **Product**

development instantiates the core asset to develop specific products according to a production plan and specific requirements. **Management** is responsible for providing technical and organizational activities to ensure the competent product development and SPL process evolution.

1.3.1.8   PLUS: Product Line UML-Based Software Engineering (2004)

The Product Line UML-based Software Engineering (PLUS) [18] is a model-driven evolutionary development approach for software product lines, mainly based on UML.

Kernel, optional, and alternative use cases are defined during requirements modeling for the software functional requirements. A feature model is then developed to represent commonality and variability in the requirements [18].

During the analysis modeling, static models, such as class diagrams, are developed for defining kernel, optional, and variant classes and their relationships. Dynamic models, such as sequence diagrams and statecharts, are developed to define state dependent aspects of the product line, as well as interaction models describe the dynamic interaction between the objects that participate in each kernel, optional, and alternative use case.

1.3.1.9   SMarty: Stereotype-Based Management of Variability (2005)

The SMarty approach [43] was created to straightforward taking advantage of the UML profiling mechanism of adding new semantics to standard meta classes via stereotypes, tagged values, and constraints. SMarty started supporting class and use case diagrams, thus evolved to incorporate activity, component, and sequence diagrams. Figure 1.8 depicts the SMartyProfile, an UML 2 profile to support representing variabilities.

SMarty interacts with the SPL development main activities based on its own process, the SMartyProcess as shown in Fig. 1.9.

As the SMartyProcess activities are performed, the SMartyProfile is applied to respective UML elements to represent variability according existing guidelines to easy the SPL engineer job.

Chapter 4 is totally dedicated to SMarty with several further exemplary excerpts. In addition, chapters of Part IV of this book are dedicated to present research works developed taking SMarty as a basis.

1.3.1.10   Pohl et al.'s SPL Framework (2005)

The Pohl et al.'s [45] framework was created in 2005 as a way to systematize the SPL development life cycle providing guidance to well-defined processes and respective artifacts. Figure 1.10 depicts the two-phase process framework for SPL engineering.

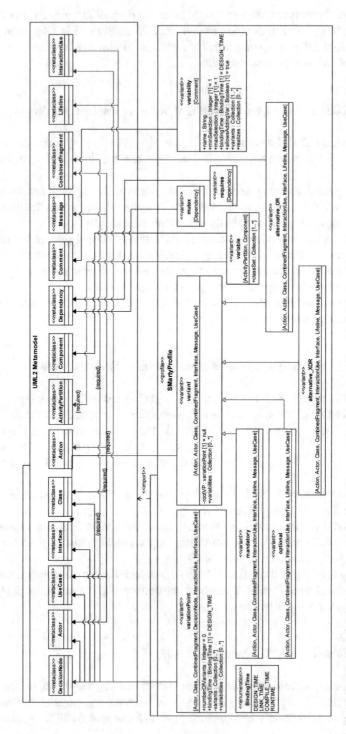

Fig. 1.8 SMartyProfile with support to use case, class, component, sequence, and activity diagrams [43]

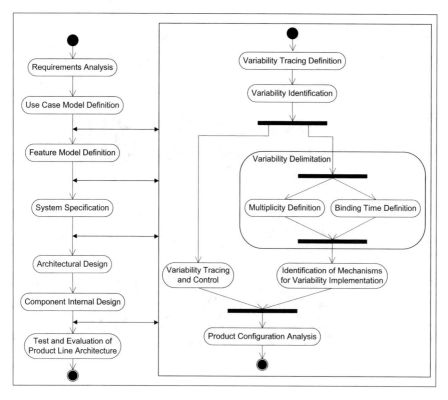

Fig. 1.9 SMartyProcess interaction with main software product line activities [43]

As we characterized in Sect. 1.1, domain engineering is mainly responsible for defining the SPL core asset. In this framework, this is done by different processes: domain engineering requirements, domain design, domain realization, and domain testing. All artifacts produced in such processes contain variability. In the application engineering, the same processes are performed, however focusing on resolving variabilities and deriving specific products according to single systems requirements and a production plan.

1.3.2 Second-Generation Software Product Line Engineering (2GPLE)

Second-generation SPL engineering (2GPLE) is characterized to be built upon methodologies and tools from previous works on SPL. It demands a more well-defined and repeatable process, most centered on a strong factory paradigm [34].

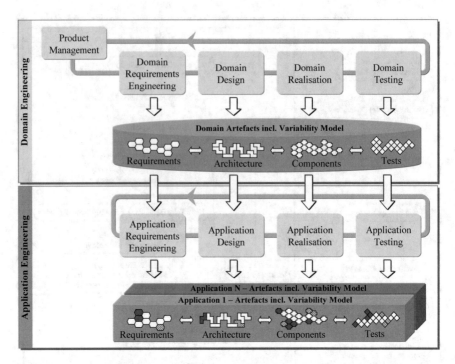

Fig. 1.10 The Pohl et al.'s SPL engineering framework [45]

What makes it different from previous efforts is that features from the core assets must be configured appropriately rather than using different languages and mechanisms for each type of artifact [13]. In addition, the shared assets come from all life cycle phases, not just from the software one, thus automation occurs in the form of a configurator.

Figure 1.11 depicts the 2GPLE factory concept. The configurator uses a feature profile for a product to exercise variation points (denoted by the gear symbols) in the shared assets, configuring them to support a product with those features.

Two interesting 2GPLE cases for the Department of Defense (DoD) of the United States are discussed by Clements et al. [13]. They used existing SPL-related tools to setup a factory for producing products for the US army and navy.

Although this book is focused mainly on first-generation SPLs life cycle, we applied certain 2GPLE techniques to build a configurator in a tool named SMartyModeling. Further details are in Chap. 5.

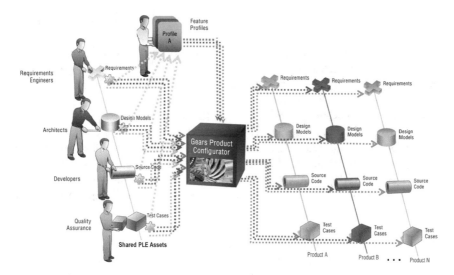

Fig. 1.11 The second-generation SPL factory concept [13]

1.3.3 ISO/IEC Standards for SPL Engineering, Management, and Tools

ISO/IEC provides a series of seven standards for:

- Software and systems engineering—Reference model for product line engineering and management (26550)
- Processes and capabilities of methods and tools for product line scoping, domain requirements engineering, and application requirements engineering (26551)
- Processes and capabilities of methods and tools for domain design and application design (26552)
- Processes and capabilities of methods and tools for domain realization and application realization (26553)
- Processes and capabilities of methods and tools for domain verification and validation and application verification and validation (26554)
- Processes and capabilities of methods and tools for technical management (26555)
- Processes and capabilities of methods and tools for organizational management (26556)

ISO/IEC 26550 is focused on presenting terms and definitions, motivation for SPL engineering, and a reference model with two life cycle engineering process: domain engineering and application engineering.

The reference model is built taking into account the other six ISO/IEC standards (26551 through 26556). The reference model is supported by two management process, such as the SEI PLP's (Sect. 1.3.1.7): Organizational Management and Technical Management.

Käkölä [26] provides several points in favor of such ISO/IEC for de facto standards to be adopted in industry especially because of the need for high levels of abstraction, the need to cope with high levels of complexity, the fragmented body of knowledge, and the lack of tools.

Käkölä [27] lists several benefits from the ISO/IEC SPL engineering series, such as they enable its users to holistically understand, adopt, and enact the domain and application engineering life cycles; enable its users to evaluate and select relevant methods and tools based on business and user-related criteria; help development teams specify, verify, and validate engineering and management practices for existing or envisioned product lines based on the product line practices described in the standard; provide a reference model for software product line engineering and management, that is, an abstract representation of the domain and application engineering life cycles and enabling core asset management, organizational management, and technical management processes that will be detailed in the other software product line standards; and help tool vendors develop interoperable tool suites and features supporting the domain and application engineering life cycles and their phases and communicate about their tools to the markets.

1.4 SPL Development Approaches

The development of SPLs from a set of systems point of view takes important steps mainly toward domain and application engineering activities. Such activities must be well established, managed, and controlled as they will provide all support for gathering, for instance, SPL requirements, production plan, core asset development and reuse, estimation, and evolution.

From this perspective, SPL stakeholders must provide a way to perform all these activities, with minimal costs and time to market, as well as maximum production and mass customization of products, justifying return on investment.

The following main approaches play an essential role at SPL development.

1.4.1 The Proactive Approach

When SPL stakeholders firstly conventionally analyze, architect, design, and implement all potential specific products on the foreseeable horizon up front, they are developing SPL in a proactive manner [10]. Such approach might be useful and valuable for companies which best known their products requirements and afford a waterfall-like SPL development life cycle.

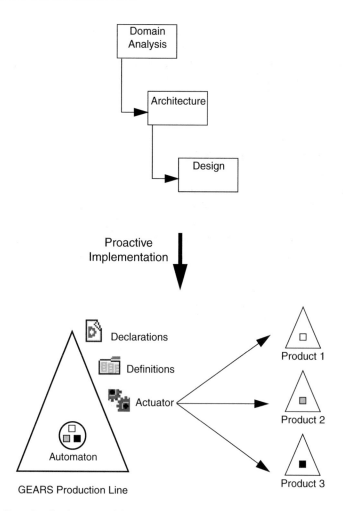

Fig. 1.12 Proactive development of GEARS SPL [32]

Krüeger [32] claims the proactive approach, illustrated in Fig. 1.12, is similar to the waterfall approach for single systems. The proactive approach requires considerably more effort up front, but this drops sharply once the SPL is complete.

To perform tasks of the proactive approach, one must [32, 36, 45]:

- Perform domain analysis and scoping to identify the variation to be supported in the SPL.
- Model the SPL architecture to support all products.
- Design the common and variant parts of the system.
- Implement the common and variant parts of the system.

Once the SPL is developed, one must create the specific products (instances). If more products are needed, they are developed from the existing scope. Therefore, maintenance and evolution are performed directly on the single production line.

The literature provides several successful examples on adopting the proactive approach [6, 16, 17, 22, 42].

1.4.2 The Extractive Approach

Krüger [32] explains the extractive approach reuses one or more existing software products as the SPL's initial baseline. To be an effective choice, the extractive approach requires lightweight SPL technology and techniques that can reuse existing software without much reengineering. This approach is very effective for an organization that wants to quickly transition from conventional to software product line engineering.

The extractive approach to software mass customization, illustrated in Fig. 1.13, is appropriate when an existing collection of customized systems can be reused. It is not necessary to perform the extraction from all of the preexisting systems at once.

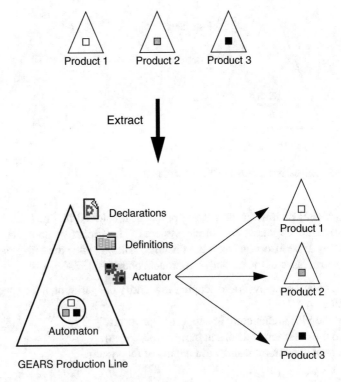

Fig. 1.13 Extractive development of GEARS SPL [32]

To perform the extractive approach tasks, one must [32, 36, 45]:

- Identify commonality and variation in the existing systems.
- Create a single copy of the common software.
- Create feature declarations that model the scope of variation among the existing systems.
- Encapsulate variation points into automata.
- Program the automata logic to map declaration parameter values to variant selections in the automata.
- Create the product definitions for the desired product instances by selecting values for each of the feature definition parameters.

After the SPL has been populated, product instances are created. Software mass customization now becomes the mode of operation as focus shifts to maintaining and enhancing the single production line.

Literature examples of this approach are [3, 33, 35, 40, 49]

1.4.3 The Reactive Approach

The reactive approach is similar to the spiral or extreme programming approach to single-software solutions. One must analyze, architect, design, and implement one or several product variations on each development spiral [32]. This approach works in situations where one cannot predict the requirements for product variations.

Figure 1.14 depicts an example of the reactive approach. It is incremental and appropriate when the requirements for new products in the SPL are unpredictable.

The reactive approach allows for rapid adoption of mass customization since a minimum number of products must be incorporated in advance.

To perform the reactive approach tasks, one must [32, 36, 45]:

- Characterize the requirements for the new product relative to what is currently supported in the SPL.
- Analyze whether the new product is currently within the scope of the current SPL. If not, perform the "delta engineering" to the SPL on any or all of the declarations, automata, common software, and definitions.
- Create the product definition for the new product by selecting values for each of the feature declaration parameters.

Literature has also several examples on the reactive approach adoption as [9, 12, 20, 39].

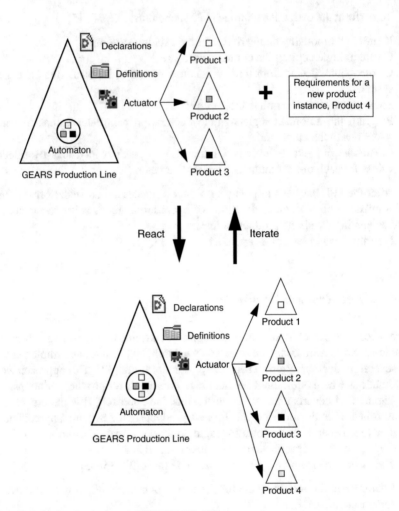

Fig. 1.14 Reactive development of GEARS SPL [32]

1.4.4 Feature-Oriented SPL Development

Feature-oriented software development (FOSD) aims at constructing, customizing, and synthesizing large-scale and variable software systems, taking into account their structures, reuse, and variations [1, 30].

The basic goal of FOSD is decomposing a software system in terms of its features. According Kang et al. [28], feature is "a prominent or distinctive user-visible aspect, quality, or characteristic of a software system or systems."

In the perspective of SPLs, a feature is defined by Apel and Kastner [2] as "a characteristic or end-user-visible behavior of a software system," and they are used

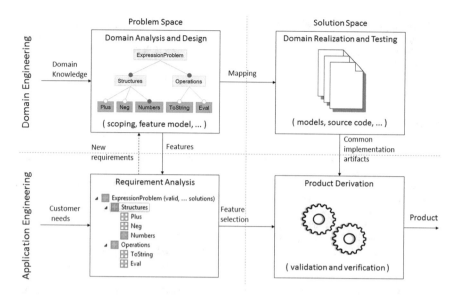

Fig. 1.15 Apel and Kastner's feature-oriented engineering process for SPLs [2]

in "SPLs to specify and communicate commonalities and differences of the products between stakeholders, and to guide structure, reuse, and variation across all phases of the software life cycle."

Figure 1.15 depicts Apel and Kastner's feature-oriented engineering process for SPLs. This approach is composed of two main processes, as well as traditional methodologies, such as domain engineering and application engineering. The main difference from this approach to the other ones is that all SPL development process is oriented to features, in the problem space, which are mapped to models, source codes, and other artifacts in the solution space of the domain engineering process. Once variabilities are represented in features and other artifacts, requirement analysis and product derivation are performed to configure (selection of features) and derive a specific SPL product in the application engineering process.

1.5 Final Remarks

In this chapter we presented concepts on software product lines which are essential to provide the reader a background to understand the rest of this book.

As SPL is an extensive subject, which encompasses other methodologies and approaches, in this book we focus our discussion on UML-based SPLs, which are perfectly understandable with the presented concepts. Potential related concepts are presented in respective chapters to avoid overlapping the ones already discussed, such as SPL variability and SPL architectures (PLA).

Acknowledgments Prof. David would like to thank the Project (RTI2018-101204-B-C22, OPHE-LIA), funded by FEDER/Ministry of Science and Innovation – State Research Agency; and the Junta de Andalucia COPERNICA (P20_01224) and METAMORFOSIS (FEDER_US-1381375) projects.

References

1. Apel, S., Kästner, C.: An overview of feature-oriented software development. J. Object Technol. **8**(5), 49–84 (2009)
2. Apel, S., Batory, D., Kstner, C., Saake, G.: Feature-Oriented Software Product Lines: Concepts and Implementation. Springer Publishing Company, New York (2013)
3. Assunção, W.K., Lopez-Herrejon, R.E., Linsbauer, L., Vergilio, S.R., Egyed, A.: Reengineering legacy applications into software product lines: a systematic mapping. Empir. Softw. Eng. **22**(6), 2972–3016 (2017). https://doi.org/10.1007/s10664-017-9499-z
4. Atkinson, C., Bayer, J., Muthig, D.: Component-based product line development: the kobra approach. In: Proceedings of the First Software Product Lines Conference SPLC, pp. 289–309. Springer, New York (2000)
5. Atkinson, C., Bayer, J., Bunse, C., Kamsties, E., Laitenberger, O., Laqua, R., Muthig, D., Paech, B., Wüst, J., Zettel, J.: Component-Based Product Line Engineering with UML. Addison-Wesley Longman Publishing Co. Inc., Boston (2002)
6. Ayala, I., Papadopoulos, A.V., Amor, M., Fuentes, L.: Prodspl: Proactive self-adaptation based on dynamic software product lines. J. Syst. Softw. **175**, 110,909 (2021). https://doi.org/10.1016/j.jss.2021.110909
7. Bayer, J., Flege, O., Knauber, P., Laqua, R., Muthig, D., Schmid, K., Widen, T., DeBaud, J.M.: Pulse: a methodology to develop software product lines. In: Proceedings of the 1999 Symposium on Software Reusability, SSR '99, pp. 122–131. ACM, New York (1999). https://doi.org/10.1145/303008.303063
8. Bjørner, D.: Domain engineering: a software engineering discipline in need of research. In: Hlaváč, V., Jeffery, K.G., Wiedermann, J. (eds.) SOFSEM 2000: Theory and Practice of Informatics, pp. 1–17. Springer, Berlin (2000)
9. Buhrdorf, R., Churchett, D., Krüeger, C.: Salion's experience with a reactive software product line approach. In: 5th International Workshop on Software Product-Family Engineering (PFE), pp. 317–322 (2003)
10. Clements, P.: Being proactive pays off. IEEE Softw. **19**(4), 28 (2002). https://doi.org/10.1109/MS.2002.1020283
11. Clements, P., Northrop, L.M.: Software Product Lines: Practices and Patterns. SEI Series in Software Engineering. Addison-Wesley, Boston (2002)
12. Clements, P.C., Jones, L.G., Northrop, L.M., McGregor, J.D.: Project management in a software product line organization. IEEE Softw. **22**(5), 54–62 (2005). https://doi.org/10.1109/MS.2005.133
13. Clements, P., Gregg, S., Krüeger, C., Lanman, J., Rivera, J., Scharadin, R., Shepherd, J., Winkler, A.: Second generation product line engineering takes hold in the dod. Crosstalk J. Def. Softw. Eng., 12–18 (2014)
14. Czarnecki, K.: Generative programming: Methods, techniques, and applications tutorial abstract. In: Gacek, C. (ed.) Software Reuse: Methods, Techniques, and Tools, pp. 351–352. Springer, Berlin (2002)
15. Dabhade, M., Suryawanshi, S., Manjula, R.: A systematic review of software reuse using domain engineering paradigms. In: 2016 Online International Conference on Green Engineering and Technologies (IC-GET), pp. 1–6 (2016). https://doi.org/10.1109/GET.2016.7916646
16. FalvoJr, V., Filho, N.F.D., OliveiraJr, E., Barbosa, E.F.: A contribution to the adoption of software product lines in the development of mobile learning applications. In: Proceedings

of the 2014 IEEE Frontiers in Education Conference (FIE), pp. 1–8 (2014). https://doi.org/10.1109/FIE.2014.7044091

17. FalvoJr, V., Filho, N.F.D., OliveiraJr, E., Barbosa, E.F.: Towards the establishment of a software product line for mobile learning applications. In: International Conference on Software Engineering and Knowledge Engineering, pp. 678–683 (2014)

18. Gomaa, H.: Designing Software Product Lines with UML: From Use Cases to Pattern-Based Software Architectures. Addison Wesley Longman Publishing Co. Inc., (2004)

19. Griss, M.L., Favaro, J., Alessandro, M.d.: Integrating feature modeling with the RSEB. In: Proceedings of the 5th International Conference on Software Reuse, ICSR '98, p. 76. IEEE Computer Society, Washington (1998)

20. Heider, W., Grünbacher, P., Rabiser, R.: Negotiation constellations in reactive product line evolution. In: 2010 Fourth International Workshop on Software Product Management, pp. 63–66 (2010). https://doi.org/10.1109/IWSPM.2010.5623862

21. Hobsbawm, E.: The Age of Revolution: Europe 1789–1848, 1 edn. Weidenfeld & Nicolson Ltd., London (1996)

22. Horcas, J.M., Pinto, M., Fuentes, L.: Software product line engineering: a practical experience. In: Proceedings of the 23rd International Systems and Software Product Line Conference, SPLC '19, vol. A, pp. 164–176. Association for Computing Machinery, New York (2019). https://doi.org/10.1145/3336294.3336304

23. ISO/IEC: ISO/IEC/IEEE 24765:2010 – Systems and software engineering: vocabulary. https://www.iso.org/standard/50518.html

24. ISO/IEC: ISO/IEC 26550:2015 – Software and systems engineering: reference model for product line engineering and management. https://www.iso.org/standard/69529.html

25. Jacobson, I., Griss, M., Jonsson, P.: Software Reuse: Architecture, Process and Organization for Business Success. ACM Press/Addison-Wesley Publishing Co., New York (1997)

26. Käkölä, T.K.: Standards initiatives for software product line engineering and management within the international organization for standardization. In: Hawaii International Conference on System Sciences, pp. 1–10 (2010). https://doi.org/10.1109/HICSS.2010.348

27. Käkölä, T.K.: ISO initiatives on software product line engineering: vision and current status invited talk for variability. In: De Troyer, O., Bauzer Medeiros, C., Billen, R., Hallot, P., Simitsis, A., Van Mingroot, H. (eds.) Advances in Conceptual Modeling. Recent Developments and New Directions, pp. 119–119. Springer, Berlin (2011)

28. Kang, K., Cohen, S., Hess, J., Novak, W., Peterson, A.: Feature-oriented domain analysis (FODA) feasibility study. Technical Report. CMU/SEI-90-TR-021, Software Engineering Institute, Carnegie Mellon University, Pittsburgh (1990). http://resources.sei.cmu.edu/library/asset-view.cfm?AssetID=11231

29. Kang, K.C., Kim, S., Lee, J., Kim, K., Shin, E., Huh, M.: Form: a feature-oriented reuse method with domain-specific reference architectures. Ann. Softw. Eng. 5(1), 143 (1998). https://doi.org/10.1023/A:1018980625587

30. Kästner, C., Apel, S., Ostermann, K.: The road to feature modularity? In: International Workshop on Feature-Oriented Software Development (FOSD), pp. 1–8. ACM Press, New York (2011). https://doi.org/10.1145/2019136.2019142

31. Kotha, S.: From mass production to mass customization: the case of the national industrial bicycle company of Japan. Eur. Manag. J. 14(5), 442–450 (1996). https://doi.org/10.1016/0263-2373(96)00037-0

32. Krüeger, C.W.: Easing the transition to software mass customization. In: van der Linden, F. (ed.) Software Product-Family Engineering, pp. 282–293. Springer, Berlin (2002)

33. Krüger, J., Berger, T.: An empirical analysis of the costs of clone- and platform-oriented software reuse. In: Proceedings of the 28th ACM Joint Meeting on European Software Engineering Conference and Symposium on the Foundations of Software Engineering, ESEC/FSE 2020, pp. 432–444. Association for Computing Machinery, New York (2020). https://doi.org/10.1145/3368089.3409684

34. Krüeger, C.W., Clements, P.C.: Second generation systems and software product line engineering. In: Proceedings of the 19th International Conference on Software Product Line, SPLC '15, pp. 388–389. Association for Computing Machinery, New York (2015). https://doi.org/10.1145/2791060.2798047
35. Krüger, J., Mahmood, W., Berger, T.: Promote-pl: a round-trip engineering process model for adopting and evolving product lines. In: Proceedings of the 24th ACM Conference on Systems and Software Product Line, SPLC '20, vol. A. Association for Computing Machinery, New York (2020). https://doi.org/10.1145/3382025.3414970
36. Linden, F.J.v.d., Schmid, K., Rommes, E.: Software Product Lines in Action: The Best Industrial Practice in Product Line Engineering. Springer, Berlin (2007)
37. Lisboa, L.B., Garcia, V.C., Lucrédio, D., de Almeida, E.S., de Lemos Meira, S.R., de Mattos Fortes, R.P.: A systematic review of domain analysis tools. Inf. Softw. Technol. 52(1), 1–13 (2010). https://doi.org/10.1016/j.infsof.2009.05.001
38. Lucas Robert E., J.: Lectures on Economic Growth, 1 edn. Harvard University Press, Cambridge (2002)
39. Neves, G.S., Vilain, P.: Reactive variability realization with test driven development and refactoring. In: The 26th International Conference on Software Engineering and Knowledge Engineering, pp. 100–105 (2014)
40. Niu, N., Easterbrook, S.: Extracting and modeling product line functional requirements. In: 2008 16th IEEE International Requirements Engineering Conference, pp. 155–164 (2008). https://doi.org/10.1109/RE.2008.49
41. Northrop, L.M.: Sei's software product line tenets. IEEE Softw. 19(4), 32–40 (2002). https://doi.org/10.1109/MS.2002.1020285
42. Oizumi, W.N., Contieri Junior, A.C., Correia, G.G., Colanzi, T.E., Ferrari, S., Gimenes, I.M.S., OliveiraJr, E., Garcia, A.F., Masiero, P.C.: On the proactive design of product-line architectures with aspects: an exploratory study. In: 2012 IEEE 36th Annual Computer Software and Applications Conference, pp. 273–278 (2012). https://doi.org/10.1109/COMPSAC.2012.38
43. OliveiraJr, E., Gimenes, I.M.S., Huzita, E.H.M., Maldonado, J.C.: A variability management process for software product lines. In: Proceedings of the 2005 Conference of the Centre for Advanced Studies on Collaborative Research, CASCON '05, pp. 225–241. IBM Press, Indianapolis (2005)
44. OliveiraJr, E., Gimenes, I.M.S., Maldonado, J.C.: Systematic management of variability in UML-based software product lines. J. Univ. Comput. Sci. 16(17), 2374–2393 (2010)
45. Pohl, K., Böckle, G., Linden, F.J.v.d.: Software Product Line Engineering: Foundations, Principles and Techniques. Springer, Berlin (2005)
46. SEI: Software Engineering Institute – Framework for Software Product Line Practice, Version 5.0. https://resources.sei.cmu.edu/asset_files/WhitePaper/2012_019_001_495381.pdf
47. WebArchive: Ford's assembly line turns 100: how it changed manufacturing and society. https://web.archive.org/web/20131130021237/http://www.nydailynews.com/autos/ford-assembly-line-turns-100-changed-society-article-1.1478331
48. Weiss, D.M., Lai, C.T.R.: Software Product-Line Engineering: A Family-Based Software Development Process. Addison-Wesley Longman Publishing Co. Inc., Boston (1999)
49. Wille, D., Runge, T., Seidl, C., Schulze, S.: Extractive software product line engineering using model-based delta module generation. In: Proceedings of the Eleventh International Workshop on Variability Modelling of Software-Intensive Systems, VAMOS '17, pp. 36–43. ACM, New York (2017). https://doi.org/10.1145/3023956.3023957

Chapter 2
Variability Implementation and UML-Based Software Product Lines

Ana Paula Allian, Elisa Yumi Nakagawa, Jabier Martinez, Wesley Klewerton Guez Assunção, and Edson OliveiraJr

Abstract Variability makes it possible to easily change and adapt software systems for specific contexts in a preplanned manner. It has been considered in several research topics, including self-adaptive systems, large-scale enterprise systems, and system-of-systems, and was mainly consolidated by the Software Product Line (SPL) engineering. SPL manages a common platform for developing a family of products with reduced time to market, better quality, and lower cost. Variability in the SPL must be clearly identified, modeled, evaluated, and instantiated. Despite the advances in this field, managing the variability of systems is still challenging for building software-intensive product families. One difficulty is that the software architecture, the cornerstone of any design process, is usually defined with notations and languages lacking accurate forms to describe the variability concerns of software systems. Hence, in this chapter, we analyze approaches used for describing software variability in SPL, paying special attention to the architecture.

A. P. Allian (✉) · E. Y. Nakagawa
Department of Computer Systems, University of São Paulo, São Carlos, Brazil
e-mail: ana.allian@usp.br; elisa@icmc.usp.br

J. Martinez
Tecnalia, Basque Research and Technology Alliance, Derio, Spain
e-mail: jabier.martinez@tecnalia.com

W. K. G. Assunção
ISSE, Johannes Kepler University Linz, Linz, Austria

OPUS, Pontifical Catholic University of Rio de Janeiro, Rio de Janeiro, Brazil
e-mail: wesley.assuncao@jku.at

E. OliveiraJr
Informatics Department, State University of Maringá, Maringá, Paraná, Brazil
e-mail: edson@din.uem.br

E. OliveiraJr (ed), *UML-Based Software Product Line Engineering with SMarty*,
https://doi.org/10.1007/978-3-031-18556-4_2

2.1 Introduction

Variability is a mechanism that allows a system, software asset, or development environment to be configured, customized, or changed for use in a specific domain in a preplanned manner [11]. This mechanism enables the mass customization of software products, which is the basis for creating Software Product Lines (SPL) [9, 26]. An advantage of managing variability is to bring flexibility when constructing families of software systems. For example, variability allows engineers to delay design decisions to later stages during the software development process by using mechanisms to define in which moment concrete design choices are bound to the software products (i.e., binding times) [10, 21, 49].

In a broader view, variability is described by three pieces of information: (i) *variation point* occurs in generic SPL artifacts, allowing the resolution of its variability in one or several locations through its associated variants; (ii) *variants*[1] represent software artifacts or possible elements, which can be chosen and resolved through a variation point; and (iii) *constraints* establish the relationships between two or more variants to resolve their respective points of variation [21, 29]. Once variability is described in an SPL, the configuration of valid products (i.e., configurations) is defined by resolving all variation points using available variants, taking into account existing constraints. As mentioned above, the resolution of variability can be in different binding times, as for example, at design time, compilation time, or runtime.

Variability involves all life cycle phases of a system development through the identification, modeling, derivation, and evaluation of variation points and variants to create specific products in an SPL [9]. Variability can then be associated with different levels of abstraction associated with different stages of software development [29, 39], for instance, at requirements level, architecture description, design documentation, source code, compiled code, linked code, or even executable code. In addition, variability can be initially identified through the concept of *feature* that can be defined as a characteristic of a system that is relevant and visible to end users [4, 26, 39]. Once the set of desired features for an SPL is established, the design of how features are configured to create products is done by defining variation points (i.e., where a feature can vary) and the variants (i.e., which are the alternatives that can be selected for a variation point).

This chapter is structured as follows. Section 2.2 presents the basics for how to model and implement variability. Given the relevance in the topic of the book, Sect. 2.3 focuses on UML-based SPL. Then, Sect. 2.4 presents a discussion, and Sect. 2.5 concludes this chapter with a summary and future directions.

---

[1] For clarification, sometimes the term "variants" is also used to refer to members of a system family (i.e., the whole product variant), as an alternative to the term "products."

2.2 Implementing Variability

This section describes key concepts for implementing variability. Notably, a family of software products can be developed by properly specifying two dimensions of decomposition, known as *variability in problem space* and *variability in solution space*. Sections 2.2.1 and 2.2.2 present the variability in the problem space and solution space, respectively. Section 2.2.3 discusses existing tooling support.

2.2.1 Variability in the Problem Space

Variability in problem space refers to identifying features that may vary to express different products during domain analysis. Domain analysis assumes the existence of an SPL infrastructure to identify variations and features that may vary according to the needs of market segments or business goals [11]. Two main techniques to support domain analysis are:

- **Questionnaire-based analysis:** it is based on surveys, questions, and meetings with domain experts aiming to identify what can vary in SPL. Questions are used to support the identification of variability: *"what does it vary?"* is used for identifying variation points; *"why does it vary?"* and *"how does it vary?"* are used for identifying variants. Extending the questions proposed in [44], Milani et al. [36] developed a framework to identify and classify variation drivers in the business architecture layer based on w-questions (how, what, where, who, and when). The variability elicitation starts with identifying branching points (variation points) from the business process model. Each branching point is classified as a decision or as a variation point. When a variation point is identified, the analysis goes to identifying variation drivers (variants) with the support of w-questions. This activity must be repeated for each branching point of the process models; however, an architectural process must be given as input.
- **Scenario-based analysis:** it supports the identification of risks by analyzing anticipated changes to be made in the software systems and architectures; as a consequence, it results in suitable mitigation actions introduced before the software system is completely designed. Park et al. [41], Moon et al. [37], Pohl et al. [44], Weiss et al. [52], Meekel et al. [34], Tekinerdogan and Aksit [50], Kim et al. [27], and Bayer et al. [7, 8] proposed solutions to identify variability in Product Line Architectures (PLAs) through scenario-based analysis. The process starts with the detection of goals, and a scenario composed of one or more actions is created for each goal with purposeful interactions. Then, a feature is attached to scenario actions, which guide the identification of domain requirements, actors, and variability during the requirements elicitation analysis.

Several notations exist to capture the configuration space defined through the domain analysis, as the well-established ones listed below:

- **Feature modeling:** Feature models offer a formal way to describe variability by defining features and their dependencies [26]. The two main components of a feature model are features and relationships. Variability is described using a hierarchical decomposition of features connected between each other that yields a tree-like structure. Figure 2.1 presents an example of a feature model with eight features connected through different relationships [46].
- **Decision modeling:** Decision models focus on capturing variability in the form of a set of requirements and engineering decisions that are mandatory to describe and construct a product [17]. Additionally, these models enable to determine the extent of possible variation among desired products of the domain [49]. Decision models are usually represented using tables or spreadsheets. Figure 2.2 illustrates a decision model [49].
- **Orthogonal variability modeling:** Orthogonal variability models (OVMs) are based on a language that defines the variability of products using a cross-sectional view across all product line artifacts [44]. For example, OVM allows modeling variability by interrelating base models such as requirement models, design

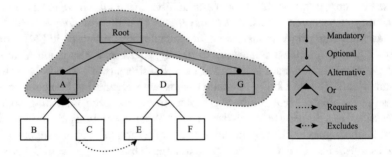

Fig. 2.1 Example of feature model, extracted from [46]

Example of a decision model

Name	Relevance	Description	Range	Selection	Constraints	Binding Times
Memory	System_Mem = True	Does the system have memory?	TRUE, FALSE	1		Compile Time
Memory_Size		The amount of memory the system has (KB)	0..100.000	1	Memory=TRUE => Memory_Size > 0	Installation, System Initialisation
Time_Measure-ment		How is time measurement done?	Hardware, Software	1		Compile Time

Fig. 2.2 Example of decision model, extracted from [49]

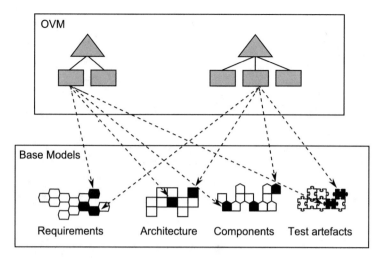

Fig. 2.3 Illustration of an orthogonal variability model, extracted from [46]

models, component models, and test models, as illustrated in Fig. 2.3. These
dependencies among base models and OVM enable traceability to support the
SPL engineering [35].

2.2.2   Variability in the Solution Space

Variability in the solution space describes the representation of features that are
used to realize the problem space. Different approaches can describe variability
in the solution space, mostly depending on the artifacts type. Existing approaches
are classified mainly into two categories [48]: (i) *negative variability* considers
one model for all products (also known as 150% models) with variant information
determining which model elements are present in which products or features, and
(ii) *positive variability* associates model fragments to features and composes them
for a given feature configuration. Negative and positive variability can be used with
any artifact during the SPL development, including hybrid approaches; however, in
this chapter, we focus on the main approaches to deal with source code and design
models.

Variability in source code.   There are two main approaches to describe variability
in the source code, namely, annotative or compositional:

- **Annotative approach**: This negative variability approach is based on annotative
  directives used to indicate pieces of code that should be compiled/included or
  not based on the value of variables [24]. The pieces of code can be marked at
  the granularity of a single line of code or to a whole file. Feature toggling is also

```
public final class DiagramFactory {
  private DiagramFactory() {
    super();
    diagramClasses.put(DiagramType.Class, UMLClassDiagram.class);
    //#if defined(USECASEDIAGRAM)
    diagramClasses.put(DiagramType.UseCase, UMLUseCaseDiagram.class);
    //#endif
    //#if defined(STATEDIAGRAM)
    diagramClasses.put(DiagramType.State, UMLStateDiagram.class);
    //#endif
    //#if defined(DEPLOYMENTDIAGRAM)
    diagramClasses.put(DiagramType.Deployment, UMLDeploymentDiagram.class);
    //#endif
    //#if defined(COLLABORATIONDIAGRAM)
    diagramClasses.put(DiagramType.Collaboration, UMLCollaborationDiagram.class);
    //#endif
    //#if defined(ACTIVITYDIAGRAM)
    diagramClasses.put(DiagramType.Activity, UMLActivityDiagram.class);
    //#endif
    //#if defined(SEQUENCEDIAGRAM)
    diagramClasses.put(DiagramType.Sequence, UMLSequenceDiagram.class);
    //#endif
  }
  ...
}
```

Fig. 2.4 Example of variability management with annotative directives (extracted from [38])

a used annotative approach [32] where there is no need for specific variability management libraries, as the annotations are based on the standard if clauses of the target programming language. Variability annotations have long been used in programming languages like C but can also be used in object-oriented languages, such as C++ [24] and Java [38]. Figure 2.4 presents a code snippet illustrating the use of preprocessor directives in ArgoUML-SPL [38]. The preprocessor directives //#if and //#endif are applied to indicate the beginning and end of each line of code belonging to a specific feature.

- **Compositional approach**: This positive variability approach is based on the addition of implementation fragments in specified places of a system [4]. The compositional approach enables SPL engineers to define separated reusable assets composed during derivation when features are selected. A widely known implementation is the superimposition approach [3]. The code snippet in Fig. 2.5 was extracted from Gruntfile,[2] which is another solution used to compose products implemented in JavaScript. The modules in the figure have a name and are followed by a brief description, if they are optional or not, and if they are replaceable by a stub version. During the building process, developers are able to define which modules they would like to exclude from their build.

---

[2] https://gruntjs.com/sample-gruntfile.

```
var modules = {
    'intro':        { 'description': 'Phaser UMD wrapper',
                      'optional': true, 'stub': false },
    'phaser':       { 'description': 'Phaser Globals',
                      'optional': false, 'stub': false },
    'geom':         { 'description': 'Geometry Classes',
                      'optional': false, 'stub': false },
    'core':         { 'description': 'Phaser Core',
                      'optional': false, 'stub': false },
    'input':        { 'description': 'Input Manager + Mouse and Touch
                      Support', 'optional': false, 'stub': false },
    'gamepad':      { 'description': 'Gamepad Input',
                      'optional': true, 'stub': false },
    'keyboard':     { 'description': 'Keyboard Input',
                      'optional': true, 'stub': false },
    'components':   { 'description': 'Game Object Components',
                      'optional': false, 'stub': false },
    'gameobjects':  { 'description': 'Core Game Objects',
                      'optional': false, 'stub': false },
    'bitmapdata':   { 'description': 'BitmapData Game Object',
                      'optional': true, 'stub': false },
    'graphics':     { 'description': 'Graphics and PIXI Mask Support',
                      'optional': true, 'stub': false },
    'rendertexture':{ 'description': 'RenderTexture Game Object',
                      'optional': true, 'stub': false },
    'text':         { 'description': 'Text Game Object (inc. Web
                      Support)', 'optional': true, 'stub': false },
    'bitmaptext':   { 'description': 'BitmapText Game Object',
                      'optional': true, 'stub': false },
    'retrofont':    { 'description': 'Retro Fonts Game Object',
                      'optional': true, 'stub': false },
    ...
};
```

Fig. 2.5 Example of variability management with compositional approach (extracted from [38])

Variability in design models. Most approaches to represent variability in design models are UML-based, ADL-based, and domain-specific [2]. Following, we present an overview of these approaches:

- **UML-based approaches:** They describe variability in software systems based on UML properties, such as stereotypes and inheritance. Different UML-based approaches have been developed to model variability in SPL. These approaches usually describe a metamodel where inheritance associations are represented as variants, and variability relationship properties are expressed as a Boolean formula.
- **ADL-based approaches:** They describe variability using code and formal representation, supporting the variability's evolution and automatic formal analysis. An example of an ADL-based approach is FX-MAN [14], a component model that incorporates variation points and composition mechanisms to handle variability in PLAs. EAST-ADL [28] is focused on a formal architecture

description and offers a complete feature model technique to represent variability in embedded system domains (automotive electronic systems). ADLARS [5], an architecture description language, captures variability information from feature models and links them to architecture structure using keyword descriptions. ArchStudio4 [16] is an open-source tool that implements an environment of integrated tools for modeling, visualizing, analyzing, and implementing software and systems architectures. For variability management, ArchStudio has a tool called product line selector with a user interface that enables graphically invoking the Selector, Pruner, and Version Pruner components. Hence, product architecture can be derived from a PLA automatically selected based on user-specified variable-value bindings. Finally, xLineMapper [15] is an Eclipse-based toolset to manage the relationships automatically (e.g., traceability, conformance) among product line features, architecture, and source code.

- **Domain-specific approaches:** They provide specific constructs and other techniques that complement UML and ADL notations. For example, Common Variability Language (CVL) models variability in architecture with metamodels combining representation of variability with its resolution [19]. The Variability Modeling Language (VML) represents variation points, features, constraints, and variants as entities in a textual language format. VML links the features in the feature model to architectural elements (e.g., components and compositions) by allowing features to be selected for specific variation points [31]. Alternatives to CVL are KCVL and BVR. KCVL[3] is bundled as a set of Eclipse plugins with a basic implementation of the OMG CVL with several additional features, namely, a textual editor for expressing variability abstraction models, variability realization models, and resolution models. Base Variability Resolution (BVR) [51] is a tool bundle to support SPL engineering and implements a language with advanced concepts for feature modeling, reuse, and realization of components in SPL. BVR covers design, implementation, and quality assurance to close the development cycle.

2.2.3   SPL Variability Tools

For nearly 30 years, industry and academia have proposed many variability tools to cope with the complexity of modeling variability in SPL [23]. Much research effort and investment have been already devoted to investigating, developing, and making available these tools [6, 30, 43].

Most tools represent variability with a graphical representation of features using *feature-oriented domain analysis* (FODA) [26] and its extensions. Examples of such tools are pure::variants, FeatureIDE, SPLOT, fmp, Clafer, GEARS, Fama, CVL, Hephaestus, CaptainFeature, PlugSPL, EASy-Producer, FW Profile, PREEVision,

---

[3] https://diverse-project.github.io/kcvl/.

Kconfig, and TypeChef [6]. Commercial tools like pure::variants and GEARS and open-source tools like FeatureIDE, CVL, and PLUM provide integration support to different tools to encompass more variability management functionalities. Some practitioners from the industry claimed that some tools fail to integrate with new technologies, including cloud and mobile applications. They stated the need for an independent application with graphical editors apart from Eclipse-based plugins.

The main concern to adopting feature models instead of UML on these tools is related to the graphical representation. UML suffers from low expressiveness to represent detailed variability concerns due to visualization to handle large variability models with multiple dependencies among them. Scalability has been a big challenge when considering millions of features (and variants) in the variability model. Ways to improve such scalability and usability of tools concerning adequate model visualization are still open research issues.

2.3 Overview of UML-Based SPL

Over the last three decades, the SPL community has witnessed a significant evolution from traditional feature-based model representation such as FODA [26] to more sophisticated languages to represent and configure variability to derive distinct products. UML is the most well-known and easier notation for modeling software systems [25] and has also been widely adopted to model variability in SPL [45]. UML can be easily extended in standardized ways; hence, generic UML models can be used to describe variability.

Some initiatives have been proposed based on the possibility of extending UML to describe variability. Ziadi et al. [53, 54] leveraged the idea that UML models can be considered reference models from which product models can be derived and created. Based on that, those authors proposed using UML extension mechanisms to specify product line variability in UML class diagrams and sequence diagrams. Basically, Ziadi et al. introduced two types of variability using stereotypes: (i) *optionality*, which indicates that a UML element is optional for the SPL members, represented by «optional», and (ii) *variation*, in which a variation point will be defined by an abstract class stereotyped «variation» and a set of subclasses stereotyped «variant». Figure 2.6 presents an example of a camera SPL with the proposed stereotypes.

Other UML-based approaches have been developed to model variability in SPL. Clauß [13] describes a metamodel where inheritance associations are represented as variants, and variability relationship properties are expressed as a Boolean formula (i.e., (component 1) XOR (component 2)). Pascual et al. [42] also made use of inheritance associations and included the use of cardinality properties to represent variability (i.e., Optional (0..*), alternatives (1..*)). Albassam and Gomaa [1, 18] introduced the Product Line UML-based Software (PLUS) method, an extension of UML to explicitly model variability and commonality in PLAs. VarSOAML [12] is another UML extension that allows modeling variability in services architectures.

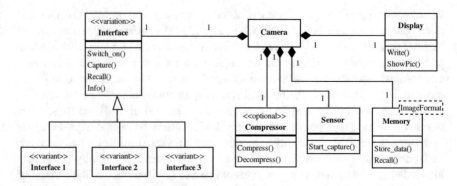

Fig. 2.6 Class diagram of a camera SPL with Ziadi et al. stereotypes, extracted from [53]

VxUML [22] models variability in architecture using many properties extracted from UML notation (i.e., stereotypes, diagrams, inheritance). Systems Modeling Language (SysML) is based on UML and can represent variability by combining SysML block diagrams with variants in the variability model. Ortiz et al. [40] present an example of a study that addresses variability with SysML. It uses thick lines to represent mandatory elements and dotted lines to represent variability elements. Guessi et al. [20] show a regular notation for SysML where optional blocks are represented with bold lines and fonts. This notation can be used to describe reference architectures and facilitate the identification of variable elements.

One of the main benefits of specifying variability in UML-based approaches is the usability for stakeholders. One disadvantage is the poor scalability of UML models when the number of variants increases [11] and the poor derivation process of variability models from UML notations to code. Besides that, maintaining the variability model embedded with UML constructs is hard when we add or remove variants and their corresponding constraints [11]. Therefore, expressing variability with UML must count on several UML diagrams, including use case, class, activity, components, and sequence diagrams. The Stereotype-based Management of Variability (SMarty), presented further in Chap. 4, explores various UML diagrams to provide a broader view of variability in SPL [39].

2.4 Discussion

This chapter summarizes the main approaches proposed to handle variability, considering its identification and representation. Most approaches for variability identification focus on SPL and were proposed in academic contexts. Domain analysis is a key process for eliciting reusable assets for SPL. Many domain analysis approaches depend on SPL infrastructure and experience from stakeholders for identifying variability and commonalities. In general, the list of features (different characteristics of a given system and relations among them) identified during the domain analysis are further modeled with feature models. Domain analysis encompasses many activities to guide stakeholders during the identification of variability in SPL, and some activities might be helpful at different architectural levels, including enterprise architecture, software architecture, and reference architecture. However, these architectures are often designed without explicitly considering information about variability. A crucial cause of this problem is that the variability information exists as tacit knowledge in architects' minds, and it is rarely documented explicitly [33, 47]. Although UML-based approaches are easy to understand, their limitations in terms of visualization and scalability to describe large variability models are major drawbacks. There is still a lack of a unique variability modeling solution that various variability modeling tools could adopt. Apart from this, the inability of graphical representations and the fact that most domain-specific languages lack support for runtime concerns or dynamic variability are another drawbacks of the existing approaches. New notations are needed to handle the changes in variability models at a post-deployment time. For the future, we believe more effort must be put into interoperability concerns among the existing tools and languages to facilitate a smooth transition from variability models to implementation and from configuration to derivation process where the variability is realized.

2.5 Final Remarks

This chapter provided a general view of existing approaches to handle variability in SPL. Such approaches offer important advantages for software development, as efforts for introducing variability in the architecture are reduced, and the reusability of architectural elements is improved. UML-based approaches simplify the variability representation through stereotypes and inheritance mechanisms, whereas ADL-, CVL-, and VML-based approaches, combined with tools, provide better support for configuration and runtime derivation capabilities.

Variability in SPL lacks a support tool capable of fully handling variability from identification, representation, and evaluation of variability and also derivation of concrete architectures. To improve such approaches, more empirical evaluations with industrial partners are needed, aiming to demonstrate the importance of handling variability in SPL. Results from such evaluations would allow other researchers to adequate their approaches to industrial needs.

Acknowledgments The work is supported by the Brazilian funding agencies FAPESP (grants 2015/24144-7, 2016/05919-0, 2018/20882-1), CNPq (Grant 313245/2021-5), and Carlos Chagas Filho Foundation for Supporting Research in the State of Rio de Janeiro (FAPERJ), under the PDR-10 program, grant 202073/2020.

References

1. Albassam, E., Gomaa, H.: Applying software product lines to multiplatform video games. In: 3rd International Workshop on Games and Software Engineering: Engineering Computer Games to Enable Positive, Progressive Change (GAS), pp. 1–7. IEEE Computer Society, San Francisco (2013)
2. Allian, A.P., Capilla, R., Nakagawa, E.Y.: Observations from variability modelling approaches at the architecture level. In: Software Engineering for Variability Intensive Systems – Foundations and Applications, pp. 41–56. Auerbach Publications/Taylor & Francis, Milton Park (2019)
3. Apel, S., Kastner, C., Lengauer, C.: FEATUREHOUSE: Language-independent, automated software composition. In: Proceedings of the 31st International Conference on Software Engineering, ICSE '09, pp. 221–231. IEEE Computer Society, Washington (2009)
4. Apel, S., Batory, D., Kästner, C., Saake, G.: Feature-Oriented Software Product Lines. Springer, Berlin (2016)
5. Bashroush, R., Brown, T.J., Spence, I.T.A., Kilpatrick, P.: ADLARS: an architecture description language for software product lines. In: 29th Annual IEEE/NASA Software Engineering Workshop (SEW), pp. 163–173. IEEE Computer Society, Greenbelt (2005)
6. Bashroush, R., Garba, M., Rabiser, R., Groher, I., Botterweck, G.: CASE tool support for variability management in software product lines. ACM Comput. Surv. **50**(1), 14:1–14:45 (2017)
7. Bayer, J., Flege, O., Knauber, P., Laqua, R., Muthig, D., Schmid, K., Widen, T., DeBaud, J.: Pulse: a methodology to develop software product lines. In: Symposium on Software reusability (SSR), Los Angeles, pp. 122–131 (1999)
8. Bayer, J., Flege, O., Knauber, P., Laqua, R., Muthig, D., Schmid, K., Widen, T., DeBaud, J.M.: Pulse: a methodology to develop software product lines. In: Proceedings of the 1999 Symposium on Software Reusability (SSR), pp. 122–131. ACM, Los Angeles (1999)
9. Bosch, J., Capilla, R., Hilliard, R.: Trends in systems and software variability. IEEE Softw. **32**(3), 44–51 (2015)
10. Capilla, R., Bosch, J.: Binding Time and Evolution, pp. 57–73. Springer, Berlin (2013). https://doi.org/10.1007/978-3-642-36583-6_4
11. Capilla, R., Bosch, J., Kang, K.C.: Systems and Software Variability Management: Concepts, Tools and Experiences. Springer, Berlin (2013)
12. Chakir, B., Fredj, M., Nassar, M.: A model driven method for promoting reuse in SOA-solutions by managing variability. Computing Research Repository (CoRR), abs/1207.2742 (2012)
13. Clauß, M.: Modeling variability with UML. In: 3rd International Conference on Generative and Component-Based Software Engineering (GCSE), pp. 1–5. Springer, Berlin (2001)
14. Cola, S.D., Tran, C.M., Lau, K., Qian, C., Schulze, M.: A component model for defining software product families with explicit variation points. In: 19th International ACM SIGSOFT Symposium on Component-Based Software Engineering (CBSE), pp. 79–84. IEEE Computer Society, Venice (2016)
15. Cu, C., Ye, X., Zheng, Y.: Xlinemapper: a product line feature-architecture-implementation mapping toolset. In: 41st International Conference on Software Engineering: Companion Proceedings, ICSE '19, pp. 87–90. IEEE Press, Piscataway (2019). https://doi.org/10.1109/ICSE-Companion.2019.00045
16. Dashofy, E., Asuncion, M., Hendrickson, S., Suryanarayana, G., Georgas, J., Taylor, R.: Archstudio 4: an architecture-based meta-modeling environment. In: 29th International Conference on Software Engineering (ICSE'07 Companion), pp. 67–68. IEEE, Piscataway (2007)
17. Dhungana, D., Grünbacher, P.: Understanding decision-oriented variability modelling. In: Software Product Line Conference – SPLC (2), pp. 233–242 (2008)
18. Gomaa, H.: Designing Software Product Lines with UML – from Use Cases to Pattern-Based Software Architectures. ACM, New York (2005)

19. Gonzalez-Huerta, J., Abrahão, S., Insfrán, E., Lewis, B.: Automatic derivation of AADL product architectures in software product line development. In: 1st International Workshop on Architecture Centric Virtual Integration and 17th International Conference on Model Driven Engineering Languages and Systems (ACVI/MoDELS), pp. 1–10. CEUR-WS.org, Valencia (2014)
20. Guessi, M., Oquendo, F., Nakagawa, E.Y.: Variability viewpoint to describe reference architectures. In: Working IEEE/IFIP Conference on Software Architecture (WICSA), pp. 14:1–14:6. ACM, Sydney (2014)
21. Halmans, G., Pohl, K.: Communicating the variability of a software-product family to customers. Softw. Syst. Model. **2**(1), 15–36 (2003)
22. He, X., Fu, Y., Sun, C., Ma, Z., Shao, W.: Towards model-driven variability-based flexible service compositions. In: 39th IEEE Annual Computer Software and Applications Conference, COMPSAC, pp. 298–303. IEEE Computer Society, Taichung (2015)
23. Horcas, J.M., Pinto, M., Fuentes, L.: Software product line engineering: a practical experience. In: Proceedings of the 23rd International Systems and Software Product Line Conference, SPLC 2019, Paris, September 9–13, 2019, vol. A, pp. 25:1–25:13. ACM, New York (2019)
24. Hu, Y., Merlo, E., Dagenais, M., Lague, B.: C/c++ conditional compilation analysis using symbolic execution. In: 30th International Conference on Software Maintenance, ICSM '00. ACM, New York (2000)
25. Júnior, E., Farias, K., Silva, B.: A Survey on the Use of UML in the Brazilian Industry, pp. 275–284. Association for Computing Machinery, New York (2021). https://doi.org/10. 1145/3474624.3474632
26. Kang, K., Cohen, S., Hess, J., Novak, W., Peterson, A.: Feature-oriented domain analysis (FODA) feasibility study. Technical Report. CMU/SEI-90-TR-021, Software Engineering Institute, Carnegie Mellon University, Pittsburgh (1990). http://resources.sei.cmu.edu/library/ asset-view.cfm?AssetID=11231
27. Kim, M., Yang, H., Park, S.: A domain analysis method for software product lines based on scenarios, goals and features. In: 10th Asia-Pacific Software Engineering Conference (APSEC), pp. 126–135. IEEE Computer Society, Chiang Mai (2003)
28. Leitner, A., Mader, R., Kreiner, C., Steger, C., Weiß, R.: A development methodology for variant-rich automotive software architectures. Elektrotechnik und Informationstechnik **128**(6), 222–227 (2011)
29. Linden, F.J.V.D., Schmid, K., Rommes, E.: Software Product Lines in Action: The Best Industrial Practice in Product Line Engineering, vol. 20. Springer, New York (2007)
30. Lisboa, L.B., Garcia, V.C., Lucrédio, D., de Almeida, E.S., de Lemos Meira, S.R., de Mattos Fortes, R.P.: A systematic review of domain analysis tools. Inf. Softw. Technol. **52**(1), 1–13 (2010)
31. Loughran, N., Sánchez, P., Garcia, A., Fuentes, L.: Language support for managing variability in architectural models. In: 7th International Symposium on Software Composition (SC), pp. 36–51. Springer, Budapest (2008)
32. Mahdavi-Hezaveh, R., Dremann, J., Williams, L.: Software development with feature toggles: practices used by practitioners. Empir. Softw. Eng. **26**(1) (2021)
33. Martínez-Fernández, S., Ayala, C.P., Franch, X., Marques, H.M.: Benefits and drawbacks of software reference architectures: a case study. Inf. Softw. Technol. **88**, 37–52 (2017)
34. Meekel, J., Horton, T.B., Mellone, C.: Architecting for domain variability. In: 2nd International ESPRIT ARES Workshop on Development and Evolution of Software Architectures for Product Families, pp. 205–213. Springer, Berlin (1998)
35. Metzger, A., Pohl, K., Heymans, P., Schobbens, P.Y., Saval, G.: Disambiguating the documentation of variability in software product lines: a separation of concerns, formalization and automated analysis. In: 15th IEEE International Requirements Engineering Conference (RE 2007), pp. 243–253. IEEE, Piscataway (2007)
36. Milani, F., Dumas, M., Matulevicius, R.: Identifying and classifying variations in business processes. In: Enterprise, Business-Process and Information Systems Modeling – 13th International Conference, BPMDS 2012, 17th International Conference, EMMSAD 2012, and 5th EuroSymposium, held at CAiSE 2012, pp. 136–150. Springer, Gdańsk (2012)

37. Moon, M., Yeom, K., Chae, H.S.: An approach to developing domain requirements as a core asset based on commonality and variability analysis in a product line. IEEE Trans. Softw. Eng. **31**(7), 551–569 (2005)
38. Moreira, R.A.F., Assunção, W.K., Martinez, J., Figueiredo, E.: Open-source software product line extraction processes: the argoUML-SPL and phaser cases. Empir. Softw. Eng. **27**(4), 1–35 (2022)
39. OliveiraJr, E., Gimenes, I.M.S., Maldonado, J.C., Masiero, P.C., Barroca, L.: Systematic evaluation of software product line architectures. J. Univer. Comput. Sci. **19**(1), 25–52 (2013)
40. Ortiz, F.J., Pastor, J.A., Alonso, D., Losilla, F., de Jódar, E.: A reference architecture for managing variability among teleoperated service robots. In: 2nd International Conference on Informatics in Control, Automation and Robotics (ICINCO), pp. 322–328. INSTICC Press, Barcelona (2005)
41. Park, S., Kim, M., Sugumaran, V.: A scenario, goal and feature-oriented domain analysis approach for developing software product lines. Ind. Manag. Data Syst. **104**(4), 296–308 (2004)
42. Pascual, G.G., Pinto, M., Fuentes, L.: Automatic analysis of software architectures with variability. In: 13th International Conference on Software Reuse (ICSR), pp. 127–143. Springer, Pisa (2013)
43. Pereira, J.A., Constantino, K., Figueiredo, E.: A systematic literature review of software product line management tools. In: 14th International Conference on Software Reuse for Dynamic Systems in the Cloud and Beyond (ICSR), pp. 73–89. Springer International Publishing, Miami (2015)
44. Pohl, K., Böckle, G., van der Linden, F.: Software product line engineering: foundations, principles, and techniques, Springer, Berlin (2005)
45. Raatikainen, M., Tiihonen, J., Männistö, T.: Software product lines and variability modeling: a tertiary study. J. Syst. Softw. **149**, 485–510 (2019)
46. Roos-Frantz, F., Benavides, D., Ruiz-Cortés, A., Heuer, A., Lauenroth, K.: Quality-aware analysis in product line engineering with the orthogonal variability model. Softw. Qual. J. **20**(3–4), 519–565 (2011). https://doi.org/10.1007/s11219-011-9156-5
47. Rurua, N., Eshuis, R., Razavian, M.: Representing variability in enterprise architecture. Bus. Inf. Syst. Eng. **61**(2), 215–227, (2019)
48. Schaefer, I.: Variability modelling for model-driven development of software product lines. In: 4th International Workshop on Variability Modelling of Software-Intensive Systems (VaMoS), pp. 85–92 (2010)
49. Schmid, K., John, I.: A customizable approach to full lifecycle variability management. Sci. Comput. Program. **53**(3), 259–284 (2004)
50. Tekinerdogan, B., Aksit, M.: Managing variability in product line scoping using design space models. In: Journal of The American Chemical Society, pp. 1–8. Elsevier, Groningen (2003)
51. Vasilevskiy, A., Haugen, Ø., Chauvel, F., Johansen, M.F., Shimbara, D.: The BVR tool bundle to support product line engineering. In: Proceedings of the 19th International Conference on Software Product Line, pp. 380–384 (2015)
52. Weiss, D.M., Lai, C.T.R.: Software Product-Line Engineering: A Family-Based Software Development Process. Addison-Wesley Longman Publishing Co. Inc., Boston (1999)
53. Ziadi, T., Hélouët, L., Jézéquel, J.: Towards a UML profile for software product lines. In: Software Product-Family Engineering, 5th International Workshop, PFE 2003, Siena, November 4–6, 2003, Revised Papers. Lecture Notes in Computer Science, vol. 3014, pp. 129–139. Springer, Berlin (2003)
54. Ziadi, T., Jézéquel, J.: Software product line engineering with the UML: deriving products. In: Software Product Lines – Research Issues in Engineering and Management, pp. 557–588. Springer, Berlin (2006)

Chapter 3
Software Product Line Architectures

Crescencio Lima, Thelma Elita Colanzi, Matthias Galster, Ivan Machado, and Edson OliveiraJr

Abstract The architecture of a Software Product Line (or Product Line Architecture, PLA) is one of the most important assets of a Software Product Line (SPL) as it represents an abstraction of all the products that can be generated in an SPL. Furthermore, the PLA is crucial for the development and evolution of an SPL. It represents the architecture of all potential products from a specific product line domain. The PLA addresses the SPL design decisions by explicitly representing similarities between product variants as well as the desired variability between them. A PLA differs from a single-product architecture in two aspects: (1) scope, i.e., the PLA describes broad design decisions relevant to related products for a given domain; (2) completeness, i.e., the PLA captures only parts of single products (which do not have unspecified or "variable" parts). Designing PLAs involves various activities and techniques, such as business case analysis, scope analysis, architectural design based on functionalities, and architecture transformation. When designing a PLA, it is important to explicitly accommodate variability (typically in the form of "variation points" in the architecture). Also, the design of a PLA needs to explicitly address quality attributes, such as complexity, extensibility, and reusability. These quality attributes are then used to evaluate the PLA to ensure (a) a PLA that supports product derivation and (b) a PLA that helps product variants meet the quality goals relevant in a domain (e.g., performance, security). Therefore, this chapter provides essential concepts on PLA, its design and variability issues.

C. Lima (✉)
Federal Institute of Bahia, Vitória da Conquista, Bahia, Brazil

T. E. Colanzi · E. OliveiraJr
State University of Maringá, Informatics Department, Maringá, Paraná, Brazil
e-mail: thelma@din.uem.br; edson@din.uem.br

M. Galster
University of Canterbury, Christchurch, New Zealand
e-mail: mgalster@ieee.org

I. Machado
Federal University of Bahia, Salvador, Bahia, Brazil
e-mail: ivan.machado@ufba.br

© Springer Nature Switzerland AG 2023
E. OliveiraJr (ed), *UML-Based Software Product Line Engineering with SMarty*,
https://doi.org/10.1007/978-3-031-18556-4_3

Finally, we present the design of a PLA aiming at illustrating the main concepts addressed in this chapter.

3.1 Software Architecture Foundations

Before discussing Product Line Architectures (PLA) in more detail, we provide an overview of the concept and relevance of software architecture in general, regardless of whether the architecture is for a product line or individual systems.

3.1.1 What Is Software Architecture

In the context of this chapter, we define software architecture as the discipline within software engineering that is responsible for designing the system organization and its components, as well as its internal and external interactions. It also indicates that software architecture considers the stakeholders priorities (e.g., in terms of functionality and quality). The software engineering community has come up with many different definitions for software architecture and what is a software architecture; see, for instance, the Software Engineering Institute's (SEI) collection of definitions.[1] However, although each definition has specific characteristics, they capture the same general idea. That is, the software architecture defines the high-level software design [3].

Shaw and Garlan consider the architecture as the top-level decomposition of a system (or a set of systems) into its main components and the design process leading to that decomposition. In other words, the architecture of a software system is defined as computational components and the interactions among those components [28]. In a different definition, Taylor et al. [30] argue that the software architecture of a system is "the set of principal design decisions made during its development and any subsequent evolution, where stakeholders decide which aspects are the principal ones" [30]. Similarly, Bass et al. [3] refer to the software architecture as "the structure of a system, consisting of software elements, externally visible properties, and the relationships among elements" [3]. ISO/IEC/IEEE 42010, a standard for software architecture description [18], defines an architecture as "a set of fundamental concepts or properties of a system in its environment embodied in its elements, relationships, and in the principles of its design and evolution."

The software architecture aids the understanding of how a system will behave and how it should be structured and implemented. This means, when making architectural design decisions, engineers need to reason about a system, its software

---

[1] http://goo.gl/wn6thh.

elements, the relations between them and properties of both, and the system's (quality) attributes, including any trade-offs [3].

Designing and evolving software architectures are collaborative activities. In this regard, Kruchten [20] has challenged one common misconception about software architecture—"the software architecture is the work of a single architect." Instead, Kruchten suggests that an architecture team is needed that offers the right mix of domain and software engineering expertise to design and maintain high quality architectures [20]. In practice, the role of the architect (or architects) is often performed by experienced developers who have the background and expertise to help development teams better understand the architecture from a development perspective [5].

3.1.2   Quality Attributes and Software Architecture

Considering quality attributes throughout software development is crucial for producing systems that meet their desired quality attribute requirements. Architectural design decisions (e.g., the choice of architectural patterns, tactics, technologies, etc.) significantly impact quality attributes. A quality attribute is a characteristic that affects the quality of software systems. Here, quality describes to which degree a system meets specified requirements [16]. The SWEBOK guide [4], which integrates other quality frameworks, such as the IEEE Standard for a Software Quality Metrics Methodology [17], or ISO standards [29], distinguishes the following types of quality attributes:

- Quality attributes discernible at runtime (e.g., performance, security, safety, availability, usability)
- Quality attributes not discernible at runtime (e.g., modifiability, reusability, portability, maintainability, deployability)
- Quality attributes related to the architecture's intrinsic qualities (e.g., conceptual integrity, correctness)

In addition, Bass et al. [3] differentiate quality attributes of the system (e.g., availability, modifiability), business quality attributes (e.g., time to market), and quality attributes that are about the architecture (e.g., correctness, consistency, conceptual integrity) [3]. This means there are quality attributes which directly apply to a system and quality attributes in term of business quality goals (e.g., time to market, cost and benefit, and targeted market) that shape a system's architecture [3].

3.1.3   Software Architecture Descriptions

The Joint Technical Committee ISO/IEC in cooperation with the Software and Systems Engineering Standards Committee of the IEEE Computer Society developed the ISO/IEC/IEEE 42010 standard for architecture description in systems and software engineering [18]. This standard addresses the creation, analysis, and evolution of systems architectures based on architecture descriptions. In this context the standard defines several fundamental concepts:

- An *architecture description* is the set of artifacts that document an architecture. It contains one or more architectural views.
- An *architectural view* represents the software architecture that addresses one or more stakeholders' concerns.
- A *viewpoint* defines the perspective from which an architecture view is taken. It specifies how to create and use an architecture view, as well as the information that should appear in the view, the modeling techniques for expressing and analyzing the information, and a rationale for these choices.
- A *concern* is an interest that stakeholders have in a system and its description. An architecture viewpoint frames one or more concerns. A concern can be framed by more than one viewpoint.
- An *architecture model* uses appropriate modeling conventions and notations to address concerns. An architectural view consists of one or more architectural models.
- A *model kind* specifies the conventions that govern architectural models. An architecture model can be part of more than one architecture view within an architecture description.

For instance, Clements et al. [8] in their approach for architecture description (which is well aligned with the ISO/IEC/IEEE 42010 standard) present three kinds of architectural views: module, component-and-connector, and allocation. The module views are concerned with documenting a system's principal units of implementation. Component-and-connector views document the system's units of execution. Allocation views document the relations between a system's software and non-software resources of the development and execution environments.

In the next subsections, we present two architecture models commonly used to represent the module view: Module Dependency Graph and Design Structure Matrix.

3.1.3.1 Module Dependency Graph

Module Dependency Graph (MDG) represents the software elements (such as packages, classes, modules, and so on) and relationships used in the architectural description of traditional systems [23]. Figure 3.1 presents the MDG for the SPL Mobile Media that describes features to handle music, videos, and photos on portable devices [36]. This MDG presents Mobile Media packages and its relationships. For instance, the package ubc.mdip.mobilephoto.core.util calls methods of the packages lancs.midp.mobilephoto.lib.exceptions and ubc.midp.mobilephoto.core.ui.datamodel. The graph represents the relationship by using arrows starting in the package that uses a method

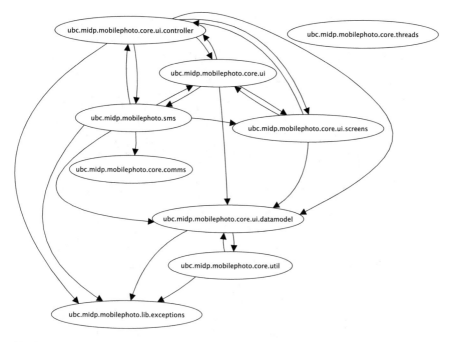

Fig. 3.1 Module dependency graph for Mobile Media [21]

(util) pointing to the packages that implements the methods (exceptions and datamodel).

MDG provides a static view of code (how classes depend on each other in source code) to support designing and maintaining the software architecture. Clean architecture leads to high maintainability and less error-prone code. On the other hand, the dynamic view is relevant for analyzing the performance and memory management purposes.

The visualization helps in the identification of issues in large and complex systems. Consequences of the lack of control on the code structure are entangled components, code smells, and architecture erosion.

3.1.3.2   Design Structure Matrix

According to Eppinger and Browning [11], "Design Structure Matrix" (DSM, also referred to as Dependency Structure Matrix) is a visual representation of a system in the form of a square matrix representing relations between the system elements" [11]. The system elements are labeled in the rows to the left of the matrix and in the columns above the matrix. These elements can represent packages, classes, modules, and product components.

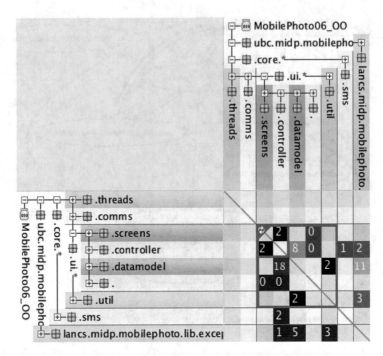

Fig. 3.2 Design structure matrix for Mobile Media created with JArchitect tool [21]

The DSM represents the same information as a graph (MDG), but it provides different details such as the number of dependencies between elements. The DSM row and column headers represent the boxes in the graph. The DSM non-empty cells represent the arrows in the graph.

Figure 3.2 presents the Mobile Media's DSM. It describes the packages' relationships. For instance, the package datamodel calls 18 methods in the package controller.

These two different methods represent the same information and complement each other. The equivalent representation in terms of a graph becomes cluttered and difficult to understand when a large amount of data is available such as in complex systems. On the other hand, the DSM scales provide information to identify architectural patterns at a glance. Moreover, problematic dependencies, such as dependencies between modules, are also straightforward to identify.

In this way, DSM is indicated to analyze large and complex systems. Some partitioning algorithms can be used on the DSM for architectural discovery and management. For software, component or reachability algorithms are recommended because they identify layering and componentization within the software system. The results of the partitioning algorithms are displayed as square boxes, called virtual partitions.

3.1.4 Variability in Software Architecture

According to Gurp et al. [33], "variability is commonly understood as the ability of a software system or software artifacts (e.g., components, modules, libraries) to be adapted so that they fit a specific context" [33]. Galster and Avgeriou [13] and Hilliard [15] stated that "variability is a relevant characteristic of the architectures of software systems [13, 15]—either single systems, product lines, product platforms and ecosystems, and system of systems. It appears in most, if not all systems and therefore a relevant concern for the architectures of those systems" [15].

Variability is facilitated through the software architecture and should therefore be treated as first-class citizen [14]. Software architecture often treats variability as a quality attribute and a cross-cutting concern [13, 14]. Since variability is a concern of different stakeholders and affects other concerns, variability should be managed early and identified during architecting rather than later [31]. Consequently, to develop the appropriate support for architects to deal with variability, we need to anticipate the various problems software architects come across when carrying out variability-related tasks [12]. Architectural variability can be summarized in an *architectural variability model*, described by a set of the *architectural variation points*. Variability is primarily addressed in the Software Product Line (SPL) domain [6, 12–14]. According to Ahmed and Capretz [1], "to address the variability at the architectural level, the community introduced the notion of product line architecture" [1]. We explore Product Line Architectures in more detail in the following sections.

3.2 Software Product Line Architectures Foundations

In this section, we describe the conceptual elements that compose product lines and Product Line Architectures. Then, we discuss about product line design and Product Line Architecture Description.

3.2.1 Product Lines and Product Line Architectures

With the increasing complexity of software-intensive systems, systematic reuse techniques have been successfully adopted in the industry. One example of systematic and non-opportunistic reuse is the adoption of SPL. An SPL is a set of systems for a specific domain sharing common and variable features in core assets [7]. As described by Weiss [35], "one of the most relevant assets of an SPL is the Product Line Architecture (PLA). It encompasses the abstraction of all SPL product software architectures" [35]. A Product Line Architecture captures the central design of all products including variability and commonalities of several product instances [34]. In the context of this chapter, we consider a PLA as a type of software architecture.

However, in contrast to a "single-system architecture," a PLA, also in following cases, systematically addresses and represents variability, variation points, variants, and mechanisms for reuse. Therefore, as stated by Pohl et al. [27], "the PLA is some kind of core architecture that represents a high-level design for all the products of an SPL, including variation points and variants documented in the variability model" [27]. Because the development of an SPL involves the implementation of different structures, processes, interfaces, and activities, it is relevant for practitioners to pay sufficient attention to its architecture.

A PLA is organized in two parts, i.e., the "core" of an SPL (elements and relationships relevant to the architecture of all SPL products) and the variable elements and relationships. In a PLA, an architectural variation point represents the architectural elements responsible for describing the product line variability. It shows parts of the architectural solution of the architectural variability. The set of architectural variation points needs to be consistently resolved and bound to concrete design options. The architecture of an SPL product is an instance of the PLA and can be considered as a single-system architecture.

Figure 3.3 shows conceptual models that link product line and software architecture concepts. Thiel and Hein [32] combined the PLA description using IEEE 1471. We updated the metamodel according to the newer standard ISO/IEC/IEEE 42010 for describing PLA. Moreover, we included an adaptation of the architecture variability extension and design element extension.

There are different terms for Product Line Architectures, such as *domain architecture*, *platform architecture*, and *configuration architecture*. These terms often carry similar meanings and describe the processes and artifacts discussed in this section. In this chapter we treat these terms as synonyms for PLA.

3.2.2   Product Line Design

In the product line design, the PLA is defined. A PLA is usually organized into components, the interfaces provided, and the interfaces required between the components. The PLA defines the scope of functionality that an SPL can handle and plays a big role in determining the quality attributes [22]. For instance, a critical step in the PLA design is the modularization of all the mandatory and variable features in separate components of an SPL. If this is not accomplished, the PLA design needs to be refactored early and hence suffer from a lack of stability over time [9, 24].

In designing the PLA, it supports on the application of architectural patterns, both architectural structure patterns and architectural communication patterns. Architectural structure patterns are applied to the design of the overall PLA structure. These patterns describe how the SPL is structured into components. A component is a unit of composition with contractually specified interfaces. Components can refer to both a high-level design unit and its physical implementation. Architectural

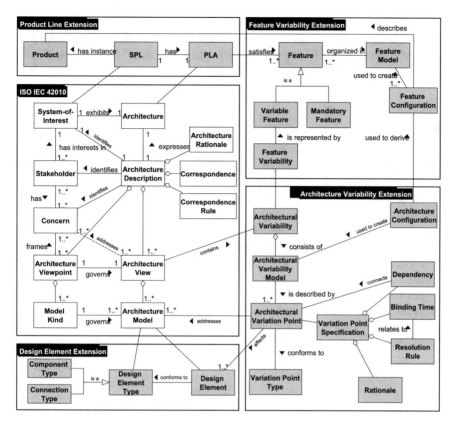

Fig. 3.3 Conceptual elements of software product lines and software architecture [21]—adapted from [32]

communication patterns address the way in which components communicate with each other. Each component is designed such that its interface is explicitly defined in terms of the operations it provides as well as the operations it uses. Communication between distributed components can be synchronous or asynchronous [22]. The adoption of architectural patterns also impacts how required quality attributes are satisfied.

The result of the product line design is a set of different views of the PLA, whereas each view may encompass different models, as presented in Fig. 3.3.

A crucial issue in designing PLAs is how to analyze and model the commonality and variability in the SPL [22]. In an SPL, an architectural element is required by at least one product of the SPL but may not be required by all derived products. The PLA must implement all the variation points of the SPL to support the right scope of products. Therefore, the PLA design contains mandatory, optional, and variant architectural elements. Some of these elements are designed to be configurable so that each element instance can implement a variability in a specific product.

Some other decisions that impact the PLA design are related to which SPL development process will be adopted; the decision of whether generic (or application-specific) components will be developed in-house or not; and the application of some framework in the SPL design.

3.2.3 Product Line Architecture Description

A *PLA Description* is an architecture description enriched with explicit information about the variability model (*Architectural Variability Model* (Fig. 3.3)) of the SPL of interest (*SPL-of-interest*). This means that PLA architecture models must be concerned with the representation of architectural variation points (*Architectural Variation Points*). For PLAs, architectural views are extended with architectural variability representation. Therefore, the architectural variability models consist of architectural variability (*Architectural Variability*) that is represented by different architecture views.

The variability information is represented in development views and architectural elements such as packages and classes. We used the variation point specification (*Variation Point Specification*) for describing the optional and mandatory elements. The former (*optional element*) represents the elements that are implemented by only some variants and the latter (*mandatory element*) represents the ones that are implemented by all the variants.

3.3 Product Line Architectures Versus Reference Architectures

According to Martinez-Fernandez et al. [25], the terms Reference Architecture (RA) and PLA are sometimes used as synonyms in the context of SPL engineering. The term RA is used to refer to "a core architecture that captures the high-level design for the application of the SPL" [27] or "just one asset, albeit an important one, in the SPL asset base" [7]. However, in an SPL context, RA and PLA are considered different types of artifacts [2, 10, 14, 26].

As Angelov et al. [2] claim, "PLAs are RAs whereas not all RAs are PLAs" [2]. PLAs are just one asset of an SPL [7]. According to Nakagawa et al. [26], "RAs provide standardized solutions for a broader domain whereas PLAs provide a standardized solution for a smaller subset of the software system of a domain" [26]. Moreover, PLAs address points of variability and more formal specification to ensure clear and precise behavior specifications at well-specified extension points [2]. In contrast, RAs have less focus on capturing variation points [2, 10, 26]. Also, while a Reference Architecture covers the knowledge in a broader domain, a PLA is more specialized and focuses on a specific set of software systems in a narrower domain [2, 14, 26].

3.4   A Product Line Architecture Example

In this section we illustrate a PLA design for Mobile Media product line [9]. The PLA of Mobile Media is a component-based design that follows the layered architectural style. By adopting this architectural style, quality attributes such as modifiability and maintainability are achieved.

Figure 3.4 presents the development view [19] of the PLA for Mobile Media. The components with suffix *Ctrl* indicate the managers that use the services available in the business layer. These components provide operations via the interface and dialog layers. The business components have the *Mgr* suffix. These components represent application independent elements to be developed. They can be further reused, contributing to the reusability of the PLA design. The system components *AlbumCtrl* and *MediaCtrl* use the interfaces provided by business components, which allow managing different types of media.

Furthermore, Fig. 3.5 presents the logical view [19] of the PLA design of Mobile Media, containing architectural elements such as packages, interfaces, classes, and their relationships. Attributes and operations of classes and interfaces are not shown in the picture for the sake of readability.

Each architectural element is associated with the feature(s) it realizes using UML stereotypes. Example of features offered by Mobile Media are *labelMedia, favourites, linkMedia,* and *SMSTransfer.*

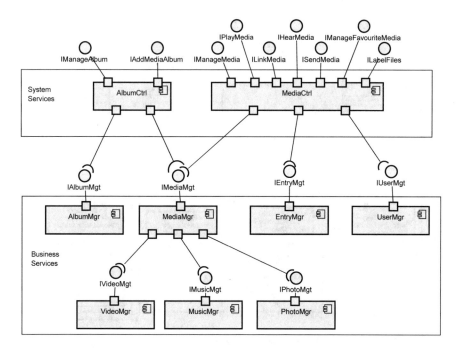

Fig. 3.4 PLA design of Mobile Media—development view [9]

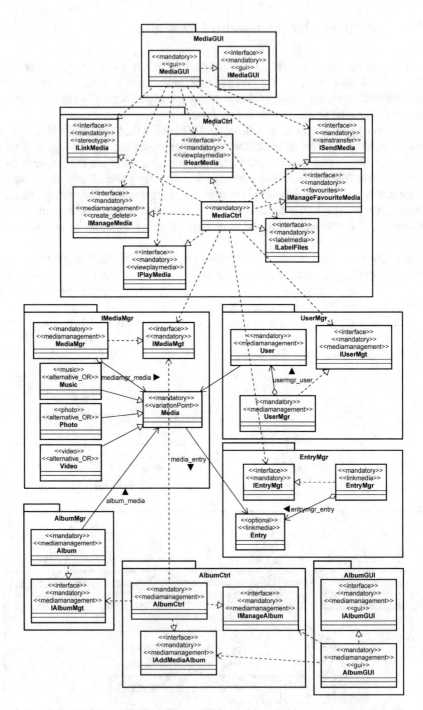

Fig. 3.5 PLA design of Mobile Media—logical view

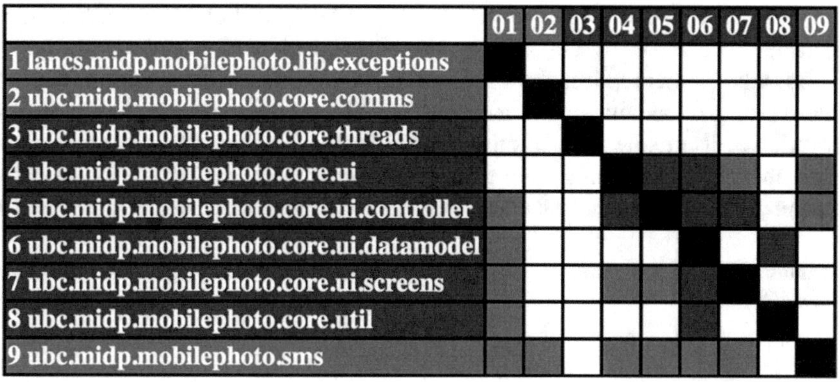

	01	02	03	04	05	06	07	08	09
1 lancs.midp.mobilephoto.lib.exceptions									
2 ubc.midp.mobilephoto.core.comms									
3 ubc.midp.mobilephoto.core.threads									
4 ubc.midp.mobilephoto.core.ui									
5 ubc.midp.mobilephoto.core.ui.controller									
6 ubc.midp.mobilephoto.core.ui.datamodel									
7 ubc.midp.mobilephoto.core.ui.screens									
8 ubc.midp.mobilephoto.core.util									
9 ubc.midp.mobilephoto.sms									

Fig. 3.6 DSM of Mobile Media with variability representation [21]

Variation points, alternative variants, optional, and mandatory elements have the stereotypes *variation Point*, *alternative_O R*, *optional*, and *mandatory*, respectively. It is noticeable that the variability of Mobile Media is associated to the *Media* and *Entry* classes. *Media* is a mandatory class that is also a variation point, whose alternative variants are *Music, Photo*, and *Video*. Each variant has the stereotype *alternative_O R*. On the other hand, *Entry* is an optional class that may not be present in some products derived from this PLA design. In addition to the variation point and variants, the architectural variability modeling includes the specification of binding time and resolution rules to be applied when deriving a product from the PLA, as presented in Fig. 3.3.

Figure 3.6 presents the Mobile Media DSM with representation of variability that is a different representation for the development view. Each line and each column represent a package. For instance, line 5 and column 5 represent the package `controller`. This package has dependencies to the packages `datamodel`, `ui`, and `screens`.

The relationship between these packages is mandatory because they are implemented by all the variants. We used the color dark gray to represent the mandatory packages and relationships (commonality). On the other hand, the relationships of `controller` with `exceptions` and `sms` are variable because they are implemented by some variants. We used the color light grey to indicate the variability.

3.5   Final Remarks

This chapter introduced general concepts of Software Architecture and SPL including detailed discussion about PLA. In a nutshell, SPL exploits commonalities among products to reduce costs and time to market and improve the software quality. On the other hand, SPL provides the variability management allowing the organization to achieve economies of scope and provides the capability of mass customization.

Because SPL comprises the implementation of different structures, processes, interfaces, and activities, it is relevant for SPL practitioners to pay sufficient attention to its architecture. In this context, the PLA enables the maximization of the architecture reuse across several products. Different PLA visualization provides information to support the understanding of the variability mechanism implemented.

Acknowledgments This work is supported by the Brazilian funding agency CNPq (Grant 428994/2018-0)

References

1. Ahmed, F., Capretz, L.F.: The software product line architecture: An empirical investigation of key process activities. Inf. Softw. Technol. **50**(11), 1098–1113 (2008)
2. Angelov, S., Grefen, P., Greefhorst, D.: A framework for analysis and design of software reference architectures. Inf. Softw. Technol. **54**(4), 417–431 (2012)
3. Bass, L., Clements, P., Kazman, R.: Software Architecture in Practice, 3rd edn. SEI Series in Software Engineering. Pearson Education, London (2012)
4. Bourque, P., Fairley, R.E., Society, I.C.: Guide to the Software Engineering Body of Knowledge (SWEBOK(R)): Version 3.0, 3rd edn. IEEE Computer Society Press, Washington (2014)
5. Brown, S.: Software Architecture for Developers, 1st edn. Leanpub, Victoria (2014)
6. Chen, L., Ali Babar, M.: A systematic review of evaluation of variability management approaches in software product lines. Inf. Softw. Technol. **53**(4), 344–362 (2011)
7. Clements, P., Northrop, L.M.: Software Product Lines: Practices and Patterns. SEI Series in Software Engineering. Addison-Wesley, Boston (2002)
8. Clements, P., Bachmann, F., Bass, L., Garlan, D., Ivers, J., Little, R., Merson, P., Nord, R., Stafford, J.: Documenting Software Architectures: Views and Beyond, 2nd edn. Addison-Wesley Professional, Boston (2010)
9. Contieri Jr, A.C., Correia, G.G., Colanzi, T.E., Gimenes, I.M., OliveiraJr, E., Ferrari, S., Masiero, P.C., Garcia, A.F.: Extending uml components to develop software product-line architectures: Lessons learned. In: Proceedings of the 5th European Conference on Software Architecture (ECSA), pp. 130–138 (2011)
10. Eklund, U., Jonsson, N., Bosch, J., Eriksson, A.: A reference architecture template for software-intensive embedded systems. In: Proceedings of the WICSA/ECSA 2012 Companion Volume, pp. 104–111. ACM, New York (2012)
11. Eppinger, S.D., Browning, T.R.: Design Structure Matrix Methods and Applications. MIT Press, Cambridge (2012)
12. Galster, M., Avgeriou, P.: Handling variability in software architecture: Problems and implications. In: Proceedings of the 2011 Ninth Working IEEE/IFIP Conference on Software Architecture, pp. 171–180. IEEE Computer Society, Washington (2011)
13. Galster, M., Avgeriou, P.: The notion of variability in software architecture: Results from a preliminary exploratory study. In: Proceedings of the 5th Workshop on Variability Modeling of Software-Intensive Systems, pp. 59–67. ACM, New York (2011)
14. Galster, M., Weyns, D., Avgeriou, P., Becker, M.: Variability in software architecture: views and beyond. SIGSOFT Softw. Eng. Notes **37**(6), 1–9 (2013)
15. Hilliard, R.: On representing variation. In: 1st International Workshop on Variability in Software Product Line Architectures. ACM, New York (2010)

16. IEEE Computer Society Software Engineering Standards Committee: IEEE standard glossary of software engineering terminology. IEEE Std 610.12-1990, pp. 1–84 (1990)
17. IEEE Computer Society Software Engineering Standards Committee: IEEE standard for a software quality metrics methodology. IEEE Std 1061-1998 (1998)
18. ISO/IEC/IEEE Systems and Software Engineering – Architecture Description. ISO/IEC/IEEE 42010:2011(E) (Revision of ISO/IEC 42010:2007 and IEEE Std 1471-2000), pp. 1–46 (2011)
19. Kruchten, P.: Architectural blueprints — the "4+1" view model of software architecture. IEEE Softw. **12**(6), 42–50 (1995)
20. Kruchten, P.: Common misconceptions about software architecture. The Rationale Edge (2001)
21. Lima Neto, C. R.: An approach for recovering architectural variability from source code. Ph.D. Thesis, Federal University of Bahia (2019)
22. Linden, F.J.v.d., Schmid, K., Rommes, E.: Software Product Lines in Action: The Best Industrial Practice in Product Line Engineering. Springer, New York (2007)
23. Mancoridis, S., Mitchell, B., Chen, Y., Gansner, E.: Bunch: a clustering tool for the recovery and maintenance of software system structures. In: IEEE International Conference on Software Maintenance Proceedings, pp. 50–59 (1999)
24. Marimuthu, C., Chandrasekaran, K.: Systematic studies in software product lines: a tertiary study. In: International Systems and Software Product Line Conference, pp. 143–152. ACM, New York (2017)
25. Martínez-Fernández, S., Ayala, C.P., Franch, X., Marques, H.M.: Proceedings of the Safe and Secure Software Reuse: 13th International Conference on Software Reuse, ICSR 2013, Pisa, June 18–20, chap. REARM: A Reuse-Based Economic Model for Software Reference Architectures, pp. 97–112. Springer, Berlin (2013)
26. Nakagawa, E.Y., Oliveira, A.P., Becker, M.: Reference architecture and product line architecture: a subtle but critical difference. In: Proceedings of the European Conference on Software Architecture (ECSA), pp. 207–211 (2011)
27. Pohl, K., Böckle, G., van der Linden, F.: Software Product Line Engineering: Foundations, Principles, and Techniques. Springer, New York (2005)
28. Shaw, M., Garlan, D.: Software Architecture: Perspectives on an Emerging Discipline. Prentice-Hall Inc., Hoboken (1996)
29. Software engineering – product quality – part 1: Quality model. ISO/IEC 9126-1:2001 (2001)
30. Taylor, R., Medvidovic, N., Dashofy, E.: Software Architecture: Foundations, Theory, and Practice. Wiley, Hoboken (2009)
31. Thiel, S., Hein, A.: Modeling and using product line variability in automotive systems. IEEE Softw. **19**(4), 66–72 (2002)
32. Thiel, S., Hein, A.: Systematic integration of variability into product line architecture design. In: Proceedings of the Software Product Lines, Second International Conference, SPLC 2, San Diego, August 19–22, 2002. Lecture Notes in Computer Science, vol. 2379, pp. 130–153. Springer, Berlin (2002)
33. van Gurp, J., Bosch, J., Svahnberg, M.: On the notion of variability in software product lines. In: Proceedings Working IEEE/IFIP Conference on Software Architecture, pp. 45–54 (2001)
34. Verlage, M., Kiesgen, T.: Five years of product line engineering in a small company. In: Proceedings of the 27th International Conference on Software Engineering, pp. 534–543. ACM, New York (2005)
35. Weiss, D.M.: Architecture of product lines. In: International Conference on Software Maintenance, pp. 6–6 (2009)
36. Young, T.: Using AspectJ to build a software product line for mobile devices. Master's thesis, University of British Columbia (2005)

Chapter 4
The SMarty Approach for UML-Based Software Product Lines

Edson OliveiraJr, Itana M. S. Gimenes, and José C. Maldonado

Abstract In this chapter we present the Stereotype Management of Variability (SMarty) approach, its UML 2 compliant profile, and its process to guide users at identifying and representing variabilities in UML-based Software Product Lines (SPL). UML plays a central role as it is the standard modeling language and it is used from now in this book, as well as it represents design decisions on SPLs. Therefore, we discuss important concepts on UML-based SPLs in the context of the SMarty supported diagrams. In addition, we present in detail the SMarty approach.

4.1 Overview of the SMarty Family

SMarty stands for _**S**tereotype-based **M**anagement of **Va**riability_. It is an approach conceived for representing variability in SPL UML diagrams by means of stereotypes (see Sect. 4.2). That is why "Stereotype-based" is its definition.

SMarty is part of what we named the **SMarty Family**. Such family is composed of:

- The **SMarty approach** itself for identifying and representing variability in UML diagrams of an SPL
- The **SMartyModeling tool** for supporting the SPL lifecycle based on requirements, features, and UML diagrams, as well as deriving product configurations and variability traceability
- The **SMartySPEM approach** for identifying and representing variability in SPEM-based Software Process Lines (SPrL)

E. OliveiraJr (✉) · I. M. S. Gimenes
Informatics Department, State University of Maringá, Maringá, Paraná, Brazil
e-mail: edson@din.uem.br; imsgimenes@uem.br

J. C. Maldonado
University of São Paulo, Department of Computer Systems, São Carlos, São Paulo, Brazil
e-mail: jcmaldon@icmc.usp.br

© Springer Nature Switzerland AG 2023
E. OliveiraJr (ed), *UML-Based Software Product Line Engineering with SMarty*,
https://doi.org/10.1007/978-3-031-18556-4_4

57

The SMartySPEM approach for SPrLs has been demonstrated in several works (see Chap. 16).

SMarty and SMartyModeling are exploited in this book as we focused on SPL engineering. Therefore, the SMarty approach is composed of different elements, which provide support for SPL lifecycles. We list such elements as follows:

- **SMartyProfile:** contains all stereotypes, tagged values, and constraints used to explicitly represent variability, variation points, and variants in use case, class, component, activity, and sequence diagrams. It is further presented in Sect. 4.2.
- **SMartyProcess:** represents the process of identifying, representing, and constraining variability in UML diagrams, according to an overall SPL lifecycle. It is further presented in Sect. 4.3.
- **SMartyModeling:** which is a tool to support most activities of the SPL lifecycle. It is further described in Chap. 5.
- **SMartyComponents:** is a process for designing SPL architectures (PLA) based on components with support to variability in components, ports, and interfaces. It is further presented and discussed in Chap. 6.
- **SMartyCheck:** is an inspection technique based on checklist to support SPL engineers at revealing defects from a catalogue in SPL artifacts with represented variability. It is further presented and discussed in Chap. 7.
- **SMartyPerspective:** is another inspection technique based on perspective in which different SPL roles perform specific activities to reveal defects in SPL artifacts. It is further presented and discussed in Chap. 7.
- **SMartyTesting:** is a testing sequence generating technique based on the representation and reuse of testing sequences for SPL artifacts. It is further presented and discussed in Chap. 8.
- **SMartyMetrics:** represents a set of ISO/IEC 25010-based metrics and guidelines to evaluate PLA independent of PLA evaluation methods. It is further presented and discussed in Chap. 9.
- **SystEM-PLA:** is a systematic method for evaluating PLAs based on metrics, the GQM paradigm, and statistical hypothesis testing. It is further presented and discussed in Chap. 10.

SMarty has evolved over the years, since its conception until current date. Figures 4.1, 4.2, and 4.3 chronologically depict all the SMarty evolution stages.

The first insights of SMarty were in 2003–2005 (version 1.0) [14], with a few stereotypes and neither tagged values nor constraints. Guidelines were defined in terms of the variability management process in relation to the SPL process itself, for instance, which variability management activity should be performed in each SPL process activity. From 2006 to 2010, SMarty (version 1.3) received its name as we conceived a proper UML-based profile in which all stereotypes were due defined for use case, class and component diagrams, as well as their proper tagged values and constraints [13]. We named the profile as SMartyProfile (see Sect. 4.2), and we created a set of specific guidelines to the profile application, named SMartyProcess (see Sect. 4.3). In the same period, we created a method to evaluate PLAs modeled with the SMarty approach [14] (see Chap. 9) and initial metrics for

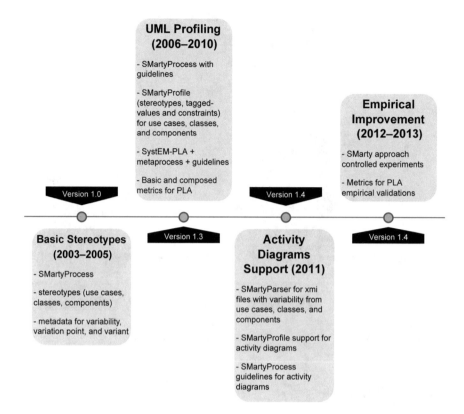

Fig. 4.1 SMarty 2003–2013

evaluating complexity and extensibility of PLAs [14, 15]. In 2011, we extended the SMartyProfile with stereotypes, tagged values, constraints, and guidelines to activity diagrams (version 1.4) [7]. We also started to experiment reading XMI files from general purpose UML tools with models annotated according to SMarty [8]. This will be later the first insights for the SMartyModeling tool. In 2012 and 2013, we performed a series of controlled experiments to evolve the SMarty approach [11, 12, 16].

In 2014 we extended the SMarty approach (version 1.5) to incorporate support to sequence diagrams [9, 10] into the SMartyProfile. We also created the SMartySPEM for representing variability in software processes [18–20]. In 2015 we added SMarty a support to package and component diagrams [2], as well as we created an inspection technique based on checklist to detect defects in use case and class SMarty diagrams [4, 6, 7]. All these modifications were empirically evaluated in 2016 and 2017 with controlled experiments and qualitative studies based on grounded theory procedures of coding. Then, in 2018 a larger set of metrics based in the ISO/IEC 25010 maintainability (see Chap. 8) attributes was created, thus allowing a more flexible trade-off analysis during SMarty-based PLAs evaluations.

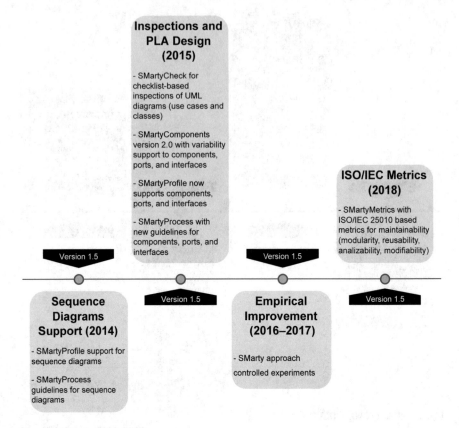

Fig. 4.2 SMarty 2014–2018

In 2019 we created our first model-based testing technique, named SMartyTesting [21, 22], to support generating testing sequences with variability, thus reusing them to test specific SPL products. In the next year, we started creating the SMartyModeling tool [23–26] to support designing SPL with MOF-based profiles (see Sect. 4.2). We also conducted several experiments for evaluating SMarty comparing it to other UML-based variability management approaches. To improve our experiments on SMarty, we created an ontology [27], which aids defining the essential elements of an SPL controlled experiments and provides a set of elements to be instantiated during an experiment. In 2021, we created our second inspection technique, named SMartyPerspective [3], based on perspective approaches to define scenarios, and different roles (perspectives) looking for detecting defects in all SMarty diagrams, including feature models. In 2022, we continued carrying out new experiments to evolve SMarty and developing new modules for the SMarty-Modeling, such as the requirements one.

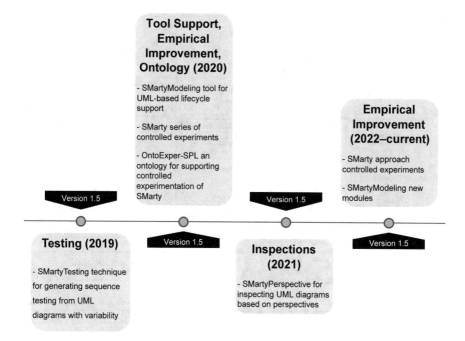

Fig. 4.3 SMarty 2019–current

4.2 The SMartyProfile

To start presenting the SMartyProfile, we will introduce essential concepts on models, metamodels and the UML Profiling Mechanism of OMG.[1] OMG is a consortium which standardizes all related specifications on several different languages, as UML and SysML. As Fig. 4.4 depicts, OMG has a standard representation to all of its languages, named Meta-Object Facility (MOF), at the M3 abstraction layer. MOF is a meta-metamodel, which describes all existing metamodels, such as the official UML metamodel and the profile one, at the M2 abstraction level. It means all metamodels at the M2 level are described by a language in a higher abstraction level. The same occurs for the M1 abstraction level, which is composed of, for instance, the UML models. Such UML models are those which designers are used to model in an UML general purpose tool, such as Astah.[2]

Examples of UML models are use cases, actor, interface, component, association, and dependency. All of these elements at the M1 level are described by UML metamodel classes at the M2 level, named metaclasses. These metaclasses, when instantiated at the M0 level, are the visual elements we used to see in an UML

---

[1] https://www.omg.org.

[2] https://astah.net.

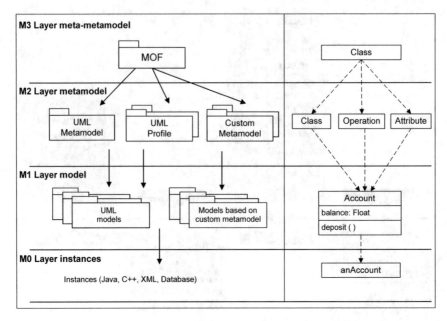

Fig. 4.4 MOF-based metamodels [1]

diagram, for instance, an actor that communicates to a use case in a use case diagram. The "actor," the "communication" relationship, and the "use case" are described by different classes from the M1 level.

UML model instances might have different semantics depending on its role in a given diagram. For instance, a use case might have a semantic which determines it is a business use case. To do so, we used to mark such use case with a stereotype. Stereotypes are a kind of signal that designates functions to an UML model instance. The function or semantics is visually represented with a name between «and ». The use case "Generate bill for the client" could be signed as business use case »to represent this use case as a business use case.

The extension mechanism, which allows this kind of new semantics incorporation, is named Profiling Mechanism,[3] and it is available for every MOF-based metamodel. For instance, we can create as many profiles as we want, since they respect the standard metamodels they are extending. OMG has a set of pre-defined profiles.[4] However, one can create his/her own profile.

SMarty adopted the UML profile mechanism to allow the identification of SPL variability elements, such variants, variation points, and constraints in use case, class, component, sequence, and activity diagrams. Figure 4.5 depicts the current version of the SMartyProfile.

---

[3] https://www.omg.org/spec/UML/2.5.1.

[4] https://www.omg.org/spec/category/uml-profile.

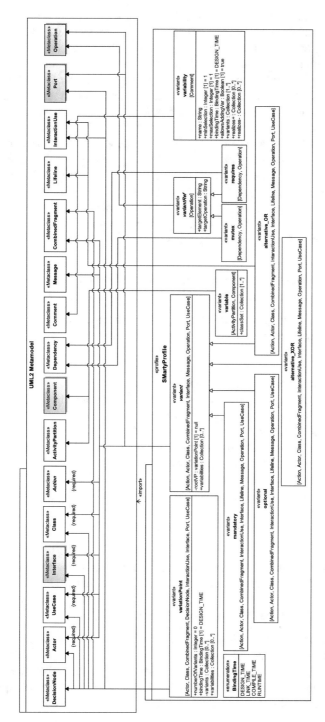

Fig. 4.5 The SMartyProfile for UML-based SPLs

At the upper part of Fig. 4.5 is the UML2 Metamodel, the same from Fig. 4.4 at the M2 level. The SMartyProfile is at the same level of UML2 Metamodel. Both are represented with an UML package, but SMartyProfile is stereotyped with «profile» to designate this package contains a profile. In addition, SMartyProfile imports metaclasses from UML2 Metamodel, which is represented by the dependency relationship, a dashed line with an arrow at the end, stereotyped as «import». It means that the new profile can add semantics to the metaclasses from the UML2 Metamodel.

To add semantics to a specific metaclass, the new stereotypes should extend the metaclass of interest. For instance, the stereotype variationPoint extends the following metaclasses: Actor, Class, CombinedFragment, DecisionNode, InteractionUse, Interface, and UseCase. It means that we one can apply such stereotype only to the extended classes. Therefore, a use case can be stereotype as an SPL variation point in a use case diagram.

The list of the stereotypes and tagged values of SMartyProfile is presented as follows [13]:

- «variability» represents the concept of SPL variability and is an extension of the metaclass Comment. This stereotype has the following tagged values:

  - name, the given name by which a variability is referred to.
  - minSelection represents the minimum number of variants to be selected to resolve a variation point or a variability.
  - maxSelection represents the maximum number of variants to be selected in order to resolve a variation point or a variability.
  - bindingTime, the moment at which a variability must be resolved, represented by the enumeration class BindingTime.
  - allowsAddingVar indicates whether it is possible or not to include new variants in the SPL development; variants represents the collection of variant instances associated with a variability.
  - variants, a collection of variants for a given variability.
  - realizes+, a collection of higher-level model variabilities that realize this variability.
  - realizes-, a collection of lower-level model variabilities that realize this variability.

- «variationPoint» represents the concept of SPL variation point and is an extension of the metaclasses Actor, Class, CombinedFragment, DecisionNode, InteractionUse, Interface, Port, and UseCase. This stereotype has the following tagged values:

  - numberOfVariants indicates the number of associated variants that can be selected to resolve this variation point.
  - bindingTime, the moment at which a variation point must be resolved, represented by the enumeration class BindingTime; variants represents the collection of variant instances associated with this variation point.

- variants, a collection of variants for a given variation point.
- variabilities represents the collection of associated variabilities.

- «variant» represents the concept of SPL variant and is an abstract extension of the metaclasses Action, Actor, Class, CombinedFragment, Interface, Message, Operation, Port, and UseCase. This stereotype is specialized in four other nonabstract stereotypes which are «mandatory», «optional», «alternative_OR», and «alternative_XOR». The stereotype variant has the following tagged values:

  - rootVP represents the variation point with which this variant is associated.
  - variabilities, the collection of variabilities with which this variant is associated.

- «mandatory» represents a compulsory variant that is part of every SPL product.
- «optional» represents a variant that may be selected to resolve a variation point or a variability.
- «alternative_OR» represents a variant that is part of a group of alternative inclusive variants. Different combinations of this kind of variants may resolve variation points or variabilities in different ways.
- «alternative_XOR» represents a variant that is part of a group of alternative exclusive variants. This means that only one variant of the group can be selected to resolve a variation point or variability.
- «mutex» represents the concept of SPL variant constraint and is a mutually exclusive relationship between two variants. This means that when a variant is selected, another variant must not be selected. This stereotype could be applied to UML dependencies and operations.
- «requires» represents the concept of SPL variant and is a relationship between two variants in which the selected variant requires the choice of another specific variant. This stereotype could be applied to UML dependencies and operations.
- «variable» is an extension of the metaclasses ActivityPartition and Component. It indicates that an activity partition or a component has a set of classes with explicit variabilities. This stereotype has the tagged value classSet which is the collection of class instances that form a component.

To represent SPL elements in a UML diagram, we need to identify variabilities first. Variability identification is an activity that depends on the domain, requiring abilities of the SPL managers and analysts. In this perspective we created the SMartyProcess to guide such roles in their respective activities.

4.3   The SMartyProcess and Guidelines

The SMartyProcess aids SPL roles to mainly identify, represent, and constrain variabilities in use case, class, component, sequence, and activity diagrams based on the stereotypes of the SMartyProfile. Figure 4.6 depicts general SPL process activities (left side) interacting to the SMartyProcess (right side).

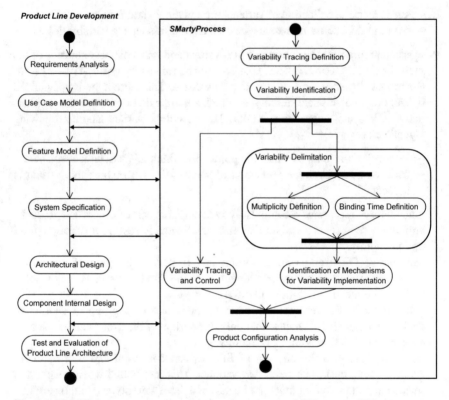

Fig. 4.6 Variability management process interacting to a general SPL process [13]

To easy the SMartyProfile application, SMartyProcess provides guidelines for each of the SMarty supported diagrams.

4.3.1 Guidelines for Use Case Diagrams

UC.1 Elements from use case diagrams with a relationship with extension mechanisms and extension points suggest variation points with associated variants. Such variants may be inclusive or exclusive.

UC.2 Use case diagram with relationship of inclusion («include») or with a relationship with an actor suggests mandatory or optional variants.

UC.3 Variants which are selected to be part of a product and the presence of other variants needed may have their dependency relationship tagged with «requires» stereotype.

UC.4 Mutually exclusive variants in specific products may have their dependency relationships tagged with the «mutex» stereotype.

4.3.2   Guidelines for Class Diagrams

CL.1 In class diagrams, variation points and their variants are identified by the following relationship:

- Generalization, the general classifiers are the variation points, while the most specific are variants.
- Interface realization, the suppliers are the variation points and the clients are the variants.
- Aggregation, the tagged instances with hollow diamonds are the variation points and the associated instances are the variants.
- Composition, the tagged instances with filled diamonds are variation points the associated instances are the variants.

CL.2 In class diagrams, the elements with relationship in which their `aggregationKing` attributes with value equals none, in other words, do not represent aggregation neither composition, suggests mandatory or optional variants.

  CL.2.1 In class diagrams, the elements with relationship in which their `aggregationKing` attributes with value equals * (zero or more) or 0..n where n is a integer number, different of zero, which suggests such class is optional.

CL.3 In class diagrams, the product selected variants which need the existence of other(s) variant(s) must have their dependency relationship tagged with the «requires» stereotype.

CL.4 In class diagrams, the product mutually exclusive variants must have their dependency relationship tagged with the «mutex» stereotype.

4.3.3   Guidelines for Component Diagrams

CP.1 Components consisting of classes and realizations with variability are tagged as «variable».

CP.2 Interfaces related to a same concern might be inclusive variants tagged as «alternative_OR» and associated with a given port tagged as «variationPoint».

CP.3 Optional interfaces («optional») should be associated directly to a component in order to avoid empty ports, except when a port is a variation point with minSelection = 1.

CP.4 Ports and operations with variability representation must be in a classifier compartment format.

CP.5 Interfaces with variabilities must be presented in the classifier format.

4.3.4   Guidelines for Sequence Diagrams

SQ.1 elements of sequence diagram such as CombinedFragment that have interactionOperator of the type "alt" (alternative) indicate that only one flow of the CombinedFragment will be performed, that is, suggests mutually exclusive variants where the points of variation will be noted as («variationPoint») and will be related to a UML comment specifying variability («variability»). The variants corresponding to the messages must be stereotyped as «alternative_XOR».

SQ.2 in sequence diagrams, the following occurrences suggest optional variants:

SQ.2.1 Elements of sequence diagrams such as CobinedFragment that have "opt" (optional) interactionOperator suggest optional variants, being stereotyped as («optional») and related to a UML comment specifying variability («variability»). The lifelines contained in this CombinedFragment and which are part of the variability must also be stereotyped as «optional».

SQ.2.2 Exchanging messages between two nonmandatory objects or between one mandatory object and another not suggest an optional variant, stereotyped as «optional» and will be related to a UML comment specifying the variability («variability»). The lifelines corresponding to this variant will also be stereotyped as «optional».

SQ.3 the interactionUse element "ref" suggests a variation point for alternative inclusive variants, being stereotyped as «variationPoint» and related to a UML comment, which identifies the elements of variability («variability»). The sequence diagrams referenced by the interactionUse "ref" corresponding to the variants of the variation point, are considered; therefore, inclusive alternatives and one or more can be related and stereotyped as «alternative_OR».

SQ.4 the messages that are independent of the flows contained in the CombinedFragment "alt" and "opt" and the interactionUse "ref" or are not directly related to a variability and its elements are kept without stereotype and considers mandatory.

SQ.5 variants in sequence diagrams that, when selected to be part of a specific product, require the presence of another or other variants must have their dependency relationships marked with the «requires» stereotype.

SQ.6 mutually exclusive variants of a sequence diagram, for a given product, must have their dependency relationships stereotyped with «mutex».

4.3.5   Guidelines for Activity Diagrams

AT.1 Elements of models of activity diagrams such as DecisionNode suggest points of variation marked as «variationPoint», as it is a place formed explicitly by possible paths for different actions.

AT.2   Action elements of activity diagrams can be defined as mandatory («manda-tory») or optional variants («optional»).

AT.3   Action elements that represent alternative outflows from a DecisionNode suggest alternative inclusive or exclusive variants.

AT.4   ActivityPartition elements that have variable elements, DecisionNode as a variation point or Action as variants, should be marked as «variable», as they are composed of elements that undergo some type of variation.

4.4   Final Remarks

In this chapter we presented the basics of the SMarty approach, its profile for representing variability in UML diagrams, and a process to guide users on how to identify and represent such variabilities.

The SMartyProfile was built extending the UML metamodel, which complies with the standard UML and the MOF specifications from OMG. Several stereotypes were created to permit representing SPL main concepts of variability, variation points, variants, and variant constraints.

The SMartyProcess guides the users on identifying and representing SPL vari-abilities throughout a set of guidelines for use case, class, components, sequence, and activity diagrams. In addition, the SMartyProcess allows one to interact directly to general phases of SPL construction, especially in the Domain Engineering.

The next chapter presents how to design, trace, and configure SPL products using SMarty.

References

1. Abdullah, M.S.: A UML profile for conceptual modelling of knowledge-based systems. Ph.D. Thesis, The University of York, Department of Computer Science (2006)
2. Bera, M.H.G., OliveiraJr, E., Colanzi., T.E.: Evidence-based SMarty support for variability identification and representation in component models. In: Proceedings of the 17th International Conference on Enterprise Information Systems—Volume 1: ICEIS, pp. 295–302. INSTICC, SciTePress (2015). https://doi.org/10.5220/0005366402950302
3. Bettin, G., OliveiraJr, E.: SMartyPerspective: a perspective-based inspection technique for software product lines. In: Brazilian Symposium on Software Engineering, pp. 90–94. Association for Computing Machinery, New York (2021)
4. Bettin, G.C.S., Geraldi, R.T., OliveiraJr, E.: Experimental evaluation of the SMartycheck techinique for inspecting defects in UML component diagrams. In: Proceedings of the 17th Brazilian Symposium on Software Quality, pp. 101–110. Association for Computing Machinery, New York (2018). https://doi.org/10.1145/3275245.3275256
5. Fiori, D.R., Gimenes, I.M.S., Maldonado, J.C., OliveiraJr, E.: Variability management in software product line activity diagrams. In: DMS, pp. 89–94 (2012)
6. Geraldi, R.T., OliveiraJr, E.: Defect types and software inspection techniques: a systematic mapping study. J. Comput. Sci. **13**(10), 470–495 (2017). https://doi.org/10.3844/jcssp.2017.470.495

7. Geraldi, R.T., OliveiraJr, E., Conte., T., Steinmacher., I.: Checklist-based inspection of SMarty variability models - proposal and empirical feasibility study. In: Proceedings of the 17th International Conference on Enterprise Information Systems—Volume 1: ICEIS, pp. 268–276. INSTICC, SciTePress (2015). https://doi.org/10.5220/0005350102680276

8. Lanceloti, L.A., Maldonado, J.C., Gimenes, I.M.S., OliveiraJr, E.: SMartyParser: a xmi parser for uml-based software product line variability models. In: Proceedings of the Seventh International Workshop on Variability Modelling of Software-Intensive Systems. ACM, New York (2013). https://doi.org/10.1145/2430502.2430516

9. Marcolino, A., OliveiraJr, E., Gimenes., I.: Towards the effectiveness of the SMarty approach for variability management at sequence diagram level. In: Proceedings of the 16th International Conference on Enterprise Information Systems—Volume 1: ICEIS, pp. 249–256. INSTICC, SciTePress (2014). https://doi.org/10.5220/0004889302490256

10. Marcolino, A., OliveiraJr, E., Gimenes, I.: Variability identification and representation in software product line UML sequence diagrams: proposal and empirical study. In: 2014 Brazilian Symposium on Software Engineering, pp. 141–150 (2014). https://doi.org/10.1109/SBES.2014.11

11. Marcolino, A., OliveiraJr, E., Gimenes, I., Conte, T.U.: Towards validating complexity-based metrics for software product line architectures. In: VII Brazilian Symposium on Software Components, Architectures and Reuse, pp. 69–79 (2013). https://doi.org/10.1109/SBCARS.2013.18

12. Marcolino, A., OliveiraJr, E., Gimenes, I.M.S., Maldonado, J.C.: Towards the effectiveness of a variability management approach at use case level. In: International Conference on Software Engineering and Knowledge Engineering, pp. 214–219 (2013)

13. OliveiraJr, E., Gimenes, I.M., Maldonado, J.C.: Systematic management of variability in uml-based software product lines. J. Universal Comput. Sci. 16(17), 2374–2393 (2010)

14. OliveiraJr, E., Gimenes, I.M.S., Huzita, E., Maldonado, J.C.: A variability management process for software product lines. In: Proceedings of the 15th Annual International Conference of Computer Science and Software Engineering, pp. 30—44. ACM, Toronto (2005)

15. OliveiraJr, E., Gimenes, I.M.S., Maldonado, J.C.: A metric suite to support software product line architecture evaluation. In: Proceedings of the XXXIV Conferência Latinoamericana de Informática, pp. 489–498. ACM, Santa Fé (2008)

16. OliveiraJr, E., Gimenes, I.M.S., Maldonado, J.C.: Empirical validation of variability-based complexity metrics for software product line architecture. In: International Conference on Software Engineering and Knowledge Engineering, pp. 622–627 (2012)

17. OliveiraJr, E., Gimenes, I.M.S., Maldonado, J.C., C. Masiero, P., Barroca, L.: Systematic evaluation of software product line architectures. J. Universal Comput. Sci. 19(1), 25–52 (2013). https://doi.org/10.3217/jucs-019-01-0025

18. OliveiraJr, E.A., Pazin, M.G., Gimenes, I.M.S., Kulesza, U., Aleixo, F.A.: SMartySPEM: a SPEM-based approach for variability management in software process lines. In: J. Heidrich, M. Oivo, A. Jedlitschka, M.T. Baldassarre (eds.) Product-Focused Software Process Improvement, pp. 169–183. Springer, Berlin, Heidelberg (2013)

19. Pazin, M.G., Allian, A.P., OliveiraJr, E.: Empirical study on software process variability modelling with SMartySPEM and vSPEM. IET Softw. 12(6), 536–546 (2018). https://doi.org/10.1049/iet-sen.2017.0061

20. Pazin, M.G., Geraldi, R.T., OliveiraJr, E.: Comparing SMartySPEM and vSPEM for modeling variability in software processes: a qualitative study. SBQS, pp. 71–80. Association for Computing Machinery, New York (2018). https://doi.org/10.1145/3275245.3275253

21. Petry, K., OliveiraJr, E., Costa, L., Zanin, A., Zorzo, A.: SMartyTesting: a model-based testing approach for deriving software product line test sequences. In: Proceedings of the 23rd International Conference on Enterprise Information Systems—Volume 2: ICEIS, pp. 165–172. INSTICC, SciTePress (2021). https://doi.org/10.5220/0010373601650172

22. Petry, K.L., OliveiraJr, E., Zorzo, A.F.: Model-based testing of software product lines: mapping study and research roadmap. J. Syst. Softw. 167, 110,608 (2020). https://doi.org/10.1016/j.jss.2020.110608

23. Silva, L., OliveiraJr, E., Zorzo, A.: Feasibility analysis of SMartymodeling for modeling uml-based software product lines. In: Proceedings of the 22nd International Conference on Enterprise Information Systems—Volume 2: ICEIS, pp. 442–449. INSTICC, SciTePress (2020). https://doi.org/10.5220/0009793404420449
24. Silva, L.F., OliveiraJr, E.: Evaluating usefulness, ease of use and usability of an uml-based software product line tool. In: Proceedings of the 34th Brazilian Symposium on Software Engineering, pp. 798–807. Association for Computing Machinery, New York (2020). https://doi.org/10.1145/3422392.3422402
25. Silva, L.F., OliveiraJr, E.: SMartyModeling: An environment for engineering uml-based software product lines. In: 15th International Working Conference on Variability Modelling of Software-Intensive Systems. Association for Computing Machinery, New York (2021). https://doi.org/10.1145/3442391.3442397
26. Silva, L.F., OliveiraJr, E.: SMartyModeling: An instance of vmtools-ra for engineering uml-based software product lines. In: XX Brazilian Symposium on Software Quality. Association for Computing Machinery, New York (2021). https://doi.org/10.1145/3493244.3493274
27. Vignando, H., Furtado, V., Teixeira, L., OliveiraJr, E.: Ontoexper-spl: an ontology for software product line experiments. In: Proceedings of the 22nd International Conference on Enterprise Information Systems—Volume 2: ICEIS, pp. 401–408. INSTICC, SciTePress (2020). https://doi.org/10.5220/0009575404010408

Part II
SMarty-Based Software Product Lines: Design, Verification and Validation

Chapter 5
Designing, Tracing, and Configuring Software Product Lines with SMarty

Edson OliveiraJr, Leandro F. Silva, Anderson S. Marcolino,
Thais S. Nepomuceno, André F. R. Cordeiro, and Rodrigo Pereira dos Santos

Abstract In this chapter we present how to design use case, class, component, activity, and sequence diagrams using the SMarty approach. Based on the SMartyProcess and its guidelines, we demonstrate how to apply the stereotypes of the SMartyProfile, as well as how to trace the modeled elements, and how to configure SPL specific products. To do so, we use the SMartyModeling, an environment created to aid users on modeling according to any MOF-based metamodel, especially using SMarty.

5.1 Quick Start to SMartyModeling

SMartyModeling[1] was developed with Java programming language—version 8. The SMartyModeling architecture was instantiated based on VMTools-RA [1]. We adapted VMTools-RA views and elements for the context of SPL aiming at identifying, constraining, representing, and tracing variabilities in the SPL context.

The SMartyModeling interface presents a menu of items with the operations organized according to the features. Figure 5.1 presents the SMartyModeling

---

[1] SMartyModeling is available at https://github.com/leandroflores/demo_SMartyModeling_tool for free using according to Creative Commons 4.0 licenses.

E. OliveiraJr (✉) · L. F. Silva · T. S. Nepomuceno · A. F. R. Cordeiro
Informatics Department, State University of Maringá, Maringá PR, Brazil
e-mail: edson@din.uem.br

A. S. Marcolino
Engineering and Exact Science Department, Federal University of Paraná, Palotina, PR, Brazil

R. P. dos Santos
Department of Applied Informatics, Federal University of the State of Rio de Janeiro, Rio de Janeiro RJ, Brazil
e-mail: rps@uniriotec.br

© Springer Nature Switzerland AG 2023   75
E. OliveiraJr (ed), *UML-Based Software Product Line Engineering with SMarty*,
https://doi.org/10.1007/978-3-031-18556-4_5

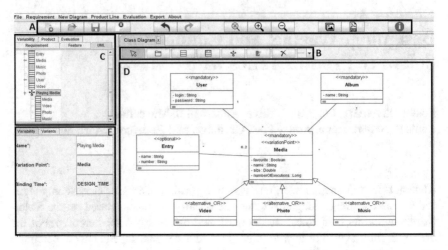

Fig. 5.1 SMartyModeling—user interface

interface for class modeling encompassing five fundamental components:

- **Operations Panel (Component A):** key system operations as new, open, save, and close Project, undo and redo, in and out zoom, and save image, save pdf, and about.
- **Buttons Panel (Component B):** features to the respective diagram. For classes, there are drag and drop diagram elements, insert new UML package, insert new UML class, insert new UML interface, insert new variability, edit, remove, and insert relationships.
- **Project Panel (Component C):** organization of the Project as a tree to display, organized into tabs: Requirement, Feature, UML, Variability, Product, and Evaluation.
- **Modeling Panel (Component D):** drawing area for diagrams.
- **Information Panel (Component E):** tabs with information on selected elements.

SMartyModeling is organized in features. For each feature, the architectural decisions were created considering the SPL context. Currently, SMartyModeling provides the following features:

- **Requirements Description:** feature responsible for describing the requirements of a Project. The description consists of the identifier, name, and description of the requirement.
- **Feature Modeling:** establishes a feature model. A feature model is a compact representation of all the products SPL.
- **Modeling of Diagrams:** defines the classes responsible for allowing the modeling of UML diagrams, including their elements and associations. The UML diagrams supported by the environment are use case, class, component, activity, and sequence.

- **Variability Management:** allows the variability management with the class structure defined based on the description of the SPL concepts. By default, the environment uses the stereotypes described by the SMarty and allows the user to redefine the profile to represent SPL concepts.
- **Product Instantiation:** feature responsible for allowing product instantiation in the environment. The instantiation has the objective at a specific Diagram. This feature is responsible for guiding the user in such a process, limiting the selection of optional elements, resolving the variability constraints, and configuring the product's instances.
- **Elements Traceability:** feature responsible for allowing the traceability of the elements modeled in different diagrams. The environment allows associating a feature, UML element, and variability to a requirement or functionality.
- **Information Export:** feature responsible for exporting the modeled diagrams and the products instantiated in the environment. The diagrams and instances can be exported in the image format. The environment also allows the export of source code of class diagrams and their instances.

5.2 Designing SMarty Diagrams

As explained in Chap. 4, SMarty consists of an UML profile, the SMartyProfile, and a process entitled SMartyProcess. While the SMartyProfile has the necessary elements to allow the modeling of variability in UML diagrams, the SMartyProcess guides the designer in the application of such profile [6].

The SMartyProcess activities are usually applied in parallel with the SPL development phases. Therefore, SMartyProcess progressively uses the output artifacts of the SPL development phases as inputs. Throughout the execution of activities, the number of variabilities tends to increase.

As SMartyProcess is iterative and incremental, variability updates are allowed from any SPL development phases or activities. SMartyProcess consumes artifacts from the SPL core assets, as well as providing it with extra information.

To exemplify how the SMartyProfile and the SMartyProcess allow the modeling of UML diagrams, we use the Mobile Media (MM) SPL [4, 5, 8]. MM generates software products for manipulating photo, music, and video on mobile devices. Figure 5.2 depicts the Mobile Media feature model.

MM uses various technologies based on the Java platform, being possible to derive around 200 products in its last release [4, 5, 8].

The next sections demonstrate how to design each of the SMarty supported UML diagrams.

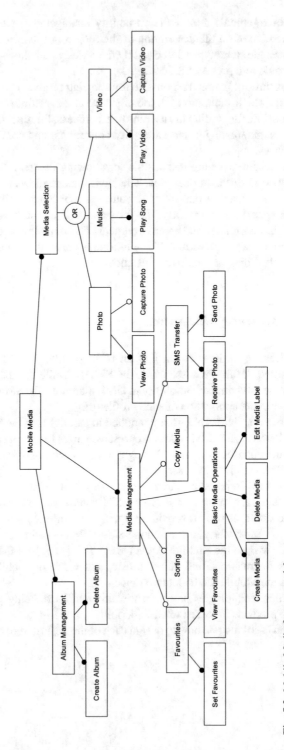

Fig. 5.2 Mobile Media feature model

5.2.1 Use Case Diagrams

Use case diagrams are referred as UML supplementary model used to describe a set of actions, represented as use cases, that systems can perform in collaboration with one or more external users of the system, represented by actors. Each use case should provide observable and valuable result to the actors or another stakeholder of the system [11].

The two selected use cases of MM for the exemplification are Play Media and Manage Media. Both use cases are variation points and mandatories. For a better understanding, Fig. 5.3 depicts such use cases with no SPL elements representation.

It is possible to observe that Play Media and Manage Media use cases have three «extend» relationships each. Play Media has relationships with Play Video, Play Music, and Visualize Photo uses cases. In addition, Manage Media has relationships with Manage Video, Manage Music, and Manage Photo. Furthermore, Manage Media has also an «include» relationship with the Log in use case.

The first step to allow the modeling of Fig. 5.3 with SMarty is to identify the different UML elements and map them according with the SMartyProcess guidelines (Chap. 4), which suggest the possible SPL roles for both graphical and textual UML elements in the target diagram.

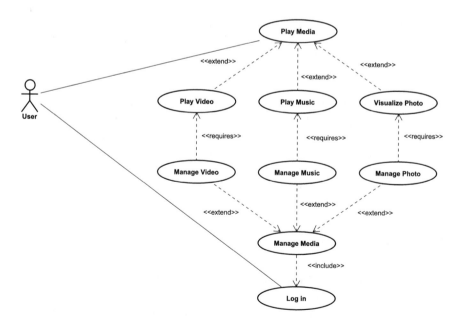

Fig. 5.3 Mobile Media use case diagram without variability

According to **UC.1**, elements from use case diagrams with a relationship with the extension mechanisms suggest variation points with associated variants. Thus, such guideline indicates that both `Play Media` and `Manage Media` are variation points and their extended use cases are variants. As soon as such variants are inclusive, the «alternative_OR» stereotype must be used for them, as well as the `variation point` stereotype for `Play Media` and `Manage Media` use cases.

Additionally, `Play Media` and `Manage Media` will receive a relationship with an UML comment. This comment has a set of tagged values to improve the SPL elements, supporting a concise product derivation

First, this comment is stereotyped as «variability», indicating that the UML graphical element related to it represents a variability.

Second, a list of tagged values is included in such comment in the SMartyModeling tool. The tagged value `name` indicates the name of such variability, for `Play Media`, for example, the value is `playing Media`. For the `minSelection` and `maxSelection`, `Play Media` and `Manage Media` have 1 and 3 values, respectively. The values indicate that at least one and at most three variants must be selected to resolve each variation point. Then, the `bindingTime` tagged value has the value of `DESIGN_TIME`, which means that the resolution of such variability occurs during the design phase. The `allowsAddingVar` tagged value is `false`, also for both use cases, indicating that none of them may have the inclusion of new variants, in a possible evolution of the SPL. For the last tagged value, named `variants`, it receives the names of the variants of their, respectively, use case, easing the traceability and relationship among them.

Third, for the `Manage Media` use case, the relationship of inclusion with the `Log in` use case needs to be analyzed in the point of view of the SMartyProcess. The **UC.2** guideline suggests that use cases with the «include» relationship or with a relationship with an actor suggest either a mandatory or an optional variant. In this case, a mandatory variant was identified, being stereotyped as «mandatory».

Forth, each selected variant of the `Manage Media` requires a `Play Media` variant. Thus, considering the SMartyProcess guideline **UC.3**, variants which are selected to be part of a product and those stereotyped as «requires» are maintained. The result of the application of the SMartyProcess lead to the modeling of the excerpt of MM use case diagram depicted in Fig. 5.4.

5.2.2 Class Diagrams

As seeing in the use case diagram modeling, the guidelines have crucial role to allow its application. SMartyProcess makes easier the process of application and use of SMarty and its profile. Going on to the design of UML diagrams, this section presents the application of SMarty to UML class diagrams.

The purpose of a class is to specify a classification of objects and to specify the features that characterize the structure and behavior of those objects. Thus, a

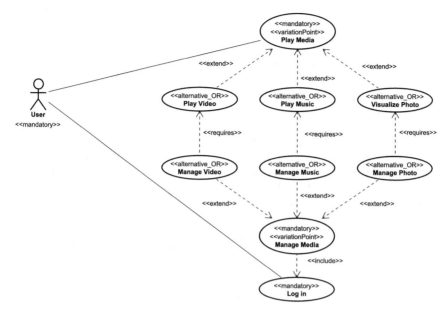

Fig. 5.4 Mobile Media use case diagram according to SMarty

class diagram is an UML structure diagram which shows structure of the designed system at the level of classes and interfaces, showing their features, constraints, and relationships—associations, generalizations, dependencies, and other classes and elements of relationship [11].

For this application, a new excerpt of the MM SPL was selected: the `MediaMgr` class, corresponding to the `Media Manage` use case diagram. This class is part of the `MediaMgr` package. In this package, besides `MediaMgr` class, there are `IMediaMgt` interface and `Media` class. The `MediaMgr` class is a concrete class and a superclass of `MusciMgr`, `PhotoMgr`, and `VideoMgr` classes. Figure 5.5 depicts the MM class diagram without variability.

First, to identify the SPL elements, the SMartyProcess and their guidelines for class diagram need to be checked. The **CL.1** guideline indicates that variation points and their variants are identified by the generalization relationship, whereas the general classifiers are the variation points, while the most specific are variants. Thus, `MediaMgr` class is the variation point, while `MusciMgr`, `PhotoMgr`, and `VideoMgr` classes are variants.

In this perspective, the `MediaMgr` class will have a relationship with an UML comment, which identifies it as a variability. It is noticed that the UML comment will depicted just in case of the adoption of a different tool from SMartyModeling, which maintains such information on specific interface. Furthermore, tagged values in such comment will provide extra information about the variability, supporting its development. The `name` tagged value receives the name of its variability. As in use case variability, the tagged values `minSelection` and `maxSelection`

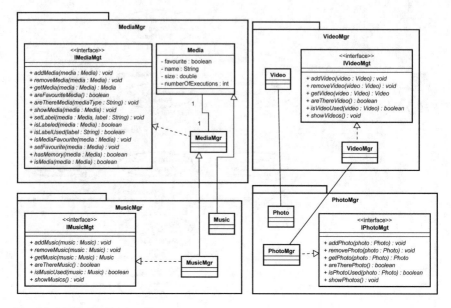

Fig. 5.5 Mobile Media class diagram

indicate the minimum and maximum values of variants. The `bindingTime` tagged value has the value of `DESIGN_TIME`, indicating that the resolution of variability occurs during the design phase. The `allowsAddingVar` tagged value is `false`, constraining the inclusion of new variants. In `variants` tagged value, the names of the variants are indicated.

As the class diagram does not indicate values in its `agregationKind` and the **CL.1** was enough to identify the type of variants the classes will be, they will be stereotyped as «alternative_OR». In consequence, other classes included in each package with an inheritance relationship with `MediaMgr` class will be also stereotyped as «alternative_OR». The same stereotype is applied for each interface, also present in their respective package. For example, in `MusicMgr` package, the `MusicMgr` class is alternative, and the same is applied for the `Music` class and the `IMusicMgr` interface. Figure 5.6 shows such classes according to SMarty.

5.2.3 Component Diagrams

A software component can be defined as a standalone, reusable, replaceable unit that encapsulates implementation details and provides services to other components of a system [10, 11].

A component influences the software architecture, either conceptually or physically [7, 10]. In component design, different quality attributes may be considered.

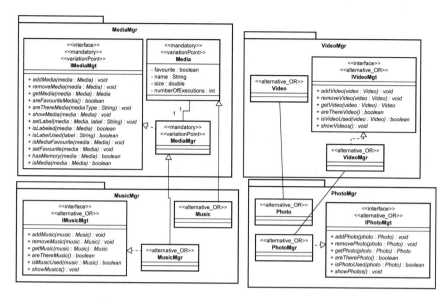

Fig. 5.6 Mobile Media class diagram according to SMarty

Possible attributes include reusability, coupling, and cohesion. Components should be designed for reuse, considering low coupling and high cohesion [12].

Each component has one or more connection points, known as the interface. Interfaces concentrate the services offered and needed by the component. An interface can be classified as required or provided. The provided interfaces represent the services offered by the component, and the required interfaces represent the services required by the same [11].

The interaction between the components of a system happens through their respective interfaces. Through this interaction, it is possible to look at existing dependency relationships. Dependencies suggest how changing one component might influence other components [7].

In UML, component and class can perform the same actions in terms of establishing associations with other components or classes, respectively, defining operations and implementing interfaces [10].

The UML component diagram has a higher level abstraction compared to an UML class diagram. One component is implemented by multiple classes [13]. Thus, even with the similarities, it is important to understand that, in general, a component has more responsibilities than a class [10].

The elaboration of an UML component diagram makes it possible to analyze the system architecture at the project level. In the analysis, one can observe the logical organization of the architecture, as well as identify the components that can be replaced, reused, partitioned, or even purchased from third parties [2].

In addition to the component and interface, other elements presented in the UML specification, version 2.5, can be used in a component diagram [11]. One

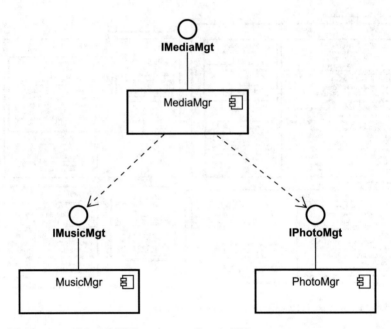

Fig. 5.7 Fragment of the MM SPL component diagram [17]

of these elements is the port. A port can be described as an element that assists in the interaction between the internal (component) and external (other elements) environments [2, 11].

Figure 5.7 illustrates a fragment of a component diagram of the MM SPL.

In Fig. 5.7, it is possible to observe three components, five interfaces, being three provided and two required.

The IMediaMgt, IMusicMgt, and IPhotoMgt interfaces offer the services of the MediaMgr, MusicMgr, and PhotoMgr components, respectively. The MediaMgr component still has two required interfaces used to receive specific media management services, such as music and photo.

The UML version 2.5 has been considered in the evolution of the Stereotype-based Management of Variability (SMarty) approach. The evolutionary version of the approach, 5.2, considers the representation of variability in different elements of a UML component diagram, specifically ports, interfaces, components, and operations. The following relationships are considered to represent variability:

- Relationships between interfaces and operations
- Relationships between ports and interfaces
- Relationships between components and ports
- Relationships between components and interfaces

Figure 5.8 illustrates the representation of variability in the MM SPL component diagram fragment.

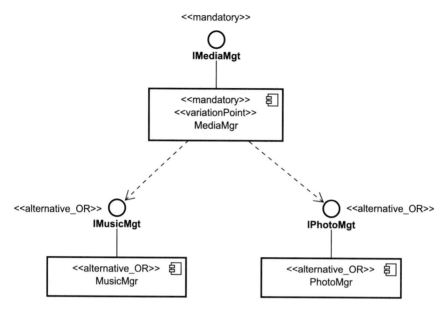

Fig. 5.8 Fragment of the MM SPL component diagram according to SMarty

In Fig. 5.8, the application of the SMartyProfile is observed. To detail the relationship between the MediaMgr, MusicMgr, and PhotoMgr components and the IMediaMgt, IMusicMgt, and IPhotoMgt interfaces, all elements of the diagram received a specific stereotype.

The MediaMgr component is a mandatory element and a variation point. The IMediaMgt interface is also a mandatory element. The IMusicMgt and IPhotoMgt interfaces as well as the MusicMgr and PhotoMgr components are optional variants associated with theMediaMgr variation point.

In Figs. 5.7 and 5.8, only the relationship between components and interfaces was considered. For more information and examples about other relationships, please refer to [2].

5.2.4 Activity Diagrams

The extension of the SMarty approach to activity diagrams was carried out by Fiori et al. [6]; thus, guidelines to identify and represent the variability in activity diagrams were created, in addition to evolving SMartyProfile metaclass.

Figure 5.9 is a representation of a fragment of a UML activity diagram, considering the SMarty approach of the saveGame() method of the Arcade Game Maker (AGM) SPL.

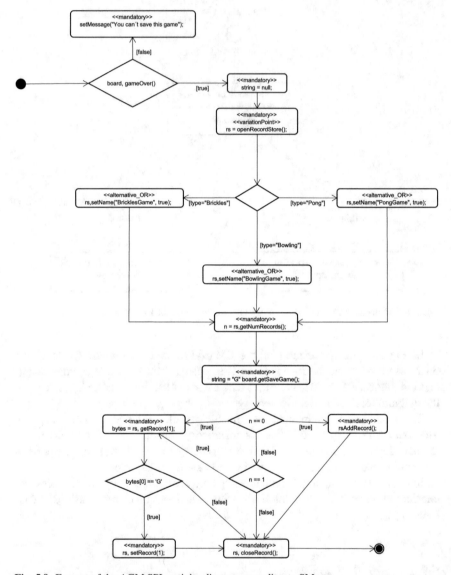

Fig. 5.9 Excerpt of the AGM SPL activity diagram according to SMarty

Instead of placing the «variationPoint» in the decision nodes to allow the choice of different flows, this stereotype must be placed in the activity prior to the decision point considered to be a point of variation.

Actions after the decision point considered «variationPoint» are considered variables, according to the AT.3 guideline. For this example, they receive stereotypes of the type «alternative_OR», since at least one of the flows must be chosen (Pong, Brickles, or Bowling).

According to the AT.2 guideline, the «mandatory» stereotype is present in all activities.

5.2.5 Sequence Diagrams

Marcolino and OliveiraJr [9] identified the elements of UML that represented the restrictions between variability, in addition to elements that are candidates for variation points and variants in sequence diagrams.

CombinedFragment of the type "alt" is defined in the UML as an element that presents the possibility of executing a single alternative flow, among several. This definition is related to the constraint that indicates mutually exclusive variants («alternative_XOR»). In this way, this element was selected to represent variation points to be tagged as «variationPoint».

The flow messages, which correspond to the variants related to the variation point identified by the CombinetFragment of the "alt" type, are annotated as variant, allowing the semantic extension with the «alternative_XOR» stereotype. Annotation with this stereotype only in the first message of the flow aims at greater readability of the model.

Optional variants are suggested through CombinedFragment with the interactionOperator "opt," being tagged as «optional» and in situations where a lifeline interacts with another lifeline, through a single message flow in a single interaction, also receiving the annotation "optional."

The CombinedFragment with interactionOperator "opt" indicates an option to choose between certain flows. The possibility to use the «optional» stereotype for messages has also been incorporated instead of using CombinedFragment with "opt."

The interactionUse graphic element "ref" is used to represent the inclusive type variability (OR). This element indicates the sharing of an interaction, thus referring a sequence diagram that can be used in more than one model. Thus, this element was selected to identify inclusive variants, as it can reference other diagrams, using «variants».

Figure 5.10 is the representation of a fragment of a UML activity diagram, considering the SMarty approach of the saveGame() method of the AGM SPL.

The diagram was modeled in the SMartyModeling tool following the criteria: Player, Menu, Board, and RecordStore are considered mandatory and, therefore, receive the «mandatory» stereotype. In addition, Menu is also a variation point, receiving the «variationPoint» stereotype. BowlingGameMenu, BricklesGameMenu, and PongGameMenu are the variants of the variation point and therefore marked with the «alternative_OR» stereotype, since at least one of these variants must be chosen.

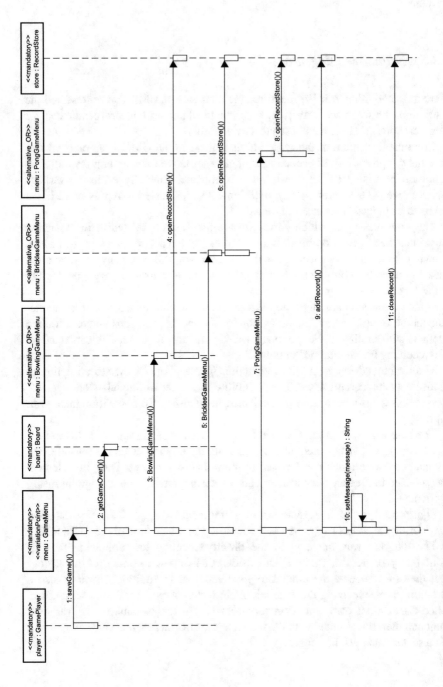

Fig. 5.10 Excerpt of an AGM sequence diagram according to SMarty

5.3 Traceability Among Designed Elements

It is known that even in organizations and projects with mature software development processes, software artifacts created as part of these processes end up being disconnected from each other [16].

Traceability allows acceptance of the system, allowing users to better understand it, and contributes to a clear and consistent documentation. According to IBM [16] this lack of traceability between software artifacts is caused by several factors, including:

- The fact that these artifacts are written in different languages.
- They describe a software system at various levels of abstraction (requirements vs. implementation).
- Processes applied within an organization do not impose maintenance of existing traceability links.
- The lack of adequate tool support to create and maintain traceability.

Consequently, one of the biggest challenges for maintainers, while performing a maintenance task, is the need to understand this myriad of frequently disconnected artifacts, originally created as part of the software development process.

Software traceability is a sought-after quality, although often elusive, in software-intensive systems, being recognized as an important factor in supporting various activities in the process of developing software systems [3, 14, 16]. It provides assurance that all necessary features have been implemented and properly tested. The easiest and most efficient way to ensure traceability is by registering the requirements traceability matrix for project [15].

Traceability supports the following aspects [14]: in analyzing the implications and integration of changes that occur in software systems, in the maintenance and evolution of software systems, when reusing components of the software system, in identifying and comparing the requirements of new and existing systems, in the testing of software system components, and system inspection, indicating alternatives and commitments made during development.

There are four steps for tracing elements among SMarty diagrams, which are:

- R.1 Identify the UML comment notation, with the «variability» stereotype in the element one wants to track. Figure 5.11 represents a comment notation used by the SMarty approach.
- R.2 To identify traceability at higher abstraction levels, look for the "realizes+" meta-attribute, which contains a set of variability names. This is identified in Fig. 5.12.
- R.3 To track elements in lower abstraction diagrams, identify the "realizes−" attribute that contains a set of variability names, as shown in Fig. 5.13.
- R.4 (Fig. 5.14) Go to the corresponding diagram, and look for the name identified in the realizes meta-attribute (+ or −).

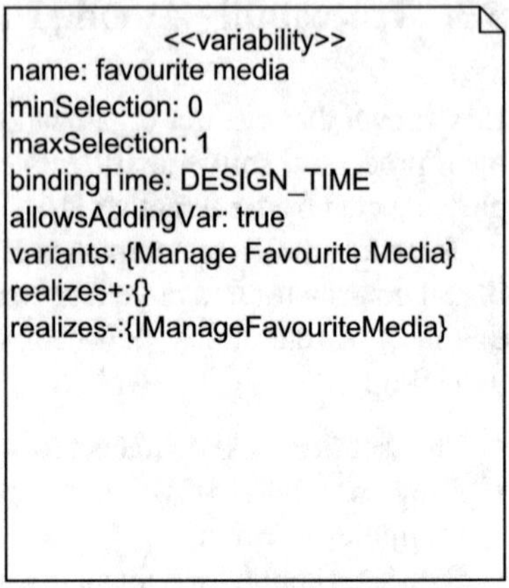

Fig. 5.11 Identifying an UM
comment variability

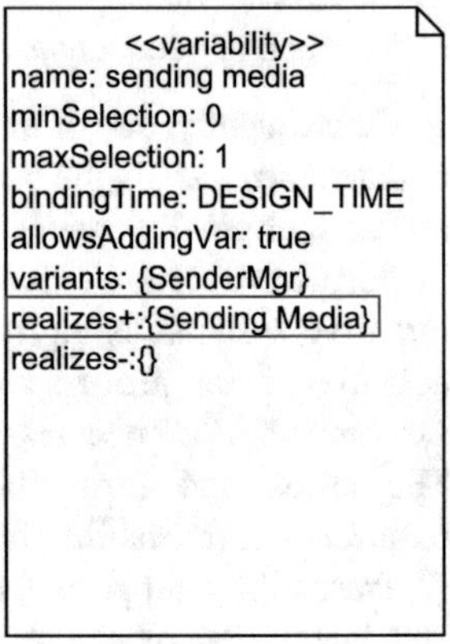

```
                    <<variability>>
name: favourite media
minSelection: 0
maxSelection: 1
bindingTime: DESIGN_TIME
allowsAddingVar: true
variants: {Manage Favourite Media}
realizes+:{}
realizes-:{IManageFavouriteMedia}
```

Fig. 5.12 Identifying the
"realizes+" attribute

```
                    <<variability>>
name: sending media
minSelection: 0
maxSelection: 1
bindingTime: DESIGN_TIME
allowsAddingVar: true
variants: {SenderMgr}
realizes+:{Sending Media}
realizes-:{}
```

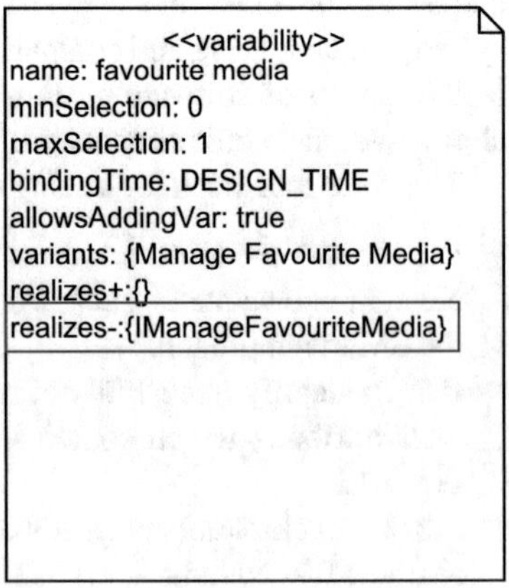

Fig. 5.13 Identifying the
"realizes−" attribute

```
                    <<variability>>
name: favourite media
minSelection: 0
maxSelection: 1
bindingTime: DESIGN_TIME
allowsAddingVar: true
variants: {Manage Favourite Media}
realizes+:{}
realizes-:{IManageFavouriteMedia}
```

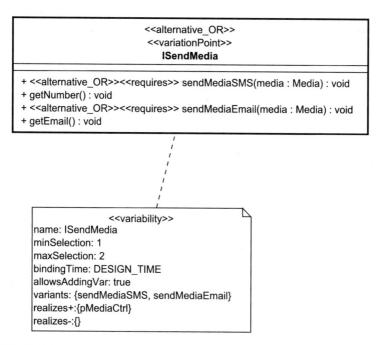

Fig. 5.14 Guideline example R.4

5.4   Configuring Specific Products

SMartyModeling supports configuring products from the SPL modeled in the environment. The environment guides the user in solving variability, taking into account the choice of optional elements and, from the variation points, selecting the variants according to the constraint rules. To support this functionality, it was necessary to define a form of representation from an architectural viewpoint.

Therefore, the product consists of a set of instances. The instantiation process starts from a specific diagram, which contains a direct reference. And similarly to the architecture defined for diagram representation, instances contain a set of artifacts, referring to the instantiated elements, and relationships, referring to the respective associations between these artifacts. Figure 5.15 presents the architecture overview defined to represent the products and instances, emphasizing the relationships, navigability, and references between the identified elements.

The first step in setting up a new product is the creation of a new product. SMartyModeling allows the creation of a new product by accessing the Product Line menu through the New Product item. A panel is presented for creating a new product, with the following attributes: name, version, and description.

As shown in Fig. 5.15, a product is composed of a set of instances. Therefore, with a product created, the next step is to instantiate a diagram, generating a new

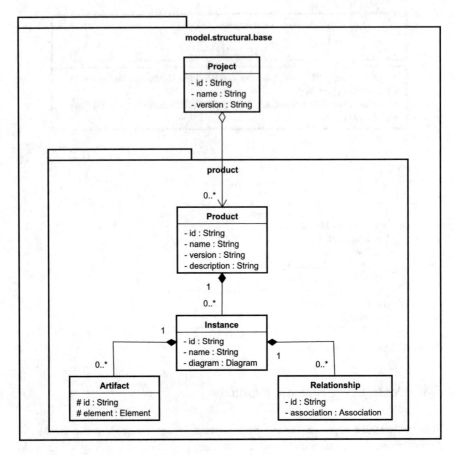

Fig. 5.15 Product architecture—overview

instance for the product. In short, SMartyModeling guides the user to instantiate a diagram through the four-step process:

- **Start Panel:** a new instance panel is presented to the user, requesting information about which Product the Instance will be part, selecting the Diagram that will be used as the basis for instantiation and the name to new instance.
- **Selecting Optional Elements:** a panel is presented with all diagram elements, with a check box associated with each element, with the required diagram elements being fixed as marked and the optional elements being marked at the user's option.
- **Variability Resolution:** a panel is presented, according to the required and optional elements selected in the previous panel, listing the elements that are marked as variation points. Thus, for all variabilities of the diagram, the following are presented:

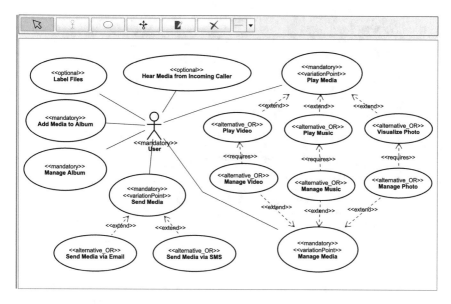

Fig. 5.16 Mobile Media adaptation

- **Inclusive Variability:** with the name of Variability, followed by its respective set of variants, associating each variant with a check box, thus allowing the user to solve the variability by choosing the variants
- **Exclusive Variability:** with the name of Variability, followed by a combo box with the variants defined for variability, thus allowing the user to select the instance variant

• **Instance Information:** finally, a panel is presented to the user, allowing the user to define the name of the new instance and showing the number of instantiated artifacts and relationships.

To exemplify the diagram instantiation process, we consider an adaptation of the Mobile Media use case model using SMartyModeling as presented in Fig. 5.16. The adaptation contains a unique mandatory user named User and 16 use cases. The mandatory use cases are Log In, Add Media to Album and Manage Album. The optional use cases are Label Files and Hear Media from Incoming Caller. Three inclusive variabilities are defined:

• *Sending Media*: optional use case Send Media as variation point and the following variants: Send Media via Email and Send Media via SMS
• *Playing Media*: mandatory use case Play Media as variation point and the following variants: Play Video, Play Music, and Visualize Photo
• *Managing Media*: mandatory use case Manage Media as variation point and the following variants: Manage Video, Manage Music, and Manage Photo.

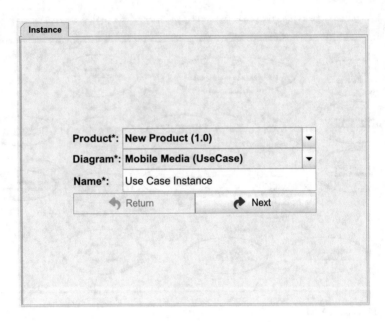

Fig. 5.17 First panel for a new instance

With the new product and modeled diagram, the next step is to instantiate the diagram by accessing the Product Line menu through the Instantiate Product item. The first panel requires the product (which instance will be part), the diagram to instantiate and a name for the new instance. Figure 5.17 presents the panel for a new instance in our example.

Following our example, the second panel presents all elements of the diagram, setting the mandatory elements to true. Optional elements can be checked as the user desires. In our example, we checked only the Label Files use case, and Send Media use case is not checked. All mandatory elements are checked automatically. Figure 5.18 presents the second panel with our example.

The third panel presents the variability to be solved by the user according to the elements selected in the previous panel. In our example, we resolve the variability as follows: *Managing Media* variability has as variation point the Manage Media use case and the Manage Video, and Manage Photo use cases were selected as variants. For the *Playing Media* variability, which has the Play Media use case as its variation point, the Play Video and Visualize Photo use cases were selected as variants. And for the *Sending Media* variability, which has the Send Media use case as the variation point, the Send Media via SMS use case as a variant. The diagram used for instantiation has only inclusive variability. Figure 5.19 presents the third panel with our example, solving the variability as mentioned.

Finally, the last panel presents a summary of the new instance, showing the following information: name of the new instance, the product that the new instance will be part of, the base diagram of the new instance, the number of resulting

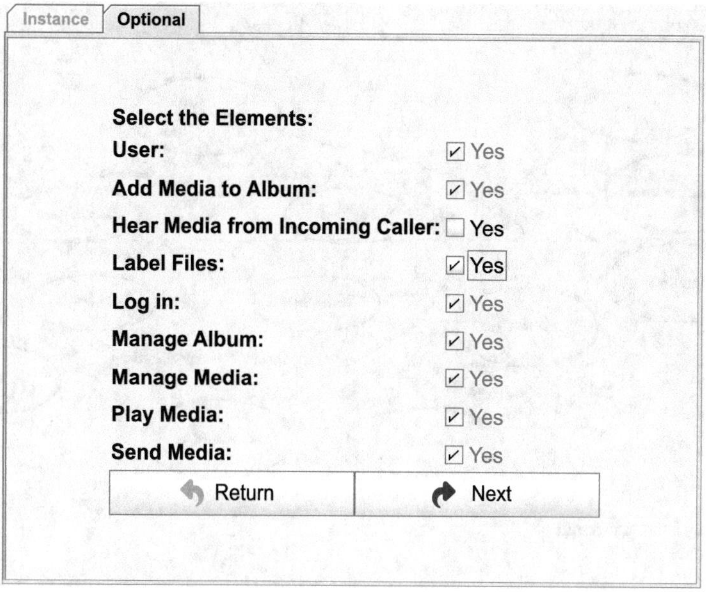

Fig. 5.18 Second panel for a new instance

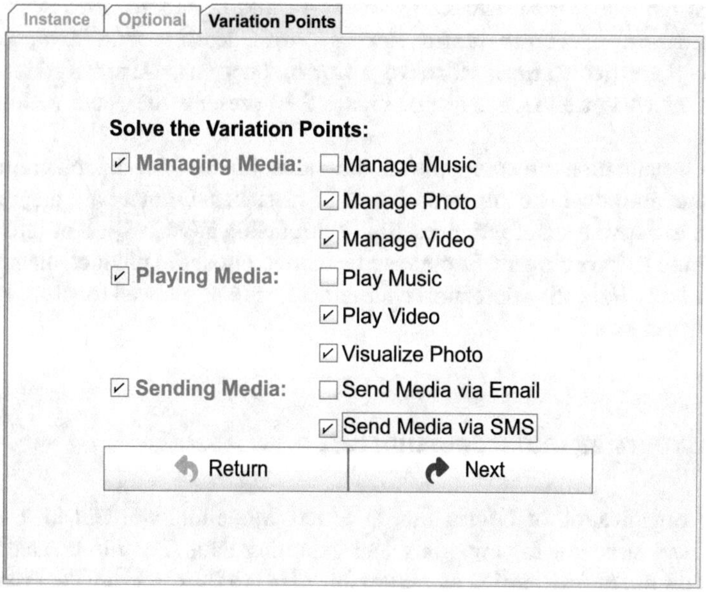

Fig. 5.19 Third panel for a new instance

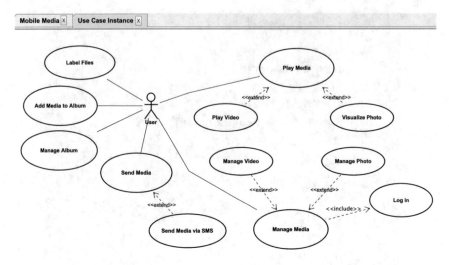

Fig. 5.20 Instance panel

artifacts (the elements derived from the base diagram), and the number of resulting relationships (the associations derived from the base diagram).

Therefore, considering our example, the new instance contains the following artifacts: the actor User and 12 use cases—Label Files, Add Media to Album, Manage Album, Send Media, Send Media via SMS, Manage Media, Manage Video, Manage Photo, Log In, Play Media, Play Video, and Visualize Photo. Figure 5.20 presents the panel with the new instance.

The instantiation process follows the same process for all diagram types. Therefore, a product is composed of a set of instances. From a base diagram, it is possible to derive a set of instances. SMartyModeling allows export of information through the Export menu. Export can be carried out at the product, diagram, and instance level. Exporting the source code structure is also allowed for class diagrams and their instances.

5.5 Exporting and Importing SPLs

For the organization of information in SMartyModeling, we defined a standard hierarchical structure for importing and exporting data. The file created for the project has the *smty* extension and is organized in tag format. From the Project root node, the other nodes with information about diagrams, variability, elements, and associations are organized, allowing defining a standard way for the environment.

From an architectural point of view, we define the *Exportable* interface and all classes written to the file implement such an interface, organizing their information in a tag format, building the complete structure of the project. All exported objects must have a unique identifier in the environment. The association of a unique identifier with objects is fundamental in the import process, both for the construction of objects and for the retrieval of elements for the definition of associations and variability.

The Project is the root node with its respective information: id, name, and version. The first objects to export are types. This group is comprised of primitive Java language types, including *lang* and *utils* package classes, as well as the classes and interfaces defined in the project class diagrams.

Next, information about the stereotypes and the profile is exported. Initially, stereotypes defined by the SMarty approach are automatically loaded; however, the user can manually enter new stereotypes. The profile by default associates SPL concepts with the SMarty approach stereotypes and can be changed by the user accessing the `Product Line` menu through the `Edit Profile` item, allowing the user to change stereotypes. For the Project it is considered a unique profile for the representation of variability.

In sequence, diagrams of the five types supported by the environment are exported. The id, name, and type values are arranged in the diagram tag. For each diagram, their respective elements are exported, containing their identifier, name, and graphical information (size and position). Associations are exported with the identifier, name, source (element id) and destination (element id) attributes, and graphical attributes (coordinate set). And at the end, the variability (according to the SMarty approach structure) is exported, containing the reference to the variation point (element id) and its variants (element set).

Traceability is also exported containing its respective attributes: identifier, name, description, and the elements. And finally the products are exported, following the structure shown in Fig. 5.15. The products contain a list of instances, with the instances having a set of artifacts (with reference to elements) and relationships (with reference to associations).

5.6 Final Remarks

This chapter presented the application of the SMarty approach to design SPLs. The SMartyModeling environment incorporates the SMartyProfile to allow the modeling of variabilities in UML diagrams. In Sect. 5.2, stereotypes and guidelines were presented for the representation of variabilities in different diagrams, such as use case, class, component, activity, and sequence.

In Sect. 5.3, specific guidelines are explained to be applied in SMarty diagrams. As a result, it is possible to maintain traceability among designed elements. Section 5.5 presented a structure for importing and exporting data from/to SMartyModeling. In these cases, traceability is also exported, containing specific attributes. The steps for configuring specific products are detailed in Sect. 5.4. The Mobile Media SPL [17] was used as example.

Considering the information presented about the design of SPLs with SMarty, it is possible to observe the feasibility of applying the SMarty approach in environments for engineering UML-based SPLs, such as in SMartyModeling.

Acknowledgments The authors would like to thank CAPES/Brazil (code 001) for funding this work.

References

1. Allian, A.P.: VMTools-RA: a reference architecture for software variability tools. Master's Thesis, Universidade Estadual de Maringá, Departamento de Informática, Programa de Pós Graduação em Ciência da Computação (2016). In Portuguese
2. Bera, M.H.G.: SMartyComponents: a process for specifying UML-based product-line architectures. Master's Thesis, Universidade Estadual de Maringá, Departamento de Informática, Programa de Pós Graduação em Ciência da Computação (2015). In Portuguese
3. Cleland-Huang, J., Gotel, O., Hayes, J., Mäder, P., Zisman, A.: Software Traceability: Trends and Future Directions, pp. 55–69 (2014). https://doi.org/10.1145/2593882.2593891
4. Ferber, S., Haag, J., Savolainen, J.: Feature interaction and dependencies: modeling features for reengineering a legacy product line. In: International Conference on Software Product Lines, pp. 235–256. Springer, Berlin (2002)
5. Figueiredo, E., Cacho, N., Sant'Anna, C., Monteiro, M., Kulesza, U., Garcia, A., Soares, S., Ferrari, F., Khan, S., Castor Filho, F., et al.: Evolving software product lines with aspects. In: 2008 ACM/IEEE 30th International Conference on Software Engineering, pp. 261–270. IEEE, Piscataway (2008)
6. Fiori, D.R., Gimenes, I.M.S., Maldonado, J.C., de OliveiraJr, E.: Variability management in software product line activity diagrams. In: DMS, pp. 89–94 (2012)
7. Fowler, M., Scott, K.: UML Distilled: A Brief Guide to the Standard Object Modeling Language. Addison-Wesley Professional (1999)
8. Kaur, M., Kumar, P.: Mobile media SPL creation by feature IDE using FODA. Global J. Comput. Sci. Technol. **14**(3), 11–16 (2014)
9. Marcolino, A., OliveiraJr, E.: Avaliação experimental da abordagem SMarty para gerenciamento de variabilidades em linhas de produto de software basedas em uml **1**, 339–353 (2015)
10. Miles, R., Hamilton, K.: Learning UML 2.0. O'Reilly Media, Sebastopol (2006)
11. OMG, O.M.G.: The unified modeling language uml. https://www.omg.org/spec/UML/2.5.1/PDF
12. Pilone, D., Pitman, N.: UML 2.0 in a Nutshell. O'Reilly Media, Sebastopol (2005)
13. Rosenberg, D., Stephens, M.: Use Case Driven Object Modeling with UML. Springer, New York (2007)
14. Spanoudakis, G., Zisman, A.: Software Traceability: A Roadmap. Handbook of Software Engineering and Knowledge Engineering, vol. 3 (2005). https://doi.org/10.1142/9789812775245_0014
15. Sundaram, S., Hayes, J., Dekhtyar, A., Holbrook, E.: Assessing traceability of software engineering artifacts. Requir. Eng. **15**, 313–335 (2010). https://doi.org/10.1007/s00766-009-0096-6
16. Traceability in software engineering—past, present and future (TR-74-211) (2007)
17. Young, T.J.: Using aspectj to build a software product line for mobile devices. Ph.D. Thesis, University of British Columbia (2005)

Chapter 6
Product-Line Architecture Designing with SMartyComponents

Márcio H. G. Bera, Thelma Elita Colanzi, Edson OliveiraJr, Nelson Tenório, Willian Marques Freire, and Aline M. M. Miotto Amaral

Abstract The SPL Architecture (PLA) is one of the main artifacts of an SPL. It represents an abstraction of all possible products that can be generated from an SPL. Important PLA requirements include (i) remain stable during the SPL lifetime, (ii) easy integration of new features during the architecture life cycle, and (iii) explicit representation of variability for providing reuse. Therefore, this chapter presents the SMartyComponents process for designing UML-based PLAs. SMartyComponents is based on the UML Components process and provides systematic activities to modeling component-based PLAs based on the SMarty approach, mainly focused on component diagram elements, such as components, interfaces, ports, and operations according to the standard UML metamodel. Workflows of SMartyComponents include: Requirements Workflow and Specification Workflow. The former is composed of activities as Develop Business Concept Model, Develop Business Processes, and Identify Use Cases. The latter activities are Component Identification, Component Interactions, and Component Specification. The main product developed using SMartyComponents is a component-based PLA with variabilities modeled in components, interfaces, ports, and operations.

6.1 The Role of SMarty in This Work

In this chapter the SMarty approach has a central role as it provides stereotypes and tagged values to represent variability in component-based PLAs. To do so, SMarty extended the standard UML profile including stereotypes for components, ports, interfaces, and operations. With variabilities in these elements, one is able

M. H. G. Bera · T. E. Colanzi · E. OliveiraJr · W. M. Freire · A. M. M. Miotto Amaral
Informatics Department, State University of Maringá, Maringá PR, Brazil
e-mail: thelma@din.uem.br; edson@din.uem.br; ammmamaral@din.uem.br

N. Tenório (✉)
Informatics Department, UniCesumar, Maringá PR, Brazil
e-mail: nelson.tenorio@unicesumar.edu.br

© Springer Nature Switzerland AG 2023
E. OliveiraJr (ed), *UML-Based Software Product Line Engineering with SMarty*,
https://doi.org/10.1007/978-3-031-18556-4_6

to provide different PLA abstractions according to a well-established component-based process, as the UML Components [5].

6.2 SMartyComponents

The Product-Line Architecture (PLA) is considered the main artifact of an SPL [1] and abstracts possible products generated [8]. The essential PLA requirements remain stable during the SPL lifetime, easy integration of new features during the architecture life cycle, and explicit representation of variability for providing reuse [4].

A well-defined component-based process was specified to provide a systematic process for designing PLA. We first carried out studies that resulted in important insights to specified SMartyComponents [6, 7].

SMartyComponents process [3] comprises the Requirements and Specification Workflows since they are the main stages for specifying PLAs. As the **workflow** term comes from the UML Components approach, the artifacts from these workflows serve as input for the SMartyProcess. In this process, variabilities from UML models are identified and represented to the PLA specifications based on components. The UML Components process is composed of two main workflows: requirements and specification.

Figure 6.1 presents the UML Components and SMartyComponents workflows divided into two parts. First section of Fig. 6.1a presents the activities of UML Components requirements and specification, and the second section of Fig. 6.1b describes the activities for the SMartyComponents.

A workflow embraces activities covered by a set of tasks, roles, and artifacts. The tasks consume and generate artifacts and are performed by roles. Each activity produces and consumes artifacts from SMartyProcess. This process is responsible for identifying and representing variabilities in UML models (Fig. 6.1).

Figure 6.2 presents the workflows supported by SMartyComponents and the roles involved in the activities and tasks of each workflow. The input and output artifacts are presented in each workflow. The next sections detailed the SMartyComponents workflows considering their activities, roles, and tasks. We used the Arcade Game Maker SPL[1] of the Software Engineering Institute (SEI) to illustrate these workflows and their task.

---

[1] Arcade Game Maker SPL (SEI) site: https://resources.sei.cmu.edu/library/asset-view.cfm?assetid=485941.

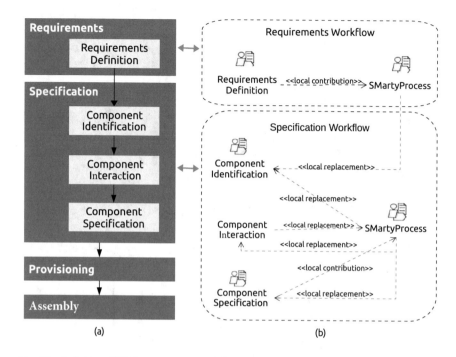

Fig. 6.1 Activities of UML components workflows interacting with SMartyProcess

6.3   Requirements Workflow

The UML Components assumes that Requirements Workflow is the user's abstraction regarding the business process. Such a business process demands project steps and a description of the business concept. Its description must include clear terms of ownership. This business process description has to be provided by the customer and adapted by the Business Analyst and Domain Expert.

This workflow has two activities: Requirements Definition with three tasks (Fig. 6.3), Describe Business Processes, Develop Business Conceptual Model, and Identify Use Cases, and SMartyProcess with four tasks Identify Variabilities, Constraint Variabilities, Represent Variabilities, and Trace and Control Variabilities.

6.3.1   Activity: Requirements Definition

This activity inputs the SPL Domain Knowledge and Business Requirements artifacts. The Domain Knowledge artifact is used by the task Developing Business Concept Model and carried out by the Domain Specialist or the Business Analyst. The Business Requirements artifact is consumed by two tasks performed by the

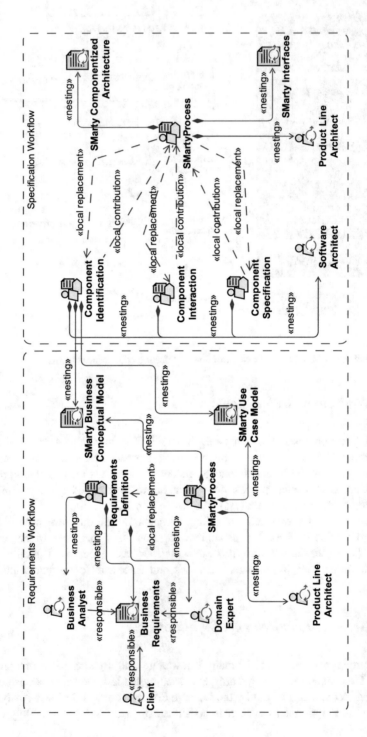

Fig. 6.2 Roles, artifacts, and activities of SMartyComponents workflows

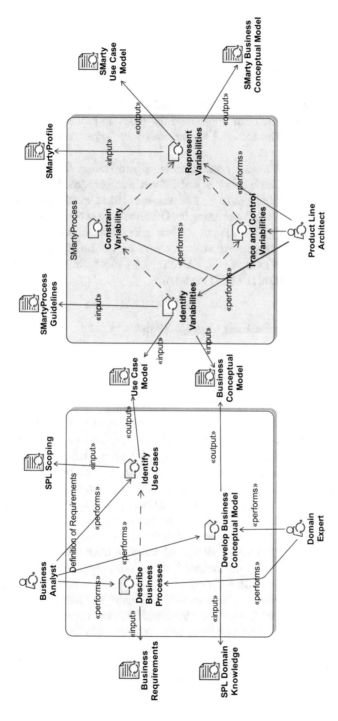

Fig. 6.3 Requirements workflow of SMartyComponents in SPEM

Business Analyst, such as Describe Business Processes and Identify Use Cases. Figure 6.3 presents the composition of the Requirements Workflow.

6.3.1.1   Task: Describe Business Processes

This task aims to understand the business processes addressed to execute the Identify Use Cases task. It is crucial to understand the business process's functionalities after describing them. The Business Requirements artifact is the key to discerning business processes.

The Business Requirements artifact contains information from meetings and workshops organized with customers and information concerned with discussion among the project stakeholders (e.g., analysts, specialists, customers, and users). This information is relevant to executing the Describe Business Processes task. The business process might be modeled as a UML activity diagram for clear business logic interpretation. This suggestion is not part of the proposed process. The stakeholders can use the models with which they are most familiar (e.g., Business Process Modeling Notation (BPMN) models).

6.3.1.2   Task: Develop Business Concept Model

The Business Analyst or the Domain Expert starts generating a business concept model based on SPL domain knowledge. This Business Concept Model (also called mapping) relates the terms contained in the description of the business process and other essential terms with no representation of variability.

As an alternative to build a Business Conceptual Model, the UML offers the class diagram [5]. However, the Business Concept Model does not necessary to be completely detailed. No raised properties or operations are during this task. Those sort of models show whether the business arises during the model creation

SPL Domain Knowledge is an artifact to store understanding and knowledge regarding how those involved understand the domain and capture the business rules from SPL knowledge. Techniques such as storyboards or mind-maps might support [2] the representation of different scenarios in the SPL domain.

The Domain Expert develops a conceptual model of the initial business through the information identified from the business process. The main idea is to be reevaluated in the next workflow. The Business Concept Model artifact is an input of SMartyProcess to execute the activities of identifying and representing the variability in such a model. Both, the guidelines of SMartyProcess (to UML classes) and guidelines of the SPL Architecture, support the variability identification and representation. The variability representation is through the set of stereotypes of SMartyProfile. SMartyProcess results in the Business Concept Model SMarty, i.e., an evolution from Business Concept Model that contains a variability representation.

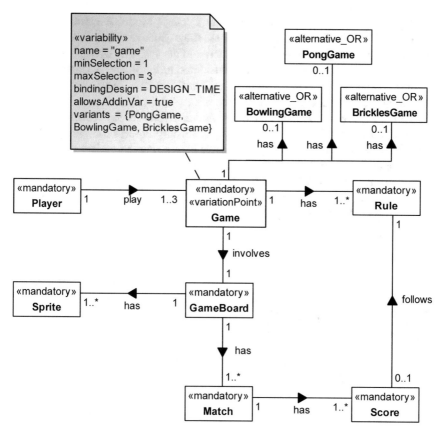

Fig. 6.4 SMarty Business Conceptual Model of the AGM SPL

Figure 6.4 shows the SMarty Business Conceptual Model produced from the SMartyProcess activities. Such artifact is based on the following concepts: a Player can play at least one and at most three Games, there must exist at least one Rule for each Game, each Rule might have a Score, each Game has one GameBoard, each GameBoard has at least one Sprite, each GameBoard might have at least one Match, and each Match might have a Score.

6.3.1.3   Task: Identify Use Cases

This task aids the Business Analyst in identifying the system's use cases. Hence, the use cases are responsible for presenting how the system fulfills its responsibilities, clarifying its limits, identifying the actors that interact with the system, and describing these interactions. The use cases are built from the events that trigger a series of steps. Therefore, all the steps make a single-use case.

After the task of Developing a Business Concept Model, a Business Analyst might assign responsibilities for each process stage. Such responsibilities may refer to the actors who manage both SPL products and the system's internal responsibilities. Some actors have probably been considered in the Business Concept Model as roles described by system components. Thus, this task deals with an artifact containing the limits and restrictions of the SPL.

At the end of this task, the Use Case Model supplies SMartyProcess for variability identification. The SPL Architect takes SMartyProcess use case guidelines as the basis for the use case diagrams. After identifying the variability contained in the use cases, the SPL Architect delimits the possible variability and represents the variability through SMartyProfile, thus, generating use cases with represented variability. Each use case produced is part of the SMarty Use Case Model. Figure 6.5 presents the AGM SPL SMarty Use Case diagram.

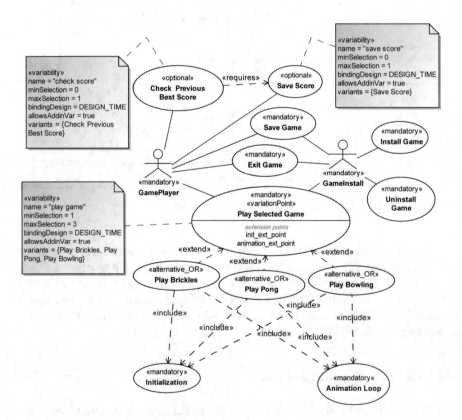

Fig. 6.5 AGM SPL SMarty use case diagram

6.4   Specification Workflow

In this workflow, information regarding business concepts and use cases are used to generate the component-based PLA specification, the Component Specification with variability, and the interfaces specification.

This workflow is divided into three activities: (i) Component Identification, (ii) Component Interaction, and (iii) Component Specification. Figure 6.6 shows the flow of workflow activities, presenting the entries to the SMartyProcess and the outputs generated at the end of the workflow. The following sections present each activity detailing its tasks, roles, and generated artifacts.

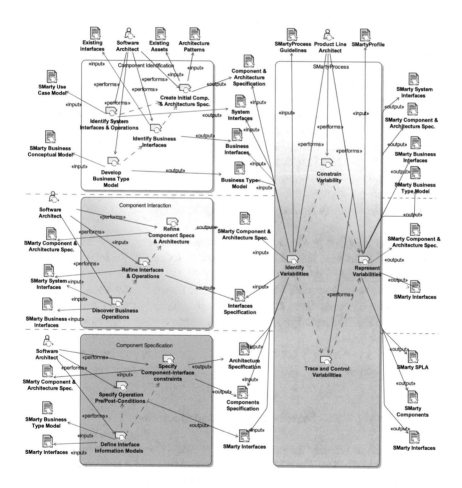

Fig. 6.6 Specification workflow of SMartyComponents in SPEM

6.4.1   Activity: Component Identification

This activity performs the Component Identification. The system interface identification and its operation are initialized based on the SMarty Use Case, thus are created the first specifications of the components and architecture. It is initialized the development of the Business Type Model and the identification of the business interfaces based on the SMarty Business Conceptual Model.

Figure 6.7 presents the artifacts, tasks, and roles, which encompass the Component Identification Activity.

6.4.1.1   Task: Develop Business Type Model

The task Develop Business Type Model aims to generate the Business Type Model using the business concepts identified in the Requirements Workflow.

The UML classes represent Business Type Model as the Business Conceptual Model but with different propose. While the Business Conceptual Model is a simple mapping of interest information of SPL domain, the Business Type Model contains the specific business information that can help to guide the PLA specification.

This task is realized through the SMarty Business Conceptual Model and results the Business Type Model artifact as output (Fig. 6.8).

6.4.1.2   Task: Identify Business Interfaces

The business interface is abstractions of information managed by the system [5]. To identify the business interface, it is required to refine the Business Type Model considering its restrictions on business rules.

One of the most important steps to define the business interfaces is to identify the business types considered core. Business interfaces to these cores are created and added to the Business Type Model. Such interfaces must be annotated by the stereotype *interface.type*.

The Software Architect performs this task generating the business interfaces (Fig. 6.9) as output.

6.4.1.3   Task: Identify System Interfaces and Operations

This task aims to identify the possible interfaces and operations of the system. Its input is the SMarty Use Case Model. A type of dialog and a system interface are identified for each use case. It is necessary to analyze all use cases considering the existing system responsibilities that must be modeled. If there are, such responsibilities must be represented as interface operations. These changes will provide an initial set of interfaces and operations.

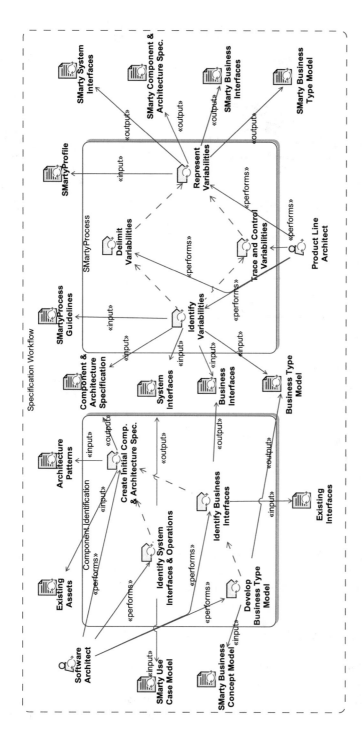

Fig. 6.7 Activity: component identification

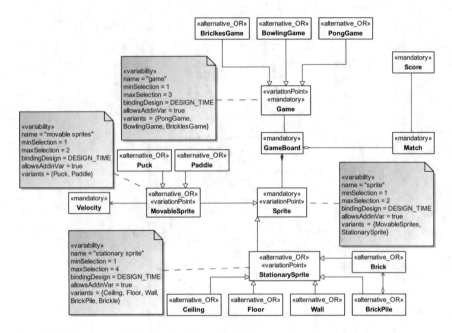

Fig. 6.8 SMarty business type model of the AGM SPL

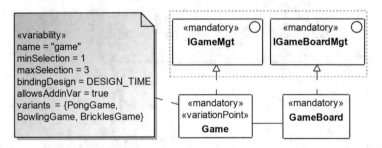

Fig. 6.9 Business interfaces of the AGM SPL

The Software Architect performs the Identify System Interfaces and Operations task using the SMarty Use Case Model. The system interfaces identified by SMarty and based on its Use Case Model is presented in Fig. 6.10.

6.4.1.4 Task: Create Initial Components and Architecture Specification

After performing the previous tasks, the task Create Initial Components and Architecture Specification is performed. In this task, an initial set of Component Specifications is created. Components can be elaborated or acquired from third parties. Cheesman and Daniels [5] highlight possible inputs to this task which are:

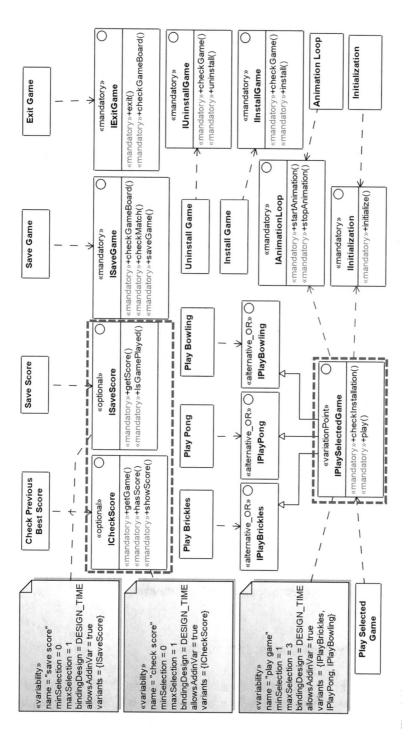

Fig. 6.10 System interfaces of the AGM SPL

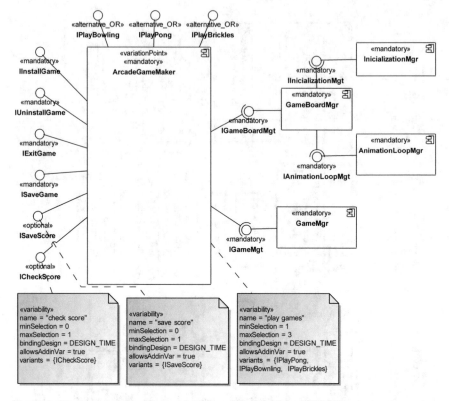

Fig. 6.11 Component and architecture initial specification of the AGM SPL

- The business and system interfaces
- Existing specification of components aiming at reuse
- A possible existing architecture of Component Specification
- The choice of architecture patterns of Component Specification

The Create Initial Components and Architecture Specification task handles as inputs Existing Assets and Architecture Patterns to creating the initial Component and Architecture Specification (Fig. 6.11).

At the end of all tasks of this activity, the SMartyProcess is performed over the resulting tasks artifacts to encompassing SPL variabilities.

6.4.2 Activity: Component Interaction

This activity aims to describe the component's interaction. The SMarty System Interfaces and the SMarty Business Interfaces define the business operations. Both identified interfaces and operations are refined to generate the artifact SMarty

Interfaces. These interfaces will support the refinement of the components and architecture specifications. Following the Interaction Components, tasks are presented. Figure 6.12 encompasses the tasks, roles, input, and output artifacts involved in this activity.

6.4.2.1   Task: Find Business Operations

The objective of this task is to reveal operations in business interfaces. This task has as inputs the SMarty Business Interfaces and the SMarty System Interfaces artifacts.

It is crucial to verify the interactions in the SMarty System Interfaces to find out such operations. One or more communication diagrams might be drawn to trace existing constraints in the execution flow resulting from the request of the operation. Operations needed for each interaction are made clear. These task input artifacts are updated and serve as input for the next task.

6.4.2.2   Task: Refine Interfaces and Operations

The responsibilities assigned to the SMarty Business Interfaces must be analyzed in this task. If necessary, an interface might be split in two toward increasing its reusability. Communication diagrams, system interfaces, and business interfaces interactions might make missing operations explicit and avoid responsibility duplicity. As a relevant output, this task generates the interfaces specification.

6.4.2.3   Task: Refine Component and Architecture Specification

The task Refine Component and Architecture Specification are performed at the end of Component Interaction Activity in which the SMarty Component and Architecture Specification artifact is the input. Thus, while interfaces and operations are discovered and refined, the Component and Architecture Specification are changed. All component and architecture specifications are refined, and reused, updating the SMarty Component and Architecture Specification artifact in this task. Thus, components are specified based on the previous tasks. Such artifact serves as input to the SMartyProcess tasks.

Figure 6.13 presents the AGM SPL component diagram representing the SMarty Component and Architecture Specification artifact with constraints in Object Constraint Language (OCL).[2]

---

[2] https://www.omg.org/spec/OCL.

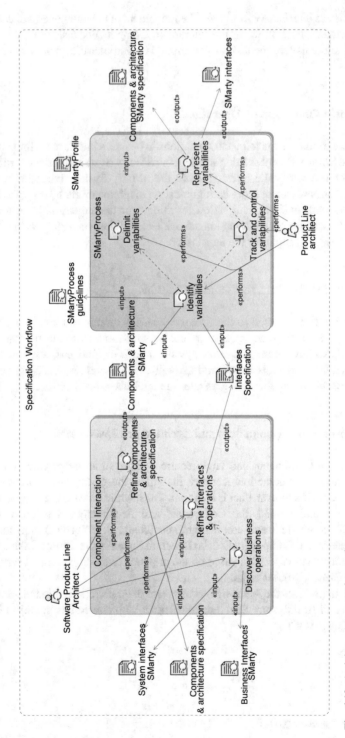

Fig. 6.12 Activity: component interaction

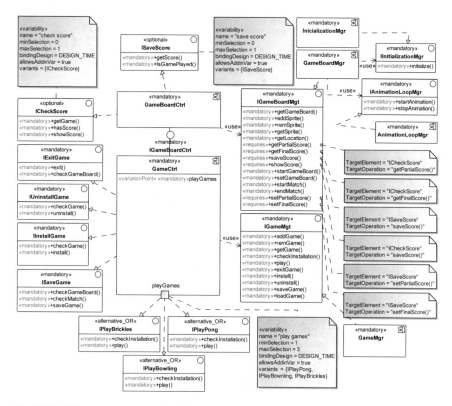

Fig. 6.13 SMarty component and architecture specification of the AGM SPL

6.4.3   Activity: Specify Components

This activity aims to define the Interfaces dependencies and constraints. It is composed of three tasks: Define Interface Information Model, Specify Operations Pre-and Post-Conditions, and Specify Component-Interface Constraints (Fig. 6.14).

6.4.3.1   Task: Define Interface Information Model

This task represents the object's state of a component on which the interface depends. For each interface must exist an Interface Information Model.

One might use an interface specification diagram to represent such information [5]. All changes in the objects state of a component generated by a certain operation can be described in terms of this definition of information model [5].

This task generates an Interface Information Model as input for the SMarty Interfaces Specification and the SMarty Business Type Model. Figure 6.15 illustrates the input Interface Information Model of AGM with variabilities.

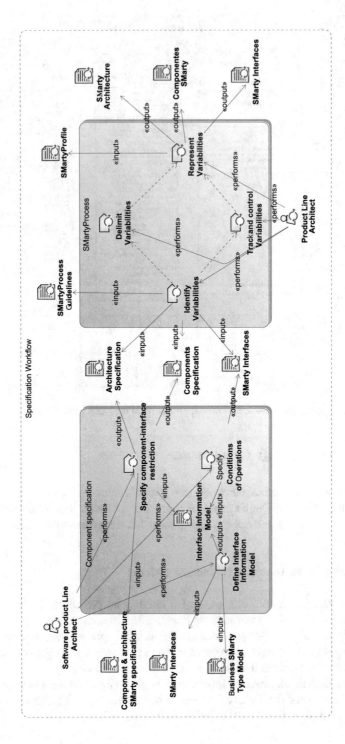

Fig. 6.14 Activity: component specification

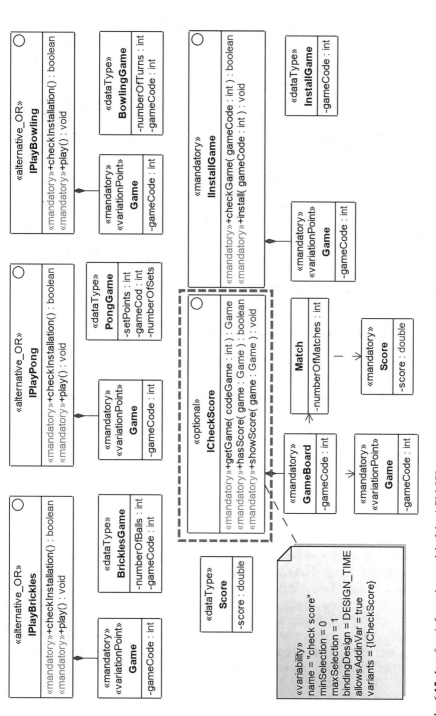

Fig. 6.15 Interface information model of the AGM SPL

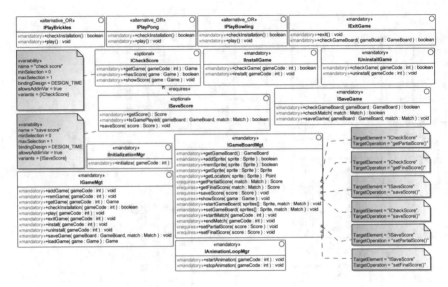

Fig. 6.16 SMarty interfaces of the AGM SPL with pre- and post-conditions

6.4.3.2 Task: Specify Operations Pre-and Post-Conditions

The Specify Operations Pre-and Post-Conditions task represent a draft of a client contract. Such a task details what the operations will perform considering a pair of pre-and post-conditions. While post-condition specifies the operation effect when the pre-conditions are true, no results must return when pre-conditions are false.

This task takes the Information Model as input and updates the SMarty Interfaces Specification artifact. Figure 6.16 shows an example of pre- and post-conditions in the AGM interfaces in OCL.

6.4.3.3 Specify Component-Interface Constraints

The last task of the Specify Components' activity is Specify Component-Interface Constraints. It takes as input the Interface Information Model to generate the Component Specification and the Architecture Specification.

There must be defined which interface realization each Component Specification supports. The architecture diagram should be decomposed into specific parts for each Component Specification. Thus, the components might be implemented by different developers to increase cohesion and reuse capability to decrease coupling.

As a final result, the PLA comes up with the logical Component-Based SMarty Architecture. Figure 6.17 represents such architecture for the AGM SPL.

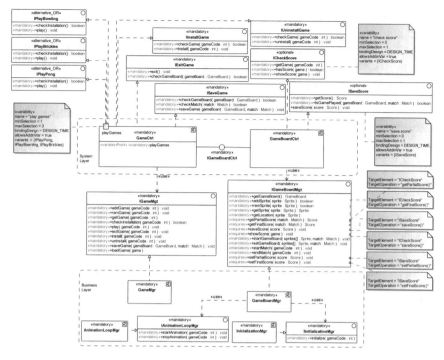

Fig. 6.17 The AGM SPL component-based SMarty architecture

6.5   Final Remarks

Since the workflows come from UML Components, the artifacts from these workflows serve as input. Software reuse is a relevant issue that has been explored both in academia and industry. Minimizing efforts in software development can reduce project costs, in addition to generating customizable products and improving the quality of the final product. Approaches such as SPL might provide mechanisms addressed to the reuse of components and artifacts. Moreover, the SPL approach allows product families to be generated, providing the reuse of artifacts and other benefits in the development process, such as development productivity in terms of time and reduction of control of risks and costs, and can also provide better time-to-market and return on investment. Therefore, the advantages and benefits provided by SPL were explored to propose a process that encompasses such characteristics, with the objective of specifying componentized PLA.

In this scenario, SMartyComponents were proposed, thus generating a systematic process for specifying componentized PLA. UML Components were properly analyzed, and modifications in its artifacts were required to provide the PLA specification process. SMarty served as the basis for managing variabilities in UML models generated by SMartyComponents, such as components, interfaces, ports, and operations.

Finally, SMartyComponents is fair to be an end solution for PLA but an opened window to the next step for easy integration of new features during the architecture life cycle and explicit representation of variability for reuse.

Acknowledgments This work is supported by the Brazilian funding agency CNPq (Grant 428994/2018-0).

References

1. Bass, L., Clements, P., Kazman, R., Safari: Software Architecture in Practice, 4th edn. SEI Series in Software Engineering. Addison-Wesley Professional a O'Reilly Media Company (2021)
2. Beel, J., Gipp, B.: Link analysis in mind maps: a new approach to determining document relatedness. In: Proceedings of the International Conference on Uniquitous Information Management and Communication, pp. 1–5. ACM, New York (2010). https://doi.org/10.1145/2108616.2108662
3. Bera, M.H.G.: SMartyComponentes: a process to specify componentized software product line architectures. Master's Thesis, State University of Maringá (2015)
4. Bera, M.H.G., OliveiraJr, E., Colanzi, T.E.: Evidence-based SMarty support for variability identification and representation in component models. In: Proceedings of the International Conference on Enterprise Information Systems, pp. 295–302. INSTICC (2015). https://doi.org/10.5220/0005366402950302
5. Cheesman, J., Daniels, J.: UML Components: A Simple Process for Specifying Component-Based Software. Addison-Wesley (2000)
6. Contieri Junior, A.C., Correia, G., Colanzi, T.E., Gimenes, I.M.S., OliveiraJr, E., Ferrari, S., Masiero, P.C., Garcia, A.F.: Extending UML components to develop software product-line architectures: lessons learned. In: European Conference on Software Architecture, pp. 130–138. Springer (2011). https://doi.org/10.1007/978-3-642-23798-0_13
7. Oizumi, W.N., Contieri Junior, A.C., Correia, G.G., Colanzi, T.E., Ferrari, S., Gimenes, I.M.S., OliveiraJr, E., Garcia, A.F., Masiero, P.C.: On the proactive design of product-line architectures with aspects: an exploratory study. In: IEEE 36th Annual Computer Software and Applications Conference, pp. 273–278. IEEE, Piscataway (2012). https://doi.org/10.1109/COMPSAC.2012.38
8. Van der Linden, F.J., Schmidt, K., Rommes, E.: Software Product Lines in Action: The Best Industrial Practice in Product Line Engineering. Springer, Berlin (2007)

Chapter 7
Model-Based Inspections of Software Product Lines

Giovanna Bettin, Ricardo Theis Geraldi, and Edson OliveiraJr

Abstract Software inspection is a rigorous special type of software review among the several verification and validation activities. It has a well-defined process that conducted all life cycle artifacts for different domains. The inspection's main objective is to detect and reduce the number of defects aiming to guarantee and control a specific SPL's quality or their products generated. Despite the several software inspection techniques available in the literature, few techniques inspect SPL modeled using UML variability diagrams. Therefore, this chapter presents SMartyCheck, a checklist-based software inspection technique that encompasses defect types taxonomy; and SMartyPerspective, a perspective-based software inspection that enables detecting defects using distinct scenarios and roles in SMarty diagrams. SMartyCheck and SMartyPerspective were evaluated in several empirical studies by undergraduate, graduate students, researchers, and experts, which provided a body of knowledge of their feasibility (quality) and effectiveness (productivity).

7.1 The Role of SMarty in This Work

SMarty differs from the others variability management approaches encompassing the software artifacts as UML models to the software inspection activity. SMarty has an original UML profile and a systematic process that supports the inspection activity through the SMartyCheck and SMartyPerspective techniques (this chapter). The main role of SMarty in this work is to aid these software inspection techniques.

SMarty provides stereotypes that also facilitate defects detection to specify and model UML models (e.g., use case, class, sequence, and components). These stereotypes are useful for delimit the variabilities of the UML diagrams elements (e.g., class) and help to identify defects. The stereotypes and meta-attributes of SMarty allow the traceability between variabilities. It is possible to verify

G. Bettin (✉) · R. T. Geraldi · E. OliveiraJr
Informatics Department, State University of Maringá, Maringá PR, Brazil
e-mail: edson@din.uem.br

© Springer Nature Switzerland AG 2023

E. OliveiraJr (ed), *UML-Based Software Product Line Engineering with SMarty*,
https://doi.org/10.1007/978-3-031-18556-4_7

inconsistency in different diagram types kept by the SMarty. This characteristic of SMarty is used by the Domain Asset Manager perspective of the SMartyPerspective to identify defects in versions of SMarty diagrams and traceability between them and different diagrams types.

The diagram types supported by SMarty collaborate for the Domain Engineering activities through the inspection of the variabilities management diagrams used in these activities by the SMartyCheck and SMartyPerspective, beyond the roles specified in the SMartyPerspective.

SMarty contributes to more targeted inspection. Its stereotypes make it easy for inspectors to find elements with SMartyCheck checklists. SMarty guide and organize SMartyPerspective scenarios narrowing inspectors' focus through instructions. Such instructions guide the inspectors in how/where to find elements in diagrams to identifying defects through specific variability management questions. SMarty adopts the variability management activity of the SPL paradigm. The models based on the UML have variabilities managed through SMarty identification and representation activities. These activities are implicit and aid during the inspections.

Overall, the SMarty considers UML models in inspections, an original UML profile, a systematic process, stereotypes, and activities for variability management. These characteristics of SMarty hold the defects detection in software inspection techniques, as in SMartyCheck and SMartyPerspective.

7.2 Software Inspection Foundations

During software development it is impossible not to inject defects into artifacts [41]. The people are prone to errors, hard days, fatigue, and have little knowledge of the project domain. Therefore, defects must be detected quickly and efficiently so that they do not propagate to other development stages, increase costs, or directly to the user [11, 41].

Software inspection is a set of methods to verify the quality properties of products to find defects by formally, efficiently, and economically reading artifacts as they are created [11, 23, 39, 41]. Thus, defects can be corrected before moving on to the next stages of development, improving not only product quality but productivity as well [11, 23, 41].

The inspection process checks the quality properties of the artifacts by identifying artifact defects by comparing them with a "set of expectations regarding structure, content, and desired qualities" [5, 11]. In this way, the inspection can help to understand the types of defects commonly found in the organization, the nature, and structure of the product [2, 39].

The first (and best known) systematic inspection process was developed in the literature by Fagan [41]. The process collaborates to organize the software inspection sessions and defines six or sequential steps [10, 39, 41]: (i) planning defines the artifacts and inspection team; (ii) overview presents the characteristics and domain of the project; (iii) preparation, inspectors individually review the artifact; (iv) inspection, inspectors review artifacts together; (v) rework, the defects are corrected; and (vi) follow-up, the artifact is re-evaluated to verify the need for a new inspection.

Inspection techniques collaborate through different approaches to the inspection process effectiveness by guiding the reader on what/how to examine the artifacts. Thus, the inspection techniques help identify defects by evaluating the several qualities and characteristics of the artifact. Often inspectors do not have a necessary understanding of the inspection process or how to read the document to extract its information for evaluation [5, 6, 29, 39].

Software inspection techniques were created to meet the specific needs of projects and quality software attributes. The techniques types differ according to the responsibility they give the inspector. The inspector must identify as many defects as possible or specific. The inspection focuses on some determined aspects, and there is a limited set of defects to be identified [16].

Ad hoc technique is the least formal and most dependent on the inspector's knowledge, skill, and experience. Ad hoc does not provide explicit guidelines on how to read the artifacts [5, 18]. The Ad hoc does not contain a specific procedure and makes it one of the most currently used along with CBR [29, 32, 33].

7.2.1   Checklist-Based Reading

In the checklist-based reading (CBR), the inspectors receive a checklist that contains questions (e.g., yes/no answers) with recommendations based on prior knowledge of the defects types recurring in previous projects of the organization [1, 41].

Inspectors detect defects properly with no instructions on how to carry out the inspection or how to use the checklist. The inspections have only "what" defects types for detection. As there is no information on how the information in the artifact should be sought, only "*what*," the CBR can be considered non-systematic. There is a generality of the questions and a lack of concrete approaches to answer them [1, 29, 31, 41].

7.2.2   Scenario-Based Reading

Scenario-based reading (SBR) has several techniques based on the scenarios during the development of distinct artifacts [41]. A scenario is a "collections of procedures for detecting particular classes of faults" [31] that provides the inspector a procedure for "how" to extract the information and "how" to examine it to detect defects [24].

These techniques are designed under two key factors: (i) active guidance, where the reader works with the document while inspecting, and (ii) separation of concerns, where the inspector restricts inspection to a specific aspect of their interest in the artifact [26].

7.2.3   Perspective-Based Reading

The perspective-based reading (PBR) technique is a type of SBR. The artifact reading separates different views and knowledge of the roles of the software development process. The roles are interested in reading the artifact and helping them to answer: "What information in this artifact should they check?" and "How do they identify defects in such information?" [34, 41].

PBR can be considered a systematic technique that provides information through the scenario procedure about how to read and verify defects in the artifacts. PBR tries to avoid overlapping defects during the inspection and establishes that each reader focuses on defects related to your perspective of the artifact [26]. By joining the perspectives, the inspection will have greater coverage of the artifact from different perspectives of the roles involved [41].

7.3   SMartyCheck

SMartyCheck is a software inspection technique conceptualized using CBR to inspect and detect defects in UML use case, class, and component SMarty variability diagrams of SPL.

SMartyCheck has positioned three SPL Domain Engineering (DE) processes [30] to inspect the UML SMarty variability diagrams in domain artifacts. SMartyCheck inputs address the following: (i) domain requirements engineering input encompasses the use case diagram inspections, (ii) domain design input comprises the class diagram inspections, and (iii) domain realization input comprehends the component diagram inspections. SMartyCheck does not inspect or generate SPL products in Application Engineering (AE) processes [12].

Figure 7.1 illustrates such inputs as UML SMarty variability diagrams for SMartyCheck inspections in the SPL DE processes.

Inspections occur in UML SMarty variability diagrams included in DE processes. SMartyCheck provides for the inspectors "what" needs to be inspected in such diagrams through a checklist, combining defect types taxonomy with assertive questions (e.g., yes or no) to guide the inspections.

This chapter follows the structure: Sect. 7.3.1 presents the defect types taxonomy; and Sect. 7.3.2 details the SMartyCheck checklists and their inspections.

7.3.1   SMartyCheck: Defect Types Taxonomy

We develop and evolve SMartyCheck defect types taxonomy from systematic literature mapping (SLM) and results obtained after three empirical studies. The defect types classification occurred by analyzing 32 primary studies from SLM

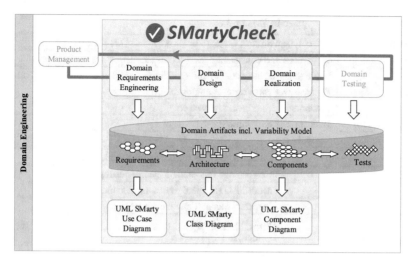

Fig. 7.1 SMartyCheck in SPL DE processes [12]. Adapted from [30]

about defect types in software inspection techniques. The primary studies in this SLM comprise different approaches, experiments, and few taxonomies that improve SMartyCheck technique over time [14].

Several defect types identified in the SLM primary studies were systematically classified and adopted in the questions of two checklists of SMartyCheck. Such defect types have solid definitions based on requirements engineering and three primary IEEE Standards related to verification and validation activities in several SLM primary studies. The most common standards adopted in SMartyCheck defect types taxonomy encompass IEEE Standard 1028-1997, Software Reviews [20]; IEEE Standard 830-1998, Recommended Practice for Software Requirements Specifications [19]; and IEEE Standard 1012-2012, System and Software Verification and Validation [21].

The next paragraphs present the updated defect types definitions of current SMartyCheck taxonomy. Table 7.1 presents the SMartyCheck taxonomy of 11 predefined defect types for checklists questions in a checklist to use case or class diagrams (Fig. 7.2) and a checklist to component diagram (Fig. 7.3).

1. **Business Rule (BR)**. It refers to the business rules wrong modeled with functionalities of a specific domain in elements of use cases/class in SMarty diagrams [12, 13].
2. **Inconsistency (Incons)**. It encompasses the lack of consistency and problems between elements that occur during the inspection of use case, class, or component SMarty diagrams. For example, the elements have pre-defined attributes of how many times are selected in a variability [3, 15].
3. **Incorrect Fact (IF)**. There are names of elements described inaccurately or used to comparison with SMarty diagrams that generate modeling mistakes of use

Table 7.1 Defect types adopted to SMartyCheck

Works	Defect types: SMarty use case or class models [12, 13, 15]	
[21]	Ambiguous and consistency (adopted as inconsistency)	
[19–21]	Stable (adopted as unstable) and modifiable (adopted as non-modifiable)	
[38]	Incorrect fact and extraneous information	
[28] *apud* [17]	Intentional deviation and infeasible	
[25] *apud* [36]	Business rule and omission	
[9]	Anomaly	
Works		Defect types: SMarty component models [3]
[21]		Consistency (adopted as inconsistency)
[19–21]		Modifiable (adopted as non-modifiable)
[38]		Incorrect fact and extraneous information
[28] *apud* [17]		Intentional deviation
[25] *apud* [36]		Omission
[9]		Anomaly

cases, class, or components. For example, the element name does not have a
description compatible with the SPL inspected [3, 15].

4. **Non-modifiable (Nm)**. It involves the organization management of customization use cases, class, and components elements through a pre-defined structure
   of variants specified as meta-attributes in variation points. Such structure is non-
   modifiable when specified to establish consistency. For example, pre-defined
   variants in a variation point may be selected as alternative (e.g., OR or XOR)
   or optional [3, 13].
5. **Omission (Om)**. Mandatory elements as use cases, class, and components are
   missing or not modeled in its SMarty diagrams. For instance, an element is no
   longer [3, 13].
6. **Extraneous Information (EI)**. There are useless or replicated elements in the
   SPL inspected. These elements are irrelevant or out of scope in the use case,
   class, or component SMarty diagrams. For example, an element model that does
   not exist [3, 15].
7. **Intentional Deviation (ID)**. It comprises the dependencies between the elements
   in the use case, class, or component SMarty diagrams. For instance, the element
   fixed needs of another element [3, 13].
8. **Ambiguous (Am)**. During the inspection, the use cases or class elements have
   different objectives, and their names influence multiple meanings. For example,
   the element title is close compared with proximate elements [12, 13].
9. **Anomaly (An)**. When there is an association of elements that not can be related
   commonly in use cases, class, or components. For example, a class extended of
   a variation point that not available [3, 13].
10. **Unstable (Uns)**. Establishes that variability associated with a variation point has
    a single and original identification in the use case or class SMarty diagrams. For
    example, a specific name that differs from another [12, 13].

Checklist Version: v2.2
Application: UML Use Case/Class SMarty Diagrams

Id. Defect Types	Checklist Items	Yes	No	Identified Defect
Comparison Category: *Compares use case or class elements with defects to use case or class elements with no defects (oracle).*				
1. Business Rule (BR)	**BR.1** The use case/class is not clear with the purpose and the desired functionalities based on defined domain.			
2. Inconsistency (Incons)	**Incons.1** Is there any use case/class specified with the stereotype <<variationPoint>> from which the number of specified variants is major or minor than defined in **maxSelection** or **minSelection** the variability (<<variability>>) associated?			
	Incons.2 Is there any use case/class specified with the stereotype <<optional>> from which the number of specified variants is major or minor than defined in **maxSelection** or **minSelection** the variability (<<variability>>) associated?			
3. Incorrect Fact (IF)	**IF.1** Is there any use case/class with incorrectly name in SPL?			
	IF.2 Is there any use case/class that it is not be compare name in SPL?			
	IF.3 Is there any use case/class with stereotype <<variationPoint>> associated with use case/class in the SPL which not <<alternative_OR>>?			
4. Non-modifiable (Nm)	**Nm.1** Is there any use case/class specified with the stereotype <<variationPoint>>, in which variants associated (<<optional>>, <<alternative_OR>> or <<alternative_XOR>>) can not be combined or selected in accordance with variants already specified in the meta-attribute variants in SPL?			
5. Omission (Om)	**Om.1** Is there any use case/class specified as mandatory (required) through the stereotype <<mandatory>> that is not specified on the SPL?			
6. Extraneous Information (EI)	**EI.1** Is there any use case/class specified besides use cases/class existing in the SPL?			
	EI.2 Is there any use case/class with its functionality duplicated in SPL?			
7. Intentional Deviation (ID)	**ID.1** Is there any use case/class which requires the selection of another (<<requires>>) and this another is not specified in the SPL?			
	ID.2 Is there any use case/class not which requires selection of another (<<mutex>>) and this another is not specified in the SPL?			
Non-comparison Category: *Inspect only use case or class diagram with defects.*				
8. Ambiguous (Am)	**Am.1** Is there any use case/class in that its name is equal to another use case/class in a manner to owning a duplicate interpretation?			
9. Anomaly (An)	**An.1** Is there any use case/class specified as <<alternative_OR>> which extend <<extend>> another use case/class that is not specified <<variationPoint>>?			
	An.2 Is there any use case/class specified as <<alternative_XOR>> which extend <<extend>> another use case/class that is not specified <<variationPoint>>?			
10. Unstable (Uns)	**Uns.1** Is there any use case/class specified with the stereotype <<variationPoint>>, in which has the stereotype associated <<variability>> from which the meta-attribute name equals to other use cases/class elsewhere specified with the stereotype <<variationPoint>>?			
11. Infeasible (Inf)	**Inf.1** Is there any use case/class specified with stereotype <<variationPoint>> which not allows you to add new variants as defined in the meta-attribute **allowsAddingVar = false**?			

Fig. 7.2 SMartyCheck v2.2 for inspection of UML use case or class SMarty diagrams [15]

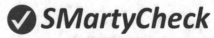

Checklist Version: v3.0
Application: UML Component SMarty Diagram

Id. Defect Types	Checklist Items	Yes	No	Identified Defect
Comparison Category: *Compares component elements with defects to component elements with no defects (oracle).*				
2. Inconsistency (Incons)	**Incons.1** Is there any component specified with the stereotype **<<variationPoint>>** from which the number of specified variants is major or minor than defined in **maxSelection** or **minSelection** the variability (**<<variability>>**) associated? **Incons.2** Is there any component specified with the stereotype **<<optional>>** from which the number of specified variants is major or minor than defined in **maxSelection** or **minSelection** the variability (**<<variability>>**) associated?			
3. Incorrect Fact (IF)	**IF.1** Is there any component with incorrectly name in SPL? **IF.2** Is there any component that it is not be compare name in SPL? **IF.3** Is there any component with stereotype **<<variationPoint>>** associated with component in the SPL which not **<<alternative_OR>>**?			
4. Non-modifiable (Nm)	**Nm.1** Is there any component specified with the stereotype **<<variationPoint>>**, in which variants associated (**<<optional>>**, **<<alternative_OR>>** or **<<alternative_XOR>>**) can not be combined or selected in accordance with variants already specified in the meta-attribute variants in SPL?			
5. Omission (Om)	**Om.1** Is there any component specified as mandatory (required) through the stereotype **<<mandatory>>** that is not specified on the SPL?			
6. Extraneous Information (EI)	**EI.1** Is there any component specified besides components existing in the SPL? **EI.2** Is there any component with its functionality duplicated in SPL?			
7. Intentional Deviation (ID)	**ID.1** Is there any component which requires the selection of another (**<<requires>>**) and this another is not specified in the SPL? **ID.2** Is there any component not which requires selection of another (**<<mutex>>**) and this another is not specified in the SPL?			
Non-comparison Category: *Inspect only component diagram with defects.*				
9. Anomaly (An)	**An.1** Is there any component specified as **<<alternative_OR>>** which extend **<<extend>>** another component that is not specified **<<variationPoint>>**? **An.2** Is there any component specified as **<<alternative_XOR>>** which extend **<<extend>>** another component that is not specified **<<variationPoint>>**?			

Fig. 7.3 SMartyCheck v3.0 for inspection of UML component SMarty diagram [3]

11. Infeasible (Inf). Define restrictions to add new variants as use cases or class elements in the variation points through variability meta-attributes of SMarty diagrams. For example, the inclusion or exclusion of new variants in such SMarty diagrams inspected [12, 13].

These defect types are used to elaborate on each question of SMartyCheck checklists (use case/class and component). The next section presents such checklists, their applications, and discussions about results obtained in the three empirical studies conducted.

7.3.2   *SMartyCheck: Inspection of SMarty SPLs*

SMartyCheck aims to detect defects using a checklist for inspecting use cases or class elements (Fig. 7.2) and another checklist for inspecting components elements (Fig. 7.3) in its UML SMarty diagrams.

The SMartyCheck v2.2 checklist for use case or class helps the inspectors to detect 11 defect types distributed in 17 questions in 2 inspections comparison situations (Fig. 7.2): (i) **Comparison Category** defines the SPL inspections in a use case or class SMarty diagrams comparing an SPL with defects (derived in SPL DE process) with another SPL with no defects (oracle/original); and (ii) **Non-comparison Category** inspects any SPL modeled with UML use case or class SMarty diagrams that can have elements with distinct defects types [13, 15].

The SMartyCheck v3.0 checklist for components has fewer defect types and questions compared with the first checklist. In this checklist for components, 7 defect types with 13 questions guide inspectors to detect defects in components elements following the same categories of first checklist for use and class. The **Comparison Category** allows inspect six defect types, and the **Non-comparison Category** has only one defect type [3].

We highlight that major checklist question items adapt the SMarty stereotypes to improve the inspection of elements in use case, class, or component diagrams. SMartyCheck inspections use its defect types taxonomy and checklist question items supported by SMarty stereotypes to guide inspectors as follows:

1. First, the inspector begins the inspection by reading the **Defect Types** field related to their **Checklist Items** field in the checklists (Fig. 7.2 or Fig. 7.3).
2. The inspector analyzes the UML uses case, class, or component SMarty diagrams after reading **Checklist Items** (first step) to detect defects using the **Comparison Category** or **Non-comparison Category** of checklists.
3. The inspector marked each defect type identified (second step, analyzing UML SMarty diagrams) with a "check" using the **Yes** or **No** answers for the **Checklist Items** of checklists.
4. In this least step, the inspector must describe the defect in **Identified Defect** field considering that the defect was "checked" in **Checklist Items** field (third step).

7.3.3   *SMartyCheck: Application Examples*

We created three inspection application examples, which model SMarty use case, class, and component diagrams in the SPL Mobile Media using the SMartyModeling tool [35]. Figures 7.4, 7.5, and 7.6 illustrate excerpts of Mobile Media diagrams using the SMartyCheck to detect different defect types.

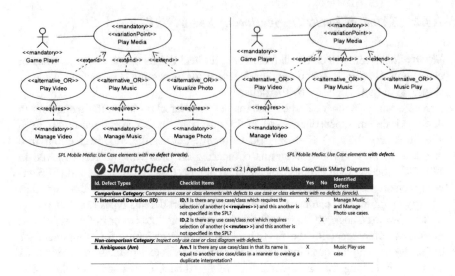

SPL Mobile Media: Use Case elements with **no defect** (oracle).   SPL Mobile Media: Use Case elements **with defects**.

Id. Defect Types	Checklist Items	Yes	No	Identified Defect
Comparison Category: *Compares use case or class elements with defects to use case or class elements with no defects (oracle).*				
7. Intentional Deviation (ID)	**ID.1** Is there any use case/class which requires the selection of another (<<**requires**>>) and this another is not specified in the SPL?	X		Manage Music and Manage Photo use cases.
	ID.2 Is there any use case/class not which requires selection of another (<<**mutex**>>) and this another is not specified in the SPL?		X	
Non-comparison Category: *Inspect only use case or class diagram with defects.*				
8. Ambiguous (Am)	**Am.1** Is there any use case/class in that its name is equal to another use case/class in a manner to owning a duplicate interpretation?	X		Music Play use case

Fig. 7.4 SMartyCheck example in SPL Mobile Media for UML use case SMarty diagram

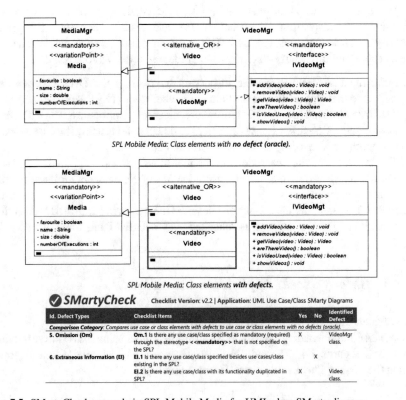

Id. Defect Types	Checklist Items	Yes	No	Identified Defect
Comparison Category: *Compares use case or class elements with defects to use case or class elements with no defects (oracle).*				
5. Omission (Om)	**Om.1** Is there any use case/class specified as mandatory (required) through the stereotype <<**mandatory**>> that is not specified on the SPL?	X		VideoMgr class.
6. Extraneous Information (EI)	**EI.1** Is there any use case/class specified besides use cases/class existing in the SPL?		X	
	EI.2 Is there any use case/class with its functionality duplicated in SPL?	X		Video class.

Fig. 7.5 SMartyCheck example in SPL Mobile Media for UML class SMarty diagram

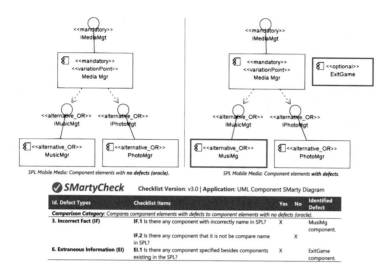

Fig. 7.6 SMartyCheck example in SPL Mobile Media for UML component SMarty diagram

7.4   SMartyPerspective

SMartyPerspective is a software inspection technique based on PBR for detecting defects in use case, class, component, and sequence UML SMarty and features diagrams. SMartyPerspective separates software reading within different SPL Domain Engineering views and goals for variability management activities [4].

SMartyPerspective was defined from two main bases adapted from Basili et al. [2] (Fig. 7.7): (i) a defect taxonomy adopted from Travassos et al. [38]: Ambiguity, Incorrect Fact, Inconsistency, Extraneous Information, and Omission and (ii) adaptation of SPL main perspectives (e.g., Domain Architect and Domain Developer) from Linden et al. [27].

The scenarios generated are to analyzing the models from the Domain Engineering roles and their goals. The scenarios were analyzed from perspectives. SMarty diagrams are essential for the task realization in the software development process and the quality levels expected for each diagram.

The SMartyPerspective technique encompasses the main defect types in UML SMarty diagrams according to their expected quality levels, context, and SPL variability management. Therefore, the questions of each technique operation scenario were defined and derived from the taxonomy Travassos et al. [38] defects and the main UML and SMarty elements expected in each diagram type.

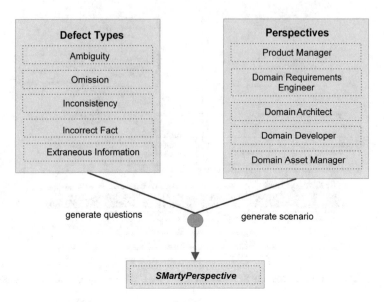

Fig. 7.7 SMartyPerspective parts. Adapted from [2]

7.4.1 SMartyPerspective: Defect Types Taxonomy

The taxonomy of the SMartyPerspective technique was defined after an analysis of the software defect classes in the literature and based on the expected quality attributes to maintain the quality of the SMarty and features diagrams for managing variability in them.

SMartyPerspective's defect taxonomy was adapted from the study of Travassos et al. [38] for object-oriented models and encompasses the defects of Ambiguity, Incorrect Fact, Inconsistency, Extraneous Information, and Omission. These classes are detailed as follows:

- **Ambiguity**: it refers to information that has not been specified enough to be understood and can generate multiple interpretations between different diagram readers.
- **Incorrect Fact**: the modeled information in the diagram is at odds with the requirements specification or knowledge of the SPL domain. This incorrectly modeled information can lead to possible configurations or incorrect input/output data in the system.
- **Inconsistency**: the information modeled in a diagram element is not consistent with another element in the same diagram or another artifact. Thus, diverging information between elements.
- **Extraneous Information**: refers to excess information in the modeled diagram, but is not necessary for the modeled context or does not belong to the SPL domain.

- **Omission**: data is absent. For example, an element or a stereotype not modeled in the diagram. This can lead to a lack of SPL functionality or a not understanding of the domain.

7.4.2 SMartyPerspective Scenarios

The SMartyPerspective scenarios consist of three main sections [4] based on the generic structure by Laitenberger and Kohler [24] and PBR scenarios [22, 33]: (i) **Introduction** presents the role and expected quality attributes; (ii) **Instruction** helps the inspector in how to read the document and find the data and information to be checked, decomposing the document in parts; and (iii) **Questions** allows the readers analyze and judge whether the element corresponds to the expected quality attributes [24].

The questions of SMartyPerspective were adapted from stereotypes, meta-attributes, and guidelines of SMarty. Defect types of SMartyPerspective taxonomy and elements of each diagram also were adapted together expected quality attributes about variability management in each perspective.

The **Introduction** segment of SMartyPerspective was defined in two paragraphs. First, is presented, the role that the inspector will assume and the diagrams that will be inspected. Second, is the same for all scenarios; it guides the inspector which step should be taken when find the defect in the inspected diagram.

Because of the number of questions, the instructions were divided into sub-instructions following Miller's law as recommended by Laitenberger and Kohler [24] for scenario development. The Law proposes that a person keeps in immediate memory 7 ± 2 pieces of information [24]. Thus, the reader could remember the current instruction, the element type, or information verified for the question.

When the inspector finds a defect using SMartyPerspective, he must inform the defect and the element of the diagram identified in the Defect Identification Form (DIF) (Fig. 7.8) [4]. First, the inspector marks in the DIF the cell corresponding to the diagram in which he identified the defect: Features (FT), Use Case (UC), Class (CL), Component (CP), and Sequence (SQ). Second, the inspector must also indicate the question number that guided him to find the defect (Question Number). Third, is the defect element name in the diagram (Element). Fourth, the description of the defect found for that element and diagram (Identified Defect). At least, inform the solution for correct the defect to the facility of the inspection phases.

The SMartyPerspective software inspection procedure consists of these steps:

1. The inspection starts with the inspector selecting the scenario that represents their role in the organization.
2. The inspector must read the introduction with the main information to start the process.

Ord.	DIAGRAM					QUESTION NUMBER	ELEMENT	IDENTIFIED DEFECT
	FT	UC	CL	CP	SQ			
1								
2								

Fig. 7.8 Defect Identification Form (DIF). Adapted from [4]

3. The inspector should look for the set of steps that correspond to the diagram that will be inspected. The set is identified with "Locate" followed by the diagram type name.
4. The first instruction contains the main instructions for the reader to start inspecting the specific diagram, such as diagrams that should be selected, and first tasks.
5. Thus, the inspector depending on the step, read the secondary instructions, which group-specific questions for a certain type of diagram element and following their instructions or read the questions referring to a specific element.
6. For each question read the inspector should look at the element to which the question refers and consider whether there is a defect in the element.
7. If the defect is detected, the inspector must complete the DIF form with the information on the defect found.
8. The inspector should repeat steps 5–7 until all questions referring to the steps for the diagram under inspection have been carried out.

7.4.3   The Product Manager Perspective

Product Manager (PMG) interacts in Application Engineering and Domain Engineering. Their efforts are significant in Domain Engineering when the portfolio is defined. The PMG must have a whole vision of the business. Its function is related to the evolution of SPL, future products, business value, and marketing strategy with attention to common and variable features [27, 30].

PMG's scenario consists of four stages (Fig. 7.9). The artifacts are inspected from the perspective of the economic view and the scope of the product developed. The feature diagrams present the inspected product features (Fig. 7.10); and the UML SMarty use case diagram has the functionality of the products generated (Fig. 7.11).

7.4.4   The Domain Requirements Engineer Perspective

Domain requirements engineer (DRE) performs the tasks known in the traditional development process: elicitation, documentation, negotiation, validation, verifica-

PRODUCT MANAGER
This perspective should plan the characteristics and business value of SPL's current and future products. To do this, you must ensure that the use cases are clear with the functionalities based on the defined domain and that the characteristics that will be common and variable for the SPL are correctly defined to be passed on to the client and the development team.
To diagrams correctly express the user requirements without inconsistencies, you must review such diagrams and elements. To achieve your goal, perform the steps outlined below to inspect each of the informed diagrams. When you find a defect in one of the steps, fill in the Defect Identification Form indicating the diagram, the step item (number question), and the element and the defect found.

LOCATE FEATURES DIAGRAM AND REQUIREMENTS SPECIFICATION	
Step 1	inspection of class diagram
Step 2	
LOCATE USE CASE DIAGRAM AND REQUIREMENTS SPECIFICATION	
Step 3	inspection of use case diagram
Step 4	

Fig. 7.9 PMG scenario structure

		LOCATE FEATURES DIAGRAM AND REQUIREMENTS SPECIFICATION
		The features diagram hierarchically describes the characteristics of all products that can be generated from an SPL, identifying the common and variable characteristics of current and future products. Read the requirements specification carefully. While reading, make a list of all the characteristics specified in the document, placing a notation with the type of stereotype of the element (mandatory, optional, etc.) and their possible relationships. Compare the list made with the feature diagram to ensure that there is no inconsistency between them. To do this, answer the questions that follow.
Step 1	1.1	Does the root node correctly represent the Domain?
		For each feature described in the features diagram, analyze it and check its relationships to answer the questions that follow. Mark the element after its analysis, to prevent it from being analyzed again.
	1.2	Does the name of the feature correctly express the characteristic it represents?
	1.3	Does the feature represent a feature that was not defined in the requirements document? If so, disregard it with your relationships for the next steps and move on to the next element.
	1.4	Has the feature described by this feature already been specified by another element? If so, disregard it with your relationships for the next Steps and move on to the next element.
	1.5	Check the edge that arrives at this feature and answer the following questions:
		1.5.1 Is there really a relationship between this characteristic and the previous node?
		1.5.2 Is the mandatory characteristic defined with a filled circle?
		1.5.3 Is the optional feature defined with a empty circle?
		1.5.4 If cardinality has been described, is it correct according to the requirements specification?
	1.6	If the edge belongs to a empty or filled arc, analyze and answer the following questions:
		1.6.1 Is this feature really an alternative feature to the previous node's feature?
		1.6.2 Are alternative features inside empty arcs or with XOR relation?
		1.6.3 Are inclusive features within filled arcs or with an OR relationship?
	1.7	If there is a line connecting this feature to another and it has not been analyzed yet. Check and answer the following questions:
		1.7.1 Is there really an inclusion/exclusion relationship between these features?
		1.7.2 If the feature requires another, is the line defined as a directed arrow?
		1.7.3 If the feature excludes another, is the line defined as a bidirectional arrow?
	1.8	Was there any lack of inclusion/exclusion relationship with another one for this feature?
Step 2		When all the features are already analyzed (all marked as visited), check if there was no missing feature important for the SPL domain under inspection. Review the following questions:
	2.1	Are there any optional or mandatory features for the SPL that are not described in the diagram?
	2.2	Check the empty or filled arches. Missing an alternative feature for the feature?

Fig. 7.10 PMG scenario for feature diagram

LOCATE USE CASE DIAGRAM AND REQUIREMENTS SPECIFICATION			
The use case diagram in Domain Engineering must correctly describe the set of features of all products that can be configured from SPL. Read the requirements specification carefully. While reading, make a list of all the requirements and actors specified in the document, placing a notation with the type of stereotype of the element (mandatory, optional, etc.) and their possible relationships. Compare the list made with the use case diagram to ensure that there is no inconsistency between them. To do this, answer the questions that follow.			
Step 3	Consider the actors and use cases as elements in this Step. For each element in the use-case diagram, check for matching elements in the list made. Mark the element after its analysis, to prevent it from being analyzed again.		
	3.1	Does the name of the element correctly express functionality?	
	3.2	Does this element correspond to a feature/actor that was not defined in the requirements document? If so, please disregard it and its relationship for the next step and go to the next element.	
	3.3	Has the functionality described by that element already been specified by another element? If so, please disregard it and its relationship for the next steps and go to the next element.	
	3.4	Is the element in the use-case diagram stereotyped?	
	3.5	In the use-case diagram, if the element is optional or mandatory, has it been specified with the correct stereotype (<<optional>> or <<mandatory>>)?	
	3.6	Were the use cases that are variation points marked with the <<variationPoint>> stereotype?	
	3.7	For each element of the diagram, check and analyze their relationships to answer the questions that follow. Remember to mark the relationships already verified to avoid re-analysis.	
		3.7.1	Does the relationship comply with the requirements specification? Check if there is really a relationship between the elements for the context.
		3.7.2	Was the relationship identified as an extension (<<extend>>) or inclusion (<<include>>) erroneously according to the requirements specification?
		3.7.3	Were the inclusion relationships between the elements specified with the <<include>> stereotype? Note: SMarty suggests that inclusion relationships are associated with mandatory (<<mandatory>>) or optional (<<optional>>) variants.
		3.7.4	If the element requires another, has the relationship between them been stereotyped with <<requires>>?
		3.7.5	If the relationship is mutual exclusion, is the relationship stereotyped in the diagram with <<mutex>>?
	3.8	Was there any relationship missing for this element that was not specified in the use case diagram?	
Step 4	When you have already visited all elements of the use case diagram (all are marked as visited), check and review the following questions:		
	4.1	For each element of the optional type or point of variation (<<optional>> or <<variationPoint>>), check and analyze their relationships and stereotypes to answer the questions that follow:	
		4.1.1	Do the variants specified for this variability have the correct variant notation (<<OR>>, <<XOR>> or <<optional>>)?
		4.1.2	Do the <<OR>> and <<XOR>> variants related to the variation point have the relationship <<extend>> to the associated variation point?
	4.2	Are there still items on your list that were not specified by any elements? That is, it is missing from the use case diagram. (If they are variants that have already been identified in the previous step, disregard)	

Fig. 7.11 PMG scenario for use case diagram

tion, and requirements management. DRE analyzes commonalities, variability, and model the requirements that satisfy all applications derived from SPL with the explicit variability documentation. It is helpful as a guide for other process activities [27, 30].

DRE must have an understanding of the business domain. DRE analyzes the diagrams about common and variable requirements in the documentation and ensures that the demands of users are specified correctly. Therefore, the DRE analyzes, identifies, and documents such requirements and may anticipate potential requirements changes for later products.

The DRE scenario consists of eight steps (Fig. 7.12) to inspect the use case (Fig. 7.13), class (conceptual view) (Fig. 7.14) and sequence (Fig. 7.15) diagrams. Provides a vision of the business domain and supports the DRE document to specify common and variable requirements, main classes, and system behavior through the message exchanges.

DOMAIN REQUIREMENTS ENGINEER
This perspective should analyze and specify the variable and common requirements of the product portfolio in order to facilitate the vision of the application that will be developed for different stakeholders. This view is given by the use case, class, activity and sequence diagrams that together define the functionalities, exchange of messages and activities of the systems.
To diagrams correctly express the user requirements without inconsistencies, you must review such diagrams and elements. To achieve your goal, perform the steps outlined below to inspect each of the informed diagrams. When you find a defect in one of the steps, fill in the Defect Identification Form indicating the diagram, the step item (number question), and the element and the defect found.

LOCATE USE CASE DIAGRAM AND REQUIREMENTS SPECIFICATION	
Step 1	inspection of use case diagram
Step 2	
LOCATE CLASS DIAGRAM AND REQUIREMENTS SPECIFICATION	
Step 3	inspection of class diagram
Step 4	
LOCATE CLASS DIAGRAM AND REQUIREMENTS SPECIFICATION	
Step 5	Inspection of sequence diagram
Step 6	
Step7	
Step 8	

Fig. 7.12   DRE scenario structure

7.4.5   The Domain Architect Perspective

Domain Architect (DAC) includes the traditional process and variability configuration activities in the architecture. The DAC encompasses configured applications and SPL architecture (PLA) rules and validates projects that adhere to this architecture. Thus, DAC structures the components and interfaces to assist as a technical guide for the implementation phase [27, 30].

The DAC needs to guarantee that the projects in the core assets meet the PLA for any application. The DAC scenario covers four steps (Fig. 7.16) in which they have inspected the UML SMarty class (Fig. 7.17) and component diagrams (Fig. 7.18). The architect must validate the class structure at the design level. Then, the architect verifies whether the main elements at the technical level are present in the components diagram, including configurations, components, interfaces, and specifications.

7.4.6   The Domain Developer Perspective

Domain Developer (DDP) must implement the weakly coupled components as part of the core asset rather than a whole application. Therefore, DDP needs to be concerned with different contexts of SPL to support variances between products

		LOCATE USE CASE DIAGRAM AND REQUIREMENTS SPECIFICATION	
		The use case diagram in Domain Engineering must correctly describe the set of features of all systems that can be configured from SPL. Read the requirements specification carefully. While reading, make a list of all the requirements and actors specified in the document, placing a notation with the type of stereotype of the element (mandatory, optional, etc.) and their possible relationships. Compare the list made with the use case diagram to ensure that there is no inconsistency between them. To do this, answer the questions that follow.	
Step 1		Consider actors and use cases as elements in this step. For each element in the use-case diagram, check for matching elements in the list made. Mark the element after its analysis, to prevent it from being analyzed again.	
	1.1	Does the name of the element correctly express functionality?	
	1.2	Does this element correspond to a feature/actor that was not defined in the requirements document? If so, disregard him and his relationships for the next steps and move on to the next element.	
	1.3	Has the functionality described by that element already been specified by another element? If so, disregard the element that is incorrect and its relationships to the next steps and move on to the next element.	
	1.4	Is the element in the use-case diagram stereotyped?	
	1.5	In the use case diagram, if the element is optional or mandatory, has it been specified with the correct stereotype (<<optional>> or <<mandatory>>)?	
	1.6	Was the element that represents a point of variation marked with the <<variationPoint>> stereotype?	
	1.7	For each element of the use case diagram, check and analyze their relationships to answer the questions that follow. Remember to mark the relationships already verified to avoid re-analysis.	
		1.7.1	Does the relationship comply with the requirements specification? Check if there is really a relationship between the elements for the context.
		1.7.2	Was the relationship identified as an extension (<<extend>>) or inclusion (<<include>>) erroneously according to the requirements specification?
		1.7.3	Were the inclusion relationships between the elements specified with the <<include>> stereotype?
			Note: SMarty suggests that inclusion relationships are associated with mandatory (<<mandatory>>) or optional (<<optional>>) variants.
		1.7.4	If the element requires another, has the relationship between them been stereotyped with <<requires>>?
		1.7.5	If the relationship is mutual exclusion, is the relationship stereotyped in the use case diagram with <<mutex>>?
	1.8	Was there any relationship missing for this element that was not specified in the use case diagram?	
Step 2		After analyzing all the elements in the previous step (all marked as visited), check and analyze the questions that follow.	
	2.1	If the element is of the optional type or point of variation (<<optional>> or <<variationPoint>>), check and analyze their relationships and stereotypes to answer the questions that follow.	
		2.1.1	Is there a variability notation (<<variability>>) associated with the element?
		2.1.2	Do the variants specified for this variability have the correct variant notation (<<OR>>, <<XOR>> or <<optional>>)?
		2.1.3	Do the <<OR>> and <<XOR>> variants related to the variation point have the relationship <<extend>> to the associated variation point?
	2.2	The <<variability>> stereotype represents variability through a UML comment. For each of these comments defined in the diagrams, locate the comment, analyze it and answer the questions below.	
		2.2.1	Are the variants defined in the variants set really variants for this element? If any are not, disregard it for the next questions.
		2.2.2	Are there any variants defined in the collection of variants that are not described in the use case diagram?
		2.2.3	Are all variants related to this element defined with (<<OR>>), (<<XOR>>) or (<<optional>>) in the collection of variants of the meta-attribute variants with their correct name?
		2.2.4	Check the type of the associated variants: • If they are of type <<optional>>, minSelection = 0 and maxSelection = 1? • If they are of type <<OR>>, minSelection = 1 and maxSelection = total of variants ? • If they are of type <<XOR>>, minSelection = maxSelection = 1?
	2.3	Are there still items on your list that were not specified by any elements? That is, it is missing from the use case diagram (If they are variants that have already been identified in the previous step, disregard).	

Fig. 7.13 DRE scenario for use case diagram

			LOCATE CLASS DIAGRAM AND REQUIREMENTS SPECIFICATION
		The class diagram for your role should, in a conceptual way, present the class structure and its relationships for all SPL systems in the business domain. Read the requirements specification carefully and, during the reading, make a list with the mentioned objects and the data that characterize this object. Compare the list made with the class diagram to ensure that there is no inconsistency between the classes and the user's requirements. To do this, answer the questions that follow.

Step 3		colspan="2"	For each class in the class diagram, check the classes, the attributes, the relationships between the classes with the list made and answer the questions that follow. Check the class after its analysis, to avoid being analyzed again.
	3.1	colspan="2"	Does the class name correctly express the objects of this class?
	3.2	colspan="2"	Does this class correspond to an object that has not been defined in the requirements document? If so, disregard him and his relationships for the next steps and move on to the next element.
	3.3		Is this class in redundancy with another one already specified in the class diagram? If so, disregard him and his relationships for the next steps and move on to the next element.
	3.4		Is the class stereotyped in the class diagram?
	3.5		If the element is optional or mandatory, has it been specified with the correct stereotype (<<optional>> or <<mandatory>>)?
	3.5		If the classes are grouped into packages, check and answer the questions that follow.
		3.5.1	Has the package name been defined and expresses the grouping correctly? If you have already filled out this defect for this package on the form you do not need to fill it out again
		3.5.2	Is the class in the correct package?
	3.6		For each relationship for this class, check the classes that make up this relationship, to ensure that the relationship between them is in accordance with the requirements specification. To do this, answer the questions that follow and mark the relationships already analyzed.
		3.6.1	Is this relationship in accordance with the requirements specification? Check if there is really a relationship between the elements for the context.
		3.6.2	Is the cardinality of this relationship correct according to the requirements specification?
		3.6.3	Check the type of relationship to ensure that the classes are stereotyped and correct according to the SMarty approach: • Generalization: Are the most general classifiers points of variation (<<variationPoint>>) and the most specific, variants? • Realization of interface: Are the specifications points of variation (<<variationPoint>>) and the implementations are variants? • Aggregation or Composition: Are the instances typed with diamonds (filled or not filled) are points of variation (<<variationPoint>>) and associated instances are variants?
		3.6.4	Are classes that require another related to the <<requires>> stereotype?
		3.6.5	Are mutually exclusive classes related to the <<mutex>> stereotype?
	3.7		Was there any relationship missing for this class that was not specified in the class diagram?
Step 4			After analyzing all the classes in the previous step (all marked as visited), check and analyze the questions that follow.
	4.1		The control classes manage the activities of the class. For each class of this type that is stereotyped with <<optional>> and/or <<variationPoint>>. Check it to ensure that the variability/variant notations are correct according to the requirements specification. To do this, go to each of these classes and answer the questions that follow.
		4.1.1	Is there a UML note that represents variability (<<variability>>) associated with the control class?
		4.1.2	Have all the variants been defined and are they with the correct variant notation (<<OR>>, <<XOR>> or <<optional>>)?
	4.2		The <<variability>> stereotype represents variability through a UML comment. For each of these comments defined in the diagrams, locate the comment, analyze it and answer the questions below.
		4.2.1	Are the variants defined in the variants set really variants for this element? If any are not, disregard it for the next questions.
		4.2.2	Are there any variants defined in the collection of variants that are not described in the class diagram?
		4.2.3	Are all variants related to this element defined with (<<OR>>), (<<XOR>>) or (<<optional>>) in the collection of variants of the meta-attribute variants with their correct name?
		4.2.4	Check the type of the associated variants: • If they are of type <<optional>>, minSelection = 0 and maxSelection = 1? • If they are of type <<OR>>, minSelection = 1 and maxSelection = total of variants ? • If they are of type <<XOR>>, minSelection=maxSelection=1?
	4.3		Are there still items on your list that were not specified by any elements? That is, it is missing from the class diagram (If they are variants that were already identified in the previous step, disregard).

Fig. 7.14 DRE scenario for class diagram

	**LOCATE THE SEQUENCE DIAGRAM AND REQUIREMENTS SPECIFICATION**

	The sequence diagram in Domain Engineering must express the interaction of the system: the exchange of messages between the objects of the systems that can be configured from an SPL. With the sequence diagram in hand, check each of the described objects/actors and look for the corresponding class in the class diagram (if defined) or in the requirements specification. For each of them, check the relationships and messages that are exchanged between the elements to ensure that they are consistent with the class diagram/requirements specification. Then answer the questions that follow.

Step 5			
		Consider the "object heads" and the lifeline actors in the sequence diagram as an element. For each one of them, check the messages and stereotypes given to them in order to answer the questions that follow.
	5.1		Does the name of the element correctly express the object/actor?
	5.2		Is the element represented in any system class?
	5.3		Is the element part of this interaction according to the Requirements Specification? If not, disregard all the lifeline and their messages for the next steps and go to the next element.
	5.4		Is the element redundant with another defined element? If so, please disregard all the lifeline and their messages for the next steps and go to the next element.
	5.5		For each of the messages defined in the lifeline of this element, analyze it and answer the questions that follow
		5.5.1	Is the message named?
		5.5.2	Is the interaction represented by this message described in the requirements specification? If not, disregard it and go to the next message.
		5.5.3	Does the name of the message correctly express the information being transmitted?
		5.5.4	Is the order of the message correct according to the requirements specification?
		5.5.5	Check the other messages on this lifeline. Is this message redundant with another? If so disregard it and go to the next message.
		5.5.6	Messages that are not directly related to a variability and its elements, do not need a stereotype and are considered mandatory. Is the message of this type stereotyped?
	5.6		Have all the important messages for this element been defined in the sequence diagram according to the requirements specification?
	5.7		Are elements that require the presence of another related to the <<requires>> stereotype?
	5.8		Are mutually exclusive elements related to the <<mutex>> stereotype?

Step 6		
		Para cada elemento alternativo no diagrama de sequência como o CombinedFragment com interactionOperator "alt" (alternative) e elemento interactionUse "ref", verifique seus estereótipos e as mensagens relacionadas a este elemento para responder as questões que seguem.
	6.1	Is the element defined with the <<variationPoint>> stereotype?
	6.2	Is there a UML notation that represents variability (<<variability>>) associated with this/CombinedFragment element?
	6.3	Are the variants corresponding to the messages stereotyped correctly? Check the stereotypes of the variant messages for this variability. • For variants of the interactionUse element "ref": <<OR>> • For variants with interactionOperator "alt": <<XOR>>

Step 7		
		For each optional element in the sequence diagram, such as: combinedFragment with interactionOperator "opt" (optional) and exchange of messages between two non-mandatory objects or between one mandatory object and one not, check their stereotypes and messages related to it to answer the questions that follow.
	7.1	Is there a UML notation that represents variability (<<variability>>) associated with this/CombinedFragment element?
	7.2	Are the variants corresponding to the/CombinedFragment messages correctly stereotyped with <<optional>>?
	7.3	For elements marked with <<optional>> are the lifelines that are part of the CombinedFragment also stereotyped with <<optional>>?

Step 8		
		The <<variability>> stereotype represents variability through a UML comment. For each of these comments defined in the diagrams, locate the comment, analyze it and answer the questions below.
	8.1	Are the variants defined in the variants set really variants for this element? If any are not, disregard it for the next questions.
	8.2	Do all variants in the variant set have an associated lifeline in the sequence diagram?
	8.3	Are all variants related to this element defined with (<<OR>>), (<<XOR>>) or (<<optional>>) in the collection of variants of the meta-attribute variants with their correct name?
	8.4	Check the type of the associated variants: • If they are of type <<optional>>, minSelection = 0 and maxSelection = 1? • If they are of type <<OR>>, minSelection = 1 and maxSelection = total of variants ?. • If they are of type <<XOR>>, minSelection=maxSelection=1?

Fig. 7.15 DRE scenario for sequence diagram. Adapted from [33]

DOMAIN ARCHITECT
This perspective should develop and maintain the SPL architecture for all products in the company's portfolio. It must ensure that the component diagrams, by means of components and interfaces, incorporate the domain classes proposed and modeled in the class diagrams, thus showing the physical structure of the system as a whole, so that the components can then be rearranged according to SPL business rules and user requirements.
To diagrams correctly express the user requirements without inconsistencies, you must review such diagrams and elements. To achieve your goal, perform the steps outlined below to inspect each of the informed diagrams. When you find a defect in one of the steps, fill in the Defect Identification Form indicating the diagram, the step item (number question), and the element and the defect found.

LOCATE THE CLASS DIAGRAM AND REQUIREMENTS SPECIFICATION	
Step 1	inspection of class diagram
Step 2	
LOCATE THE COMPONENT AND CLASS DIAGRAM	
Step 3	inspection of component diagram
Step 4	

Fig. 7.16 DAC scenario structure

generated from configurations in the Application Engineering by the customer's choices [27, 30]. (Fig. 7.19)

The DDP perspective can review class (Figs. 7.20 and 7.21), sequence (Fig. 7.22), and component (Fig. 7.18) diagrams in eight steps (Fig. 7.19) in order to get an overview of the product range and functionality of the SPL. In addition, it includes the activities that a user can perform to implement the interfaces and components of the platform.

7.4.7 The Domain Asset Manager Perspective

Domain Asset Manager (DAM) is responsible for domain asset management and traceability between assets through version control. This role keeps the valid version and configuration of the domain assets. The traceability is done in all steps in the development process by the other Domain Engineering roles [27, 30].

The manager analyzes the inconsistencies between versions of the same diagram and reviews the traceability between different diagrams. The DAM role reads the following inspected diagrams to remove the defects incorporated in the latest version: use case, class, component, sequence, and feature diagrams. Most questions are common for all diagram types because the comparison should be performed during the reading between diagrams and their elements.

DAM's perspective encompasses four steps (Fig. 7.23), including the three standard steps of the SMartyPerspective. The fourth step is specific for SMarty diagrams (Fig. 7.25). Such step deals with the traceability between elements, supported by SMarty through meta-attributes as $realizes+$ and $realizes-$ of the <<variability>> stereotype (Fig. 7.24). This <<variability>> groups the information in a UML *comment* element.

			LOCATE THE CLASS DIAGRAM AND REQUIREMENTS SPECIFICATION
			The class diagram for your role should present the class structure and its relationships for all SPL systems in the project domain, paying attention to the application interfaces and their main methods. To ensure that this diagram describes the design classes in the correct way, carefully read the specification of requirements and while reading, make a list with the mentioned objects, the data that characterize this object and the possible methods. Compare the list made with the class diagram to ensure that there is no inconsistency between classes and user requirements. To do this, answer the questions that follow.
Step 1			For each class in the class diagram, check the classes, the attributes, the relationships between the classes with the list made and answer the questions that follow. Check the class after its analysis, to avoid being analyzed again.
	1.1		Does the class name correctly express the objects of this class?
	1.2		Does this class correspond to an object that has not been defined in the requirements document? If so, please disregard it and their relationships to the next steps and go to the next class.
	1.3		Is this class in redundancy with another one already specified in the class diagram? If so, please disregard it and their relationships to the next steps and go to the next class.
	1.4		Is the class stereotyped in the class diagram?
	1.5		If the classes are grouped into packages, check and answer the questions that follow.
		1.5.1	Has the package name been defined and expresses the grouping correctly? If you have already filled out this defect for this package on the form you do not need to fill it out again
		1.5.2	Is the class in the correct package?
	1.6		For each relationship for this class, check the classes that make up this relationship, to ensure that the relationship between them is in accordance with the requirements specification. To do this, answer the questions that follow and mark the relationships already analyzed.
		1.6.1	Is this relationship in accordance with the requirements specification? Check if there is really a relationship between the elements for the context.
		1.6.2	Is the cardinality of this relationship correct according to the requirements specification?
		1.6.3	Check the type of relationship to ensure that the classes are stereotyped and correct according to the SMarty approach: • Generalization: Are the most general classifiers points of variation (<<variationPoint>>) and the most specific, variants? • Realization of interface: Are the specifications points of variation (<<variationPoint>>) and the implementations are variants? • Aggregation or Composition: Are the instances typed with diamonds (filled or not filled) are points of variation (<<variationPoint>>) and associated instances are variants? • Association: Check the AgregationKind attribute • if none: variants suggest to be mandatory (<<mandatory>>) or optional (<<optional>>). Check against the requirements specification. Is the stereotype correct? • whether the value * or 0..n are optional (<<optional>>)?
		1.6.4	Are classes that require another related to the <<requires>> stereotype?
		1.6.5	Are mutually exclusive classes related to the <<mutex>> stereotype?
	1.7		Was there any relationship missing for this class that was not specified in the class diagram?
	1.8		Interfaces specify methods that are externally visible to others. If the interface is of this type, analyze each of the defined methods and answer the questions that follow.
		1.8.1	Is the interface stereotyped with <<interface>>?
		1.8.2	Does the method match a functionality that actually exists in the system?
		1.8.3	Does the name of the method correctly express its function?
		1.8.4	Is the method redundant with another method previously defined for this class?
	1.9		Have the main methods been defined?
Step 2			After analyzing all the classes in the previous step (all marked as visited), check and analyze the questions that follow.
	2.1		The control classes manage the activities of the class. For each class of this type that is stereotyped with <<optional>> and/or <<variationPoint>>. Check it to ensure that the variability/variant notations are correct according to the requirements specification. To do this, go to each of these classes and answer the questions that follow.
		2.1.1	Is there a UML notation that represents variability (<<variability>>) associated with the control class?
		2.1.2	Have all the variants been defined and are they with the correct variant notation (<<OR >>, <<XOR>> or <<optional>>)?
	2.2		The <<variability>> stereotype represents variability through a UML comment. For each of these comments defined in the diagrams, go to the comment, analyze it and answer the questions below.
		2.2.1	Are the variants defined in the variants set really variants for this element? If any are not, disregard it for the next questions.
		2.2.2	Are there any variants defined in the collection of variants that are not described in the class diagram?
		2.2.3	Are all variants related to this element defined with (<<OR>>), (<<XOR>>) or (<<optional>>) in the collection of variants of the meta-attribute variants with their correct name?
		2.2.4	Check the type of the associated variants: • If they are of type <<optional>>, minSelection = 0 and maxSelection = 1? • If they are of type <<OR>>, minSelection = 1 and maxSelection = total of variants ? • If they are of type <<XOR>>, minSelection=maxSelection=1?
	2.3		Are there still items on your list that are not in any class? That is, it is missing from the class diagram (If they are variants that were already identified in the previous step, disregard).

Fig. 7.17 DAC scenario for class diagram

	LOCATE THE COMPONENT AND CLASS DIAGRAM		
	The component diagram in Domain Engineering should show the physical structure of the implementation through components, interfaces and their relationships to all system components, since some will be mandatory for all products and others will be arranged according to needs user-specific. To inspect it, make a list from the class diagram with all the classes in the system (remember to inspect the class diagram before). Compare the list with the component diagram to ensure that there is no inconsistency between them and that all classes are grouped into components. To do this, answer the questions that follow.		
Step 3	Consider an element as a component or interface for the next steps. For each of them specified in the component diagram, check its correspondence with the list made, analyze it to answer each of the questions that follow. Remember to mark the elements of your list that have already been defined in any of the components.		
	3.1	Does the name correctly express the element?	
	3.2	Is the element redundant with another one previously specified? If so, disregard it for the next steps and go to the next element	
	3.3	Is the element on your list? If not, disregard it for the next steps and go to the next element.	
	3.4	Is the element stereotyped in the component diagram?	
	3.5	If the component is mandatory, is it marked with the <<mandatory>> stereotype?	
	3.6	For each list of this element, check it and answer the questions that follow.	
		3.6.1	Does the component/interface relationship with another element really exist?
		3.6.2	If the relationship is of the type of contract, is the order provided/required or required/provided correct?
		3.6.3	Are variants that require the presence of another related to the <<requires>> or <<use>> stereotype?
		3.6.4	Are mutually exclusive variants related to the <<mutex>> stereotype?
	3.7	If the element is of the optional type, check it and answer the questions that follow.	
		3.7.1	Was the <<optional>> stereotype defined for the element?
		3.7.2	Is there a UML notation that represents variability (<<variability>>) associated with the element?
	3.8	If the element represents a variation point, check it and answer the questions that follow.	
		3.8.1	Was the <<variationPoint>> stereotype defined for the element?
		3.8.2	Is there a UML notation that represents variability (<<variability>>) associated with the element?
		3.8.3	Have all the variants been defined and are they with the correct variant notation (<<OR>> or <<XOR>>)?
		3.8.4	Are there any variants described in the component diagram that do not belong to this element?
		3.8.5	Is there a variant in redundancy with another one already specified?
		3.8.6	Is there a variant related to the element that was defined with (<<OR>>) or (<<XOR>>) that was not specified in the requirements? If so, remove it from the diagram and disregard this variant and its relationships for the next questions.
Step 4	After analyzing all the elements in the previous step (all marked as visited), check and analyze the questions that follow.		
	4.1	The <<variability>> stereotype represents variability through a UML comment. For each of these comments defined in the diagrams, go to the comment, analyze it and answer the questions below.	
		4.1.1	Are the variants defined in the *variants* set really variants for this element? If any are not, disregard it for the next questions.
		4.1.2	Are there variants defined in the collection of variants that are not described in the component diagram?
		4.1.3	Are all variants related to this element defined with (<<OR>>), (<<XOR>>) or (<<optional>>) in the collection of variants of the meta-attribute *variants with* their correct name?
		4.1.4	Check the type of the associated variants: • If they are of type <<optional>>, minSelection = 0 and maxSelection = 1? • If they are of type <<OR>>, minSelection = 1 and maxSelection = total of variants ? • If they are of type <<XOR>>, minSelection=maxSelection=1?
	4.2	For components and interfaces described in the classifier format. Go to the classifier compartment and check the described operations.	
		4.2.1	Does the component/interface have the <<variationPoint>> stereotype defined?
		4.2.2	Are all component/port/interface variants to resolve this variation point visible in the operations compartment?
		4.2.3	Is there a port/component/interface specified in the operations compartment that does not belong to this element?
		4.2.4	Is there any redundancy for the ports/components/interfaces specified in the operations compartment?
		4.2.5	Are the stereotypes in the operations compartment correct according to each of the elements described there?
	4.3	Are there still items on your list that do not belong to any component? That is, it is missing from the component diagram (If there are variants that have already been identified in the previous step, disregard).	

Fig. 7.18 DAC scenario for component diagram

DOMAIN DEVELOPER
This perspective should implement and test the components and interfaces that will be reusable throughout the product portfolio. You must develop according to the requirements of a range of products, for this you must ensure that the elements represented in the SMarty diagrams of class, sequence and component are not in disagreement with the requirements, contemplate the expected functions and allow you to have a vision implementation of reusable components.
To diagrams correctly express the user requirements without inconsistencies, you must review such diagrams and elements. To achieve your goal, perform the steps outlined below to inspect each of the informed diagrams. When you find a defect in one of the steps, fill in the Defect Identification Form indicating the diagram, the step item (number question), and the element and the defect found.

LOCATE CLASS DIAGRAM AND REQUIREMENTS SPECIFICATION	
Step 1	inspection of use case diagram
Step 2	
LOCATE THE COMPONENT AND CLASS DIAGRAM	
Step 3	inspection of component diagram
Step 4	
LOCATE THE SEQUENCE DIAGRAM, CLASS AND REQUIREMENT SPECIFICATION	
Step 5	
Step 6	Inspection of sequence diagram
Step7	
Step 8	

Fig. 7.19 DDP scenario structure

7.4.8 SMartyPerspective: Application Examples

For each perspective of the SMartyPerspective, there are specific defect classes by roles that will be assumed by the inspector. Thus, defect types can be detected from different perspectives in the same diagram.

Three inspection examples for the **SenderMgr** package are presented (Fig. 7.26) from the SPL Mobile Media class diagram. The main objective is to illustrate the differences between the defects detected from the DAC (design view), DDP (implementation view), and DAM (traceability view) perspectives.

7.4.8.1 Domain Architect Example

The objective of the DAC is to have a technical structure view of the system design and no implementation specifications to identify the main methods developed. Therefore, how classes are analyzed based on the design view is necessary to highlight the defects in specifications.

For example, in the **ISendMedia** interface, no defect will be detected until Question 1.3. Such class correctly expresses the objects in the domain, and it's not redundant with another class. However, the interface was not stereotyped using the SMarty approach (Question 1.4—Step 1).

Considering the **ISendMedia** interface, the reader should analyze whether the methods represent functions expressed in the SPL domain in Question 1.10.2 (Fig. 7.27). For this example (Fig. 7.26), the **sendMediaBluetooth** method was

			LOCATE CLASS DIAGRAM AND REQUIREMENTS SPECIFICATION
			The class diagram for your role should present the class structure and its relationships for all SPL systems in the project domain, including specific details for implementation, such as types of attributes and method parameters. To ensure that this diagram describes the design classes in the correct way, carefully read the specification of requirements and while reading, make a list with the mentioned objects, the data that characterize this object and the possible methods. Compare the list made with the class diagram to ensure that there is no inconsistency between the classes and the user's requirements. To do this, answer the questions that follow.
Step 1			For each class in the class diagram, check the attributes, the relationships between the classes with the list made and answer the questions that follow. Make an appointment in the class after its analysis, to avoid being analyzed again.
	1.1		Does the class name correctly express the objects of this class?
	1.2		Does this class correspond to an object that has not been defined in the requirements document? If so, please disregard it and their relationships to the next steps and go to the next class.
	1.3		Is this class in redundancy with another one already specified in the class diagram? If so, disregard her and her relationships for the next steps and move on to the next class.
	1.4		Is the class stereotyped in the class diagram?
	1.5		If the classes are grouped into packages, check and answer the questions that follow.
		1.5.1	Has the package name been defined and expresses the grouping correctly? If you have already filled out this defect for this package on the form you do not need to fill it out again
		1.5.2	Is the class in the correct package?
	1.6		For each relationship for this class, check the classes that make up this relationship, to ensure that the relationship between them is in accordance with the requirements specification. To do this, answer the questions that follow and mark the relationships already analyzed.
		1.6.1	Is this relationship in accordance with the requirements specification? Check if there is really a relationship between the elements for the context.
		1.6.2	Is the cardinality of this relationship correct according to the requirements specification?
		1.6.3	Check the type of relationship to ensure that the classes are stereotyped and correct according to the SMarty approach: • Generalization: Are the most general classifiers points of variation (<<variationPoint>>) and the most specific, variants? • Realization of interface: Are the specifications points of variation (<<variationPoint>>) and the implementations are variants? • Aggregation or Composition: Are the instances typed with diamonds (filled or not filled) are points of variation (<<variationPoint>>) and associated instances are variants? • Association: Check the AgregationKind attribute • if none: variants suggest to be mandatory (<<mandatory>>) or optional (<<optional>>). Check against the requirements specification . • whether the value * or 0..n are optional (<<optional>>)?
		1.6.4	Are classes that require another related to the <<requires>> stereotype?
		1.6.5	Are mutually exclusive classes related to the <<mutex>> stereotype?
	1.7		Was there any relationship missing for this class that was not specified in the class diagram?
	1.8		Entity classes store data that identifies real-world concepts. If the data compartment and/or its types have been defined in the attribute compartment, analyze this information and for each attribute of this class answer the questions below.
		1.8.1	Does the attribute name correctly express the real-world data?
		1.8.2	Does the attribute really belong to that class?
		1.8.3	Is the attribute redundant with another one already defined for this class?
		1.8.4	Is the attribute type correct?
		1.8.5	Is the visibility of the attribute in the class correct?
	1.9		Were the main attributes defined for this class?
	1.10		The interfaces specify the methods externally visible to others. If the class is of this type, analyze each of the defined methods and answer the questions that follow.
		1.10.1	Is the class stereotyped with <<interface>>?
		1.10.2	Does the method match a functionality that actually exists in the system?
		1.10.3	Does the name of the method correctly express its function?
		1.10.4	Is the method redundant with another method previously defined for this class?
		1.10.5	Check the input parameters for the method and answer the following questions: • Was any input parameter missing for the method? • Has a parameter been specified beyond what is necessary? • Have the parameter types been specified correctly?
		1.10.6	Check the output parameters for the method and answer the following questions: • Is the return value correct? • Is the return type correct?
		1.10.7	Is the visibility of the method correct?
	1.11		Was there a lack of an important method for the implementation to be defined?

Fig. 7.20 DDP scenario for class diagram—part 1

		After analyzing all the classes in the previous step (all marked as visited), check and analyze the questions that follow.	
Step 2	2.1	The control classes manage the activities of the class. For each class of this type that is stereotyped with <<optional>> and/or <<variationPoint>>. Check it to ensure that the variability/variant notations are correct according to the requirements specification. To do this, go to each of these classes and answer the questions that follow.	
		2.1.1	Is there a UML notation that represents variability (<<variability>>) associated with the control class?
		2.1.2	Have all the variants been defined and are they with the correct variant notation (<<OR>>, <<XOR>> or <<optional>>)?
	2.2	The <<variability>> stereotype represents variability through a UML comment. For each of these comments defined in the diagrams, go to the comment, analyze it and answer the questions below.	
		2.2.1	Are the variants defined in the variants set really variants for this element? If any are not, disregard it for the next questions.
		2.2.2	Are there any variants defined in the collection of variants that are not described in the class diagram?
		2.2.3	Are all variants related to this element defined with (<<OR>>), (<<XOR>>) or (<<optional>>) in the collection of variants of the meta-attribute variants with their correct name?
		2.2.4	Check the type of the associated variants: • If they are of type <<optional>>, minSelection = 0 and maxSelection = 1? • If they are of type <<OR>>, minSelection = 1 and maxSelection = total of variants ?. • If they are of type <<XOR>>, minSelection = maxSelection = 1?
	2.3	Are there still items on your list that are not in any class? That is, it is missing from the class diagram. (If they are variants that have already been identified in the previous step, disregard)	

Fig. 7.21 DDP scenario for class diagram—part 2

specified. However, there is no specification for **sending media via bluetooth** but via SMS and email.

Step 1 was completed for all diagram elements. Step 2 will analyze the control classes, the UML notations (represent the variability), and the class missing from the diagram. For example, in Fig. 7.26 the inspector will check that Sender is optional and *maxSelection* should be set to 1.

7.4.8.2 Domain Developer Example

The reader has a full view of the class diagram for the DDP role, unlike the DAC and DRE roles. In addition to the defects detected from the DAC perspective, DDP will detect other defect types (Fig. 7.28). DDP scenario inspects the class diagram highlighting the solution to the problem, including checking for defects in the classes, attributes, parameters, types, and others.

The **Sender** class presents a defect type detected by the DDP perspective. It refers to the attribute types specified for the objects. For **Sender** two attributes have been defined: Date and Time. The latter expresses the **media shipping time** and is correct as per the requirements specification. However, the Date attribute (**sent date**) was set to Time incorrectly.

7.4.8.3 Domain Asset Manager Example

In the DAM scenario, the inspector receives the oracle diagram and a diagram with no defects of the core asset of the SPL. The diagram will be inspected from the DAM

		LOCATE THE SEQUENCE DIAGRAM, CLASS AND REQUIREMENT SPECIFICATION	
	The sequence diagram in Domain Engineering should express the interaction of the system: the exchange of messages between the objects of the systems that can be configured from an SPL from a technical point of view, close to the implementation that you must perform. With the sequence diagram in hand, check each of the described objects/actors and look for the corresponding class in the class diagram (if defined) or in the requirements specification. For each of them, check the relationships and messages that are exchanged between the elements to ensure that they are consistent with the class diagram/requirements specification. Then answer the questions that follow.		
Step 5		Consider the "object heads" and the lifeline actors in the sequence diagram as an element. For each one of them, check the messages and stereotypes given to them in order to answer the questions that follow.		
	5.1		Does the name of the element correctly express the object/actor?	
	5.2		Is the element represented in any class in the class diagram?	
	5.3		Is the element part of this interaction according to the Requirements Specification? If not, disregard all the lifeline and their messages for the next steps and go to the next element.	
	5.4		Is the element redundant with another defined element? If so, please disregard all the lifeline and their messages for the next steps and go to the next element.	
	5.5		For each of the messages defined in the lifeline of this element, analyze it and answer the questions that follow.	
		5.5.1	Is the message named?
		5.5.2	Is the interaction represented by this message described in the requirements specification? If not, disregard it and go to the next message.
		5.5.3	Is the order of the message correct according to the requirements specification?
		5.5.4	Does the message name match the method name in the class diagram?
		5.5.5	If specified, are the input parameters correct according to the class diagram?
		5.5.6	If specified, are the output parameters correct according to the class diagram?
		5.5.7	Messages that are not directly related to a variability and its elements, do not need a stereotype and are considered mandatory. Is the message of this type stereotyped?
	5.6		Have all messages for this element been defined in the sequence diagram according to the requirements specification and the class diagram?	
	5.7		Are there redundant messages on this lifeline? If so, disregard it and move on to the next message.	
	5.8		Are elements that require the presence of another related to the <<requires>> stereotype?	
	5.9		Are mutually exclusive elements related to the <<mutex>> stereotype?	
Step 6		For each alternative element in the sequence diagram such as the CombinedFragment with interactionOperator "alt" (alternative) and interactionUse "ref" element, check its stereotypes and messages related to this element to answer the questions that follow.		
	6.1		Is the element defined with the <<variationPoint>> stereotype?	
	6.2		Is there a UML notation that represents variability (<<variability>>) associated with this/CombinedFragment element?	
	6.3		Are the variants corresponding to the messages stereotyped correctly? Check the stereotypes of the variant messages for this variability. • For variants of the interactionUse element "ref": <<OR>> • For variants with interactionOperator "alt": <<XOR>>	
Step 7		For each optional element in the sequence diagram, such as: combinedFragment with interactionOperator "opt" (optional) and exchange of messages between two non-mandatory objects or between one mandatory object and one not, check their stereotypes and messages related to it to answer the questions that follow.		
	7.1		Is there a UML notation that represents variability (<<variability>>) associated with this/CombinedFragment element?	
	7.2		Are the variants corresponding to the/CombinedFragment messages correctly stereotyped with <<optional>>?	
	7.3		For elements marked with <<optional>>, are the lifelines that are part of the CombinedFragment also stereotyped with <<optional>>?	
Step 8		The <<variability>> stereotype represents variability through a UML comment. For each of these comments defined in the diagrams, review the questions below.		
	8.1		Are the variants defined in the variants set really variants for this element? If any are not, disregard it for the next questions.	
	8.2	colspan="2"	Do all variants in the variant set have an associated lifeline in the sequence diagram?	
	8.3	colspan="2"	Are all variants related to this element defined with (<<OR>>), (<<XOR>>) or (<<optional>>) in the collection of variants of the meta-attribute variants with their correct name?	
	8.4	colspan="2"	Check the type of the associated variants: • If they are of type <<optional>>, minSelection = 0 and maxSelection = 1? • If they are of type <<OR>>, minSelection = 1 and maxSelection = total of variants ?. • If they are of type <<XOR>>, minSelection=maxSelection=1?	

Fig. 7.22 DDP scenario for sequence diagram. Adapted from [33]

DOMAIN ASSET MANAGER
This perspective interacts with all Domain Engineering activities to manage the versions and variants of the artifacts produced in this phase. Therefore, the Domain Asset Manager must ensure that the versions of the use case, class, component, sequence, and features diagrams are valid and traceable.
To diagrams correctly express the user requirements without inconsistencies, you must review such diagrams and elements. To achieve your goal, perform the steps outlined below to inspect each of the informed diagrams. When you find a defect in one of the steps, fill in the Defect Identification Form indicating the diagram, the step item (number question), and the element and the defect found.

LOCATE THE DIAGRAM TO BE INSPECTED	
Step 1	
Step 2	inspection all SMarty diagrams and feature diagram
Step 3	
LOCATE ALL SMARTY DIAGRAMS TO BE INSPECTED	
Step 4	inspection all SMarty diagrams

Fig. 7.23 DAM scenario structure

perspective to analyze (using *realizes+*) if it is possible to trace the variability in this set to the use case diagram.

Figure 7.26 represents **sending media** the variability related to the **SenderMgr** class. Assuming that there are two variabilities in the use case diagram named **sending**, the inspector will detect this duplicated by Question 4.1. Thus, the inspection must verify which is traceable to the **sending media** (Fig. 7.29).

In this example, two variabilities have the same name: one variability is named "wrong"; and one will be missing. This defect is detected by Questions 4.1 and 4.3 of the DAM scenario (Fig. 7.29).

7.5 Final Remarks

SMartyCheck is a CBR software inspection technique used to detect defects in common UML diagrams (use case, class, and component) during design-time, but not runtime. SMartyCheck defines the checklist as the main precondition for inspection and the inspector has any SPL based on the UML models.

SMartyCheck detects the "what" must be inspected depending on a checklist format with questions (e.g., yes or no) and a well-defined defect types taxonomy. The SMartyCheck inspections can occur from UML SMarty diagrams following such checklist and their taxonomy. In contrast to SMartyPerspective, SMartyCheck does have not scenarios, perspectives, and specific roles to systematically define how the inspections happen.

SMartyPerspective is a PBR technique that uses scenarios for each perspective of the SPL Domain Engineering. Therefore, PBR collaborates with the inspection of artifacts about "how" to detect the elements to be inspected. PBR has instructions and scenario questions to collaborate with a more detailed inspection and specific defects for each function within an SPL organization.

LOCATE THE DIAGRAM TO BE INSPECTED			
Please locate the first version of the SPL diagram (oracle), check the change log for the new version of the SPL. Correct the diagram by deleting or adding the new elements as described in the record (remember the guidelines for defining the diagrams). Then, locate the version that will be inspected and compare it with the oracle to avoid inconsistency between them, marking the elements as they are being inspected. To do this, answer the questions that follow.			
Step 1	For each element of the diagram being inspected, check it and mark it as visited when you finish the questions about it from Step 1:		
	1.1	Is it possible to trace the element to the oracle? If not, disregard it with your relationships and move on to the next element (remember that elements added in the change log will not appear in the oracle)	
	1.2	Does the name of the element in the second version differ/is abbreviated from the first version?	
	1.3	In the second version, was the element's stereotype defined?	
	1.4	Is the element stereotype in the second version correct?	
	1.5	For each relationship/message in this element, check and answer the questions that follow. Remember to mark the relationships already analyzed.	
		1.5.1	Does this relationship/message exist in the oracle? If not, skip the next questions and move on to the next one.
		1.5.2	If so, has the relationship/message stereotype been defined correctly?
		1.5.3	For the sequence diagram, check the messages: • Is the order of the message correct according to the oracle? • If defined, are the input and output parameters correct according to the oracle?
	1.6	If you are inspecting the class diagram, analyze the attributes and methods of the classes to answer the following questions:	
		1.6.1	If so, are the attributes of this class correct according to the oracle? Check the name and type to answer the question.
		1.6.2	If so, are the methods of this class correct according to the oracle? Check the input and output parameters and their types to answer the question.
	1.7	If you are inspecting the component diagram, review the interfaces and components defined in the classifier format to answer the following question:	
		1.7.1	Are all component/door/interface variants visible in the operating compartment as well as in the oracle? Also check for stereotypes
Step 2	If you are inspecting any SMarty diagram. For each element with a related variability (<<variability>>), go to UML notation and look for it in the second version:		
	2.1	Is the variability notation present in the inspected version?	
	2.2	Is the name (meta-attribute name) of the variability redundant with another already defined?	
	2.3	Does the name (meta-attribute name) of the variability a reflect correctly?	
	2.4	Are minSelection and maxSelection set correctly? Remember to check if a new variant has been inserted according to the change log.	
	2.5	Check the associated variants. Are they present with their correct name as in the oracle?	
	2.6	Check the alllowsAddingVar meta-attribute. Is it correct according to the oracle?	
	2.7	Check the bindingTime meta-attribute. Is it correct according to the oracle?	
	2.8	Check the realizes + and realizes- meta-attributes. Are they specified in the second version, as well as in the first?	
Step 3	After analyzing all the elements in the previous steps (all elements of the inspected diagram marked as visited), check and analyze the questions that follow in the oracle diagram.		
	3.1	Is any element of the oracle not present in the inspected version?	
	3.2	Is there any relationship of the oracle not present in the previewed version?	

Fig. 7.24 DAM scenario for all diagrams

Comparing the SMartyCheck related to SMartyPerspective inspections, SMartyCheck may be easy to detect defect types because of its simplicity. To adopt SMartyCheck is necessary UML SMarty diagrams (SPL) and their checklist to conduct inspections. Perhaps a disadvantage of the SMartyCheck is that just the pre-defined defect types of its checklist are verified during the inspections through checklist format.

SMartyPerspective makes the inspection more specific and less general when compared to SMartyCheck. Since inspectors are assisted from the scenario and

	LOCATE ALL SMARTY DIAGRAMS TO BE INSPECTED	
	The realizes+ and realizes- meta-attributes allow traceability in SMarty diagrams. For each inspected diagram, check which diagrams it is traceable to. To ensure that it is really possible to trace these elements from one diagram to another, please review the diagram and answer the following questions.	
Step 4	Locate the diagram to be inspected. For each variability (UML comment stereotyped with <<variability>>), locate the elements realizes+ and realizes-. • realizes+ should contain the name of variability(ies), thus locate the higher level diagrams with such variability(ies) • realizes- should contain the name of variability(ies), thus locate the lower level diagrams with such variability(ies)	
	4.1	Did you find (match) the variability(ies) informed in the realizes+ or realizes- attributes?
	4.2	Does the variability in the corresponding diagram(s) realizes the variability of source inspected diagram?
	4.3	Is there any missing variabilities in the corresponding diagram(s), informed in the source inspected diagram?

Fig. 7.25 DAM scenario for SMarty diagram

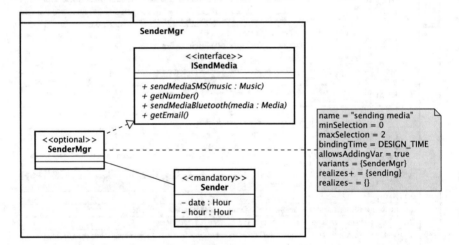

Fig. 7.26 Class diagram part of SPL Mobile Media with defects

nº	DIAGRAM					QUESTION NUMBER	ELEMENT	IDENTIFIED DEFECT
	FT	UC	CL	CP	SQ			
1			X			1.4	ISendMedia	The "ISendMedia" interface has not been stereotyped. Because it is an optional class in the system, it should include the stereotype <<optional>>
2			X			1.8.4	ISendMedia	The "sendMediaBluetooth" method does not belong to the SPL Mobile Media domain. Well, there is no media sending via bluetooth, only via SMS or email.
3			X			1.6.3	Sender	Was defined as mandatory, but should be optional according to SPL.
4			X			2.2.4	SenderMgr	The "sending media" variability related to the SenderMgr class has its maxSelection meta-attribute incorrect. The correct is maxSelection=1.

Fig. 7.27 Defect Identification Form for Fig. 7.26 by DAC

perspective associated with different roles and together they cover the inspection of the artifact in its entirety. SMartyPerspective inspections depend on the scenario and perspective associated with distinct roles. This SMartyPerspective panorama can make the inspections complete, richer, and detailed but extensive, complex, and exhausting when compared to SMartyCheck.

Finally, the techniques presented in this chapter are complementary and aid to detect different defect types in UML SMarty diagrams. SMartyPerspective

n°	DIAGRAM					QUESTION NUMBER	ELEMENT	IDENTIFIED DEFECT
	FT	UC	CL	CP	SQ			
1		X				1.10.2	Sender	The "Date" attribute refers to the date the media was sent. So its type should be set to Date and not Hour as modeled in this diagram.
2		X				1.10.5	ISendMedia	The method "sendMediaSMS" has music as input parameter, however, it is possible to send music, photo and video according to SPL domain.

Fig. 7.28 Defect Identification Form for Fig. 7.26 by DDP

n°	DIAGRAM					QUESTION NUMBER	ELEMENT	IDENTIFIED DEFECT
	FT	UC	CL	CP	SQ			
1		X				4.2	sending media	The "sending" variability related to the "Manage Favorite Media" use case does not realize the "sending media" variability of the class diagram.

Fig. 7.29 Defect Identification Form for Fig. 7.26 by DAM

is useful when proceeds necessary to identify "how" the defects emerge using distinct scenarios, and SMartyCheck defines "what" should be inspected based on its checklist. Both techniques must be used by inspectors manually. As future works, SMartyCheck was automated through a tool that is under development (SMartyCheckTool [37]) aiming to accelerate the inspection process. Furthermore, we intend to automate the SMartyPerspective to contribute to this automation cycle related to the model-based inspections of SPL considering UML SMarty diagrams.

Acknowledgments The authors would like to thank CAPES/Brazil (code 001) for funding this work.

References

1. Alshazly, A.A., Elfatatry, A.M., Abougabal, M.S.: Detecting defects in software requirements specification. Alexandria Eng. J. **53**(3), 513–527 (2014). https://doi.org/10.1016/j.aej.2014.06.001
2. Basili, V.R., Green, S., Laitenberger, O., Lanubile, F., Shull, F., Sørumgård, S., Zelkowitz, M.V.: The empirical investigation of perspective-based reading. Empirical Softw. Eng. **1**(2), 133–164 (1996)
3. Bettin, G.C.S., Geraldi, R.T., OliveiraJr, E.: Experimental evaluation of the SMartyCheck techinique for inspecting defects in UML component diagrams. In: Proceedings of the Brazilian Symposium on Software Quality, pp. 101–110. ACM Press (2018). https://doi.org/10.1145/3275245.3275256
4. Bettin, G.C.S., OliveiraJr, E.: SMartyPerspective: a perspective-based inspection technique for software product lines. In: Proceedings of the Brazilian Symposium on Software Engineering, pp. 90–94. ACM Press (2021). https://doi.org/10.1145/3474624.3474626
5. Biffl, S., Halling, M.: Investigating the defect detection effectiveness and cost benefit of nominal inspection teams. IEEE Trans. Softw. Eng. **29**(5), 385–397 (2003). https://doi.org/10.1109/TSE.2003.1199069
6. Ciolkowski, M., Differding, C., Laitenberger, O., Münch, J.: Empirical investigation of perspective-based reading: a replicated experiment. Fraunhofer Institute for Experimental Software Engineering (1997)

7. Corbin, J.M., Strauss, A.L.: Basics of Qualitative Research: Techniques and Procedures for Developing Grounded Theory. Sage Publishing (2008)
8. Creswell, J.W., Clark, V.L.P.: Designing and Conducting Mixed Methods Research. Sage Publishing (2010)
9. Cunha, R., Conte, T., de Almeida, E.S., Maldonado, J.C.: A Set of inspection techniques on software product line models. In: Proceedings of the 24th International Conference on Software Engineering and Knowledge Engineering, pp. 657–662 (2012)
10. Fagan, M.: Advances in software inspections. IEEE Trans. Softw. Eng. **12**(1), 744–751 (1986). https://doi.org/10.1109/TSE.1986.6312976
11. Fagan, M.: Design and code inspections to reduce errors in program development. In: Software Pioneers, 575–607, Springer, Berlin (2002). https://doi.org/10.1007/978-3-642-59412-0_35
12. Geraldi, R.T.: SMartyCheck: a checklist-based inspection technique for use case and class diagrams of SMarty approach. Master Dissertation, State University of Maringá (2015). http://repositorio.uem.br:8080/jspui/handle/1/2558
13. Geraldi, R.T., OliveiraJr, E., Conte, T., Steinmacher, I.: Checklist-based inspection of SMarty variability models—proposal and empirical feasibility study. In: Proceedings of the 17th International Conference on Enterprise Information Systems, pp. 268–276. Scitepress (2015). https://doi.org/10.5220/0005350102680276
14. Geraldi, R.T., OliveiraJr, E.: Defect types and software inspection techniques: a systematic mapping study. J. Comput. Sci. **13**(10), 470–495 (2017). https://doi.org/10.3844/jcssp.2017.470.495
15. Geraldi, R.T., OliveiraJr, E.: Towards initial evidence of SMartyCheck for defect detection on product-line use case and class diagrams. J. Softw. **12**(5), 379–392 (2017). https://doi.org/10.17706/jsw.12.5.379--392
16. Halling, M., Biffl, S., Grechenig, T., Kohle, M.: Using reading techniques to focus inspection performance. In: Proceedings 27th EUROMICRO Conference: A Net Odyssey, pp. 248–257. IEEE, Piscataway (2001). https://doi.org/10.1109/EURMIC.2001.952461
17. Hayes, J., Raphael, I., Holbrook, E., Pruett, D.: A case history of International Space Station requirement faults. In: Proceedings of the 11th IEEE International Conference on Engineering of Complex Computer Systems, p. 10. IEEE Computer Society (2006). https://doi.org/10.1109/ICECCS.2006.1690351
18. Höhn, E.: Técnicas de leitura de especificação de requisitos de software: estudos empíricos e gerência de conhecimento em ambientes acadêmico e industrial. Master Dissertation, Universidade de São Paulo (2003)
19. IEEE: Recommended Practice for Software Requirements Specifications, Standard 830–1998 (1998). http://standards.ieee.org/findstds/standard/830-1998.html
20. IEEE: Software Reviews, Standard 1028–1997 (1998). http://ieeexplore.ieee.org/stamp/stamp.jsp?tp=&arnumber=663254
21. IEEE: System and Software Verification and Validation, Standard 1012–2012 (2012). https://standards.ieee.org/standard/1012-2012.html
22. Laitenberger, O, Atkinson, C.: Generalizing perspective-based inspection to handle object-oriented development artifacts. In: Proceedings of the International Conference on Software Engineering, pp. 494–503. ACM Press (1999). https://doi.org/10.1145/302405.302680
23. Laitenberger, O.: Cost-effective detection of software defects through perspective-based inspections. Empirical Softw. Eng. **6**, 81–84 (2001). https://doi.org/10.1023/A:1009805707387
24. Laitenberger, O., Kohler, K.: The systematic adaptation of perspective-based inspections to software development projects. In: 1st Workshop on Inspection in Software Engineering, McMaster University, pp. 105–114 (2001)
25. Lamsweerde, A.: Requirements Engineering: From System Goals to UML Models to Software Specifications. Wiley, London (2009)
26. Lanubile, F., Mallardo, F., Calefato, F., Denger, C., Ciolkowski, M.: Assessing the impact of active guidance for defect detection: a replicated experiment. In: Proceedings of the 10th International Symposium on Software Metrics, pp. 269–278. IEEE, Piscataway (2004). https://doi.org/10.1109/METRIC.2004.1357909

27. Linden, F.J., Schmid, K., Rommes, E.: Software Product Lines in Action: The Best Industrial Practice in Product Line Engineering. Springer, Berlin (2007)
28. Mirsky, S., Hayes, J., Miller, L.: Guidelines for the verification and validation of expert system software and conventional software. Technical report (1995). https://doi.org/10.2172/42512
29. Oladele, R., Adedayo, H.: On empirical comparison of checklist-based reading and adhoc reading for code inspection. Int. J. Comput. Appl. **87**(1) (2014). https://doi.org/10.5120/15174--3251
30. Pohl, K., Böckle, G., Linden, F.: Software Product Line Engineering: Foundations, Principles, and Techniques. Springer, Berlin (2005)
31. Porter, A., Votta, L.G., Basili, V.R.: Comparing detection methods for software requirements inspections: a replicated experiment. IEEE Trans. Softw. Eng. **21**(6), 563–575 (1995). https://doi.org/10.1109/32.391380
32. Rombach, D., Ciolkowski, M., Jeffery, R., Laitenberger, O., McGarry, F., Shull, F.: Impact of research on practice in the field of inspections, reviews and walkthroughs: learning from successful industrial uses. ACM SIGSOFT Softw. Eng. Notes **33**(6), 26–35 (2008). https://doi.org/10.1145/1449603.1449609
33. Sabaliauskaite, G., Matsukawa, F., Kusumoto, S., Inoue, K.: Further investigations of reading techniques for object-oriented design inspection. Inform. Softw. Technol. **45**(9), 571–585 (2003). https://doi.org/10.1016/S0950-5849(03)00044-2
34. Shull, F., Rus, I., Basili, V.: How perspective-based reading can improve requirements inspections. Computer **33**(7), 73–79 (2000). https://doi.org/10.1109/2.869376
35. Silva, L.F., OliveiraJr, E.: SMartyModeling: an environment for engineering UML-based software product lines. In: 15th International Working Conference on Variability Modelling of Software-Intensive Systems, pp. 1–5. ACM, New York (2021). https://doi.org/10.1145/3442391.3442397
36. Souza, I.S., da Silva Gomes, G.S., da Mota Silveira Neto, P.A., do Carmo Machado, I., de Almeida, E.S., de Lemos Meira, S.R.: Evidence of software inspection on feature specification for software product lines. J. Syst. Softw. **86**(5), 1172–1190 (2013). https://doi.org/10.1016/j.jss.2012.11.044
37. Taroda, M.H., OliveiraJr, E., Geraldi, R.T.: SMartyCheckTool: uma Ferramenta para Detecção e Remoção de Defeitos em Modelos SMarty de Linhas de Produto de Software. In: XXVI Encontro Anual de Iniciação Científica, pp. 1–4. State University of Maringá (2017)
38. Travassos, G., Shull, F., Fredericks, M., Basili, V.R.: Detecting defects in object-oriented designs: using reading techniques to increase software quality. In: Proceedings of the 14th ACM SIGPLAN Conference on Object-Oriented Programming, Systems, Languages, and Applications, vol. 34, no. 10, pp. 47–56. ACM Press, New York (1999). https://doi.org/10.1145/320384.320389
39. Travassos, G. H.: Software defects: stay away from them. do inspections! In: Proceedings of the 9th International Conference on the Quality of Information and Communications Technology, pp. 1–7. IEEE, Piscataway (2014). https://doi.org/10.1109/QUATIC.2014.8
40. Wohlin, C., Runeson, P., Höst, M., Ohlsson, M.C., Regnell, B., Wesslén, A.: Experimentation in Software Engineering. Springer, Berlin (2012)
41. Zhu, Y.: Software Reading Techniques: Twenty Techniques for More Effective Software Review and Inspection. Apress (2016)

Chapter 8
Model-Based Testing of Software Product Lines

Kleber Lopes Petry, Edson OliveiraJr, Leandro Teodoro Costa, Aline Zanin, and Avelino Francisco Zorzo

Abstract The use of test approaches in software development to ensure quality and safety has grown considerably among model processes in recent decades. Software Product Line (SPL) as seen in previous chapters aims at reusing software components, thus obtaining greater productivity, reducing time and cost. The characteristic that differentiates a product from the others in a core of a product line is called variability. To test a set of products from an SPL is a great challenge since to cover all the functions or variabilities of a group of products could be exhaustive, and this might not be feasible, regardless of the size of the generated products. The analysis and management of variabilities are important since a variability represents different types of variations under different levels and with different types of dependencies. One of the management approaches to deal with variability is Stereotype-based Management of Variability (SMarty), which has been discussed in previous chapters. In order to deal with testing of the wide variety of variations, Model-Based Testing (MBT) has been an approach that can be used in conjunction with SPL. MBT is a software testing technique to generate test cases based on system models that describe aspects (usually functional) of the system under test. The use of MBT in SPL can provide several advantages, for example, contributes to reduce the likelihood of misinterpretation of system requirements by a test engineer, decreases testing time in SPL projects, brings greater traceability between functional requirements and generated test cases, and facilitates the maintenance of test artifacts. In this chapter, we present two MBT approaches to generate functional test cases and scripts to test products derived from SPLs: SPLiT-MBt

K. L. Petry (✉) · E. OliveiraJr
Informatics Department, State University of Maringá, Maringá, Paraná, Brazil
e-mail: edson@din.uem.br

L. T. Costa
Unisinos, São Leopoldo RS, Brazil
e-mail: lteodoroc@unisinos.br

A. Zanin · A. F. Zorzo
Pontifical Catholic University of Rio Grande do Sul, Porto Alegre, Rio Grande do Sul, Brazil
e-mail: avelino.zorzo@pucrs.br

© Springer Nature Switzerland AG 2023
E. OliveiraJr (ed), *UML-Based Software Product Line Engineering with SMarty*,
https://doi.org/10.1007/978-3-031-18556-4_8

and SMartyTesting. Thus, test cases to verify products common functionalities are generated based on the reuse inherent to SPLs. In order to demonstrate the applicability of our two methods, we perform examples of use to test academic SPLs.

8.1 The Role of SMarty in This Work

The SMarty approach has already been adopted for Model-Based Testing of UML-based SPLs. Since SMarty allows to represent variabilities in UML diagrams, especially in Use Case and Activity Diagrams, in this work it has been used also to generate testing sequences in the SPLiT-MBt method and in the SMartyTesting approach.

Therefore, SMarty contributes to provide a way to graphically represent variabilities, variation points, variants, and variant constraints that are used to automatically generate testing sequences in the SPL Domain Engineering with variabilities. Such variabilities are then resolved, and sequences are generated for specific products, thus reusing them.

8.2 SPLiT-MBt: A Model-Based Testing Method for Software Product Lines

It is known that software testing in an autonomous development process is a complex and challenging activity. Therefore, as commented earlier, the testing activity in an SPL context is even more complex, as common and specific artifacts must be tested, as well as the interaction between these artifacts. Consequently, in order to test SPL products, it is necessary to develop and apply approaches and methods differently from those used in a stand-alone development process, where single applications must be tested. With the purpose of improving the testing of applications derived from SPLs, we proposed a method to test SPL products named Software Product Line Testing Method Based on System Models (SPLiT-MBt) [6].

This work was developed in the context of an academy-industry collaboration, in which, our research group has worked closely to a Technology Development Laboratory (TDL) of Dell Computer, Brazil. Their development and testing teams are located in different regions worldwide and develop and test in-house solutions in order to attend their own demand systems on a global scale of sales of computer assets. The aim of this cooperation was to experiment and develop new strategies and approaches for software testing. In this collaboration we developed new strategies and approaches for software testing, e.g., an SPL by Costa et al. [7] and Rodrigues et al. [35] to generate testing products for different testing techniques, i.e., performance testing by Macedo et al. [24] and Rodrigues et al. [34], structural testing by Costa et al. [8], and functional testing by Laser et al. [22].

8.2.1   SPLiT-MBt Characterization

In this section, we present the SPLiT-MBt method, which provides the reuse of test artifacts based on adapting Model-Based Testing (MBT) by Utting and Legeard [1] for automatic generation of functional test cases and scripts from models/notations that represent the SPL functionalities and variability information.

To provide reuse of test artifacts, SPLiT-MBt is applied in two steps. The first one occurs during Domain Engineering, when test and variability information are extracted from SPL models. We assume that these models were previously designed by the SPL analyst using a variability management approach. For example, if the models were designed using UML, then SMarty (Chap. 3) [31] could be used. SMarty aims to manage variability in UML models supported by a profile and a set of guidelines. This approach could be applied to manage variability present in Use Cases, Classes, Components, Activities, and Sequence Diagrams, as well as to Packages. Therefore, a test analyst uses SPLiT-MBt to add test information[1] on two UML diagrams: Use Case and Activity Diagrams. The test information is added, by the test analyst, on these two diagrams in the form of stereotypes and tags. Then, once the Use Case and Activity Diagrams are annotated with test information, the test analyst uses SPLiT-MBt to generate Finite State Machines (FSMs) study by Gill et al. [15] from these UML diagrams.

These FSMs are extended in an SPL context and are used as input, in a specific step of the SPLiT-MBt method, to generate test sequences with variability information. These test sequences are generated through extending conventional test sequence generation methods in an SPL context, e.g., Transition Tour (TT) by Naito et al. [30], Unique Input/Output (UIO) by Sabnani et al. [36], Distinguishing Sequence (DS) by Gonenc et al. [17], W by Chow et al. [4], or Harmonized State Identification (HSI) by Petrenko et al. [32].

SPLiT-MBt supports extended versions of these methods, which are modified to generate test sequences considering variability information present in FSMs. An advantage of extending these methods to handle variability in a SPL context is they provide some benefits, such as prioritization and minimization of test cases. The test sequences generated through applying these modified methods are stored in a test repository, and the variability present in these sequences is resolved by the SPLiT-MBt during Application Engineering.

The second step of SPLiT-MBt takes place during Application Engineering, when the variability present in those test sequences is resolved to meet the specific requirements of each system. We assume that the variability is resolved at design time by the SPL analyst from a Traceability Model containing information about the resolved variability. Thus, the Traceability Model is the main artifact to resolve variability present in the test sequences. Once the variability is resolved, the test sequences are reused to test the specific functionalities of several products. More-

---

[1] It corresponds to test data for functional testing, e.g., test input data or expected results.

over, at this phase, models that represent specific functionalities of each product are generated, and they are annotated with test information by the test analyst. Similarly as it occurs during Domain Engineering, these models are converted into FSMs, and the conventional methods of test sequence generation are applied in order to generate specific test sequences for each product. Finally, all these sequences (from Domain Engineering and Application Engineering) are converted into a description equivalent to test cases in natural language, i.e., abstract test cases.

An abstract test case is a text file describing the interaction of the user with the system. Since its format is generic, the abstract test cases can easily be used as a reference for generating scripts for different functional testing tools, e.g., HP Quick Test Professional (QTP) [25], IBM Rational Functional Tester (RFT) [10], Selenium WebDriver [19], Microsoft Visual Studio (VS) [23], and Microsoft Test Manager (MTM) [26]. SPLiT-MBt allows that test data used to generate test scripts are selected through any existing functional testing criteria, e.g., Boundary Value Analysis and Equivalence Partitioning study by Delamaro et al. [11] and Myers et al. [29]. These criteria contribute to a testing process more systematic and effective, since they avoid testing all system inputs, which would make the testing process impractical. The idea is that test artifacts developed during Domain Engineering are reused to test products during Application Engineering.

Therefore, the adoption of our method presents several benefits from the reuse inherent to SPLs. For instance, through the set of test sequence generation methods that are extended using SPLiT-MBt, it is possible to reduce the amount of test cases, provide a full coverage of the product functionalities, and contribute to select relevant test cases (prioritization and minimization of test cases). Another advantage of our method is that it is based on MBT, since all test information is annotated on systems models, for example, UML Use Case and Activity Diagrams. Thereby, for being based on MBT, SPLiT-MBt contributes to reduce the likelihood of misinterpretation of the system requirements by a test engineer and decreasing testing time in SPL projects.

Furthermore, SPLiT-MBt saves testing effort, since we reuse the test sequences generated in Domain Engineering to test several products derived from Application Engineering. Therefore, if we have, for example, ten products sharing several functionalities, our method will generate test sequences to test the common functionalities for these ten products just once. Therefore, the set of test sequences generated during Domain Engineering is used to test just those products sharing common functionalities.

In a nutshell, SPLiT-MBt aims to answer the following questions: (i) How to test SPL products with the benefits of reusing test artifacts? (ii) How to test, in a systematic manner, products from an SPL? (iii) How to reduce the number of test cases and still find the same amount of system failures? (iv) How to generate test scripts to be executed by different functional testing tools?

To answer these questions, the SPLiT-MBt method:

- Produces test cases that are reused to generate scripts based on system models. Thus, test cases to test common functionalities for different products are generated just once (Question i).
- Is implemented through an application named SPLiT-MBt Tool, which supports the activities of the SPLiT-MBt method. Thus, the testing process of products derived from SPLs can be performed automatically (Question ii).
- Adapts test sequence generation methods in an SPL context. Thus, it is possible to reduce the number of test cases through applying prioritization and minimization of test cases, which contributes to select the relevant ones (Question iii).
- Defines a generic structure representing test cases in pseudo-natural language. Thus, it is possible to generate test scripts that can be executed by different functional testing tools (Question iv).

8.2.2   SPLiT-MBt Phases

As mentioned before, the idea of SPLiT-MBt is to generate test artifacts during Domain Engineering and to reuse them during Application Engineering. In order to make this possible, SPLiT-MBt is applied in two steps: first, we add test information on UML models that were previously designed using a variability management approach, to generate test sequences during Domain Engineering. Second, we add test information on UML models (during Application Engineering) and resolve variability present in the test sequences. Finally, test scripts are generated to be executed for a specific testing tool. Next, we present the main topics that encompass these steps:

- Testing activity during Domain Engineering:

  - Extracting test information and variability from extended UML models based on SPL requirements
  - generating Finite State Machines (FSMs) with test and variability information from UML models
  - Generating test sequences with variability through applying a chosen test sequence generation method (over FSMs), which is adapted/extended to SPL context

- Testing activity during Application Engineering:

  - Resolving variability present in test sequences
  - Extracting test information from UML models based on software requirements of a specific product, since it is possible to exist functionalities of products that are represented only in Application Engineering
  - Generating FSMs from information annotated on UML models of a specific product

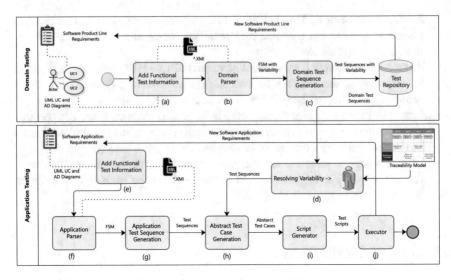

Fig. 8.1 SPLiT-MBt steps for generating functional test cases [6]

- Generating test sequences to a specific product through applying a chosen test sequence generation method (over FSMs)
- Generating test cases to test SPL products
- Generating test scripts for a chosen functional testing tools based on test sequences generated on Domain Engineering and Application Engineering

Next, we present in details the steps to generate test cases and scripts based on the SPLiT-MBt (see Fig. 8.1):

(a) Add Functional Test Information The first step of our method consists of annotating, with test information, an UML model previously designed with a variability management approach. This UML model is generated by an SPL analyst that uses a specific variability management approach and is responsible to extract information from the SPL requirements specification to design the model. SPLiT-MBt can be integrated to several variability management approaches, e.g., *Product Line UML-based Software Engineering* (PLUS), *Triangle Notation* by Halmans et al. [18], or *Stereotype-based Management of Variability* (SMarty) by OliveiraJr et al. [31]. However, we have adopted the SMarty approach, since it can be easily extended, it has a low learning curve, and it represents variability information in several UML models. Although SMarty approach could manage variability in different UML models, it is still necessary to add functional test information on models representing the SPL functionalities, i.e., Activity Diagrams.

We have chosen UML Activity Diagrams (AD) as functional testing model, since they are the most widely used models to represent the behavior and functionalities of a system study by Booch et al. [3]. Basically, stereotypes and tagged values are added to these diagrams, and some specific UML elements are annotated with test information study by Rodrigues et al. [35] and Silveira et al. [38]. The use of stereotypes and tags allows describing functional test information necessary to generate test scripts. Moreover, stereotypes and tagged values can be used to enhance the specification documents, improving the quality of models and test artifacts study by Apfelbaum et al. [2].

Based on the analysis of several scientific papers, as well as the ad hoc experience, observations, and practices developed in our research group,[2] we have defined one stereotype that has three tags to describe test information. Their description is as follows: *FTstep*, stereotype annotated in the *ControlFlow* (transition) element of an Activity Diagram. It has three associated tags, i.e., *TDactionDomain*, that specify the action data to be performed by the user to test a specific functionality. Test information present in this tag is used to perform a specific system functionality, *TDexpectedResultDomain*, that specifies the expected result data used to check whether a specific functionality is working as described in the functional requirements. The information present in this tag is compared to the result obtained from the system execution for the data described in *TDactionDomain* tag and *TDfunctionalCriterion* that specifies information about the functional test criterion used to test some system functionality, e.g., Boundary Value Analysis and Equivalence Partitioning study by Delamaro et al. [11] and Myers et al. [29]. The tester who is using SPLiT-MBt Tool could choose among different functional criterion to test different functionalities of the same system.

When the Activity Diagrams is fully annotated[3] with test information, the test analyst must export the models to an XMI file, which is the input of the next step of our method.

(b) Domain Parser This step consists of automatically extracting variability and test information from Activity Diagrams (XMI file) to generate a formal model, e.g., FSM. We have chosen FSMs, since they are among the most used formal models applied in MBT by Halmans et al. [9]. FSMs are a good alternative to design software testing components, since they may be applicable in any specification model by Chow et al. [4]. The problem is that FSMs were essentially designed to test software based on single system paradigm, and only few works by Gomaa et al. [16] and Millo et al. [28] extend FSMs to an SPL context. Therefore, an extension of FSMs to represent variability information is required. In order to deal with this issue, SPLiT-MBt adds all variability information extracted from Activity Diagrams to the input transitions of the FSM states. FSMs are the outcome of *Domain Parser*, and it is used as input in the next steps of SPLiT-MBt.

---

[2] We experimented several functional testing tools, such as QTP, RFT, Selenium, VS, and MTM.

[3] The test analyst could annotate the actual test data directly in a specific tag or use an external file (for great volume of data) to describe the test information. In the case of using an external file, the tag describes only a reference to this file.

(c) Domain Test Sequence Generation The FSM previously generated is used to create test sequences with variability information. These sequences are produced through the use of a specific test sequence generation method, e.g., W, Wp, UIO, or HSI. These methods are able to generate fewer amounts of test sequences. The idea is to test products with less effort (time spent), as well as to generate less test cases when comparing with other approaches. However, they must be adapted in an SPL context to handle variability information present in FSMs, since they were originally created to test applications developed from the single system paradigm. Therefore, they are inefficient to reduce the number of test cases for products generated from SPLs. In a nutshell, in an SPL context, these methods must be able to determine the location of a variation point and then generate distinct sequences to test all variants associated to a particular variation point. Furthermore, test sequence generation methods have several characteristics in common. For instance, joining the Q, P, and HI (partial sequences) produces as result the HSI final test sequence.

After identifying the characteristics these methods have in common, we chose the most suitable method, i.e., HSI. The reason for choosing this method was due to the fact that it is one of the least restrictive methods regarding the properties that FSMs must have. For instance, the HSI is able to interpret complete and partial FSMs study by Petrenko et al. [32]. Moreover, the HSI method allows full coverage of existing failures, and it generates test sequences smaller than other methods, which contributes to a testing process optimization. These factors are very relevant in SPL context, because when an SPL grows, the number of test cases necessary to test SPL products could increase exponentially study by Engstrom et al. [13].

We have adopted the HSI as a method to generate test sequences with variability information. However, the process to adapt other test sequence generation methods in an SPL context occurs similarly, and it is described as follows:

1. Variants can also be a variation point. In this case, FSM's states (variants) associated to a variant (that is also a variation point) are "separated" from the FSM. In this context, a new FSM is produced, i.e., a sub-FSM. Sub-FSMs can be generated in another situation. For instance, they can also be created when exist "Nested Activities" in UML Activity Diagrams, i.e., when an action element (activity) of an Activity Diagram makes a reference to another Activity Diagram. It is important to highlight that a sub-FSM will be replaced by a state that represents the sub-FSM in the main FSM.

2. Variants associated to the same variation point are assumed to be a single state in the FSM. Furthermore, the input transition of this single state must have the input/output information of all states (variants). This state is a concatenation of *VP_* plus *a unique identifier*, e.g., VP_S1. This state represents a specific variation point and has information about its variants. This occurs because it is not possible to determine which variants associated to a particular variation point will be resolved, since a variation point is not resolved in Domain Engineering. Thus, a solution would be to increase the abstraction level through a state representing variants. Therefore, the test sequence generation methods can be applied and still

preserve variability, which will be resolved only in Application Engineering. A concrete example representing this situation is shown in Sect. 8.2.3.

3. After executing the criteria 1 and 2, it is necessary to generate a set of *partial test sequences*, which is performed by the application of a test sequence generation method under an FSM. As described earlier, the *partial test sequences* corresponds to a set of sequences that are joined to form the *final set of test sequence* of a specific test sequence generation method. For instance, the final test sequence generated by the HSI method is formed by the combination of three *partial test sequences*, i.e., *State Cover* (Q), *Transition Cover* (P), and *Harmonized Identifier* (HI).

4. In Domain Engineering the goal is to preserve variability. Therefore, variants having dependency relationship (*depends/requires*) or mutually exclusive ones (*excludes/mutex*) among themselves, as well as optional variants and variants that are part of a group of alternative inclusive variants (`alternative_OR`) or exclusive ones (`alternative_XOR`), are not considered when performing the methods but will be resolved in Application Engineering, in which concrete test cases are derived to test specific products [5].

5. The output of this SPLiT-MBt step is a set of test sequences generated from the application of a chosen method, e.g., HSI. These sequences still contain variability information, which is represented by the following alphabet:

- Op = represents optional variants
- VP_or = represents a variant that is part of a group of inclusive alternative variants (`alternative_OR`)
- VP_xor = represents a variant that is part of a group of exclusive alternative variants (`alternative_XOR`)
- { } = defines the set of variants associated to a variation point
- () = defines the set of test sequences generated by the application of a test sequence generation method under an FSM
- [] = defines the set of test sequences generated by the application of a test sequence generation method under sub-FSMs
- $Req_{->}$ = represents the dependency relationship (*depends/requires*) among variants
- $Ex_{->}$ = represents the mutually exclusive relationship (*excludes/mutex*) among variants

Once the test sequences are generated, they are stored in a repository (`test repository`) to be later reused (when variability was already resolved) to test specific products during Application Engineering (Fig. 8.1). In Sect. 8.2.3, we demonstrate how SPLiT-MBt supports the HSI adaptation to generate test sequences during Domain Engineering.

(d) Resolving Variability This step describes how to resolve the variability in test sequences generated in Domain Engineering in order to reuse them to test specific products. To provide that, this step receives as input two types of artifacts, i.e.,

the test sequences stored in the test repository and a Traceability Model. We assumed that this model was previously designed by the SPL analyst based on the SMarty approach.[4] It describes, in a tabular format, a correlation between an SPL feature model and UML model elements, such as Use Case and action elements from Activity Diagrams. This Traceability Model also describes information about the features that were selected to resolve the variability. Therefore, the variability present in the test sequences is resolved by crossing information present in the Traceability Model with the test sequences present in the test repository.

For instance, consider a hypothetic test sequence, i.e., (ab{d;e;c}$_{VP\_or}$fff). It is possible to realize three inputs (d;e;c) associated to variants type OR. When this sequence is compared with information present in a Traceability Model (e.g., activity *shopping cart* with data input = 'e'), it is possible to determine which variant (d;e;c) will be selected to resolve the variability present in that sequence. In this case, the selected variant was 'e', and as result we have the corresponding test sequence: *abefff*.

(e) Add Functional Test Information This step has some similarities when comparing to its equivalent step from Domain Engineering, i.e., test information is added to UML models. However, the model depicts functionalities of a specific product. For example, during Application Engineering it could be necessary to add a specific functionality to an existing product when a new version of this product is required. As this functionality is specific to a single product, it is, usually, not added to models during Domain Engineering. In this context, a new model representing the specific functionalities for a particular product must be designed from scratch during Application Engineering. For this SPLiT-MBt step, we assumed that these models (Activity Diagrams) were previously designed based on information extracted from Software Application Requirements. Thus, a test analyst is only responsible for annotating, with test information, those UML models. This annotation process is almost the same as that performed during Domain Engineering. Therefore, the same tags used to annotate *ControlFlow elements* (transitions) during Domain Engineering are used at this step, i.e., *TDactionDomain*, *TDexpectedResultDomain*, and *TDfunctionalCriterion*. The difference is that, during Application Engineering, the Activity Diagrams have no variability information.

When the Activity Diagrams are fully annotated, with test information, the test analyst must export the models to an XMI file, which is the input of the next step of our method.

(f) Application Parser and (g) Application Test Sequence Generation These steps are very similar to their equivalent ones from Domain Engineering, just differing in some aspects. For instance, the Application Parser is applied to models

---

[4] More details about the smart approach can be found at study by OliveiraJr et al. [31].

that contain only test information, since the variability has been previously resolved. Therefore, the `Application Parser` receives, as input, an XMI file describing test information to generate FSMs. These formal models are the input of the `Application Test Sequence Generation` step, from which are applied a specific test sequence generation method, i.e., traditional HSI. In this step, there is no need to adapt the HSI, since there is no variability information to be handled. Therefore, a set of test sequences is, automatically, generated through applying the HSI under FSMs describing functionalities of a specific product. These sequences are the input of the next SPLiT-MBt step.

(h) Abstract Test Case Generation This step aims to, automatically, convert the test sequences, generated in `Application Test Sequence Generation` and `resolving variability` steps, into abstract test cases. An abstract test case is a text file structured in a technology independent format that describes the activities to be performed by the user (or a tool) during the interaction with the system under test (SUT). It uses the test data to define the user or their actual data inputs/outputs and the functional criteria. These data input/output and functional criteria present in the abstract test case correspond to the test information, previously added to the Activity Diagrams.

The motivation for generating abstract test cases is that they can be reused to, automatically, produce scripts to several functional testing tools. Thus, SPLiT-MBt provides greater flexibility by allowing products derived from an SPL to be tested using different testing tools. For instance, consider an IT company that has adopted SPLiT-MBt to test the products of its SPL. This company can be motivated by technical or managerial decision to easily migrate from a testing tool A to a testing tool B without the need to manually create new scripts. Thus, all test cases and scripts previously created can be reused. Furthermore, the abstract test case has a clear representation where the test data are presented in a high level language (for more details see Sect. 8.2.3).

(i) Script Generator and (j) Executor These steps (`Script Generator`) consist of, automatically, creating scripts based on the abstract test cases generated in previous step. It is a tool-dependent step, since the scripts are "strongly" associated to a specific functional testing tool, i.e., MTM. In this context, SPLiT-MBt Tool supports the instantiation of abstract test cases into test scripts to be used to the test execution. Although we have chosen the MTM, SPLiT-MBt allows the integration of other functional testing tools, e.g., VS and QTP and RFT.

It is important to highlight these steps are performed by a prototype tool supporting the SPLiT-MBt activities, i.e., SPLiT-MBt Tool. It is a plugin-based tool that provides automatic test sequence generation using different test sequence generation methods, e.g., W, Wp, and HSI. Furthermore, in order to automate test scripts generation, as well as the test execution, our tool can also be integrated with different functional testing tools e.g., QTP, RFT, Selenium, VS, and MTM.

Furthermore, the scripts generated by SPLiT-MBt Tool have a tabular format and are imported by the MTM to perform the test. Once the test scripts are generated, the SPLiT-MBt Tool performs its last functionality (`Executor`), which aims to launch the testing tool and to start the test execution. This initialization consists of an internal system call, where the test engineer (through the SPLiT-MBt Tool interface) provides the testing tool installation path and the scripts path. Thus, the MTM environment is initialized, and the test can be finally performed.

8.2.3 SPLiT-MBt Application Example

This section describes how our method was applied to generate test cases for 336 products that could be derived from an actual SPL, i.e., Product Line of Testing Tools (PLeTs) [34] study by Elder et al. [35]. This SPL was developed in the context of a collaboration project between PUCRS (Brazil) and a global IT company.

PLeTs was designed and developed to automate the generation of MBT Tools (products) study by Rodrigues et al. [35] and by Bernardino et al. [38]. These testing tools automate the generation of test cases based on the system models, i.e., products derived from PLeTs accept a system model as an input and generate test cases. Actually, PLeTs could be used to generate MBT Tools that perform three type of tests, i.e., performance, functional or structural testing. Table 8.1 summarizes the main functionalities of PLeTs products, which are used to explain our method.

8.2.3.1 Add Test Information to SPL Models

Based on PLeTs requirements presented in Table 8.1, the SPL analyst has to design the Use Case and Activity Diagrams that describe the functionalities of

Table 8.1 PLeTs SPL requirements [6]

ID	Requirement	Description
RF-01	Choose type of test	The system should allow the user to select the type of testing that will be performed
RF-02	Functional	The MBT Tools must support automatic generation of testing data for functional testing. These tools must support integration with other functional testing tools
RF-03	Performance	The MBT Tools must support automatic generation of testing data for performance testing. These tools must support integration with other performance testing tools
RF-04	Structural	The MBT Tools must support automatic generation of testing data for structural testing. These tools must support integration with other structural testing tools
RF-05	Functionalities Functional	The MBT Tools must allow users to create a log file, edit an configuration file, and close the system interface
RF-06	Functionalities Performance	The MBT Tools must allow users to set performance test environment (scripts and scenarios) and test case generation

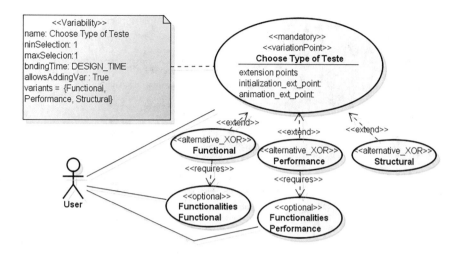

Fig. 8.2 PLeTs use case model [6]

the PLeTs products. Thus, the SPL analyst has to build these diagrams and add variability information in accordance with the SMarty approach. Figure 8.2 presents an Use Case model with one actor and six Use Case elements describing several operations that can be performed by the user, such as select the type of testing to be executed (*Choose Type of Test*), to perform one of three types of test (*Functional, Performance,* or *Structural*).

The PLeTs *Structural* Use Case element (see Fig. 8.2) was chosen as an example to demonstrate how the test case generation is performed using SPLiT-MBt and how these test artifacts are reused to test the product functionalities. The reason for choosing this Use Case element is that it is decomposed into an Activity Diagram (see Fig. 8.3) that presents more variability elements, e.g., *optional* and *mandatory* variants, dependency relationship (*requires*), mutually exclusive relationship (*mutex*), and inclusive variants (*alternative_OR*).[5]

This PLeTs Activity Diagram describes the user interactions with some PLeTs products, specifically those used to perform structural testing. Firstly, the user must import an XMI file (*Load XMI File*) that has information related to structural testing. Next, the user click on "Parser button" (*Submit the XMI File to a Parser*) in order to generate test cases. Then, the user chooses the path (*Type the Path to Save Abstract Structure and Data File*) where the test cases will be saved (*Saving the Abstract Structure and Data File*), and selects the tool that will perform the structural testing (*Informing the Tool Path*). Next, the user generates test scripts for one of the three

---

[5] We have generated test cases for all Activity Diagrams related to the other Use Case elements. These diagrams and all test artifacts generated in this Case Study (e.g., test sequences with variability, test sequences with variability already resolved, abstract test cases, and test scripts) can be found in study by Costa et al. [6].

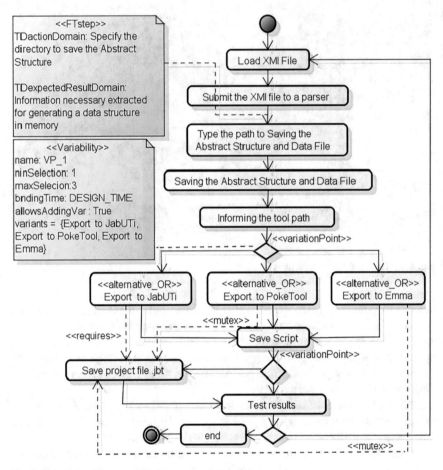

Fig. 8.3 Activity diagram of PLeTs structural tools [6]

available tools (*Export to JaBUTi, Export to PokeTool, Export to Emma*). Finally, the user chooses a directory to save the scripts (*Save Scripts*), executes the test, and presents the test results (*Test Results*). In case the user generates test cases for JaBUTi, a project file will be created (*Save Project File .jbt*), since this tool needs to create an additional configuration file.

The *Load XMI File, Submit the XMI File to a Parser, Type the Path to Save Abstract Structure and Data File, Saving the Abstract Structure and Data File, Informing the Tool Path, Save Scripts,* and *Test Results* activities represent mandatory variants (mandatory), i.e., they have to be present in all generated products. The *Export to JaBUTi, Export to PokeTool,* and *Export to Emma* activities, on the other hand, correspond to inclusive variants (alternative_OR), since a product derived from PLeTs may have the combination of one, two, or even three structural testing tools. This Activity Diagram has also dependency and mutually exclusive relationships, i.e., *Export to JaBUTi* requires the *Save Project File .jbt*

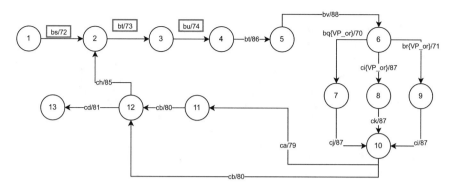

Fig. 8.4 FSM with variability information [6]

activity, while the *Export to PokeTool* and *Export to Emma* will exist in a product configuration only whether the *Save Project File .jbt* activity won't be selected to make part of a specific product.

It is important to highlight that when the Use Case and Activity Diagrams have been modeled and the variability information has been added to these models, our method can be applied. As described in Sect. 8.2.2, the first SPLiT-MBt step consists of annotating *ControlFlow* elements in Activity Diagrams, with test information, through the use of `TDactionDomain` and `TDexpectedResultDomain` tags and their respective tagged values.

Therefore, to make it clearer, we inserted a UML note element, in the Activity Diagram depicted in Fig. 8.3, to show some tagged values annotated in a *ControlFlow* element. In this example, all tags we have defined for our method and their corresponding tagged values are showed. Each of these tags has a value that is bounded to the transition between the *Load XMI File* and *Submit the XMI File and Save* activities.

8.2.3.2 Generate Test Sequences with Variability

After the SPL analyst modeled and exported the PLeTs models to an XMI file,[6] this file must be loaded using the SPLiT-MBt Tool, and then seven FSMs, with variability information, are generated. As described in Sect. 8.2.2, the step b (Domain Parser) of SPLiT-MBt is responsible for converting an Activity Diagram into a FSM with variability information. In Fig. 8.4, we show an example of FSM, which depicts information related to input/output transitions. Input (e.g., bs, bt, bu) corresponds to the input data used to test the system functionalities, and output (e.g., 72, 73, 74) corresponds to the expected result. This information is just a set of identifiers, and the actual test data is described in study by Costa et al. [6].[7] This

---

[6] Most of the UML modeling environments export models to an XMI file. Here we used Astah Professional modeling tool [33].

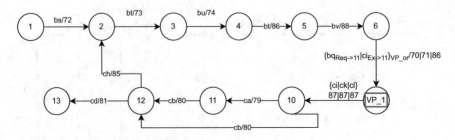

Fig. 8.5 FSM with a state representing a variation point [6]

table also presents information regarding the source/target states of the FSM, as well as variability, which corresponds to the variant type associated with a given state (Target State).

Considering that FSM with variability, the HSI method must generate test sequences during Domain Engineering. In order to make it possible, the states (variants) associated to the same variation point are assumed to be a single state in the FSM (state VP_1 in Fig. 8.5), in which the input transition of this state must have the input/output information of all states (variants).

As a result of this step, the FSM depicted in Fig. 8.4 is converted into the FSM from Fig. 8.5. It is possible to notice, in this FSM, that the input transition of **VP_1** has input and output information from the states (variants) *7*, *8*, and *9* as well as information related to dependency ($bq_{req->11}$) and mutually exclusive ($ci_{ex->11}$, $br_{ex->11}$) relationship.

Once the FSM is modified, the HSI method will generate test sequences for FSMs with transitions containing a set of inputs instead of transitions with just one input, as those used to test single applications. In order to apply the modified HSI, we must consider and adapt the three steps used by this method to generate partial test sequences, i.e., Q, P, and HI. These steps produce, as result, a set of partial test sequences that are combined with each other to compose the HSI final test sequence. Table 8.2 presents a sample of test sequences with variability information, in which we describe the partial test sequences generated through applying P, Q, and HI as well as HSI final test sequence. It is important to highlight that we present just a limited sample of test sequences. The test sequences are stored in a repository to be resolved during Application Engineering.

8.2.3.3 Resolving Variability

Through applying the adapted HSI for all FSMs (7 FSMs) that correspond to the entire PLeTs functionalities in Domain Engineering, 18 test sequences with

---

[7] Table available at https://doi.org/10.5281/zenodo.6792389.

Table 8.2 Some examples of test sequences Q, P, HI, and HSI [6]

State	State cover (Q)
1	ϵ, bs, bt
VP_1	ϵ, bs, bt, bu, bv{bq;ci;br\}$_{VP\_or}$
11	ϵ, bs, bt, bu, bv{bq;ci;br\}$_{VP\_or}$, {bs;bs;bs},ca

State	Transition cover (P)
1	ϵ, bs, bt, bu
VP_1	ϵ, bs, bt, bu, bv,{bq;ci;br\}$_{VP\_or}$, {bs;bs;bs}
1	ϵ, bs, bt, bu, bv,{bq;ci;br\}$_{VP\_or}$, {bs;bs;bs},cb

State	Harmonized identifier (HI)
1	bt
1	bt
1	Null

HSI final test sequence: bs,bt,bu ,bt,bv,{$bq_{req->11}$; $ci_{ex->11}$; $br_{ex->11}$\}$_{VP\_or}$,{cj;ck;cl},ca, cb

variability information were generated. During Application Engineering, when the variability is resolved through the use of the `Traceability Model`, 3257 test sequences were produced. In order to illustrate an example of test sequence with variability already resolved, we consider the following test sequences: *"bu bt bv ci bs cb cd"* and *"bu bt bv br bs cb cd."* These sequences were generated when the variability present in the test sequence *"bs bu bt bv* {$bq_{req->11}$;$ci_{ex->11}$;$br_{ex->11}$}$_{VP\_or}$ *{bs;bs;bs} cb cd"* was resolved. All the 3257 test sequences were reused to test the functionalities of 336 products derived from PLeTs, and based on these numbers, the reuse percentage was obtained by a metric called *Size and Frequency* (R_{sf}) study by Devanbu et al. [12]. Considering this metric, the reuse percentage for the generated test sequences is given by:

$$R_{sf} = \frac{Size_{sf} - Size_{act}}{Size_{sf}} = \frac{3257 - 18}{3257} = 0.99$$

This value determines that 99% of test sequences generated in Domain Engineering were reused to test the functionalities of all products derived from PLeTs. Therefore, the SPLiT-MBt allowed the test artifacts generation with a considerable reuse percentage for this example. Thus, it demonstrates a possible gain when comparing with approaches that do not consider reuse as a strategy for generating test artifacts, where test cases are individually generated for each product. Furthermore, the use of methods for generating test sequences, such as HSI, contributes to an effort reduction in the test activity, since they allow full coverage of the failures. These features are essential in the SPL context, because the increasing of variabilities has influenced the amount of tests needed to validate the quality of products. SPLiT-MBt can also be useful to adapt several test sequence generation methods, from which test sequences are converted into abstract test cases and test scripts.

```
#Abstract Test Case: bu bt bv ci ck cb cd
1. Load XMI File
<<TDactionDomain = "Type the path of the XMI
file on console" >>
<<TDexpectedResultDomain = "File XMI loaded">>
2. Submit the XMI file to a Parser
<<TDactionDomain = "Press Enter">>
<<TDexpectedResultDomain = "Information necessary
 extracted for generating a data structure
in memory">>

                      .....
<<TDexpectedResultDomain = "Java class is saved">>
8. Test results
<<TDactionDomain = "Application will open on screen">>
<<TDexpectedResultDomain = "Tests results on screen">>
9. end
<<TDactionDomain = "Press on Close">>
<<TDexpectedResultDomain = "Application is closed">>
```

Fig. 8.6 Snippet of an abstract test case [6]

8.2.3.4 Abstract Test Case Generation

The test sequences generated in the last step were converted into an equivalent description to test cases in natural language, i.e., abstract test cases. Figure 8.6 presents an abstract test case generated from a set of test sequences in the previous step, i.e., "*bu bt bv ci bs cb cd*." Each element of this sequence has information related to the input data (TDactionDomain) and output (TDexpectedResultDomain), as well as definition of the functional test criterion (TDfunctionalCriterion) used for selecting test data. The input/output information and functional criteria present in the abstract test case have actual test data, which corresponds to the test information present in the Activity Diagram from Fig. 8.3. This abstract test case represents user activities (e.g., (1) Load XMI File and (2) Submit the XMI file to a Parser), and its related tagged values are presented between double angle quotation marks (e.g., ≪TDactionDomain≫: "Press Enter").

In the example presented in Fig. 8.6, no functional testing criteria was used, since for each tested functionality, only one input was set and not data domain. It is important that SPLiT-MBt supports the use of the Boundary Value Analysis criterion to select a set of test data, since it is one of the most known criteria in the literature and can be easily automated. It is important to highlight that SPLiT-MBt allows the use of other criteria, such as Equivalence Partitioning. Finally, once the abstract test cases are generated, they are instantiated to concrete test cases, i.e., test scripts.

	A	B	C	D	E	F
1	Test case #	Work Item ID	Test Title	Test Step	Action/Description	Expected Result
2	TC001	Test Case 259121	Sequence 4	1	S0 - 20, 21, 100, 101	"Age must be in the range between 21 and 100 years old"
3				2	S1 - "", "a", "abcdefghij", "abcdefghijk"	"The field must have at least 1 and at most 10 characters"
4				3	S8 - 0, 1, 1638, 1639	"The font size must be a value between 1 and 1638"
5				4	S3 - 1929, 1930, 2005, 2006	"Birth date accepts values from 1930 to 2005"
6				5	S4 - R$ 999,99, R$ 1.000,00, R$ 85.000,00, 85.000,01	"Authorized lending to values between R$ 1.000,00 and R$ 85.000,00"
7				6	S6 - -1, 0, 5, 6	"Age must be in the range between 21 and 5 years old"
8				7	End - 11, 12, 24, 25	"Contract period from 12 to 24 months"

Fig. 8.7 Script to test the functionalities of a PLeTs product [6]

8.2.3.5   Test Script Generation and Test Execution

The next step to be performed by SPLiT-MBt Tool is to instantiate scripts to MTM from the abstract test cases previously generated. As described in Sect. 8.2.2, the scripts generated by SPLiT-MBt Tool have a tabular format, and for this case study 3257 scripts were automatically generated. Figure 8.7 shows an snippet script with test information generated from the abstract test case illustrated in Fig. 8.6. In this example, it is possible to notice that the values of the fields TDactionDomain and TDexpectedResultDomain correspond respectively to the input data and expected results present in cells Action/Description and Expected Results. The information present in Action/Description cells corresponds to the test data.

Finally, once the test scripts were generated, we use the SPLiT-MBt Tool to perform the test execution. Thereunto, we have used our tool to launch the interface of the MTM, load the scripts previously generated, and start the test execution. This initialization consists of an internal system call, where through the SPLiT-MBt Tool interface, we provided the scripts and the MTM installation path. Thus, the MTM's environment is initialized and the test is performed.

It is important to highlight that one of the main advantages of our method is related to the possibility of reusing test information described in SPL models to generate, during Domain Engineering, test sequences using an extended version of a test sequence generation method, i.e., HSI. This extended version is able to handle variability information present in FSMs and then generate test sequences with variability information. Moreover, using the extended version of the HSI, it is possible to reduce the amount of test cases (since it is a feature inherent to HSI and one of the purposes of this method has been created) providing full coverage of the product functionalities.

Another advantage of SPLiT-MBt is related to the possibility of generating, during Application Engineering, an abstract structure that can be used to generate test scripts to different functional test technologies, such as QTP, RFT, Selenium, VS, and MTM. Therefore, a company that is using tool A can, motivated by a technical or managerial decision, easily change to a testing tool B without having to create new test cases. Hence, SPLiT-MBt provides benefits not only during Domain Engineering but also during Application Engineering when the SPL products can be tested using the functional test technology available for a specific company.

Finally, our method provides a considerable reuse percentage of the test artifacts generated for this Application Example, i.e., PLeTs. Therefore, we can claim that SPLiT-MBt is, in this specific context, a useful method to provide reusable test artifacts, full functional test coverage, and flexibility to generate test scripts for different test technologies.

8.3 SMartyTesting: MBT on Use Case and Sequence Diagrams

This topic presents an approach that helps to generate test sequences in SPL Domain Engineering from SMarty models. Such test sequences can be used to generate test cases, which later on can be used in Application Engineering. This approach is called SMartyTesting and assists in the generation of test sequences from Sequence Diagrams. These Sequence Diagrams are based on Use Cases and their basic and alternative flows. These diagrams are converted to Activity Diagrams, which is the input of the SPLiT-MBt approach. Hence, test sequences containing variability are generated and reused for each product to be tested, taking advantage of the benefits of SPLiT-MBt.

8.3.1 SMartyTesting Characterization

This section addresses the elements that characterize the SMartyTesting approach, i.e., models, processes, and tools.

After the Use Case and Sequence Diagrams are modeled using SMarty, the conversion to an intermediate artifact is performed, i.e., an Activity Diagram. This conversion is mandatory for the SMartyTesting approach. Basically, SMarty manages the variability, while SPLiT-MBt is responsible for the generation of test sequences.

8.3.2 Used Models

The SMartyTesting approach uses the following models to support SPL testing:

- **Use Case Diagrams:** These diagrams represent the modeling of the requirements of an SPL containing variability in the graphical representation and consider the

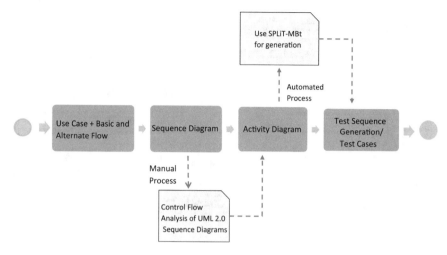

Fig. 8.8 Steps for generating test sequences using SMartyTesting

basic and alternative flows as a source of information for modeling Sequence Diagrams.

- **Sequence Diagrams:** These diagrams are used because they allow the representation of flows and procedures at a low level of abstraction, very close to the source code and with more details on the variability.
- **Activity Diagrams:** used as a input artifacts for conversion to FSM but with a higher level of abstraction than Sequence Diagrams.

Figure 8.8 illustrates the process with emphasis on the diagrams used by our approach. This initial proposal consists of the use of Use Case Diagrams and Sequence Diagrams, which will be converted to an Activity Diagram to later be used in the SPLiT-MBt Tool.

8.3.3 Converting Sequence Diagrams to Activity Diagrams

Our approach uses Garousi et al. [14] proposal to convert Sequence Diagrams into Activity Diagrams, since, as mentioned before, SPLiT-MBt Tool has Activity Diagrams as input. Although the Activity Diagram is also a communication diagram, it also shows the control flow from one activity to another as well as the competition of activities. Actually, both diagrams are equivalent when it comes to elements of representation.

Furthermore, Garousi et al. [14] also mention that there is no risk of losing properties in the mapping, maintaining the characteristics of variability that were extended in the Sequence Diagram. This mapping was validated by Swain et al. [40]. This kind of validation can also be used to validate products generated by SMartyTesting.

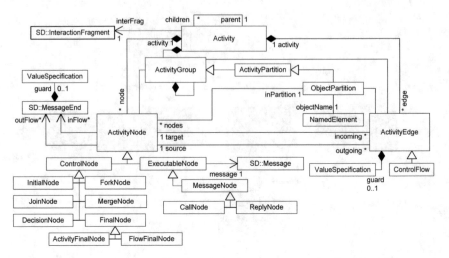

Fig. 8.9 CCFG, control flow analysis of UML 2.0 Sequence Diagrams metamodel (Extended activity diagrams) study by Garousi et al. [14]

The Garousi et al. [14] proposal consists of a control flow analysis methodology based on UML 2.0 Sequence Diagrams. This technique can be used during the development cycle and in other testing approaches. For example, this technique can be used on systems based on Sequence Diagrams.

Based on well-defined Activity Diagrams, the control flow analysis of UML 2.0 Sequence Diagrams study by Garousi et al. [14] brings a metamodel of the extended activity diagram (Fig. 8.9), to support analysis of the control flow of Sequence Diagrams. Thus, it is possible to define a mapping based on Object Constraint Language (OCL) study by Warmer et al. [41], which is a declarative language to describe the rules that apply to UML models.

The application of OCL is carried out formally and verifiable with rules of consistency between a Sequence Diagram and a control flow analysis (CCFG) (extended activity diagrams), in which CCFG has all the necessary classes and associations, as well as support for simultaneous control flow paths (concurrency), which are a generalization of the conventional concept of control flow path study by Garousi et al. [14].

The mapping consists of the use of a Sequence Diagram metamodel and a set of rules that must be used in the conversion, in which the CCFG metamodel is considered as a validator. For example, we have a Sequence Diagram that contains asynchronous messages. To perform the mapping for activities, a set of rules created from the study by Garousi et al. [14] metamodels was used. The rules are presented in Table 8.3. As a result, the mapping process produces the Activity Diagram (Fig. 8.10).

To validate the SMartyTesting approach, manual and limited conversion from Sequence Diagrams to Activity Diagrams was performed using the Astah profes-

Table 8.3 Rules used for converting Sequence Diagrams to Activity Diagrams study by Garousi et al. [14]

Rule #	SD feature	CCFG resource (activities)
1	Interaction	Activity
2	First message end	Flow between InitialNode and first control node
3	SynchCall/SynchSignal	CallNode
4	AsynchCall or AsynchSignal	(CallNode+ForkNode) or ReplyNode
5	Message SendEvent and ReceiveEvent	ControlFlow
6	Lifeline	ObjectPartition
7	par CombinedFragment	ForkNode
8	loop CombinedFragment	DecisionNode
9	alt/opt CombinedFragment	DecisionNode
10	break CombinedFragment	ActivityEdge
11	Last message ends	Flow between end control nodes and FinalNode
12	InteractionOccurrence	Control Flow across CCFGs
13	Polymorphic message	DecisionNode
14	Nested InteractionFragmen	Nested CCFGs

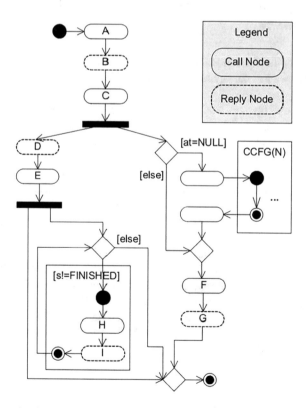

Fig. 8.10 Example of result of SD mapping study. Adapted from Garousi et al. [14]

sional tool.[8] At the end of the creation of the diagrams, they were exported with the XML extension to be used by SPLiT-MBt.

8.3.4 Used Tool

To validate part of our approach, we used the SPLiT-MBt Tool presented in Section 8.1.

8.3.5 SMartyTesting Phases

This section presents each step of the SMartyTesting approach. In this work, it is assumed that the modeling of Use Cases Diagrams is used to generate Sequence Diagrams.

8.3.6 Step 1: Mapping Sequence Diagrams to Activity Diagrams

In this first step, the Sequence Diagrams are mapped to the extended activities. To exemplify this, we use the Arcade Game Maker (AGM) SPL. Step 1 is illustrated in Fig. 8.11.

The Sequence Diagram was modeled considering the SMarty approach using the Cameo Enterprise Architecture tool version 19.[9] After modeling the Sequence Diagram and all its properties (Fig. 8.12), the software engineer must then perform a new construction of an Activity Diagram but taking into account the rules of Table 8.3 and the properties of the created Sequence Diagram.

In this work, Astah version 6 was used to create the model converted from Sequence Diagram to Activity Diagram. We chose this version since it allows showing that different tools can be used and the same result can be produced.

The creation of the Activity Diagram must take into account the use of the mapping rules contained in Table 8.3. The variability properties are maintained without resolution, in order to be transported to the test sequences to be reused. Figure 8.13 shows the Sequence Diagrams conversion result from Fig. 8.12.

When executing the construction of the Activity Diagram, we must take into consideration the necessary requirements that will be used in Step 2. The modeled artifact file must be exported from the tool in XML format, which is the input format supported by SPLiT-MBt.

---

[8] Available at http://astah.net/download.

[9] https://www.nomagic.com/products/cameo-enterprise-architecture.

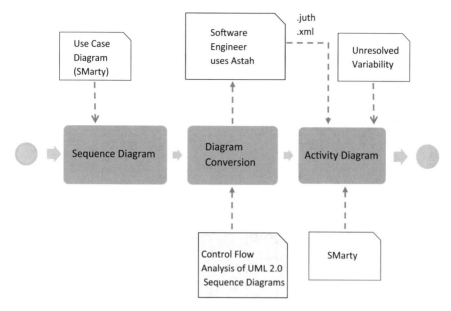

Fig. 8.11 Step 1—initial phase of SMartyTesting

Before exporting the Activity Diagram, some features must be taken into account. One of them is the parameterization of the Activity Diagram transitions, which will be needed by the SPLiT-MBt Tool. The stereotype of the activity being modeled using SMarty must also be taken into account.

These parameters are information regarding the transitions in the Activity Diagram. Actually, it contains the tag identifying the action (TDaction), the expected result (TDexpectedResult), and, finally, the values (Values) that are added according to the specifications of the Activity Diagram. Figure 8.14 presents a view of this configuration.

Table 8.4 presents all the parameters of the AD transitions resulting from the mapping.

8.3.7 Step 2: Generating Test Sequences

In the second step, it is considered that the Sequence Diagram has already been mapped and converted to an Activity Diagram, according to the flow shown in Fig. 8.15. Given the conversion mapping performed, test case sequences are generated.

Once the XML file was generated, it is loaded and checked by the application. After the validation is completed, it is possible to visualize its structure and the test cases can be generated. At the time of generation, the tool converts Activity

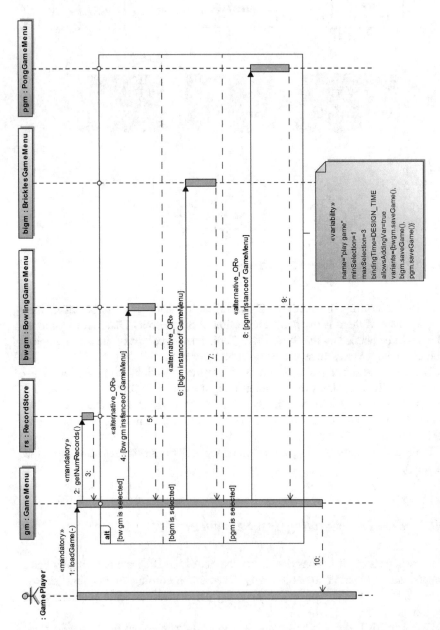

Fig. 8.12 Sequence Diagram illustrating the AGM Use Case game menu

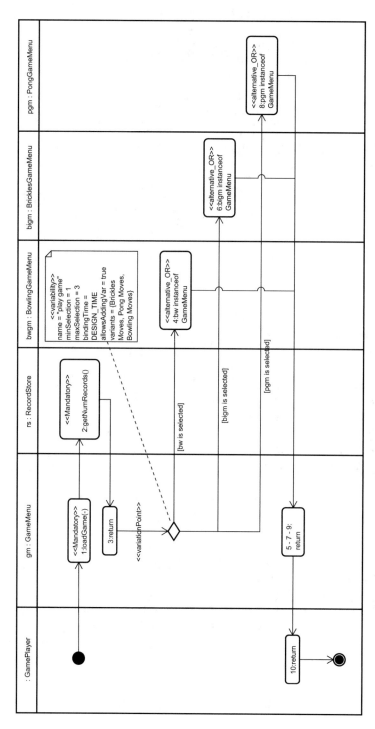

Fig. 8.13 Activity Diagrams resulting from the DS mapping of Fig. 8.12

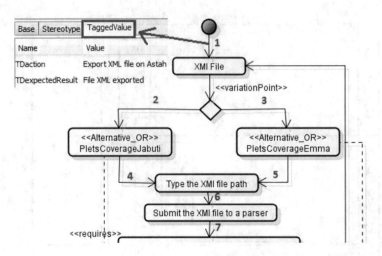

Fig. 8.14 Example of the parameterization of the control flows of an Activity Diagram using SPLiT-MBt study by Costa et al. [6]

Table 8.4 Values of AD parameterization attributes for use in SPLiT-MBt

Transition of activities	Tags	Values
1. Early stage to	TDaction	Game player loads the game
LoadGame	TDexpectedResult	Game loads
2. LoadGame to	TDaction	Game menu accesses score data
getNumRecords	TDexpectedResult	Gets access to score data
3. getNumRecords	TDaction	recordStore returns data
to return	TDexpectedResult	Score data is returned
4. Decision node to bw	TDaction	Option bw is selected
instance of GameMenu	TDexpectedResult	Access to resources of option bw
5. Return	TDaction	Return of the bw option
	TDexpectedResult	Return to the options menu
6. Decision node to bigm	TDaction	Bigm option is selected
instance of GameMenu	TDexpectedResult	Access to bigm option features
7. Return	TDaction	Return of the bigm option
	TDexpectedResult	Return to the options menu
8. Decision node to pgm	TDaction	Pgm option is selected
instance of GameMenu	TDexpectedResult	Access to pgm option resources
9. Return	TDaction	Return of the pgm option
	TDexpectedResult	Return to the options menu
10. Return	TDaction	Return of information to the Game Player
	TDexpectedResult	Player receives return of the chosen action

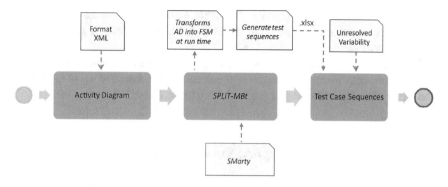

Fig. 8.15 Step 2 of SMartyTesting

Diagrams into extended FSMs to support variability. This conversion is performed at run time. Thus, there is no access to any file or process, making the execution an internal process of the tool. After the generation, it is possible to export an XLSX file that can be used in test tools that use scripts.

8.3.8   Variability Resolution

SMartyTesting initially addresses the resolution of variability in the same format as SPLiT-MBt, where the test case strings are generated containing the variability without resolution. This is important to reuse the test cases, since when we generate new products, the variability can change, or there are more points of variation.

8.3.9   Limitations on the Use of SPLiT-MBt

Since third-party support tools were being used, limitations were found in both steps described previously.

In the first step, regarding the use of SMarty notation in the conversion mapping, control flow analysis of UML 2.0 Sequence Diagrams does not mention solutions to deal with variability. Nonetheless, there are no obstacles to use that notation, since the limitation occurs only because there is explicit rule to variability notation.

In the second step, involving the application of SPLiT-MBt, the limitations are more significant, although they have not influenced the validation. The limitations are directly linked to the metamodel structure of the Activity Diagram (Fig. 8.9).

SPLiT-MBt does not support two items of ControlNode, i.e., ForkNode and JoinNode, when testing concurrent activities. Another limitation is regarding the continuity of an activity after a DecisionNode in which sub-activities are not accepted unless it is a merge activity. Thus, this is considered a noncompliance with sub-systems represented in the input artifact; an example would be an InitialNode (see Fig. 8.9).

In a process that is not automated, there may be threats to its functioning, in this case the first step. For this reason, it is recommended in future work to implement and automate all processes from the beginning to the end of the cycle.

8.3.10 SMartyTesting Application Example

After analyzing the possibility of generating the test sequence with Activity Diagrams as input artifacts from SPLiT-MBt, Sequence Diagrams created by Marcolino et al. [27] are used. These Activity Diagrams are equivalent to the ones created by Costa et al. [6]. Figures 8.16 and 8.17 show some examples of the Activity Diagrams.

After that, Sequence Diagrams were used in SMartyTesting to generate test strings for comparison. In the initial step, the conversion to Activity Diagrams (Fig. 8.17) was performed, which in the next step were used to generate the test sequences (Table 8.5).

Figure 8.16 presents a Sequence Diagram of the SPL AGM that was used by SMartyTesting for the conversion to an Activity Diagram. Based on this diagram, the manual conversion to the Activity Diagram was carried out. This validation is important to be able to verify that all points of the origin diagram are presented in a logical way.

Figure 8.17 presents a diagram of the activities of the SPL AGM that was converted by SMartyTesting for the generation of test sequences. This validation is important to observe whether all elements of the artifact are included.

Table 8.5 shows the results of the test sequence generated from Fig. 8.17.

8.4 Final Remarks

In this chapter, we presented two methods to provide reuse of test artifacts based on adapting Model-Based Testing (MBT) for automatic generation of functional test cases from models that represent SPL functionalities and variability information.

SPLiT-MBt provides testing artifacts generation based on the adaptation of Utting and Legeard [1] work for automatic generation of functional test cases and scripts from models/notations that represent the SPL functionalities and variability information. SMartyTesting uses SPLiT-MBt to generate test sequences but using Sequence Diagrams rather than activity ones.

Both SPL testing sequence generation methods complement each other as a way to increase defect detection and correction by reusing SPL artifacts, thus resolving variability of the sequences to testing individual derived SPL products.

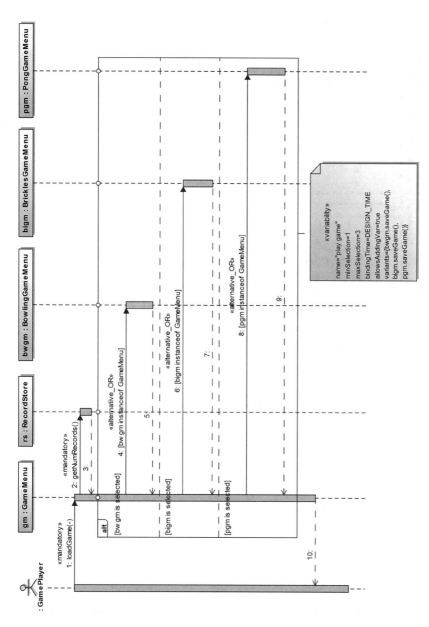

Fig. 8.16 Sequence Diagram Play Selected Game study by Marcolino et al. [27]

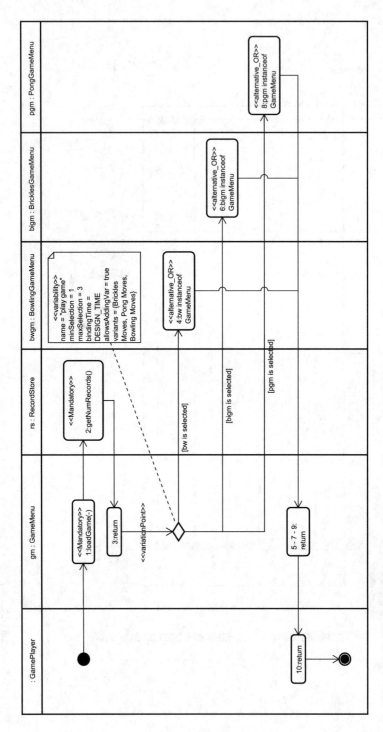

Fig. 8.17 Activity Diagram resulting from the Sequence Diagram of Fig. 8.16

Table 8.5 Sequences of activity diagram test cases from Fig. 8.17 generated by SMartyTesting

Test sequence	Step	Action/description	Expected result
Test case 1	1	1:loadGame(-) – Game Player fire method loadGame{Mandatory};	loadGame is load
Test case 1	2	2:getNumRecords() – Game menu after loaded it makes use of the method getNumRecords{Mandatory};	Access data from recordStore
Test case 1	3	3:return – recordStore send bounce messages;	Score data is returned by getNumrecords for GameMenu.
Test case 1	4	VP_3:return – {; – Option bw is selected {alternative_OR}; – Option bigm is selected – {alternative_OR}; – Option pgm is selected {alternative_OR}};	{. Instantiate option feature bowling. Instantiate option feature bigm brickles. Instantiate option feature pong}.
Test case 1	5	5 - 7 - 9:return – {; – Option return bw; – Option return bigm; – Option return pgm};	{. Returns after bw instance of GameMenu is performed. Returns after bigm instance of GameMenu is performed. Returns after pgm instance of GameMenu is performed.}.
Test case 1	6	10:return – Return of information to the Game Player	Player receives action return choice return choice

Acknowledgments This work is partially supported by the Brazilian funding agency CNPq (Grant 306250/2021-7).

References

1. Utting, M., Legeard, B.: Practical Model-Based Testing: A Tools Approach. Elsevier, Amsterdam (2006)
2. Apfelbaum, L., Doyle, J.: Model-based testing. In: Proceedings of the 10th Software Quality Week Conference, pp. 296–300 (1997)
3. Booch, G., Rumbaugh, J., Jacobson, I.: The Unified Modeling Language User Guide, 2nd edn. Addison-Wesley Professional, Reading (2005)

4. Chow, T.S.: Testing software design modeled by finite-state machines. IEEE Trans. Softw. Eng. **4**, 178–187 (1978)
5. Clements, P., Northrop, L.: Software Product Lines: Practices and Patterns. Addison-Wesley, Reading (2001)
6. Costa, L.T.: SPLiT-MBt: A Model-based Testing Method for Software Product Lines. Ph.D. Thesis, Pontifícia Universidade Católica do Rio Grande do Sul (2017)
7. Costa, L.T., Czekster, R.M., Oliveira, F.M., Rodrigues, E.M., Silveira, M.B., Zorzo, A.F.: Generating performance test scripts and scenarios based on abstract intermediate models. In: Proceedings of the 24th International Conference on Software Engineering & Knowledge Engineering, pp. 112–117 (2012)
8. Costa, L.T., Zorzo, A.F., Rodrigues, E.M., Silveira, M.B., Oliveira, F.M.: Structural test case generation based on system models. In: Proceedings of the 9th International Conference on Software Engineering Advances, pp. 276–281 (2014)
9. Cristiá, M., Santiago, V., Vijaykumar, N.L.: On comparing and complementing two MBT approaches. In: Proceedings of the 11th Latin American Test Workshop, pp. 1–6 (2010)
10. Davis, C., Chirillo, D., Gouveia, D., Saracevic, F., Bocarsley, J.B., Quesada, L., Thomas, L.B., Lint, M.v.: Software Test Engineering with IBM Rational Functional Tester: The Definitive Resource. IBM Press (2009)
11. Delamaro, M.E., Maldonado, J.C., Jino, M.: Introdução ao Teste de Software. Elsevier, Amsterdam (2007)
12. Devanbu, P., Karstu, S., Melo, W., Thomas, W.: Analytical and empirical evaluation of software reuse metrics. In: Proceedings of the 18th International Conference on Software Engineering, pp. 189–199 (1996)
13. Engström, E., Runeson, P.: Software product line testing—a systematic mapping study. Inform. Softw. Technol. **53**(1), 2–13 (2011)
14. Garousi, V., Briand, L.C., Labiche, Y.: Control flow analysis of UML 2.0 sequence diagrams. In: Proceedings of the European Conference on Model Driven Architecture-Foundations and Applications, pp. 160–174. Springer, Berlin (2005)
15. Gill, A.: Introduction to the Theory of Finite State Machines. McGraw-Hill, New York (1962)
16. Gomaa, H.: Designing Software Product Lines with UML: From Use Cases to Pattern-Based Software Architectures. Addison-Wesley, Reading (2005)
17. Gonenc, G.: A method for the design of fault detection experiments. IEEE Trans. Comput. **19**, 551–558 (1970)
18. Halmans, G., Pohl, K.: Communicating the variability of a software-product family to customers. Softw. Syst. Model. **2**, 15–36 (2003)
19. Holmes, A., Kellogg, M.: Automating functional tests using selenium. In: Proceedings of the 9th International Conference on Agile, pp. 270–275 (2006)
20. OliveiraJr, E.: SystEM-PLA: um Método para Avaliação de Arquitetura de Linha de Produto de Software Baseada em UML. Ph.D. Thesis (in Portuguese), Instituto de Ciências Matemáticas e Computação, Universidade de São Paulo, Brasil (2010)
21. Krishnan, P.: Uniform descriptions for model based testing. In: Proceedings of the 15th Australian Software Engineering Conference, pp. 96–105 (2004)
22. Laser, M., Rodrigues, E.M., Domingues, A.R., de Oliveira, F.M., Zorzo, A.F.: Research notes on the architectural evolution of a software product line. Int. J. Softw. Eng. Knowl. Eng. **20**, 1753–1758 (2015)
23. Levinson, J.: Software Testing With Visual Studio 2010. Pearson Education (2011)
24. Rodrigues, E.M., Oliveira, F.M., Costa, L.T., Bernardino, M., Zorzo, A.F., Souza, S.R.S, Saad, R.: An empirical comparison of model-based and capture and replay approaches for performance testing. Empirical Softw. Eng. **20**, 1831–1860 (2015)
25. Mallepally, S.R.: Quick Test Professional (QTP) Interview Questions and Guidelines: A Quick Reference Guide to QuickTest Professional. Parishta (2009)
26. Manager, M.T.: Running Tests in Microsoft Test Manager (2016). http://www.msdn.microsoft.com/en-us/library/dd286680

27. Marcolino, A.S., OliveiraJr, E., Gimenes, I.M., Barbosa, E.F.: Variability resolution and product configuration with SMarty: an experimental study on UML class diagrams. J. Comput. Sci. **13**(8), 307–319 (2017)
28. Millo, J.V., Ramesh, S., Krishna, S.N., Narwane, G.: Compositional verification of software product lines. In: Proceedings of the 10th Integrated Formal Methods, pp. 109–123 (2013)
29. Myers, G.J., Sandler, C.: The Art of Software Testing. Wiley, London (2004)
30. Naito, S., Tsunoyama, M.: Fault detection for sequential machines by transitions tours. In: Proceedings of the 11th IEEE Fault Tolerant Computing Conference, pp. 283–243 (1981)
31. OliveiraJr, E., Gimenes, I.M.S., Maldonado, J.C.: Systematic management of variability in UML-based software product lines. J. Universal Comput. Sci. **16**, 2374–2393 (2010)
32. Petrenko, A., Yevtushenko, N., Lebedev, A., Das, A.: Nondeterministic state machines in protocol conformance testing. In: Proceedings of the 6th International Workshop on Protocol Test Systems, pp. 363–378 (1993)
33. Professional, A.: Astah Professional (2016). http://www.astah.net/editions/professional
34. Rodrigues, E.M., Bernardino, M., Costa, L.T., Zorzo, A.F., Oliveira, F.: PLeTsPerf–a model-based performance testing tool. In: Proceedings of 8th IEEE International Conference on the Software Testing, Verification and Validation, 2015, pp. 1–8 (2015)
35. Rodrigues, E.M., Viccari, L.D., Zorzo, A.F., Gimenes, I.M.S.: PLeTs tool—test automation using software product lines and model-based testing. In: Proceedings of the 22th International Conference on Software Engineering and Knowledge Engineering, pp. 483–488 (2010)
36. Sabnani, K., Dahbura, A.: A protocol test generation procedure. Comput. Netw. ISDN Syst. **15**, 285–297 (1988)
37. Silveira, M.B., Rodrigues, E.M., Zorzo, A.F.: Performance testing modeling: an empirical evaluation of DSL and UML-based approaches. In: Proceedings of the 31st ACM Symposium on Applied Computing, pp. 1660–1665 (2016)
38. Silveira, M.B., Rodrigues, E.M., Zorzo, A.F., Costa, L.T., Vieira, H.V., de Flavio Moreira Oliveira: Generation of scripts for performance testing based on UML models. In: Proceedings of the 23rd International Conference on Software Engineering and Knowledge Engineering, pp. 258–263 (2011)
39. Silveira, M.B., Zorzo, A.F., Rodrigues, E.M.: Canopus: a domain-specific language for modeling performance testing. In: Proceedings of the 9th IEEE International Conference on Software Testing, Verification and Validation, pp. 157–167 (2016)
40. Swain, S.K., Mohapatra, D.P., Mall, R.: Test case generation based on use case and sequence diagrams. Int. J. Softw. Eng. **3**(2), 21–52 (2010)
41. Warmer, J.B., Kleppe, A.G.: The Object Constraint Language: Getting your Models Ready for MDA. Addison-Wesley Professional, Reading (2003)

Part III
Product-Line Architecture Evolution

Chapter 9
Maintainability Metrics for PLA Evaluation Based on ISO/IEC 25010

André F. R. Cordeiro, Leandro F. Silva, and Edson OliveiraJr

Abstract In software product line (SPL), metrics are used to evaluate different artifacts such as the product-line architecture (PLA). When the PLA's evaluation is conducted using metrics, it allows for the analysis of quality attributes (QAs). The QAs are represented in an isolated way or using quality models (QM). There are different QM published in the literature. ISO/IEC 25010 is one of these models that considers the following QAs: functional suitability, reliability, performance efficiency, usability, security, compatibility, maintainability, and portability. For instance, maintainability is an important attribute in the SPL context. According to the literature, 92% of the measures defined to evaluate the SPL's artifacts consider attributes related to maintainability. Despite the number of measures related to maintainability, it is observed a lack of measures and metrics associated with QA and QM. These metrics could aid in the PLA's evaluation. The observed lack motivates the development of the SMartyMetrics, a framework with measures and metrics associated with the attribute maintainability to support PLA evaluations. A structure with attributes was developed, to systematize the association between attributes and measures/metrics. The framework also provides a set of guidelines to use it at the level of SPL, PLA, measures/metrics, and constraints.

9.1 The Role of SMarty in This Work

Different artifacts are necessary in the context of the evaluation of a product-line architecture (PLA). SMartyMetrics can help the evaluation methods of PLAs with guidelines, measures, and metrics. To use SMartyMetrics, the PLA must

A. F. R. Cordeiro (✉) · L. F. Silva
Informatics Department, Maringá, PR, Brazil

E. OliveiraJr
Informatics Department, State University of Maringá, Maringá, Paraná, Brazil
e-mail: edson@din.uem.br

© Springer Nature Switzerland AG 2023
E. OliveiraJr (ed), *UML-Based Software Product Line Engineering with SMarty*,
https://doi.org/10.1007/978-3-031-18556-4_9

consider the Unified Modeling Language (UML). Information about variability also is necessary.

The Stereotype-based Management of Variability (SMarty) approach makes it possible to complement the UML-modeled PLA with details about variabilities, variation points, and variants. After finishing the variability management of the PLA in UML, it is possible to apply the measures and metrics described in this chapter. The following sections present more information.

9.2 SMartyMetrics Characterization

A measure can be described as a value, obtained as a result of a measurement process. A metric represents a quantitative measure, associated with an attribute, to evaluate a system, component, or process [5, 7].

SMartyMetrics is a framework with measures and metrics to support PLA evaluation, based on the ISO/IEC 25010 attribute maintainability. The framework also provides guidelines related to the planning and design of software product line (SPL); creation, evaluation, and selection of measures and metrics; and conditions to use the framework. In the context of SMartyMetrics, a guideline is a recommendation to consider during PLA's evaluation.

SMartyMetrics measures and metrics are associated with the ISO/IEC 25010 quality model [6]. The association is based on quality attribute (QA). The following sections introduce the SMartyMetrics framework structure, QAs, measures and metrics, and guidelines.

9.3 SMartyMetrics: Quality Attributes

SMartyMetrics incorporates measures and metrics selected after performing a systematic mapping (SM) [4]. These measures and metrics are associated with one or more attributes. Some of the selected attributes are described as quality attributes (QAs). Each QA is calculated according to the attributes of its subcategory known as quality sub-attributes (QSAs). Figure 9.1 shows the relationship between QAs and their QSAs.

We analyzed the maintainability attribute in the development of SMartyMetrics. For this attribute, we investigated the following QSAs: modularity, reusability, modifiability, and testability. Moreover, we associated the selected SMartyMetrics measures and metrics with the maintainability QSA present in ISO/IEC 25010. Figure 9.2 presents the established association in detail.

The structure shown in Fig. 9.2 establishes a hierarchy, where a QA evaluation considers a set of QSAs. Different QSAs can be associated, in terms of the first and second levels. QSAs associated with ISO 25010 [6] were classified as the first

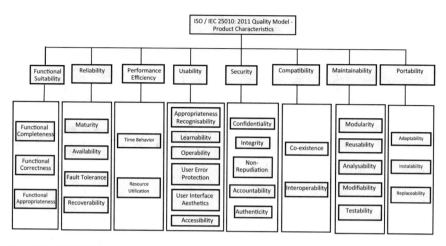

Fig. 9.1 ISO/IEC 25010 quality model

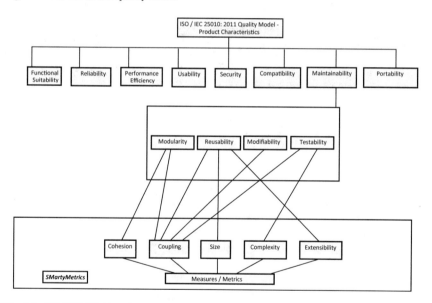

Fig. 9.2 ISO/IEC 25010 attributes and sub-attributes associated with the selected SMartyMetrics measures and metrics

level. QSAs associated with selected measures and metrics to SMartyMetrics were classified as the second level.

Figure 9.3 presents the association of `Maintainability` with the QSA in the first level: `Modularity`, `Reusability`, `Modifiability`, and `Testability`. These QSAs are associated with the QSA in the second level: `Cohesion`, `Coupling`, `Size`, `Complexity`, and `Extensibility`. These QSAs are specific to one or more measures and metrics.

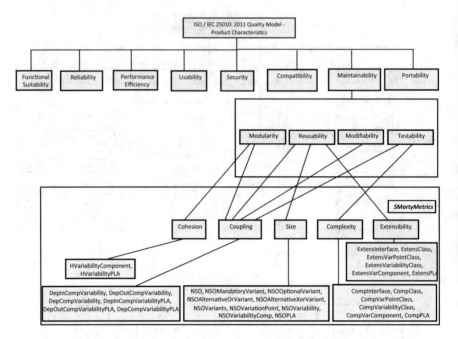

Fig. 9.3 QA and QSA association structure according to SMartyMetrics

9.4 SMartyMetrics: Metrics

This section presents the measures and metrics selected for SMartyMetrics. They were organized according to the following QSAs: modularity, reusability, modifiability, and testability. We described each measure and metric, even if they were associated with more than one QSA.

We described application examples for each group of measures and metrics. The SPL considered in the examples of this chapter is *Mobile Media* (*MM*) [15]. In this section, the examples consider two PLA fragments. Figure 9.4 presents a PLA fragment represented in the UML class diagram. The fragment contains three classes (*Photo*, *Media*, and *Video*), an interface (*IVideoMgt*), and a representation of the variability (*select media*). These elements allow the representation of characteristics evaluated by measures and metrics of complexity, extensibility, and size.

Figure 9.5 presents a PLA fragment represented in the UML component diagram. Three components (*MediaMgr*, *PhotoMgr*, and *VideoMgr*), three interfaces provided (*IMediaMgr*, *IPhotoMgt*, and *IVideoMgr*), two required interfaces (*IPhotoMgt* and *IVideoMgr*), and a representation of the variability. The components allow the understanding of the characteristics evaluated by the measures and metrics of cohesion and coupling. In the next subsections, we present the measures and metrics associated with first-level QSA.

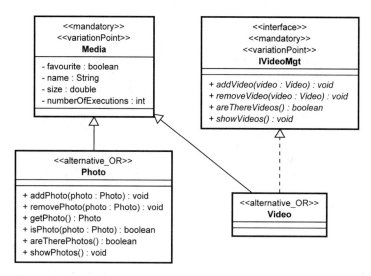

Fig. 9.4 PLA fragment represented in an UML class diagram

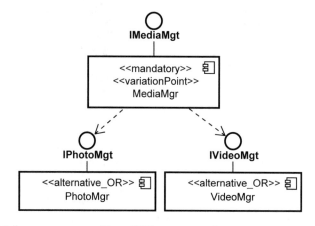

Fig. 9.5 PLA fragment represented in an UML component diagram

9.4.1 Modularity

Modularity is the degree to which a system is made up of independent components, trying to ensure that the removal of one component does not impair the functionalities of other components [6, 7, 14].

The modularity of a system can be achieved by maximizing the relationships between elements of the same module and minimizing the relationship between the external modules[7, 11]. The concepts presented in [11] correspond to `cohesion` and `coupling` attributes definition. According to ISO/IEEE/IEC 24765 [7],

Table 9.1 Modularity measures and metrics

Attribute	Measure/metric	Description
Cohesion	Relational cohesion (H)	Ratio between the number of dependency relationships and the number of classes and interfaces in a package or component
Cohesion	Relational cohesion variability component (HVariabilityComponent)	Sum of the values of **H**, for all the components that has variation points associated with a given variability
Cohesion	Relational cohesion variability PLA (HVariabilityPLA)	Sum of the values of the **HVariabilityComponent**, for all components associated with PLA variability
Coupling	DepIn	Number of elements that depend on a component
Coupling	DepOut	Number of elements on which a component depends
Coupling	DepInCompVariability	Sum of the values of the **DepIn** for all components that has variation points associated with a variability
Coupling	DepOutCompVariability	Sum of the values of the **DepOut** for all components that has variation points associated with the variability
Coupling	DepCompVariability	Sum between **DepInCompVariability** and **DepOutCompVariability**
Coupling	DepInCompVariabilityPLA	Sum of the values of **DepInCompVariability**, for all the variation points? associated with the PLA components
Coupling	DepOutCompVariabilityPLA	Sum of the values of the **DepOutCompVariability**, for all the variabilities associated with the PLA components
Coupling	DepCompVariabilityPLA	Sum between **DepInCompVariabilityPLA** and **DepOutCompVariabilityPLA**

cohesion is the level at which software modules are related to other modules, and coupling is the level of interdependence between software modules.

Maximizing relationships between elements of the same module enables centralization of operations and gets a higher level of module independence from other modules in the [11] system. In addition, minimizing relationships between external system modules avoids possible dependency relationships between these modules. Table 9.1 presents measures and metrics associated with modularity.

Table 9.2 Cohesion metrics application

Metrics	Elements			
	Select media	MediaMgr	PhotoMgr	VideoMgr
H	N/A	1.5	1.5	1.5
HVariabilityComponent	1.5	N/A	N/A	N/A
HVariabilityPLA	1.5	N/A	N/A	N/A

Table 9.1 presents 11 modularity measures and metrics. Relational cohesion (**H**), **DepIn**, and **DepOut** are measures and metrics focused on general purpose. The others are specific to SPL context.

Tables 9.2 and 9.3 present an application example using the measures and metrics from Table 9.1. Table 9.2 illustrates the values collected by applying the **HVariabilityComponent** and **HVariabilityPLA** for the PLA represented in Fig. 9.5.

Table 9.2 presents the values of the **H**, **HVariabilityComponent**, and **HVariabilityPLA** metrics. We collected **H** for all the PLA components. Variation point components are evaluated for variability. We evaluated the variability *select media* using **HVariabilityComponent** and **HVariabilityPLA**. The expression N/A represents not applicable. It means that the metric was not applied to the specific element.

Figure 9.5 presents the variation point *MediaMgr* that is considered by the metric **HVariabilityComponent**. This metric accounts for the relational cohesion value for all variation point components associated with a given variability. There is only one variation point in Fig. 9.5 that explains the value of 1.5. For a given variability with two components, the metric value would be the sum of the two **H** values.

The presented PLA fragment considers only one variability. For this reason, the **HVariabilityPLA** value is equal to the **HVariabilityComponent** value. If there were two or more variabilities, the value obtained would be the sum of the **HVariabilityComponent** values.

Table 9.3 shows the values collected by applying coupling metrics in the PLA of Fig. 9.5. We calculated the metrics **DepIn** and **DepOut** for all PLA components. Moreover, we collected other metrics such as **DepInCompVariability**, **DepOutCompVariability**, **DepCompVariability**, **DepInCompVariabilityPLA**, **DepOutCompVariabilityPLA**, and **DepCompVariabilityPLA**, PLA components, and the components associated with them.

Table 9.3 shows the results considering only *MediaMgr* associated with metrics that evaluate the variability. We obtained the value 3 for the metrics **DepCompVariability** and **DepCompVariabilityPLA**. The existence of one variability in PLA and a one variation point component associated with it influenced the equality of the collected values.

Table 9.3 Coupling metrics application

	Elements			
Metrics	MediaMgr	PhotoMgr	VideoMgr	Select media
DepIn	1	1	1	N/A
DepOut	2	0	0	N/A
DepInCompVariability	N/A	N/A	N/A	1
DepOutCompVariability	N/A	N/A	N/A	2
DepCompVariability	N/A	N/A	N/A	3
DepInCompVariabilityPLA	N/A	N/A	N/A	1
DepOutCompVariabilityPLA	N/A	N/A	N/A	2
DepCompVariabilityPLA	N/A	N/A	N/A	3

9.4.2   Reusability

Reusability is defined as the degree to which parts of the system are used in the development of other systems [14]. Coupling is the level of interdependence between software modules [7]. According to Chidamber and Kemerer [3], a high level of coupling is detrimental to modularity and prevents module reuse.

The module size is also an important attribute for evaluating reusability. According to Fenton and Pfleeger [5], in a software context, the attribute size is composed of the attribute's length, functionality, and complexity. Length describes the physical size of the product or artifact. Functionality describes the functions provided by this product, and complexity is interpreted through some aspects, such as the problem, the algorithm, the structure, the product, or the artifact cognitive complexity.

Larger modules can become more application-specific, limiting the capability to reuse the module [3].

The attribute extensibility is also considered when evaluating reusability. In the context of SMartyMetrics, we analyzed extensibility considering the proportion of abstract methods in the classes [12]. We already presented coupling metrics in Sect. 9.4.1. Moreover, Table 9.4 presents the other measure and metric attributes.

QSA reusability considers 28 measures and metrics, distributed among coupling (8), size (14), and extensibility (6) QSAs. Size and extensibility are considered in the application example for reusability. Tables 9.5 and 9.6 present the results.

In Table 9.5, we observed that the element *Photo* presented five specific operations. On the other hand, zero operations have been defined for the element *Media*. The elements *Video* and *IVideoMgt* had four operations each. The same value for both elements is explained by the realization relationship that exists between them.

Only the element *Media* was considered in the application of the metric **NSO-VariationPoint**. In total, nine operations are associated with the variation point. Specifically on the evaluation of variabilities and PLA, respectively, associated with **NSOVariability** and **NSOPLA**, we observed a total of nine operations. We

Table 9.4 Reusability measures and metrics

Attribute	Measure/metric	Description
Size	NumOps	Number of operations in each class/interface
Size	NumberOfGetsSets	Total number of operations that start with get or set
Size	NumberOfConstructors	Total number of constructors (own or inherited) of the class
Size	NumberOfOverwrittenOperations	Total number of superscript operations of the class/interface
Size	NumberOfSpecificOperations (NSO)	Total number of operations, disregarding get, set, overwritten operations, and class/interface constructors
Size	NSOMandatoryVariant	**NSO** value of a required class/interface variant
Size	NSOOptionalVariant	**NSO** value of an optional variant class/interface
Size	NSOAlternativeOrVariant	**NSO** value of an inclusive variant class/interface
Size	NSOAlternativeXorVariant	**NSO** value of a class/interface variant unique
Size	NSOVariants	Sum of the metrics **NSOMandatoryVariant**, **NSOOptionalVariant**, **NSOAlternativeOrVariant**, and **NSOAlternativeXorVariant**
Size	NSOVariationPoint	Value of **NSO** for a variation point class/interface plus the sum of the value of **NSOVariants** for all associated variants
Size	NSOVariability	Sum of the values of **NSOVariationPoint**, for all the variation points associated with variability
Size	NSOVariabilityComp	Sum of the values of **NSOVariability**, for all variabilities associated with component's classes/interfaces
Size	NSOPLA	Sum of the values of **NSOVariability**, for all the variabilities associated with classes/interfaces of a PLA
Extensibility	ExtensInterface	Ratio between the number of abstract operations of an interface and the total number of operations of an interface

(continued)

Table 9.4 continued

Attribute	Measure/metric	Description
Extensibility	ExtensClass	Ratio between the number of abstract operations of the class and the total number of operations of the class
Extensibility	ExtensVarPointClass	Value of **ExtensClass** for a variation point class plus the sum of the values of **ExtensClass** for all variants associated with that variation point
Extensibility	ExtensVariabilityClass	Sum of the values of **ExtensVarPointClass**, for all variation points associated with variability
Extensibility	ExtensVarComponent	Sum of the values of **ExtensVariabilityClass**, for all the variabilities associated with the component's classes
Extensibility	ExtensPLA	Sum of the values of **ExtensVariabilityClass**, for all classes and interfaces of a PLA, associated with variabilities

Table 9.5 Size metrics application

Metrics	Elements				
	Select media	Media	Photo	Video	IVideoMgt
NSO	N/A	0	5	4	4
NSOVariants	N/A	0	5	4	4
NSOVariationPoint	N/A	9	N/A	N/A	N/A
NSOVariability	9	N/A	N/A	N/A	N/A
NSOVariabilityComp	N/A	N/A	N/A	N/A	N/A
NSOPLA	9	N/A	N/A	N/A	N/A

Table 9.6 Extensibility metrics application

Metrics	Elements				
	Select media	Media	Photo	Video	IVideoMgt
ExtensInterface	N/A	N/A	N/A	N/A	1
ExtensClass	N/A	0	0.5	0	N/A
ExtensVarPointClass	N/A	0.5	N/A	N/A	N/A
ExtensVariabilityClass	0.5	N/A	N/A	N/A	N/A
ExtensVarComponent	N/A	N/A	N/A	N/A	N/A
ExtensPLA	0.5	N/A	N/A	N/A	N/A

identified the same value for both metrics due to PLA characteristics, which present only one variability associated with one variation point class.

In Table 9.6, we considered the metric **ExtensInterface** to the interface *IVideoMgt*. In applying the metrics **ExtensClass** and **ExtensVarPointClass**, we only considered the classes. We evaluated the classes *Media*, *Photo*, and *Video* using the metric **ExtensClass**. Except for *Photo*, which had an extensibility of 0.5, the other classes had a value of 0 for the extensibility level.

In evaluating the metric values of **ExtensVarPointClass**, we considered only the variation point of the class *Media* and obtained value 0.5. The value of **ExtensVariabilityClass** and **ExtensPLA** was also 0.5. Considering these values, we can conclude that for this PLA, the extensibility level is in 50%.

Regarding the application of the metric **ExtensVarComponent**, no value was obtained due to the lack of components present in the PLA fragment related to the classes, interface, and architecture variability.

9.4.3 Modifiability

Modifiability is the ability to detect and correct errors, trying to avoid those new modifications introducing new errors in the system [14].

In the context of SMartyMetrics, modifiability is associated with coupling. As already mentioned previously, coupling evaluates the level of interdependence between software modules. This interdependence can hamper numerous activities such as maintenance and testing [2, 3].

As noted in Sect. 9.4.3, modifiability is associated with coupling. We presented the coupling metrics in Sect. 9.4.1.

9.4.4 Testability

Testability allows the identification of expected or unexpected situations. To identify these cases, metrics can be used, in a testing software process [14].

QA of the software, such as cyclomatic complexity or modular cohesion, can affect testability [3]. In the context of SMartyMetrics, testability is associated with coupling and complexity.

In addition to the impact on modularity, reusability, and modifiability, coupling also influences testability. A coupling measure is used to determine a module test complexity. The larger the coupling of a software module, the more rigorous it must be to test [3]. Table 9.7 presents the testability measures and metrics.

The testability QSA is associated with 14 measures and metrics, distributed between coupling (8) and complexity (6). We presented the coupling measures and metrics in the modularity Sect. 9.4.1. Therefore, Table 9.7 shows only the complexity measures and metrics.

Table 9.7 Testability measures and metrics

Attribute	Measure/metric	Description
Complexity	`CompInterface`	It is the value of the metric `Weighted Methods per Class` (WMC) for an interface
Complexity	`CompClass`	It is the value of **WMC** for a class
Complexity	`CompVarPointClass`	It is the value of **CompClass** for a class that is a variation point plus the sum of the values of **CompClass** of all variants associated with that variation point
Complexity	`CompVariabilityClass`	Sum of the values of **CompVarPointClass**, for all variation points associated with the variability
Complexity	`CompVarComponent`	Sum of the values of **CompVariabilityClass**, for all variabilities associated with the component's classes
Complexity	`CompPLA`	Sum of values of **CompVariabilityClass**, for all classes and interfaces of a PLA, associated with variabilities

Table 9.8 Complexity metrics application

Metrics	Elements				
	Select media	Media	Photo	Video	IVideoMgt
CompInterface	N/A	N/A	N/A	N/A	5
CompClass	N/A	0	6	5	N/A
CompVarPointClass	N/A	11	N/A	N/A	N/A
CompVariabilityClass	11	N/A	N/A	N/A	N/A
CompVarComponent	N/A	N/A	N/A	N/A	N/A
CompPLA	11	N/A	N/A	N/A	N/A

Table 9.8 presents the results of complexity metrics and measures application in the context of testability.

In applying the metric **CompInterface**, we considered only the element *IVideoMgt*. A complexity value of 5 was collected for the interface. We analyzed the classes *Media*, *Photo*, and *Video* to collect the metric **CompClass**. We used the metric **CompVarPointClass** to evaluate the variation point class Media. The value 11 was obtained to the element complexity level.

The variability *select media* was considered by the **CompVariabilityClass** and **CompPLA** metrics. In applying both metrics, the value 11 was collected. The equal value collected can be explained by the characteristics of the PLA fragment, composed of one variability associated with one variation point.

9.5   SMartyMetrics Guidelines

During the SMartyMetrics development, we identified different recommendations for SPL, PLA, and measures/metrics. In assessing such recommendations, some were incorporated. In the context of SMartyMetrics, these recommendations are called guidelines.

As already mentioned in Sect. 9.2, one or more guidelines can be considered in evaluating PLAs. Tables 9.9, 9.10, 9.11, and 9.12 present the framework guidelines.

Table 9.9 presents guidelines related to SPL planning and design. Such guidelines may assist in the SPL development, especially in understanding the domain, scope, and main stakeholders.

Table 9.10 presents guidelines for PLA design. Such guidelines may assist in the design of an adequate PLA with the SPL domain and scope considering the main stakeholder's interests.

Table 9.11 presents guidelines for measures and metrics. Such guidelines may assist in the creation, evaluation, and selection of measures and metrics to be considered in a PLA evaluation.

Table 9.12 presents the constraint guidelines. These guidelines indicate the most appropriate conditions for using SMartyMetrics in the evaluation of PLAs.

9.6   Applying Metrics in SMartyModeling

One of the SMartyModeling (Chap. 5) modules is responsible for defining metrics and applying measurements in PLAs. The SMartyModeling environment defines an architecture to represent the metric and the measures. The *Project* class centralizes navigation and stores metrics and measures. The class *Metric* is the model for all metrics supported by SMartyModeling, being composed of measures. The class *Measure* serves as a model for all measures. Figure 9.6 depicts the evaluation view of SMartyModeling.

As shown in Fig. 9.6, the class *Metric* contains the following attributes: *id*, the unique identifier of metric in the tool; *name*, metric name; *label*, metric label; *description*, metric description; *target*, metric target, in this case, if it covers the whole project or a specific type of diagram or just for SPL; and *operation*, describes the operation to be performed by the metric, consisting of the keyword and filter. The class *Measure* contains the following attributes: *id*, the unique identifier of measure; *name*, measure name; *date*, measure application date; *target*, measure target (project or diagram); and *value*, value obtained by measure.

Table 9.9 SPL guidelines

ID	Guideline	Source
G.SPL.1	The domain of the SPL should be identified before the architecture development	Software and Systems Engineering—Reference model for product line engineering and management [9]
G.SPL.2	The scope of the SPL should be defined after the domain identification and before the architecture development. The domain represents a set of characteristics and rules observed in a given context. Scope represents the possible products, services, and results of a project	Framework for Evaluation of Reference Architectures (FERA) [13]; VMTools-RA: A Reference Architecture for Software Variability Tools [1]; Systems and software engineering—Vocabulary [7]
G.SPL.3	The possible SPL market segments, related to the domain and scope, should be analyzed	Software and Systems Engineering—Reference model for product line engineering and management [9]
G.SPL.4	Competing companies, considering the domain and scope of the SPL, should be studied and analyzed	Software and Systems Engineering—Reference model for product line engineering and management [9]
G.SPL.5	The SPL main stakeholders should be identified. They are directly benefited or affected by the SPL	Framework for Evaluation of Reference Architectures (FERA) [13]; VMTools-RA: A Reference Architecture for Software Variability Tools [1]; Systems and software engineering—Architecture description [8]
G.SPL.6	The interests of the main SPL stakeholders should be identified	Framework for Evaluation of Reference Architectures (FERA) and VMTools-RA: A Reference Architecture for Software Variability Tools [1, 13]
G.SPL.7	It should be possible to change, modify, and evolve communalities and SPL variabilities	Software and Systems Engineering—Reference model for product line engineering and management [9]
G.SPL.8	The SPL commonalities and variabilities should be represented in textual, graphic, or tabular mode	Software and Systems Engineering—Reference model for product line engineering and management [9]
G.SPL.9	The SPL domain should be documented in textual, tabular, or graphical mode	Framework for Evaluation of Reference Architectures (FERA) and VMTools-RA: A Reference Architecture for Software Variability Tools [1, 13]
G.SPL.10	The SPL scope should be documented in textual, tabular, or graphical mode	Framework for Evaluation of Reference Architectures (FERA) and VMTools-RA: A Reference Architecture for Software Variability Tools [1, 13]

Table 9.10 SPL architecture guidelines

ID	Guideline	Source
G.PLA.1	A domain architecture should be developed, considering the SPL domain and scope	Software and Systems Engineering—Reference model for product line engineering and management [9]
G.PLA.2	The domain architecture should represent all the identified and analyzed SPL commonalities and variabilities	Software and Systems Engineering—Reference model for product line engineering and management [9]
G.PLA.3	The architecture under development should represent the understanding of the SPL domain and the scope, as well as satisfy the possible requirements established for both	Software and Systems Engineering—Reference model for product line engineering and management [9]
G.PLA.4	The SPL architecture should represent the interests of the main stakeholders	Framework for Evaluation of Reference Architectures (FERA) [13] and VMTools-RA: A Reference Architecture for Software Variability Tools [1]; Systems and software engineering—Architecture description [8]
G.PLA.5	The architecture should represent all the identified and analyzed commonalities and variabilities	Software and Systems Engineering—Reference model for product line engineering and management [9]; Framework for Evaluation of Reference Architectures (FERA) [13] and VMTools-RA: A Reference Architecture for Software Variability Tools [1]
G.PLA.6	The architecture should enable the modification or evolution of commonalities and variabilities	Software and Systems Engineering—Reference model for product line engineering and management [9]
G.PLA.7	The architecture should contribute to the application of a variability management approach	Software and Systems Engineering—Reference model for product line engineering and management [9]

(continued)

Table 9.10 (continued)

ID	Guideline	Source
G.PLA.8	The architecture should be traceable through artifacts related to the domain, scope, stakeholders, commonalities, and variabilities	Software and Systems Engineering—Reference model for product line engineering and management [9]
G.PLA.9	The architecture should be developed to assist in the research and analysis of implementation technologies for the SPL, if necessary. The PLA can be used as a criterion to evaluate the selected implementation technologies	Software and Systems Engineering—Reference model for product line engineering and management [9]
G.PLA.10	The architecture should allow the extraction of technical and technological details, such as interfaces and components. It is understood that the representation of the functional modules in the architecture helps in the extraction of these details	Software and Systems Engineering—Reference model for product line engineering and management [9]
G.PLA.11	The architecture should allow the identification and relationship between functional modules of the system	Framework for Evaluation of Reference Architectures (FERA) [13] and VMTools-RA: A Reference Architecture for Software Variability Tools [1]
G.PLA.12	The process of instantiating products through the architecture should be specified in textual, graphic, or tabular mode	Framework for Evaluation of Reference Architectures (FERA) [13] and VMTools-RA: A Reference Architecture for Software Variability Tools [1]
G.PLA.13	The architecture should allow the instantiation of different products, by specifying the product instantiation process	Framework for Evaluation of Reference Architectures (FERA) [13] and VMTools-RA: A Reference Architecture for Software Variability Tools [1]
G.PLA.14	The architecture should be described or documented in textual, graphic, or tabular mode	Framework for Evaluation of Reference Architectures (FERA) [13] and VMTools-RA: A Reference Architecture for Software Variability Tools [1]

9.7 Application Example

This section presents examples of applying metrics using SMartyModeling. We present as an application example an adaptation of the Mobile Media (*MM*) class diagram. The elements are organized in four packages: *MediaMgr*, *VideoMgr*,

Table 9.11 Guidelines for measures and metrics

ID	Guideline	Source
G.Measure.1	The measure should be related to a specific attribute .	Framework for evaluation and validation of software complexity measures [10]
G.Measure.2	The measure should reflect the attribute considered	Framework for evaluation and validation of software complexity measures [10]
G.Measure.3	The measure should be language-independent, not considering specific details of implementation or development	Framework for evaluation and validation of software complexity measures [10]
G.Measure.4	The measure should be developed on a scale that favors its measurement and comparison with other existing measures for the same attribute	Framework for evaluation and validation of software complexity measures [10]
G.Measure.5	The measure should provide a justification to be elaborated/created/developed. The measure should evaluate an attribute differently from the existing measures for the same attribute	Framework for evaluation and validation of software complexity measures [10]

Table 9.12 Use constraints guidelines

ID	Guideline
G.Constraint.1	SMartyMetrics considers architectures represented in SMarty UML diagrams using class and component diagrams
G.Constraint.2	Each quality attribute/sub-attribute, different than those considered by SMartyMetrics, should have at least one associated metric or measure
G.Constraint.3	Architecture evaluation methods to be aided by SMartyMetrics should allow the representation of architectures in UML diagrams. The class and component diagrams must be among the UML diagrams considered by the method

PhotoMgr, and *MusicMgr*. The *MediaMgr* package contains the basic elements for the media components: the *Media* class with 4 attributes and the *MediaMgr* class which implements the *IMediaMgt* interface, which describes 13 operations for media management. The three forms of media available are defined similarly. Thus, the *VideoMgr* package contains the *Video* and *VideoMgr* classes, the latter implementing the *IVideoMgt* interface, which describes specific operations for video manipulation. The *PhotoMgr* package contains the *Photo* and *PhotoMgr* classes, the latter implementing the *IPhotoMgt* interface, which describes specific operations for photo manipulation. And the *MusicMgr* package contains the *Music* and *MusicMgr* classes, the latter implementing the *IMusicMgt* interface, which describes specific operations for music manipulation. The *Video*, *Photo*, and *Music* classes extend

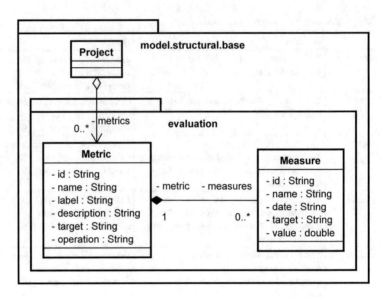

Fig. 9.6 SMartyModeling—evaluation view

the *Media* class, and the *VideoMgr, PhotoMgr,* and *MusicMgr* classes extend the *MediaMgt* class.

SMartyModeling adopts the SMarty approach as a standard for representing variability. In the example, three variabilities are defined:

Media Interface, with the *IMediaMgt* as a variation point and the following inclusive variants: *IVideoMgt, IPhotoMgt,* and *IMusicMgt*

Managing Media, with the *MediaMgr* class as a variation point and the following inclusive variants: *VideoMgr, PhotoMgr,* and *MusicMgr*

Playing Media, with the *Media* class as a variation point and the following inclusive variants: *Video, Photo,* and *Music*

Figure 9.7 shows the example described and adapted from MM.

SMartyModeling supports the definition and application of metrics on modeled PLAs. Formally, it is possible to define metrics and import and export them. In the *Evaluation* menu, accessing the *New Metric* item, a view is presented with the attributes shown in Fig. 9.6, and the metric is saved in the project. To apply the metric and save a metric, it is necessary to access the item *New Measure* in the *Evaluation* menu. The first panel presents basic information about the measurement, *name, date,* and *metric,* to be applied. The second panel presents information about the measurement target; in this case, it can be applied to the whole project, a type of diagram, or a specific diagram. The number of elements, associations, and variability is also presented. And finally, the third panel presents the result of the application of the metric, the operation attribute of the metric, the target of

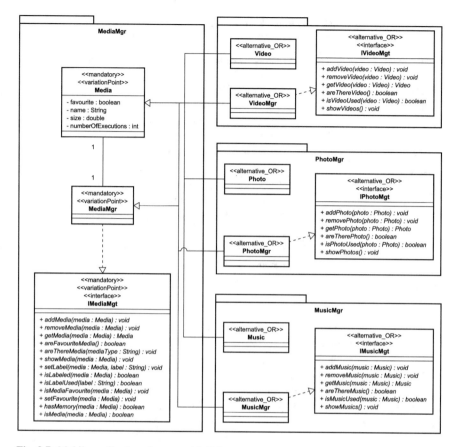

Fig. 9.7 Mobile media class diagram with SMarty

the measure, the collected value, and the items returned in the execution of the expression.

SMartyModeling also allows the application of metrics freely through the *Evaluation* menu. The target can be the Project (*Evaluate Project*), Diagram (*Evaluate Diagram*), or Product (*Evaluate Product*). In this case, it is not necessary to formally insert a new metric but to describe the operation attribute and execute the expression, and the value is calculated.

The operation attribute is an expression composed of clauses formed from a **<keyword>**(**<filter>**). The keywords are responsible for indicating which elements one is looking for, and the filter is responsible for selecting the elements by some criterion. The combination of mathematical operators with clauses is allowed. Table 9.13 presents the keywords for elements identified by SMartyModeling.

The filter is built from a set of attributes described by SMartyModeling. The selection of elements is made by the attributes of the filter. Table 9.14 presents the filter attributes available to elements.

Table 9.13 SMartyModeling—keywords for elements

Keyword	Description
Elements	Returns all elements, including the features and objects of the UML metamodel
Feature	Returns the features of the feature diagrams
Actor	Returns the UML actors of the use case diagrams
Usecase	Returns the UML use cases of the use case diagrams
Package	Returns the UML packages of the class diagrams
Class	Returns the UML classes of the class diagrams
Interface	Returns the UML interfaces of the class diagrams
Attribute	Returns the UML attributes/properties of the class diagrams
Method	Returns the UML methods/operations of the class diagrams
Component	Returns the UML components of the component diagrams
Activity	Returns the UML activities of the activity diagrams
Decision	Returns the UML decisions of the activity diagrams
Lifeline	Returns the UML lifelines of the sequence diagrams
Instance	Returns the UML instances of the sequence diagrams

Table 9.15 presents the keywords for associations identified by SMartyModeling. Table 9.16 presents the filter attributes available to associations.

Table 9.17 presents the keywords for SPL identified by SMartyModeling.

To exemplify the application of metrics with SMartyModeling, we chose to do it freely, using the *Evaluate Diagram* item in the *Evaluation* menu. Figure 9.8 presents the panel for evaluating the diagram in SMartyModeling. The diagram presented in Fig. 9.7 was used to apply the metrics. The operation applied was the total number of operations of the *VideoMgr* class, resulting in a total of 19, including the methods inherited from the *MediaMgr* class and implemented in the *IVideoMgt* interface.

To exemplify the application of metrics, we consider the metrics of modularity (Table 9.1), reusability (Table 9.4), and testability (Table 9.7). Table 9.18 presents examples of modularity metrics using SMartyModeling.

Table 9.19 presents examples of reusability metrics using SMartyModeling.

Table 9.20 presents examples of testability metrics using SMartyModeling.

9.8   Final Remarks

This chapter introduced SMartyMetrics, a framework with measures and metrics associated with the ISO/IEC 25010 standard [6], to assist in the evaluation of PLAs.

Section 9.2 presented an overview of the framework. In Sect. 9.3, QA and QSA are described. In the context of SMartyMetrics, the attribute `Maintainability` and the sub-attributes `Modularity`, `Reusability`, `Modifiability` and `Testability` were considered.

Table 9.14 SMartyModeling—filter attributes for elements

Filter attributes	Description
[name$_1$, ..., name$_n$]	Select elements by names: name$_1$, ..., name$_n$
<stereotype$_1$, ..., stereotype$_n$>	Select elements by associated stereotypes: stereotype$_1$, ..., stereotype$_n$
{parent}	Select elements by parent name. It is applied to attributes and methods
Mandatory	Select the mandatory elements
Optional	Select the optional elements
Abstract/no-abstract	Select the elements by abstract Flag [abstract=TRUE, no-abstract=FALSE]. It is applied to features, classes, and methods
Final,leaf/no-final,no-leaf	Select the elements by final flag [final,leaf=TRUE, no-final,no-leaf=FALSE]. It is applied to classes, attributes, and methods
Static/no-static	Select the elements by static flag [static=TRUE, no-static=FALSE]. It is applied to classes, attributes, and methods
Constructor/no-constructor	Select the methods by constructor flag [constructor=TRUE, no-constructor=FALSE]. It is applied to methods
Private, protected, public, default/package	Select the elements by visibility. It is applied to attributes and methods
Getter/no-getter	Select the methods starts with "get." It is applied to methods
Setter/no-setter	Select the methods starts with "set." It is applied to methods
Overwritten	Select the methods overwritten in class. It is applied to methods
Specific	Select the specific methods of a class/interface. It is applied to methods

The framework measures and metrics are presented in Sect. 9.4. Each measure or metric is associated with one or more of the following attributes: Cohesion, Coupling, Size, Complexity, and Extensibility. Such attributes are associated with the sub-attributes of ISO 25010.

In addition to measures and metrics, SMartyMetrics also considers sets of guidelines, related to SPL, PLA, measures, and metrics, and use restrictions. Each guideline represents an orientation or condition for using an artifact or performing an activity.

The SPL guidelines (Table 9.9) provide guidance on the planning and design involved in creating and maintaining an SPL. We understand that such stages influence the development of the PLA. The PLA guidelines consider aspects related to the design and development of architecture, in terms of domain, scope, and stakeholder interests.

Table 9.15 SMartyModeling—keywords for associations

Keyword	Description
Associations	Returns all associations, including the features and associations of the UML metamodel
Dependency	Returns the project dependencies
Generalization	Returns the project generalizations
Connection	Returns the feature diagrams connections
Communication	Returns the use case diagrams communications
Extends	Returns the use case diagrams extends
Include	Returns the use case diagrams includes
Association	Returns the associations of the class diagrams
Realization	Returns the class diagrams realizations
Communication	Returns the component diagrams communication
Flow	Returns the activity diagrams flows
Message	Returns the sequence diagrams messages

Table 9.16 SMartyModeling—filter attributes for associations

Filter attributes	Description
$[name_1, \ldots, name_n]$	Select the associations by names of element source: $name_1, \ldots, name_n$
$\{name_1, \ldots, name_n\}$	Select the associations by names of element target: $name_1, \ldots, name_n$
$<name_1, \ldots, name_n>$	Select the associations by names of element source or target: $name_1, \ldots, name_n$

Table 9.17 SMartyModeling—keywords for SPL

Keyword	Description
Variability	Returns all variability of the project
Variants	Returns the variants of the project
Variation point	Returns the variation points of the project

Regarding the measures and metrics guidelines, recommendations are presented about the creation, evaluation, and selection of measures and metrics with SMartyMetrics. Use restrictions guidelines present conditions for using SMartyMetrics during PLA evaluation.

Once we presented measures, metrics, and guidelines, we focused at presenting an application example using the SMartyModeling tool.[1]

---

[1] SMartyModeling is available at https://github.com/leandroflores/demo_SMartyModeling_tool for free using according to Creative Commons 4.0 licenses.

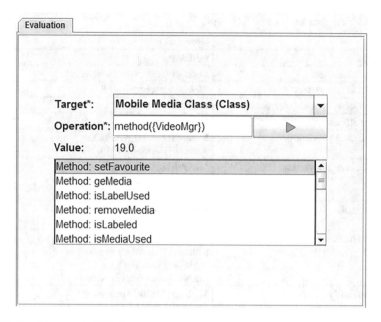

Fig. 9.8 Panel to evaluate MM diagram

Table 9.18 Application of modularity metrics

Metric	Operation	Result
Relational cohesion (H)	Associations(*) / (class(*) + interface(*))	0.9166
DepIn	Associations({Media})	4
DepOut	Associations([Video, Photo, Music])	3
DepInCompVariability	Associations({Media, Video, Photo, Music})	4
DepOutCompVariability	Associations([Media, Video, Photo, Music])	3
DepCompVariabiltyPLA	Associations({Media, Video, Photo, Music}) + associations([Media, Video, Photo, Music])	7

Table 9.19 Application of reusability metrics

Metric	Operation	Result
NumOps	method(*)	31
NumberOfGetsSets	Method(getter) + method(setter)	5
NumberOfConstructors	Method(constructor)	0
NumberOfOverwrittenOperations	Method(overwritten)	0
NumberOfSpecificOperations (NSO)	Method(specific)	25
NSOMandatoryVariant	Method({Media} specific) + method({IMediaMgt} specific)	10
NSOAlternativeOrVariant	Method({Photo} specific) + method({PhotoMgr} specific) + method({IPhotoMgt} specific)	5
NSOVariants	Method({Media} specific) + method({IMediaMgt} specific)	10
NSOVariationPoint	Method({MediaMgr} specific) + method({VideoMgr} specific) + method({PhotoMgr} specific) + method({MusicMgr} specific)	0
NSOVariability	Method({Media} specific) + method({MediaMgr} specific) + method({IMediaMgt} specific)	10
ExtensInterface	Method({IMediaMgt} abstract) / method({IMediaMgt} *)	1
ExtensClass	Method({MediaMgr} abstract) / method({MediaMgr} *)	1
ExtensVarPointClass	Method({MediaMgr} abstract) / method({MediaMgr} *) + method({VideoMgr} abstract) / method({VideoMgr} *) + method({PhotoMgr} abstract) / method({PhotoMgr} *) + method({MusicMgr} abstract) / method({MusicMgr} *)	4
ExtensVarPointClass	Method({MediaMgr} abstract) / method({MediaMgr} *) + method({VideoMgr} abstract) / method({VideoMgr} *) + method({PhotoMgr} abstract) / method({PhotoMgr} *) + method({MusicMgr} abstract) / method({MusicMgr} *)	4

Table 9.20 Application of testability metrics

Metric	Operation	Result
CompInterface	method({IMediaMgt} getter) + method({IMediaMgt} setter) + 2 * method({IMediaMgt} specific)	23
CompClass	method({PhotoMgr} getter) + method({PhotoMgr} setter) + 2 * method({PhotoMgr} specific)	34
CompPLA	method(getter) + method(setter) + 2 * method(specific)	56

Acknowledgments The authors would like to thank CAPES/Brazil (code 001) for funding this work.

References

1. Allian, A.P.: VMTools-RA: A reference architecture for software variability tools. Master's thesis, Universidade Estadual de Maringá, Departamento de Informática, Programa de Pós Graduação em Ciência da Computação (2016). In Portuguese
2. Chidamber, S.R., Kemerer, C.F.: Towards a metrics suite for object oriented design. In: Conference Proceedings on Object-Oriented Programming Systems, Languages, and Applications, pp. 197–211 (1991)
3. Chidamber, S.R., Kemerer, C.F.: A metrics suite for object oriented design. IEEE Trans. Softw. Eng. **20**(6), 476–493 (1994)
4. Cordeiro, A.F.R.: SMartyMetrics: A contribution to the ISO/IEC 25010 standard in the perspective of maintainability of software product lines. Master's thesis, Universidade Estadual de Maringá, Departamento de Informática, Programa de Pós-Graduação em Ciência da Computação (2018). In Portuguese
5. Fenton, N., Bieman, J.: Software Metrics: A Rigorous and Practical Approach, 3rd edn. CRC Press, Boca Raton (2014)
6. ISO: ISO/IEC 25010, Systems and Software Engineering. Systems and Software Quality Requirements and Evaluation (SQuaRE). System and Software Quality Models. International Organization for Standardization (ISO) (2011). http://www.iso.org/iso/catalogue_detail.htm?csnumber=35733
7. ISO/IEEE/IEC: ISO/IEC/IEEE 24765:2017(e) - systems and software engineering – vocabulary (2010). https://ieeexplore.ieee.org/document/8016712
8. ISO/IEC/IEEE: ISO/IEC/IEEE 42010:2011 - revision of ISO/IEC 42010:2007 (2011). https://ieeexplore.ieee.org/document/6129467
9. ISO/IEC 26550: software and systems engineering - reference model for product line engineering and management - ISO/IEC 26550. (2015). https://www.iso.org/standard/69529.html
10. Misra, S., Akman, I., Colomo-Palacios, R.: Framework for evaluation and validation of software complexity measures. IET Softw. **6**(4), 323–334 (2012)
11. Myers, G.J.: Reliable Software Through Composite Design. Wiley, Hoboken (1976)
12. OliveiraJr, E., Gimenes, I.M.S.: Empirical validation of product-line architecture extensibility metrics. In: Proceedings of the 16th International Conference on Enterprise Information Systems, pp. 111–118 (2014)

13. Santos, J.F.M., Guessi, M., Galster, M., Feitosa, D., Nakagawa, E.Y.: A checklist for evaluation of reference architectures of embedded systems (s). In: SEKE, pp. 1–4 (2013)
14. Sommerville, I.: Software Engineering. Pearson, London (2015)
15. Toung, T.J.: Using aspectj to build a software product line for mobile devices. Master's thesis, University of British Columbia, Department of Science, Faculty of Computer Science (2005)

Chapter 10
The SystEM-PLA Evaluation Method

Edson OliveiraJr, André F. R. Cordeiro, Itana M. S. Gimenes,
and José C. Maldonado

Abstract The architecture of a software product line is an important artifact which represents an abstraction of the products that can be generated. It is crucial to evaluate the quality attributes of a product line architecture to improve the product line process, in terms of productivity and reduction of the time to market. The evaluation of PLA can serve as a basis to analyze the managerial and economical values of a product line for software managers and architects. Current research on the evaluation of product line architecture does not take into account metrics directly obtained from UML models and their variabilities. In this context, used metrics are difficult to be applied in general and to be used for quantitative analysis. This chapter presents a Systematic Evaluation Method for UML-based Software Product Line Architectures (SystEM-PLA), which provides a methodology to (i) estimate and analyze products; (ii) use UML-based metrics in a composition related to quality attributes; (iii) perform feasibility and trade-off analysis, and (iv) facilitate the evaluation of product line architecture. An example using the SEI's Arcade Game Maker (AGM) software product line is presented and illustrates SystEM-PLA activities. Metrics for complexity and extensibility quality attributes are used to perform a trade-off analysis.

10.1 The Role of SMarty in This Work

As described in previous chapters, the Stereotype-based Management of Variability (SMarty) approach [11] was developed to deal with the management of variability represented in Unified Modeling Language (UML). Variability management is performed from a UML profile (SMartyProfile) and a process (SMartyProcess).

E. OliveiraJr (✉) · A. F. R. Cordeiro · I. M. S. Gimenes
State University of Maringá, Informatics Department, Maringá, PR, Brazil
e-mail: edson@din.uem.br; imsgimenes@uem.br

J. C. Maldonado
University of São Paulo, Institute of Mathematical and Computer Sciences, São Carlos, SP, Brazil
e-mail: jcmaldon@icmc.usp.br

© Springer Nature Switzerland AG 2023
E. OliveiraJr (ed), *UML-Based Software Product Line Engineering with SMarty*,
https://doi.org/10.1007/978-3-031-18556-4_10

Such elements present distinct and complementary contributions. The profile makes it possible to represent variabilities and associated elements, such as variation points and variants, in UML models. The process organizes the execution of different activities related to the variability, in terms of identification, delimitation, implementation, tracking, and control mechanisms.

Once the variability has been managed in the UML models, efforts can be directed toward developing and evaluating the product-line architecture (PLA). Metrics and quality attributes (QA) can be considered during PLA evaluation. The Systematic Evaluation Method for UML-based Software Product Line Architectures (SystEM-PLA) is used in this scope.

10.2 Characterization of SystEM-PLA

The SystEM-PLA is a method for evaluating software product line (SPL) architectures represented in UML. When evaluating a PLA with SystEM-PLA, the following possibilities are viable:

- estimate and analyze potential products of an SPL according to its respective architecture;
- use metrics related to quality attributes (QA) in the evaluation of PLA;
- perform PLA trade-off analyses, considering two or more QA;
- make architecture evaluation more flexible in terms of QA and metrics.

In SystEM-PLA, the PLA evaluation is carried out during the following evaluation phases: (1) planning, (2) data collection, and (3) data analysis and documentation. An illustration of these phases is found at [12]. Each phase of SystEM-PLA has a specific purpose.

During the planning phase, important artifacts to evaluate are selected. The selection of artifacts takes place in the instantiation of the evaluation metaprocess (EMP) [13]. The EMP represents a structure, which presents the activities to be carried out in the planning. More information about the metaprocess is presented in Sect. 10.3.

During the data collection phase, metrics are applied in the selected UML diagrams. Metrics are used to evaluate basic elements of SPL or QA. Variabilities, variation points, and variants are understood as basic elements. In addition to considering the metrics, PLA configurations must be generated in the collection phase. Such configurations are generated in a manual or automatized way.

In the data and documentation analysis phase, the collected data are analyzed, and the results are recorded. Quantitative and qualitative analyses can be performed. After analysis, it is possible to prepare one or more reports, considering different purposes. Some purposes are related to the description of the results or packaging the obtained information for future replications.

Each phase of SystEM-PLA presents a set of guidelines to help in the activities and in the development of the artifacts. More information about the guidelines is presented in Sect. 10.4.

10.3   Evaluation Metaprocess (EMP)

The evaluation metaprocess (EMP) presents the activities that must be carried out during the evaluation planning. Before instantiating the EMP, the features and UML models of the SPL to be evaluated must be available.

In the case of UML models, they must be specified based on the SMarty [11]. Figure 10.1 illustrates the EMP.

Figure 10.1 shows the EMP activities. SPL and QA models enable metaprocess instantiation. The activities are carried out and artifacts are developed once the EMP is instantiated. During the execution of the EMP, questions and metrics are defined. Both are used in the following steps.

In the instantiation and execution of the EMP, different artifacts are considered by the activities performed. The artifacts and activities presented in Fig. 10.1 are detailed in Tables 10.1, 10.2, and 10.3. Table 10.1 presents the following EMP artifacts: business drivers (BD), defined scenarios (DS), classified scenarios (CS), selected quality attributes (SQA), management and technical questions (MTQ), and quality attribute metrics (QAM). Each artifact is described in Table 10.1.

To develop the artifacts presented in Table 10.1, different activities are carried out. Table 10.2 presents such activities. For each activity, there is a related description.

Each activity in Table 10.2 receives one or more input artifacts. When the activity is finished, one or more output artifacts are completed. For example, in the Scenario Classification activity, the DS artifact is an input. After the activity, the CS artifact is made available. Once the activity has been carried out, it is possible to use the artifact developed in other activities, such as the Activity of Selecting Quality Attributes Based on Scenarios. All EMP activities receive at least one input artifact and return at least one output artifact. Table 10.3 presents the artifacts associated with each activity.

Input or output artifacts associated with each EMP activity can be developed during EMP or originated in activities performed before EMP instantiation. For example, BD, FM, and DS were developed in the context of EMP. MLP and QA artifacts were developed before instantiation.

As mentioned in Table 10.2, different professionals participate in the instantiation of the EMP. Each professional has a responsibility. In the context of the EMP, the responsibilities are understood as roles. SPL manager, SPL architect, and developer are role examples. More information about EMP roles is presented in Table 10.4.

Each professional has one or more associated questions, which must be answered during the evaluation. In the case of the SPL manager, a possible question is "What

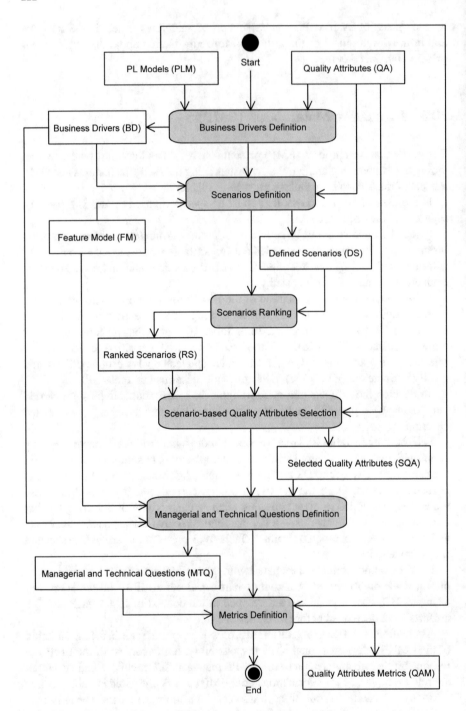

Fig. 10.1 Evaluation metaprocess [12]

Table 10.1 Artifacts for instantiation of the evaluation metaprocess [12]

Artifact	Description
Business drivers (BD)	The business objectives that a PLA must satisfy
Defined scenarios (DS)	Set of scenarios defined for the QA of a PLA to support their selection in a given evaluation
Classified scenarios (CS)	Set of classified scenarios for the evaluation of PLAs
Selected quality attributes (SQA)	A non-empty subset of QA are to be considered in the evaluation
Management and technical questions (MTQ)	Questions to be answered in the evaluation of PLAs. These questions are related to the definition of quantitative metrics
Quality attribute metrics (QAM)	Metrics defined to support the prioritization of QA

Table 10.2 Activities for instantiation of the evaluation metaprocess [12]

Activity	Description
Defining business drivers	Setting goals to support the definition of scenarios and questions
Defining scenarios	Establishment of scenarios for the QA associated with the PLA. The scenarios influence the selection of QA
Classification of scenarios	Classification performed according to defined factors for PLA
Attribute selection based on scenarios	Establishment of the QA that will be considered
Definition of management and technical questions	Elaboration of questions to be answered by the professionals who participate in the evaluation
Defining metrics	Use of QA metrics, to answer the established questions

Table 10.3 Input and output artifacts for the activities in the evaluation metaprocess [12]

Activity	Input(s)	Output(s)
Defining business drivers	PLM and QA	BD
Defining scenarios	BD, FM, and QA	DS
Classification of scenarios	DS	CS
Attribute selection based on scenarios	CS and QA	SQA
Definition of management and technical questions	BD, FM. and SQA	MTQ
Defining metrics	PLM, SQA, and MTQ	QAM

configurations are most viable in a given domain?". The SPL architect may be concerned with knowing "How much effort is required to develop an SPL product, based on its artifacts and variability?". The developer, in turn, may be interested in knowing "What SPL implementation techniques can be used considering the

Table 10.4 Roles defined in the EMP [12]

Role	Description
SPL manager	Responsible for SPL planning, monitoring, and control
SPL architect	Responsible for managing the evolution of the PLA
Developer	Responsible for the implementation and maintenance of variability in SPL

estimated effort?". All questions defined for the selected roles must be answered after evaluation. When evaluating PLAs, it is necessary to consider the EMP and the evaluation guidelines. These guidelines are presented in the next section.

10.4   Evaluation Guidelines

There are sets of guidelines to each phase of the SystEM-PLA. These guidelines help in the activities related to the phase. Tables 10.5, 10.6, and 10.7 present the guidelines.

Table 10.5 presents specific guidelines for the planning phase of SystEM-PLA. Such guidelines help in the establishment of the artifacts necessary for the evaluation. The planning guideline PG.1, related to BD, presents the user's responsibility in defining goals.

The planning guidelines PG.2, PG.3, and PG.4 are related to scenarios. In PG.2, there is a recommendation associated with the definition of scenarios. It is the user who must define scenarios for the QA of a PLA. Each scenario is expected to indicate the QA that it affects.

PG.3 presents a necessity to classify each scenario. Such classification may be carried out in terms of certain criteria or attributes of interest. Some examples of attributes are the general importance of PLA, the generality of the scenarios, cost, risk, and several variabilities contained in each scenario.

Table 10.5 Planning guidelines [12]

ID	Guideline
PG.1	Define business drivers
PG.2	Define scenarios
PG.3	Classify scenarios
PG.4	Select quality attributes based on classified scenarios
PG.5	Define managerial and technical questions
PG.6	Define quality attribute metrics

Table 10.6 Data collection guidelines [12]

ID	Guideline
DCG.1	Create PLA configurations
DCG.2	Apply and collect metrics from PLA configurations

Table 10.7 Data analysis and documentation guidelines

ID	Guideline
DAG.1	Plot the collected data in one or more forms of graphical representation
DAG.2	Analyze the descriptive statistics of the data collected
DAG.3	Identify how many scenarios satisfy the selected QA
DAG.4	Identify which selected QA(s) satisfy the PLA
DAG.5	Perform trade-off analysis
DAG.6	Write a final evaluation report
DAG.7	Store all artifacts produced in the repository

In PG.4, the selection of the QA to the PLA is considered based on the classified scenarios. In the selection of QA, different strategies can be used. An example is the voting system [1, 5].

PG.5 is related to the definition of MTQ. To elaborate on the questions, it is recommended to consult the BD, the FM, and the selected QA. To facilitate the elaboration of the questions, the GQM method may be used [2]. In the SystEM-PLA method, it is possible to map the BD, the QA, and the FM for GQM goals and questions. PG.6 is associated with the definition of metrics for the QA selected in the evaluation. Each metric should indicate which attributes are associated with itself.

Regarding the specific guidelines for the data collection phase, called data collection guidelines (DCG), Table 10.6 presents such guidelines.

Two guidelines are presented in Table 10.6. The DCG.1 presents the need to create PLA configurations. There is a condition to create the configurations in a manual or automated way. Manual creation requires the participation of one or more people. In this creation mode, care must be taken not to generate invalid configurations or configurations that do not respect constraints, such as those existing between variants. Automated creation happens with the help of tools. In general, this creation method is considered more reliable, as long as all the functionalities of the tools used are known. Among the tools used are Captor-AO [15], pure::variants [3], and Software Product Line Online Tools (SPLOT) [8].

DCG.2 presents the application and collection of data from the PLA configurations. After the creation of configurations, it is necessary to apply metrics and collect data. Different tools may be used in this task. Among the main ones is the SDMetrics tool [16], which considers UML models exported to XML files Metadata Interchange (XMI) [14].

About the guidelines for the data analysis and documentation phase, Table 10.7 presents more information.

According to Table 10.7, DAG.1 presents a recommendation related to different forms of graphical representation. Among the representation, possibilities are measures of descriptive statistics and histogram of dispersion. Such representations are used for statistical analysis, providing information on the total values of a measure and comparing the behavior of two or more different sets of measures.

Regarding descriptive statistics, DAG.2 presents the need to analyze measures calculated from the collected data. After analysis, it interestingly identifies how many scenarios satisfy the selected QA.

DAG.3 considers the number of scenarios. DAG.4 presents the need to identify which selected QA satisfies the PLA. From these attributes, it is possible to decide which attributes should be prioritized during the development and evolution of the products of an SPL. This decision is recommended by DAG.5.

In the DAG.6, the writing of a final evaluation report is recommended. The report is expected to present a record of all evaluation activities, the artifacts produced, data collected, and graphs or tables generated. A report ATAM style may be considered [5]. The DAG.7 guideline presents the recommendation to store all produced artifacts in a repository. The existence of a repository facilitates replication evaluations.

The guidelines described in Tables 10.5, 10.6, and 10.7 guide the application of the SystEM-PLA method. After presenting these guidelines and the phases of the method, it is possible to illustrate its application. An example is described in the next section.

10.5 Application Example

The application example presented in this section is a variation of application examples described in [12] and [13]. The following subsections detail the application of the method.

10.5.1 Product Line Architecture

The SPL to be evaluated in this example is the Arcade Game Maker (AGM) [17]. This SPL is related to electronic games. It was developed by the Software Engineering Institute (SEI). Figure 10.2 shows the use case diagram of the AGM.

Figure 10.2 describes features and games supported by AGM. There are elements related to the physical environment of the games. Such elements are shown in Fig. 10.3.

Figure 10.3 presents essential elements for the games supported by SPL in a class diagram. The GameMenu, MovableSprite, and StationarySprite classes are associated with the game menu (GameMenu), with the elements that move (MovableSprite), and with the elements that do not move (StationarySprite). The classes

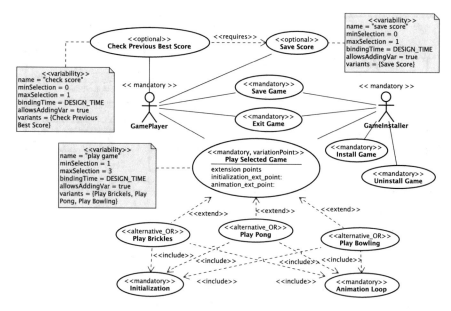

Fig. 10.2 Use case diagram for SPL AGM [12]

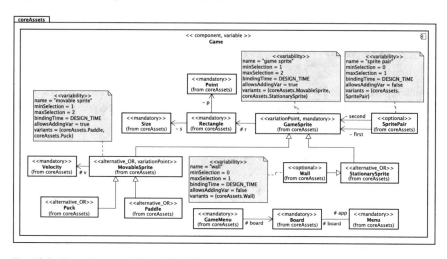

Fig. 10.3 Class diagram of SPL AGM [12]

shown in Fig. 10.3 are organized into components. Some necessary components are described in Fig. 10.4.

A logical view of the base architecture of the SPL is established through the components described in Fig. 10.4. In addition, it is necessary to consider possibilities of interaction in the games to the specific elements of the SPL.

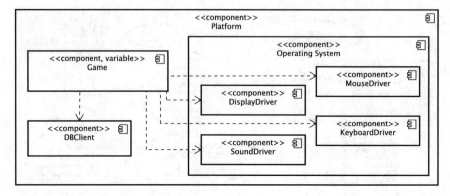

Fig. 10.4 Component diagram of SPL AGM [12]

Interactions via mouse and keyboard are shown in Fig. 10.4. The driver associated with each possibility is presented.

Once representations of PLA have been presented, it is necessary to present the phases of the SystEM-PLA method. The next subsection presents the evaluation planning.

10.5.2 Planning

As described in Sect. 10.4, the planning phase considers six guidelines, presented in Table 10.5. The guidelines influence the description of the artifacts presented below.

10.5.2.1 Business Drivers

The first PG.1 shows the need to establish BD. For such an evaluation, the defined goals are represented in Table 10.8.

Table 10.8 Business drivers are established in the evaluation

Identifier	Business driver (BD)	Description
BD.1	Keep game complexity degree lower than 0.7 (70%), compared to PLA complexity, for at least 50% of produced products	The level of complexity can indicate a difficulty to maintain products derived from an PLA. In this way, the greater the degree of complexity of a product, the more difficult it is to maintain it
BD.2	Keep game extensibility degree higher than 0.75 (75%), compared to PLA extensibility, for at least 50% of produced products	The level of extensibility can indicate the product's reusability in terms of its components. In this way, the more extensible a product is, the higher its reusability level

Table 10.8 presents the two goals established for the evaluation. Such goals are associated with the QA complexity and extensibility. Complexity can be defined as the degree of difficulty in understanding or verifying system elements. Extensibility may be defined as the ability of an element to be modified to help other system elements [6].

The BD.1 considers the interest to keep the degree of complexity of the games below 70% for at least 50% of the products produced. It is understood that the greater the degree of complexity of a product, the more difficult it will be to maintain it throughout the life cycle of an SPL.

The BD.2 considers the interest to keep the level of extensibility of games between 50 and 75% for all products produced. It is understood that the higher the level of extensibility of a product, the higher its reusability rate and the lower its maintenance cost.

The definition of BD.1 and BD.2 makes it possible to define scenarios associated with QA. The scenarios defined in the evaluation are presented below.

10.5.2.2   Scenarios

There are six scenarios related to QA complexity and extensibility. These scenarios are presented in Tables 10.9 and 10.10.

Table 10.9 describes three scenarios associated with complexity. Scenario Sc.1 shows the maintenance of BD.1, even with the addition, modification, and removal of variation points or variants. Scenario Sc.2 considers the maintenance of BD.1 even with the removal of 50% of the variabilities. Scenario Sc.3 presents that environments that have a game must have a maximum complexity of 65% of the AGM architecture.

The other three remaining scenarios are associated with extensibility. Scenario Sc.4 shows that BD.2 must remain true even with the addition, removal, or modification of variation points or variants. Scenario Sc.5 shows that BD.2 must remain true even after removing 50% of the variability. Scenario Sc.6 presents that

Table 10.9 Scenarios established for complexity [12, 13]

	AGM—Quality attribute utility tree
Quality attribute	Complexity
Related business driver(s)	BD.1: keep game complexity level lower than 0.7 (70%), compared to the overall PLA complexity, for at least 50% of produced products
Scenario(s)	Sc.1: Variation points or variants are added, modified, or removed maintaining the BD.1 true
	Sc.2: 50% of variabilities are removed. The BD.1 is maintained true
	Sc.3: One-game environments have complexity values at most 0.65 (65%) compared to the total AGM PLA complexity

Table 10.10 Scenarios established for extensibility [12, 13]

	AGM—Quality attribute utility tree
Quality attribute	Extensibility
Related business driver(s)	BD.2: keep game extensibility level higher than 0.75 (75%), compared to the total PLA extensibility, for at least 50% of produced products
Scenario(s)	Sc.4: Variation points or variants are added, modified, or removed, maintaining the BD.2 true
	Sc.5: 50% of variabilities are removed. The BD.2 is maintained true
	Sc.6: Two-game environments have extensibility values of at least 0.8 (80%) compared to the total AGM PLA extensibility

environments that have two games must have minimum extensibility of 80% of the AGM architecture.

After establishing the scenarios, it is important to classify them. Classification information is presented below.

10.5.2.3 Classified Scenarios

To classify scenarios, it is possible to establish criteria or attributes of interest. Some attributes are importance, generality, cost/risk, and several variabilities. The importance describes how much such a scenario should be considered from the established BD. The generality evaluates how generic such a scenario is for PLA. The cost/risk evaluates the effort involved to satisfy requirements related to the scenarios, as well as the perceived risk. The number of variabilities presents the total of them, present in each scenario.

During classification, the user must classify each scenario as high (H), medium (M), or low (L), for each selected attribute of interest. Table 10.11 presents the classification of the scenarios defined in Sect. 10.5.2.2. Based on classified scenarios, it is possible to select QA.

10.5.2.4 Selected Quality Attributes

The selection of the QA from the classified scenarios can be performed based on a strategy. A possible strategy is the voting system [1]. In this evaluation, the scenarios were selected from the following analyses:

1. it is understood that the scenarios Sc.1, Sc.4, and Sc.5 are of general importance for PLA to consider a high number of variabilities. Such scenarios are considered mandatory with a cost/risk defined as average;

Table 10.11 Classification of established scenarios [12, 13]

Business drivers		BD.1			BD.2		
Quality attributes		Complexity			Extensibility		
Scenarios		Sc.1	Sc.2	Sc.3	Sc.4	Sc.5	Sc.6
Overall importance	H	X		X	X	X	X
	M		X				
	L						
Generality	H	X			X		
	M		X			X	
	L			X			X
Cost/risk	H		X			X	
	M	X			X		
	L			X			X
Number of variability	H	X	X		X	X	X
	M			X			
	L						

Table 10.12 Selected quality attributes [12]

Business driver	Quality attribute	Scenario	Selection order
BD.1	Complexity	Sc.1	1st
BD.2	Extensibility	Sc.4	2nd
BD.2	Extensibility	Sc.5	3rd
BD.2	Extensibility	Sc.6	4th
BD.1	Complexity	Sc.2	5th
BD.1	Complexity	Sc.3	6th

2. it is understood that the Sc.6 is optional since its respective cost/risk was analyzed as low (even though it has a high number of variabilities and high importance for PLA);
3. to Sc.2, it is understood that it has a high number of variabilities involved, a high cost/risk, and average significance. Therefore, such a scenario is considered an alternative type;
4. the Sc.3 is an alternative, even though it understands that it has a high preference for PLA, a low cost/risk, and a low number of variabilities involved.

After analyzing the scenarios classified for complexity and extensibility, a ranking was created. This ranking is presented in Table 10.12. Table 10.12 presents the selection order of the classified scenarios. After analysis, it was concluded that scenarios Sc.1, Sc.4, and Sc.5 are the most important for SPL AGM. The Sc.1 scenario is related to BD.1 and the complexity attribute. The Sc.4 and Sc.5 scenarios are related to BD.2 and the extensibility attribute. In this way, the selection of the QA complexity and extensibility was considered.

It is interesting to notice that in this example, all QA were selected based on the classified scenarios. In other evaluations, involving more QA, it would be possible that not all were selected. After solving the scenarios and the QA selected, it is necessary to define the managerial and technical questions to be considered. This is done in the next subsection.

10.5.2.5 Management and Technical Questions

To elaborate on questions about management and technical aspects, it is recommended to consider BD and QA. Goals and attributes may be inserted in the application of the Goal Question Metric (GQM) method [4]. Thus, it is necessary to establish the associated questions. Table 10.13 presents the questions related to the evaluation.

In Table 10.13, each question has a unique identifier. Ten questions were established. The questions from Q.01 to Q.05 are related to BD.1 (low complexity). The questions from Q.06 to Q.10 are related to BD.2 (high extensibility).

10.5.2.6 Quality Attribute Metrics

During the application of GQM, there is an association between goals, questions, and metrics. In the context of SystEM-PLA, metrics are associated with QA. The selected metrics are shown in Table 10.14.

Table 10.14 describes all metrics used in this application example. In addition to the metrics, the question identifiers are also presented. In this way, it is easier to understand the association between questions and metrics. It is also possible to observe the association between goals, questions, and metrics from Tables 10.12, 10.13, and 10.14.

The metrics associated with QA present in Table 10.14 have been validated experimentally. These metrics are calculated from basic metrics for SPL. More information about validation and basic metrics is found at [7, 10] and [9].

Table 10.13 Questions related to complexity [12, 13]

ID	Question
Q.01	What is the complexity of a class/interface in a class model?
Q.02	What is the complexity of a variation point class/interface in a class model?
Q.03	What is the complexity of a variability class/interface in a class model?
Q.04	What is the complexity of a variable component in a model?
Q.05	What is the complexity of a PLA based on its class model?
Q.06	What is the extensibility of a class/interface in a class model?
Q.07	What is the extensibility of a variation point class/interface in a class model?
Q.08	What is the extensibility of a variability class/interface in a class model?
Q.09	What is the extensibility of a variable component in a model?
Q.10	What is the extensibility of a PLA based on its class model?

Table 10.14 Metrics of complexity and extensibility [12]

Quality attribute	Metric Question	Name	Description
Complexity	Q.01	CompInterface	Value of the Weighted Methods per Class (WMC) complexity metric for an interface. It is always 0.0 as interfaces do not have concrete methods
Complexity		CompClass	Returns the value of the Weighted Methods per Class (WMC) complexity metric for a class
Complexity	Q.02	CompVarPointClass	Returns the sum of the CompClass or CompInterface value of all its associated variants plus the CompClass or CompInterface value of the variation point
Complexity	Q.03	CompVariabilityClass	Returns the sum of the CompVarPointClass associated with all variabilities in class models
Complexity	Q.04	CompVarComponent	Returns the sum of the CompVariabilityClass value for all the variabilities associated with classes that form a component
Complexity	Q.05	CompPLA	Returns the sum of the CompVarComponent value for all of a PLA
Extensibility	Q.06	ExtensInterface	Returns the number of abstract methods divided by the number of methods of an interface. It is always 1.0
Extensibility		ExtensClass	Returns the number of abstract methods divided by the number of methods (concrete plus abstract) of a class
Extensibility	Q.07	ExtensVarPointClass	Returns the value of the ExtensClass or ExtensInterface of an abstract class or interface multiplied by the number of its subclasses or implementation classes
Extensibility	Q.08	ExtensVariabilityClass	Returns the sum of ExtensVarPointClass associated with all variabilities in class models
Extensibility	Q.09	ExtensVarComponent	Returns the sum of ExtensVariabilityClass value for all the variabilities associated with classes that form a component
Extensibility	Q.10	ExtensPLA	Returns the sum of ExtensVarComponent value for all the components in class models of a PLA

10.5.3   Data Collection

The data collection phase considers two guidelines in Table 10.6. Information about the application of such guidelines is described below. According to this table, it is possible to generate PLA configurations manually or automatically, using a tool (DCG.1). In this example, the configurations were generated manually. For an automated generation, different tools may be considered. Some examples are Captor [15], pure::variants [3], and SPLOT [8].

After generating the configurations, it is necessary to apply metrics and perform data collection based on the DCG.2. The metrics used were described in Table 10.14. The results of the application of the metrics are presented in Table 10.15. With the collected data, the data analysis and documentation phase can start.

10.5.4   Data Analysis and Documentation

The data analysis and documentation phase consider the application of the seven guidelines, presented in Table 10.7. Different artifacts associated with the guidelines are described below.

10.5.4.1   Graphical Representation of Data

After applying the metrics, it is necessary to represent the collected data. Different representations are possible. Figures 10.5 and 10.6 present box graphs, which are related to the used metrics.

10.5.4.2   Analysis of Collected Data

The collected data represented in Figs. 10.5 and 10.6 may be analyzed, according to the metrics CompPLA and ExtensPLA. In analysis 1, related to the CompPLA metric (Fig. 10.5), it is observed that the median value is 0.5895. This means that:

- 15 configurations (50%) have values less than or equal to 0.5895;
- 15 configurations (50%) have values greater than 0.5895;

In analysis 2, related to the ExtensPLA metric (Fig. 10.6), it is observed that the median value is 0.7060. This means that:

- 15 configurations (50%) have values less than or equal to 0.7060;
- 15 configurations (50%) have values greater than 0.7060.

After the analysis conclusion, the number of scenarios that satisfy the selected QA may be identified.

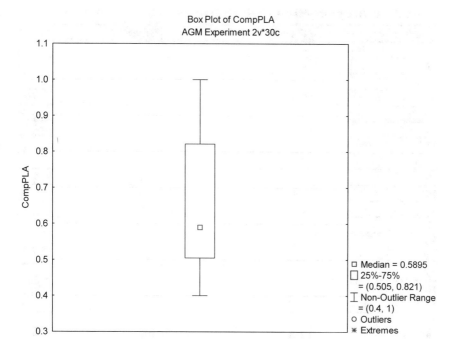

Fig. 10.5 Configuration analysis, according to the CompPLA metric [12]

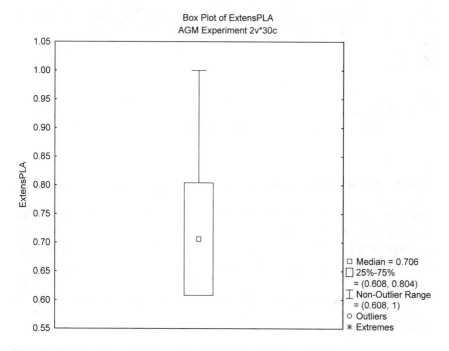

Fig. 10.6 Configuration analysis according to the ExtensPLA metric [12]

Table 10.15 PLA configurations considered in the evaluation [12]

Configuration#	CompPLA	ExtensPLA
1	0.51	0.61
2	0.56	0.61
3	0.51	0.81
4	0.83	0.80
5	0.91	1.00
6	0.50	0.61
7	0.47	0.61
8	0.53	0.61
9	0.67	0.80
10	0.90	1.00
11	0.53	0.61
12	0.97	1.00
13	0.48	0.61
14	0.69	0.61
15	0.74	0.80
16	0.98	1.00
17	0.77	0.80
18	0.82	0.80
19	0.52	0.61
20	0.82	0.80
21	0.49	0.61
22	1.00	1.00
23	0.52	0.61
24	0.42	0.61
25	0.62	0.80
26	0.47	0.61
27	0.53	0.61
28	0.70	0.80
29	0.40	0.61
30	0.78	0.80

10.5.4.3 Scenarios That Satisfy Quality Attributes

After carrying out the analysis, it is possible to identify the mandatory scenarios that satisfy the selected QA. Such identification is done to verify that the scenarios are appropriate to the QA. If the scenarios are evaluated as inadequate, the professionals can rewrite them. In this context, it is understood that at least 50% of the scenarios must satisfy the selected QA. Thus, it is viable to carry out trade-off analyses. Analyses 1 and 2, presented in Sect. 10.5.4.2, are considered. Based on analysis 1 (DAG.2 guideline), it is observed that scenario Sc.1 is satisfied for the complexity attribute. During the creation of the configurations, there were modifications or removal of variation points and variants. Still, the scenario kept BD.1 true, wherein 18 of the 30 configurations (60%) have CompPLA values less than 0.70.

Based on analysis 2 (DAG.2 guideline), it is observed that scenarios Sc.4 and Sc.5 are satisfied for the extensibility attribute. When creating configurations, variation points and variants were manipulated. Even with the changes, both scenarios kept the BD.2 true. In 15 of the 30 configurations (50%), ExtensPLA values greater than 0.75 were observed.

10.5.4.4 Quality Attributes That Satisfy the PLA

Based on the analysis of mandatory scenarios, it is possible to conclude that both complexity and extensibility meet the PLA, since 100% of its scenarios have been satisfied.

10.5.4.5 Trade-Off Analysis

To carry out a trade-off analysis, it is necessary to consider the QA that satisfies the PLA (DAG.4) and decide which attribute(s) will be prioritized. In this evaluation, the analysis was performed from the values plotted for the metrics CompPLA and ExtensPLA. Figure 10.7 presents a dispersion histogram. The results presented on the histogram are associated with the generated configurations.

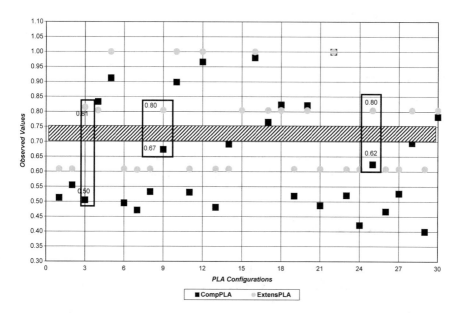

Fig. 10.7 Scatter histogram for the generated configurations [12]

When analyzing Fig. 10.7, it is possible to notice that 19 configurations present a value of CompPLA < 0.7. Regarding the ExtensPLA metric, it is observed that 15 configurations have a value of >0.75. The shaded region in the histogram, with values ranging from 0.7 to 0.75, presents the configurations that are not interesting, since they are not in compliance with the BD (low complexity and high extensibility), established in the evaluation.

Among the configurations considered in the evaluation, three are described in detail in Fig. 10.7. For the first configuration, the values of CompPLA = 0.50 and ExtensPLA = 0.81 are observed. The second presents the values 0.67 for CompPLA and 0.80 for ExtensPLA. The third configuration has a result of 0.62 for CompPLA and 0.80 for ExtensPLA.

When analyzing the three configurations, it is noticed that the ExtensPLA level is practically the same (0.80). This similarity of results can represent an indicator that, for similar products, complexity may be preferred in comparison with extensibility.

Another indicator is related to satisfying the scenarios. In the case of the SPL AGM, it is observed that 60% of the generated products satisfy the complexity scenario (Sc.1), while 50% of the generated products satisfy the extensible scenarios (Sc.4 and Sc.5).

Considering these two indicators presented, it is possible to conclude that for SPL AGM, complexity must be prioritized in comparison with extensibility.

10.5.4.6   Evaluation Report

When the evaluation is finished, it is necessary to prepare a report. In this report, all activities related to producing artifacts, collected data, generated data, generated tables, and other information considered relevant must be recorded. As a suggestion for report style, there is the ATAM style [5], widely known by the software architecture community.

10.5.4.7   Storage of Artifacts

After the preparation of the evaluation report, it is recommended that all evaluation artifacts be stored in a repository to allow future consultations and replications.

10.6   Final Remarks

In this chapter, we introduced the SystEM-PLA method to evaluate PLAs according to the SMarty approach. We defined three phases for this method: planning, data collection, data analysis and documentation. When evaluating a PLA with SystEM-PLA, it is possible to estimate potential products of an SPL, as well as apply associated metrics and perform trade-off analyses with one or more QA. As a result, greater flexibility in the evaluation can be observed.

We presented an overview of the method in Sect. 10.2 and its forming elements. An evaluation metaprocess is detailed in Sect. 10.3.

To guide the application of SystEM-PLA, guidelines are presented in specific sets (Tables 10.5, 10.6 and 10.7) related to each phase of the method.

Finally, an application example illustrated the presented method in Sect. 10.5.

References

1. Barbacci, M.R.: SEI Architecture Analysis Techniques and When to Use Them. Technical Report, Carnegie Mellon University, Software Engineering Institute, Pittsburgh, Pennsylvania, USA (2002)
2. Basili, V.R., Rombach, H.D.: The TAME project: towards improvement-oriented software environments. IEEE Trans. Softw. Eng. **14**(6), 758–773 (1988)
3. Beuche, D.: Pure:: variants. In: Systems and Software Variability Management, pp. 173–182. Springer, New York (2013)
4. Caldiera, V., Rombach, H.D.: The goal question metric approach. In: Encyclopedia of Software Engineering, , vol. 1, no. 6, pp. 528–532 (1994)
5. Clements, P., Kazman, R., Klein, M.: Evaluating Software Architectures: Methods and Case Studies. Addison-Wesley Reading, Boston (2002)
6. 24765, I.: ISO/IEC/IEEE Systems and Software Engineering - Vocabulary, ISO/IEC/IEEE Core Team (2022). https://ieeexplore.ieee.org/document/8016712
7. Marcolino, A., OliveiraJr, E., Gimenes, I.M.S., Conte, T.U.: Towards validating complexity-based metrics for software product line architectures. In: Proceedings of the VII Brazilian Symposium on Software Components, Architectures and Reuse, pp. 69–79. IEEE, New Jersey (2013)
8. Mendonca, M., Branco, M., Cowan, D.: SPLOT: Software product lines online tools. In: Proceedings of the 24th ACM SIGPLAN Conference Companion on Object-Oriented Programming Systems Languages and Applications, pp. 761–762, ACM, New York (2009)
9. OliveiraJr, E., Gimenes, I., Maldonado, J.: A metric suite to support software product line architecture evaluation. In: Proceedings of the XXXIV Conferencia Latinaoamericana de Informática, pp. 489–498, Santa Fe, AR (2008)
10. OliveiraJr, E., Gimenes, I.M.S.: Empirical validation of product-line architecture extensibility metrics. In: Proceedings of the 16th International Conference on Enterprise Information Systems, pp. 111–118, SCITEPRESS, Setúbal, PT (2014)
11. OliveiraJr, E., Gimenes, I.M.S., Maldonado, J.C.: Systematic management of variability in UML-based software product lines. J. Univer. Comput. Sci. **16**(17), 2374–2393 (2010)
12. OliveiraJr, E., Gimenes, I.M.S., Maldonado, J.C., Masiero, P.C., Barroca, L.: Systematic evaluation of software product line architectures. J. Univer. Comput. Sci. **19**(1), 25–52 (2013)
13. OliveiraJr, E., Gimenes, I.M.G., Maldonado, J.C.: A meta-process to support trade-off analysis in software product line architecture. In: Proceedings of the Twenty-Third International Conference on Software Engineering e Knowledge Engineering, pp. 687–692. Flórida (2011)
14. OMG, O.M.G.: XML Metadata Interchange (2022). Available at https://www.omg.org/spec/XMI/About-XMI/. Accessed 03 Jun 2022

15. Project, C.A.: Captor-AO application generator (2022). Available at https://code.google.com/archive/p/captor/. Accessed 03 Jun 2022
16. SDMetrics: Sdmetrics: The software design metrics tool for UML (2022). Available at https://www.sdmetrics.com/. Accessed 03 Jun 2022
17. SEI, S.E.I.: The arcade game maker pedagogical product line (2022). Available at https://resources.sei.cmu.edu/asset_files/WhitePaper/2009_019_001_485943.pdf. Accessed 03 Jun 2022

Chapter 11
Optimizing Product-Line Architectures with MOA4PLA

Thelma Elita Colanzi, Mamoru Massago, and Silvia Regina Vergilio

Abstract One of the main core assets of a software product line (SPL) is the product-line architecture (PLA). PLA design can be modeled as a multi-objective problem, influenced by many factors, such as feature modularization, extensibility, and other architectural properties. Due to this, PLA design has been properly optimized in the search-based software engineering (SBSE) field, by taking into account key factors and by continuously evaluating the architecture according to certain metrics. In this chapter, we present an approach, named MOA4PLA (Multi-Objective Approach for Product-Line Architecture Design). MOA4PLA encompasses a process to give a multi-objective treatment to the design problem, based on specific SPL metrics. It introduces a meta-model to represent the PLA and specific search operators to improve architectural properties of the PLA design, such as feature modularization. We also discuss certain implementation aspects and present an application example.

11.1 Introduction

Software product line (SPL) engineering is an approach which has been widely adopted by software industry to ease reuse. Some successful case studies include Boeing, Philips, Bosch, Nokia, and Toshiba [39]. An SPL consists of core assets that have explicit common and variable features [27], which are used to derive the products. A feature is an end-user-visible program characteristic that is relevant to the stakeholders of the application domain [25]. The product-line architecture (PLA) comprises the SPL core design model. Hence, a PLA needs to be generic and flexible enough to support the configuration of many products.

T. E. Colanzi (✉) · M. Massago
Informatics Department, State University of Maringá, Maringá, PR, Brazil
e-mail: thelma@din.uem.br

S. R. Vergilio
Informatics Department, Federal University of Paraná, Curitiba, PR, Brazil
e-mail: silvia@inf.ufpr.br

© Springer Nature Switzerland AG 2023
E. OliveiraJr (ed), *UML-Based Software Product Line Engineering with SMarty*,
https://doi.org/10.1007/978-3-031-18556-4_11

To satisfy such needs and evaluate PLA designs, some works [3, 8] often taken into account a set of metrics that indicates quality attributes, such as design stability, feature modularization, and extensibility [3, 19, 29, 36]. However, there is a lack of automated support for the modeling and evaluation of the diverse attributes of a PLA design. Modularizing features is difficult because they usually cut across many PLA components. In addition, feature modularization is related to important modularity concepts, such as cohesion, coupling, feature crosscutting, and tangling [16]. A higher feature modularization implies in a lower functionality scattering in PLA design. Scattered Functionality [22] is one of the most relevant architectural bad smells because it negatively impacts on the PLA reusability and extensibility. In particular, these properties are important for PLA design.

Thus, to obtain a modular and extensible PLA design might be very difficult to the architect, being necessary considering a large range of possible competing metrics during the modeling. Thus, finding the best trade-off among the used metrics makes the PLA design a people-intensive task. Furthermore, some metrics can be in conflict, and architects need to choose which metric should be prioritized. In this context, to recognize a good design can be easy for architects, but it is difficult to obtain.

In this context, we can model the PLA design as an optimization problem influenced by several factors (metrics). Such kind of complex problem of software engineering has been effectively solved in the search-based software engineering (SBSE) field [1, 23, 31]. The idea is to use search-based algorithms (meta-heuristics), such as genetic algorithms, to find near-optimal solutions that satisfy pre-defined objectives. Search-based algorithms can provide automated evaluation to reason about and improve a PLA design, thus reducing the design flaw propagation throughout the SPL development.

Taking into account the promising results obtained by using SBSE techniques to solve several software engineering problems, we introduced an approach named MOA4PLA (Multi-Objective Approach for Product-Line Architecture Design) [13]. It uses search-based algorithms to optimize the PLA design and gives a multi-objective treatment to the PLA design problem including feature-driven metrics. Experimental results showed that MOA4PLA produces a set of potential solutions with the best trade-off between different objectives, such as feature modularization, SPL extensibility, and basic design principles like coupling and cohesion.

MOA4PLA has four main characteristics. It encompasses (i) a meta-model to represent the PLA, allowing its symbolic manipulation by a search-based algorithm; (ii) search operators to improve feature modularization; (iii) an evaluation model, composed of metrics, which are specific for PLA; and (iv) a process to apply multi-objective algorithms, composed of a set of steps for MOA4PLA application and automation.

In this chapter, we reproduce the MOA4PLA definition, which was firstly published in [13], present the crossover operator published in [12], and add an application example using the Mobile Media product line. To enable a better comprehension of our approach, in the next sections, we present the main concepts on multi-objective optimization and provide an overview about the use of SBSE for the SPL context. Later, we present a detailed description of MOA4PLA and illustrate its application for PLA design optimization.

11.2 Introduction to Multi-Objective Optimization

When an optimization problem is influenced by many factors, it is called multi-objective. To obtain a solution, it is necessary to optimize all objectives simultaneously, generally following the Pareto dominance concepts [30]. The objective functions are usually in conflict with each other; hence, almost ever there is not a single solution to the problem. In such a context, the aim is to find a set of solutions which represents the trade-off among the objectives. In most applications, the search for the Pareto optimal is NP-hard. For these applications, the goal is to find an approximation set (PF_{approx}), as close as possible to the Pareto front. PF_{approx} is composed of the non-dominated solutions. "Given a set of possible solutions, the solution A dominates B if the value of at least one objective in A is better than the corresponding objective value in B, and the values of the remaining objectives in A are at least equal to the corresponding values in B. A is non-dominated if it is not dominated by any other solution" [13].

The general multi-objective minimization problem with no restrictions can be stated as to minimize Eq. 11.1, subjected to $\overrightarrow{x} \in \Pi$, where $\overrightarrow{x}$ is a vector of decision variables and Π is a finite set of feasible solutions.

$$\overrightarrow{f}(\overrightarrow{x}) = (f_1(\overrightarrow{x}), ..., f_B(\overrightarrow{x})) \tag{11.1}$$

Let $\overrightarrow{x} \in \Pi$ and $\overrightarrow{y} \in \Pi$ be two solutions. For a minimization problem, the solution $\overrightarrow{x}$ dominates $\overrightarrow{y}$ if Eqs. 11.2 and 11.3 are satisfied; $\overrightarrow{x}$ is a non-dominated solution if there is no solution $\overrightarrow{y}$ that dominates $\overrightarrow{x}$.

$$\forall f_i \in \overrightarrow{f}, i = 1...B, f_i(\overrightarrow{x}) \leq f_i(\overrightarrow{y}) \tag{11.2}$$

$$\exists f_i \in \overrightarrow{f}, f_i(\overrightarrow{x}) < f_i(\overrightarrow{y}) \tag{11.3}$$

Figure 11.1 illustrates a multi-objective problem with two factors (decision variables). The problem consists on choosing a type of vehicle minimizing cost and transportation time. There are seven solutions in this picture. The non-dominated are depicted in black and form the Pareto front. Solutions b and e are not in the Pareto front because they are dominated solutions. Solution b is dominated by solution c, while solution e is dominated by solutions f and g.

To solve a multi-objective problem, multi-objective algorithms have been successfully applied in SBSE [14, 23, 28]. Variants of genetic algorithms are widely used. They are named multi-objective evolutionary algorithms (MOEAs). A genetic algorithm (GA) is a heuristic inspired by the theory of natural selection and genetic evolution [9]. The search starts with an initial population composed of a pre-defined

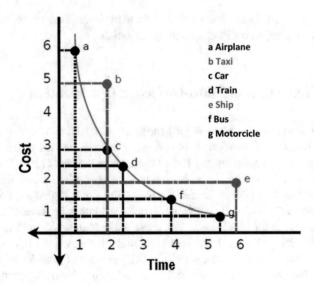

Fig. 11.1 Example of multi-objective problem with two factors

number of solutions from the search space. Search operators are applied for every population. These operators are selection, crossover, and mutation, and they must be specific for the representation adopted for the problem. GA iteratively generates new solutions from existing ones, until some stopping condition is reached. The selection operator selects the individuals with the best values of the objective function to be parent. Hence, the best individuals will survive in the next population. The crossover operator creates a new individual by combining parts of two parent solutions. Then, the mutation operator performs changes in a solution at random. The descendent population created through the application of the three search operators replaces the parent population. At the end, the best solution found is returned. During the evolution process, some constraints, associated with the validity of the solutions, can be used. Invalid solutions, which do not satisfy the constraints, can be repaired or discarded. It is relevant to notice that, in the context of SBSE, each objective function is associated with the one or a composition of several software metrics.

NSGA-II (non-dominated sorting genetic algorithm) [17] is one of the most used MOEAs [14, 23]. NSGA-II uses a strong elitism strategy. For each generation, it sorts the individuals from parent and offspring populations aiming to create fronts of non-dominated solutions. After the sorting, solutions with lower dominance are discarded. These fronts characterize the elitism strategy adopted by NSGA-II. This algorithm also uses a diversity operator (crowding distance) that sorts the individuals according to their distance from the neighbors of the border for each objective, in order to ensure greater spread of solutions.

11.3 Search-Based SPL Optimization

Search-based techniques have been applied to address problems related to SPL engineering in several studies. Recent surveys [24, 28] show a growing number of papers on this subject. Most of them focus on the following: automated feature model construction [37], configuration of products [42], feature selection for SPL development and evolution [26, 34], reverse engineering of feature models [5, 6], and SPL testing [4, 40]. Since they usually work with the feature model, their optimization goal is not PLA design.

Some works apply SBSE techniques to optimize software architecture at the component-connector level and deployment level [1, 2, 33]. Their optimization goal is also different from ours.

The works on search-based software design [31] are the most related to our approach. They focus on the architectural design outset by addressing two problems: the application of design patterns to software design [32] and the class responsibility assignment [7, 38]. Most of them use MOEAs and coupling and cohesion metrics [7, 32, 38]. The search operators move methods and attributes from one class to another and also add new classes [7, 38].

Design transformations based on search operators are applied in some studies directly to software design models [38], such as class diagrams. Thus, the possible design alternatives form the search space. Some studies perform a genotype-phenotype mapping where search operators are applied to integer vectors [7] or supergene representations [32].

There are some limitations [10] that make the use of such approaches not suitable to PLA design. They are:

- PLA representation at class diagram level was not used in related work. In a previous work [11], we analyzed how to adapt each representation used in the literature to the PLA design context. Based on this analysis, we concluded that the direct object-oriented representation adopted in [38] is more suitable than others. It is easier to extend it in order to represent variabilities and features. Thus, we proposed a novel representation (described in Sect. 11.5.1) that comprises SPL needs aiming at PLA design optimization.
- The approaches do not apply search operators to promote feature modularization, and the used search operators do not include specific characteristics of PLA;
- They do not use specific SPL metrics to evaluate the solutions.

Our approach, named MOA4PLA, was proposed for solving those limitations and enabling PLA design optimization through search-based algorithms. It is presented in Sect. 11.5.

11.4   The Role of SMarty in This Work

The SMarty approach is used to represent the SPL variabilities of PLA designs that are provided as input to MOA4PLA. The main stereotypes of SMarty applied in PLA design in the context of MOA4PLA are *variability*, *variationPoint*, and *variant*, including the non-abstract stereotypes that specialize *variant*: *mandatory*, *optional*, *alternative_OR*, and *alternative_XOR*. The explicit use of SMarty can be seen in the PLA design depicted in Fig. 11.4.

11.5   MOA4PLA

The focus of MOA4PLA is the PLA design since PLA is one of the most important artifacts in the SPL approach. In addition to basic architectural properties like coupling and cohesion, MOA4PLA aims at optimizing other factors such as feature modularization and SPL extensibility.

According to Harman et al. [23], two key ingredients are necessary to tackle a problem using search-based algorithms: (1) a representation of the problem to allow symbolic manipulation and (2) an objective function, defined in terms of the representation and metrics, to evaluate the quality of the solutions. To obtain such ingredients, MOA4PLA encompasses a process that includes a set of activities as depicted in Fig. 11.2. The first ingredient is generated in the activity named Construction of the PLA Representation. The second one is defined in the activity Definition of the Evaluation Model. Then, the search-based algorithm is applied, and a set of solutions (PLAs representations) is obtained. In the last activity, the solutions are transformed and presented to the architect, who can select one of them. These activities are better explained below.

Construction of the PLA Representation   The input for this activity is the PLA design, a UML class diagram. In such a diagram, each architectural element is

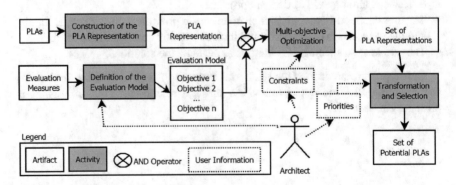

Fig. 11.2   MOA4PLA process

associated with the feature(s) that it realizes. The output of this activity is a representation of the PLA containing architectural elements, their inter-relationships, the variabilities, the variation points, and the variants. This representation is obtained by using a meta-model, explained in Sect. 11.5.1.

Definition of the Evaluation Model The input for this activity is the metrics to be used in the objective function. MOA4PLA proposes a set of metrics, but the user can select only some of them or include new ones. MOA4PLA aims to optimize SPL intrinsic characteristics, PLA attributes that can lead to a better design, such as feature modularization [3, 19, 36] and SPL extensibility [29]. Thus, it takes into account SPL-specific metrics in addition to the conventional ones. A high extensibility level indicates that a greater number of products can be generated from the PLA, which leads to maximizing the market share. Given that a feature can be considered a concern in an SPL, concern-driven measures [19, 36] support the analysis of feature-based cohesion and feature scattering and interlacing. Component cohesion can also be measured by cohesion metrics specific for SPL [3]. These metrics provide modularity indicators, which can be used to achieve more modular, reusable, and maintainable PLA designs. The evaluation model is described in Sect. 11.5.2.

Multi-Objective Optimization The PLA representation obtained in the first activity is optimized according to pre-defined constraints. An example of a constraint is to consider classes without attributes or methods as invalid. Each obtained alternative PLA is evaluated following the evaluation model defined in the previous activity. The output is a set of PLA representations, that is, solutions with the best trade-off between the objectives. Different algorithms can be used in this activity, such as multi-objective evolutionary algorithms (MOEAs), Pareto ant colony optimization (PACO), and multi-objective particle swarm optimization (MPSO).

Transformation and Selection Each PLA representation, from the set obtained in the Multi-Objective Optimization, is converted to a UML class diagram containing the PLA design. Thus, one PLA representation should be selected to be adopted as the PLA of the SPL. This choice can be based on one metric to be prioritized according to the SPL needs or organizational goals. Another option is to select the solution with the best trade-off between the objectives. Both input and output of MOA4PLA are XMI files containing the PLA design in order to ease the interchangeable use of the approach artifacts.

MOA4PLA is independent of the method adopted for mapping features to the architectural elements. It is also a generic approach that may be instantiated by using different search algorithms and metrics.

The next subsections present details on the two key ingredients to adopt search-based algorithms in PLA design, namely, the PLA representation and the evaluation model used to define the objective functions. The search operators proposed for MOA4PLA are also presented. Finally, we discuss the aspects of the MOA4PLA implementation.

11.5.1 Product-Line Architecture Representation

The meta-model proposed to represent the PLA is shown in Fig. 11.3. The meta-model consists of a class diagram of PLA elements associated with the respective description of variabilities, using SMarty approach. This allows the handling of the architectural elements by the search operators.

A PLA contains architectural elements such as components, interfaces, operations, and their inter-relationships. Each architectural element is associated with feature(s) by using UML stereotypes. It can be either common to all SPL products or variable, appearing only in some product(s). Variable elements are associated with variabilities that have variation points and their variants.

Figure 11.4 depicts an example of a PLA for the SPL Mobile Media [15] represented by this meta-model. Mobile Media is an application for mobile devices which encompasses features that handle music, video, and photo [43]. There are seven variabilities detailed in UML notes associated with the classes that realize the variabilities in the PLA. Variation points, alternative variants, and optional and mandatory features are shown by the SMarty stereotypes *variationPoint*, *alternative_OR*, *optional*, and *mandatory*, respectively. Features, such as *favourites, linkmedia*, and *SMSTransfer*, are also shown through stereotypes. Architectural components

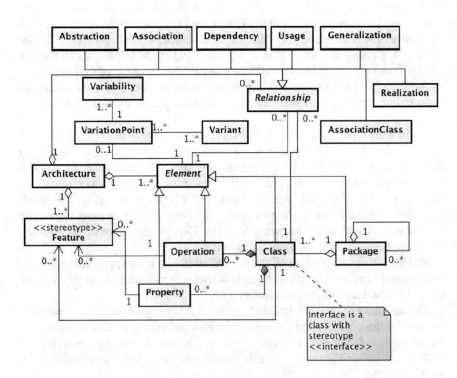

Fig. 11.3 Meta-model of a PLA design [18]

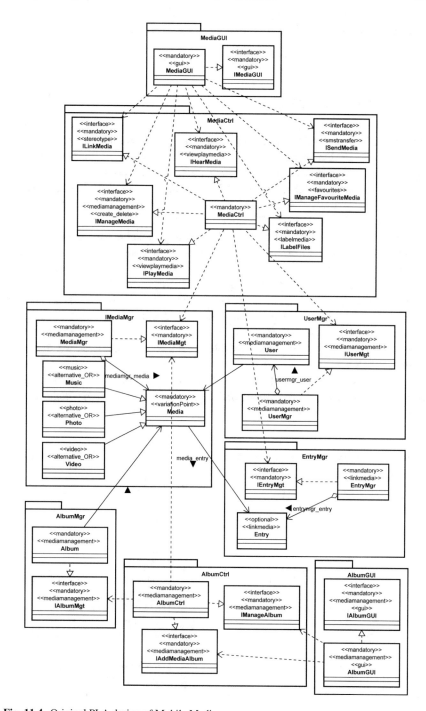

Fig. 11.4 Original PLA design of Mobile Media

were represented by packages of their classes. Attributes and operations were omitted in the picture.

11.5.2 Evaluation Model

The evaluation model is established according to the architects' priorities and needs. To accomplish MOA4PLA goals, we suggest the use of both conventional and specific SPL metrics. Conventional metrics (CM) (see Table 11.1) provide indicators on basic design principles. The cohesion measure H indicates which components have weak cohesion since it measures to what extent do the components have strongly related elements. The size metric NumOps indicates the number of operations of each interface of the PLA. This is important because small interfaces are, in general, easier to reuse. The other metrics evaluate the coupling between architectural elements.

The feature-driven metrics (FM) [19, 35] are used to evaluate the changes caused by the feature-driven operator, proposed in the next section. However, specific metrics for SPL are more appropriate. Since the feature-driven operator aims at better modularizing features, it is important to use metrics sensitive to this kind of change in the design. FMs are effective to do this. They evaluate the degree of feature modularization of a PLA. Inaccurate feature modularization has a negative impact on PLA reusability and maintainability. It can also lead to a wide range of design flaws, such as feature tangling and scattering to specific code smells, such as feature envy or god class [20].

Table 11.1 Conventional metrics suite (CM) [41]

Attribute	Metric	Definition
Cohesion	Relational cohesion (H)	Average number of internal relationships per class in a component
Coupling	Dependency of packages (DepPack)	Number of packages on which classes and interfaces of this component depend
	ClassDependencyIn (CDepIn)	Number of elements that depend on this class
	ClassDependencyOut (CDepOut)	Number of elements on which this class depends
	DependencyIn (DepIn)	Number of UML dependencies where the package is the supplier
	DependencyOut (DepOut)	Number of UML dependencies where the package is the client
Size	Number of operations by interface (NumOps)	Number of operations in the interface

Table 11.2 Feature-driven metrics suite (FM) [19, 35]

Attribute	Metric	Definition
Feature scattering	Feature diffusion over architectural components (CDAC)	Number of architectural components which contributes to the realization of a certain feature
	Feature diffusion over architectural interfaces (CDAI)	Number of interfaces in the system architecture which contributes to the realization of a certain feature
	Feature diffusion over architectural operations (CDAO)	Number of operations in the system architecture which contributes to the realization of a certain feature
Feature interaction	Component-level interlacing between features (CIBC)	Number of features with which the assessed feature share at least a component
	Interface-level interlacing between features (IIBC)	Number of features with which the assessed feature share at least an interface
	Operation-level overlapping between features (OOBC)	Number of features with which the assessed feature share at least an operation
Feature-based cohesion	Lack of feature-based cohesion (LCC)	Number of features addressed by the assessed component

Table 11.2 presents the metrics that allow the evaluation of the feature modularization in PLA design solutions evolved by the proposed search operators. The metrics CDAC, CDAI, and CDAO take into account that a feature scattered on a high number of elements harms modularity. The metrics CIBC, OOBC, and IIBC measure the feature interaction that happens by the presence of different features in the same architectural element. This interaction is measured in three levels: component, interface, and operation. The metric called lack of feature-based cohesion (LCC) indicates that a component that addresses many features is not stable since changes in any of the associated features may impact the other ones.

The evaluation model relies on feature-driven and conventional metrics aiming at assessing feature modularization, reusability, and stability of a PLA. However, other metrics can be included and used since the evaluation model is extensible.

11.5.3 Search Operators

Search operators modify the initial population and force the search-based algorithms to explore new regions in the space of solutions. To do this, the operators need to consider the adopted PLA representation. Search operators from related work on software design can be applied in MOA4PLA as mutation operators. They are MoveMethod [7, 38], MoveAttribute [7, 38], AddClass [7, 38], MoveOperation [10], and AddComponent [10]. MoveMethod and MoveAttribute move a method or an attribute, respectively, for a randomly selected class. AddClass moves a method or an attribute to a new class. The creation of classes is necessary as optimal class assignments may require additional classes that were not identified in the design. The class that receives the moved attribute/method becomes client of the original class of the element. MoveOperation moves operations between interfaces. AddComponent creates a new interface to a new component and moves an operation to this interface. When an operation is moved, the component that receives the moved operation becomes client of the original interface of the operation.

However, according to the MOA4PLA goals and its evaluation model, which considers feature modularization, specific operators to improve feature modularization are mandatory. In this order, MOA4PLA has a mutation operator, named feature-driven mutation operator [13], and a crossover operator, named feature-driven crossover operator [12].

Algorithm 1: Pseudocode of feature-driven mutation operator [13]

---

1 begin
2 | $C \leftarrow A.getAllComponents()$
3 | $E \leftarrow$ set of architectural elements of A
4 | $c_x \leftarrow$ a randomly selected component from C
5 | $F_c \leftarrow c_x.getAllFeatures()$
6 | **if** $F_c.size()>1$ **then**
7 | | $f_x \leftarrow$ a randomly selected feature from F_c
8 | | $c_f \leftarrow A.getAllComponentsAssociatedWithFeature(f_x)$
9 | | **if** $c_f.size()==0$ **then**
10 | | | $c_z \leftarrow A.createComponent()$
11 | | | $c_z.addFeature(f_x)$
12 | | **else**
13 | | | **if** $c_f.size()==1$ **then**
14 | | | | $c_z \leftarrow c_f.get(0)$
15 | | | **else**
16 | | | | $c_z \leftarrow$ a randomly selected component from c_f
17 | | | **for** *each* $e \in E \mid (e \neq c_z \ or \ e \notin c_z)$ **do**
18 | | | | **if** $e.getFeatures.size()==1 \ and \ e.isAssociatedWithFeature(f_x)$ **then**
19 | | | | | Move e to c_z
20 | | | | | $A.addRelationship \ (c_z,$ original component of $e)$
21 | | | **end for**
22 | | **return** A;
23 **end**

The pseudocode of feature-driven mutation operator is presented in Algorithm 1. It aims to modularize a feature tangled in a component, considering that a feature is usually realized by a group of architectural elements. The operator receives as input a PLA design A and returns its improved design as output. It selects an arbitrary component (c_x), and, if c_x has architectural elements (e.g., interfaces, classes, operations, methods, and attributes) associated with different features, an arbitrary feature (f_x) is selected to be modularized to the component c_z; c_z is chosen according to the size of the set c_f, which contains all components of A associated with f_x. When the size is equal to 0, a new component c_z is created. When the size is 1, c_z receives the single component of c_f. Or, if the size is greater than 1, c_z receives a randomly selected component of c_f. The architectural elements of c_x associated with f_x are moved to c_z. c_z becomes client of the original components from the moved architectural elements.

This operator helps to obtain PLA designs with less scattered and tangled features, improving the feature cohesion of the architectural components. The operator also contributes to avoiding the presence of the architectural bad smell Scattered Functionality [22]. To exemplify how this operator works, consider Fig. 11.4. The operations are not shown; however, either the feature *labemmedia* or *favourites* are spread over operations of two interfaces, where they are tangled with other features. Nevertheless, the interfaces *ILabelFiles* and *IManageFavourite-Media* (package *MediaCtrl*) are associated only with the feature *labemmedia* and *favourites*, respectively. By applying the operator, operations associated with each of these features would be properly modularized into one of these two interfaces.

The goal of feature-driven crossover operator is to improve the feature modularization of a PLA design. This operator selects a feature at random and then creates children by swapping the architectural elements (classes, interfaces, operations, etc.) that realize the selected feature. In this way, we hypothesize that children might combine groups of architectural elements that better modularize some feature(s) inherited from their parents.

The pseudocode of feature-driven crossover operator is presented in Algorithm 2. Feature-driven crossover randomly selects a feature (f_x) at line 3. From two parents

---

Algorithm 2: Pseudocode of feature-driven crossover operator [12]

1 begin

    Input: *Parent*1, *Parent*2

2 $F \leftarrow$ Parent1.getAllFeatures()

3 $f_x \leftarrow$ a randomly selected feature from F

4 $c_1 \leftarrow$ Parent1.getAllElementsAssociatedWithFeature(f_x)

5 $c_2 \leftarrow$ Parent2.getAllElementsAssociatedWithFeature(f_x)

6   Child1 $\leftarrow$ new Solution(*Parent*1)

7   Child1.removeElementsRealizingFeature(c_1, f_x)

8   Child1.addElementsRealizingFeature(c_2, f_x)

9   Child1.updateVariabilities()

10   Child2 $\leftarrow$ new Solution(*Parent*2)

11   Child2.removeElementsRealizingFeature(c_2, f_x)

12   Child2.addElementsRealizingFeature(c_1, f_x)

13   Child1.updateVariabilities()

    Output: *Child*1, *Child*2

14 end

(*Parent*1 and *Parent*2), two offspring are generated in lines 6 and 10 (*Child*1 and *Child*2). Then, the elements associated with f_x are removed from *Child*1 and *Child*2 (lines 8 and 12). The next step is to add the elements (and their relationships) of *Parent*2 associated with f_x in *Child*1 (line 9) and the same for *Child*2 (line 13). After completing each child, relationships related to the SPL variabilities are updated (lines 10 and 15). Thus, it is possible to obtain children that better realize f_x.

Figure 11.5 illustrates the application of feature-driven crossover operator. The solutions presented are alternative designs for Mobile Media [15]. Due to lack of space, only excerpts of solutions are presented, and several details were omitted. In *Parent*1, the feature *linkMedia* is modularized in the system layer into the component *LinkMediaCtrl*. In *Parent*2, the feature *SMSTransfer* is modularized in the system component *SMSTransferCtrl*. Given the selected feature *SMSTransfer*, after the application of the feature-driven crossover operator, two child solutions are generated: *Child*1 and *Child*2. In terms of fitness, *Child*1 is

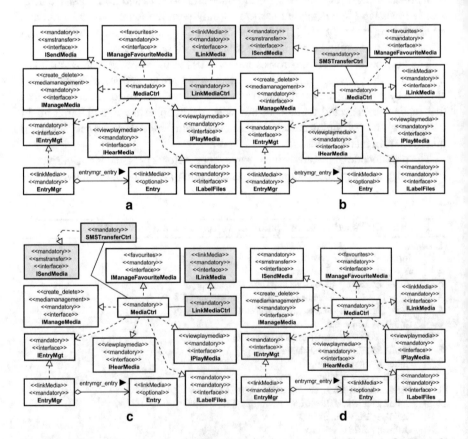

Fig. 11.5 Feature-driven crossover operator: an application example. (**a**) Parent 1. (**b**) Parent 2. (**c**) Child 1. (**d**) Child 2

better than *Parent*1, *Parent*2, and *Child*2 because the component *MediaCtrl* has higher feature-driven cohesion and the feature *SMSTransfer* is less tangled with other features in the PLA design. On the other hand, *Child*2 is worse than the other three solutions in terms of both (i) modularization of the feature *SMSTransfer* and (ii) cohesion of *MediaCtrl*. *Child*2 probably will not survive in the next generation.

Feature-driven crossover operator aims at maintaining and improving the feature modularization of a PLA design. Thus, its application generates solutions by swapping architectural elements associated with a randomly selected feature. It may combine architectural elements that better modularize some SPL features that were inherited from their parents. As crossover may be performed in several generations, the number of obtained children with better feature modularization tends to improve over time. Parents, in turn, have often suffered mutations from feature-driven mutation operator in previous generations. In such cases, parents may contain well-modularized features. Thus, the feature-driven crossover operator complements feature-driven mutation operator.

We establish some constraints to ensure that each solution generated by MOA4PLA is consistent as follows: (i) classes and their subclasses cannot be separated; (ii) the moved element must maintain the original associated feature even if it was moved to an element associated with a different feature; and (iii) components, interfaces, and classes cannot be empty.

11.5.4 Implementation Aspects

OPLA-Tool [21] is a web-based tool created to automate the application of MOA4PLA. Its usage documentation is available in the tool website.[1] OPLA-Tool allows the configuration and execution of a PLA design optimization experiment as well as the visualization of the experiment's results.

Before an experiment execution in OPLA-Tool, a set of parameters needs to be configured, such as (i) the PLA design to be optimized; (ii) the multi-objective algorithm to perform the optimization; (iii) selection of the objective functions to be optimized during the search process, and (iv) setting of several algorithm parameters, such as population size, stopping criterion, mutation and crossover rates, and mutation and crossover operators to be applied during the search.

---

[1] https://github.com/otimizes/OPLA-Tool.

After the experiment execution, the results can be visualized. OPLA-Tool presents to users a list of all experiments carried out. Thus, they can obtain experiment's information, such as the input PLA, details of the optimization runs, and information about the PLA designs generated as output. OPLA-Tool enables the download of all pieces of information regarding the generated solutions as well as the analysis through graphics.

11.6   Application Example

In this section, we present some other examples of the application of MOA4PLA, especially regarding its search operators, intending to show how the search-based approach makes changes in the PLA design during the optimization process.

Taking into account the PLA design of Mobile Media presented in Fig. 11.4, we illustrate the application of *Move Operation* mutation operator, when it selects the operation *hasMemory* of *IMediaMgt* interface to move to the *ILabelFiles* interface. Figure 11.6 depicts the excerpt of the original design impacted by the operator changes, whereas Fig. 11.7 depicts the excerpt of the resulting PLA design.

The search operators of MOA4PLA make changes in the PLA design that can (a) impact the cohesion and coupling degrees; (b) change the size of classes and interfaces; (c) influence the design elegance; and (d) improve or damage the PLA extensibility. In the example presented in Fig. 11.7, the PLA extensibility was not changed; however, it could be impacted if the *Move Method* operator moves an abstract method of a class which is a variation point to some class that is not a variation point. The conventional mutation operators can also impact the values of feature-driven metrics when the movement of the architectural elements changes, for instance, the feature diffusion or feature interlacing.

Note that in the original PLA design of Mobile Media (Fig. 11.4), the *MediaCtrl* component has interfaces associated with several features: *Favourites, SMSTransfer,* and *LinkMedia*. The application of **Feature-driven Mutation Operator** to *MediaCtrl* aiming at modularizing the *SMSTransfer* feature involves the following steps:

1. Create the *SMSTransferCtrl* component (highlighted in Fig. 11.8);
2. Move the *ISendMedia* interface to *SMSTransferCtrl* (highlighted in Fig. 11.8);
3. Add relationships between *SMSTransferCtrl* and *EntryMgr, UserMgr,* and *MediaMgr* interfaces;
4. Associate the *SMSTransferCtrl* component to the *SMSTransfer* feature.

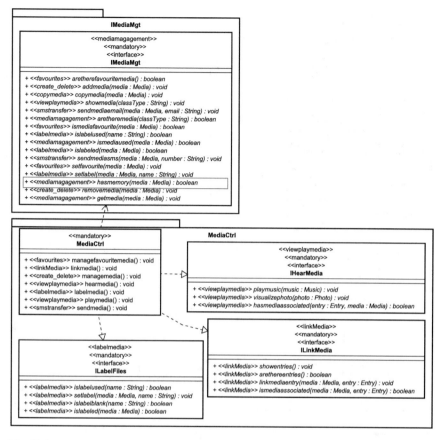

Fig. 11.6 Application example 1: Move operation operator (excerpt of the original PLA design)

Figure 11.8 depicts the excerpt of the PLA design changed after the feature-driven mutation operator application. If there were other architectural elements associated with the *SMSTransfer* feature, they would be moved to the *SMSTransferCtrl* component during the operator application.

After the feature-driven mutation operator application, the values of the metrics LCC, CDAC, CDAI, OOBC, and CIBC (see Sect. 11.5.2) tend to decrease. Taking into account the *SMSTransfer* feature, there was a beneficial change in the values of LCC and CIBC of this feature, indicating that the *SMSTransfer* cohesion increased and its interlacing with other features decreased. Furthermore, this operator can contribute to deflating overloaded components, such as *MediaCtrl* in the example of Fig. 11.8. Hence, this operator also impacts metrics related to size, elegance, coupling, and cohesion.

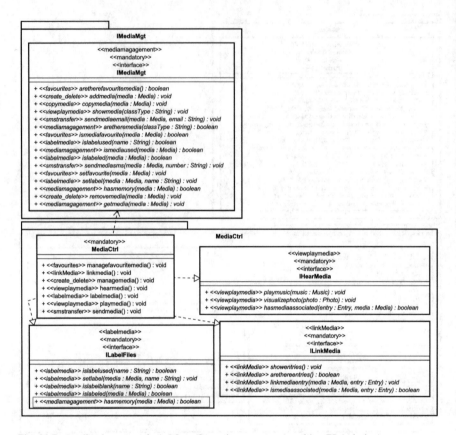

Fig. 11.7 Application example 1: Move Operation operator (resulting PLA design)

In general, the solutions generated by MOA4PLA using OPLA-Tool after the complete optimization process have features less tangled and scattered than the original PLA design (Fig. 11.4) which leads to lower feature-based cohesion and lower coupling. Such kind of optimization in the PLA design is provided by the search operators related to feature modularization: *Feature-driven Mutation Operator* and *Feature-driven Crossover Operator*.

To illustrate this, Fig. 11.9 shows an excerpt of one solution generated by MOA4PLA during the optimization of objective functions related to conventional and feature-driven metrics: CM and FM (see Sect. 11.5.2). It is possible to see that there are components to modularize the features *create_delete* and *viewplayMedia* in the system layer (components with the suffix Ctrl). In this solution (Fig. 11.9), $SMSTransfer$ was modularized into $Component3679Ctrl$ increasing feature-based cohesion of the features *create_delete* and *viewplayMedia*. Operations associated with *linkMedia* are

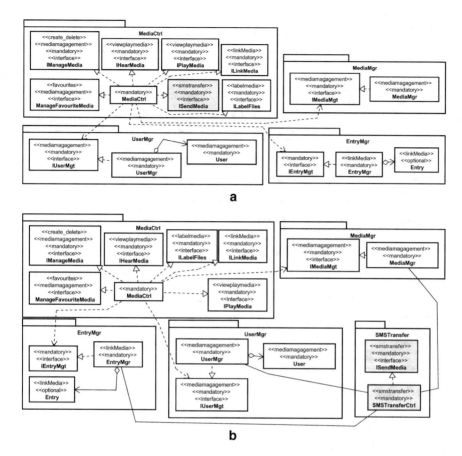

Fig. 11.8 Application example 2: *Feature-driven Mutation Operator.* (**a**) Excerpt of the original PLA design. (**b**) Resulting PLA design

not shown to improve the design readability, but they were modularized into another component. Furthermore, there are other points in this solution (not shown here) in favor of MOA4PLA, which means that MOA4PLA can generate solutions better than the original PLA design given as input to the optimization. Architectural element names such as $Interface2510$ were automatically generated by feature-driven mutation operator and should be redefined by the architect before the PLA design adoption.

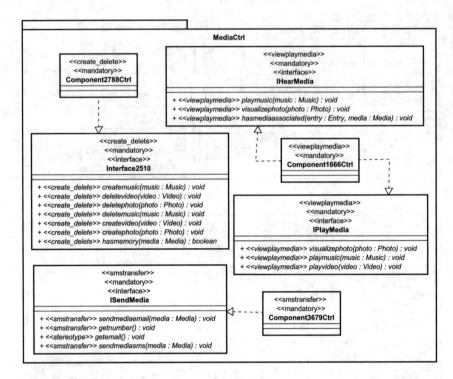

Fig. 11.9 Application example 3: *Feature-driven Mutation* and *Feature-driven Crossover Operators*

11.7   Final Remarks

This chapter presented MOA4PLA, a systematic and computer-aided approach to improve PLA design. The approach treats the PLA design as a multi-objective problem, to be solved by search-based algorithms. It includes a meta-model to represent the PLAs, thus allowing direct transformations of the original PLA design by the algorithms. It encompasses search operators to produce such transformations in order to improve PLA design, especially for feature modularization improvement. MOA4PLA includes an evaluation model, which is composed by conventional and feature-driven metrics, to evaluate the solutions.

MOA4PLA generates PLA designs with lower scattered and lower interlaced features than the original PLAs provided as input to the approach. Hence, the approach has the potential to contribute to reducing the SPL architect's effort to obtain and evaluate PLA designs with respect to feature modularization, PLA reusability and extensibility, and conventional architectural properties, such as coupling, cohesion, and size.

Acknowledgments This work is supported by the Brazilian funding agencies CNPq (Grants 428994/2018-0 and 305968/2018-1) and CAPES (Grant 88887.464499/2019-00).

References

1. Aleti, A., Buhnova, B., Grunske, L., Koziolek, A., Meedeniya, I.: Software architecture optimization methods: a systematic literature review. IEEE Trans. Softw. Eng. **39**(5), 658–683 (2013)
2. Andrade, S.S., Macêdo, R.J.A.: A search-based approach for architectural design of feedback control concerns in self-adaptive systems. In: 2013 IEEE 7th International Conference on Self-Adaptive and Self-Organizing Systems, pp. 61–70. IEEE, Philadelphia, PA (2013)
3. Apel, S., Beyer, D.: Feature cohesion in software product lines: An exploratory study. In: Proceedings of the International Conference on Software Engineering (ICSE'11), pp. 421–430 (2011)
4. Arrieta, A., Wang, S., Sagardui, G., Etxeberria, L.: Search-based test case selection of cyber-physical system product lines for simulation-based validation. In: Mei, H. (ed.) Proceedings of the 20th International Systems and Software Product Line Conference, SPLC 2016, Beijing, September 16–23, 2016, pp. 297–306 (2016)
5. Assunção, W.K., Lopez-Herrejon, R.E., Linsbauer, L., Vergilio, S.R., Egyed, A.: Multi-objective reverse engineering of variability-safe feature models based on code dependencies of system variants. Empir. Softw. Eng. **22**(4), 1763–1794 (2017)
6. Assunção, W.K., Lopez-Herrejon, R.E., Linsbauer, L., Vergilio, S.R., Egyed, A.: Reengineering legacy applications into software product lines: a systematic mapping. Empir. Softw. Eng. **22**(6), 2972–3016 (2017)
7. Bowman, M., Briand, L.C., Labiche, Y.: Solving the class responsibility assignment problem in object-oriented analysis with multi-objective genetic algorithms. IEEE Trans. Softw. Eng. **36**(6), 817–837 (2010)
8. Chang, S.H., La, H.J., Kim, S.D.: Key issues and metrics for evaluating product line architectures. In: Proceedings of the 18th International Conference on Software Engineering & Knowledge Engineering (SEKE), pp. 212–219 (2006)
9. Coello, C.A.C., Lamont, G.B., Veldhuizen, D.A.V.: Evolutionary Algorithms for Solving Multi-Objective Problems, 2nd edn. Springer, New York (2007)
10. Colanzi, T.E., Vergilio, S.R.: Applying search based optimization to software product line architectures: Lessons learned. In: Symposium on Search Based Software Engineering (SSBSE'12), vol. 7515, pp. 259–266 (2012)
11. Colanzi, T.E., Vergilio, S.R.: Representation of software product line architectures for search-based design. In: Proceedings of the 1st International Workshop on Combining Modelling and Search-Based Software Engineering (CMSBSE), ICSE'13, pp. 28–33 (2013)
12. Colanzi, T.E., Vergilio, S.R.: A feature-driven crossover operator for multi-objective and evolutionary optimization of product line architectures. J. Syst. Softw. **121**, 126–143 (2016)
13. Colanzi, T., Vergilio, S., Gimenes, I.M.S., Oizumi, W.N.: A search-based approach for software product line design. In: International Systems and Software Product Line Conference, SPLC 2014, pp. 237–241 (2014)
14. Colanzi, T.E., Assunção, W.K., Vergilio, S.R., Farah, P.R., Guizzo, G.: The symposium on search-based software engineering: past, present and future. Inf. Softw. Technol. **127**, Article 106372 (2020)
15. Contieri Jr, A.C., Correia, G.G., Colanzi, T.E., Gimenes, I.M., OliveiraJr, E., Ferrari, S., Masiero, P.C., Garcia, A.F.: Extending uml components to develop software product-line architectures: Lessons learned. In: Proceedings of the 5th European Conference on Software Architecture (ECSA), pp. 130–138 (2011)

16. Czarnecki, K.: Variability in software: State of the art and future directions. In: International Conference on Fundamental Approaches to Software Engineering, FASE'13, pp. 1–5 (2013)

17. Deb, K.; Pratap, A.; Agarwal, S.; Meyarivan, T.: A fast and elitist multiobjective genetic algorithm: NSGA-II. IEEE Trans. Evol. Comput. **6**(2), 182 –197 (2002). https://doi.org/ 10.1109/4235.996017

18. Federle, E. L.: A Tool to Support the Design of Software Product Line Architecture. (In Portuguese) Master's thesis, Federal University of Parana, Brazil (2014)

19. Figueiredo, E., Cacho, N., Sant'Anna, C., Monteiro, M., Kulesza, U., Garcia, A., Soares, S., Ferrari, F., Khan, S., Castor Filho, F., Dantas, F.: Evolving software product lines with aspects: An empirical study on design stability. In: Proceedings of the International Conference on Software Engineering (ICSE'08), pp. 261–270. ACM (2008)

20. Figueiredo, E.; Sant'Anna, C.; Garcia, A.; Lucena, C.: Applying and evaluating concern-sensitive design heuristics. J. Syst. Softw. **85**(2), 227–243 (2012)

21. Freire, W.M., Massago, M., Zavadski, A.C., Amaral, A.M.M.M., Colanzi, T.E.: OPLA-Tool v2.0: A tool for product line architecture design optimization. In: Proceedings of the Brazilian Symposium on Software Engineering, SBES 2020. ACM, New York (2020)

22. Garcia, J., Popescu, D., Edwards, G., Medvidovic, N.: Toward a catalogue of architectural bad smells. In: Proceedings of the 5th International Conference on the Quality of Software Architectures (QoSA), pp. 146–162. Springer, Berlin (2009)

23. Harman, M., Mansouri, S.A., Zhang, Y.: Search-based software engineering: trends, techniques and applications. ACM Comput. Surveys **45**, 1, Article 11 (2012)

24. Harman, M., Jia, Y., Krinke, J., Langdon, W.B., Petke, J., Zhang, Y.: Search based software engineering for software product line engineering: a survey and directions for future work (keynote paper). In: International Systems and Software Product Line Conference, SPLC 2014, SPLC '14, pp. 5–18 (2014)

25. Kang, K.C., Cohen, S., Hess, J.A., Novak, W.E., Peterson, A.S.: Feature-Oriented Domain Analysis (FODA) Feasibility Study. Technical Report CMU/SEI-90-TR-21 SEI CMU (1990) http://resources.sei.cmu.edu/library/asset-view.cfm?AssetID=11231

26. Karimpour, R., Ruhe, G.: Bi-criteria genetic search for adding new features into an existing product line. In: 2013 1st International Workshop on Combining Modelling and Search-Based Software Engineering (CMSBSE), ICSE'13, pp. 34–38 (2013)

27. Linden, F.v.d., Schmid, F., Rommes, E.: Software Product Lines in Action: The Best Industrial Practice in Product Line Engineering. Springer, Berlin (2007)

28. Lopez-Herrejon, R.E., Linsbauer, L., Egyed, A.: A systematic mapping study of search-based software engineering for software product lines. Inf. Softw. Technol. **61**, 33–51 (2015)

29. OliveiraJr, E., Gimenes, I.M.S., Maldonado, J.C., Masiero, P.C., Barroca, L.: Systematic evaluation of software product line architectures. J. Univer. Comput. Sci. **19**, 25–52 (2013)

30. Pareto, V.: Manuel D'Economie Politique. Ams Press, Paris (1927)

31. Räihä, O.: A survey on search-based software design. Comput. Sci. Rev. **4**(4), 203–249 (2010)

32. Räihä, O., Koskimies, K., Mäkinen, E.: Generating software architecture spectrum with multi-objective genetic algorithms. In: 2011 Third World Congress on Nature and Biologically Inspired Computing (NaBIC), pp. 29–36 (2011)

33. Ramírez, A., Romero, J.R., Ventura, S.: On the performance of multiple objective evolutionary algorithms for software architecture discovery. In: Proceedings of the 2014 Annual Conference on Genetic and Evolutionary Computation, GECCO '14, pp. 1287–1294. ACM, New York (2014)

34. Saber, T., Brevet, D., Botterweck, G., Ventresque, A.: Is seeding a good strategy in multi-objective feature selection when feature models evolve? Inf. Softw. Technol. **95**, 266–280 (2018)

35. Sant'Anna, C.N.: On the modularity of aspect-oriented design: A concern-driven measurement approach. Ph.D. Thesis, PUC-Rio, Brazil (2008)

36. Sant'Anna, C., Figueiredo, E., Garcia, A., Lucena, C.J.P.: On the modularity of software architectures: A concern-driven measurement framework. In: Proceedings of the 1st European Conference on Software Architecture (ECSA), pp. 207–224 (2007)

37. Segura, S., Parejo, J.A., Hierons, R.M., Benavides, D., Ruiz-Cortés, A.: Automated generation of computationally hard feature models using evolutionary algorithms. Expert Syst. Appl. **41**(8), 3975–3992 (2014)
38. Simons, C., Parmee, I., Gwynllyw, R.: Interactive, evolutionary search in upstream object-oriented class design. IEEE Trans. Softw. Eng. **36**(6), 798–816 (2010)
39. SPLC: Product line hall of fame (2021). http://www.splc.net/fame.html
40. Wang, S., Ali, S., Gotlieb, A.: Minimizing test suites in software product lines using weight-based genetic algorithms. In: Proceedings of the 15th Annual Conference on Genetic and Evolutionary Computation, GECCO '13, pp. 1493–1500. ACM, New York (2013)
41. Wüst, J.: SDMetrics (2020). Available at http://www.sdmetrics.com/
42. Xiang, Y., Zhou, Y., Zheng, Z., Li, M.: Configuring software product lines by combining many-objective optimization and SAT solvers. ACM Trans. Softw. Eng. Methodol. **26**(4), 1–46 (2018)
43. Young, T.: Using AspectJ to build a software product line for mobile devices. Master's Thesis, University of British Columbia (2005)

Chapter 12
Preventing Feature Interaction with Optimization Algorithms

Luciane Nicolodi Baldo, Aline M. M. Miotto Amaral, Edson OliveiraJr, and Thelma Elita Colanzi

Abstract Feature interaction (FI) can be defined as a situation in which a feature influences positively or negatively on the behavior of another feature. The FI problem has been a challenging subject for decades because it is not easy to predict, identify, and resolve interactions among features. A common occurrence is the impact of a feature on another one, leading to unexpected behavior, for instance, a feature can influence, activate, or replace the behavior of other feature, or even an unwanted behavior, known as bad feature interaction. In this chapter, we present an approach to identify possible feature interaction in the software product-line architecture design as well as an automatic way to prevent feature interaction by means of search-based algorithms. Such kind of algorithm is used to improve the feature modularization degree of the product-line architecture leading to low feature interaction on the architectural elements.

12.1 Introduction

Each product of a software product line (SPL) is derived through a configuration of features. To achieve an efficient delivery of an SPL product, its features have to work in harmony, i.e., the features have to be compatible with each other [29]. Otherwise, issues related to feature interaction might arise and affect the SPL product, leading to unexpected behaviors. "A feature interaction is a situation in which two or more features exhibit unexpected behavior that does not occur when the features are used in isolation" [2]. Such unexpected behaviors can be, for instance, the interference, the activation, or the replacement of the effect of other features. "While it is easy to identify the behavior of a feature in isolation, specifying and resolving interactions among features may not be a straightforward task" [20]. In the literature, undesired feature interactions are also called as "feature interference" or "bad

L. N. Baldo · A. M. M. M. Amaral · E. OliveiraJr · T. E. Colanzi (✉)
State University of Maringá, Informatics Department, Maringá, PR, Brazil
e-mail: ammmamaral@uem.br; edson@din.uem.br; thelma@din.uem.br

© Springer Nature Switzerland AG 2023
E. OliveiraJr (ed), *UML-Based Software Product Line Engineering with SMarty*,
https://doi.org/10.1007/978-3-031-18556-4_12

feature interaction." We will simply use the expression "feature interactions" (FI) when referring to unwanted interactions.

It is possible to certify that all the interactions are known and properly resolved by generating each valid product configuration. However, as soon as the number of features of an SPL grows, it becomes increasingly difficult to identify and resolve all the interactions. The number of feature interaction candidates is exponential in the number of features, and this statement is known as the feature interaction problem [4].

On the other hand, FI could be analyzed in domain engineering to anticipate unwanted interaction between features, before the selection of features for the configuration of specific products. Some approaches to detect and resolve FI in domain engineering are based on behavioral models, requirement models, or aspect-oriented analysis techniques [1, 6, 20, 24].

The focus of some works is either to modularize features that are scattered in several components or to modularize crosscutting features [1, 24]. A useful artifact to identify such kind of situation is the product-line architecture (PLA) because it encompasses a common design to all the SPL products including variable and mandatory features. However, to the best of our knowledge, there are no works that deal with such possibility. The FI detection in a PLA design and preventive actions are ways to soften the FI problem before the PLA instantiation to the product generation.

This chapter presents a strategy to detect and prevent potential FI in PLA design—represented in UML class diagrams—with the goal of taking early preventive actions in the domain engineering in order to soften unexpected behavior (see Sect. 12.3). This strategy includes an initial set of points where it is likely to find potential feature interactions. The strategy focus is the logical view of the PLA since it captures implementation concerns, with traceability links to the feature model and SPL products. The logical view describes the main classes of the design with their organization in service packages and subsystems [10].

The strategy is based on two patterns whose goal is identifying the set of classes and the set of features that are likely to be involved in a potential FI. Furthermore, for each pattern, we present steps to modularize the identified features in an alternative design in order to prevent FI in the products or, at least, to ease the analysis of potential FI since the features will be better modularized in the PLA design. The assumption underlying the strategy is that the better the feature modularization, the easier to detect and prevent the FI occurrence. For instance, classes or packages that comprise more than one feature are architectural elements prone to FI. Considering that a feature is a concern in an SPL, this assumption is corroborated by Zhang et al. [30] which states that the lack of systematically handling of crosscutting concerns leads to scattering and tangling in the architectural elements, which affects the components and connectors and makes the final architecture solution complex and uneasy to understand. Therefore, it is even more crucial to separate the crosscutting concerns at the architecture level that would form suitable approach for identifying, representing, and composing all the concerns.

We implemented our strategy as part of MOA4PLA, a search-based approach described in Chap. 11. An example of the application of our strategy in the SPL Mobile Media is presented in Sect. 12.4. The necessary concepts to understand the strategy as well as related work are presented in the next section.

12.2 Background

This section briefly describes approaches to detect and resolve FI as well as PLA design optimization with search-based algorithms.

12.2.1 Approaches to Detect and Resolve Feature Interaction

Feature interaction has been widely discussed in the telecommunications domain [29]. However, it has been recognized as a general problem in different fields, including software engineering, and the goal is to predict, detect, and resolve interactions [29]. A widespread feature interaction example is related to the features *call waiting* and *call forwarding* of a telephone system. When both are present at the same time, the system behavior is ill-defined. Call waiting allows managing two interleaved calls—one is suspended, while another one is being answered. Call forwarding requires specifying a phone number to forward new calls that arrive when the phone is busy. If these features are used together, and a new call is received when the phone is busy, it does not know how to proceed: it can either forward or suspend the new call. FI can cause unexpected situations and may even go against the system specification [7].

In the literature, there are several approaches to detect and resolve FI in SPL engineering [29]. Around 40% of them deal with FI in the code level (e.g., [25–28]). Other ones use different SPL models, such as use case or state models, to detect, analyze, and resolve FI (e.g., [1, 21]). Several studies focus on the FI detection in the domain engineering, including domain analysis, specification, design, and implementation, and, in the application engineering, studies are concentrated in the product configuration and generation [3, 6, 8, 9, 11, 15, 18, 27]. Studies that focus on the domain engineering are more related to ours. However, the majority of them verify behavior models or dependency models, such as [21, 24].

Liu et al. [21], for instance, analyze fault trees to detect FI in safety-critical SPL. Firstly, the architectural behavioral nodes are detected, considering that each node represents the behavior of one feature. Secondly, each feature is modeled in a state diagram. When a new feature appears in a node previously modeled, the state diagram must be updated. The DECIMAL tool is used to analyze the dependency violations between the SPL features.

Razzaq and Abbasi [24] use aspect-oriented techniques to analyze how features are related in the SPL. Their goal is to provide separation of concerns at the feature level. To accomplish such a goal, they identify features that have crosscutting relations with other features using dependency models aiming at providing early feature modularization and separation of concerns. In the work of Mosser et al. [22], the way an interaction is resolved is considered as a variation point in the configuration process. Thus, they help developers to resolve FI during the product configuration. They use the feature model and dependency model to identify the feature interactions. Kato et al.'s work [19] aims to detect FI using a feature model and a mapping between features and components. For each derived product, each new FI is documented in a cumulative approach to simplify the product configuration process.

Our work is also focused on domain engineering, but it does not include product configuration activities as in the previously mentioned studies. Meantime, we rely on the orthogonal relation between features and components/classes as well as in [19]. Similar to the proposal presented in [24], our strategy is concerned with feature modularization. However, our focus is on the design (classes) level, and theirs is on the requirements (feature) level.

Alférez et al. [1] also addressed the FI detection at the requirements level. Two FI detection strategies are discussed in their work. The first one presents a catalog of patterns that includes the possibilities of interference of more than one feature in a particular use case, taking into account the *includes* and *extends* relationships to identify feature dependencies as potential points to the FI occurrence. The second strategy aims at detecting feature overlapping in behavioral models. They use UML use case and activity models to model the requirements behavior of each feature. They aim to find the specific model elements in the whole set of the activity models, in which the behavior of one feature influences the behavior expressed in the models of other features.

Similar to [1], we also have patterns to identify potential FI despite our patterns being applied to the UML class model in our strategy. We decide to focus on PLA design because it allows traceability between the feature model and the SPL products. Furthermore, the classes of the logical view of the PLA design capture implementation issues that can impact the product architecture. Despite the common characteristics with related work, such as traceability link between features and models elements (use case, components, etc.) [1, 19], detection of potential FI [1, 19, 21, 22, 24], and focus on feature modularization [24], our work also suggests steps to achieve an alternative design to obtain pieces of PLA less prone to the FI occurrence during the product generation. Our strategy is presented in Sect. 12.3. The next section addresses the main concepts of an approach to PLA design optimization, which was used to implement our strategy.

12.2.2 PLA Design Optimization

The approach named *Multi-Objective Approach for Product-Line Architecture Design* (MOA4PLA) [12] optimizes PLA design by means of multi-objective search algorithms. MOA4PLA, described in detail in Chapter 11, does not deal with the FI problem. However, it evaluates a PLA design given as input and generates improved alternative PLA designs. MOA4PLA can be extended to implement the strategy introduced in this chapter (see next section) because potential FI can be identified and alternative solutions can be generated to soften the FI problem during the PLA design optimization.

In MOA4PLA [12], the PLA design is treated as an optimization problem to be solved by search algorithms, as happens in the research field named search-based software engineering [17]. Software metrics are used in the objective functions that guide the search algorithm. The metrics provide indicators of several architectural properties. At the end of the optimization process, the algorithm returns a set of solutions that are alternative designs to the PLA given as input. This set contains the solutions with the best trade-off between the objectives that were optimized, being different modeling possibilities for the PLA design.

The mutation operator named feature-driven operator, presented in Chap. 11, is one of the search operators of MOA4PLA specific for the PLA design domain. This operator aims to modularize a feature tangled in a component, considering that a feature is usually realized by a group of architectural elements. This operator helps to obtain PLA designs with less scattered and tangled features, improving the feature cohesion of the architectural components. This operator plays an important role in our strategy since it improves feature modularization at the component level contributing to preventing potential FI.

The tool named OPLA-Tool [16] automates the application of MOA4PLA. It is an open-source tool that was extended to implement our strategy to prevent potential FI.

12.2.3 The Role of SMarty in This Work

SMarty is used in this work to manage the variabilities of the SPL in the PLA design. As our strategy is an extension of MOA4PLA, the role of SMarty is the same described in Chap. 11.

MOA4PLA uses SMarty to represent variabilities in PLA design. This approach applies the following SMarty stereotypes:

- *«variability»*, an extension of the UML meta-class Comment, which represents the concept of SPL variability;
- *«variationPoint»*, an extension of the meta-classes Actor, UseCase, Class, and Interface, which represents the variation points;
- *«variant»*, an extension of the meta-classes Actor, UseCase, and Class, which represents the variants. The variant stereotype is specialized in four non-abstract variants, *«mandatory»*, *«optional»*, *«alternative_OR»*, and *«alternative_XOR»*;

- *«mutex»* to represent the concept of exclusion constraint between two variants;
- *«requires»* to represent the concept of inclusion constraint between two variants.

12.3   A Search-Based Approach to Prevent Feature Interaction

This section presents the strategy proposed to detect and prevent FI in the logical view of PLA design represented using class diagrams. When conceiving the strategy, we assumed that the decrease of feature tangling in the PLA design contributes to softening the FI problem. The strategy includes (a) two patterns to detect an initial set of pieces of PLA design where there are feature tangling (such pieces are considered potential elements to the FI occurrence) and (b) suggestions to change those pieces of design detected by the patterns as they are prone to the FI occurrence to decrease feature tangling.

The patterns to detect FI and the actions suggested preventing FI are presented in Sects. 12.3.1 and 12.3.2. Some implementation aspects of our strategy are addressed in Sect. 12.3.3.

12.3.1   Potential Feature Interaction Detection Patterns

Kato and Yamaguchi [19] noticed that there is some kind of orthogonal relation between features and components/classes. Considering this statement and taking into account some PLA designs, related work, and the FI definition [2], we realize that it is possible to happen some interaction among the realized features when one class realizes more than one feature, which might be a potential FI problem during the PLA design optimization. Such an observation inspired two potential FI detection patterns for the classes context: (1) *Pattern of Class Detection* (PCD), when two or more features are realized by the same class, and (2) *Pattern of Inheritance Detection* (PID), when two or more features are realized by the superclass and one or more features are realized by a subclass of this superclass. In the case of the latter pattern, the subclass inherits the architectural elements of its superclass becoming a candidate to the FI occurrence.

Figure 12.1 depicts generic examples of both patterns. In Fig. 12.1a, the PCD pattern is illustrated in Class1 which have attributes and methods to realize two features, *«feature1»* and *«feature2»*, denoted in the picture using UML stereotypes. As both features have different behavior, this is a candidate situation to the occurrence of some FI, because it is possible that the elements of Class1 interfere with the expected behavior of each feature.

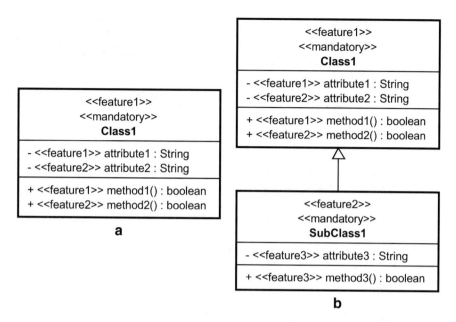

Fig. 12.1 Illustration of the FI detection patterns. (**a**) PCD. (**b**) PID

The PID pattern is illustrated in Fig. 12.1b. The superclass Class1 realizes *«feature1»* and *«feature2»*, and the subclass SubClass1 realizes *«feature3»*. By means of the inheritance, the subclass inherits the superclass's attributes and methods. Thus, SubClass1 is the design point prone to the FI occurrence since it inherits the behavior of *«feature1»* and *«feature2»*. Hence, there may be feature interaction among the three features in SubClass1.

12.3.2 Feature Interaction Preventive Actions

In the context of our strategy, the preventive action to soften the FI occurrence is improving the modularity of the features tangled with other ones in the context of the PCD and PID patterns. For doing that, the strategy suggests the creation of new classes to realize every single feature in the pieces of design prone to the FI occurrence.

The steps suggested as preventive actions to be applied when the PCD pattern is detected are presented below. These steps aim to improve the feature modularization in the piece of design where PCD was identified. Hereafter, we refer to this set of steps as **PCD pattern resolution**:

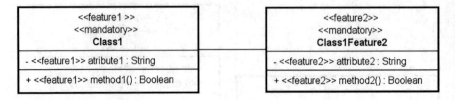

Fig. 12.2 PCD pattern resolution

1. Select the feature realized by the largest number of architectural elements (methods and attributes). In case of a tie between the number of elements, select the first feature found with the largest number of architectural elements;
2. Keep in the source class all architectural elements that realize the feature selected in Step 1;
3. Create a new class using the name format:
   source class name + name of the feature to be modularized;
4. Move to the new class all architectural elements that realize the feature being extracted from the source class;
5. Insert a bidirectional association between the new class and the source class;
6. Repeat Steps 3–5 while the source class contains architectural elements to realize at least two features.

In Fig. 12.2, we illustrate the PCD pattern resolution for the original design of Class1 presented in Fig. 12.2a. Following the steps of the PCD pattern resolution, «feature1» is selected in Step 1, and the architectural elements that realize «feature1» are maintained in Class1. In Step 3, a new class named Class1Feature2 is created, and attribute2 and method2 are moved to Class1Feature2 (Step 4). In Step 5, an association between Class1Feature2 and Class1 is added, achieving the design presented in Fig. 12.2.

Regarding the **PID pattern resolution**, the suggested steps for modifying the design in order to improve the feature modularization are:

1. Search for common homonym elements (attributes and methods) between the superclass and the subclass(es). If homonym elements are found, stop the steps application to prevent damages in procedures, such as method overriding or overloading;
2. Select the feature realized by the largest number of architectural elements of the superclass. In case of a tie between the number of elements, select the first feature found with the largest number of elements;
3. Keep in the superclass all architectural elements that realize the feature selected in Step 2;

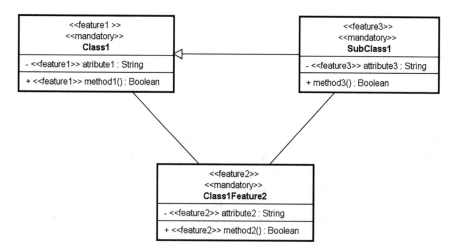

Fig. 12.3 PID pattern resolution

4. Create a new class using the name format:
   <u>superclass name + name of the feature to be modularized</u>;
5. Move to the new class all architectural elements that realize the feature being extracted from the superclass;
6. Insert a bidirectional association between the new class and the superclass;
7. Insert a unidirectional association from the subclass to the new class;
8. Repeat Steps 4–8, while the source class contains architectural elements to realize at least two features.

In Fig. 12.3, we illustrate the PID pattern resolution for the original design of Class1 and SubClass1 presented in Fig. 12.3. As no homonym element was identified in Step 1, in Step 2, *«feature1»* is selected to be maintained in Class1. In Step 4, a new class named Class1Feature2 is created, and attribute2 and method2 are moved to Class1Feature2 (Step 5). An association between Class1Feature2 and Class1 is added in Step 6, and a unidirectional association between SubClass1 and Class1Feature2 is added in Step 7. Thus, feature2 is modularized in Class1Feature2 without interference in the inheritance between Class1 and SubClass1. The class SubClass1 still accesses method2 of Class1Feature2 by the new association.

Regarding the homonym elements, a possible solution would be multiple inheritance. Thus, *«feature1»* and *«feature2»* could be modularized in different superclasses, and SubClass1 inherits architectural elements from both superclasses. However, such a solution is not feasible for all SPL since several programming languages do not implement multiple inheritance. This alternative is not addressed in the scope of the present work.

12.3.3   Implementation Aspects

The strategy could be manually applied, but this task could be unfeasible for a real PLA design due to the design size. An automatic application is better, which is corroborated by Soares et al. [29] who stated that tools would suggest ways to resolve the detected FI to developers.

Thus, an implementation alternative to our strategy would be to write an exact (deterministic) algorithm to apply the steps to detect the PCD and PID patterns and suggest an alternative design to prevent the potential detected FI to developers. On the other hand, the MOA4PLA approach (see Sect. 12.2.2) uses multiobjective search-based algorithms to generate alternatives of PLA design that optimize the selected objectives, including feature modularization. Furthermore, this approach contains a mutation operator to improve feature modularization at the component level: the *feature-driven operator*. After a previous analysis of the PLA designs generated by MOA4PLA in the study of Perissato et al. [23], no potential FI was found at the component level. We infer that this is due to the *feature-driven operator*. However, such an operator does not change feature modularization at the class level as it is proposed in this work.

Similar to the *feature-driven operator*, the implementation of our strategy was conceived as a new search operator to be added to MOA4PLA, named *feature-driven operator for class*. In this operator, a class is randomly selected, and, if it has elements to realize more than one feature, the steps of the PCD and PID patterns are performed in order to find pieces of design willing to become a FI. The pseudocode of this operator is presented in Algorithm 1. A is the PLA design given as input. In line 3, C_x class is randomly selected from the C set which contains all classes of A. In line 4, the number of features realized by elements of A is verified. If A realizes more than one feature and it is a superclass (line 5), the steps related to PID pattern are performed (line 6). If A realizes more than one feature, but it has no subclasses (line 8), the steps of the PCD pattern are performed (line 9).

The pseudocode for PID and PCD pattern resolutions is presented in Algorithms 2 and 3, respectively. Regarding the PID pattern, the algorithm searches for homonym elements in either superclass or subclasses (line 3). The execution is stopped if homonym elements are found. Otherwise, the feature (F_s) that is realized by the highest number of elements of C_x is verified (line 4); in line 7, new class(es) NC_x is(are) created to modularize every other feature; an appropriate name is given to each NC_x class, and the elements (attributes/methods) are moved to NC_x (line 8); new relationships are added between C_x and NC_x classes (line 9); and in line 10, new relationship is added between each subclass and the new class NCx.

The pseudocode for the PCD pattern resolution (Algorithm 3) searches for the feature (F_s) that is realized by the highest number of elements of C_x (line 2). In line 5, new class(es) NC_x is(are) created to modularize every other feature; an appropriate name is given to each NC_x class, and the elements (attributes/methods) are moved to NC_x (line 6); and new relationships are added between C_x and NC_x (line 7).

Algorithm 1: Pseudocode for FI detection

```
1  begin
2  |    C ← A.getAllClasses()
3  |    Cx ← randomly selected class from C
4  |    Fc ← Cx.getAllFeatures()
5  |    if (Fc.size()>1) and (Cx is a superclass) then
6  |    |    run PID(Fc, Cx)
7  |    else
8  |    |    if (Fc.size()>1) then
9  |    |    |    run PCD(Fc, Cx)
10 |    return A
11 end
```

Algorithm 2: Pseudocode for the PID pattern resolution

```
1  begin
2  |    SBx ← Cx.getAllSubclasses()
3  |    if !(isThereHomonymElements(Cx, SBx)) then
4  |    |    Fs ← findFeatureWithHighestElementsNumber(Cx)
5  |    |    Fc ← Fc − Fs
6  |    |    for each Fx ∈ Fc do
7  |    |    |    NCx ← createClass(Cx.getName()+Fx.getName())
8  |    |    |    Move elements that realizes Fx to NCx
9  |    |    |    A.AddRelationship(Cx, NCx)
10 |    |    |    for each subClass ∈ SBx do
11 |    |    |    |    A.AddRelationship(subClass, NCx)
12 |    |    |    end for
13 |    |    end for
14 end
```

Algorithm 3: Pseudocode for the PCD pattern resolution

```
1  begin
2  |    Fs ← findFeatureWithHighestElementsNumber(Cx)
3  |    Fc ← Fc − Fs
4  |    for each Fx ∈ Fc do
5  |    |    NCx ← createClass(Cx.getName()+Fx.getName())
6  |    |    Move elements that realizes Fx to NCx
7  |    |    A.AddRelationship(Cx, NCx)
8  |    end for
9  end
```

Given the non-determinism of search algorithms, there is a randomness factor in the search operators application. In the context of MOA4PLA, the application of the search operator *feature-driven operator for class* would be in randomly selected classes. The evolutionary aspect of genetic algorithms used by MOA4PLA can lead to feature modularization at class level over generations, which combined with the *feature-driven operator* application can significantly impact the FI prevention.

12.4   Application Example

In this section, we present excerpts of the PLA design obtained for Mobile Media after running an experiment using our strategy implemented as a search operator of MOA4PLA.

Such an experiment was carried out using the algorithm NSGA-II [14] available at MOA4PLA. NSGA-II was executed using the population size of 200 individuals, and the fitness evaluation number equals to 30,000 (300 generations), which was the stopping criterion. We executed 30 independent runs, as recommended by Arcuri and Fraser [5]. All the search operators of MOA4PLA were applied together with the *feature-driven operator for class* that implements our strategy. The objective functions optimized during the optimization process were related to feature modularization and class coupling because they are the most relevant architectural properties for the context and goal of our strategy.

The solution analyzed in this section is that one that has the best trade-off between the optimized objectives, i.e., the solution that has the best balance between maximizing the feature modularization and minimizing the class coupling. In comparison with the original design of Mobile Media [13], given as input to the experiment, ten features are better modularized, namely, *«labelMedia»*, *«create_Delete»*, *«favourites»*, *«albumManagement»*, *«viewPlayMedia»*, *«photo»*, *«copyMedia»*, *«music»*, *«smsTransfer»*, and *«video»*, in the optimized solution.

Figure 12.4 shows an example of such situation involving the IManageMedia interface, where the action of *feature-driven operator for class* for PCD pattern is noticed. Figure 12.4a presents the original version of the referred interface, where the IManageMedia class had only methods to realize two features. These features are represented using the UML stereotypes *«mediaManagement»* and *«create_Delete»*. The design of the optimized solution is depicted in Fig. 12.4b, where it is possible to see that the *«mediaManagement»* feature is modularized in the IManageMedia interface. The IManageMediaCreateDelete inter-face was created to modularize the *«create_Delete»* feature. It is important to observe that all interfaces in Fig. 12.4 have the mandatory stereotype. All the methods associated with *«create_Delete»* were moved from IManageMedia to IManageMediaCreateDelete. Association between IManageMedia and the new IManageMediaCreateDelete class was added.

Figure 12.5 illustrates another excerpt of the design regarding the MediaMgr class of Mobile Media. The original version of the MediaMgr class is depicted in Fig. 12.5a   containing methods to realize three features, represented by the stereotypes *«mediaManagement»*, *«favourites»*, and *«labelMedia»*. Figure 12.5b depicts the design of the optimized design.   The *«mediaManagement»* feature was modularized in the   mediaMgr class.   Two new classes were created (MediaMgrFavourites and MediaMgrLabelMedia) to modularize the *«favourites»* and *«labelMedia»* features. MediaMgrLabelMedia contains the methods associated with *«labelMedia»*.   Similarly,   methods   associated with *«favourites»* were moved to MediaMgrFavourites. New associations were

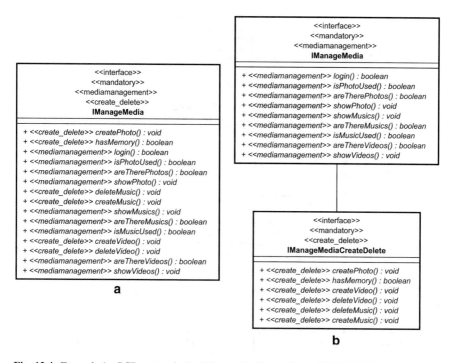

Fig. 12.4 Example 1—PCD pattern in the IManageMedia interface of Mobile Media. (**a**) Original design. (**b**) Optimized design

added between `MediaMgr` and the new classes. In this figure, we can notice the SMarty mandatory stereotype in the `mediaMgr` class.

The third example of the PCD pattern resolution is presented in Fig. 12.6. In the original design, Fig. 12.6a, the `IManageMedia` interface is associated with five features: *«mediaManagement»*, *«create_Delete»*, *«viewPlayMedia, «photo»*, and *«music»*. In the optimized design shown in Fig. 12.6b, most operations of the original interface `IManageMedia` were modularized in four new interfaces: `IManageViewPlayMedia`, `IManageMediaManagement`, `IManageMediaPhoto`, and `IManageMediaMusic`. Two of these new interfaces (`IManageMediaPhoto` and `IManageMediaMusic`) are provided by the new packages `Package54570Ctrl` and `Package54724Ctrl` that were created to modularize the «photo» and «music» features. Both packages were created by *feature-driven operator*—the operator that improves feature modularization at the component level. As this operator creates packages with automatic generated names, the architect needs to rename these packages using meaningful names, at the end of the optimization process.

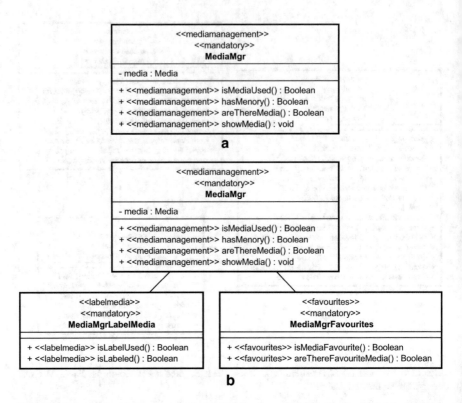

Fig. 12.5 Example 2—PCD pattern in the MediaMgr class of Mobile Media. (**a**) Original design. (**b**) Optimized design

Regarding the PID pattern, we did not observe any instance of its application in the optimized design. Thus, we manually checked the original design searching for opportunities to apply the PID pattern. Only one instance of the PID pattern was detected in original design of Mobile Media. However, only the first step was carried out due to the presence of homonym elements, in this situation. Figure 12.7 depicts an excerpt of the original design of Mobile Media where PID was detected. Such an example shows the Media superclass and its three subclasses. During the application of the first step to resolve PID (see Sect. 12.3.2), homonym methods were found: getMedia. Hence, the original design was maintained in order to avoid damages during the method overriding/overlapping.

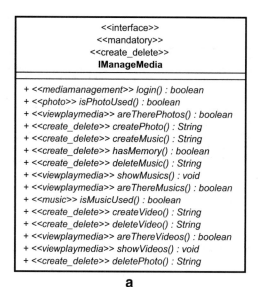

a

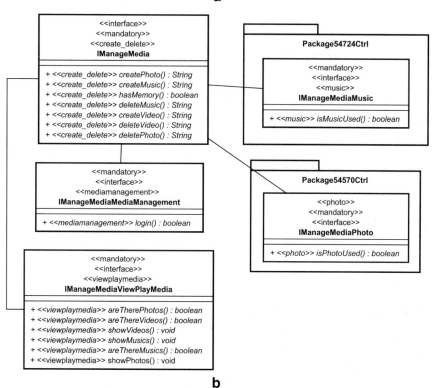

b

Fig. 12.6 Example 3—PCD pattern in the IManageMedia interface of Mobile Media. (**a**) Original design. (**b**) Optimized design

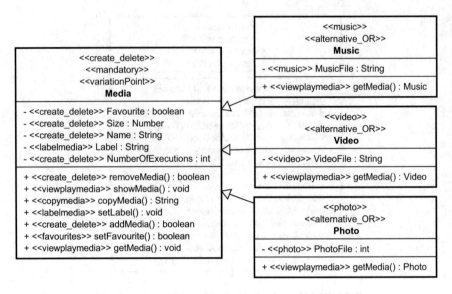

Fig. 12.7 Example 4—PID pattern detected in the Media class of Mobile Media

This design excerpt (Fig. 12.7) depicts a typical variability in SPL. Media is a mandatory class that is also a variation point (notice the SMarty stereotypes *«mandatory»* and *«variationPoint»*). The variants for this variation point are the classes music, video, and photo, which in turn have the SMarty stereotype *«alternative_OR»*, representing variants in a variant set, which can be combined to solve the variability.

Although it was not possible to resolve PID in the PLA design of Mobile Media, we conjecture it can be applicable in other PLA designs.

12.5 Limitations

This section addresses aspects that require further research in the implementation of our strategy.

One principle considered in the conception of our strategy is that the semantics of the design obtained after feature modularization needs to be maintained equals to the original design. As such, we observed that the visibility of attributes and methods needs to be carefully analyzed as well as the type of classes relationships, which can lead to some improvements in the implemented version of our strategy.

We conjecture that an interesting way to modularize the features realized by the Media class (Fig. 12.7) could be multiple inheritance. However, another alternative to resolve the PID pattern is needed because multiple inheritance is not a feasible solution for all programming languages. In the SPL context, a superclass is usually a variation point, whereas its subclasses are the variants, increasing the possibilities to have homonym elements to realize the variant behavior.

Another point to be considered is the inclusion of the SPL developer's opinion about the feature modularization alternatives during the optimization process. The developer approval in certain moments can lead to more appropriate solutions in the context of the SPL under development.

The current implementation of our strategy considers only the proactive SPL development. In further studies, it is necessary to reason about its applicability and adaptation to extractive and reactive development.

12.6 Final Remarks

In this chapter, we presented a strategy to detect and prevent situations that are potential FI in the logical view of the PLA design. The strategy includes either two patterns to detect pieces of design that are likely to the FI occurrence or steps to improve the modularity of the features realized by the classes identified by the FI detection patterns aiming at softening FI during the SPL product generation.

The proposed strategy was implemented as an extension of an optimization approach that uses search-based algorithms. We presented an application example using the PLA design of Mobile Media.

Overall, the main contribution is the early detection of potential FI. This enables taking preventive actions in the domain engineering in order to both (i) minimize the FI occurrence in the product generation in the application engineering and (ii) ease the analysis of feature behavior by improving feature modularization.

Acknowledgement This work is supported by the Brazilian funding agency CNPq (Grant 428994/2018-0).

References

1. Alférez, M., Moreira, A., Kulesza, U., Araújo, J.A., Mateus, R., Amaral, V.: Detecting feature interactions in SPL requirements analysis models. In: Proceedings of the First International Workshop on Feature-Oriented Software Development, FOSD '09, pp. 117–123. ACM, New York (2009)
2. Apel, S., Kästner, C.: An overview of feature-oriented software development. J. Obiect Technol. **8**(5), 49–84 (2009)
3. Apel, S., Scholz, W., Lengauer, C., Kastner, C.: Detecting dependences and interactions in feature-oriented design. In: 2010 IEEE 21st International Symposium on Software Reliability Engineering, pp. 161–170 (2010)
4. Apel, S., Kolesnikov, S., Siegmund, N., Kästner, C., Garvin, B.: Exploring feature interactions in the wild: The new feature-interaction challenge. In: Proceedings of the 5th International Workshop on Feature-Oriented Software Development, FOSD '13, pp. 1–8. ACM, New York (2013)

5. Arcuri, A., Briand, L.: A hitchhiker's guide to statistical tests for assessing randomized algorithms in software engineering. Softw. Testing Verif. Reliab. **24**(3), 219–250 (2014). https://doi.org/10.1002/stvr.1486
6. Bass, L., Clements, P., Kazman, R.: Software Architecture in Practice, 3rd edn. Addison-Wesley Professional, Boston (2012)
7. Batory, D., Höfner, P., Kim, J.: Feature interactions, products, and composition. In: Proceedings of the 10th Intl. Conf. on Generative Programming and Component Engineering, GPCE '11, pp. 13–22. ACM, New York (2011)
8. Ben-David, S., Sterin, B., Atlee, J.M., Beidu, S.: Symbolic model checking of product-line requirements using sat-based methods. In: Proceedings of the 37th International Conference on Software Engineering - Volume 1, ICSE '15, pp. 189–199. IEEE Press, Piscataway, NJ (2015)
9. Blundell, C., Fisler, K., Krishnamurthi, S., Van Hentenrvck, P.: Parameterized interfaces for open system verification of product lines. In: Proceedings of the 19th International Conference on Automated Software Engineering, 2004, pp. 258–267 (2004)
10. Bowen, T.F., Dworack, F.S., Chow, C.H., Griffeth, N., Herman, G.E., Lin, Y..: The feature interaction problem in telecommunications systems. In: 7th International Conference on Software Engineering for Telecommunication Switching Systems, pp. 59–62 (1989)
11. Classen, A., Heymans, P., Schobbens, P.Y.: What's in a feature: A requirements engineering perspective. In: International Conference on Fundamental Approaches to Software Engineering, pp. 16–30 (2008)
12. Colanzi, T.E., Vergilio, S.R., Gimenes, I.M.S., Oizumi, W.N.: A search-based approach for software product line design. In: Proceedings of the 18th International Software Product Line Conference - Volume 1, SPLC '14, pp. 237–241. ACM, New York, NY (2014)
13. ContieriJr, A.C., Correia, G.G., Colanzi, T.E., Gimenes, I.M.S., OliveiraJr, E., Ferrari, S., Masiero, P.C., Garcia, A.F.: Extending UML components to develop software product-line architectures: Lessons learned. In Proceedings of 5th European Conference on Software Architecture pp. 130–138 (2011)
14. Deb, K., Pratap, A., Agarwal, S., Meyarivan, T.: A fast and elitist multiobjective genetic algorithm: Nsga-ii. IEEE Trans. Evolution. Comput. **6**(2), 182–197 (2002)
15. Dietrich, D., Shaker, P., Atlee, J.M., Rayside, D., Gorzny, J.: Feature interaction analysis of the feature-oriented requirements-modelling language using alloy. In: Proceedings of the Workshop on Model-Driven Engineering, Verification and Validation, MoDeVVa '12, pp. 17–22. ACM (2012)
16. Féderle, E.L., do Nascimento Ferreira, T., Colanzi, T.E., Vergilio, S.R.: OPLA-Tool: A support tool for search-based product line architecture design. In: Proceedings of the 19th International Conference on Software Product Line, SPLC '15 pp. 370–373 (2015)
17. Harman, M.: The current state and future of search based software engineering. In: Future of Software Engineering (FOSE '07), pp. 342–357 (2007)
18. Hu, H., Yang, D., Xiang, L.F.H., Sang, C.F.J., Li, C.Y.R.: Semantic Web-based policy interaction detection method with rules in smart home for detecting interactions among user policies. IET Commun. **5**, 2451–2460 (2011)
19. Kato, S., Yamaguchi, N.: Variation management for software product lines with cumulative coverage of feature interactions. In: 2011 15th International Software Product Line Conference, pp. 140–149 (2011)
20. Kim, C.H.P., Kästner, C., Batory, D.: On the modularity of feature interactions. In: Proceedings of the 7th International Conference on Generative Programming and Component Engineering, GPCE '08, pp. 23–34 (2008)
21. Liu, J., Dehlinger, J., Sun, H., Lutz, R.: State-based modeling to support the evolution and maintenance of safety-critical software product lines. In: 14th Annual IEEE International Conference and Workshops on the Engineering of Computer-Based Systems (ECBS'07), pp. 596–608 (2007)

22. Mosser, S., Parra, C., Duchien, L., Blay-Fornarino, M.: Using domain features to handle feature interactions. In: Proceedings of the 6th Intl. Workshop on Variability Modeling of Software-Intensive Systems, VaMoS '12, pp. 101–110. ACM, New York (2012)

23. Perissato, E.G., Choma Neto, J., Colanzi, T.E., Oizumi, W., Garcia, A.: On identifying architectural smells in search-based product line designs. In: Proceedings of the VII Brazilian Symposium on Software Components, Architectures, and Reuse, SBCARS '18, pp. 13–22. ACM (2018)

24. Razzaq, A., Abbasi, R.: Automated separation of crosscutting concerns: Earlier automated identification and modularization of cross-cutting features at analysis phase. In: 2012 15th International Multitopic Conference (INMIC), pp. 471–478 (2012)

25. Rodrigues, I., Ribeiro, M., Medeiros, F., Borba, P., Fonseca, B., Gheyi, R.: Assessing fine-grained feature dependencies. Inf. Softw. Technol. **78**, 27–52 (2016)

26. Santos, A.R., Ivan do Carmo Machado, Almeida, E.S.: RiPLE-HC: Visual support for features scattering and interactions. In: ACM International Conference Proceeding Series, pp. 320–323 (2016)

27. Scholz, W., Thüm, T., Apel, S., Lengauer, C.: Automatic detection of feature interactions using the java modeling language: An experience report. In: Proceedings of the 15th International Software Product Line Conference, Volume 2, SPLC '11, pp. 1–8. ACM, New York (2011)

28. Siegmund, N., Kolesnikov, S.S., Kästner, C., Apel, S., Batory, D., Rosenmüller, M., Saake, G.: Predicting performance via automated feature-interaction detection. In: 34th International Conference on Software Engineering (ICSE), pp. 167–177 (2012)

29. Soares, L.R., Schobbens, P.Y., do Carmo Machado, I., de Almeida, E.S.: Feature interaction in software product line engineering: a systematic mapping study. Inf. Softw. Technol. **98**, 44–58 (2018)

30. Zhang, L., Ying, S., Ni, Y., Wen, J., Zhao, K.: An approach for multi-dimensional separation concerns at architecture level. In: 2008 Workshop on Power Electronics and Intelligent Transportation System, pp. 541–545 (2008)

Part IV
SMarty-Related Research

Chapter 13
M-SPLearning: A Software Product Line for Mobile Learning Applications

Venilton FalvoJr, Anderson S. Marcolino, Nemésio F. Duarte Filho, Edson OliveiraJr, and Ellen F. Barbosa

Abstract The advent of mobile devices in all social classes leads us to new possibilities of interaction, including in the educational context, where mobile learning (m-learning) applications have become powerful teaching and learning tools. Such applications, even having many benefits and facilities, also present problems and challenges, especially regarding their development, reuse, and architectural standardization. On the other hand, the adoption of the systematic reuse concept has been consolidated, making approaches such as software product lines (SPL) interesting alternatives for these gaps. This paradigm favors the abstraction of the similarities and variabilities of a domain and its products, promoting the reuse of core assets and, consequently, reducing the development time and cost (from the break-even point) of the generated solutions. Thus, to systematically explore the variabilities of m-learning applications domain, an SPL, called M-SPLearning, was proposed. First, we analyze the existing adoption models in the literature, allowing us to identify the most appropriate approach to the context of our SPL. Then, the main features of m-learning applications were defined with the support of a previously defined requirements catalog. As a result, the domain engineering and application engineering phases were conducted for M-SPLearning. In the context of domain engineering, the Stereotype-based Management of Variability (SMarty)

V. FalvoJr (✉) · E. F. Barbosa
Department of Computer Systems, University of São Paulo, São Carlos, São Paulo, Brazil
e-mail: falvojr@usp.br; francine@icmc.usp.br

A. S. Marcolino
Engineering and Exact Science Department, Federal University of Paraná, Palotina, Paraná, Brazil
e-mail: anderson.marcolino@ufpr.br

N. F. Duarte Filho
Federal Institute of Education, Science and Technology of São Paulo, Informatics Department, Sertãozinho, São Paulo, Brazil
e-mail: nemesio@ifsp.edu.br

E. OliveiraJr
Informatics Department, State University of Maringá, Maringá, PR, Brazil
e-mail: edson@din.uem.br

© Springer Nature Switzerland AG 2023
E. OliveiraJr (ed), *UML-Based Software Product Line Engineering with SMarty*,
https://doi.org/10.1007/978-3-031-18556-4_13

approach was fundamental in the representation of similarities and variabilities with regard to architecture, components, and production plan, synthesizing the features of this domain through UML diagrams. Regarding application engineering, we present the dynamics of M-SPLearning's operation, generating m-learning applications according to the selected variabilities through a web application, in other words, a user interface (UI) for the generation of products. Finally, M-SPLearning had its products experimentally evaluated in the context of a real software development company, providing statistical evidence that SPL can improve time-to-market and quality (measured by the number of bugs) in the domain of m-learning applications. Therefore, in this chapter, M-SPLearning is presented from the analysis and design phases to the generation of its products. In particular, we highlight the use of SMarty and its importance in M-SPLearning application engineering. In this sense, we discussed the importance of managing variability and how approaches such as SMarty can contribute to SPL design and demystify the adoption of this reuse strategy.

13.1   M-Learning Domain and the Role of SMarty in This Work

The advance of hardware technologies and their reduced costs have been capable to turn mobile devices into a more essential technology than computers, increasing the worldwide widespread of such devices and making them an attractive platform in several scenarios and tasks, as in professional/personal routines and even in educational activities [40, 42, 50].

While in professional and daily routines several applications can be found to support them, the educational scenario still needs more research about how such devices may support and improve the teaching and learning processes. Furthermore, besides both hardware and software specifications of mobile devices, there are also the diversity of elements (e.g., human resources, educational theories, disciplines) and challenges in such domain [42]. One of the initiatives to overcome such limitations arose with the adoption of information and communications technologies (ICT).

These new technologies relate to processes and products that are constantly changing, coming especially from electronics, microelectronics, and the telecommunications area. The scope of action of these technologies is virtual, and they use information as the main input. Therefore, different areas of knowledge tend to benefit from the use of these technologies [39].

Consequently, the ICT has favored the emergence of innovative ways for facing the shortcomings of traditional education [49]. Mobile learning (m-learning), for instance, has provided a strong interaction between learners and instructors, enabling them to actively participate in the knowledge construction process anytime and anywhere [31, 39].

In m-learning applications, students not only access a virtual learning environment but also actively participate in the knowledge construction process through the ubiquity of mobile devices, which enable interactions anytime and anywhere [31].

However, the use of m-learning brings benefits that go beyond accessibility, convenience, and communication. For example, with mobile devices define apprentices can use the most different types of applications (e.g., text processors, photos, games), specific environments for learning, web access, collaboration tools, and social networks, among others [30].

Despite the benefits provided in the context of teaching and learning, the development of m-learning apps is still a process that requires an expert team of developers and demands high investments and comprehension of the functionalities of the device's components (i.e., sensors, cameras) and their libraries in order to make them possible to be explored and to be used correctly [7, 31].

Furthermore, the identification and understanding of guidelines for m-learning applications is also a complex task [45]. Due to its educational components, attributes of ubiquitous computing, criteria of mobile usability, performance, security, portability, and communication, among others, should also be taken into consideration.

M-learning is still considered a new and incipient concept, having some limitations in its construction and use [2, 45]: (1) teacher training; (2) limited energy (battery dependent); (3) modeling of educational content; (4) adequacy to usability aspects; (5) and lack of architectural patterns, among others.

In this context, considering such diversity of features, and educational and developmental issues that need to be investigated, understood and mitigated to allow the development of proper educational tools, the adoption of methodologies that support the overcome of such challenges is needed.

In the traditional development process, there are challenges related with the conception phase of applications, reuse of components, and adoption of architectural patterns. The diversity of hardware components and also the specificity of software in mobile devices, due to its several versions, are reasons that further increase the number of challenges. Also, many of the artifacts are used into a unique project and need to be refactored to allow its reuse in another.

In this perspective, reuse-based software engineering methodologies may mitigate such problems, besides allowing the establishment of a higher number of applications, broadening the portfolio of software development industries. As a consequence, such methodologies allow the creation of m-learning apps which attend more precisely to the educational process, facilitating also the adoption and modification of existing components.

Based on such need and on the identification of a few studies that aimed at the adoption of systematic reuse methodologies, this adoption may allow a further investigation in such domain. One of such methodologies, known as software product lines (SPL), has gained prominence and can be a good opportunity to turn possible the exploration of m-learning applications and the reuse of their components.

In this sense, Krueger [29] presents three adoption strategies, aiming to demystify the use of SPL through the following construction approaches: extractive, reactive, and proactive. Basically, the extractive approach reuses one or more existing software for the SPL baseline. In the reactive approach, SPL evolves incrementally considering the new demands for products or requirements. Finally, the proactive approach is appropriate when the requirements for the set of products to be created are stable and can be defined in advance.

In this context, SPL proactive approach can be considered a viable alternative in the development process, as long as it is possible to delimit a domain and the importance of its respective features. Thus, this adoption strategy proved to be viable in the context of developing m-learning applications, due to the variability and variants identified through a catalog of requirements for the m-learning domain [15].

Therefore, the proactive approach guided the entire process of conception of our SPL, called M-SPLearning. In addition, mechanisms for the discovery, representation, and organization of variabilities were considered, among which SMarty was selected.

SMarty was crucial in the development of M-SPLearning, primarily through SMartyProfile. In practice, SMartyProfile contains a set of stereotypes and notations for the management of variability in SPL design. Furthermore, SMartyProfile is extremely flexible, supporting multiple UML diagrams: use case, class, component, activity, and sequence [36]. Thus, this approach has great synergy with most software development processes, as long as they exploit the UML.

To support the usage of both profile and process, a tool entitled SMartyModeling is available. Such tool is an environment for engineering UML-based SPL with modeling process functionalities using any compliant UML profile [46]. However, any computer-aided software engineering (CASE) tool with the capability to import UML profiles can also be used, since the SMartyProfile is one of such profiles. In this sense, the UML diagrams of M-SPLearning were modeled with SMarty in a CASE market tool, due to researchers' familiarization with it and its availability.

Finally, SMarty has also the SMartyCheck technique, capable to support the inspection of use case and class UML diagrams of SPLs, which bring more concise models to be implemented [20]. In this context, despite the abstract nature of such diagrams, SMarty can provide concise and standardized domain information about variabilities.

In this perspective, SMarty makes possible better support in the representation and the establishment of several configurations of products and also a better standardization and design of the SPL architecture, capable to support the creation of software with higher quality than the singular methodology. Such evidence was obtained by conducting an experimental evaluation, which collected positive evidence for SPL, when compared with the singular development methodology [11–13].

The development of M-SPLearning and its evaluation are presented in this chapter, which is structured as follows. In Sect. 13.2, we discussed the M-SPLearning conception, design, and implementation through the adoption of

SMarty. In Sect. 13.3, we discussed the conception of a m-learning application developed in the conduction of an experimental evaluation comparing the singular development with the SPL methodology supported by SMarty. In Sect. 13.4, we discussed the contributions and final considerations about how SMarty improved the establishment of M-SPLearning.

13.2 M-SPLearning Domain Engineering

Aiming at presenting how the management of variabilities can improve the development of m-learning applications, we have established M-SPLearning [11–13]. The idea is to investigate how the variabilities of this domain can accelerate time-to-market and reduce product faults. In this section, the activities conducted in the conception of M-SPLearning are detailed.

During the domain engineering (DE) activity, similarities and variabilities must be specified for the development of the SPL and for the establishment of a systematic reusable platform. The result is a set of assets from which the SPL should be implemented, which characterizes its product family [43, 48]. In general, the activities that characterize the DE are the most critical in the conception of an SPL, since the delimitation of a domain of study is not a trivial task.

Mobile applications can be implemented through different development platforms, but currently only two operating systems (OS) are relevant: Android and iOS. Thus, the m-learning domain also includes these OS implicitly. We selected the Android OS for the definition of an acceptable domain in terms of scope, based on the number of devices each OS control. Android owns approximately 86.1% (against 13.9% of iOS) of the forecasts worldwide smartphone shipments, which is equivalent to 1339 billion units in 2020 [8]. Therefore, considering potential users, we built our SPL to generate Android apps.

After defining a feasible domain, a requirements catalog for m-learning applications, based on Duarte and Barbosa's work [15] and on the ISO/IEC 25010 quality model, was proposed.

This catalog aims to reflect the experience acquired by developers and researchers in the field of m-learning applications. Also, since it is generic and comprehensive, its adoption can benefit different learning approaches besides m-learning.

For the management of variabilities, the development of M-SPLearning was based on the SMarty approach, due to (i) the cognitive ease provided by SMarty, supported by several modeling tools; (ii) its full compliance with UML, which facilitates the development and validation of SPL; and (iii) the existence of experimental evidence on its use [5, 33–35, 37].

In practical terms, the activities for the SPL implementation are not trivial and require significant time and effort which undermines its acceptance in industry. In order to define an appropriate adoption strategy to the concept of SPL, the proactive, reactive, and extractive techniques can be considered [29].

Each technique was analyzed considering the context of our work, and the proactive approach was chosen.

This strategy proved to be more coherent in the context of M-SPLearning, as it is recommended when the requirements for the products are stable and can be previously defined. In this sense, this condition was satisfied by the proposed requirements catalog.

In this context, domain engineering was divided into the following formal steps: (i) domain analysis, where features and their variabilities are analyzed; (ii) architecture definition, in which architectural elements are modeled; (iii) component design, focusing on the details of the software components defined in the architecture; and (iv) production plan, which presents SPL's product creation dynamics.

13.2.1 Domain Analysis

According to the proactive model, the domain and scope analysis should be summarily performed, so that the variation of the products supported by an SPL can be explored [29]. The requirements catalog proposed by Duarte and Barbosa [15] was refined in relation to the ISO/IEC 25010 quality model, which helped us to identify missing or disconnected quality requirements. Some requirements were regrouped, renamed, and, in a few cases, added to and removed from the catalog. The final requirements catalog is shown in Fig. 13.1.[1]

According to the catalog, most requirements originally proposed were directly or indirectly equivalent to the characteristics and sub-characteristics of ISO/IEC 25010 [23]. In structural terms, the resulting catalog has 10 primary and 35 secondary requirements. For instance, the *Support* element has common features, such as internationalization of messages (provided by *Customization* requirement) and frequently asked questions (*Help*).

Despite the generic requirements, the catalog also has specific features for m-learning applications. For instance, most requirements derived from *Pedagogical* and *Communication* represent essential requirements to the m-learning domain.

In pedagogical terms, the management of educational content is essential for the development of educational activities. Furthermore, multimedia resources can provide access to information in a more attractive way. Such peculiarities summarize the requirements classified by the *Pedagogical* item.

The requirements from *Communication* represent features related to the exchange of messages, alerts, and sharing results or feedback, which make the learning process more collaborative and dynamic. Another important feature is the synchronization of data from a m-learning application, since users can have more than one mobile device or platform.

---

[1] All images of this chapter are available in high resolution at https://doi.org/10.5281/zenodo.6662488.

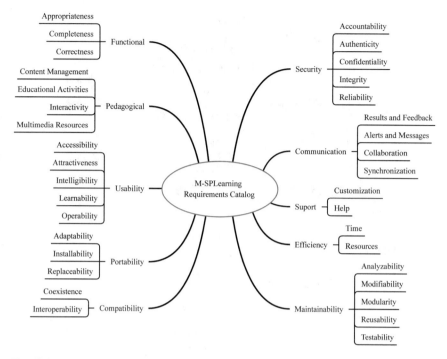

Fig. 13.1 M-SPLearning requirements catalog. Adapted from [12]

An additional validation activity was conducted for evaluating the requirements catalog proposed for the M-SPLearning. An online form was prepared for informally checking the main technical issues related to the catalog. It was structured as a checklist, with 12 multiple-choice questions so that it could measure the experts' opinions in the software engineering area.

The first two questions were related to the participants' experience in the concepts of SPL and m-learning. The options were "Advanced," "Intermediate," and "Novice." The remaining ten questions concern the requirements catalog created for M-SPLearning, for example, "Does the catalog contain requirements suitable for the m-learning domain?". The options were "Adequate," "Regular," and "Unsatisfactory."

The form/checklist was answered by 11 participants, and the results showed that the requirements catalog was evaluated as "Adequate" (60.90%) or "Regular" (39.10%), considering the average of the questions related to it. Therefore, none of the questions related to M-SPLearning were answered as "Unsatisfactory." Although preliminary, this validation was an important positive feedback from experts on the set of requirements elicited for M-SPLearning.

The next stage of the domain analysis activity was the identification of variabilities in the M-SPLearning products. The variabilities represent the range of differences between the products of an SPL, enabling the generation of products

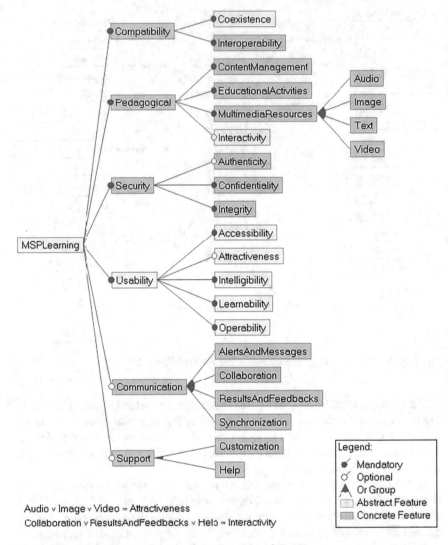

Fig. 13.2 M-SPLearning feature model. Adapted from [11–13]

with specific functionalities, respecting the SPL's assets [6, 18]. In practical terms, variabilities are generally identified and represented through the features concept [3].

We used this requirements catalog as a reference for the creation of an adherent feature model for M-SPLearning (Fig. 13.2), designed using FeatureIDE.[2] The interpretation of the feature model is simple and follows the traditional represen-

---

[2] Tool available at https://featureide.github.io.

tation conceived by the feature-oriented domain analysis (FODA) [28]. Basically, each requirement was mapped as a primary feature, generating its respective secondary features, obviously respecting the domain variabilities, which provide thousands of product configuration possibilities. Clarifying our feature model, its primary features and their responsibilities for m-learning applications are detailed as follows:

- *Compatibility*: includes the *Coexistence* and *Interoperability*. Both are mandatory for m-learning applications, given the need for multiple devices to interact in the same ecosystem, which often interoperates with other systems and solutions. In particular, *Coexistence* is intrinsic in the mobile domain, so this feature was defined as abstract;[3]
- *Pedagogical*: it has the educational and pedagogical requirements, providing the main features of m-learning applications. In particular, the *Interactivity* is optional and depends on the constraint: *(Collaboration or ResultsAndFeedbacks or Help) implies Interactivity*. Lastly, *Content Management, Educational Activities*, and *Multimedia Resources* are mandatory; the latter offers a choice of one or more multimedia resources to support teaching;
- *Security*: this is a critical feature because any mobile app must send/receive information securely. Subfeatures *Integrity* and *Confidentiality* were defined as mandatory, as they are essential for data consistency and integrity. On the other hand, the *Authenticity* is optional because not every m-learning application has explicit authentication of its users;
- *Usability*: addresses the essential visual interface features of m-learning applications, abstracting the user interface (UI) and user experience (UX) platform standards. It is fundamental for the acceptance of the app in the market, because the products generated by SPL must adopt usability standards that offer an attractive experience to the end users. Therefore, all features were defined as mandatory, with the exception of *Attractiveness*, which has a constraint: *(Audio or Image or Video) implies Attractiveness*. Furthermore, all subfeatures are abstract because the guidelines are provided by the development platform itself, such as Material Design for Android;
- *Communication*: responsible for exchanging information between users, making the teaching ecosystem more collaborative and cohesive, due to the interactivity of learners and synchronization of activities. Anyway, this feature and subfeatures are optional and accept any possible combinations;
- *Support*: offers interesting features for some m-learning applications, such as user support and internationalization. In this context, all elements were classified as optional because they are not mandatory for all applications.

---

[3] Abstract features represent those features which do not have direct impact in the products' code.

13.2.2 Architecture Definition

From the feature model, it is necessary to define an adherent software architecture to the needs of the m-learning domain. Such an architecture and its components represent, in an abstract way, the core assets of M-SPLearning. Accordingly, most of the approaches developed to assist in the management of variability involve several concepts and representation models. SMarty, in particular, is based on UML, widely known the SPL community [41]. Due to its ease of use and results (experimentally evaluated), SMarty was chosen to support the design of the M-SPLearning architecture.

SMarty played an important role in the development of M-SPLearning, as it provided guidelines to represent the similarities and, especially, the variabilities of this SPL. The diagram of architectural components illustrated in Fig. 13.3 represents a high-level perspective of the M-SPLearning. In this context, the SMarty-based component diagram was used because it provides component and feature representations at different levels of abstraction.

Based on the architecture diagram, it is possible to visualize the structural abstraction used for the implementation of M-SPLearning. The package *Core Assets* comprises its concrete features from Fig. 13.2.

The components that represent the specific features of the m-learning domain were grouped into package *core*. Therefore, the fundamental modules for products generated by M-SPLearning could be unified. We could also identify some of the elements of SMarty that represent the variabilities at a component level.

The *Application Layer* contains a component that characterizes the M-SPLear ning, identifying its association with core assets and enabling product derivation.

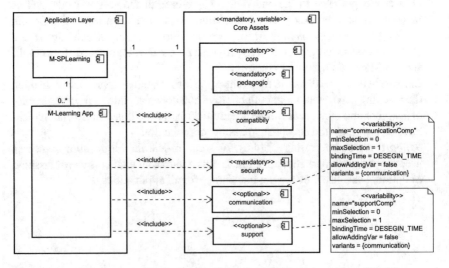

Fig. 13.3 M-SPLearning: SMarty-based architecture diagram. Adapted from [11–13]

Each product should include the components available in the *Core Assets*, making each m-learning application able to use different features according to its configurations, defined in m-learning.

13.2.3 Component Design

In this phase, the variabilities and similarities identified in the domain analysis are designed. Thus, the core assets' elements were visually represented by another SMarty-based component diagram (Fig. 13.4).

The diagram shows all concrete features covered by M-SPLearning. The resulting components are labeled with the characteristic stereotypes of SMarty approach. This diagram presents the possible component configurations, based on features, for m-learning applications covered by the SPL.

For example, the *multimedia* component was modeled with variability stereotype, i.e., the SPL can be configured for creating custom m-learning applications with such features. Therefore, a product can be configured to have among one and four *multimedia* resources (audio, image, text, and video), according to notations "minSelection" and "maxSelection." Any component formed for other components with variability should be tagged with the variable stereotype.

Considering our target domain, the *pedagogical* and *communication* components stand out, just like their domain requirements. In this sense, most *pedagogical* subcomponents are mandatory, with possible variabilities in terms of *interactivity* and *multimedia* features, whereas the *communication* subcomponents are alternative, and at least one of them must provide its functionalities to the generated products.

Dependency relationships between modeled components can also be observed. As previously defined, the *core* component unifies the mandatory features for the m-learning domain, being necessary, directly or indirectly, to the *security, communication*, and *support* components. Particularly, the *communication* component depends on the *security* component, which is related to the *core* component. As a consequence, the *communication* component also knows the *core*.

From the component design, it is possible to define a production plan to transform the abstract representations in concrete software products, with their respective variabilities.

13.2.4 Production Plan

The production plan prescribes how the products should be generated from the core assets identified for the SPL. An activities' diagram using the SMarty approach and exposing the possible variabilities in the creation of a product (Fig. 13.5) was modeled. Basically, this plan can be considered a core asset of M-SPLearning, as any other artifact contributes to the systematic creation of its products.

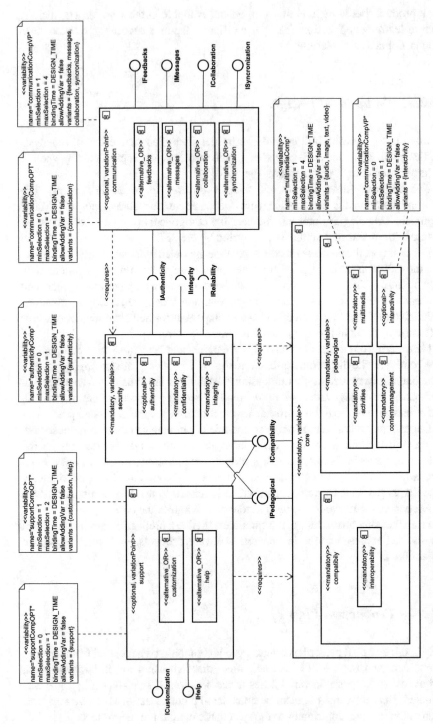

Fig. 13.4 M-SPLearning: SMarty-based component diagram. Adapted from [11–13]

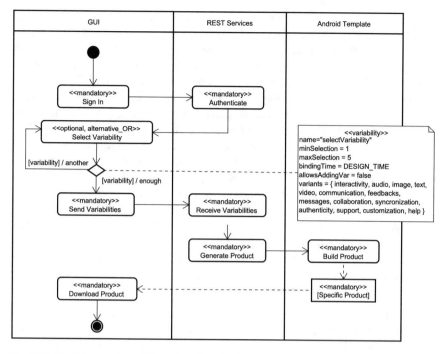

Fig. 13.5 `M-SPLearning`: SMarty-based production plan. Adapted from [12]

The variation point defined in the production plan exposes all variabilities elicited for `M-SPLearning`. Therefore, the customization of the products was centralized at a single point, facilitating the configuration process and generation of m-learning applications by the SPL proposal.

Each swimlane of the diagram represents a specific module and enables the identification of some architectural characteristics of the `M-SPLearning`. An important technical highlight is the use of the REpresentational State Transfer (REST) [14] architectural style. Through this concept, web services can be created and consumed by the Hypertext Transfer Protocol (HTTP), and emerging software architectures, as service-oriented architecture (SOA), can be also used in the context of mobile applications.

Each module represented in Fig. 13.5 is synthesized according to its main characteristics in technical terms:

- **Graphical User Interface (GUI):** a module that provides the visual representations from which users interact to generate the products supported by `M-SPLear ning`. Variabilities can be configured for the generation of a customized product. This module was implemented through front-end technologies, especially HTML, JavaScript, and CSS. The idea was to demonstrate interoperability in a SOA architecture, since all services were implemented using REST.

- **REST Services:** module developed based on the REST architectural style and characterized by the use of web technologies and protocols to create and expose services/endpoints through an application programming interface (API). This style is fully adherent to the SOA architectural pattern and ensures the availability and consumption of web services in a simple and efficient way. It is the main interface among the products generated by the M-SPLearning and their features and accesses a remote database where all the information is stored, including features (similarities and variabilities) configured from the GUI. The centralization of data in the *REST Services* module is essential for other modules (GUI and *Android Template*), since both consume the web services provided.
- **Android Template:** provides a generic template, natively developed for Android, in order to allow the customization of apps in your installation package. Therefore, the *REST Services* module executes a custom build, according to the variabilities configured in the GUI. The result is an Android Application Package (APK) with all pre-configured features for the installation of a custom product on any Android device. To conclude, we know that each Android device manufacturer has its particularities, so we prefer to follow a native approach to creating this template, which tends to be more stable.

M-SPLearning was elaborated from a process based on relevant practices and concepts of software engineering and has used an incremental process for its definition, addressing the difficulties of domain analysis and the architectural definitions necessary for a proactive implementation. The next section addresses the subsequent SPL activity, i.e., the application engineering (AE).

13.3 M-SPLearning Application Engineering

In this section, the EA activity will be detailed, highlighting the dynamics of product generation and, mainly, their experimental evaluation in the corporate environment of a software development company. Therefore, the process of selection of variabilities to the availability and evaluation of m-learning applications will be presented.

13.3.1 Product Generation

This activity depends on the output artifacts of DE, which now act as input devices. A specific set of features with such artifacts was selected for the implementation of M-SPLearning. This reduction in scope was defined for an experimental evaluation of the M-SPLearning. Therefore, the SPL could be implemented with a limited number of features.

In our study, features related to teaching and security activities were prioritized and implemented since they represent the minimum functional requirements of an m-learning application: (i) *Pedagogical*, includes learning activities through the management of interactive and multimedia content; (ii) *Security*, provides confidentiality and integrity of data, which includes user authentication; and (iii) *Communication*, includes features related to data synchronization.

In technical terms, M-SPLearning is an SPL that provides the configuration and generation of m-learning applications on the Android platform. For this, we provide a GUI for the selection of variables, which are sent to a REST API that orchestrates the generation and download of native Android Apps customized with features from the m-learning domain. M-SPLearning's source code, from its REST API to its GUI, is available in this open-source Git repository.[4]

By definition, the AE instantiates the core assets of SPL to generate specific products. The production plan was used for the construction of the respective concrete modules. In such activity, the GUI module is inevitably the most exploited, because all products are generated through it.

The first interaction between the user and M-SPLearning occurs through a webpage. Users can sign up and access the application. This interface also introduces the domain and the main objectives of M-SPLearning. Another important aspect refers to the construction of the webpages completely based on the concept of responsive layouts, which makes the visual representation of SPL even more dynamic and flexible.

With an authenticated user, the resulting interface represents the M-SPLearning, as it enables the visual management of all variabilities provided by SPL. At this point, the user (e.g., a teacher) simply performs a few clicks to generate a specific product that creates an APK, which encapsulates a custom m-learning application for any Android device. The page for this procedure is illustrated in Fig. 13.6, which also shows the visual interface for the management of products generated by M-SPLearning. Furthermore, variabilities related to features prioritized during this implementation can be configured in the product generation.

When the generation of an APK is required, the *REST Services* and *Android Template* modules are triggered simultaneously. This integration results in the creation of an adherent product for user's selected variabilities. The m-learning application generated can be installed in the Android device of any teacher or student, who must register with the mobile application if feature *Authentication* has been selected in the creation of the APK.

Figure 13.7 shows two products generated with *Authenticity* and *Interactivity* variabilities configured in different ways: (a) the product was configured with only the *Authenticity* feature; and (b) the product was generated with both variabilities, which explains the authentication form with the possibility of interaction with some social network.

According to Fig. 13.7, the common button for products also provides the possibility of registering. To do so, the user should fill his/her email and password in the fields available for the application to verify whether the user exists (Fig. 13.8a).

---

[4] https://github.com/falvojr-msc/msplearning

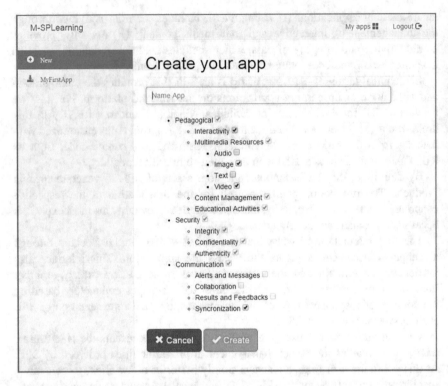

Fig. 13.6 M-SPLearning: main GUI product generation

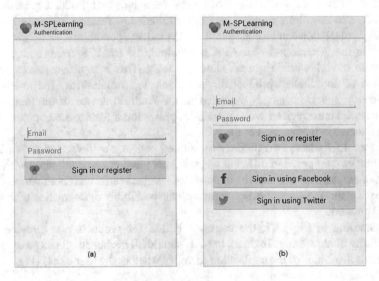

Fig. 13.7 M-SPLearning: product login—configurations of the features:
(**a**) *Authenticity* and (**b**) *Authenticity* and *Interactivity*

Fig. 13.8 M-SPLearning: product registration—steps for user registration:
(**a**) confirmation message and (**b**) registration form

If not, the registration form is displayed with the information previously typed
(Fig. 13.8b).

An user can select the type of access, teacher, or student in the registration
form. For security reasons, all registered users must be approved by the user who
generated the APK. At the time of the APK creation, the user is associated with
an administrative profile. This aspect clarifies the feature *Content Management*,
since each user's profile provides specific and well-defined accesses. Figure 13.9
illustrates a possible scenario with (a) teacher's view and (b) student's view, but
with no content, since the access to this feature is disabled.

After the user has been properly authenticated, the m-learning application is
ready for storage and sharing of its main asset, i.e., the educational content. The
teacher can register his/her courses and lessons and finally the content of each
lesson. These functionalities are an usage sample of the *Educational Activities* and
Multimedia Resources shown in Fig. 13.10.

According to the features provided by M-SPLearning, audio, text, image, and
video can be selected. Specifically, Fig. 13.10 illustrates from the registration of a
video (Teacher profile, screenshots "a" and "b") to displaying it in an embedded
player (Student profile, screenshot "c")

Finally, the design of M-SPLearning involved from analysis and design to
functional implementation. A formal evaluation of the M-SPLearning along with
this approach, as well as the main results obtained, is described in Sect. 13.3.2.

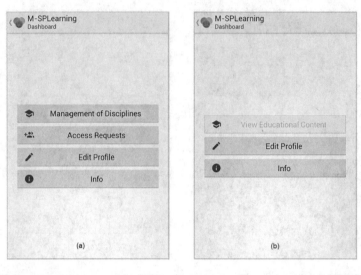

Fig. 13.9 M-SPLearning: product dashboard—access profiles: (a) teacher and (b) student

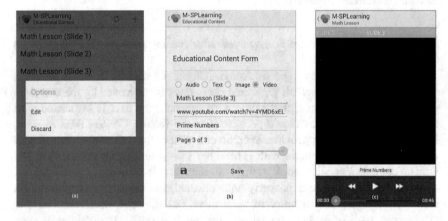

Fig. 13.10 M-SPLearning: product educational content management –
(a) listing of educational content and context menu; (b) editing form; and (c) displaying video content

13.3.2 Product Evaluation

To evaluate the product generation, allowing the comparison among the traditional software development and an SPL (supported by SMarty), an experimental evaluation was conducted. Thus, the M-SPLearning was compared to a singular software development methodology. The term "singular methodology" is defined in this evaluation as the process of software development in which developers use only their own knowledge to develop m-learning applications from scratch, without any reuse or support technique.

The guidelines proposed by Wohlin et al. [51] and the report template suggested by Jedlitschka and Pfahl [27] were followed for the conduction of the controlled experiment. The experiment aimed at **comparing** a singular software development (SSD) and the software product line (SPL) methodologies, **for the purpose of** identifying the most efficient, **with respect to** the time spent on the creation of software products and the number of faults found, **from the point of view** of software engineers **in the context of** practitioners from a software development company.

In this context, two research questions based on the research objective were raised:

- Which methodology is more efficient regarding time-to-market in the m-learning domain: SSD or SPL?
- Which methodology presents more quality, in terms of number of faults, in the m-learning domain: SSD or SPL?

Two software product configurations for m-learning applications (using Android platform) were considered to evaluate the SSD and SPL methodologies, named Product 1 (P1) and Product 2 (P2). P1 provides support to image-based educational content, and P2 provides support to video-based educational content.

The participants in the evaluation were employees from a Brazilian software development company. In this context, 18 developers participated as volunteers and had at least 1 year of experience on software development (Java, Microsoft .NET, and/or PHP).

The main assessment tools were the products developed based on two software specifications (P1 and P2) for m-learning applications. A specific niche of features was used for the evaluation. The variabilities related to multimedia resources enabled the creation of up to 15 different products. P1 and P2 were specified and implemented by SSD and SPL methodologies.

Based on the results obtained in the development of the two m-learning products during the experimental sessions, we submitted the collected data, in both methodologies (SSD and SPL), to the Shapiro-Wilk normality test [44] and the Mann-Whitney-Wilcoxon hypothesis test [32]. Such tests validated the statistical power of the sample, allowing to test the hypotheses.

Results related with the efficiency in the time of implementation indicated that SPL is more efficient than the SSD to implement software products for mobile platform taking into account the product P1 and P2 specification. The implementations of the base project and of the SPL were also considered in the experiment.

The participants received the base project of the two software products to be developed with SSD or SPL. It consisted of similarities of the products and was developed to reduce the experimental execution duration. It was implemented in 480 minutes (8 hours). The base project included also, for the SSD, a set of UML diagrams and, for the SPL, the SMarty diagrams and feature model. The base project is available in an open-source repository.[5]

Based on the time spent in the development of each software product, it is possible to make some estimates related with the time efforts for both SSD and SPL methodologies evaluated. If we considered the time required for the implementation of each base project adopting the SSD methodology, plus the total development time to each participants (480 minutes), the total time would be 10680 minutes or 178 hours ($total_{time}$((subjects(18) × minutes(480)) + 2040 = 10,680 minutes).

On the other hand, taking into account the base project developing with SPL methodology, the time spent by the 18 participants was 81 minutes (1 hour and 21 minutes), and the total time would be 11,361 minutes or 189 hours and 35 minutes ($total_{time}$((participants(18) × minutes(4.5)) + 10,599 = 11,361 minutes).

Comparing the values, we can notice that the SPL development spent 621 minutes (11 hours and 35 minutes) more than SSD. However, after the SPL implementation, this approach allows the evolution and insertion of new variabilities, assuring the faster generation of new products in addition to other advantages of the adoption of SPL approach, as mentioned in Chap. 4.

Regarding the number of faults of the created software products, they were identified based on test cases defined with a group of quality analysts from a software industry encompassing both SPL and SSD methodologies. These test cases considered the main functionalities of the expected software products. Two types of faults were found for two participants that received the SPL methodology, one for each configuration (P1 and P2). In both test cases, it was expected the system to display a list of educational content, video or image, but nothing was displayed.

For the SSD methodology, the faults were more serious. All the participants presented faults somehow. For the image (P1) and video (P2) software product, the faults where found in the same test cases: (i) the data was expected to be validated before being stored by the application to the database in the content creation process; (ii) the application should present a form with the selected educational content, but nothing was displayed; and (iii) the informational messages were not displayed on some screens. Table 13.1 summarizes the main results of the normality and statistical tests, used to allow the collection of evidences for the research objectives.

It is important to highlight that, even with a small number of participants and a reduced statistical power, the experimental evaluation is crucial since it allows the collection of initial evidence about the compared methodologies. Besides, the sample can be increased in future replications [10, 21].

Both the time spent on the creation of software products and the reduced number of faults found were positive for SPL methodology. Finally, with the SPL defined and its first evaluation results, replications and new evaluations can be conducted. Furthermore, the implementation of all the elicited features could provide broader investigations in the domain of m-learning applications, targeting from the SPL itself to its respective products and their similarities and variabilities.

---

[5] https://github.com/falvojr-msc/msplearning-experiment.

Table 13.1 SSD and SPL normality and statistical test results

Element	SSD	SPL
Selection of participants	N(SSD) = 18	N(SPL) = 18
Time to implementation		
Mean	113.33	4.5
Shapiro-Wilk	p = 0.0274 (p <0.05) non-normal	p = 0.0014 (p <0.05) non-normal
Mann-Whitney-Wilcoxon	326.5	0
Result	SPL has a smaller time-to-market than SSD, based on evidenced statistical difference of the time to implementation	
Number of faults		
Mean	7.11	1
Shapiro-Wilk	p = 0.0006 (p <0.05) non-normal	p = 0.00000007 (p <0.05) non-normal
Mann-Whitney-Wilcoxon	282	42
Result	SPL has a smaller fault in the products than SSD, based on evidenced statistical difference of the number of faults	

13.3.3 Related Work

This research includes three main perspectives: m-learning applications, SPL and the variability management benefits, and experimental software engineering. Based on such perspectives, a small number of related works were found [4, 9, 17, 19, 22, 26, 38].

Neither [19] nor [38] allowed us to conduct a direct comparison with respect to our research, because these works explore a more generic SPL domain: SPL for mobile systems and SPL for mobile and context-aware applications, respectively. On the other hand, the works of [9, 22], and [4] proposed the specification of variabilities through language and graphical representations in industry case studies. In our research, the representation of variability was made by using the SMarty approach.

Only two studies addressed some quality issues and tests. Ardis et al. [4] defined a testing approach based on modeling test cases. However, the proposed method was applied only in the context of SPL, not considering the SSD methodology. Gacek et al. [17] adopted twofold strategies in a case study to test the SPL products. Firstly, single components were tested by the developers themselves; secondly, the system was tested at runtime in the target environment. Similar to the [4] study, only the SPL methodology was considered, unlike our experiment, where quality analysts defined and executed test cases on products generated by two different development methodologies.

Finally, although all related works have been applied in the industry, none of them compare development methodologies, highlighting variables such as quality and time-to-market. This lack of research in the area motivated our work.

13.4   Final Remarks

According to UNESCO [47], there are approximately 6 billion mobile subscribers worldwide. Based on these numbers, in 2019, the octave "UNESCO *Mobile Learning Week*" pointed out mobile learning as a viable alternative to the global need for 8.2 million new teachers, something impossible to achieve using traditional methods.

On the other hand, according to the International Telecommunication Union (ITU) [24, 25], almost the entire world population (about 93%) has access to a mobile cellular network. Therefore, the development of increasingly connected and resilient m-learning applications tends to occur naturally.

The Android platform, in turn, showed to be more relevant in the domain of m-learning applications, due to its notorious amount of potential users [8]. The Android OS market is extremely consolidated, which benefits the development of m-learning applications. Therefore, this ease of access to mobile devices can enable the use of m-learning in different teaching contexts.

Despite the benefits of m-learning, this concept is still considered incipient, with problems and challenges, especially with regard to development, reuse, and architectural standardization. On the other hand, there is a growing adoption of the SPL concept in research related to reuse. This paradigm allows organizations to abstract the similarities and variabilities of their products, increasing the reuse of artifacts and, consequently, reducing costs and development time [1].

In this scenario, the time required for the development of m-learning applications is essential so that they arrive more quickly to their end users. So, our work aimed at proposing an SPL, called *M-SPLearning*, exploiting the existing needs in the mobile learning domain. The main objective was to provide a greater reuse and standardization for these applications. Thus, the study of the concept of SPL converged with the need of the m-learning applications and resulted in the conception of *M-SPLearning*.

In general, through the *M-SPLearning*, a completely designed SPL was obtained, being possible to abstract most of the difficulties encountered in the definition of this concept. According to van der Linden et al. [48], abstractions such as SPL allow the development process to be documented and reused systematically, contributing to the better comprehension of the target domain. Therefore, from the results obtained in this research we can offer valuable insights for any other SPL in domains similar to m-learning. In this context, in view of the world's educational needs, SPLs can be powerful tools for creating large-scale teaching solutions.

M-SPLearning was developed in accordance with a proactive adoption model [29] and explored the concept of SOA to standardize access to assets using a REST

API. Particularly, we focused on technical aspects of *M-SPLearning*, evaluating two products generated from its GUI, which explored the main features of the m-learning domain. Thus, the main contribution of the proposed SPL is to provide benefits with regard to overall quality, domain understanding, and reduction of time spent on developing and maintaining m-learning applications.

The *M-SPLearning* proposal has also made possible several contributions to the context of m-learning applications. At first, it was possible to identify and analyze different works that investigated the themes of SPL and m-learning, verifying within the scientific community the approaches that have already been studied and applied, ensuring greater reliability of the *M-SPLearning*.

Another important point of *M-SPLearning* refers to the definition of characteristics and requirements related to the domain of m-learning applications. This definition was based on a generic requirements catalog, whose elements were confronted by a quality standard ISO. As a result, a new requirements catalog was derived that conforms to the needs of the m-learning domain.

In addition, the requirements defined in the new catalog have been summarized into representations adhering to the SPL concept. In this context, similarities and variabilities could be better defined by means of a feature model. It is noteworthy that, with the support of experts in the domain, the requirements included in the new catalog were evaluated to complement its shortcomings and limitations. The evaluation of the requirements by experts was important to really verify if such requirements are satisfactory in relation to the domain in question, mobile learning applications.

Another contribution was the formalization of the entire SPL development process, in addition to the UML-based variability management provided by SMarty. This supports the management of variabilities, since the correct representation and identification of these assets are fundamental for SPL to reach its business objectives. It is also possible to design previously modeled features, ensuring the necessary inputs for SPL implementation.

Regarding the contributions of SMarty in the current work, we highlight some points. From the point of view of the feature model, it was possible to define a software architecture that adheres to the needs of the mobile learning domain. Such architecture and its components represent, in abstract form, the core assets of the *M-SPLearning*. During the architecture definition activity arose the need to elaborate an architectural representation for the proposed SPL. In this sense, the SMarty approach particularly contributed due its roots in UML, widely accepted by the scientific community.

The SMarty approach was essential throughout the development process of the proposed SPL, mainly because it adds its profile to UML models to represent the similarities and the variabilities of the *M-SPLearning*. SMarty was also useful at the component design stage, because in this stage there is a need to design variabilities and similarities identified by domain analysis. In this perspective, the architectural components were synthesized into core assets, having their respective features visually represented with the support of SMarty component diagram.

Another contribution of SMarty was in the development of the production plan of *M-SPLearning*. The production plan is important as it prescribes how products should be generated from the SPL core assets. For this, an activity diagram using the SMarty approach was modeled, exposing the possible variability during the process of creating a product. Basically, this plan can be considered a core asset of the *M-SPLearning*, just like any other artifact that contributes to the systematic creation of its products.

The variation point defined in the production plan exposes all elicited variability for *M-SPLearning* with the help of the SMarty approach. In this way, product customization was centralized at a single point, streamlining the process of setting up and generating mobile learning applications from the proposed SPL.

In general, in the current work, we basically used the components' and activities' diagrams, both having a profile defined in SMarty. Therefore, it is important to note that SMarty has great flexibility with respect to different UML diagrams. Furthermore, SMartyProfile and SMartyProcess may be appropriate in other contexts, emphasizing their flexibility in the management of variabilities.

In order to evaluate the proposed SPL, a subset of its functionalities was experimentally measured. Thus, an implementation of an SPL was performed based on all the knowledge obtained through the activities of this work. Prioritized modules were building in a functional way in their software project. For this, a specific group of features were prioritized for the conduction of an evaluation in real industry environment, which had the main variabilities (*Audio* and *Video*), provided by *Pedagogical* feature. These assets were considered to represent some relevant features to m-learning applications.

The obtained results were positive to the *M-SPLearning*, showing a reduction in *time-to-market* and better quality (in terms of faults) considering the products evaluated. At the end of the experimental evaluation, it was possible to verify, through statistical tests, that the time-to-market means and faults for application development m-learning, using the *M-SPLearning*, were smaller when compared to the traditional software development methodology.

We also noticed that SMarty approach was crucial to the development of M-SPLearning since it was easy to import SMartyProfile in a UML tool and apply such profile, by the SMartyProcess guidelines. Furthermore, with the experimental evaluations performed, improvements were applied in their elements, making SMarty a more complete and concise approach to be used. Improvements were made in relation to the requirements of the domain of mobile learning applications and requirements related to aspects of variability. Modeling upgrades were also performed, improving and facilitating the understanding of the SPL.

As a limitation of the present study, we highlight that the empirical evaluation that was performed on a limited number of features does not cover the SPL in its totality. Therefore, a part of the features that were modeled in the SPL was implemented, being more specific in the teaching and learning part. In addition to this limitation, essentially, only the products generated by SPL were evaluated experimentally, which does not statistically assess the effectiveness of this reuse approach.

Another limitation is related to the possibility of evolution of products in the SPL, since the Android version evolves quickly, implying in the development of Android applications based on an outdated architecture. This needs further analysis for the architectural evolution/restructuring of M-SPLearning's assets, considering the latest technologies recommended for the development of the Android platform.

As future work, we intend to evolve M-SPLearning based on the inputs provided by the experimental evaluation performed. Actually, there is still a significant amount of information that can lead to new research lines and experimental evaluations. In this sense, new experimental evaluations can be planned from two perspectives: (i) replication of the experimental evaluation presented here, in order to increase the statistical power of the initial sample, and (ii) design and execution of experiments, aiming to evaluate the SPL itself and not just its respective products, as explored in this work. For this, there are currently well-defined guidelines to promote SPL experiments [16], which can structure even more effective evaluations.

The conceptual model developed has also been evaluated and evolved, considering the specific domain of programming teaching. More studies on the adoption of M-SPLearning in different contexts should enable improvements in our proposal, making it more suitable for the use in both academia and industry. Moreover, for a complete evaluation of M-SPLearning, all features elicited by the catalog requirements must be properly implemented. Therefore, an experimental study involving the SPL itself should be also conducted.

Finally, considering the limitations and future work presented, perhaps an adequate approach to evolution would be the reactive strategy proposed by Krueger [29]. Thus, we could evolve *M-SPLearning* incrementally considering its new requirements (functional and non-functional) and features.

Considering the reactive approach, we also intend to incorporate the recent evolutions of SMarty, in order to continuously improve our management of variability. For example, through the usage of SMartyCheck technique [20], it would be possible to validate and explore new design perspectives (class and use case diagrams). Therefore, future work on *M-SPLearning* can benefit from the consistent improvements in the SMarty approach.

Acknowledgments The authors would like to thank CAPES/Brazil (PROCAD Grant number 071/2013) and FAPESP/Brazil (Grant number 2012/04053-9) for supporting this work.

References

1. Almeida, E. S.: Software Reuse and Product Line Engineering: Handbook of Software Engineering, pp. 825–847. Springer, Berlin (2019)
2. Aluko, R.: Applying unesco guidelines on mobile learning in the south african context: Creating an enabling environment through policy. Int. Rev. Res. Open Distributed Learn. **18**(7), 1–21 (2017)
3. Apel, S., Batory, D.S., Kästner, C., Saake, G.: Feature-Oriented Software Product Lines – Concepts and Implementation. Springer, Berlin (2013)

4. Ardis, M., Daley, N., Hoffman, D., Siy, H., Weiss, D. (2000). Software product lines: a case study. Softw. Pract. Exper. **30**(7), 825-847
5. Bera, M.H.G., OliveiraJr, E., Colanzi, T.E.: Evidence-based SMarty support for variability identification and representation in component models. In: Proceedings of the 17th International Conference on Enterprise Information Systems - Volume 2, ICEIS 2015, pp. 295–302. SCITEPRESS – Science and Technology Publications, Lda (2015)
6. Capilla, R., Bosch, J., Kang, K.C.: Systems and Software Variability Management: Concepts, Tools and Experiences. Springer Publishing Company, Incorporated, Berlin (2013)
7. Castrillo, M.D., Martín-Monje, E., Bárcena, E.: Mobile-based chatting for meaning negotiation in foreign language learning. In: Proceedings of the 10th International Conference on Mobile Learning (ML), pp. 49–59. Madrid, ES (2014)
8. Chau, M., Reith, R.: Smartphone market share (2020). https://www.idc.com/promo/smartphone-market-share/os. Accessed 29 May 2022
9. Eriksson, M., Börstler, J., Borg, K. Managing requirements specifications for product lines an approach and industry case study. J. Syst. Softw. **82**(3), 435–447 (2009)
10. Falessi, D., Juristo, N., Wohlin, C., Turhan, B., Münch, J., Jedlitschka, A., Oivo, M.: Empirical software engineering experts on the use of students and professionals in experiments. Empir. Softw. Eng. **23**(1), 452–489 (2018)
11. FalvoJr, V., Duarte Filho, N.F., OliveiraJr, E., Barbosa, E.F.: Towards the establishment of a software product line for mobile learning applications. In: International Conference on Software Engineering and Knowledge Engineering, pp. 678–683. Vancouver, CA (2014)
12. FalvoJr, V., Duarte Filho, N.F., OliveiraJr, E., Barbosa, E.F.: A contribution to the adoption of software product lines in the development of mobile learning applications. In: IEEE Frontiers in Education Conference. Madrid, ES, pp. 1–8 (2014)
13. FalvoJr, V., Marcolino, A.S., Duarte Filho, N.F., OliveiraJr, E., Barbosa, E.F.: Development and evaluation of a software product line for M-learning applications. J. Univers. Comput. Sci. **28**(10), 1058–1086 (2022)
14. Fielding, R.T.: Architectural styles and the design of network-based software architectures. Ph.D. Thesis, University of California, Irvine, CA (2000)
15. Filho, N.F.D., Barbosa, E.F.: A requirements catalog for mobile learning environments. In: Annual ACM Symposium on Applied Computing, pp. 1266–1271. New York, NY (2013)
16. Furtado, V., OliveiraJr, E., Kalinowski, M.: Guidelines for promoting software product line experiments. In: 15th Brazilian Symposium on Software Components, Architectures, and Reuse (SBCARS), pp. 31–40. Joinville (2021)
17. Gacek, C., Knauber, P., Schmid, K., Clements, P.: Successful software product line development in a small organization. Fraunhofer IESE, IESE-Report No. 013.01/E (2001). https://www.researchgate.net/publication/237262870. Accessed 18 Jun 2022
18. Galster, M., Weyns, D., Tofan, D., Michalik, B., Avgeriou, P.: Variability in software systems: a systematic literature review. IEEE Trans. Softw. Eng. **40**(3), 282–306 (2014)
19. Gamez, N., Fuentes, L., Troya, J.M.: Creating selfadapting mobile systems with dynamic software product lines. IEEE Softw. **32**(2), 105–112 (2015)
20. Geraldi, R.T., OliveiraJr, E.: Towards initial evidence of SMartycheck for defect detection on product-line use case and class diagrams. J Softw. **12**(5), 379–392 (2017)
21. Höst, M., Regnell, B., Wohlin, C.: Using students as subjects – a comparative study of students and professionals in lead-time impact assessment. Empir. Softw. Eng. **5**(3), 201–214 (2000)
22. Hubaux, A., Boucher, Q., Hartmann, H., Michel, R., Heymans, P.: Evaluating a textual feature modelling language: Four industrial case studies. In Malloy, B., Staab, S., van den Brand, M. (eds.) Software Language Engineering, pp. 337–356. Springer, Berlin (2011)
23. ISO/IEC: ISO/IEC 25010:2011 – Systems and software engineering – Systems and software Quality Requirements and Evaluation (SQuaRE) – System and software quality models. International Organization for Standardization, pp. 1–34 (2011). https://www.iso.org/standard/35733.html. Accessed 18 Jun 2022

24. ITU: Report on the implementation of the strategic plan and the activities of the union for 2018-2019. https://bit.ly/2UF6Q1o (2019). https://itu.foleon.com/itu/annual-report-2018/home/. Accessed 29 May 2022
25. ITU: Measuring digital development. https://bit.ly/3aHBbC1 (2019). https://itu.foleon.com/itu/measuring-digital-development/home/. Accessed 29 May 2022
26. Jaring, M., Bosch, J.: Representing variability in software product lines: A case study. In International Conference on Software Product Lines, pp. 15-36. Springer, Berlin (2002)
27. Jedlitschka, A., Pfahl, D.: Reporting guidelines for controlled experiments in software engineering. In: International Symposium on Empirical Software Engineering, pp. 1–10 (2005)
28. Kang, K.C., Cohen, S.G., Hess, J.A., Novak, W.E., Peterson, A.S.: Feature-oriented domain analysis (FODA) feasibility study. Technical Report, Software Engineering Institute, Carnegie Mellon University (1990). https://resources.sei.cmu.edu/library/asset-view.cfm?assetid=11231. Accessed 18 Jun 2022
29. Krueger, C.W.: Easing the transition to software mass customization. In: International Workshop on Software Product-Family Engineering, pp. 282–293. London (2002)
30. Kukulska-Hulme, A.: Mobile and personal learning for newcomers to a city. Electron. J. Foreign Language Teach. 17(1), 93–103 (2020)
31. Kukulska-Hulme, A., Traxler, J.: Mobile learning: A handbook for educators and trainers (2005). http://oro.open.ac.uk/6109/. Accessed 29 May 2022
32. Mann, H.B., Whitney, D.R.: On a test of whether one of two random variables is stochastically larger than the other. Ann. Math. Statist. 18(1), 50–60 (1947)
33. Marcolino, A., OliveiraJr, E., Gimenes, I., Maldonado, J.C.: Towards the effectiveness of a variability management approach at use case level. In: Proceedings of the 25th International Conference on Software Engineering and Knowledge Engineering (SEKE), pp. 214–219. Boston, MA (2013)
34. Marcolino, A., OliveiraJr, E., Gimenes, I., Barbosa, E.: Empirically based evolution of a variability management approach at uml class level. 38th Annual International Computers, Software & Applications Conference, vol. 1, pp. 354–363 (2014)
35. Marcolino, A., OliveiraJr, E., Gimenes, I.: Towards the effectiveness of the SMarty approach for variability management at sequence diagram level. In: Proceedings of the 16th International Conference on Enterprise Information Systems - Volume 2, ICEIS 2014, pp. 249–256. SCITEPRESS – Science and Technology Publications, Lda (2014)
36. Marcolino, A., OliveiraJr, E., Gimenes, I., Barbosa, E.F.: Empirically based evolution of a variability management approach at uml class level. In: 2014 IEEE 38th Annual Computer Software and Applications Conference, pp. 354–363. IEEE, Piscataway (2014)
37. Marcolino, A., OliveiraJr, E., Gimenes, I., Barbosa, E.: Variability resolution and product configuration with SMarty: An experimental study on uml class diagrams. J. Comput. Sci. 13, 307–319 (2017)
38. Marinho, F., Costa, A., Lima, F., Neto, J., Filho, J., Rocha, L., Dantas, V., Andrade, R., Teixeira, E., Werner, C.: An architecture proposal for nested software product lines in the domain of mobile and context-aware applications. In: Proceedings of the 4th Brazilian Symposium on Software Components, Architectures and Reuse (SBCARS), pp. 51–60. Salvador, BA (2010)
39. Moreira, F., Rocha, Á.: A special issue on disruption of higher education in the 21st century due to ICTs. Telematics Inf. 35(4), 930–932 (2018)
40. Nah, K.C., White, P., Sussex, R.: The potential of using a mobile phone to access the internet for learning efl listening skills within a Korean context. ReCALL 20(03), 331–347 (2008)
41. OliveiraJr, E., Gimenes, I., Maldonado, J.C.: Systematic management of variability in UML-based software product lines. J. Univer. Comput. Sci. 16(17), 2374–2393 (2010)
42. O'Malley, C., Vavoula, G., Glew, J.P., Taylor, J., Sharples, M., Lefrere, P.: Guidelines for learning/teaching/tutoring in a mobile environment. Technical Report, MOBIlearn/UoN/UoB/OU (2012). https://hal.archives-ouvertes.fr/hal-00696244/document. Accessed 18 Jun 2022
43. Pohl, K., Böckle, G., Linden, F.J.v.d.: Software Product Line Engineering: Foundations, Principles and Techniques. Springer, New York (2005)

44. Shapiro, S.S., Wilk, M.B.: An analysis of variance test for normality (complete samples). Biometrika **52**, 591–611 (1965)
45. Sharples, M.: Making sense of context for mobile learning. In: Mobile Learning, pp. 140–153. Routledge, Milton Park (2015)
46. Silva, L.F., OliveiraJr, E.: Empirical evaluation of VMTools-RA: A reference architecture for software variability tools. In: Anais Estendidos da X Conferência Brasileira de Software: Teoria e Prática, pp. 17–23. SBC (2019)
47. UNESCO: Report of the unesco mobile learning week 2019. Technical Report, United Nations Educational, Scientific and Cultural Organization (2019). https://en.unesco.org/mlw/2019. Accessed 18 Jun 2022
48. Van der Linden, F.J., Schmid, K., Rommes, E.: Software Product Lines in Action: The Best Industrial Practice in Product Line Engineering. Springer, New York (2007)
49. West, M.: Mobile learning for teachers: Global themes (2012). http://unesdoc.unesco.org/images/0021/002164/216452E.pdf. Accessed 29 May 2022
50. Wexler, S., Brown, J., Metcalf, D., Rogers, D., Wagner, E.: Mobile learning: What it is, why it matters, and how to incorporate it into your learning strategy. The Learning Guild Research (2008). https://www.elearningguild.com/showfile.cfm?id=2467. Accessed 18 Jun 2022
51. Wohlin, C., Runeson, P., Höst, M., Ohlsson, M., Regnell, B., Wesslén, A.: Experimentation in Software Engineering. Springer Science & Business Media, Berlin (2012)

Chapter 14
PLeTs: A Software Product Line for Testing Tools

Elder M. Rodrigues, Avelino F. Zorzo, and Luciano Marchezan

Abstract Software testing is a fundamental activity to improve software quality. However, software testing is one of the most time-consuming and expensive activities of the software development process. Therefore, several testing tools have already been developed to support software testing, including tools for model-based testing (MBT), which is a testing technique to automatically generate testing artifacts from the system model. Some of the advantages of MBT include lower cost and less effort to generate test cases. Therefore, in the last years, a diversity of commercial, academic, and open-source tools to support MBT has been developed to better explore these advantages. Although several testing tools to support MBT were produced in the past years, most of them have been individually and independently developed based on a single architecture. Therefore, it is difficult to integrate, evolve, maintain, and reuse them. One strategy that could minimize those problems would be to use software product lines (SPL), which allows to systematically generating software products at lower costs, in a shorter time, and with higher quality. Therefore, this chapter presents an SPL for testing tools that support MBT (PLeTs (This chapter is an expanded version of previously published paper Rodrigues et al. (PLeTs - Test Automation using Software Product Lines and Model-Based Testing. In: Proceedings of the 22th International Conference on Software Engineering and Knowledge Engineering, pp. 483–488, 2010.))) and how we applied the Stereotype-based Management of Variability (SMarty) approach to manage and resolve the dependencies among components and to represent the variability in PLeTs architecture. PLeTs is a component-based SPL developed to automatically generate MBT tools. The PLeTs MBT tools aim to automate any of

E. M. Rodrigues (✉) · L. Marchezan
Department of Computer Systems, Federal University of Pampa, Alegrete, Rio Grande do Sul, Brazil
e-mail: elderrodrigues@unipampa.edu.br

A. F. Zorzo
School of Technology, Pontifical Catholic University of Rio Grande do Sul (PUCRS), Porto Alegre, Rio Grande do Sul, Brazil
e-mail: avelino.zorzo@pucrs.br

© Springer Nature Switzerland AG 2023
E. OliveiraJr (ed), *UML-Based Software Product Line Engineering with SMarty*,
https://doi.org/10.1007/978-3-031-18556-4_14

315

the test activities of MBT, for example, the generation of test cases and/or test scripts based on the system model. Basically, PLeTs MBT tools receive, as input, a system model, generate the test cases/scripts, execute the test scripts, and then compare the produced results. Since PLeTs can generate tools that connect to any commercial testing tool, a software testing team can incorporate their own testing tools, hence reducing effort and investment. In a nutshell, the main PLeTs goal is to reuse SPL artifacts and use existing testing tools to ease the development of new MBT tools.

14.1 The Role of SMarty in This Work

Stereotype-based Management of Variability (SMarty) approach [31] was used to manage the dependencies among components and to represent the variability in the PLeTs architecture. Our main motivations to choose the SMarty approach, among other approaches to manage variability using UML models, are the fact that it can be easily extended, it has a considerable amount of supporting documentation, and it has a low learning curve [31]. Figure 14.1 shows the PLeTs component model based on SMarty, which reflects the PLeTs feature model presented in Fig. 14.4. Since we are using a component replacement mechanism, each provided interface represents a variation point, and each variable component implementation represents a variant. The interfaces provided by the *PLeTs* components are shown in Fig. 14.1.

14.2 Model-Based Testing

Model-based testing (MBT) supports the (semi)-automatic generation of test case/scripts from the system under test (SUT) models [13]. Usually, the SUT can be modeled from three different views: data model, which represents the data

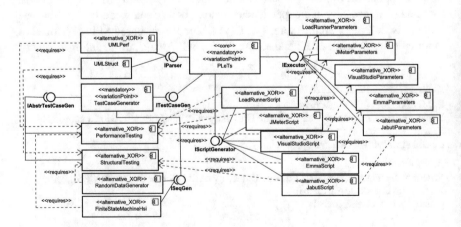

Fig. 14.1 PLeTs UML component diagram modeled with SMarty [23]

input to the SUT; tester model, which represents the interaction between the user and SUT, and design model, which represents the dynamic behavior of the SUT. A wide amount of languages that describe system models can be used as input to MBT, for example, Unified Modeling Language (UML) [32], state diagrams, or Specification and Description Language (SDL).

MBT adoption requires more activities than the traditional activities of software testing [24]. For instance, MBT adoption requires that test engineers adjust their testing process and activities and invest in the training of the testing team. The main activities of the MBT process are Build Model, Generate Expected Inputs, Generate Expected Outputs, Run Test, Compare Results, Decide Further Actions, and Stop Testing [13]. Figure 14.2 presents an overview of these activities.

- *Build Model*: consists of constructing a model based on the specification of a system. This step defines the choice of model, according to the application being developed;
- *Generate Expected Inputs*: uses the model to generate test inputs (test cases, test scripts, application input data);
- *Generate Expected Outputs*: generates some mechanism that determines whether the results of test execution are correct. This mechanism is a test oracle, and it is used to determine the correctness of the output;

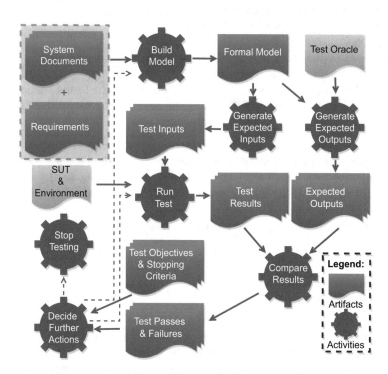

Fig. 14.2 MBT main activities [13]

- *Run Tests*: executes test scripts and stores the results of each test case. This execution can be performed on the system under test (SUT) and/or system's environment;
- *Compare Results*: compares the test results with expected outputs (test oracle), generating reports to alert the test team about failures;
- *Decides Further Actions*: based on the results, it is possible to estimate the software quality. Depending on the achieved quality, it is possible to stop testing (quality achieved), to modify the model to include further information to generate new inputs/outputs, to modify the system under test (to remove remaining faults), or to run more tests;
- *Stop Testing*: concludes the testing and releases the software system.

As the MBT process supports the (semi)-automation of the testing activities, it helps to reduce the cost of software testing since this cost is related to the number of interactions and test cases that are executed during the testing phase. As the testing phase costs between 30 and 60% of software development effort [29], MBT is a valuable approach to mitigate these problems [46]. Furthermore, the MBT adoption can bring several other advantages to the test team, such as [13]:

- Shorter schedules, lower cost, and better quality;
- Early identification of ambiguities in the model specification;
- Enhanced communication among developers and testers;
- Automatic test script generation from test cases;
- Test mechanisms to automatically run generated scripts;
- Easiness to update the test cases when the requirements are changed;
- Less effort to perform regression tests;
- Capability to assess software quality and reliability (due to the possibility of comparing quality and reliability using the same formal model, e.g., Markov chains).

Although a testing team takes all advantages proportioned by MBT adoption, tool support is mandatory. For some time, it has been possible to find several commercial, academic, and open-source MBT tools [24]. However, it is not an easy task for a testing engineer to choose a tool since several tools can be based on a variety of models, coverage criteria, approaches, and notations. For this reason, some works have been published to help to compare MBT tools and approaches [6, 12, 24, 37, 39].

14.3   PLeTs Project

The cost and effort of the software testing activities are related to many factors, such as the definition of the coverage criteria used to generate the test cases that will be executed during the testing process and the tool support. As mentioned before, the MBT technique and their supporting tools can be used to mitigate this problem by automating the process of generating testing data, e.g., test cases and scripts. However, although can be found in the literature several works of MBT tools [1, 8, 15, 27, 43], and most of these tools have similar features (e.g., coverage criteria and modeling notations), the effort to design and develop a new MBT tool is high since, usually, it has to be constructed from scratch. In addition, most of the available MBT tools are limited to generate testing data in a proprietary format and to a specific technology or domain [18, 19].

Another issue that a testing team has to face is that in some situations, it could be necessary to adopt complementary testing technology and consequently use a different testing tool to test an application. Moreover, the necessity to adopt a different testing tool could also be motivated by non-technical factors, such as the tool's cost, available features, and market decisions. Furthermore, in these situations, it is usual that a large investment is made in a software license and to train the testing team. Besides that, a lot of pressure is put on the testing team to quickly learn the new technology and then explore all the tool's features. Furthermore, sometimes, the testing team is already motivated to move from some testing approach to an MBT approach and its supporting tools, but when they realize that the already purchased tools and the related team knowledge are almost useless for apply MBT, they give up or postpone MBT adoption.

To overcome these issues, during the design and development of an MBT tool, the *Build Model*, *Generate Expected Inputs*, and *Generate Expected Outputs* steps should be designed and developed bearing in mind that an external tool, e.g., LoadRunner [16] or JaBUTi [47], or even an in-house tool could be used to execute the *Run Test* step. Thus, the testing team could reuse these testing tools to apply MBT, reducing the time and cost of the development of an MBT tool. Although the possibility of using an external tool to execute MBT is useful to the testing community, this approach does not systematize the reuse of software artifacts already developed to support each MBT step. Another point is that it is necessary to control and plan the variability between the artifacts.

Based on this, an approach to mitigate these limitations and systematize the artifact's reuse could be to design and develop an SPL that could be used to generate MBT tools to cover all steps of the MBT process [13], i.e., a tool that allows to describe the system model, to generate test cases/scripts, to execute test scripts, and also to compare the results. An even better situation would be if the test team could generate a testing tool for each different application domain or different testing level and then execute it over the same application. Furthermore, it is desirable that the testing team reuse previously implemented artifacts, e.g., models, software components, and scripts.

Therefore, based on the context and motivation presented above, which in turn are based on information about MBT tools extracted from the mapping study depicted in [6] and our expertise on the design and development of an MBT tool in collaboration with a technical development laboratory (TDL) from a big global IT company, we defined the basic requirements of our SPL of MBT tools. In the next section, we introduce the MBT tool requirements, our approach to develop PLeTs, and their variability identification.

14.3.1 Requirements

During the domain engineering, an SPL engineer uses the product roadmap and the requirements of desired systems to define and document the common and variable requirements of the SPL [25]. Thus, our starting point in the development of our SPL was to define the PLeTs requirements and identify whether they are common or variable.

However, identifying the MBT tools' requirements is a challenging task since, to the best of our knowledge, there are few updated contributions in the MBT literature about tools characteristics [12, 39], and there are a significant number of MBT tools available. Because of this, we performed a systematic mapping study (SMS) [6] to map out the available MBT tools and their main features. Furthermore, we resorted to a TDL of an industrial partner to discuss the requirements and validate the identified tools' features.

Based on this, we defined the following basic requirements to design our SPL of MBT tools:

(RQ1) *The MBT tools must support automatic generation of testing data*
        Reducing effort and investment and at the same time improving software quality are always the goals of a testing team. Thus, the PLeTs MBT tools should support the automatic generation of test cases and/or test scripts based on the system model. These MBT tools should accept a system model as an input, generate test cases/scripts (*Generate Expected Inputs*), execute test scripts, and then allows for the comparison of results. Those generated tools should also load the generated scripts and start the test (*Run Tests*). Certainly, in some situations, it could be desirable that a tool supports only some of these activities. For example, a functional MBT tool could be used to generate only a set of abstract test cases. It is important to note that the full automation of the testing process is still a dream [7]. Thus, the use of the MBT tools generated from PLeTs requires that some activities must be performed manually, such as the creation of system models and result analyses.

(RQ2) *Tools generated from PLeTs must support integration with other testing tools*
        The generation of MBT tools must take advantage of the integration with other testing tools to run the test scripts that were generated using MBT. Therefore, the last activities of the MBT process (*Generate Expected Outputs* and *Run Test*) should be designed to support an external tool, such as LoadRunner [16] or JaBUTi [47], or even an in-house tool. This requirement addresses the reduction of development time and costs in the development of MBT tools since the SPL engineer only has to design and develop components related to the testing script generation. Another motivation to include this requirement is that the testing team's knowledge about an already used testing tool is still a valuable skill since in some situations the use of an MBT tool would not be desirable. For instance, in some scenarios,

it is required that a specific feature must be implemented in an MBT tool to test an application. However, this kind of application or technology is not common in the company's portfolio. Thus, a test engineer could decide to save effort and investment necessary to implement this new feature and just use the legacy testing tool to test the application.

(RQ3) *PLeTs artifacts must be designed and developed to support automatic generation of MBT tools*

Based on the fact that MBT tools generated from PLeTs could be adopted by a company as an alternative to reducing their testing effort and that nowadays it is common for a company to have geographically distributed testing teams, changes to SPL artifacts must be easily documented and self-contained to facilitate the development and maintenance. Furthermore, usually, testers evolve a tool (e.g., by adding an extra tool capability). It must not require any knowledge about other tool's artifact's inner structure nor require any change in the source code of the previously developed artifacts. This means that the feature implementation must extend a tool in just one place [21]. Furthermore, distributed teams can access the same PLeTs repository and generate their own tools using these components developed by different teams. To alleviate the effort required by a testing team that wants to reuse components developed by other teams, such as understand the components' inner structure, we also defined that the use of these components on the generation of an MBT tool from PLeTs must require minimal manual intervention.

(RQ4) *PLeTs must not be bound to any proprietary SPL supporting environment or tool*

One particular concern regards the use of *off-the-shelf* tools, such as FeatureIDE [45], to support a company development life cycle since sometimes these tools do not meet the specific requirements of the companies aiming to adopt them. Furthermore, the adoption of an *off-the-shelf* tool would require specific platform expertise that could limit the company potential and also lead to high training costs. Moreover, most of the available tools require a reasonable financial investment in a software license and, in some cases, an expensive investment in SPL consulting. Thus, the decision to adopt a tool to support the automatic generation of a product from PLeTs might not cause a meaningful extra investment and should not require complex expertise.

It is important to note that the requirements *RQ3* and *RQ4* do not directly address the definition of features to MBT tools, but they address how we design our SPL and our choice of an SPL variability mechanism. In the following section, we present and discuss our design decisions, which are based on the requirements presented in this section. Furthermore, requirements *RQ1* and *RQ2* are high-level requirements, which could be decomposed into more specific ones. To facilitate the understanding and readability of this thesis, we introduce and discuss the specific requirements along with the text without mentioning it as a specific *RQ*.

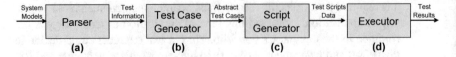

Fig. 14.3 MBT tool process

14.3.2 Design Decisions, Process, and Variability Control

The basic requirement *RQ1* defines that MBT tools generated from PLeTs must support the automatic generation of cases and scripts from system models. Although El-far [13] has initially presented and discussed MBT steps, we used the SMS results to identify the tool's common and variable characteristics. Based on that, we noticed that MBT tools share the following set of basic characteristics: extract test information from system models, generate the test cases/scripts, and run the test. Since the requirement *RQ2* defines that MBT tools must take advantage of the integration with other testing tools, it leads us to split the generation of test cases and scripts into two features. The first generates abstract test cases, which are not related to technology, and then the latter instantiates them to executable test scripts of a testing tool. Thus, an MBT tool generated from PLeTs could have the following basic features: extract test information from system models, generate abstract test cases, generate scripts, and run the test.

Figure 14.3 shows the adopted MBT process, which is based on the MBT process proposed by El-far [13]. Thus, an MBT tool generated from PLeTs must parse testing information from a file[1] (Fig. 14.3a) and based on this information generate the abstract test cases (Fig. 14.3b). After that, the MBT tool can instantiate the abstract test to a tool format (Fig. 14.3c) and then run the test (Fig. 14.3d).

After the identification of the basic features and the definition of the MBT tools' process, we focus on the analysis of the MBT tools, recovered from the SMS, to identify which set of features are related to each basic feature. For instance, some MBT tools use typical test case generation techniques to generate test cases, e.g., random generation [22] or graph search algorithms [48], or could deal with common modeling notations, e.g., UML or labeled state transition system (LSTS). It is important to highlight that we did not focus on identifying fine-grained features, such as common classes or methods necessary to parse a file, but rather identifying coarse-grained variabilities, such as a parser to extract the test information from some common modeling notations or a common test case generator implementation. This decision partially met the requirement *RQ3*, which defines that each feature implementation must be self-contained and extend a tool in just one place.

Since we have identified the tools' basic and specific features, we use an extend feature-oriented domain analysis (FODA) model [20] to represent the relationship

---

[1] Most software modeling tools export/store model's information using a structure file format, e.g., XML.

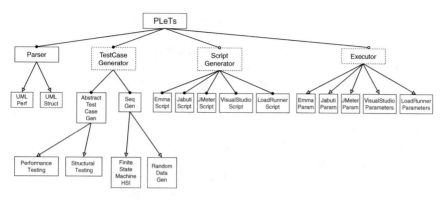

Fig. 14.4 PLeTs feature model [23]

between the child features and their parent feature and the dependency between features (cross-tree constrains). Figure 14.4 presents the PLeTs four basic features: *Parser, TestCaseGenerator, ScriptGenerator,* and *Executor* (notice that each basic feature represents a step in the MBT tool process—see Fig. 14.3). One important characteristic of PLeTs is that, even though the current feature model has a well-defined number of features, its feature model can be expanded to include new features whenever necessary. A description of the main PLeTs features is as follows:

- *Parser* is similar to the *Build Model* step in the MBT main activities (see Fig. 14.3). This is a mandatory feature with two child features, *UmlPerf* and *UmlStruct.* The former is related to extract performance testing information from UML diagrams, and the latter is related to extract structural testing information from UML diagrams. UML models were chosen as a feature since it is a well-established notation and has been used by several researchers [2, 8, 14, 15, 17, 18, 26, 30, 38, 42]. Furthermore, in several companies, UML notation has been used by their development and testing teams.
- *TestCaseGenerator* represents the *Generate Expected Inputs* step in the MBT process. It is a mandatory feature since every MBT tool must support the generation of test cases and has two child features: *AbstrTestCaseGen* and *SeqGen.* The former has two features: *PerformanceTesting* and *StructuralTesting.* The latter has two child features: *FiniteStateMachineHSI* and *RandomTestData.* The *AbstrTestCaseGen* feature encompasses the generation of the abstract test cases: for performance testing if the SPL engineer/testing engineer selected the *PerformanceTesting* feature or structural test if the *StructuralTesting* feature is selected. The *SeqGen* feature encompasses the generation of the test sequences. The test sequence generation can be based on the harmonized state identifiers' (HSI) sequence generator method when the *FiniteStateMachineHSI* feature is selected or based on random test data generation when the *RandomTestData* feature is selected. It is important to note that the definition of a test sequence

method and the generation of abstract test cases were based on our investigation of MBT tools. Furthermore, the decision to include the feature *FiniteStateMachineHSI*, among other sequence generator methods, was also motivated by a collaboration project with a research group from ICMC-US (Instituto de Ciências e Matemáticas e de Computação da Universidade de São Paulo), which has expertise in the development of test sequence methods. Thus, the *FiniteStateMachineHSI* feature was developed by a master student in the context of this collaboration project.

- *ScriptGenerator* is an optional feature, since some MBT tools can just generate abstract test cases that encompass the instantiation of the abstract test cases into executable scripts for a testing tool that will be used to run the test over the SUT. The *ScriptGenerator* feature has five child features: *VisualStudioScript*, *LoadRunnerScript*, *JMeterScript*, *JabutiScript*, and *EmmaScript*. These features encompass the instantiation of abstract test cases to concrete test scripts to the following testing tools: Visual Studio [33], LoadRunner [16], and JMeter [3] for performance testing and EMMA [36] and JaBUTi [47] for structural testing. Based on the assumption that a testing team should use at least one testing tool for each testing level, we expected that new script generator features will be continuously added reactively.
- *Executor* is an optional feature that embraces the automatic execution of the external testing tool and also the automatic execution of the tests. This feature also has five features: *VisualStudioSParameters*, *LoadRunerParameters*, *JMeterParameters*, *JabutiParameters*, and *EmmaParameters*. These features encompass the automatic execution of the testing tool and running the test scripts to the respective external testing tools: Visual Studio, LoadRunner, and JMeter for performance testing and EMMA and JaBUTi for structural testing.

Figure 14.4 shows several dependencies among features, which are denoted using propositional logic. For example, if feature *LoadRunnerParameters* is chosen to be integrated in an MBT tool, feature *LoadRunnerScript* must also be selected, since the generated tool will not able to run tests without test scripts. In turn, the selection of *LoadRunnerScript* implies the selection of feature *PerformanceTesting*, which encompasses the generation of abstract test cases for performance testing, which in turn requires the *SeqGen* feature. Furthermore, since our SPL adoption approach is proactive and reactive, the PLeTs feature model will evolve, and new features will be included. For instance, if the SPL owner/manager wants to support the generation of scripts to another external testing tool and also to support the automatic execution of the testing, it will have to include two new features, one to the parent *ScriptGenerator* and another to *Executor*. Moreover, it might be necessary to define their dependencies on other features.

Due to requirement *RQ3*, PLeTs artifacts must be designed and developed to support the automatic generation of MBT tools. Thus, the following design decisions were taken:

- The PLeTs feature model must support the definition of abstract and concrete features (green features on Fig. 14.4 are abstract and blue are concrete) [44]. Abstract features on PLeTs are used only for readability purposes, and concrete features must be mapped to exactly one component, as it does not require maintaining explicit traceability links and reduces mistakes, development effort, and costs. The PLeTs engineer can rely on *#ifdef*-based notations in case of feature interaction. Binding is done by matching feature and component names, in a 1:1 mapping

- To use a component replacement as a variability mechanism. Choosing this variability mechanism will require that the PLeTs engineer implements several versions of a component, where each version follows a different component specification, e.g., several parser implementations, where each implementation parses a different set of information. The component replacement mechanism allows the substitution, at compiling time, of a standard component by each implementation of the components (since it implements the same interface). Thus, a test engineer can derive an MBT tool just by selecting the desired tools' features, which are directly mapped to components.

Requirement *RQ4* defines that PLeTs artifacts must not be bound to any proprietary SPL supporting environment or tool. This requirement led us to design and develop an environment to support the design, development, and product generation of an SPL using a component replacement mechanism. Furthermore, the adoption of our environment does not require complex tool expertise or extra costs. Chapter 15 presents more details about the environment-specific requirements, design decisions, and their implementation. Besides, Chap. 15 also presents how the environment influences the support for the automatic generation of MBT tools from PLeTs.

14.3.3   Architecture and Implementation

As presented in Sect. 14.3.2, we defined the use of a replacement mechanism to develop each concrete feature of the PLeTs feature model. Thus, a PLeTs MBT tool is composed of a set of components and a common software base. PLeTs uses this approach to generate PLeTs products since it presents some advantages, for example, a high level of modularity and a simple one-to-one feature to code mapping.

- *IParser* is a mandatory variation point that has two exclusive variant components, *UmlPerf* and *UmlStruct*. It is important to notice that the associated variability indicates that the minimum and maximum number of variants is one (*minSelection = 1* and *maxSelection = 1*, respectively).
- *ITestCaseGen* is a mandatory variation point that has one mandatory component: *TestCaseGenerator*. This component provides two interfaces: *IAbstractTestGen* and *IseqGen*. The former interface can be implemented by one of the following components: *PerformanceTesting* or *StructuralTesting*. The latter interface can be implemented by one of the following components: *FiniteStateMachineHsi* or *RandomDataGenerator*. The minimum and maximum number of variants that

can implement the interface is one (*minSelection* = *1* and *maxSelection* = *1*, respectively).

- *IScriptGenerator* is an optional variation point that can be implemented by one of the following components: *VisualStudioScript, LoadRunnerScript, EmmaScript, JabutiScript*, and *JmeterScript*. Thus, the minimum number of variants that can implement the interface is zero (*minSelection* = *0*), while the maximum is one (*maxSelection* = *1*).
- *IExecutor* is an optional variation point that can be implemented by one of the following components: *VisualStudioScript, LoadRunnerScript, EmmaScript, JabutiScript*, and *JmeterScript*. The minimum number of variants that can implement the interface is zero (*minSelection* = *0*), while the maximum is one (*maxSelection* = *1*).

Each associated variability, in all components, indicates that one variant can be exclusively selected to resolve the variability. This can be solved using SMarty since it allows representing scenarios where the selection of a variant constrains the selection of another variant, as a constraint among the variants. For example, if component *LoadRunnerParameters* is selected to compose a PLeTs product, this will require that component *LoadRunnerScript* should also be selected. Furthermore, that selection will require that the *PerformanceTesting* component must be also selected. Besides, the constraints presented in the variability component model are used as input to resolve the dependencies among features when generating a product. For example, a valid configuration of a product derived from PLeTs could have the following components: *PLeTs, UmlParser, TestCaseGenerator, PerformanceTesting, FiniteStateMachineHsi, LoadRunnerScript*, and *LoadRunnerParameters*.

14.4 Example of Use: Generating Performance MBT Tools

In this section, we present two performance MBT tools generated from PLeTs using the PlugSPL [35] environment (see more in Chap. 15). Those MBT tools generate performance scripts and scenarios from UML use case and activity diagrams. They also have some common features and use the same approach: receive annotated UML use case and activity diagrams as input and automatically derive abstract test cases. After that, the abstract test cases can be instantiated to a script format (concrete test cases and scripts), and then the scripts can be executed using an existing load generator tool (e.g., LoadRunner) to test a web application. It is important to note that the main use of MBT has been directed to the test of functional aspects of software and only lately researchers have applied MBT to investigate techniques toward non-functional testing [4, 11, 34, 41].

Bernardino et al. [41] discuss how to apply MBT and UML models to automatically generate performance test cases and scripts. Most of them apply MBT in conjunction with a UML profile, such as Modelling and Analysis of Real-Time and Embedded Systems (MARTE) [5] or Schedulability Performance and Time (SPT), which are extensions of UML for modeling performance requirements. The use of these profiles provides modeling patterns with clear semantics allowing the automated generation of test cases and scripts.

Based on UML models, one can extract information for tests and then analyze the performance counters (e.g., throughput, transactions per second, and response time). Such information is distributed throughout several UML diagrams, e.g., use cases (UC), activity (AD), and sequence diagrams (SD). An approach that depicts how these diagrams are used to represent the information of performance testing is presented by Demathieu et al. [11], in which a model designed in SPT and composed of UML diagrams was tagged with specific properties such as probabilities on the incidence of use cases, response times for each activity, and resource availability.

Usually, the first step adopted by industry when testing applications for non-functional properties is to choose a given workload generator among the various available tools. The decision on which tool to better test an application involves several factors such as familiarity (has been used before), price, or target software platform. Furthermore, every workload generator has its peculiarities, configurations, and tweaks as well as common operations to be performed when mimicking user behavior within the SUT. Thus, test scenarios and scripts generated for some tools cannot be reused by another tool.

Figure 14.5 shows our approach, in which the main idea is to receive as an input the UML diagrams (Fig. 14.5a) and generate abstract test cases and scenarios (Fig. 14.5b) suitable for the derivation of test scenarios and scripts to a workload generator (Fig. 14.5c) and then execute the test (Fig. 14.5d). The main difference between our approach and MBT abstract test suites is the fact that we focus on creating intermediate models to use for performance testing rather than functional testing. Another contribution is that we apply MBT to construct a performance abstract test scenario. Based on that, test scenarios and scripts can be generated for a wide range of workload generators. Thus, to generate an MBT tool, from PLeTs, that generates scripts to a workload generator, the SPL engineer can reuse the previously developed components (e.g., parser and test case generator) and only design and develop the script generator and the executor components.

To apply our approach, we used an application scenario. For this purpose, we used the TPC-W benchmark [28] as an application example. TPC-W is a transactional web service benchmark that implements an e-commerce application that is used by the benchmark (or by any other workload generator). Thus, to generate scripts and scenarios to test the performance of the TPC-W application, we derived two performance MBT tools from PLeTs: PLeTsPerfLR and

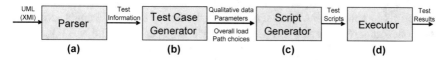

Fig. 14.5 An approach for generating performance scripts and scenarios

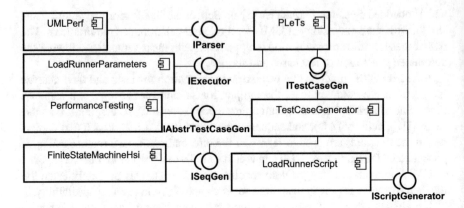

Fig. 14.6 PLeTsPerfLR tool architecture

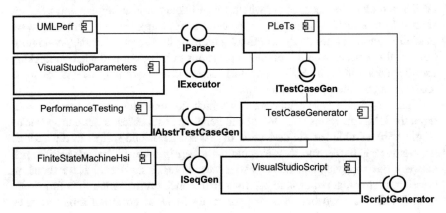

Fig. 14.7 PLeTsPerfVS tool architecture

PLeTsPerfVS. Figures 14.6 and 14.7 present the tool architecture, which depicted the common components shared by these tools (i.e., UmlPerf, PerformanceTesting, TestCaseGenerator, and FiniteStateMachineHsi). Since the tools share a set of common components and each step of our methodology is implemented in a component, both tools accepted UML models as input (UMLPerf component in Figs. 14.6 and 14.7) and automatically generate the abstract scenarios (components FiniteStateMachine, PerformanceTesting, and TestCaseGenerator—see Figs. 14.6 and 14.7).

The tools' specific components, which are load generator-oriented because they generate specific test scripts, are related to the script generation and test execution. Therefore, to generate the PLeTsPerfLR, we developed the LoadRunnerScript and the LoadRunnerParameters components, which are specific to the MBT tool that generates scripts and scenarios to the LoadRunner load generator (Fig. 14.6). To derive the MBT tool that generates scripts to the Visual Studio, the PLeTsPerfVS, we had to develop two specific components: VSScripts and VSParameters

(Fig. 14.7). It is important to highlight that the common components were coded with 1646 lines of code, the PLeTsPerfLR-specific components have 258 lines of code, and the PLeTsPerfVS-specific components have 344 lines of code. These numbers illustrate that the use of our SPL to generate MBT tools can reduce the development effort of MBT tools, e.g., the effort to develop the PLeTsPerfLR was decreased by almost 80%.

14.5 Example of Use: Generating Structural MBT Tools

This section presents two model-based testing tools, generated by PLeTs, to produce structural test cases from UML sequence diagrams. Since these tools are derived from PLeTs, they have common features and use the same approach: accept a system model as an input and automatically derive test cases using a random technique. After that, the test cases can be executed to test the corresponding code, i.e., measure structural coverage using existing testing tools. Our structural MBT tools are composed of the following features (see Fig. 14.8): (a) parser, extracts test information about the classes and methods to be tested from UML sequence diagrams; (b) test case generator, applies a random test data generation technique to generate an abstract structure, which has a technology-independent format (abstract test cases) and describes the test case information; (c) script generator, generates script/test driver for a specific testing tool from information contained in the abstract structure; and (d) executor, represents the test execution for a specific testing tool using the test driver generated in the previous step [9, 10].

It is important to notice that during the domain implementation, we first developed the common structural components, and then we focused on the development of the specific components (application implementation) required to generate the PletsStructJabuti tool, which generates script/test drivers and executes them using the JaBUTi tool. After that, we developed the specific structural components required to generate the PletsStructEmma MBT tool, which generates a script/test driver and executes it using the EMMA tool. In summary, both generated tools extract test information from annotated UML sequence diagrams (test models), generate an abstract structure, and instantiate the information present in this structure to generate and execute concrete test cases/test drivers, respectively, for

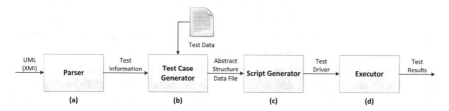

Fig. 14.8 An approach for generating structural test cases

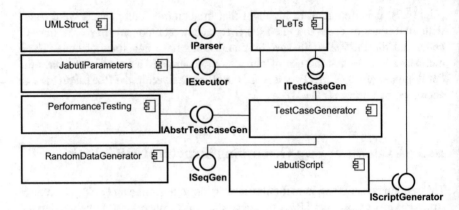

Fig. 14.9 PLeTsStructJabuti tool architecture

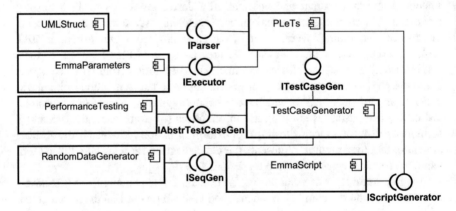

Fig. 14.10 PLeTsStructEmma tool architecture

the target tools: JaBUTi or EMMA. Furthermore, once the common components are developed and the first tool was generated, it was easy to generate the second one, because both tools share several features, which in turn are mapped to components, e.g., parser and test data generation. Therefore, we were able to develop the second tool with less effort due to the reuse of components already developed for the first tool.

Figures 14.9 and 14.10 present the architecture for the two structural testing tools: PletsStructJabuti and PletsStructEmma. The figures also show the tools' common (UmlStruct, TestCaseGenerator, RandomDataGenerator, and Structural-Testing) and specific components (JabutiScript, EmmaScripts, JabutiParameters, and EmmaParameters) used to implement the steps of our approach. The first two steps of our approach are related to the extraction of information from the UML sequence diagram and to generate an abstract test structure. The abstract test structure contains test case information and is used to generate scripts to different structural testing tools, in this case, the PletsStructJabuti and PletsStructEmma. The last two steps are technology-dependent, one to extract information from the abstract structure and to generate scripts and scenarios and the other to execute scripts and collect results from the execution of a structural testing tool. Thus, to generate the MBT tools from PLeTs, we reused the common components and developed two components, which support the two last steps of our approach.

14.6 Final Remarks

This chapter presented the requirements, the design decisions, and the development of a software product line of model-based testing (PLeTs). This SPL was used to generate a set of MBT tools that used the SMarty approach in their design. The main benefits and issues identified while developing our SPL are as follows.

The management of the whole MBT process can be performed by the tools that are generated by PLeTs SPL. The derived tools accept SUT models as input and, based on that, generate an output, which can be a test case suite or a script to a specific testing tool. Therefore, PLeTs was designed to allow a company, which already have a testing process, to adapt their environment to use the MBT tools generated by PLeTs.

Furthermore, to design and develop an MBT tool from scratch might be time-consuming and expensive. Therefore, we designed/developed PLeTs to support the automatic creation and execution of the scripts to any kind of testing tools that are able to import scripts or use template files. As we mentioned in this chapter, several different tools have already been developed using this approach.

Another important aspect to mention is that our collaboration with a technology development laboratory (TDL) from a big IT company gave us valuable feedback about using our SPL in an industrial setting. This feedback was used to update the MBT tools' requirements and then adjust the tools' features. Although we have had success in our collaboration, we know that other companies may have different tool requirements. Nonetheless, we believe that our SPL is flexible enough to support changes to meet these different requirements.

As we tried to show in this chapter, a feature can be easily incorporated to PLeTs to allow a new MBT tool functionality. This is allowed since PLeTs was developed using a component-based variability mechanism. Based on that, a new component can be developed and easily added to the PLeTs repository. Furthermore, we can select an existent component and modify it to support a different functionality. Figure 14.1 represents the situation where new components have a dependency relationship with another component, denoted by ≪*requires*≫. An undesired consequence of that is that managing dependency becomes more complex. Furthermore, manual selection of the features, which are mapped to components during the product generation, and resolving their constraints is an error-prone activity and requires highly skilled SPL engineers. Thus, to mitigate this issue, we defined a simple mapping to map features to components (1:1) and implemented features in a self-contained and code replacement way, to support the automatic generation of the products. The downside of the use of this coarse-grained variability is that during the development of some components, we cannot take full advantage of their common class and methods. For instance, components *UmlPerf* and *UmlStruct* extract testing information from a UML diagram, and then they can share some common methods, such as a method used to open a UML file. Therefore, these two components could be developed as a single component, reusing common methods. However, as currently we identify and manage variability at the component level, we lose fine-grained reuse. A solution would be to use another variability mechanism, in combination with the actual mechanism, to support fine-grained variability, such as preprocessor directives. Actually, *#ifdef*-based notations already can be used as a variability mechanism inside the PLeTs components, but the PlugSPL environment must be changed to support the SPL design and the automatic product generation.

Finally, in this chapter, we also discussed a set of requirements and our design decisions addressing the development of PlugSPL (see Chap. 15) to support the SPL development life cycle. Furthermore, we presented how the PlugSPL environment can be used to support the design, product configuration, and generation of component-based SPLs. Besides the products generated for the TDL, some of the generated tools have also been used in some case studies and student projects to support the generation of testing tools to support different testing techniques and approaches [9, 40].

Acknowledgement This work is partially supported by the Brazilian funding agency CNPq (Grant 306250/2021-7).

References

1. Abbors, F., Backlund, A., Truscan, D.: MATERA - An integrated framework for model-based testing. In: Proceedings of the 17th IEEE International Conference and Workshops on the Engineering of Computer-Based Systems, pp. 321–328 (2010)
2. Andaloussi, B.S., Braun, A.: A test specification method for software interoperability tests in offshore scenarios: A case study. In: Proceedings of the IEEE International Conference on Global Software Engineering, pp. 169–178 (2006)
3. Apache: JMeter Performance Test. https://jmeter.apache.org/. Accessed 20 March 2020
4. Barna, C., Litoiu, M., Ghanbari, H.: Model-based performance testing. In: Proceedings of the 33rd International Conference on Software Engineering, pp. 872–875 (2011)
5. Bernardi, S., Merseguer, J.: A UML profile for dependability analysis of real-time embedded systems. In: Proceedings of the 6th International Workshop on Software and Performance, pp. 115–124 (2007)
6. Bernardino, M., Rodrigues, E.M., Zorzo, A.F., Marchezan, L.: Systematic mapping study on MBT: tools and models. IET Software **11**, 141–155(14) (2017)
7. Bertolino, A.: Software testing research: achievements, challenges, dreams. In: Proceedings of the Future of Software Engineering, pp. 85–103 (2007)
8. Cartaxo, E., Neto, F., Machado, P.: Test case generation by means of UML sequence diagrams and labeled transition systems. In: Proceedings of the IEEE International Conference on Systems, Man and Cybernetics, pp. 1292–1297 (2007)

9. Costa, L.T.: Conjunto de Características para Teste de Desempenho: Uma Visão a Partir de Ferramentas. Master's Thesis (in Portuguese), Pontifícia Universidade Católica do Rio Grande do Sul, Porto Alegre, Brazil (2012)
10. Costa, L.T., Czekster, R.M., Oliveira, F.M., Rodrigues, E.D.M., Silveira, M.B., Zorzo, A.F.: Generating performance test scripts and scenarios based on abstract intermediate models. In: Proceedings of the 24th International Conference on Software Engineering and Knowledge Engineering, pp. 112–117 (2012)
11. Demathieu, S., Thomas, F., André, C., Gérard, S., Terrier, F.: First experiments using the UML profile for marte. In: Proceedings of the 11th IEEE Symposium on Object Oriented Real-Time Distributed Computing, pp. 50–57 (2008)
12. Dias Neto, A.C., Subramanyan, R., Vieira, M., Travassos, G.H.: A survey on model–based testing approaches: A systematic review. In: Proceedings of the 1st ACM international Workshop on Empirical Assessment of Software Engineering Languages and Technologies, pp. 31–36 (2007)
13. El-Far, I.K., Whittaker, J.A.: Model-based software testing. In: Marciniak, J. (ed.) Encyclopedia of Software Engineering, pp. 825–837. Wiley, Hoboken (2001)
14. Farooq, Q., Lam, C.P.: Evolving the quality of a model-based test suite. In: Proceedings of the IEEE International Conference on Software Testing, Verification, and Validation Workshops, pp. 141–149 (2009)
15. Farooq, Q., Iqbal, M., Malik, Z., Riebisch, M.: A model-based regression testing approach for evolving software systems with flexible tool support. In: Proceedings of the 17th IEEE International Conference and Workshops on Engineering of Computer Based Systems, pp. 41–49 (2010)
16. Focus, M.: LoadRunner Professional.   https://www.microfocus.com/en-us/products/loadrunner-professional/. Accessed 20 Feb 2020
17. Gonczy, L., Heckel, R., Varro, D.: Model-based testing of service infrastructure components. In: Proceedings of the 7th International Workshop Testing of Software and Communicating Systems, pp. 155–170 (2007)
18. Hasling, B., Goetz, H., Beetz, K.: Model-based testing of system requirements using UML use case models. In: Proceedings of the 1st International Conference on Software Testing, Verification, and Validation, pp. 367–376 (2008)
19. Heiskanen, H., Jääskeläinen, A., Katara, M.: Debug support for model-based GUI testing. In: Proceedings of the 3rd International Conference on Software Testing, Verification and Validation, pp. 25–34 (2010)
20. Kang, K.C, Cohen, S.G., Hess, J.A., Novak, W.E., Peterson, A.S. Feature-Oriented Domain Analysis (FODA) Feasibility Study. Carnegie-Mellon University, Pittsburgh Software Engineering Institute (1990)
21. Kästner, C., Apel, S., Kuhlemann, M.: Granularity in software product lines. In: Proceedings of the 30th International Conference on Software Engineering, pp. 311–320 (2008)
22. Korel, B.: Automated software test data generation. IEEE Trans. Softw. Eng. **16**, 870–879 (1990)
23. Laser, M.S., Rodrigues, E.M., Domingues, A., Oliveira, F., Zorzo, A.F.: Research notes on the architectural evolution of a software product line. Int. J. Softw. Eng. Knowled. Eng. **25**, 1753–1758 (2015)
24. Legeard, B., Utting, M.: Practical Model-Based Testing: A Tools Approach. Morgan Kaufmann Publishers, Burlington (2006)
25. Linden, F.J., Schmid, K., Rommes, E.: Software Product Lines in Action: The Best Industrial Practice in Product Line Engineering. Springer, New York (2007)
26. Löffler, R., Meyer, M., Gottschalk, M.: Formal Scenario-based requirements specification and test case generation in healthcare applications. In: Proceedings of the Workshop on Software Engineering in Health Care, pp. 57–67 (2010)
27. Memon, A.M.: An event-flow model of GUI-based applications for testing: Research articles. Softw. Testing Verif. Reliab. **17**, 137–157 (2007)
28. Menascé, D.A.: TPC-W: A benchmark for e-Commerce. IEEE Int. Comput. **6**(3), 83–87 (2002)

29. Myers, G.J., Sandler, C., Badgett, T.: The Art of Software Testing. Wiley, Hoboken (2011)
30. Olimpiew, E.M.: Model-based testing for software product lines. Ph.D. Thesis, George Mason University, Washington (2008)
31. OliveiraJr, E., Gimenes, I.M.S., Maldonado, J.C.: Systematic management of variability in UML-based software product lines. J. Univer. Comput. Sci. **16**, 2374–2393 (2010)
32. OMG: Unified Modeling Language - UML. http://www.uml.org/. Accessed 30 April 2020
33. Perez, J., Guckenheimer, S.: Software Engineering with Microsoft Visual Studio Team System. Pearson Education, London (2006)
34. Rodrigues, E.M., Viccari, L.D., Zorzo, A.F.: PLeTs - Test automation using software product lines and model-based testing. In: Proceedings of the 22th International Conference on Software Engineering and Knowledge Engineering, pp. 483–488 (2010)
35. Rodrigues, E.M., Zorzo, A.F., OliveiraJr, E, Gimenes, I.M.S., Maldonado, J.C., Domingues, A.R.: PlugSPL: An automated environment for supporting plugin-based software product lines. In: Proceedings of the 24th International Conference on Software Engineering and Knowledge Engineering, pp. 647–650 (2012)
36. Roubtsov, V.: EMMA: a Free Java Code Coverage Tool. http://emma.sourceforge.net. Accessed 20 March 2020
37. Sarma, M., Murthy, P., Jell, S., Ulrich, A.: Model-based testing in industry: A case study with two MBT tools. In: Proceedings of the 5th Workshop on Automation of Software Test, pp. 87–90 (2010)
38. Schulz, S., Honkola, J., Huima, A.: Towards model-based testing with architecture models. In: Proceedings of the 14th Annual IEEE International Conference and Workshops on the Engineering of Computer-Based Systems, pp. 495–502 (2007)
39. Shafique, M., Labiche, Y.: A systematic review of model-based testing tool support. Technical Report, Department of Systems and Computer Engineering, Carleton University, Ottawa, Canada (2010). http://squall.sce.carleton.ca/pubs/tech_report/TR_SCE-10-04.pdf
40. Silveira, M.B.: Conjunto de Características para Teste de Desempenho: uma Visão a partir de Modelos. Master's thesis (in Portuguese), Pontifícia Universidade Católica do Rio Grande do Sul, Porto Alegre, Brazil (2012)
41. Silveira, M.B., Rodrigues, E.M., Zorzo, A.F., Vieira, H., Oliveira, F.M.: Model-based automatic generation of performance test scripts. In: Proceedings of the 13th International Conference on Software Engineering and Knowledge Engineering, pp. 258–263 (2011)
42. Stefanescu, A., Wieczorek, S., Kirshin, A.: MBT4Chor: A model-based testing approach for service choreographies. In: Proceedings of the 5th European Conference on Model Driven Architecture - Foundations and Applications, pp. 313–324 (2009)
43. Stefanescu, A., Wieczorek, S., Wendland, M.F.: Using the UML testing profile for enterprise service choreographies. In: Proceedings of the 36th Euromicro Conference on Software Engineering and Advanced Applications, pp. 12–19 (2010)
44. Thum, T., Kastner, C., Erdweg, S., Siegmund, N.: Abstract features in feature modeling. In: Proceedings of the 15th International Software Product Line Conference, pp. 191–200 (2011)
45. Thüm, T., Kästner, C., Benduhn, F., Meinicke, J., Saake, G., Leich, T.: FeatureIDE: An extensible framework for feature-oriented software development. Sci. Comput. Programm. **1**, 1–16 (2012)
46. Veanes, M., Campbell, C., Grieskamp, W., Schulte, W., Tillmann, N., Nachmanson, L.: Model-based testing of object-oriented reactive systems with spec explorer. In: Formal Methods and Testing, pp. 39–76. Springer, Berlin (2008)
47. Vincenzi, A., Maldonado, J., Wong, W., Delamaro, M.: Coverage testing of Java programs and components. Sci. Comput. Programm. **56**, 211–230 (2005)
48. Yuan, Y., Li, Z., Sun, W.: A graph-search based approach to BPEL4WS test generation. In: International Conference on Software Engineering Advances, pp. 1–9 (2012)

Chapter 15
PlugSPL: An Environment to Support SPL Life Cycle

Elder M. Rodrigues and Avelino F. Zorzo

Abstract In recent years, software product line engineering (SPLE) has emerged as a promising reusability approach that brings out some important benefits, e.g., it increases the reusability of its core assets while decreasing the time to market. The SPL approach focuses mainly on a two-life cycle model: domain engineering, where the SPL core asset is developed for reuse, and application engineering, where the core asset is reused to generate specific products. It is important to highlight that the success of the SPL approach depends on several principles, in particular variability management. Although the SPL engineering brings out important benefits, it is clear the lack of environments aimed at automating the overall SPL life cycle, including (i) configuration of feature model (FM); (ii) configuration of products; and (iii) generation of products. Literature and industry present several important tools that encompass part of the SPL development life cycle, such as SPLOT and pure::variants. The plugin approach has also received an increasing attention in the development of SPLs. Some SPL-based approaches are characterized by the development of different applications through the selection/development of different sets of plugins. Although the use of plugins to develop SPL products is a promising approach and several works have been published in recent years, there is no tool to fully support plugin-based SPLs. This chapter presents PlugSPL (This chapter is an expanded version of a previously published paper Rodrigues et al. (Plugspl: An automated environment for supporting plugin-based software product lines. In: SEKE, pp. 647–650, 2012).), an automated environment to support the overall plugin-based SPL life cycle. PlugSPL is a modular environment, written in C#, in which a test manager can design an SPL using the SMarty approach, configure

E. M. Rodrigues (✉)
Department of Computer Systems, Federal University of Pampa, Alegrete, Rio Grande do Sul, Brazil
e-mail: elderrodrigues@unipampa.edu.br

A. F. Zorzo
Department of Computer Systems, Pontifical Catholic University of Rio Grande do Sul, Porto Alegre, Rio Grande do Sul, Brazil
e-mail: avelino.zorzo@pucrs.br

E. OliveiraJr (ed), *UML-Based Software Product Line Engineering with SMarty*,
https://doi.org/10.1007/978-3-031-18556-4_15

and develop its components, define a valid product configuration, and generate a product. Although there are tools that partially give support to the SPL life cycle as, for instance, pure::variants, to the best of our knowledge, there was no tool that supported plugin-based SPLs and the overall SPL life cycle. Furthermore, there are tools to design FMs, but most of them use different notations and file formats. PlugSPL provides capabilities with regard to creating or import/export FMs from/to other tools and uses a commonly used file format. Therefore, there is no need to incorporate other tools/environments into PlugSPL. Although PlugSPL is a flexible environment for modeling FMs, its most significant benefit is supporting the generation of SPL products based on its FM. Moreover, PlugSPL automatically generates an abstract class structure, which can be used to develop third-party plugins. A PlugSPL application example is presented for deriving MBT tools from the PLeTs product line.

15.1   The Role of SMarty in This Work

PlugSPL is a tool that is built initially for the PLeTs product line (see Chap. 14). Since PLeTs used SMarty to manage the dependencies among components and to represent the variability in the PLeTs architecture, the main role of SMarty in this work is related to the PLeTs product line (see Chap. 14).

15.2   Introduction

Software product line (SPL) has emerged as a promising technique to achieve systematic reuse and, at the same time, decrease development costs and time to market [21]. Although the use of SPL practices has significantly increased in recent years, with an extensive list of successful cases,[1] there are still many challenges when implementing SPLs in industrial settings [12].

One particular concern relates to the use of *off-the-shelf* tools, e.g., pure::variants [3] and Gears [13], to support the SPL development life cycle, since frequently these tools do not meet specific requirements of companies aiming to adopt them. To overcome this, many companies set to develop in-house solutions to support their specific needs.

The SPL community, however, currently lacks evidence on the driving factors around custom-based solutions, which hinders tool vendors and developers from having feedback from industrial clients outside their clientele. To mitigate this, we report our experience in implementing an SPL to derive testing tools for a laboratory of a global IT company. In particular, we describe the specific requirements of that

---

[1] http://www.sei.cmu.edu/productlines/casestudies/.

company and argue that existing tools fail to support them. We also present the design decisions in creating a customized solution supporting the target SPL. Our contribution is twofold: (i) we identify a set of requirements that, although specific to our research context, already point needs currently not addressed by existing tools, either commercial or open-source. Thus, we elicit practical scenarios that tool vendors and/or developers may consider supporting; (ii) we report our design decisions in fulfilling these requirements for an in-house solution developed for our partner company. These decisions, in turn, may be reused or adapted to improve existing tools or when devising solutions targeting similar needs.

This chapter is organized as follows. Section 15.3 presents some context relative to the company, from which Sect. 15.5 builds on. The latest one then enumerates the elicited requirements, which we address with specific design decisions, discussed in Sect. 15.6. Section 15.7 briefly presents our custom-made tool and its usage workflow. Section 15.8 revisits related work, while Sect. 15.9 concludes this chapter and points out final remarks.

15.3 Context

This research was performed in cooperation with the technology development lab (hereafter referred to as TDL) of a global IT company, whose development and testing teams are located in different regions worldwide.

In the partner IT company, development is performed over different programming languages and IDEs (integrated development environments), including Visual Studio (for Microsoft-based solutions), Eclipse (for Java-based implementations), Flash Builder, PHP, and packaged applications (e.g., Siebel and Oracle).

Testing teams use commercial and open-source frameworks and tools to partially automate their testing activities. Frequently, however, due to the complexity of the testing in place, these teams create custom components to enable testing non-trivial applications. For example, testers may need to create web service-based scripts to test back-end components that provide interfaces to the front-end of a given application or components that simulate asynchronous messages for offline business processes. Currently, due to the distributed nature of the testing teams, custom components are rarely shared, thus leading to redundancy, little reuse, coding inconsistencies, higher development costs, etc.

To eliminate the effort of repeatedly creating custom infrastructure, we started a pilot study on SPL adoption with the TDL of our partner company. Upon success, we aim to replicate or apply it in different testing teams, if not all of them. In particular, we used an SPL called PLeTs [6] (see Chap. 14) that supports the derivation of a particular testing infrastructure from a set of shared components (product configuration), which are then glued together (product derivation). In this SPL, derived products are testing tools that take behavioral models as input; these models denote specific test cases, thus leveraging testing teams to follow a model-based approach [29], a process that we describe elsewhere [6].

Before creating any tool to support product configuration and derivation in the target SPL, the TDL first considered the use of off-the-shelf solutions, provided that specific requirements were met. We describe this requirements list in Sect. 15.5.

15.4 Background

In recent years, the plugin concept has emerged as an interesting alternative for reusing software artifacts de facto [16]. Moreover, plugins are a useful way to develop applications in which functionalities must be extended at runtime.

To take advantage of the plugin concept for developing software, it is necessary to design and implement a system as a core application that must be extended with features implemented as software components. A successful example of the plugin approach is the Eclipse platform [11], which is composed of several projects to which plugins are developed and incorporated to improve both the platform and the providing services.

The plugin approach has also received increasing attention in the development of SPLs [4, 31]. The SPL approach has emerged over the last years due to competitiveness in the software development segment. The economic considerations of software companies, such as cost and time to market, motivate the transition from single-product development to the SPL approach, in which products are developed in a large-scale reuse perspective [14]. Whereas an SPL can be defined as a set of applications that share a common set of features and are developed based on a common set of core assets, the plugin approach can be easily applied to build new applications by plugging different sets of plugins to a core application [26]. Although the use of plugins to develop products is a promising approach and several works have been published in recent years, there is no tool to support plugin-based SPLs.

15.5 Requirements

This section presents the requirements we identified with regard to enabling the configuration (component selection) and derivation of products (gluing selected components).

(RQ. 1) The adopted tool must not be bound to any IDE. Based on the fact that in most companies the development and testing teams, usually, take advantage of a significant number of different solutions, e.g., IDEs, programming language, and version control system, they use solutions from different distributors/vendors (e.g., Eclipse for Java and Visual Studio for C#). The adopted tool must not impose any IDE, as that would require specific platform expertise that could limit the company's potential and also lead to training costs unrelated to the adoption of an SPL-based solution alone.

(RQ. 2) The adopted tool must support a graphical-based notation for designing feature models. Following the fact that features are an effective communication medium across different stakeholders and feature model-based notations are a widespread mechanism to capture variability, to support for variability modeling, we use feature models (FMs). For example, in a company, the FMs can be used as the main communication mechanism with stakeholders outside testing teams and possibly non-technical staff (e.g., project managers). Also, we consider that FMs provide testers with a quick visualization of the existing features in the current snapshot of the testing infrastructure and how each feature relates to one another. In some cases, stakeholders could state a preference toward graphical notations, as they consider textual ones to be linear, i.e., one element is only known when another one ends and, as such, hinders an immediate grasp of the underlying structure.

(RQ. 3) The adopted tool must support a graphical-based notation for designing structural architectural models. Since testing teams could be geographically distributed, changes to the underlying test infrastructure must be documented at all times to facilitate communication and future maintenance. Furthermore, both models should be kept in sync with each other, to facilitate the communication between the teams.

(RQ. 4) Structural architectural models must be kept in synchronization with the FM and codebase (and vice versa). In addition to keeping FMs, changes should also be documented in terms of structural architectural models that closely resemble the coding artifacts in the testing infrastructure (e.g., UML component diagrams). These models capture what feature models alone would otherwise miss (e.g., a class method). In addition, both models should be kept in sync with each other and the codebase (full round-tripping). As before, models should be presented/edited graphically.

(RQ. 5) The tool must be extensible to support different structural architectural models and FM notations. The TDL states that structural architectural modeling should be centered on UML diagrams (see (RQ. 3)), but they point out the benefit of supporting other notations in the future (e.g., domain-specific languages). Likewise, one should also account for different FM notations, with extensions added as needed.

(RQ. 6) FMs should be derivable from structural architectural models. Since SPL is something new for most companies, testers are familiar with standard UML structural models, while less so with feature models. To prevent initial mistakes and to minimize the effort in extending the testing infrastructure, the tool must be able to recover an FM from the defined structural architecture, which in turn can be tuned accordingly.

(RQ. 7) Structural architectural models should be derivable from FMs. As time progresses and FMs become more common among stakeholders, testers can start extending the testing infrastructure by first changing the FM and then deriving the corresponding structural architectural model, which can be tuned accordingly (round-trip is already requested by (RQ. 4).

(RQ. 8) For each product of the testing infrastructure, it should be possible to derive its corresponding structural architectural model. Testing tools (products) are the result of selecting and combining components. For each product, it should be possible to generate its structural architectural model, which results from selecting specific elements from the architectural model of the whole SPL.

(RQ. 9) Traceability links among models and implementation assets/elements should require minimal human intervention/effort. Traceability is an important concern for the TDL, as FMs and structural architectural models need to be mapped to implementation assets, and vice versa. To prevent a high burden on manually keeping such links, any adopted solution must automate traceability as fully as possible.

(RQ. 10) When extending the existing infrastructure with new features (components), their implementation must adhere to specific interfaces. To decrease coding effort and avoid human mistakes while enforcing coding styles, an initial skeleton implementation should be automatically derived from specific code templates. Currently, when testers evolve the testing infrastructure (e.g., when implementing the interface of a core capability of the testing infrastructure), they often copy and adapt an existing implementation or write a new one from scratch.

(RQ. 11) The adopted tool must allow the creation of new glue code generators that should be pluggable into the system without intrusiveness changes. The adopted tool must allow hooking code generators to produce glue code for specific target languages. This is aligned with the need to integrate with non-Microsoft solutions.

Summary by evaluating existing tools for SPL adoption, we found that no existing off-the-shelf tool (either commercial or open-source) meets all of the presented requirements. Therefore, we and the TDL set to create an in-house component-based tool to support the target SPL. In Sect. 15.6, we describe our design decisions in building such a tool.

15.6 Design Decisions

In this section, we report our design decisions (DDs) in creating an in-house tool supporting the requirements previously discussed. For each design decision, we refer to the associated requirements.

(DDT1) We define an extensible environment for using different feature models. The tool includes a feature model editor that currently supports a modified FODA notation together with abstract features [27]. (RQT 1, 2, 5)

(DDT2) We define an extensible environment for using different structural models. Currently, we use UML component models as structural models, as they are the one most used modeling notation. Therefore, this adoption mitigates a need for extensive training, as it is the standard notation taught in universities in our country. The editor supports SMarty notation [20] to capture underlying variability in the model. (RQT 3, 5)

(DDT3) Every concrete feature is mapped to exactly one component, as it dispenses maintaining explicit traceability links, and thus reduces mistakes, development effort, and costs. We rely on *#ifdef*-based notations in case of feature interaction. Binding is done by matching feature and component names, in a 1:1. (RQT 4, 9)

(DDT4) We synchronize the feature and structural models to maintain consistency after performing changes in each of them. Consistency, in this case, is eased, by relying on the 1:1 mapping, which transforms models straightforward. (RQT 4, 6, 7, 9)

(DDT5) Every component corresponds to a single compilation unit. Again, the binding is done by matching names. Based on the product configuration and relying on the 1:1 mapping, we create a program that instantiates the components of the given configuration. (RQT 8)

(DDT6) Each component corresponds to a project (e.g., Visual Studio). The environment supports the generation of an initial code skeleton (classes realizing the designed components), to which developers must complete, i.e., provide implementation to current empty methods. (RQT 10)

(DDT7) We define an extensible environment for using different target languages. Currently, we use C# (RQT 11).

15.7 PlugSPL Environment: Supporting Plugin-Based Software Product Lines

In this section, we present the PlugSPL environment that has been developed to support the design, product configuration, and generation of plugin-based SPLs [23, 31, 32]. Although there are many tools focused on SPL modeling, consistence checking [18, 25], and product generation support [2], currently, there is no tool that integrates all SPL development phases. Moreover, there is no tool to support the automated product configuration and product generation from a plugin-based SPL. Therefore, we designed and developed PlugSPL to support all plugin-based SPL development phases. Figure 15.1 presents the PlugSPL modules and activities, as follows:

15.7.1 SPL Design Activity

The SPL design activity is the starting point in PlugSPL and aims to support the design of the SPL utilizing a graphical FM notation or a UML component diagram.

Although PlugSPL supports FMs, the tool ultimately operates on the level of components and requires the understanding of concepts such as components,

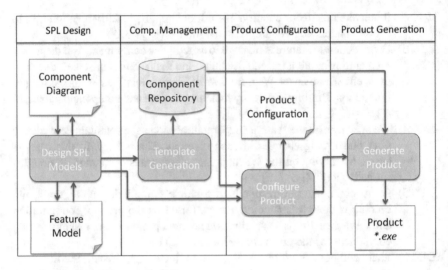

Fig. 15.1 The PlugSPL modules [24]

interfaces, and realization, as these drive later activities. For domain engineers with a strong background on FMs, but less so in component diagrams, the tool alleviates the modeling activity by supporting the automatic generation of a component diagram from the designed FM. In such a case, engineers still manipulate components in other activities but do not perform any modeling activity in terms of UML component diagrams. Similarly, for those with a strong background in UML component diagrams, but less so in FMs, the tool also supports the automatic generation of an FM from an existing component diagram. In both cases, edits in generated models are automatically synchronized with the models from which they are created, and vice versa, along with their constraints (full round-tripping). By supporting both FMs and component diagrams and automatic conversion between them, PlugSPL allows effective communication among different stakeholders in the TDL, with different modeling expertise.

To design an SPL using FMs, domain engineers rely on the FM graphical editor plugin (see Fig. 15.2). Besides supporting FODA elements (except or-groups), the editor allows marking features as abstract [28] (features are set to be concrete by default). Abstract features exist only to improve the organization of the FM and are not mapped to any implementation element (class, interface, macro, etc.). Concrete features, on the other hand, follow a 1:1 mapping to a corresponding implementation component and ultimately to a whole compilation unit. This mapping allows PlugSPL to trace a feature throughout its life cycle.

For the cases where domain engineers choose to model the SPL using component diagrams, they first select that diagram type (the UML component diagram editor is shown in Fig. 15.3). In this modeling approach, features are represented as components, which connect to other components by realizing their required interfaces. Since more than one component can implement a given interface, a required

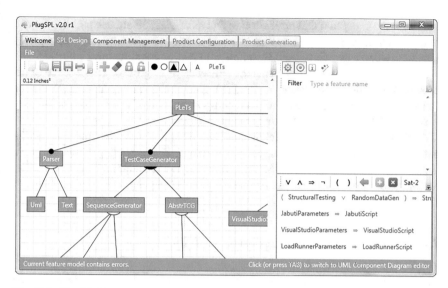

Fig. 15.2 PlugSPL feature model editor [24]

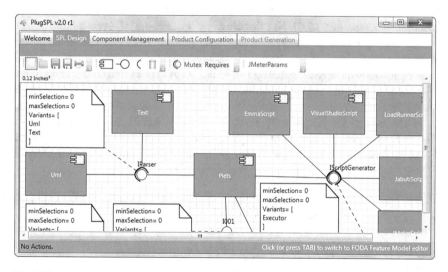

Fig. 15.3 PlugSPL component diagram editor [24]

interface defines a variation point, and connecting components denote specific variants. These variation points can be further detailed by means of *tags* (UML comments, shown in Fig. 15.3) and *stereotypes* (e.g., <<Mutex>> group and <<Requires>> dependencies), allowing a fine-grained control over the variability in place. Tags allow engineers to control the cardinality of instances of each connecting component (captured as *minSelection* and *maxSelection*) and specify the set of possible variants. The value of *minSelection/maxSelection* is either zero or one, with the exception that *minSelection* and *maxSelection* are never both zero and that *minSelection* is always less than or equal to *maxSelection*. Hence, this captures mandatory (*minSelection* = *maxSelection* = 1) and optional features (*minSelection* = 0, *maxSelection* = 1), but prevents the existence of or-groups. The absence of or-groups is currently a limitation, as PlugSPL cannot resolve which variant instance to use when integrating it with a given component. PlugSPL relies on the SMarty variability UML profile [20] as an annotation scheme.

Following a plugin-based architecture, the design activity in PlugSPL can be extended with other plugins supporting different FM modeling notations (e.g., cardinality-based FM [7]) or UML diagrams (e.g., class diagram). It can also be extended to support different file formats (e.g., SPLOT [19]).

15.7.2 Component Management Activity

In PlugSPL, the component management activity assists domain engineers in the implementation of the SPL components. Given the set of previously defined interfaces, domain engineers define their method signatures (operations) by importing external files (see Fig. 15.4). Not favoring any specific editor, even a built-in one, allows testing teams to continue using their preferred IDE or editor. Once the interfaces are defined, given the set of declared components, their interfaces, and their connections, PlugSPL generates an initial set of classes that conforms to them; still, these classes are not runnable, but rather skeletons whose associated methods are empty.

In the current C# plugin supporting this activity, each component results in a Visual Studio project, and each interface/class matches exactly one component. These projects are then distributed among different developers and/or testing teams,

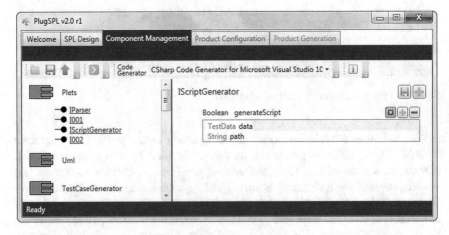

Fig. 15.4 PlugSPL component management [24]

which then complete their implementation. In this process, developers instantiate interfaces through *fake* statements that are later replaced during *Product Generation*. This is due to the fact that developers cannot (and should not) predict which component can provide the contract of any given interface. Figure 15.6 illustrates this: instantiation of an `IParser` is done by instantiating the `DummyIParser` interface, a semantically incorrect statement, as interfaces cannot be directly instantiated (they only state a contract and thus lack any behavior on their own). This resembles the dependency injection pattern [22], while avoiding the burden of keeping XML configuration files, as required by many existing frameworks (e.g., Spring [30]). The penalty, in this case, is that variability is resolved at an early stage (during *Product Generation*) and not during runtime. Once the implementation of components is completed (they are now in the form of complete Visual Studio projects), they are fed back to PlugSPL, which in turn saves them in the component repository, provided no integration problem occurs.

15.7.3 Product Configuration Activity

In this activity, application engineers select the components that should comprise a target product (see Fig. 15.5). To allow such configuration, PlugSPL relies on the feature or component models previously designed, along with the components stored in the project workspace.

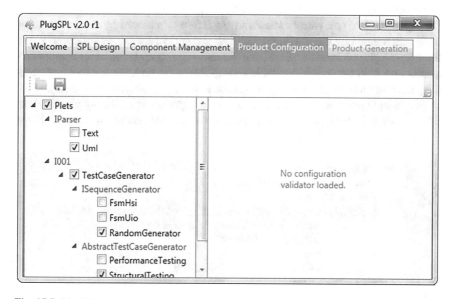

Fig. 15.5 PlugSPL product configuration [24]

PlugSPL generates a tree view of the project's components and their interfaces, along with the set of components that can connect to each such interface. For instance, following the UML component diagram in Fig. 15.3, two components implement IParser and serve as its variants: UML and Text. In that case, UML and Text appear as child nodes of IParser in the tree view in Fig. 15.5.

During configuration, application engineers select one component for each provided interface. In accordance with the constraints defined during the SPL design, PlugSPL automatically manages dependencies for selected components. The only exception occurs when configuration conflicts arise, which are then reported and must be manually fixed. Once a product is configured, the configuration is saved in the project workspace, and application engineers proceed to generate target products.

15.7.4 Product Generation Activity

In the product generation activity, from an existing product configuration and its chosen components, PlugSPL selects the corresponding Visual Studio projects generated during *Component Management*. PlugSPL then copies the source code of the selected components from the project workspace to a specified output folder, where components are then glued together. Gluing is performed by replacing extension points that instantiate interfaces (*fake* statements as previously discussed) by the instantiation of the concrete components in the configuration that support such interfaces. Figure 15.7 illustrates this: on line 5, the instantiation of DummyIParser (previously shown in Fig. 15.6) is replaced by the instantiation of the UML concrete class. Gluing also sets dependencies among different Visual Studio projects, i.e., among related components. The compilation of all components results in a final product (executable testing infrastructure). As in other activities, the plugin supporting this activity is specific to C#-based projects (Fig. 15.7).

Plugin implementation granularity [10] is an important issue during plugin-based SPL design and development phases. To improve the code reuse and to simplify the

```
1   public class PLeTs{
2       string fileName, newFileName;
3       //ommited code
4       Console.WriteLine("Initializing <Parser> component...");
5       IParser parser = new DummyIParser();
6       parser.LoadDocument(fileName);
7       parser.ConvertStructures();
8       parser.SaveDocument(newFileName);
9       //ommited code
10  }
```

Fig. 15.6 Code before the replacement

```
1   public class PLeTs{
2       string fileName, newFileName;
3       //ommited code
4       Console.WriteLine("Initializing <Parser> component...");
5       IParser parser = new Uml();
6       parser.LoadDocument(fileName);
7       parser.ConvertStructures();
8       parser.SaveDocument(newFileName);
9       //ommited code
10  }
```

Fig. 15.7 Code after the replacement [24]

automatic mapping between features and plugins, PlugSPL implements each feature as a plugin.

15.8 Related Work

There are several mechanisms to implement variability in an SPL, for instance, preprocessor directives [9]. Such mechanisms are directly related to plugin-based mechanisms as in [4, 31].

Cervantes and Charleston-Villalobos [4] proposed an SPL architecture in which applications are assembled by installing a set of plugins on a common software base. Such work presents the advantages promoted by plugin-based systems, as the high level of modularity and decoupling between the base application and plugins. Furthermore, they claim that the plugin-based SPL presents other benefits as, for instance, it can be developed independently and geographically distributed, reducing time to market and costs.

Wolfinger et al. [31] present an approach to integrate plugin-based techniques to SPLs. They present several usage scenarios developed in the industry and validate the approach with an ERP system.

Although the literature proposes a relevant number of works on integrating SPL and plugin mechanisms to develop software, there is no tool to support and integrate all phases of a plugin-based SPL development. On the other hand, there is a wide amount of tools focused only on the design of a SPL [18, 25] and supporting the product generation and different variability mechanisms as, for instance, conditional compilation and configuration file. Therefore, PlugSPL effectively contributes to supporting the overall plugin-based SPL life cycle.

The SPL community lacks studies that explicitly state the requirements surrounding tool adoption and the corresponding design decisions in the case of custom-made solutions. The few studies attempting to tackle the first part (requirements) are based on collected interviews and surveys [1, 5] and aim to undercover particular challenges that could be the starting point for better tools and methodologies.

Our study, although restricted to a single company and its specific requirements, provides an in-depth discussion over its requirements and context at the place. Such requirements have not been fully exploited in the SPL literature, nor have they been fully addressed by existing tools (most notably, full traceability and round-trip over different models). Some teams report some of their design decisions when creating SPL-related tools, e.g., Feature IDE [17]. However, decisions are not explicitly backed up by any industry-set requirements, but, rather, from the creators' experience [17].

Other researchers investigate differences among existing tools [8, 15], but do not collect feedback based on industrial cases where these tools are used or to which extent they succeed or fail when supporting SPL adoption.

On the tool development side, different solutions have been proposed, including both commercial and open-source. The two most popular commercial products today are pure::variants [3], from pure::systems, and Gears [13], from Big Lever Software Inc. Although they represent the most complete toolset for product line adoption, the specificity of the TDL's requirements makes them unsuitable. The open-source arena is no different, although a plethora of solutions exist, ranging from web-based solutions [19] to Eclipse plugins [17]. A comprehensive list of existing tools, either commercial or open-source, is presented in [15].

15.9   Final Remarks

In this chapter, we discussed a set of requirements and our design decisions addressing the development of PlugSPL to support the SPL development life cycle. We also presented how the PlugSPL environment can be used to support the design, product configuration, and generation of component-based SPLs. It is important to highlight that this environment has been successfully applied to generate several model-based testing tools for a TDL of a global IT company. Thus, the tool has also been used in some case studies and student projects to support the generation of testing tools to support different testing techniques and approaches. Furthermore, the user's feedback indicates that the tool usage requires low investment in the user's training and presents a low learning curve. However, we have to better investigate and understand the effort of the learning curve when using our environment, e.g., an empirical experiment to compare the effort an learning curve when using our environment and an off-the-shelf environment.

Acknowledgement This work is supported by the Brazilian funding agency CNPq (Grant 306250/2021-7).

References

1. Berger, T., Rublack, R., Nair, D., Atlee, J.M., Becker, M., Czarnecki, K., Wkasowski, A.: A survey of variability modeling in industrial practice. In: Proceedings of the Seventh International Workshop on Variability Modelling of Software-intensive Systems (2013)
2. Beuche, D.: Modeling and building software product lines with pure::Variants. In: Proeedings of the International Software Product Line Conference, p. 358. ACM, New York (2011)
3. Beuche, D.: Modeling and building software product lines with pure::variants. In: Proceedings of the 16th International Software Product Line Conference, vol. 2 (2012)
4. Cervantes, H., Charleston-Villalobos, S.: Using a lightweight workflow engine in a plugin-based product line architecture. Lecture Notes Comput. Sci. **4063**, 198–205 (2006)
5. Chen, L., Babar, M.: Variability management in software product lines: An investigation of contemporary industrial challenges. In: Software Product Lines: Going Beyond, Lecture Notes in Computer Science. Springer, Berlin (2010)
6. Costa, L., Rodrigues, E., Czekster, R., Oliveira, F., Silveira, M., Zorzo, A.: Generating performance test scripts and scenarios based on abstract intermediate models. In: Proceedings of the 24th International Conference on Software Engineering and Knowledge Engineering (2012)
7. Czarnecki, K., Helsen, S., Eisenecker, U.W.: Formalizing cardinality-based feature models and their specialization. In: Software Process: Improvement and Practice. Wiley, Hoboken (2005)
8. Dammagh, M., Troyer, O.: Feature modeling tools: Evaluation and lessons learned. In: Advances in Conceptual Modeling. Recent Developments and New Directions. Lecture Notes in Computer Science. Springer, Berlin (2011)
9. Fritsch, C., Lehn, A., Strohm, T., Gmbh, R.B.: Evaluating variability implementation mechanisms. In: Proc. Int. Workshop on Product Line Engineering, pp. 59–64. Springer, Seattle, USA (2002)
10. Kästner, C., Apel, S., Kuhlemann, M.: Granularity in software product lines. In: Proceedings of the International Conference on Software Engineering, pp. 311–320. ACM, New York (2008)
11. Kempf, M., Kleeb, R., Klenk, M., Sommerlad, P.: Cross language refactoring for eclipse plugins. In: Proceedings of the Workshop on Refactoring Tools, pp. 1–4. ACM, New York (2008)
12. Krueger, C.W.: New methods in software product line practice. Commun. ACM **49**, 37–40 (2006)
13. Krueger, C., Clements, P.: Systems and software product line engineering with BigLever software Gears. In: Proceedings of the 16th International Software Product Line Conference (2012)
14. Linden, F.J.v.d., Schmid, K., Rommes, E.: Software Product Lines in Action: The Best Industrial Practice in Product Line Engineering. Springer, New York (2007)
15. Lisboa, L.B., Garcia, V.C., Lucrédio, D., de Almeida, E.S., de Lemos Meira, S.R., de Mattos Fortes, R.P.: A systematic review of domain analysis tools. Inf. Softw. Technol. **52**(1), 1–13 (2010)
16. Mayer, J., Melzer, I., Schweiggert, F.: Lightweight plug-in-based application development. In: Proceedings of the International Conference on NetObjectDays on Objects, Components, Architectures, Services, and Applications for a Networked World, pp. 87–102. Springer, London (2003)
17. Meinicke, J., Thüm, T., Schröter, R., Benduhn, F., Leich, T., Saake, G.: Mastering Software Variability with FeatureIDE. Springer, Cham (2017)
18. Mendonça, M., Branco, M., Cowan, D.: S.P.L.O.T.: Software product lines online tools. In: Proceedings of the Conference on Object Oriented Programming, Systems, Languages, and Applications, pp. 761–762. ACM, New York (2009). https://doi.acm.org/10.1145/1639950.1640002
19. Mendonça, M., Branco, M., Cowan, D.: S.P.L.O.T.: Software product lines online tools. In: OOPSLA Companion (2009)

20. OliveiraJr, E., Gimenes, I.M.S., Maldonado, J.C.: Systematic Management of Variability in UML-based Software Product Lines. Journal of Universal Computer Science **16**(17), 2374–2393 (2010)
21. Pohl, K., Böckle, G., Linden, F.J.v.d.: Software Product Line Engineering: Foundations, Principles and Techniques. Springer, Berlin (2005)
22. Prasanna, D.R.: Dependency Injection, 1st edn. Manning Publications, Shelter Island (2009)
23. Rodrigues, E.M., Zorzo, A.F., OliveiraJr, E., Gimenes, I.M.S., Maldonado, J.C., Domingues, A.R.: Plugspl: An automated environment for supporting plugin-based software product lines. In: SEKE, pp. 647–650 (2012)
24. Rodrigues, E.M., Passos, L.T., Teixeira, L., Zorzo, A.F., Oliveira, F.M., Saad, R.S.: On the requirements and design decisions of an in-house component-based SPL automated environment. In: SEKE, pp. 492–407 (2014)
25. Segura, S., Galindo, J., Benavides, D., Parejo, J.A., Cortés, A.R.: BeTTy: Benchmarking and testing on the automated analysis of feature models. In: VaMoS, pp. 63–71 (2012)
26. Silveira, M.B., Rodrigues, E.M., Zorzo, A.F., Costa, L.T., Vieira, H.V., de Oliveira, F.M.: Model-based automatic generation of performance test scripts. In: Proceedings of the Software Engineering and Knowledge Engineering Conference, pp. 258–263. IEEE Computer Society, Miami (2011)
27. Thum, T., Kastner, C., Erdweg, S., Siegmund, N.: Abstract features in feature modeling. In: International Software Product Line Conference, pp. 191–200 (2011)
28. Thum, T., Kastner, C., Erdweg, S., Siegmund, N.: Abstract features in feature modeling. In: Proceedings of the 15th International Software Product Line Conference (2011)
29. Utting, M., Legeard, B.: Practical Model-Based Testing: A Tools Approach. Morgan Kaufmann, Burlington (2006)
30. Walls, C., Breidenbach, R.: Spring in Action. Manning Publications, Shelter Island (2007)
31. Wolfinger, R., Reiter, S., Dhungana, D., Grunbacher, P., Prahofer, H.: Supporting runtime system adaptation through product line engineering and plug-in techniques. In: International Conference on Commercial-off-the-Shelf (COTS)-Based Software Systems pp. 21–30 (2008)
32. Zhu, J., Yin, Q., Zhu, R., Guo, C., Wang, H., Wu, Q.: A plugin-based software production line integrated framework. In: International Conference on Computer Science and Software Engineering, vol. 2, pp. 562–565 (2008)

Chapter 16
SyMPLES: Embedded Systems Design with SMarty

Rogério F. da Silva, Alexandre A. Giron, and Itana M. S. Gimenes

Abstract The evolution of hardware platforms has led to the move of a large amount of functionality to embedded software systems. Thus, the software has become increasingly complex. Several techniques have been proposed over the years for dealing with this complexity. Software product line (SPL) and model-driven engineering (MDE) can enhance the development of complex embedded systems by using different specification languages according to the abstraction levels and controlling variability across development. This chapter describes SyM-PLES: an approach that combines MDE and SPL to deal with the complexity of embedded systems software. SyMPLES includes two SysML extensions, created using UML profiling mechanism both to associate SysML blocks with the main classes of functional blocks and to express SPL variability concepts using SMarty approach. SyMPLES also provides a model transformation that transforms the SysML SPL into Simulink models, speeding up the development process. Lastly, this chapter shows how an approach like SyMPLES can be validated to ensure the quality of its products.

16.1 The Role of SMarty in This Work

The benefits of SPL to the software development process have been pointed out in this book. In summary, the SPL concept aims the reuse of common software artifacts to create customized new applications. In the context of embedded systems, the

R. F. da Silva (✉)
Federal University of Paraná, Jandaia do Sul, PR, Brazil
e-mail: rogerio.ferreira@ufpr.br

A. A. Giron
Federal Technology University of Paraná, Toledo, Paraná, Brazil
e-mail: alexandregiron@utfpr.edu.br

I. M. S. Gimenes
Informatics Department, State University of Maringá, Maringá, PR, Brazil
e-mail: itana@din.uem.br

© Springer Nature Switzerland AG 2023
E. OliveiraJr (ed), *UML-Based Software Product Line Engineering with SMarty*,
https://doi.org/10.1007/978-3-031-18556-4_16

software development process must deal with restrictions like energy consumption, performance, software-hardware integration, costs, user demands, and security, among others [3, 15]. Even small modifications to the product design would give an impact in terms of costs. Due to its SPL design capabilities, the viability of the SMarty approach was investigated in the context of embedded systems development.

An SPL designed for an embedded system would give the ability to provide different configurations to the product being developed. In this perspective, designers and engineers must deal with the comprehensibility of the system under development. Therefore, using an SPL modeling tool could help in the design process. An example is shown in Fig. 16.1, created with the *pure::variants* tool [4] (the figure is a visual representation of it). The feature model is designed for a mini-UAV (unmanned aerial vehicle), where the product variabilities were resolved (marked with a checkbox).

The usage of the SPL capabilities to improve the embedded systems design is relevant. However, several tools are specific for embedded systems in the development process. For example, Simulink models are frequently used in the engineering of embedded systems [6]. In addition, SysML is a modeling language for the analysis, design, verification, and validation of complex and dynamic systems [21]. But how do you integrate all of the design choices and the SPL configurations with those embedded systems development tools? This is the main question discussed in this chapter, and it is where the SyMPLES approach is inserted.

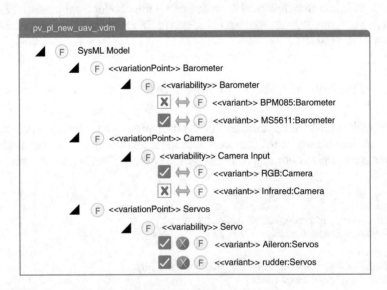

Fig. 16.1 Feature model of the mini-UAV (adapted from [10])

16.2   The SyMPLES Approach

The SysML-based product line approach for embedded systems (SyMPLES) [19] supports the embedded systems development process by combining in its structure MDE and the SPL concepts provided by SMarty. Model-driven engineering (MDE) is a development methodology that could be of benefit in the embedded systems context. The MDE concept aims to speed up the development process with fast model transformation at distinct abstraction levels [16]. By joining these two concepts, the benefits of both SPL and MDE can be exploited for the development of embedded systems.

SyMPLES provides two profiles and two processes. The profiles are extensions of the SysML language created to support the representations of the SPL artifacts, and the processes guide the user in the application of the profiles to specify the SPL artifacts. The profiles and processes are described in the next sections.

16.2.1   SyMPLES Profiles

The SPL in SyMPLES is specified with SysML models with stereotypes from the profiles *SyMPLES-ProfileFB* and *SyMPLES-ProfileVar*, described as follows:

- The SyMPLES profile for functional blocks (SyMPLES-ProfileFB) provides additional semantics to SysML blocks. It is composed of a group of stereotypes to support the mapping of the SysML elements to the main classes of functional block languages, such as Simulink. This supports the association of behavior with SysML models, thus facilitating the transformation process from specification to implementation.
- The SyMPLES profile for representation of variability (SyMPLES-ProfileVar) is based on the UML profile defined in the SMarty approach. It defines a set of stereotypes and tagged values that allow the association of SysML elements such as block, interfaces, dependency, and comment with variability concepts. It enables the specification of the structural, behavioral, and variability aspects by using a single notation. Figure 16.2 presents the SyMPLES-ProfileVar and its stereotypes. We can see, for instance, that the `variable` stereotype is applied to the `Block` metaclass.

16.2.2   SyMPLES Processes

SyMPLES processes are composed of a set of activities as follows:

- The SyMPLES process for product lines (SyMPLES-ProcessPL) defines a set of generic and tool-independent activities that support SPL domain engineering.

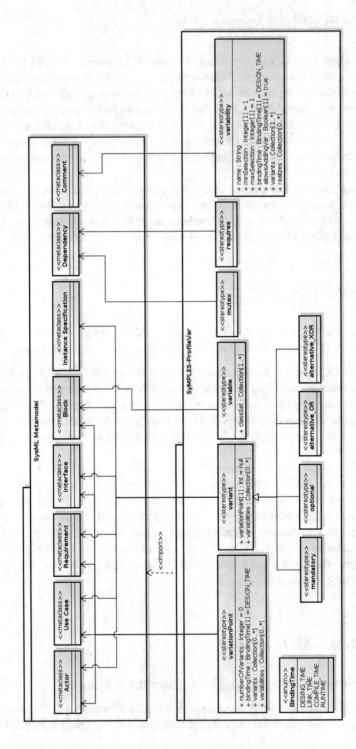

Fig. 16.2 Stereotypes of the SyMPLES-ProfileVar profile (adapted from [19])

- The SyMPLES process for identification of variabilities (SyMPLES-ProcessVar) is an iterative and incremental process for representing and managing SPL variability in application engineering. Each SyMPLES-ProcessPL activity requires iteration with the SyMPLES-ProcessVar. Its goal is to support the user in the identification, delimitation, representation, and configuration of variability.

Figure 16.3 shows an activity diagram representing the interaction between SyMPLES-ProcessPL, represented by the rectangle activities on the left side, and SyMPLES-ProcessVar, represented by the rectangle activities on the right side. These processes run in parallel during SPL domain engineering.

The activities of SyMPLES-ProcessPL were extended from OOSEM [1], as follows:

- `Requirements analysis` performs analysis of both the systems environment and user needs to generate a list of requirements and the systems use case diagram.
- `Requirements refinement` takes a list of requirements and the use case diagram produced in the previous activity and generates a SysML requirements diagram as output.
- `Feature model definition` identifies the externally visible features of products that compose the SPL and organizes them into a feature model.
- `Architecture definition`, which decomposes the system into blocks to create the SysML block diagram and therefore defines how such blocks interact to meet the systems requirements.
- `Architecture refinement`, which defines the internal structure of the blocks by creating SysML internal block diagrams; moreover, in this activity, it can define the parametric diagram and state machine diagrams.
- `Map requirements` onto the architecture, which associates previously created artifacts with the requirements defined in the requirements diagram. This activity produces tracing reports between the requirements and the architecture, which support the analysis of the SPL evolution. SysML uses, at this level, the requirements diagram instead of the use case model as this diagram allows the representation of nonfunctional requirements and better mapping of them to the elements of the architecture.

SyMPLES-ProcessVar activities are described as follows:

- `Variability Identification` is performed in every interaction between SyMPLES-ProcessPL and SyMPLES-ProcessVar taking as input the feature model, use cases, requirements, blocks, state machine, and parametric diagram. This activity aims to identify the variabilities associated with these models. SyMPLES-ProfileVar supports this activity by applying their stereotypes to SysML models and associating values with tagged values.
- `Variability Delimitation` sets values for the following variability tagged values: *minSelection*, *maxSelection*, *bindingTime*, *allowsAddingVar*, and *variants*.

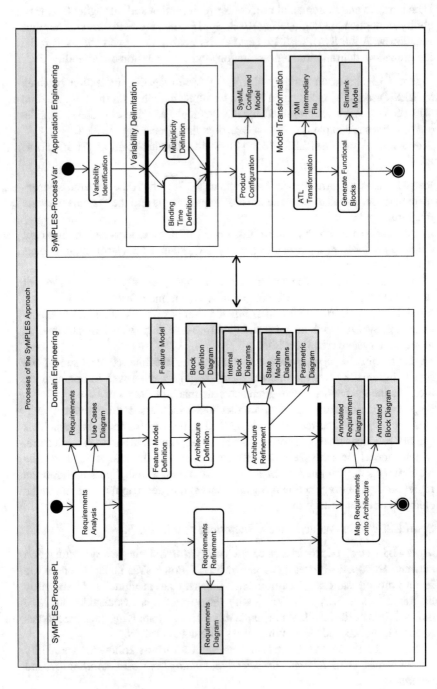

Fig. 16.3 Interaction between SyMPLES-ProcessPL and SyMPLES-ProcessVar (adapted from [19])

- Product Configuration contains specific block models (e.g., block and block definition diagrams). This activity leads to the resolution of SysML model variabilities for generating a specification for a specific product. The product configuration can be performed manually or automatically, for instance, using the tool *pure::variants* [4].

Other activities in the SyMPLES-ProcessVar are related to model transformation using MDE techniques. Such activities are described in the next subsections.

16.2.3 SyMPLES Model Transformation

Following the arrows in Fig. 16.3, after the product configuration, the SyMPLES model transformation comes into place. This transformation can be applied to the configured SysML models to obtain corresponding Simulink models.

The main purpose of the SyMPLES model transformation is to generate Simulink models from the configured SPL model. In other words, the transformation lowers the abstraction level toward the implementation, which is the main goal of MDE. Generating Simulink models is also useful because in MATLAB they can be used to generate C/C++ code.

The model transformation of SyMPLES, represented in Fig. 16.4, is divided into two steps: (i) perform an ATL (Atlas Transformation Language) transformation and (ii) generate functional blocks. The product configuration can be seen as a requirement of the model transformation: the SPL must be modeled with SyMPLES stereotypes—in short, with SysML and SMarty.

In the SyMPLES approach, the configured model can be composed of four annotated SysML diagrams: block definition, internal block, state machine, and parametric. The root diagram is the block definition, used to describe the main blocks of the system, the internal block represents the internal relationship of a

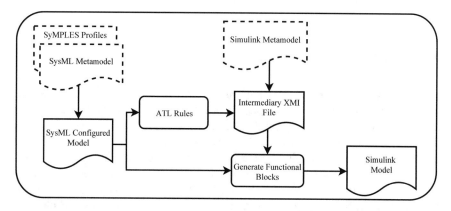

Fig. 16.4 SyMPLES model transformation

block based on block instances from the block definition diagram, the state machine diagram specifies the behavior of the system, and the parametric diagram specifies block constraints, values, and properties. The product configuration is concluded when the variabilities are resolved and the product is configured.

Step (i) of the transformation uses the ATL [13]. ATL is used to develop model transformations in the MDE context. In the SyMPLES model transformation, ATL rules are used to select relevant information about the SysML model, like element attributes, SMarty stereotypes, and graphic data (i.e., element position and size), and map them to an XMI intermediary model. This intermediate transformation using this intermediary model makes the process more flexible to deal with EMF-based editors, but that is not the main reason for it. In the MDE context, all model transformations generate models from one metamodel to another. Therefore, to map SysML elements to Simulink, it requires a SysML metamodel to describe the input and a Simulink metamodel to describe the output. That is why an intermediary representation is used, which maps the elements from the SysML domain to the Simulink domain.

Step (ii) of the transformation of SyMPLES is called generate functional blocks. It is implemented in Java and uses the XMI model produced by step (i) and part of the SysML configured model, defined here as the UML file. The UML file must be used because it contains values and the SyMPLES stereotypes that are referenced by the XMI model. In this step, a MATLAB script is generated and it represents the Simulink model. The Simulink model can be visualized with its execution in a MATLAB environment.

16.3   Application Example

This section describes the SyMPLES model transformation application example, divided in three steps: product configuration, ATL transformation, and generate functional blocks.

16.3.1   Product Configuration

An application example is presented as a proof of concept of the SyMPLES approach based on part of the autopilot Yapa 2 [9]. The autopilot software executes on a controller board for Paparazzi mini-unmanned aerial vehicles (mini-UAVs). The activities defined by SyMPLES-ProcessPL were executed to create the core of an SPL for the navigation and flight control subsystems of the mini-UAV. The stereotypes of SyMPLES-ProfileFB were used to represent the main blocks recovered from the Simulink models in the SysML models. The block definition was specified with their respective variabilities following the SyMPLES-ProfileVar.

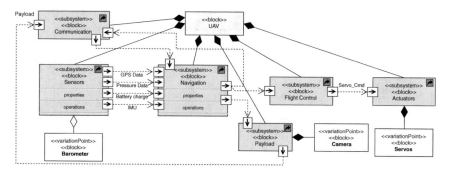

Fig. 16.5 Initial mini-UAV SPL architecture represented in SysML [9]

The models created by the SyMPLES processes were represented with the support of the Papyrus tool [12].

Figure 16.5 shows an example of an initial SPL architecture for the mini-UAV. The architecture is represented by a SysML block definition diagram. Blocks with stereotypes «subsystem» are mapped to subsystems in Simulink. This shows that SyMPLES-ProfileFB supports the establishment of straightforward correspondence between SysML blocks and Simulink implementation blocks. After executing the variability identification activity of SyMPLES-ProcessVar, the stereotypes «variationPoint» were used to represent elements that have variants to be resolved in the SyMPLES SPL. In this figure, three variation points were defined: barometer, servos, and camera. SyMPLES approach defines that for each variation point, there must be one internal block diagram to complete the specification of the variabilities.

The SysML model with SyMPLES stereotypes can be imported to the *pure::* *variants* tool, which creates a variant model descriptor (VDM). Figure 16.1 in the first section of this chapter shows a feature model example with three variabilities: two options mutually exclusive for the barometer sensors, two options mutually exclusive for the camera, and two options for the servos. The variabilities are resolved in this model, and then they are reflected in an output SysML model, automatically.

Each block presented in Fig. 16.5 can be detailed internally. Figure 16.6 is the SysML internal block diagram for the "payload block." There is an example of variability resolution in SyMPLES. In this case, the chosen configuration was the RGB camera, and therefore the infrared camera was removed from the diagram, automatically, using SyMPLES. When all the variabilities are resolved and the SysML model is properly configured, the model transformation can be started.

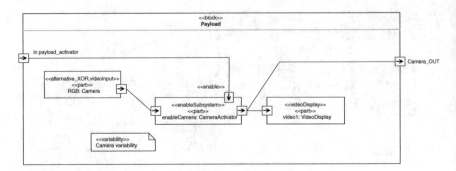

Fig. 16.6 Internal block diagram for payload block [9]

16.3.2 ATL Transformation

The SyMPLES transformation begins with the ATL step of the transformation, which produces an intermediary output. This output model has the elements from the SysML model transformed into elements belonging to the Simulink metamodel. Besides, SMarty stereotypes and graphic data are also collected in this step of the transformation. For example, in Fig. 16.6, the «enabledSubsystem», «videoDisplay», and «videoInput» stereotypes, input/output ports, and connections are mapped to the corresponding elements in the Simulink metamodel. The result is an XMI model with the elements transformed, which is used in the next step of the transformation.

16.3.3 Generate Functional Blocks

To produce the final MATLAB/Simulink model, the second step of the SyMPLES transformation reads the previous XMI model along with the SysML configured model and generates a MATLAB script. This script, when executed, generates the Simulink model in MATLAB. As an example, Fig. 16.7 shows the Simulink model generated from the diagram in Fig. 16.6.

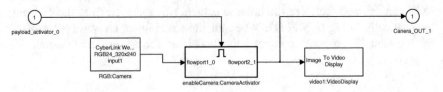

Fig. 16.7 Simulink model generated by the transformation of the payload internal block diagram [9]

16.4   Validation of MDE Transformations

A question that arises from the development of the SyMPLES model transformation is how to determine if its output is correct. The answer is in the context of the validation of MDE transformations, and it is an important way to ensure quality. If the models are derived automatically by the MDE transformations, then their quality will depend on the correctness of the transformation [8, 14]. In the following sections, concepts and techniques of MDE validation are presented, as well as how the SyMPLES model transformation was validated.

The validation of MDE transformations has been investigated in some studies. Some examples are techniques based on model-based testing, formal verification, and validation based on common software testing techniques. In addition, two main types of testing can be applied: black box (functional) testing or white box (structural) testing. The first compares the input models to the output models after the transformation, and the second type analyzes the internal aspects of the model transformation.

The specific characteristics of MDE transformations must be taken into account for their validation. An example of these singularities is that a transformation can be written in different MDE languages (e.g. ATL, QVT) or even common programming languages. SyMPLES uses ATL and Java in its model transformation. This could increase the complexity of a white box approach for testing.

Another characteristic of the MDE validation is when the output model (or code) produced is executable. So the output can be validated statically (i.e., model checkers) or dynamically, with the execution of the model [20].

The analysis process from the execution of the tests in model transformations is also important. This is due to the fact that despite the common programming errors (i.e., syntax errors), the wrong implementation of a model transformation may lead to specific errors, classified as follows [14]:

- **(Type 1)** Metamodel Coverage: the transformation rules have been implemented, but they are not sufficient to map all elements that the metamodel possesses. An example is when the rules can only be applied to certain kinds of elements, so other kinds of elements are not mapped.
- **(Type 2)** Syntactically incorrect models: when the transformation rule causes generation of an output model to not comply with the output metamodel.
- **(Type 3)** Semantically incorrect models: when the transformation rules are applied to an input model and the output model is syntactically correct, but it does not produce a model with the expected elements, for example, when an input model with elements is transformed but some elements are missing in the output model. Therefore, the output model is not a correct transformation of the input model.
- **(Type 4)** Ambiguity: the same transformation rule produces different results from the same input model.

- **(Type 5)** Common errors: here are all of other types of errors and the codification errors. Examples are the incorrect primitive types (integer, floating point) and memory references out of bounds.

A methodology to validate model transformations is proposed in [14]. The methodology includes test case generation, which generates test cases based on a coverage criterion; oracle definition, which defines the expected result of a test; and test execution, which determines and analyzes testing results.

Regarding the test case generation activity, two factors must be taken into account: the size of one test case and the size of the set of test cases. The size of one test case is determined by the number of elements in the model. A test case with few elements facilitates both its comprehension and an efficient diagnostic when an error is found. However, decreasing the size of the test case may result in an increase in the set of test cases. When the size of the set of test cases is too big, the test becomes unfeasible. It is possible to control the size of the set by using coverage criteria and generation policies. Reducing the size of the set is important to reduce the test time [7, 8].

The effectiveness of a set of test cases is an interesting metric for comparing test case generation approaches: the proportion of effective test cases (which found errors) over the total number of test cases. Thus, if an approach generates sets with high effectiveness, the time spent on testing is used more efficiently.

The above concepts must be considered when validating a model transformation. In this context, the methodology chosen in order to validate SyMPLES model transformation contains the following choices:

- As previously mentioned, the SyMPLES model transformation is implemented with two different languages (ATL and Java). Thus, a black box approach can be a better choice.
- Due to the specificity of SyMPLES, two approaches can be used to generate test cases: test case generation based on the (SysML) metamodel and based on the (SyMPLES) SPL.
- A dynamic test can also be performed because the output of the SyMPLES model transformation is executable (MATLAB script which produces the Simulink model).

Regarding the two possibilities for the test case generation, the first one is generic: since the input metamodel of the SyMPLES transformation is the SysML metamodel, this metamodel can be used to generate a set of generic SysML models to test the transformation. The second possibility is specific to SyMPLES: since the input model is a configured SysML model from an SPL, it is possible to perform a feature analysis on the SPL to generate a set of configured models to test the transformation. Both of the test case generation possibilities and their results are presented in the following sections.

16.4.1 Test Case Generation Based on the Metamodel

It is worth mentioning that the concept of test case generation based on the metamodel is generic, but for SyMPLES this approach is generic only for SysML model transformations. This "generic" characteristic of this approach can lead to problems:

- Hardly all of the elements from a metamodel are used in an MDE transformation [8]. Thus, an approach based on metamodel coverage could generate several useless test cases. To alleviate this problem, heuristics and/or an analysis of the transformation mapping could be performed. On average, it has been found that SyMPLES uses 60% of the SysML metamodel [10].
- When testing a model transformation, generally there are specific restrictions that could increase or decrease the number of test cases. SyMPLES also has restrictions on transforming SysML models:

  - The block definition and internal block diagram require stereotypes of the SyMPLES profile for functional blocks, which are 48 stereotypes mapping SysML blocks to Simulink blocks. Therefore, each one must be tested;
  - Ports must be used to connect blocks only.
  - In/outports are not considered in the transformation.
  - Ports with more than one connection will not be transformed.
  - The parametric diagram (if any) must have at least one element of type constraint property.

It is worth mentioning that the test case generation must comply with the restrictions of the model transformation, or the test would not be fit for its purpose.

One last thing to consider when generating test cases is the generation policy [5]. A problem when automating this generation is that the models can be difficult to interpret by a human tester, due to the size of the set (too many input models) or the size of the model (too many elements in the model) [18]. Thus, if a test case shows an error, the tester/developer must understand the model to discover which part of the model transformation is the cause of the error. Typically, the one-to-one policy means that each new element is created in a new model, and the N-to-one policy means that a set of N elements (at most) is inserted in a new model.

16.4.2 Test Case Generation Based on the SPL

Specifically for the SyMPLES model transformation, the test case generation based on the SPL can be used. This happens because SyMPLES requires an SPL to provide the configured models, which are the input of the model transformation. Therefore, a hypothesis raised is whether the SPL-based generation approach is more specific and then more effective for testing the transformation.

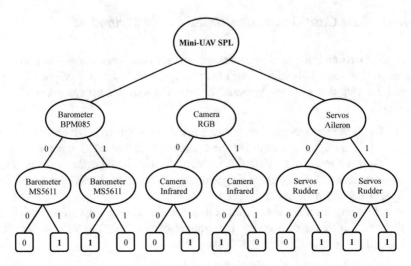

Fig. 16.8 Feature analysis of the mini-UAV SPL using BDD (adapted from [11])

It is worthy to note that the focus is to test the SyMPLES model transformation, **not the SPL**. The SPL-based approach here cannot be confused with any SPL testing techniques. This means that a premise for this approach is that the (real) SPL modeled with SyMPLES and its software components have already been tested. The SPL is used only to generate a family of SysML models as input to test the model transformation.

While the metamodel-based approach generates models without semantics, because those models are not from a real SPL modeled with SyMPLES, the SPL-based generation is more specific. Since SyMPLES has variability management, the possibility of generating test cases from the SPL was identified. In order to do so, a feature analysis of the SPL must be performed.

The feature analysis of an SPL can be performed with a binary decision diagram (BDD). BDD uses a logic structure to represent a Boolean function composed of decision nodes and terminal nodes (0 and 1). Thus, each path in the BDD leading to 1 is a valid configuration in the SPL. According to comparative studies in feature analysis, BDD is efficient in terms of execution time [2, 17].

Options for SPL features in SyMPLES are *alternative_OR*, *alternative_XOR*, *optional*, and *mandatory*. The SPL constraints of the application example (Sect. 16.3) are mapped to Boolean functions in a BDD, presented in Fig. 16.8. Note that not all paths lead to a one-terminal node.

The feature analysis in Fig. 16.8 shows three variation points: "barometer," "camera," and "servos." The first variability shows two mutually exclusive options, BPM085 and MS5611, mapped to the BDD as an XOR function. The "camera" variability is also mapped as an XOR function, and the "servos" variability is mapped as an OR function. The calculus of the number of possible configurations is done with a simple multiplication of the number of paths leading to the one terminal in each variation point. Two paths lead to the one terminal in both the barometer and the camera and three paths in the servos. Therefore, 12 possible configurations can be generated as products to test the model transformation. This means that the set of test cases generated by this approach tends to be as small as the SPL in use.

16.5 Final Remarks

This chapter presented the SyMPLES approach designed to facilitate the embedded systems development process. The approach deals with the high complexity of the development process by combining SPL and MDE concepts. SyMPLES supports the generation of platform-specific models of SPL through the refinement of abstractions which facilitates code generation. SysML configured models are used as input for transformation process and represent embedded systems at the initial levels of development. A validation of MDE transformations was carried out considering two possibilities for the test case generation: generic *vs.* specific. In order to compare them, experiments were conducted in [11]. However, it is hard to conclude if the SPL-based or metamodel-based approach is better because of the nature and design of the approaches.

The effectiveness observed in [11] for the SPL-based approach was about 92%: 11 of the 12 test cases were useful to find errors. However, these errors were type 5 (common errors, see Sect. 16.4). On the other hand, errors of type 3 were found using metamodel-based approach, and the effectiveness of the approach was 18% (using 1-to-1 policy) and 22% (N-to-1). Both effectiveness rates are lower compared to the SPL-based approach, but the quantity of errors found is higher with the metamodel-based technique.

The high variety of technologies related to MDE transformations can make it difficult to automate the testing process. When testing the SyMPLES model transformation, a considerable amount of time was spent on performing both test case generation approaches. The singularities of the model transformations also contribute to the complexity of the testing process. It seems that the automation of the testing process is the key to minimize testing time.

Acknowledgments Authors would like to thank CAPES/Brazil (code 001) for supporting this work.

References

1. Bassi, L., Secchi, C., Bonfe, M., Fantuzzi, C.: A sysml-based methodology for manufacturing machinery modeling and design. IEEE/ASME Trans. Mechatron. **16**(6), 1049–1062 (2010). https://doi.org/10.1109/TMECH.2010.2073480.
2. Benavides, D., Segura, S., Trinidad, P., Cortés, A.R.: FAMA: Tooling a framework for the automated analysis of feature models. VaMoS **2007**, 01 (2007)

3. Berger, A.S.: Embedded Systems Design: An Introduction to Processes, Tools, and Techniques. CRC Press, Boca Raton (2001). https://doi.org/10.1201/9781482280715

4. Beuche, D.: Industrial variant management with pure:: variants. In: Proceedings of the 23rd International Systems and Software Product Line Conference-Volume B, pp. 37–39. ACM (2019). https://doi.org/10.1145/3307630.3342391

5. Brottier, E., Fleurey, F., Steel, J., Baudry, B., Le Traon, Y.: Metamodel-based test generation for model transformations: An algorithm and a tool. In: Software Reliability Engineering, 2006. ISSRE'06. 17th International Symposium on, pp. 85–94. IEEE (2006). https://doi.org/10.1109/ISSRE.2006.27

6. Chaturvedi, D.K.: Modeling and Simulation of Systems Using MATLAB and Simulink. CRC Press, Boca Raton (2017). https://doi.org/10.1201/9781315218335

7. Fawaz, K., Zaraket, F., Masri, W., Harkous, H.: Pbcov: a property-based coverage criterion. Softw. Qual. J. **23**(1), 171–202 (2015). https://doi.org/10.1007/s11219-014-9237-3

8. Fleurey, F., Steel, J., Baudry, B.: Validation in model-driven engineering: Testing model transformations. In: Proceedings of the 2004 First International Workshop on Model, Design and Validation, 2004, pp. 29–40. IEEE (2004). https://doi.org/10.1109/MODEVA.2004.1425846

9. Fragal, V.H., Silva, R.F., Gimenes, I.M.S., OliveiraJr, E.: Application engineering for embedded systems-transforming sysml specification to Simulink within a product-line based approach. In: 15th International Conference on Enterprise Information Systems (ICEIS), 2013, no. 2, pp. 94–101 (2013). https://doi.org/10.5220/0004402600940101

10. Giron, A.A., Gimenes, I.M.S., OliveiraJr, E.: Case study of test case generation based on metamodel for model transformations. J. Softw. **12**(5), 364–378 (2017). https://doi.org/10.17706/jsw.12.5.364-378

11. Giron, A.A., Gimenes, I.M.S., OliveiraJr, E.: Evaluation of test case generation based on a software product line for model transformation. J. Comput. Sci. **14**(1), 108–121 (2018). https://doi.org/10.3844/jcssp.2018.108.121

12. Guermazi, S., Tatibouet, J., Cuccuru, A., Dhouib, S., Gérard, S., Seidewitz, E.: Executable modeling with fuml and alf in papyrus: tooling and experiments. Strategies **11**, 12 (2015)

13. Jouault, F., Allilaire, F., Bézivin, J., Kurtev, I.: Atl: A model transformation tool. Sci. Comput. Programm. **72**(1–2), 31–39 (2008). https://doi.org/10.1016/j.scico.2007.08.002

14. Küster, J.M., Abd-El-Razik, M.: Validation of model transformations – First experiences using a white box approach. In: In Proceedings of MODEVA'06 (Model Design and Validation Workshop Associated to MODELS'06), pp. 193–204. Springer (2006). https://doi.org/10.1007/978-3-540-69489-2_24.

15. Marwedel, P.: Embedded System Design, vol. 1. Springer, Berlin (2006). https://doi.org/10.1007/978-3-030-60910-8

16. Mellor, S.J., Scott, K., Uhl, A., Weise, D.: MDA Distilled: Principles of Model-Driven Architecture. Addison-Wesley Professional, Boston (2004)

17. Mendonça, M., Branco, M., Cowan, D.: Splot: software product lines online tools. In: Proceedings of the 24th ACM SIGPLAN Conference Companion on Object Oriented Programming Systems Languages and Applications, pp. 761–762. ACM (2009). https://doi.org/10.1145/1639950.1640002

18. Sen, S., Baudry, B., Mottu, J.M.: Automatic model generation strategies for model transformation testing. In: Theory and Practice of Model Transformations, pp. 148–164. Springer, Berlin (2009). https://doi.org/10.1007/978-3-642-02408-5_11

19. Silva, R.F., Fragal, V., OliveiraJr, E., Gimenes, I.M.S., Oquendo, F.: SyMPLES: a SysML-based approach for developing embedded systems software product lines. In: 15th International Conference on Enterprise Information Systems (ICEIS), 2013, no. 2, pp. 257–264 (2013). https://doi.org/10.5220/0004446802570264

20. Tiso, A., Reggio, G., Leotta, M.: Early experiences on model transformation testing. In: Proceedings of the First Workshop on the Analysis of Model Transformations, pp. 15–20. ACM (2012). https://doi.org/10.1145/2432497.2432501
21. Weilkiens, T.: Systems Engineering with SysML/UML: Modeling, Analysis, Design. Morgan Kaufmann OMG Press. Elsevier, Amsterdam (2011)

Chapter 17
Variability Representation in Software Process with the SMartySPEM Approach

Maicon Pazin, Jaime Dias, Edson OliveiraJr, Fellipe Araújo Aleixo, Uirá Kulesza, and Eldânae Nogueira Teixeira

Abstract Different notations can be used to model software processes. This set of notations typically does not have constructs that are appropriate for expressing process variability. Variability in software process models justifies tailoring them to meet the specific goals and characteristics of organizations and projects. Recent studies propose techniques and tools based on software process line (SPrL) to systematically manage the variability found during the maintenance and reuse of software processes. Although this research area is still not consolidated, some approaches found in the literature can be considered promising, as SMartySPEM. This chapter presents an overview of the SPrL by highlighting important aspects for variability management. In this context, an approach called SMartySPEM is presented. It extends the SPEM profile to specify variabilities in SPrLs considering the SMarty approach for variability management.

M. Pazin · J. Dias (✉) · E. OliveiraJr
Informatics Department, State University of Maringá, Maringá, PR, Brazil
e-mail: edson@din.uem.br

F. A. Aleixo
Federal Institute of Rio Grande do Norte, Academic Department of Administration and Information Technology, Natal, RN, Brazil
e-mail: fellipe.aleixo@ifrn.edu.br

U. Kulesza
Informatics and Applied Mathematics Department, Federal University of Rio Grande do Norte, Natal, RN, Brazil
e-mail: uira@dimap.ufrn.br

E. N. Teixeira
Federal University of Rio de Janeiro, Rio de Janeiro, RJ, Brazil
e-mail: eldany@ic.ufrj.br

© Springer Nature Switzerland AG 2023
E. OliveiraJr (ed), *UML-Based Software Product Line Engineering with SMarty*,
https://doi.org/10.1007/978-3-031-18556-4_17

17.1   The Role of SMarty in This Work

Software process line (SPrL) [2, 3, 32] applies software product line principles and techniques to the software process context. It aims to provide techniques and mechanisms to (i) the modeling of existing commonalities and variabilities of a software process family and (ii) the automatic derivation of customized software processes that address specific needs of a given software development project.

Approaches from the product line research area have been used as base of SPrL studies. One of them, the SMarty approach [27, 28], which is composed of a UML profile and a set of guidelines developed to support variability management in software product lines, was used as part of the definition of the stereotype-based variability management for SPEM (SMartySPEM) [29] approach for SPrL. SMartySPEM introduces the profiling mechanism based on the SMarty approach for representing variability in SPEM modeled elements with specific stereotypes [12].

SMartySPEM is an annotative approach that provides the separation of elements and their management by using a visual annotation that associates notes and stereotypes to each type of process element variability [12]. It supports both the identification and the representation of variabilities in SPEM-based software process elements [29].

17.2   Software Process Line (SPrL) Fundamentals

Process definition, management, and improvement are important activities to reach software products with high quality. However, software process definition deals with high levels of complexity. It involves diverse factors including the need for dealing with a variety of organizational aspects and for complying with project and product contexts. This diversity implies that there is not a general process that can be applied in all software development scenarios. "A process engineer usually defines a specific process for each project in an ad-hoc fashion, which is expensive, unrepeatable and error prone" [1, 21]. An optimized definition for each process becomes a challenge considering that processes need to fit several particular characteristics of each scenario and lead to a large set of constraints.

One common approach is to customize a new software process from an existing general process specification [18]. However, such approach requires a large experience and knowledge of software engineering, which can be difficult to be addressed even for expert professionals [5].

A systematic and intentional reuse of software process can be viewed as a way to reuse past experiences supporting new process definitions aiming to reduce the time, costs, and effort involved in this complex activity and to improve process and product quality. Many existing product reuse techniques started to be adapted to the context of software process reuse [22], based on valid analogies between software products and processes. In this scenario, process reuse techniques are emerging such as software process lines (SPrLs) [4, 33, 40] and the definition of software processes by using smaller and reusable units, called as process components. Software product line (SPL) concepts [7, 26] are being applied to develop SPrL approaches. A SPrL can be defined as a process family that maps the needs of a particular domain with specific purposes, defining common characteristics represented as common and reusable process assets [40]. It involves to model and specify the common process core and respective variable process elements to address specific needs [4].

The SPrL engineering main characteristics include two separate development processes [33]: (i) domain engineering process, where processes for reuse are created, and (ii) application engineering process, where project-specific processes are defined based on the selection of the reusable process artifacts developed in the domain engineering and on the resolution of their respective variability.

Variability management is a key requirement in SPrL approaches. This concept refers to the variable aspects of the process family of a SPrL [29]. It involves providing support to SPrL specification, implementation, variability resolution, and customized process generation [12]. Therefore, SPrL representation is a relevant topic where process modeling languages, and therefore the metamodels which support them, need to include variability constructors [24].

Software process modeling languages (SPMLs) have been created from different sources, aiming to address different problems. Due to the large number of users, it is difficult to establish the best language to be used. Software organizations have not still adopted existing processing modeling languages [16]. The variability aspect is one of the main concerns that can affect the SPML expressiveness and comprehension, which are considered as some of the most relevant factors that affect the adoption of SPrL by companies [35].

This section aims to overview the basics of SPrL (see Sect. 17.2.1) and to highlight important aspects considering SPrL variability management topic (see Sect. 17.2.2).

17.2.1 Software Process Line Overview

The creation of a process that is usable on different software development projects involves the application of a method that captures the common and variant process elements to allow the creation of reusable process definitions that can be customized to address several specific scenarios [19]. In this context, systematic process reuse techniques are being developed, such as software process lines (SPrLs). These techniques are based on analogies among software products and software processes.

The first publications of SPrLs were identified in 1996, with introductory concepts in the area. The notion of process family with relations and analogies among product and process were outlined by Sutton and Osterweil [37]. In the same year, an initial practical application of a process domain engineering method in one organization was published [19, 20].

The notion of family viewpoint emphasizes both the commonality among family members and the differences between them, and it draws attention to their interrelationships [37]. In this context, an SPrL can be defined as a set of software processes with a managed set of characteristics that satisfy the specific needs of a particular organization and that are developed from a common set of core processes in a prescribed way [4]. The SPrL research area aims to provide techniques and mechanisms for (i) modeling existing similarities and variabilities in a family of software processes and (ii) the customization of software processes according to specific needs of software process domain [29]. According to a systematic literature review focused in characterizing the *state of the art* of SPrL area [25], which identified 49 primary studies in the field, the main concentration of publications occurred in recent years—from 2014 to 2018. This data demonstrates the interest of researchers in the systematic process reuse area in the SPrL as a recent research topic. This fact can be reinforced by the concentration of papers in conferences (31) and a lower number of publications in journals (8), which indicates it as a maturing area and that there are few consolidated works.

The main characteristics of SPrL are (Fig. 17.1): (i) two separate development processes, the domain engineering process, where processes for reuse are being created, and the application engineering process, where project-specific processes are being developed, (ii) a process repository where reusable processes are made available, (iii) a systematic reuse process to select process components for predefined variability, and (iv) a systematic process management process where, for each exception, it will be decided whether this exception will be factored into generic process or not [33].

The domain engineering (Fig. 17.2) stage involves different activities to create the process reusable artifacts that are going to be used in application engineering stage. Some of these activities are (1) domain identification, (2) knowledge acquisition, (3) domain similarity and variability analysis, and (4) domain modeling with variability representation [39].

The domain identification activity starts with the scope definition with a domain feasibility study. The SPrL scope definition is responsible for the identification of process family characteristics to be covered by the process line. The scope definition activity should analyze the organization's current and future products and projects by eliciting process needs in the organization [4]. The analysis should consider time and resource availability constraints versus the domain expected results.

The knowledge acquisition activity includes some tasks as knowledge source(s) identification and knowledge capture and storage. These can be conducted by bottom-up or top-down strategy and possibly even a combination of both. Top-down establishment reflects the typical standardization process, and bottom-up approaches look at commonalities and variabilities across a number of projects [33]. This means that in the first strategy, existing knowledge in organizational process models or running instances of software projects are recovered to create the process line. In the second, process line starts from scratch, based on reference models, which is most appropriate when there are no predefined processes in the organization [23]. Process discover is an area being investigated as a basis to

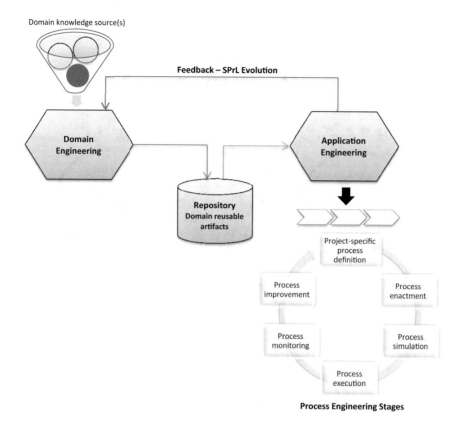

Fig. 17.1 SPrL engineering overview

implement techniques of process mining using project logs as inputs to derive mechanism for domain knowledge acquisition and SPrL derivation [6]. Other process reengineering techniques still need to be developed, based on process mining and possibly on other techniques of software reengineering.

The domain similarity and variability analysis activity determines points where the domain processes are similar (mandatory elements) and points where they diverge (optional and alternative elements), which represent adaptation points during the specific process derivation [39]. The concept of commonality and variation is intrinsic of domains and family viewpoint. According to Rombach [33], commonalities are functionalities that are contained in all (or at least a large number of) systems within that domain. On the other hand, variabilities are functionalities that are unique to one (or some number of) system(s) within that domain. The success of an SPrL depends on the accuracy of its variability management activity [33]. Therefore, variability management is a key requirement in the development of SPrLs to provide support to specification, implementation,

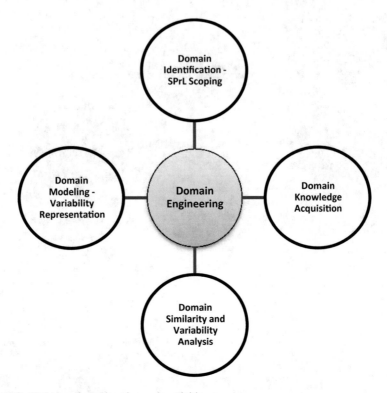

Fig. 17.2 SPrL domain engineering main activities

variability resolution, and customized process generation [12]. This topic is better described in Sect. 17.2.2.

The organization and storage of domain knowledge and reusable artifacts need to consider the development of a repository. Retrieval mechanisms should be defined in order to capture the information required and to provide the artifacts that address specific contexts. Software process repository development and management are still topics not frequently discussed by SPrL approaches [25] and need more research attention. This is the same case of implementation or adaptation of software tools to support the SPrL approaches. Although it is considered an important topic, the development of a reuse infrastructure with integrated tools that provides support to all reuse stages is still a limitation and can be considered an opportunity for future research efforts.

Most of SPrL approaches identified in literature focus on domain engineering stage, defining how to develop an SPrL and the reuse infrastructure [25]. This can lead to the fact that without reusable process artifacts and domain representation, it is more difficult to propose support to use and apply strategies to better combine and adapt the reusable artifacts during new process definitions during application

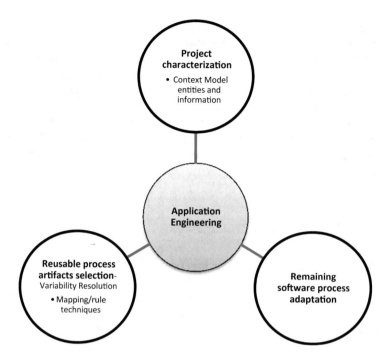

Fig. 17.3 SPrL application engineering main activities

engineering [25]. In the literature, this phase started to be more directly treated back in 2014, with approaches that deal specifically with it being detected [25].

The application engineering (Fig. 17.3) phase involves different activities to create project-specific software process based on the reusable process artifacts produced in the domain engineering phase. Some of these activities are (1) project characterization, identifying its requirements, (2) selection of reusable process artifacts by mapping variation points, and (3) adaptation of remaining software process to address specific needs [8]. During this phase, specific activities need to be accomplished involving decision-making analysis and verification and validation of element composition and compliance with domain constraints.

Project-specific features are characterized by context entities and information in most of SPrL approaches. A context corresponds to any information used to characterize the situation of an entity (i.e., dimensions) considered relevant [10]. Each entity is described by a specific set of information which should be monitored to detect changes in the context [9].

We observe a predominance of SPrL approaches that use mapping and rule techniques to address project-specific software process definition [8]. Feature mapping and rule-based system have some emphasis. Feature mapping involves identification of context information, features, or goals that regulate the inclusion or deletion of reusable process elements [9]. The rule-based systems store and manipulate knowledge to interpret information, emulating decision-making ability of a human expert for variability resolution during project-specific process derivation [9]. Other techniques were identified in the literature to support variability management during application engineering phase such as fuzzy inference systems, analytic hierarchy process (AHP), and genetic algorithms [9]. It is important to consider that the knowledge acquisition process required by this kind of techniques is not trivial, due to the unavailability of experts and overhead in domain engineering [8].

It is important to consider the impacts in process execution, as the adequacy of the derived process in the specific context application. Simulation and optimization areas can be further explored to provide more insights in variability resolution activity.

17.2.2 SPrL Variability Management

Variability management (Fig. 17.4) defines how common and variable artifacts are represented and processed during the process instance generation stage from an SPrL [12]. An SPrL represents commonalities and variabilities associated with process elements such as activities, artifacts, roles, and actions [29]. Different approaches and techniques for variability management can be found in the literature. Each one can be classified as compositional, annotative, transformational, and model-driven [14]. Some desirable requirements for a software process variability representation can be outlined such as [38]: (i) graphical representation; (ii) support to model configurable process elements (variation points), their alternatives

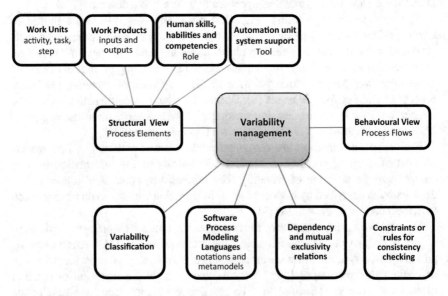

Fig. 17.4 SPrL variability management main topics

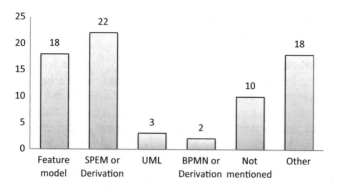

Fig. 17.5 Process variability modeling proposals for SPrL approaches

(variants), and artifact optionally; (iii) support to specify relationships among elements and behavior variation designed by alternative or optional control flows; and (iv) support to specify relationships of dependency and mutual exclusivity among elements.

Analyzing the SPrL area [25], it is possible to identify what are the existing variability modeling proposals and how they provide support to variability representation considering (i) which process elements are involved in process variation, (ii) the type of variation that can be applied (optionally, variability, adaptation actions, evolving variations, parameterization; use of components) and (iii) the type of constraints and consistency rules that can be defined.

Considering 49 primary studies identified in the SLR mentioned [25] (see Fig. 17.5), the main modeling notations identified were SPEM-based models (22) and feature models (18). UML-based models were pointed by three approaches, and BPMN-based notations were pointed out by only two approaches. Other SPrL representations are present in 18 approaches, such as component models, V-model XT metamodel, and their own notations, such as Little-JIL and WebAPSEE languages. A combination of representation proposals are used by 13 studies.

The process elements involved in variations are activities (41 citations), tasks (33 citations), work products (29 citations), roles (26 citations), tools (11 citations), and steps (3 citations). Additional elements cited were guidance, discipline, stages, iterations, and practices. Control flows are represented by 25 approaches, generally using SPEM or UML (activity diagram) notations. Considering specifically variability classification, two types were observed: (i) optional (32 citations), which refers to elements that may or may not be present in the process, or (ii) variation point (34 citations), which refers to elements in which several alternatives are placed.

Explicit dependency and mutually exclusive relationships of process elements are addressed by some existing approaches. Twenty-one approaches mentioned the representation of dependence relationships, which describe composition process elements that should be selected together. Eighteen approaches cited exclusive relation representation, which treat process elements that do not have a meaning to be combined. A total of 21 approaches did not mention support for representing constraints or rules for consistency checking. Contextual models were cited as a supplementary representation by 15 approaches.

Some important issues identified are as follows: (i) in general, the approaches do not focus on the behavioral aspect of processes (flows), addressing variability only in process elements, especially in work units (activities and tasks); (ii) the whole set of process elements that are indicated as variables in a process family (i.e., activity, task, role, work product, tool, and relations) are generally not completely addressed in the same approach; (iii) the variability of process elements is not always defined together with their options; and (iv) special notations to represent variability in different process perspectives were only presented in a few works [25].

17.3 The SMartySPEM Approach

The SMartySPEM approach [29] aims to support the identification and representation of variability in SPEM-based software process elements. In addition, it provides support to the derivation of specific processes by resolving variabilities. Currently, SMartySPEM does not support automatic derivation of specific processes.

SMartySPEM consists of a UML profile (SMartySPEMProfile) and a set of guidelines that contributes to identifying and representing variability. Figure 17.6 depicts the activities that need to be carried out to model SPrL and deriving specific processes based on SMartySPEM. The `Apply SMartySPEM Guidelines` activity takes as input `SPEM-based Process Models`. These models are previously created for a given software process based on the SPEM metamodel. Thus, SMartySPEM guidelines (presented next) contain directions to identify and represent variabilities in such process models. As an output of this activity, `SMartySPEM-based Process Models` are generated. These models contain variabilities represented and are taken as input for the next activity, `Resolve Variabilities/Derive Specific Process`. In this activity, several specific processes (`Process 1, Process 2... Process n`) are derived [29]. This derivation occurs by resolving the variation points found in SPrL, based on the project or domain in which the derived process will be used.

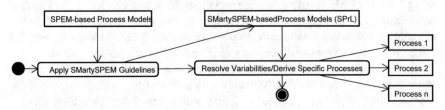

Fig. 17.6 Modeling SPrLs and deriving specific processes based on the SMartySPEM approach SMartySPEM [29]

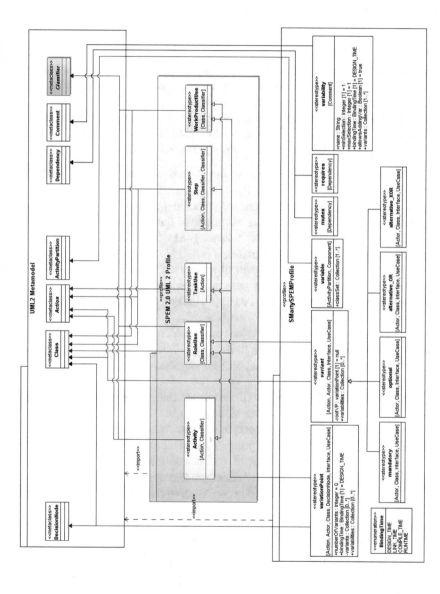

Fig. 17.7 The SMartySPEMProfile and its stereotypes [29]

The SMartySPEM guidelines basically provide directions on how to identify variabilities and model them into SPEM-based process elements by applying UML stereotypes from the SMartySPEMProfile [29]. Figure 17.7 provides an overall view of the SMartySPEMProfile and its related packages. The SMartySPEMProfile (first bottom-up) stereotypes extend UML metaclasses or are extensions of the SPEM metamodel. Therefore, one can apply such stereotypes directly to UML elements or SPEM elements.

SMartySPEMProfile takes into account the following SPEM stereotypes: ≪Step≫, ≪Activity≫, ≪RoleUse≫, ≪TaskUse≫, and ≪Work ProductUse≫. Such stereotypes represent the elements activity, role use, task use, and work product step and use, respectively, which are taken into consideration for modeling software processes. Thus, only a specific subset of the UML metaclasses is extended by the SPEM and SMartySPEM profiles.

The stereotypes that form the SMartySPEMProfile are as follows (Fig. 17.7):

- ≪variability≫ is an extension of the *Comment* metaclass that represents variability in SPrL.
- ≪variationPoint≫ represents the specific points where variation on process elements can occur. It is an extension of the *DecisionNode* and *Class* metaclasses, and it specializes the following SPEM 2.0 profile stereotypes *RoleUse*, *TaskUse*, and *WorkProductUse*.
- ≪variant≫ represents the concept of a variant process element in a SPrL, and it is an abstract extension of the class and action, and a specialization of the SPEM stereotypes ≪Activity≫, ≪RoleUse≫, ≪TaskUse≫, ≪Step≫, and ≪WorkProductUse≫.
- ≪mandatory≫ represents mandatory process elements that must be present in all specific derived processes of a SPrL.
- ≪optional≫ represents optional process elements that might be part of an instantiated process.
- ≪alternative_OR≫ represents different possible combinations of elements for resolving a variation point or a variability.
- ≪alternative_XOR≫ represents the selection of only one process element from a set for resolving a variation point or a variability.
- ≪mutex≫ represents the concept of variant constraint, and it is a mutually exclusive relationship between two variant process elements. It means that the selection of a variant requires the deselection of another variant for a specific process.
- ≪requires≫ represents the concept in which the selection of a variant implies the selection of another variant for a specific process.
- ≪variable≫ is an extension of the metaclass *ActivityPartition*. It indicates that a partition in an activity diagram contains a set of process elements with explicit variabilities.

SMartySPEM provides a set of guidelines to support the identification and representation variability in modeled process elements by taking into consideration the SMartySPEMProfile stereotypes. These guidelines help identify possible elements that may vary depending on the domain of application of a software process, which are:

- G1. *DecisionNode* elements in activity diagrams suggest variation points tagged as ≪variationPoint≫ as they explicitly represent different paths.
- G2. SPEM *Activity* elements in activity diagrams might be defined as mandatory or optional variants tagged as ≪mandatory≫ and ≪optional≫, respectively.
- G3. SPEM *Activity* elements which represent alternative path flows of a *DecisionNode* suggest variant activities inclusive (≪alternative_OR≫) or exclusive (≪alternative_XOR≫).
- G4. *ActivityPartition* in activity diagrams that contain elements with associated variability, *DecisionNode* as a variation point and/or *Activity* as a variant, must be tagged as ≪variable≫;
- G5. *Role Use*, *Task Use*, and *Work Product Use* SPEM elements suggest variation points tagged as ≪variationPoint≫ as they might be selected for different specific processes.
- G6. *RoleUse*, *TaskUse*, *Step*, and *WorkProductUse* SPEM elements might be tagged as mandatory or optional variants, respectively, by applying the stereotypes ≪mandatory≫ and ≪optional≫.
- G7. *RoleUse*, *TaskUse*, *Step*, and *WorkProductUse* SPEM elements that specialize or are composition/aggregation of ≪variationPoint≫ elements suggest inclusive (≪alternative_OR≫) or exclusive (≪alternative _XOR≫) variant elements.
- G8. Selected variant elements which require the presence of another element must have a dependency relationship tagged as ≪requires≫.
- G9. Mutually exclusive variant elements for a specific process must have a dependency relationship tagged as ≪mutex≫.

The SMartySPEM approach provides the same set of icons of the SPEM metamodel. These icons are annotated to assist in identifying variation points and variants in models that use them. The annotated elements are *Activity*, *TaskUse*, *WorkProductUse*, *RoleUse*, and *Step*. They have several variant icons tagged with one of the following acronyms (see Fig. 17.8): MDT for mandatory, OPT for optional, OR for inclusive variants, XOR for exclusive variants, and VP for variation points. It means that each SPEM icon receives one of these acronyms to improve the readability of a SMartySPEM-based SPrL model [29].

17.4   Application Example

This section presents a Scrum-based SPrL represented by the SMartySPEM approach. Scrum [34] is an agile methodology for the management and planning of software projects, in which project development are divided into cycles called

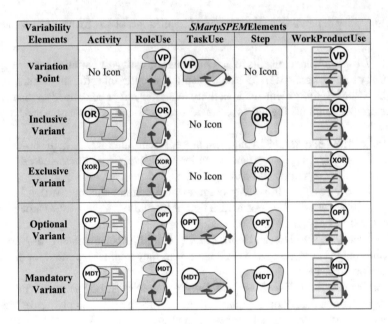

Variability	*SMartySPEM*Elements				
Elements	Activity	RoleUse	TaskUse	Step	WorkProductUse
Variation Point	No Icon	VP	VP	No Icon	VP
Inclusive Variant	OR	OR	No Icon	OR	OR
Exclusive Variant	XOR	XOR	No Icon	XOR	XOR
Optional Variant	OPT	OPT	OPT	OPT	OPT
Mandatory Variant	MDT	MDT	MDT	MDT	MDT

Fig. 17.8 The SMartySPEM icons

Sprints. A Sprint represents a time interval where a series of activities must be carried out.

All functionality for project development is stored in a list called Product Backlog. At the beginning of each Sprint, a planning meeting called Sprint Planning Meeting is held, where the Product Owner (a profile that represents the interests of the stakeholders for the team) prioritizes the tasks of the Product Backlog and the team selects the tasks that can be developed during the Sprint, thus transferring the selected tasks from the Product Backlog to the Sprint Backlog.

Throughout the Sprint, the team usually participates in a daily meeting, called Daily Scrum. The objective of this meeting is to share knowledge regarding the work that was developed the previous day, discussing business rules, solutions, difficulties, doubts, and impediments and prioritizing the tasks of the current day.

At the end of each Sprint, the team presents the features developed for the Product Owner in a delivery meeting called Sprint Review Meeting. Finally, the Sprint Retrospective is held, discussing the positive and negative points that occurred during the Sprint. Figure 17.9 illustrates the Scrum life cycle.

The main elements of Scrum are:

- Daily Scrum—a daily meeting to share knowledge about what was developed the day before, discussing impediments and prioritizing the tasks of the current day.

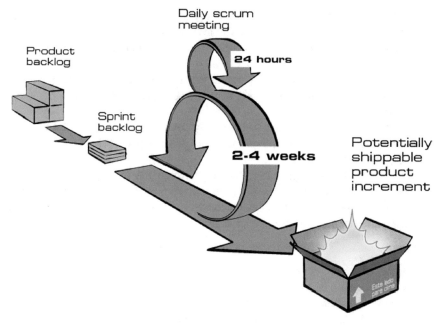

Fig. 17.9 Scrum life cycle [34]

- Product Backlog—list of all functional and nonfunctional requirements of the product to be developed. This list is defined by the product owner.
- Product Owner—role that defines the items that make up the product backlog and prioritizes them at Sprint planning meetings.
- Release Burndown Chart—in a Scrum project, the team monitors its progress by a Release Burndown Chart. The horizontal axis of a Release Burndown Chart represents the Sprints, and the vertical axis represents the amount of work that remains to be done.
- Scrum Master—role that ensures that the team respects and follows the values and practices of Scrum. It also protects the team by ensuring that it is not overly committed to what it is capable of doing during a Sprint. The Scrum master has the role of facilitating the Daily Scrum and is responsible for removing any impediments that are pointed out by the team.
- Scrum Team—represents the entire development team working on the project. There is not necessarily a functional division through traditional roles, such as programmer, designer, test analyst, or architect. Everyone works together to complete the set of tasks they have committed to deliver at the end of the Sprint.
- Sprint Backlog—represents a list of tasks that the Scrum team has committed to deliver at the end of the Sprint. The Sprint Backlog tasks are taken from the Product Backlog based on the priorities defined by the product owner, in addition to the estimated work time of each task made by the team.
- Sprint Planning Meeting—meeting attended by the product owner, Scrum master, and the entire Scrum team, as well as anyone interested in the

Sprint. During the Sprint planning meeting, the product owner outlines the highest priority tasks for the team. The team asks questions during the meeting so that it is able to break features into technical tasks after the meeting. These tasks will give rise to the Sprint Backlog.

- `Sprint Retrospective`—ceremony that occurs at the end of a Sprint and serves to identify what worked well, what can be improved, and what actions will be taken to improve it.
- `Sprint Review Meeting`—ceremony held at the end of each Sprint. In this meeting, the Scrum team presents to the product owner what was developed during the Sprint.
- `Scrum of Scrum`—planning meeting between the teams, necessary when there is more than one team working on the same project, aims to integrate the work performed. It usually takes place two or three times a week and has the participation of one member of each team.

The main variations in Scrum practice are according to [15]:

- The role of the project manager is optional.
- The Daily Scrum task is optional.
- Ask three questions at the daily meeting: What did you do yesterday, what are you going to do today, and any impediments in your way are optional.
- The release planning task is optional.
- The Scrum of Scrum task is optional.
- Estimation techniques, being able to select only 1:

  - T-shirt size
  - Planning Poker

- Taskboard types, being able to select 1 or more:

  - Task table (physical)
  - Spreadsheet
  - Redmine tool

- The Burndown Chart work product is optional.
- The Release Burndown Chat work product is optional.
- Time for the Daily Scrum, being able to select only 1:

  - In the morning
  - After lunch
  - Late afternoon

- Sprint duration, being able to select only 1:

  - 1 day
  - 1 week
  - 15 days
  - 1 month

- Break user stories into tasks is optional.

- Backlog prioritization, being able to select only 1:

  - Table of importance X complexity
  - MoSCoW prioritization
  - Kano model

A complete list of Scrum variations from the literature and practitioners can be found in [15].

Figure 17.10[1] is a Scrum-based SPrL represented with the SMartySPEM [13] approach, in which we can identify all Scrum elements such as roles, ceremonies, artifacts, tasks, and methods, as well as the variabilities found. The Enterprise Architect tool [36] was used to model this SPrL. This tool allows you to import the SMartySPEM profile into model diagrams.

Figure 17.11 presents an example of a process derivation from the Scrum-based SPrL presented in Fig. 17.10. It was accomplished by solving the variabilities and choosing the optional elements.

The Scrum-based SPrL derivation of Fig. 17.11 has the following elements:

- Roles:

  - Product owner
  - Scrum team
  - Scrum master

- Artifacts:

  - Product backlog
  - Sprint backlog
  - BurnDown chat
  - Taskboard
  - Increment of usable product

- Tasks and methods:

  - Backlog estimation by Planning Poker
  - Backlog prioritization
  - Weekly Sprint planning with breaking stories into tasks, organized in the Redmine tool and visible when tasks are done
  - Sprint review meeting
  - Daily morning meeting with planned questions

---

[1] This figure is available in high resolution at https://doi.org/10.5281/zenodo.6570981.

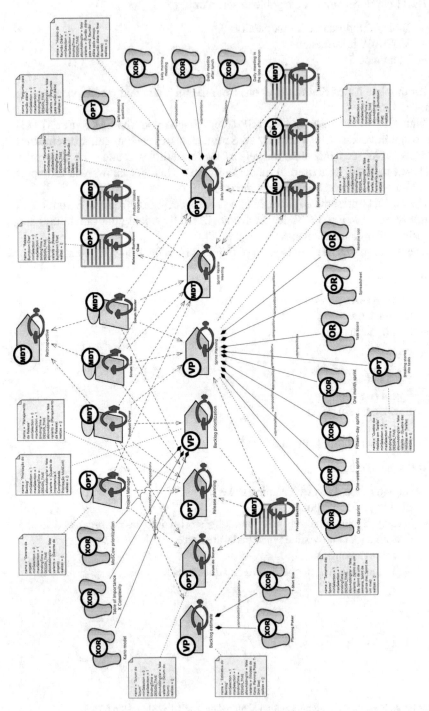

Fig. 17.10 SPrL based on Scrum [11]

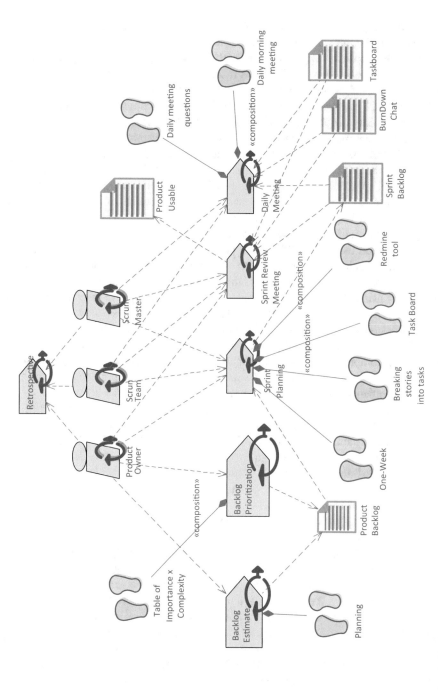

Fig. 17.11 Process derived from the SPrL of Fig. 17.10 based on Scrum [11]

17.5   Final Remarks

Several approaches such as SMartySPEM can be found to assist in identifying similarities and managing variability in SPrLs, as we presented in Sect. 17.2.2. Recent studies present positive evidence on SMartySPEM, showing to be a promising approach. However, SMartySPEM lacks more studies that may bring evidence of the viability and effectiveness of its variability mechanisms.

Dias et al. [12] presented an empirical qualitative study comparing the representation of variability in compositional and annotative approaches. The compositional approach was represented by the Eclipse Process Framework (EPF) and its composer tool, and the annotative approach was represented by the SMartySPEM approach for variability representation in software process elements. As a result, the compositional approach was better evaluated for the criteria modularity and error detection, whereas the annotative approach was better evaluated for the criteria traceability, granularity, adoption, and systematic variability management. Such a study provided, although initial, evidence that the annotative approach, in this study represented by SMartySPEM, has more advantages over the compositional approach, represented by EPF composer. Although the criteria of modularity and detection errors had lower results in the annotative approach, they might be improved by using UML packages for modularity and applying inspection activities for error detection such as in Geraldi et al. [17].

Pazin et al. [30] empirically compared the SMartySPEM and vSPEM approaches in terms of representing variability in software process models. The objective was to compare the comprehensibility of diagrams and variability mechanisms by means of correctness, time, and efficiency. The experiment performed provides evidence that the participants took more time to understand and interpret the diagrams modeled with SMartySPEM. However, analyzing the correction of the SMartySPEM diagrams, it can be seen that it had a superior result, with greater efficiency. Regarding the variability mechanisms, the diagrams modeled with SMartySPEM had lower efficiency and took longer to be modified; however, the correction of the SMartySPEM diagrams obtained a superior result. Therefore, an initial body of knowledge evidenced a positive efficiency of SMartySPEM for representing variability in process models. Potential points for improvement were also found to reduce the complexity of modeling SMartySPEM diagrams, which can significantly contribute to its evolution.

Pazin et al. [31] presents an empirical study, which qualitatively compares SMartySPEM and vSPEM approaches based on traceability, modularity, granularity, error detection, adoption, and systematic variability management. Experts were invited to contribute to our study. Results provided initial evidence SMartySPEM has better results compared to vSPEM, except for the adoption criterion. In addition, several points of improvement for SMartySPEM were highlighted. It was also identified the need to study or propose support tools that can assist in the modularization of processes and to verify the viability of SMartySPEM from the point of view of coarse granularity modeling. Another point of improvement was to identify possible directions to reduce the complexity of the approach.

Acknowledgments The authors would like to thank CAPES/Brazil (PROCAD Grant number 071/2013) and FAPESP/Brazil (Grant number 2012/04053-9) for supporting this work.

References

1. Agh, H., García, F., Piattini, M.: A checklist for the evaluation of software process line approaches. Inf. Softw. Technol. **146**, 106864 (2022). https://doi.org/10.1016/j.infsof.2022.106864
2. Alegría, J.A.H., Bastarrica, M.C.: Building software process lines with casper. In: 2012 International Conference on Software and System Process (ICSSP), pp. 170–179 (2012). https://doi.org/10.1109/ICSSP.2012.6225962
3. Aleixo, F.A., Freire, M.A., dos Santos, W.C., Kulesza, U.: Automating the variability management, customization and deployment of software processes: a model-driven approach. In: 12th International Conference on Enterprise Information Systems, pp. 372–387 (2010). https://doi.org/10.1007/978-3-642-19802-1_26
4. Armbrust, O., Katahira, M., Miyamoto, Y., Münch, J., Nakao, H., Ocampo, A.: Scoping software process lines. Softw. Process. **14**(3), 181–197 (2009). https://doi.org/10.1002/spip.v14:3
5. Barreto, A.S., Murta, L.G.P., da Rocha, A.R.C.: Software process definition: a reuse-based approach. J. Univer. Comput. Sci. **17**(13), 1765–1799 (2011)
6. Blum, F., Simmonds, J., Bastarrica, M.: Software process line discovery. In: ICSSP 2015: Proceedings of the 2015 International Conference on Software and System Process, pp. 127–136 (2015). https://doi.org/10.1145/2785592.2785605
7. Clements, P.C., Northrop, L.: Software Product Lines: Practices and Patterns. SEI Series in Software Engineering. Addison-Wesley, Boston (2001)
8. Costa, D., Teixeira, E., Werner, C.: Odyssey-processcase: A case-based software process line approach. In: SBQS: Proceedings of the 17th Brazilian Symposium on Software Quality, pp. 170–179 (2018). https://doi.org/10.1145/3275245.3275263
9. Costa, D., Teixeira, E., Werner, C.: Software process definition using process lines: A systematic literature review. In: 2018 XLIV Latin American Computer Conference (CLEI), pp. 110–119 (2018). https://doi.org/10.1109/CLEI.2018.00022
10. Dey, A., Abowd, G., Salber, D.: A conceptual framework and a toolkit for supporting the rapid prototyping of context-aware applications. Human-Comput. Interact. **16**(2-4), 97–166 (2001). https://doi.org/10.1207/S15327051HCI16234_02
11. Dias, J.W., OliveiraJr, E.: Empirical evidence of compositional and annotative approaches to managing variability in software process lines. Master's Thesis, State University of Maringá, Maringá, Paraná (2015)
12. Dias, J.W., OliveiraJr, E.: Modeling variability in software process with EPF composer and SMartyspem: An empirical qualitative study. In: Proceedings of the 18th International Conference on Enterprise Information Systems, ICEIS 2016, pp. 283–293. SCITEPRESS - Science and Technology Publications, Lda (2016). https://doi.org/10.5220/0005771502830293
13. Dias, J.W., OliveiraJr, E., Silva, M.A.G.: Preliminary Empirical Evidence on SPrL Variability Management with EPF and SMartySPEM. In: Proceedings of the 30th Brazilian Symposium on Software Engineering, SBES 2016, Maringá, Brazil, September 19–23, 2016, pp. 133–142 (2016). https://doi.org/10.1145/2973839.2973850
14. Galster, M., Weyns, D., Tofan, D., Michalik, B., Avgeriou, P.: Variability in software systems-a systematic literature review. IEEE Trans. Softw. Eng. **40**(3), 282–306 (2014). https://doi.org/10.1109/TSE.2013.56
15. Garcia, L.A., OliveiraJr, E., Morandini, M.: Tailoring the Scrum framework for software development: Literature mapping and feature-based support. Inf. Softw. Technol. **146**, 106814 (2022)

16. García-Borgoñón, L., Barcelona, M., García, J., Alba, M., Escalona, M.: Software process modeling languages: A systematic literature review. Inf. Softw. Technol. **56**(2), 103–116 (2014). http://dx.doi.org/10.1016/j.infsof.2013.10.001

17. Geraldi, R.T., OliveiraJr, E., Conte, T., Steinmacher, I.: Checklist-based inspection of SMarty variability models - proposal and empirical feasibility study. In: Proceedings of the 17th International Conference on Enterprise Information Systems - Volume 1: ICEIS, pp. 268–276. INSTICC, SciTePress (2015). https://doi.org/10.5220/0005350102680276

18. Ginsberg, M., Quinn, L.: Process tailoring and the software capability maturity model. Technical Report CMU/SEI-94-TR-024, Software Engineering Institute, Carnegie Mellon University, Pittsburgh, PA (1995). http://resources.sei.cmu.edu/library/asset-view.cfm?AssetID=12261

19. Hollenbach, C.R.: Experiences in process domain engineering at PRC inc. In: Proceedings 10th International Software Process Workshop pp. 78–79 (1996)

20. Hollenbach, C., Frakes, W.: Software process reuse in an industrial setting. In: Proceedings of Fourth IEEE International Conference on Software Reuse, pp. 22–30 (1996). https://doi.org/10.1109/ICSR.1996.496110

21. Hurtado Alegría, J.A., Bastarrica, M.C., Quispe, A., Ochoa, S.F.: An mde approach to software process tailoring. In: Proceedings of the 2011 International Conference on Software and Systems Process, ICSSP '11, pp. 43–52. ACM, New York, NY (2011). https://doi.org/10.1145/1987875.1987885

22. Kellner, M.I.: Connecting reusable software process elements and components. In: Proceedings 10th International Software Process Workshop, pp. 8–11 (1996). https://doi.org/10.1109/ISPW.1996.654356

23. Magdaleno, A., de Araujo, R., Werner, C.: COMPOOTIM: An approach to software processes composition and optimization. In: CIbSE (2012).

24. Martinez-Ruiz, T., Garcia, F., Piattini, M., Munch, J.: Modelling software process variability: an empirical study. IET Softw. **5**(2), 172–187 (2011). https://doi.org/10.1049/iet-sen.2010.0020

25. Nogueira Teixeira, E., Aleixo, F., Amâncio, F., OliveiraJr, E., Kulesza, U., Werner, C.: Software process line as an approach to support software process reuse: a systematic literature review. Inf. Softw. Technol. **116**, 106175 (2019). https://doi.org/10.1016/j.infsof.2019.08.007

26. Northrop, L.M.: Sei's software product line tenets. IEEE Softw. **19**(4), 32–40 (2002). https://doi.org/10.1109/MS.2002.1020285

27. OliveiraJr, E., Gimenes, I.M.d.S., Maldonado, J.C.: Systematic management of variability in UML-based software product lines. J. Univer. Comput. Sci. **16**, 2374–2393 (2010). https://doi.org/10.3217/jucs-016-17-2374

28. OliveiraJr, E., Gimenes, I., Maldonado, J.: systematic management of variability in UML-based software product lines. J. Univer. Comput. Sci. **16**(17), 2374–2393 (2010)

29. OliveiraJr, E., Pazin, M.G., Gimenes, I.M.S., Kulesza, U., Aleixo, F.A.: SMartyspem: A spem-based approach for variability management in software process lines. In: Heidrich, J., Oivo, M., Jedlitschka, A., Baldassarre, M.T. (eds.) Product-Focused Software Process Improvement, pp. 169–183. Springer, Berlin (2013)

30. Pazin, M.G., Allian, A.P., OliveiraJr, E.: Empirical study on software process variability modelling with SMartySPEM and vSPEM. IET Softw. **12**, 536–546 (2018)

31. Pazin, M.G., Geraldi, R.T., OliveiraJr, E.: Comparing SMartyspem and vSPEM for modeling variability in software processes: A qualitative study. In: Proceedings of the 17th Brazilian Symposium on Software Quality, SBQS, p. 71–80. Association for Computing Machinery, New York, NY (2018). https://doi.org/10.1145/3275245.3275253

32. Rombach, D.: Integrated software process and product lines. In: International Conference on Unifying the Software Process Spectrum, pp. 83–90 (2005). https://doi.org/10.1007/11608035_9

33. Rombach, D.: Integrated software process and product lines. In: Li, M., Boehm, B., Osterweil, L.J. (eds.) Unifying the Software Process Spectrum, pp. 83–90. Springer, Berlin (2006)

34. SCRUM: Agile Software Development (2014). http://www.desenvolvimentoagil.com.br/scrum/

35. Simmonds, J., Bastarrica, M.C., Silvestre, L., Quispe, A.: Variability in software process models: Requirements for adoption in industrial settings. In: 2013 4th International Workshop on Product LinE Approaches in Software Engineering (PLEASE), pp. 33–36 (2013). https://doi.org/10.1109/PLEASE.2013.6608661
36. Sparxs: Enterprise Architect (2014). https://sparxsystems.com/products/ea/
37. Sutton Jr., S.M., Osterweil, L.J.: Product families and process families. In: Proceedings 10th International Software Process Workshop, pp. 109–111 (1996)
38. Teixeira, E.: A component-based software process line engineering with variability management in multiple perspectives. In: 18th International Software Product Line Conference Doctoral Symposium, pp. 1–10 (2014)
39. Teixeira, E., Vasconcelos, A., Werner, C.: Odyssey process reuse: A component-based software process line approach. In: ICEIS, pp. 231–238 (2018).
40. Washizaki, H.: Building software process line architectures from bottom up. In: Münch, J., Vierimaa, M. (eds.) Product-Focused Software Process Improvement, pp. 415–421. Springer, Berlin (2006)

Chapter 18
Reengineering UML Class Diagram Variants into a Product Line Architecture

Wesley Klewerton Guez Assunção, Silvia R. Vergilio, and Roberto E. Lopez-Herrejon

Abstract Software reuse is a way to reduce costs and improve the quality of products. In practice, software reuse is commonly done by opportunistic strategies. In these strategies, the artifacts are simply copied/cloned and modified/adapted to fulfill existing needs. Opportunistic reuse leads to a set of system variants developed independently, generating technical debts. The maintenance and evolution of these independent variants are a costly and difficult task since most of the times the practitioners do not have a global view of such variants nor a clear understanding of the actual structure of the system. In such a case, a systematic reuse approach is paramount. Software product line engineering (SPLE) is a well-established approach to deal with a set of product variants in a specific domain, including systematic reuse in the software development process. One of the main design assets generated during the SPLE is the product line architecture (PLA), which describes how commonalities and variabilities are implemented in an SPL. Designing a PLA from scratch is challenging, since it must contemplate a detailed description of a whole family of products. PLAs can be obtained from existing product variants, requiring less effort and time from practitioners. Commonly, UML class diagrams of system products are available or can be reverse engineered easily. These UML class diagrams are a rich source of information to support PLA creation. In this chapter, we describe our method of reengineering UML class diagram of variants into an initial version of a PLA. Our method relies on a search-based technique to merge a set of UML model variants and insert annotations in model elements to describe

W. K. G. Assunção (✉)
ISSE, Johannes Kepler University Linz, Linz, Austria

OPUS, Pontifical Catholic University of Rio de Janeiro, Rio de Janeiro, Brazil
e-mail: wesley.assuncao@jku.at

S. R. Vergilio
DInf, Federal University of Paraná, Curitiba, Brazil
e-mail: silvia@inf.ufpr.br

R. E. Lopez-Herrejon
LOGTI, ETS, University of Quebec, Montreal, QC, Canada
e-mail: roberto.lopez@etsmtl.ca

© Springer Nature Switzerland AG 2023
E. OliveiraJr (ed), *UML-Based Software Product Line Engineering with SMarty*,
https://doi.org/10.1007/978-3-031-18556-4_18

the system features they belong to. The output of our method is an annotated UML class diagram that shows the whole structure of product variants that allows practitioners to reason better about the adoption of SPLE, aiding communication among stakeholders, supporting SPLE planning, and helping estimate maintenance, evolution, and testing activities.

18.1 Introduction

The development of a software system from scratch is a complex and high-cost activity. Software reuse, which is based on the use of existing artifacts to develop new software systems, is a well-established strategy to reduce costs, improve productivity, and increase quality [13]. The reuse of artifacts can be performed in different levels of abstraction and in different phases of the software development life cycle. Artifacts that can be reused include source code, design models, and test cases, to cite some.

In practice, software reuse is generally carried out using an opportunistic reuse strategy, which is also known as clone-and-own reuse, copy-and-paste reuse, or ad hoc reuse [10]. In this strategy, existing software artifacts are cloned/copied and adapted/modified to fulfill the new requirements. The opportunistic reuse strategy offers a simple way to reuse software artifacts. It does not require an upfront investment and quickly obtains adequate short-term results. However, the extensive use of opportunistic software reuse quickly becomes problematic. For example, opportunistic reuse results in extensive refactoring, adding technical debt, and eventually leading to unanticipated behavior, violated constraints, conflicts in assumptions, fragile structure, and software bloat [14]. To make matters even worse, the simultaneous maintenance of many independent variants of the same system is a complex activity, as duplicated functionalities must be managed individually [7].

We can find several studies in the literature dealing with the reengineering of multiple system variants into SPLs [2, 15]. Only a few of them focus on the definition of a product line architecture (PLA) from existing product variants. Software architectures are artifacts that provide a high-level view of functional parts of systems, allowing analysis of their structure and supporting design decisions [5]. In addition, PLAs describe how commonalities and variabilities are implemented in an SPL. To recover or discover a PLA that best represents an existing family of software products demands high human effort [21]. Furthermore, the few existing approaches to recover/discover are based on source code [8, 11, 12].

Taking into account the aforementioned limitations of existing work, in a previous study, we presented an approach to automatically merge multiple UML model variants to obtain a documented software architecture that is a step toward the definition of a PLA [3]. The goal of our approach is to discover a global model that contains an overview of all the implementation elements spread across the different variants. The input of our approach is a set of UML model variants, and the output is a complete model, the most similar to all variants. The proposed merging process relies on a search-based technique, in which the evolutionary process is in charge of dealing with domain-specific constraints of systems under consideration and possible conflicts among models merging operations. We implemented our approach with a genetic algorithm and evaluated it using four case studies from different domains and with different sizes. The evaluation of the proposed approach showed that the merging of UML class diagram variants represented good documented architectures to support the maintenance, evolution, and testing of system variants.

In this book chapter, we describe our approach of merging UML models to obtain a documented architecture [3] and introduce an additional step of variability annotations, where UML model elements are annotated to describe existing variability. The goal is to provide a UML-based PLA to aid practitioners to reengineer independent variants into SPLs.

The remainder of this chapter is as follows: In Sect. 18.2, we describe in detail the proposed search-based approach. The evaluation of the proposed approach and the results are presented in Sect. 18.3. Finally, Sect. 18.5 presents the final remarks and suggestions of future work.

18.2 Proposed Approach

In this section, we describe our approach to reengineer UML class diagram variants into PLAs. The proposed approach has two steps: (i) a search-based algorithm to merge UML class diagram variants to obtain a global UML model having as many as possible of the features contained across the variants and (ii) the process to annotate variability information in the UML models.

The input for the proposed approach is a set of UML class diagrams, which is used for the search-based algorithm, and traceability information of features implemented in the products and the model elements mapped to them, which is used for variability annotation. This traceability[1] should be provided by practitioners based on their knowledge or discovered by using automated tools. The output is a PLA, composed of a global UML model and annotated elements that describe variability information. To illustrate how our approach works, we rely on three variants of a banking system [19]. These variants[2] are presented in Fig. 18.1.

---

[1] Traceability links describe where features are implemented in the source code. The definition or reverse engineering of traceability links is out of the scope of this work. For further details, see [16].

[2] Available at https://github.com/but4reuse/but4reuse/wiki/Examples.

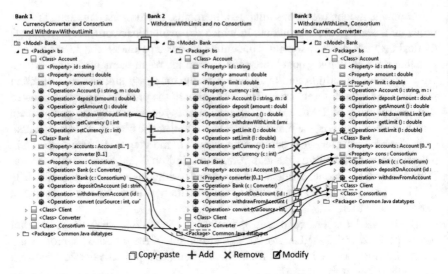

Fig. 18.1 Three banking system model variants, adapted from [19]

18.2.1 Step 1: Search-Based Model Merging

The first step of our approach relies on a genetic algorithm with the goal of merging UML class diagram variants. In what follows, we present the representation of individuals and generation of the initial population, the fitness function, and the genetic operators.

18.2.1.1 Representation of Individuals and Initial Population

Our search-based approach deals with models created with the well-known and widely used Eclipse Modeling Framework (EMF) [22]. We represent the models using EMF-based UML2[3] implementation of the UML^{TM} 2.x metamodel for the Eclipse platform. When models are represented using EMF-based UML2 data types, they can be compared and modified. These operations enabled by EMF tools are the basis of our search-based approach.

Based on the proposed representation and considering the set of UML class diagram variants used as input, the initial population is created by duplicating every variant until reaching the population size. For example, consider a population of 90 individuals for the search-based algorithm and the three variants of Fig. 18.1. The initial population will be composed of 30 copies/duplicates of each input model. Each duplicated mode variant is an individual.

---

[3] http://wiki.eclipse.org/MDT/UML2.

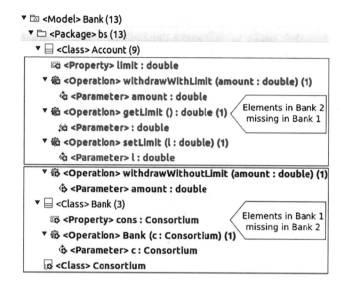

Fig. 18.2 Differences between variants Bank 1 and Bank 2

18.2.1.2   Fitness Function

The fitness function of our approach is based on differences among UML models of system variants. The computation of these differences is based on the Eclipse EMF Diff/Merge tool.[4] EMF Diff/Merge compares two models and returns the differences between them. EMF Diff/Merge computes three essential types of differences between models: (i) presence of an unmatched element, which refers to an element in a model that has no match in the opposite model; (ii) presence of an unmatched reference value, which means that a matched element references another element in only one model; (iii) presence of an unmatched attribute value, where a matched element owns a certain attribute value in only one model.

Figure 18.2 presents the output of EMF Diff/Merge when comparing differences between variants Bank 1 and Bank 2 (Fig. 18.1). The total number of differences is 13, but it is composed of two sets of differences. At the top of the figure, we have seven differences that are elements present in Bank 2 but missing in Bank 1, and at the bottom of the figure, we have six elements that belong to Bank 1 but do not appear in Bank 2.

EMF Diff/Merge tool is able to compare only two or three models at once. However, to evaluate a candidate architecture, we have to compute differences from one model to many model variants. Considering this, we propose a fitness function composed of the sum of differences from one model to all input model variants. Definition 18.1 presents the fitness function called here *model similarity*. The

---

[4] http://www.eclipse.org/diffmerge/.

function *diff* represents the number of differences found by using EMF Diff/Merge, but here we sum only the set of differences that indicate the elements that exist in the variant *v* but are missing in the *candidate_model*. There are no distinctions among the three essential types of differences.

Definition 18.1 (Model Similarity (MS)) Model similarity expresses the degree of similarity of the candidate architecture model to a set of model variants:

$$MS = \sum_{v \in Variants} diff(candidate\_model, v) \qquad (18.1)$$

To illustrate the computation of MS, we consider the candidate architecture model presented in Fig. 18.3a and the input models in Fig. 18.1. Using EMF Diff/Merge tool, we obtain the sets of differences presented in Fig. 18.3b,c, and d, corresponding to Bank 1, Bank 2, and Bank 3, respectively. For our fitness function, only the differences from the candidate architecture to each variant are relevant, which are highlighted in the figures. There are no differences from the candidate model to Bank 1. From the candidate model to Bank 2, there exist six differences. From the candidate model to Bank, 3 we have also six differences. We can observe 12 differences from the candidate model to all input variants and then MS = 12. The goal is to minimize the value of MS. An ideal solution has MS equal to zero, which indicates that the candidate architecture has all elements from the variants for which we want to discover the corresponding architecture.

18.2.1.3   Genetic Operators

The set of differences returned by EMF Diff/Merge is used to perform crossover and mutation. This result of EMF Diff/Merge also allows duplication and/or modification of models to incorporate the changes done by the operators. The mechanisms of the operators of crossover and mutation are described next.

Crossover
The crossover operator starts with two candidate architectures. From these two models, we generate two children: one with the differences merged and one without the differences. For instance, let us consider any parent models X and Y. The children will be:

- *Crossover Child Model 1*: This model has differences between its parents merged. For example, the elements of X that are missing on Y are merged in this later, or vice versa. Both ways will produce the same child.
- *Crossover Child Model 2*: This child is generated by removing the differences between the parents. For example, the differences of X that are missing on Y are removed, or vice versa. Both ways will produce the same child.

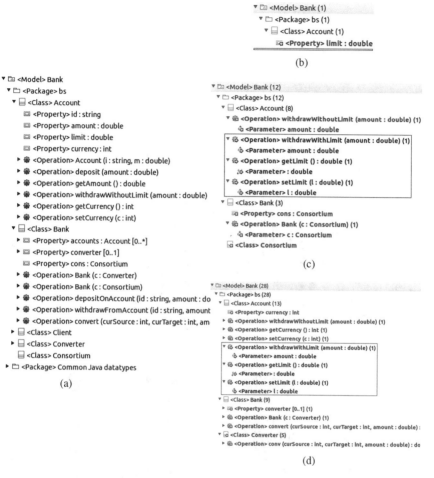

Fig. 18.3 Example of fitness evaluation. (**a**) Candidate model. (**b**) Differences to Bank $1 = 0$. (**c**) Differences to Bank $2 = 6$. (**d**) Differences to Bank $3 = 6$

The strategy adopted by Child Model 1 aims at creating a model that has more elements, going toward a more complete system architecture. On the other hand, the strategy used by Child Model 2 has the goal of eliminating possible conflicting elements from a candidate architecture.

To illustrate the crossover operator, let us consider as parents Bank 1 and Bank 2 presented in Fig. 18.1 and the differences between them, presented in Fig. 18.2. The offspring generated by crossover is presented in Fig. 18.4. In Fig. 18.4a, we have the child with all differences merged (highlighted) and in Fig. 18.4b the child with the differences removed.

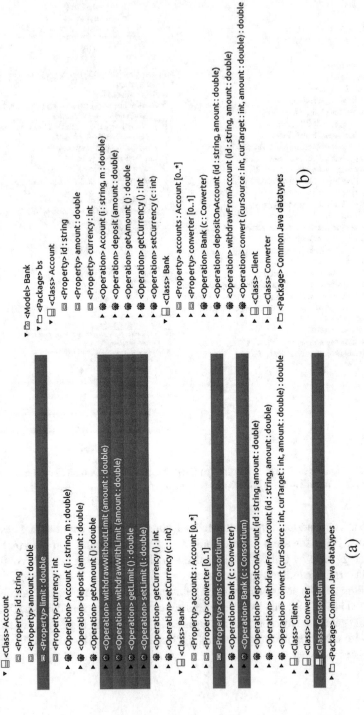

Fig. 18.4 Example of crossover between Bank 1 and Bank 2. (a) Crossover Child 1. (b) Crossover Child 2

Mutation

The mutation operator aims at applying only one modification in each model parent. The start point of the mutation is two candidate architectures, and the result is also two children. Let us again consider any parent models X and Y. The children are:

- *Mutation Child Model 1*: The first child is created by merging one difference from model Y to model X. After randomly selecting one element of model Y but missing on model X, this element is added into model X.
- *Mutation Child Model 2*: The same process described above is performed again, but in the opposite direction, namely, including one element of model X into model Y.

An example of mutation between Bank 1 and Bank 2 (Fig. 18.1) is presented in Fig. 18.5. Considering the differences shown in Fig. 18.2, we have seven differences to select one to be included in Bank 1 and six differences to select one to be included in Bank 2. As highlighted in Fig. 18.5a, the attribute `limit` was chosen to be included in Bank 1. In the child of Fig. 18.5b we can see that the class `Consortium` was selected to be included in Bank 2.

The mutation process can select a difference that is part of another difference. In such cases, the entire owning difference is moved to the child. For example, when a mutation selects a parameter owned by an operation, the entire operation is moved to the child.

Selection

The genetic algorithm of our approach uses the binary tournament strategy whereby a set of individuals are randomly selected from the population. Among the randomly selected individuals, the ones with the best fitness are chosen to undergo crossover and mutation [9].

18.2.2   Step 2: Variability Annotation

The best solution found during the evolutionary process in Step 1 is the basis for this step. Since in our context a PLA is a global UML class diagram with annotations regarding variabilities, to generate such representation the traceability information provided as input for our approach is used to annotate the class diagram. To include annotation of variability information in the PLA, we decided to use UML-owned comments which are available for each element of a UML class diagram. By adopting this strategy, the obtained PLA can be viewed in any UML editor.

The process of variability annotation is presented in Algorithm 1. Basically, the algorithm goes through all the UML elements comparing them to the traceability links. When there is a matching between the model element of the class diagram and the model element in the traceability information, an owned comment is assigned to the UML element with the name of the feature obtained from the traceability information.

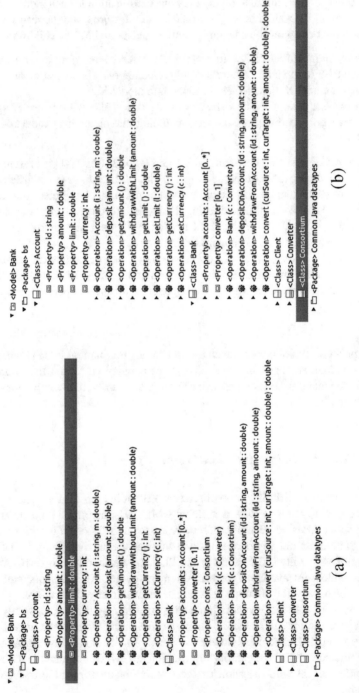

Fig. 18.5 Example of mutation between Bank 1 and Bank 2. (**a**) Mutation Child 1. (**b**) Mutation Child 2

Algorithm 1: Variability annotation

Input: UML class diagram, traceability information
Output: PLA
1 $modelElements \leftarrow$ all UML model elements from the UML class diagram;
2 $traceLinks \leftarrow$ all trace link tuples (feature, modelElement) from the Traceability information;
3 **for** *each* $element \in modelElements$ **do**
4   **for** *each* $trace \in modelElements$ **do**
5   **if** $modelElements.name = trace.modelElement.name$ **then**
6              $modelElements.ownedComment \leftarrow trace.feature.name$;
7   **end if**
8   **end for**
9 **end for**

Figure 18.6 presents a PLA constructed using the merged model obtained in the first step of our approach. The figure presents the variability information of an attribute of `Bank` with the comment that indicates it belongs to `Converter`.

18.3   Evaluation

In this section, we present the setup and the subject systems used to evaluate the proposed approach, along with the results obtained and their analysis.

18.3.1   Implementation Aspects and Experimental Setup

We implemented our work using JMetal[5] framework which provides several algorithms for multi-objective and mono-objective optimization [6]. We selected the mono-objective generational genetic algorithm (GA) [9]. Our GA was designed to deal with a minimization problem; recall that an ideal solution for our architecture recovery problem is an individual (i.e., candidate architecture) with fitness equal to zero (0).

EMF framework was used to load and save models. For the evolutionary process, where we compare and modify models, we used EMF Diff/Merge. Despite of EMF Diff/Merge having many functionalities, we needed to develop a customized match policy. The default match policies of EMF Diff/Merge only perform comparisons based on XMI:ids. However, model variants could have similar semantics even with different structures. Our customized match police considers qualified names, data types, and relationship types.

---

[5] Available at: http://jmetal.sourceforge.net/.

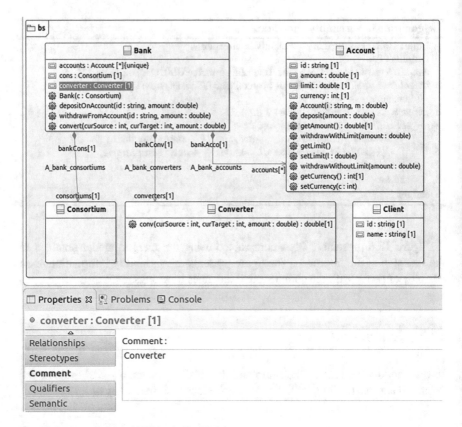

Fig. 18.6 Example of variabilities in the PLA

The GA parameters were population size = 200, crossover probability = 0.95, mutation probability = 0.2, and number of fitness evaluations = 8000. We set the parameters of crossover and mutation based on default values used in other discrete problems available on JMetal. Population size and the number of evaluations were set based on hardware's limitation. When we tried to use greater values for these two latter parameters, they caused limited memory exceptions. The elitism strategy adopted in the generational GA is to copy the best four individuals of one generation to the next one. The number of fitness evaluations is the stop criterion. The experiments were run on a machine with an Intel® Core^{TM} i7-4900MQ CPU with 2.80 GHz, 16 GB of memory, and running a Linux platform.

Table 18.1 Banking system

Variant	Features				#Cl	#Attr	#Op	#Rel
	BS	WL	CON	CC				
1	✓				3	5	6	1
2	✓		✓		4	6	7	3
3	✓	✓			3	6	8	1
4	✓			✓	4	7	11	2
Baseline	✓	✓	✓	✓	5	9	14	4

BS, base; WL, withdraw limit; CON, consortium; CC, currency converter

Table 18.2 Draw product line

Variant	Features						#Cl	#Attr	#Op	#Rel
	DPL	L	R	C	W	F				
1	✓	✓					4	13	26	3
2	✓	✓	✓				5	24	37	4
3	✓		✓				4	18	29	3
4	✓	✓		✓			4	22	27	3
5	✓		✓	✓			4	27	30	3
6	✓	✓			✓		4	15	27	3
7	✓		✓		✓		4	20	30	3
8	✓		✓	✓		✓	4	33	32	3
Baseline	✓	✓	✓	✓	✓	✓	5	42	41	4

DPL, base; L, line; R, rectangle; C, color; W, wipe; F, fill

18.3.2   Subject Systems

In our experiment, we used four subject systems, where each one is a set of UML model variants implementing different system features, and composed of classes, attributes, operations, and relationships. The subject systems are banking system (BS), a small banking application composed of four features [18]; draw product line (DPL), a system to draw lines and rectangles with six features [1]; video on demand (VOD), which implements 11 features for video-on-demand streaming [1]; and ZipMe (ZM), a set of tools to file compression with 7 features [1]. The variants are presented in Tables 18.1, 18.2, 18.3, and 18.4, respectively. These tables show the features, number of classes (#Cl), number of attributes (#Attr), number of operations (#Op), and number of relationships (#Rel) for each variant. This information was computed using SDMetrics.[6] Only BS is originally a set of UML model variants; for other subject systems, we reverse engineered the models from Java code using the Eclipse MoDisco.[7]

---

[6] http://www.sdmetrics.com.

[7] https://eclipse.org/MoDisco.

Table 18.3 Video on demand

Variant	Features VOD	SP	SelM	StaM	PI	VRC	P	StoM	QP	CS	D	#Cl	#Attr	#Op	#Rel
1	✓	✓	✓	✓	✓	✓						32	362	217	75
2	✓	✓	✓	✓	✓	✓	✓					32	362	217	75
3	✓	✓	✓	✓	✓	✓		✓				33	364	221	77
4	✓	✓	✓	✓	✓	✓	✓	✓				33	364	221	77
5	✓	✓	✓	✓	✓	✓			✓			33	364	221	77
6	✓	✓	✓	✓	✓	✓	✓		✓			33	364	221	77
7	✓	✓	✓	✓	✓	✓		✓	✓			34	366	225	79
8	✓	✓	✓	✓	✓	✓				✓		37	377	232	87
9	✓	✓	✓	✓	✓	✓	✓			✓		37	377	232	87
10	✓	✓	✓	✓	✓	✓		✓		✓		38	379	236	89
11	✓	✓	✓	✓	✓	✓			✓	✓		38	379	236	89
12	✓	✓	✓	✓	✓	✓					✓	35	374	226	82
13	✓	✓	✓	✓	✓	✓	✓				✓	35	374	226	82
14	✓	✓	✓	✓	✓	✓		✓			✓	36	376	230	84
15	✓	✓	✓	✓	✓	✓			✓		✓	36	376	230	84
16	✓	✓	✓	✓	✓	✓				✓	✓	40	389	241	94
Baseline	✓	✓	✓	✓	✓	✓	✓	✓	✓	✓	✓	42	393	249	98

VOD, base; SP, start player; SelM, select movie; StaM, start movie; PI, play Imm; VRC, VRC interface; P, pause; StoM, stop movie; QP, quit player; CS, change server; D, details

We have variants with all possible feature combinations for every subject system. However, we selected only variants that implement at most half of the non-mandatory features. To select these variants, we followed the rule:

$$threshold = \left(RoundUp\left(\frac{\#all\_features - \#mandatory\_features}{2}\right) + \#mandatory\_features\right)$$

We selected for our experiment only variants that implement a number of features below the threshold. The reason to select only a subset of variants is to have the combinations of features spread on different variants, to assess the ability of our approach to merge the models and get good system architectures. For each subject system, we also had a variant that implements all features, i.e., the most complete variants. We use this variant as a baseline for our analysis, since we consider this variant as the most similar model to a known system architecture. In the last line of Tables 18.1, 18.2, 18.3, and 18.4, there is information about the baseline.

Observing the information in the subject system tables (Tables 18.1, 18.2, 18.3, and 18.4), we can see that there are no variants with as many features as the baselines. Furthermore, the number of classes, attributes, operations, and relationships in the variants of all systems is smaller than the baselines.

Table 18.4 ZipMe

Variant	Features							#Cl	#Attr	#Op	#Rel
	ZM	C	CRC	AC	GZIP	A32	E				
1	✓	✓						22	212	241	64
2	✓	✓	✓					23	215	251	66
3	✓	✓		✓				22	212	243	66
4	✓	✓	✓	✓				23	215	253	68
5	✓	✓			✓			25	223	263	68
6	✓	✓	✓		✓			26	229	282	72
7	✓	✓		✓	✓			25	223	265	70
8	✓	✓				✓		23	216	263	69
9	✓	✓	✓			✓		24	219	273	71
10	✓	✓		✓		✓		23	216	265	71
11	✓	✓		✓		✓		26	227	285	73
12	✓	✓					✓	23	219	262	70
13	✓	✓	✓				✓	24	223	279	74
14	✓	✓		✓			✓	23	219	264	72
15	✓	✓			✓		✓	26	230	284	74
16	✓	✓				✓	✓	24	223	284	75
Baseline	✓	✓	✓	✓	✓	✓	✓	28	241	334	87

ZM, ZipMe; C, compress; CRC, CRC-32 checksum; AC, archive check; GZIP, GZIP format support; A32, Adler32 checksum; E, extract

18.3.3 Results and Analysis

Figure 18.7 shows the evolution of the best candidate architecture in each GA generation during the first step of our approach. The best individual of each system after the first 200 fitness evaluations is an input model from the initial population that has the least difference from other input models. For BS, the best individual is variant 4 that has 25 differences from the input. For DPL, the best initial individual is variant 2 with 127 differences. For VOD, the best initial candidate architecture is variant 16 with 315 differences. Finally, variant 11 of ZM is the best individual of the initial population having 854 differences from the input. These individuals are the first solutions presented in the charts in Fig. 18.7. Observing the figures, we can see how the evolutionary process is able to find better candidate architectures by reducing the number of differences. On average, the best solution is found after 1400 fitness evaluations. VOD is the simplest subject system, since the best solution was reached with approximately 1000 fitness evaluations. On the other hand, ZM is the most complex system, needing approximately 1800 fitness evaluations to reach the best solution. As expected for a GA, in all subjects, there is a great improvement in the number of found solutions in the initial generations, and then the search remains stable.

Fig. 18.7 Evolution of the best individual. (**a**) Banking system. (**b**) Draw product line. (**c**) Video on demand. (**d**) ZipMe

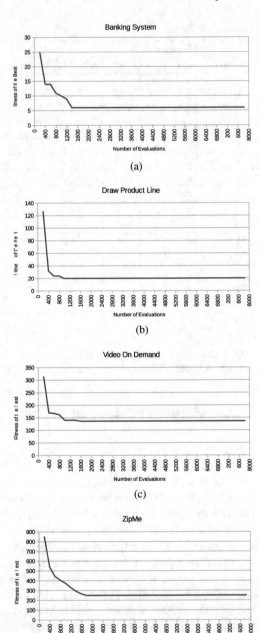

Table 18.5 Candidate architectures

System	Model	MS	#Cl	#Attr	#Op	#Rel
BS	Baseline	20	5	9	14	4
	Best individual	6	5	9	14	3
DPL	Baseline	40	5	42	41	4
	Best individual	20	5	42	41	4
VOD	Baseline	162	42	393	249	98
	Best individual	136	42	393	249	98
ZM	Baseline	633	28	241	334	87
	Best individual	250	28	241	381	79

#Cl, number of classes; #Attr, number of attributes; #Op, number of operations; #Rel, number of relationships

Another piece of information gathered during the evaluation of the first step of our approach is the runtime. The amount of time spent by the GA to perform the entire evolutionary process was BS = 55 s 740 ms, DPL = 6 m 13 s 17 ms, VOD = 1 h 46 m 55 s 698 ms, and ZM = 2 h 10 m 29 s 267 ms. GA ran very fast for BS, which has the smallest number of features, classes, attributes, operations, and relationships. DPL has more features and model elements (Table 18.2) than BS, and for this system, the GA took a little more than 6 min. A huge difference in the runtime is observed for VOD and ZM. VOD needed almost 2 h to be finished. ZM is the subject system that required the biggest amount of time; it took more than 2 h.

Now, let us consider the details of the best candidate architecture found, i.e., global UML class diagram. Table 18.5 shows the information of candidate architectures and baseline models. The values of MS presented in the third column are based on the input models. Regarding the number of classes, attributes, operations, and relationships, the baseline model and the best individual model are very similar. For BS, there is only a single difference in the number of relationships, where the best individual has one relationship less. In DPL and VOD, the number of model elements is the same. For ZM, the number of model elements is different in operations and relationships. Despite having a similar number of model elements, we can observe that the values of MS are not similar. As mentioned before in Sect. 18.2.1.2, the fitness function EMF Diff/Merge computes the presence of elements, presence of attributes values, and presence of reference values. This latter difference happens when a model element references to, or belongs to, different model elements. This explains the reason why baselines and best individuals have a similar number of model elements but different values of MS.

Table 18.6 presents the differences between baseline and the best individuals for each system. Since the comparison of EMF Diff/Merge has two directions, we show the number of differences existing from baseline to the best individual (candidate architecture), and vice versa. For example, considering BS, there are seven differences needed for baseline having all elements of the candidate architecture. On the other hand, candidate architecture needs 14 existing differences to have all elements of baseline. In the values of Table 18.6, we can observe that the baseline is less different for systems BS, DPL, and VOD. This means that it is easier to transform

Table 18.6 Differences between baseline and candidate architectures

System	From baseline to best	From best to baseline
BS	7	14
DPL	5	451
VOD	20	3425
ZM	4155	200

baseline in the best than vice versa. For ZM, the solution obtained by the GA is the most similar to the baseline.

The analysis of Tables 18.5 and 18.6 reveals that a model having all features does not imply that it is the most similar to a set of model variants. We can infer this by considering that the best individual obtained by the GA for each system is the most similar to the model variants than the baseline (third column in Table 18.5) and, on the other hand, baseline is more similar to the best individual when comparing these two models (second and third columns of Table 18.6). To illustrate this situation, let us use the models of BS presented in Fig. 18.8. In Fig. 18.8a, the baseline has all features implemented, and in Fig. 18.8b, the best solution found is the most similar to the input models. Observe that in the best solution there exists an operation `withdrawWithoutLimit(amount: double)`. This operation is present in the variants that do not implement the feature WL (see Fig. 18.1), i.e., it is present in three out of four variants. This operation is not present in the baseline model, so this baseline model does not provide a global overview of the variants. The baseline would not serve as a reference for maintaining variants that do not have the feature WL. However, in the architecture, we can find out where the operation `withdrawWithoutLimit` is located.

The results of the second step of our approach, namely, variability annotation, are presented in Table 18.7. The number of model elements annotated with the traceability information is presented in the second column. The runtime for each application is in the last column. Applications VOD and ZM have the largest models; therefore, the variability grafting algorithm took the largest runtime. However, the runtime did not take more than 10 s.

18.4 UML-Based SPLs

Our approach to merge UML class diagrams in order to obtain a documented UML-based PLA is a step toward the reengineering of independent variants into SPLs. On one hand, we used the standard UML class diagram model and widely adopted modeling tools, such as Eclipse Modeling Framework and Eclipse EMF Diff/Merge tool. These tools are commonly adopted for designing of single-product development, which can ease the extractive adoption of SPLs. On the other hand, this same tolling support is limited on covering the whole SPL development life cycle and dealing with variability management [4].

Fig. 18.8 Baseline and best
solution for banking system.
(**a**) Baseline. (**b**) Best solution

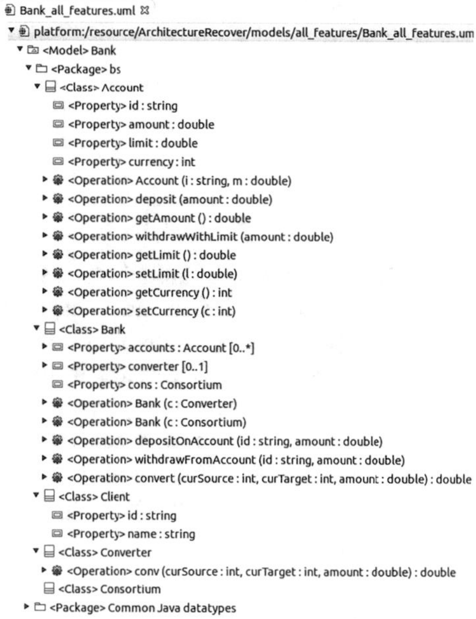

📄 Bank_all_features.uml ⊠
▼ 📄 platform:/resource/ArchitectureRecover/models/all_features/Bank_all_features.um
  ▼ 📰 <Model> Bank
    ▼ 📂 <Package> bs
      ▼ 🗒 <Class> Account
          ▭ <Property> id : string
          ▭ <Property> amount : double
          ▭ <Property> limit : double
          ▭ <Property> currency : int
        ▶ ⚙ <Operation> Account (i : string, m : double)
        ▶ ⚙ <Operation> deposit (amount : double)
        ▶ ⚙ <Operation> getAmount () : double
        ▶ ⚙ <Operation> withdrawWithLimit (amount : double)
        ▶ ⚙ <Operation> getLimit () : double
        ▶ ⚙ <Operation> setLimit (l : double)
        ▶ ⚙ <Operation> getCurrency () : int
        ▶ ⚙ <Operation> setCurrency (c : int)
      ▼ 🗒 <Class> Bank
        ▶ ▭ <Property> accounts : Account [0..*]
        ▶ ▭ <Property> converter [0..1]
          ▭ <Property> cons : Consortium
        ▶ ⚙ <Operation> Bank (c : Converter)
        ▶ ⚙ <Operation> Bank (c : Consortium)
        ▶ ⚙ <Operation> depositOnAccount (id : string, amount : double)
        ▶ ⚙ <Operation> withdrawFromAccount (id : string, amount : double)
        ▶ ⚙ <Operation> convert (curSource : int, curTarget : int, amount : double) : double
      ▼ 🗒 <Class> Client
          ▭ <Property> id : string
          ▭ <Property> name : string
      ▼ 🗒 <Class> Converter
        ▶ ⚙ <Operation> conv (curSource : int, curTarget : int, amount : double) : double
          🗒 <Class> Consortium
    ▶ 📂 <Package> Common Java datatypes

(a)

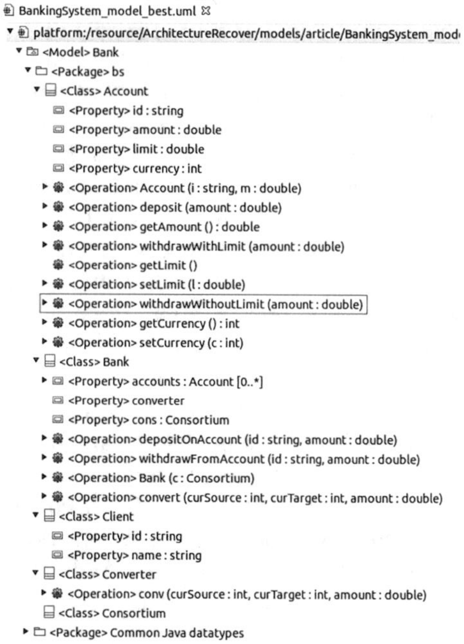

📄 BankingSystem_model_best.uml ⊠
▼ 📄 platform:/resource/ArchitectureRecover/models/article/BankingSystem_mod
  ▼ 📰 <Model> Bank
    ▼ 📂 <Package> bs
      ▼ 🗒 <Class> Account
          ▭ <Property> id : string
          ▭ <Property> amount : double
          ▭ <Property> limit : double
          ▭ <Property> currency : int
        ▶ ⚙ <Operation> Account (i : string, m : double)
        ▶ ⚙ <Operation> deposit (amount : double)
        ▶ ⚙ <Operation> getAmount () : double
        ▶ ⚙ <Operation> withdrawWithLimit (amount : double)
          ⚙ <Operation> getLimit ()
        ▶ ⚙ <Operation> setLimit (l : double)
        ▶ ⚙ <Operation> withdrawWithoutLimit (amount : double)
        ▶ ⚙ <Operation> getCurrency () : int
        ▶ ⚙ <Operation> setCurrency (c : int)
      ▼ 🗒 <Class> Bank
        ▶ ▭ <Property> accounts : Account [0..*]
          ▭ <Property> converter
          ▭ <Property> cons : Consortium
        ▶ ⚙ <Operation> depositOnAccount (id : string, amount : double)
        ▶ ⚙ <Operation> withdrawFromAccount (id : string, amount : double)
        ▶ ⚙ <Operation> Bank (c : Consortium)
        ▶ ⚙ <Operation> convert (curSource : int, curTarget : int, amount : double)
      ▼ 🗒 <Class> Client
          ▭ <Property> id : string
          ▭ <Property> name : string
      ▼ 🗒 <Class> Converter
        ▶ ⚙ <Operation> conv (curSource : int, curTarget : int, amount : double)
          🗒 <Class> Consortium
    ▶ 📂 <Package> Common Java datatypes

(b)

Table 18.7 Variability
annotation results

System	Model elements annotated	Runtime s	ms
BS	44	1	481
DPL	103	1	811
VOD	728	8	972
ZM	857	9	31

Considering the above limitations, we envisage the use of SPL-based tools for dealing better with the design and management of variability. For example, SMarty is an approach to manage variabilities in UML diagrams based on a profile and respective guidelines [20]. SMarty is flexible for use since it relies on profile stereotypes to represent variability in use case diagrams, class diagrams, component diagrams, activity diagrams, and sequence diagrams [17]. As tool support, we can mention SMartyModeling[8] that is an environment for engineering UML-based SPLs in which variabilities are modeled using the SMarty approach.

18.5 Final Remarks

This chapter presented our approach to reengineer UML class diagram variants into PLAs. The approach is composed of two steps, in which firstly a model-based software architecture is discovered by merging UML model variants and secondly variability annotation is included based on traceability information. The first step relies on a search-based technique that does not require information regarding domain constraints or conflicting model elements in advance. The variability annotation is a basic matching between UML model elements and traces information, using the name of the features to include UML-owned comments.

We performed an evaluation of our approach with four case studies from different domains and of different sizes. The results show that our approach is able to find good PLAs even when features are spread across multiple variants. Furthermore, we could observe that having a variant that implements all features of a system does not imply that this variant has all model elements of all individual variants.

We acknowledge that some results could be influenced by internal aspects of the subject systems; however, our approach is an easy way to support the reengineering of UML model variants into PLAs. Furthermore, the PLAs found by using our approach can help practitioners during maintenance by (i) providing a global view of a set of variants that supports the identification of bad smells and refactoring activities, (ii) allowing design reconciliation of different variants (potentially inconsistent) implemented by many designers, and (iii) showing clearly which product will be affected by modifications, since commonalities and variabilities are explicitly

---

[8] https://github.com/leandroflores/demo_SMartyModeling_tool.

shown. The documented architecture supports evolution by (i) being a start point to transform artifacts into an SPL and (ii) reducing the time to produce products with a new combination of features.

Acknowledgments The work is supported by the Brazilian funding agencies CAPES and CNPq (Grant 305968/2018), by the Carlos Chagas Filho Foundation for Supporting Research in the State of Rio de Janeiro (FAPERJ), under the PDR-10 program, grant 202073/2020, and by the Natural Sciences and Engineering Research Council of Canada (NSERC) grant RGPIN-2017-05421.

References

1. Assunção, W.K.G., Lopez-Herrejon, R.E., Linsbauer, L., Vergilio, S.R., Egyed, A.: Extracting variability-safe feature models from source code dependencies in system variants. In: Genetic and Evolutionary Computation Conference (GECCO), pp. 1303–1310. ACM, New York (2015). https://doi.org/10.1145/2739480.2754720
2. Assunção, W.K.G., Lopez-Herrejon, R.E., Linsbauer, L., Vergilio, S.R., Egyed, A.: Reengineering legacy applications into software product lines: a systematic mapping. Empir. Softw. Eng. 1–45 (2017). https://doi.org/10.1007/s10664-017-9499-z
3. Assunção, W.K.G., Vergilio, S.R., Lopez-Herrejon, R.E.: Discovering software architectures with search-based merge of UML model variants. In: Botterweck, G., Werner, C. (eds.) Mastering Scale and Complexity in Software Reuse, pp. 95–111. Springer International Publishing, Berlin (2017)
4. Berger, T., Steghöfer, J.P., Ziadi, T., Robin, J., Martinez, J., et al.: The state of adoption and the challenges of systematic variability management in industry. Empir. Softw. Eng., 1755–1797 (2020)
5. Dobrica, L., Niemela, E.: A survey on software architecture analysis methods. IEEE Trans. Softw. Eng. 28(7), 638–653 (2002). https://doi.org/10.1109/TSE.2002.1019479
6. Durillo, J.J., Nebro, A.J.: jmetal: a Java framework for multi-objective optimization. Adv. Eng. Softw. 42, 760–771 (2011). https://doi.org/10.1016/j.advengsoft.2011.05.014. http://jmetal.sourceforge.net/
7. Faust, D., Verhoef, C.: Software product line migration and deployment. Softw. Pract. Exp. 33(10), 933–955 (2003)
8. Garcia, J., Ivkovic, I., Medvidovic, N.: A comparative analysis of software architecture recovery techniques. In: International Conference on Automated Software Engineering (ASE), pp. 486–496. IEEE, Piscataway (2013)
9. Goldberg, D.E., Deb, K., Clark, J.H.: Genetic algorithms, noise, and the sizing of populations. Complex Syst. 6, 333–362 (1992)
10. Holmes, R., Walker, R.J.: Systematizing pragmatic software reuse. ACM Trans. Softw. Eng. Methodol. 21(4), 1–44 (2013). https://doi.org/10.1145/2377656.2377657
11. Hussain, I., Khanum, A., Abbasi, A.Q., Javed, M.Y.: A novel approach for software architecture recovery using particle swarm optimization. Int. Arab J. Inf. Technol. 12(1), 32–41 (2015)
12. Jeet, K., Dhir, R.: Software architecture recovery using genetic black hole algorithm. ACM SIGSOFT Softw. Eng. Not. 40(1), 1–5 (2015)
13. Krueger, C.W.: Software reuse. ACM Comput. Surv. 24(2), 131–183 (1992). https://doi.org/10.1145/130844.130856
14. Kulkarni, N., Varma, V.: Perils of opportunistically reusing software module. Softw. Pract. Exp. 47(7), 971–984 (2017). https://doi.org/10.1002/spe.2439
15. Laguna, M.A., Crespo, Y.: A systematic mapping study on software product line evolution: from legacy system reengineering to product line refactoring. Sci. Comput. Program. 78(8), 1010–1034 (2013). https://doi.org/10.1016/j.scico.2012.05.003

16. Linsbauer, L., Lopez-Herrejon, E.R., Egyed, A.: Recovering traceability between features and code in product variants. In: 17th International Software Product Line Conference, SPLC'13, pp. 131–140. ACM, New York (2013). https://doi.org/10.1145/2491627.2491630
17. Marcolino, A.S., OliveiraJr, E.: Comparing SMarty and plus for variability identification and representation at product-line uml class level: a controlled quasi-experiment. J. Comput. Sci. 13(11), 617–632 (2017). https://doi.org/10.3844/jcssp.2017.617.632
18. Martinez, J., Ziadi, T., Klein, J., Traon, Y.L.: Identifying and visualising commonality and variability in model variants. In: 10th European Conference Modelling Foundations and Applications (ECMFA), pp. 117–131 (2014). https://doi.org/10.1007/978-3-319-09195-2_8
19. Martinez, J., Ziadi, T., Bissyandé, T.F., Klein, J., l. Traon, Y.: Automating the extraction of model-based software product lines from model variants. In: International Conference on Automated Software Engineering (ASE), pp. 396–406 (2015)
20. OliveiraJr, E., Gimenes, I.M.S., Maldonado, J.C.: Systematic management of variability in uml-based software product lines. J. Univ. Comput. Sci., 2374–2393 (2010). https://doi.org/10.3217/jucs-016-17-2374
21. Pohl, K., Böckle, G., van Der Linden, F.J.: Software Product Line Engineering: Foundations, Principles And Techniques. Springer Science & Business Media, Berlin (2005)
22. Steinberg, D., Budinsky, F., Merks, E., Paternostro, M.: EMF: eclipse modeling framework. Pearson Education, London (2008)

Part V
Software Product Line Experimentation

Chapter 19
Controlled Experimentation of Software Product Lines

Viviane R. Furtado, Henrique Vignando, Carlos D. Luz, Igor F. Steinmacher, Marcos Kalinowski, and Edson OliveiraJr

Abstract The process of experimentation is one of several scientific methods that can provide evidence for a proof of a theory. This process is counterpoint to the real world observation method, thus providing a reliable body of knowledge. However, in the experimentation for emerging areas and in the consolidation process in scientific and industrial communities, such as the software product line (SPL), there has been a constant lack of adequate documentation of experiments that makes it difficult to repeat, replicate, and reproduce studies in SPL. Therefore, this chapter presents a set of guidelines for the quality assessment of SPL experiments with its conceptual model to support the understanding of the proposed guidelines, as well as an ontology for SPL experiments, called OntoExper-SPL, in addition to support the teaching experimentation in SPL. Thus, these points aim to improve the planning, conduction, analysis, sharing, and documentation of SPL experiments, supporting the construction of a reliable and reference body of knowledge in such a context in addition to enabling improvement in the teaching of SPL experiments.

V. R. Furtado (✉) · H. Vignando · C. D. Luz
State University of Maringá, Informatics Department, Maringá, Paraná, Brazil

I. F. Steinmacher
Northern Arizona University, Flagstaff, AZ, USA

Federal University of Technology, Campo Mourão, Paraná, Brazil
e-mail: igor.steinmacher@nau.edu

M. Kalinowski
Pontifical Catholic University of Rio de Janeiro, Informatics Department, Rio de Janeiro, Brazil
e-mail: kalinowski@inf.puc-rio.br

E. OliveiraJr
State University of Maringá, Informatics Department, Maringá, Paraná, Brazil
e-mail: edson@din.uem.br

© Springer Nature Switzerland AG 2023
E. OliveiraJr (ed), *UML-Based Software Product Line Engineering with SMarty*,
https://doi.org/10.1007/978-3-031-18556-4_19

417

19.1   Experimentation in Software Engineering

An experiment investigates a link between a cause and an effect, through which there is a "theoretical" model of how the two phenomena are related, aiming to determine the extent to which the model is correct. Thus, the model is used to create a hypothesis in relation to particular changes in phenomena (the "cause") that will lead to changes in the other (the "effect"). Therefore, the role of the experiment is to test the hypothesis to decide whether it is true or false [21]. Figure 19.1 presents the idea of a cause and effect relationship in theory [43], in which the theory is at the top, and the observation at the bottom.

The process of carrying out an experiment can be divided into five activities [43], as shown in Fig. 19.2 and described below:

- **Experiment Scoping:** This is the first activity of the experiment, where the problem, goals, and objectives of the experiment are defined. If not properly established, rework may occur, or the experiment may not be used to study what was desired [31].
- **Experiment Planning:** It is an activity that prepares the way the experiment will be conducted, in which the context of the experiment is established, the hypotheses are formulated, the variables are selected (dependent and independent), the participants are selected, the experiment is designed, and the instrumentation and the validity are assessed.

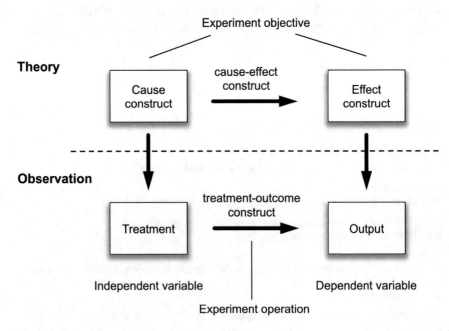

Fig. 19.1 Essential concepts of an experiment [43]

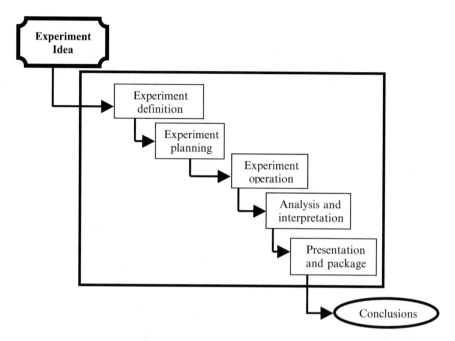

Fig. 19.2 Overview of the experimental process [43]

- **Experiment Operation:** This activity consists of preparing the necessary materials, execution of tasks according to different treatments and data collection, and data validation so that the results of the experiment are valid.
- **Analysis and Interpretation:** The data collected in the previous activity are analyzed using descriptive statistics. After that, the need to reduce the data set is verified, in order to ensure that the data represents correct and/or expected information. Finally, the hypothesis test is performed to statistically assess whether the null hypothesis could be rejected or correlations between samples are established and the effect size is evaluated.
- **Presentation and Package:** In this activity, the results are documented, for example, as conference and/or journal articles, decision-making reports, replication packages, and educational material, among others. In addition, whenever possible, data is made available.

19.2 Quality of Experiments in Software Engineering

The quality of SE experiments can be observed from two different points of view: the first one is to consider quality as the result of the internal validity of a good experiment, and the second one refers to the amount of bias in the experimental results [7]. External validity also has a key function in analyzing whether an experiment has quality, but this function is subordinate to internal validity [8].

According to Dieste et al. [8] and Dieste and Juristo [7], "Good-quality experiments are free of bias. Bias is considered to be related to internal validity (e.g., how well experiments are planned, designed, executed, and analyzed)."

As bias cannot be measured, there are approaches to evaluate it [7, 8, 40], such as:

- **Simple approaches:** A set of validity criteria, which can be answered in a qualitative way, by means of a rating scale.
- **Checklists:** Based on quality items, which are not scored numerically and which have a considerable number of quality-related questions that are answered with "Yes/No."
- **Quality scales:** Based on a set of quality items, scored numerically with the purpose of providing a quantitative assessment of the quality study. Scoring tends to be subjective, as it can be generated by weighing all items equally or by assigning them different weights in relation to the importance of the criteria assessed.
- **Expert opinion:** One or several experts provide an evaluation of the quality of an experiment based on its nominal value, i.e., a subjective evaluation of the overall quality of the paper based on an ordinal scale of 5 points (excellent (5), very good (4), acceptable (3), poor (2), and unacceptable (1)), being able to distinguish experiments with high and low quality.

The experimental quality in SE can also be evaluated considering the design and analysis of experiments as described [17]:

- **Statistical power** is the probability the statistical test rejects the null hypothesis correctly [6]. Thus, a test without sufficient statistical power will not provide the researcher with enough information to draw the conclusions to accept or reject the null hypothesis, making the results of the experiment insignificant.
- **Effect size** is the degree to which the phenomenon under investigation is present in the population, that is, it is the relationship between the treatment variables and the outcome variables. It is possible to measure the effect size by means of correlation, odds ratios, and the difference between means, for example. "If the effect size is not judged as part of the experimental results, incorrect or imprecise conclusions might be drawn" [17].
- **Quasi-experimentation** is when there is no randomness of participants and/or objects in the experiment. The nonrandom assignment process might result in selection bias, that is, a threat to internal validity.
- **Experiment report** is important to prioritize the information included in the experiment report. The SE literature presents guidelines on important elements to be reported in the experiments. The study of Kampenes [17] presents important information that should be reported to understand and judge experiment results, but they are reported by less than half of experiments: (i) selection of participants; (ii) environment (academic/industrial); (iii) well-defined population for testing

hypotheses who use statistics; (iv) sample size mortality rate, which is the number of participants initially included in the experiment and the number of participants included in the data analysis, in addition to the reasons for dropouts and exclusions; (v) statistical power not included in test information of incomplete significance; (vi) effect size, which is recommended to always use to report both standardized and nonstandardized effect size measurements as they serve different supplementary purposes; (vii) randomization method so the reader can judge whether the process is in accordance with the recommendations of randomization processes; and (viii) threats to validity which should be evaluated in all experiments, but not necessarily discussed because of the space limit in report document.

19.3 Software Product Line Experiments

We carried out a systematic mapping study (SMS) following the guidelines proposed by Kitchenham et al. [21] and Petersen et al. [29] to identify SPL experiments reported in the literature. The SMS presented an overview of experiments performed in the area of SPL. Based on the search strategy, a total of 1,039 studies were retrieved, from which 211 were identified for data extraction. The SMS study is target of a different publication, currently under review at a journal. The search strategy, the 211 identified studies, and their extracted data can be found in our Zenodo package[1] prepared to support this submission.

Through the analysis of the obtained studies, we provided evidence that the most used guidelines were the textbook by Wohlin et al. [43]. Considering the quality evaluation of experiments, none of the selected studies were concerned with carrying out such evaluation. We also found that only 37% of studies reported the experimental package, which is an important element to facilitate replications. As for the context in which the experiment was executed, 96% were in vitro. We also observed that 95% were new experiments (i.e., not replications). Another important point, 93% were quasi-experiments (i.e., without random assignment to treatments), which we interpret as a need to improve experimental designs applied in the area. Regarding the experimental study designs, the SMS revealed that the most used ones in SPL experiments are "one factor with two treatments" and "one factor with more than two treatments."

With regard to the selection of participants and/or experimental objects, 92% was by convenience sampling. Only 11% of studies conducted pilot studies, which are a common way to improve the instrumentation and validate the experimental design. With regard to the analysis of collected data, most of the studies have performed different hypothesis tests. Concerning the research topics investigated in the experiments, the studies were mainly focused on feature model configuration,

---

[1] https://doi.org/10.5281/zenodo.3893302.

feature model test, SPL test, and SPL architecture design optimization. As for the artifacts used in the studies, the feature model was the most common one, being used in 29.7% of the experiments. Regarding threats to validity, we observed that most of the experiments discuss internal and external validity, such as SPL size and selection, participants' experience, and used instruments.

19.4 Guidelines to Report SPL Experiments

This section presents guidelines for quality evaluation of SPL experiments developed for users to appropriately document an experiment in SPL as well as to allow sharing of experimental data, replication, and auditing of the experiments.

The elaboration of guidelines was based on two approaches to quality evaluation of experiments in SE, Kampenes [17] and Kitchenham et al. [20]. These approaches obtained the highest correlation and best results in a controlled experiment comparing quality evaluation of experiment approaches in Furtado et al. [10] and also considering the practices observed in SPL experiments identified in 211 studies in our SMS study, whose extracted data can be found in our Zenodo package.[2]

The guideline contains 25 items. Table 19.1 presents the source for each guideline item. Possible sources are detailed below:

- **Approach:** When the guideline was based on the SE experiment quality evaluation approach, thus it is reported with the abbreviation KI
  [20] and/or KA [17] plus the quality criteria (QC) corresponding to the questions of such an approach, for example, KI.QC4, wherein QC4 refers to "*Do the authors describe the data collection procedures and define the measures?*," and KA.QC1.5, wherein QC1.5 refers to "*Some kind of background information.*"
- **Systematic Mapping:** when the guideline was based on SPL elements obtained in systematic mapping, presented with the abbreviation SM.
- **Author**: when the guideline was elaborated by the authors of this paper.

In addition, we constructed a conceptual model (Sect. 19.4.2) to support the understanding of the relationships among experimental elements mentioned in the definition of each guideline.

19.4.1 Proposed Guidelines

The following items present such guidelines (G), as well as application examples. The examples of each guideline have the source from which it was taken and when it was prepared by the author.

---

[2] https://doi.org/10.5281/zenodo.3893302.

Table 19.1 Source of guideline items [11]

Guideline item (G)	Source
[G.1]	KI.QC1
[G.2]	KI.QC1.2
[G.3]	KI.QC3.2
[G.4]	KI.QC2.4 and KA.QC1.1
[G.5]	KI.QC2.1 and KA.QC1.3, KA.QC1.4, KA.QC1.5, KA.QC1.5.1, KA.QC1.5.2, KA.QC1.5.3, and KA.QC1.5.4
[G.6]	SMS
[G.7]	KI.QC3.1
[G.8]	KI.QC2.1 and KA.QC2.4 and KA.QC2.6
[G.8.1]	SMS
[G.8.1.1]	SMS
[G.8.2]	SMS
[G.9]	Author
[G.10]	KA.QC2.1 and KA.QC2.2
[G.11]	KI.QC6.3
[G.12]	SMS
[G.13]	KA.QC2.5
[G.14]	SMS
[G.15]	SMS
[G.16]	KI.QC4
[G.17]	KI.QC5
[G.18]	KA.QC1.2
[G.19]	SMS
[G.20]	KI.QC5.2 and KA.QC3.3
[G.21]	Author
[G.22]	KI.QC6.1
[G.23]	KA.QC4.1, KA.QC4.2, KA.QC4.3, KA.QC4.4, KA.QC4.5, and SMS
[G.24]	Author
[G.25]	SMS

G.1 **Define the aim of the experiment:** Use GQM (*goal-question-metric*) [4]. An example taken from Basili and Rombach [38]: "The goal of this evaluation was to **analyze** the regression testing approach **for the purpose of** evaluation **with respect to** understandability, usability, completeness, applicability, and effectiveness **from the point of view of** SPL researchers and test engineers **in the context of** an SPL project."

G.2 **State the hypotheses of the experiment:** Establish a null hypothesis and alternative hypotheses, as proposed in Wohlin et al. [43]. The following example is from Rodrigues et al. [34]:

- **"Null Hypothesis H0:** The representativeness is the same, when using the Odyssey-Fex or UI-Odyssey-Fex notations, to represent UI elements."
- **"Alternative Hypothesis H1:** The use of the UI-Odyssey-Fex notation better represents UI elements when compared with the Odyssey-Fex notation."

G.3 **Define the variables of the experiment:** establish independent and dependent variables [43]. The example given below was taken from Reinhartz-Berger et al. [32]: "The **independent variable**, in this case, was familiarity with feature modeling, while the **dependent variables** were comprehension scores (measured using the percentage of correct solution), time spent to complete tasks, and difficulty perception using the self-rated difficulty of specific element types."

G.4 **Inform the sample size:** (1) For human subjects, it is essential to inform the size of the sample, because size can be a threat to the experiment, and (2) for algorithms/software, inform the number of executions performed. Examples are from Santos et al. [36] and Lopez-Herrejon et al. [24], respectively:

1. "Nineteen senior undergraduate students enrolled in a Software Engineering course acted as subjects."
2. "We executed 30 independent runs for each feature model input set for each of the three algorithms and for each objective function. The total number of independent runs is thus: $74(featuremodels) \times 3(algorithms) \times 2(objectivefunctions) \times 30$ runs $= 13{,}320$."

G.5 **Describe how participants/experimental objects were selected:** (1) Important information to be described in the case of human participants are their type (student or professionals), recruitment (voluntary or mandatory), experience in relation to programming, work, tasks, and grades, for example; (2) experimental objects refer to experiments that are not performed with participants, but with algorithms, thus if the algorithm used was developed by the authors or was taken from the literature and if the source code is available for download and the configurations of the machine and parameters to run it, for example; and (3) describe their selection in relation to the chosen sampling technique proposed by Wohlin et al. [43], such as simple random sampling, systematic sampling, stratified random sampling, convenience sampling, and quota sampling. Examples for cases 1 and 3 were taken from Silveira Neto et al. [38] and 2 from LiZhang [23] and Lopez-Herrejon et al. [24], respectively:

1. and 3. "This evaluation involved eight participants. All of them had completed a post-graduate course in the software testing area prior to this evaluation. The subjects were either upper-level computer science majors or graduate students. They were selected by convenience sampling, which means that the nearest and most convenient persons were selected as participants [13] (...)."

2. "In this paper, we designed MOOFHD and MOOFε+ by introducing our SolutionRevise operator into IBEA suggested by [6]. Our two algorithms with NSGAII[8], SPEA2[9], IBEAHD[10] and IBEAε+[10] were experimented on the four models. All of these algorithms were implemented in jMetal[11], a popular framework for multi-objective optimization. The parameters of these algorithms are default values in jMetal: population size $= 100$, single-point crossover, crossover probability $= 0.90$, bit-flip mutation, mutation probability $= 1/$NumberOfVariables."

2. "We ran our experiments on an array of different machines with 4–16 cores with clock speeds between 2 and 4 GHz with 4–16 GBs of memory."

G.6 **Identify the research topic of the experiment:** The mind map of research topics [11] from our SMS can be used. The following example was elaborated by the authors: "The experiment was conducted in the research topic of regression testing in product line architecture."

G.7 **Describe the chosen experimental design:** It is necessary to know if the experiment was able to adequately test the hypotheses, thus using the experimental design proposed by Wohlin et al. [43]: blocking, randomization, and balancing. Depending on the experimental context, a design may have specific arrangements, such as one factor with two treatments, one factor with more than two treatments, two factors with two treatments, and more than two factors each with two treatments. In addition, it is important to describe how groups, objects, tasks, and treatments relate. An example taken from Machado et al. [25] is presented below: "One factor with two treatments. We compared the two treatments against each other [16]. Factor in this experiment was the RiPLE-TE unit testing process and treatments were: (1) Testing with the process; and (2) testing without it (...)."

G.8 **Describe how the experimental materials were defined and selected:** There are three types of experimental materials, objects (specifications or code documents), guidelines (process descriptions and checklists), and measurement instruments (performed by data collection such as interviews and manual forms), according to Wohlin et al. [43]. For example, inform the size of materials and the tools used. To illustrate this guideline, an example was taken from Machado et al. [25]: "Objects used in this experiment were as follows: Consent Form, Background Questionnaire, Test Assets, and Component Source Code, RiPLE-TE Documentation—including guidelines and usage samples, Error Reporting Form, Feedback Questionnaire (...)."

G.8.1 **Describe the SPL used:** It is important to present the description of the SPL used in the experiment, besides its name. An example taken from Eyal-Salman et al. [9] is given below: "To validate our approach, we have applied it to a collection of seven variants of a large-scale system, ArgoUML-SPL modeling tool, and five variants of a small-scale system, MobileMedia. The

ArgoUML-SPL is a Java open-source which supports all standard UML 1.4 diagrams (...)."

G.8.1.1 **Inform the source where the SPL was found:** If available, it is important to present the source, either from the literature or from a website, to enable future replication, for example. The example below is from LiZhang [23]: "Four feature models including two realistic models and two syntheses were selected from SPLOT[7], a popular feature model repository."

G.8.2 **Describe the SPL artifacts used in experiment:** The mind map of SPL artifacts [11] from our SMS can be used to assist in their selection. The following is the example taken from Reinhartz-Berger et al. [32]: "The objects of the experiment were two CVL models describing different sets of features of Skoda Yeti cars. The CVL models for the experiment were built by Prof. Haugen, who is the founder of CVL and is familiar with the possible Skoda Yeti configurations from the Norwegian Skoda public web pages (...)."

G.9 **Validate the materials used in experiment:** Validate materials used such as questionnaires, forms, and interviews to verify the reliability and provide insight into the type of knowledge requested by the experiment. One technique that can support such validation for questionnaires is principal component analysis (PCA) [16].

G.10 **Describe the tasks of experiment:** Describe the tasks to be performed by participants with a level of detail to enable replication without the need to consult the authors of the original experiment. If possible, provide the duration and schedule to perform such tasks. An example of Santos et al. [36] is presented below: "In the tasks, the subjects had to find the code of both, modular (when the feature is implemented in a single file or in a set of files placed together) and scattered (when the code of a single feature is spread over several source files) features (...)."

G.11 **Describe the training requirements for participants:** It is necessary to provide appropriate training to participants in all treatment conditions. The example shown below was taken from Silveira Neto et al. [38]: "The subjects were trained in several aspects of SPL, and control flow graphs, besides the use of the following tools: Junit(http://www.junit.org/), Eclemma plugin(http://www.eclemma.org/), and JDiff tool [5]. The analyzed approach was also another training topic. Next, they performed the regression testing approach in the code provided (...)."

G.12 **Describe the conduct of pilot project:** It is essential to carry out a pilot project, which is a simplified version of the experiment, to evaluate materials and experimental design, for example. In addition, it is suggested to apply the pilot project to evaluate the materials to experts in the area. Such a guideline is illustrated by the example of Silveira Neto et al. [38] below: "Before performing the evaluation, two pilot projects were conducted with the same structure defined in this planning phase. The first pilot was performed by a single subject, aiming to detect problems and calibrate the evaluation process before its real execution (...)."

G.13 **Describe the environment of conducting the experiment:** Inform if the experiment was conducted in an academic or industrial environment, for example. Below is an example taken from Asadi et al. [3]: "The experiment was executed at Simon Fraser University (...)."

G.14 **Inform the date the experiment was performed:** It is important to inform the date the experiment was performed, because it may take some time for the experiment to be published. The following is the example of Machado et al. [25]: "The experiment was conducted from November to December in 2009, according to the definition and planning documented."

G.15 **Describe the conduct of experiment:** It is necessary to describe how the experiment was carried out to allow its replication, including the preparation of materials and participants/objects. Also, report any changes in the execution and schedule of the experiment. Such a guideline is illustrated with an example taken from Silveira Neto et al. [37]: "The experiment was performed using a set of eight subjects, where each one applied the approach in both scenarios. Firstly, both code versions were provided with a set of change requests (three), as well as a set of previously designed integration test cases, for the subjects to validate the approach considering the corrective scenario. The subjects needed to apply the approach aiming to find the seeded faults, as well as to classify the integration test cases (...)."

G.16 **Describe how the data collection was performed:** Data collection can be performed through specific tools, APIs, and log files, among others. An example of Silveira Neto et al. [38] is shown below: "The results of the evaluation were collected using measurement instruments. Thus, time-sheets were used to collect the time spent in each activity (...)."

G.17 **Describe the procedures for analyzing the collected data:** The analysis of the collected data can use descriptive statistics, normality tests, parametric or nonparametric hypothesis tests, and correlations, for example. In addition, it is important to justify the choice and provide references to the descriptions of procedures. The examples of descriptive statistics and hypothesis testing were taken from Machado et al. [25], as shown below:

- "**Test case effectiveness.** In terms of valid defects found, in group 1 (G-1) (without run the process), the mean value was 6.188 with an standard deviation (sd) of 3.187, while in group 2 (G-2) (with the process), the mean was 3.857, with a sd of 3.505 (...)."
- "**Hypothesis Testing.** Regarding TCE, t-test (unpaired, two-tailed) was applied and resulted in a p-value higher than 0.05, which indicates that the Null Hypothesis H01 could not be rejected. H02 could not also be rejected, since calculated p-value was higher than 0.05. Thus, we can conclude that there was no gain using the process instead of an ad hoc fashion, regarding QDF (...)".

G.18 **Describe the mortality rate:** There are two types of sample size—the initial number of participants or executions and the number of participants or executions included in the analysis of data. Thus, describe both numbers and the reasons for dropouts or exclusions. An example of Silveira Neto et al. [38] is shown below: "Corrective Scenario: Table II shows the raw data collected after the experiment execution, where "not considered (NC)" means that the step was not reported correctly and "not reported (NR)" means that no time was reported by the subject. Before analyzing the collected data, some issues were observed: Test Design and Test Selection steps needed to be refined, subjects ID 1 and 3 were removed from the analysis since they did not correctly report the data regarding to this item (…)."

G.19 **Inform the statistical tool for data analysis:** It is important to inform the statistical tool used in data analysis, whether or not it is free to there are no divergences in the results when replicating the experiment in another sample. The example given below was taken from Rodrigues et al. [34]: "We performed hypothesis testing for all data sets using the R Studio statistical environment for R [12]."

G.20 **Inform the effect size:** Effect size is a technique to check for gain in the experimental group. In addition, the hypothesis test can be supported by the effect size. Such a guideline is illustrated with an example of Lopez-Herrejon et al. [24]: "Even when differences in the performance of the algorithms are statistically significant as in our case, it is also crucial to assess the magnitude of such a difference, in order to ensure that such difference has practical value.6 Following the guidelines provided in [2], we use Vargha and Delaney's Â12 statistic to evaluate the effect size. Specifically, Â12 measures the probability that using one algorithm yields higher values than the other for a comparison metric (…)."

G.21 **Discuss the results obtained from the point of view of researchers and practitioners:** It is necessary the results obtained are also discussed for industry practitioners to be able to identify whether the experiment has practical relevance and whether the technique, for example, evaluated in the experiment is feasible.

G.22 **Discuss the implications of treatments developed:** When the treatments were developed, it is necessary to discuss the implications of treatments, in order to mitigate their threats in the experiment.

G.23 **Discuss the threats to validity identified in experiment:** Discuss the threats to validity in internal, external, construct, and conclusion, as proposed by Wohlin et al. [43]. Most common threats to SPL validity can be found in [11]. An example taken from Santos et al. [36] is shown below:

- **"External validity:** We identified some threats that may limit the ability to generalize the results. For example, the study was carried out in an in-vitro setting, which means a sample selected pseudo-randomly (…)."

- **"Internal validity:** There are possible threats that may happen without the researcher's knowledge affecting individuals from different perspectives, such as (i) the maturation and learning effects, (ii) the testing repetition since several tasks were carried out, and (iii) the experiment instrumentation. These threats were mitigated by choosing different features for each task, as well as by randomizing the sequence of task's execution to omit possible relationships (...)."
- **"Construct Validity:** Confounding constructs may affect the findings. For instance, the presence or the absence of knowledge about a particular programming language may not explain the causes of failures in the feature location tasks. In fact, the differences may depend on the subjects' experience, which was controlled with the characterization form, to ensure that subjects had substantial experience to accomplish the tasks."
- **"Conclusion Validity:** We observed from the results a likely low statistical power, which concerns to the power of used tests to reveal a true pattern in the data. Employing well-known measures mitigated such a threat. Another observed threat is the fishing for a specific result, which we mitigated by relying the analysis only on the gathered data (...)."

G.24 **Inform the source of experimental package:** The experimental package contains experimental materials, raw data, and data analysis scripts, for example. Thus, it is important to present the permanent and public source of the experimental package to enable auditing or future replication, using repositories such as Zenodo,[3] for example. Such a guideline is illustrated below with an example of Ribeiro et al. [33]: "All data, materials, tasks, plug-ins, and R scripts are available at http://twiki.cin.ufpe.br/twiki/bin/view/SPG/EmergentInterfaces."

G.25 **Inform the experimental template used to conduct, plan or report the experiment:** examples of experimental templates that were found in SM performed are: Jedlitschka et al. [14]; Kitchenham et al. [18]; Kitchenham et al. [19]; Sjøberg et al. [39]; and Wohlin et al. [43]. The following is an example taken from [35]: " The experimental study was based on the process proposed by Wohlin [11]."

19.4.2 Conceptual Model to Support Guidelines

The conceptual model presents the concepts of experiments for the context of SPL addressed in guidelines defined in the previous section. Figure 19.3 presents the

---

[3] https://zenodo.org/.

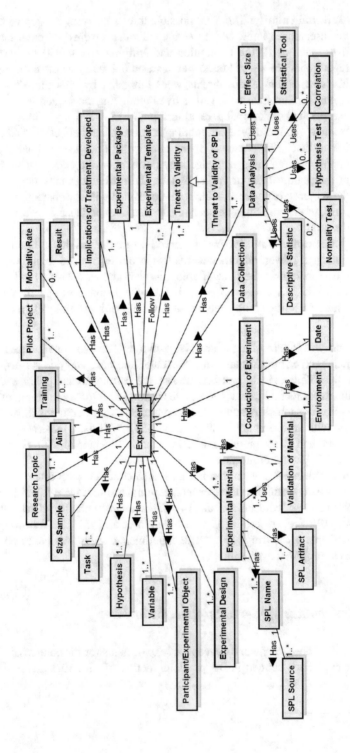

Fig. 19.3 The conceptual model for supporting SPL experiment guidelines [10]

direct relationships between concepts using a UML class diagram. It is possible to observe there are more general concepts about experiments, such as aim, variables, and hypothesis, but also specific to the SPL domain, such as threat to validity of SPL, SPL artifact, SPL name, SPL source, and research topic.

The conceptual model relationships are described as follows:

- The experiment has an aim.
- The experiment has zero or more training sessions.
- The experiment has one or more pilot projects.
- The experiment has zero or more mortality rates.
- The experiment has one or more results.
- The experiment has one or more implications of treatment developed.
- The experiment has an experimental package.
- The experiment follows one or more experimental templates.
- The experiment has one or more threats to validity.
- The threat to validity of SPL is a specialization of threat to validity.
- The experiment has one or more data analysis.
- Data analysis uses one or more descriptive statistics and statistical tools. Also, it uses zero or more normality tests, hypothesis tests, effect size, and correlations.
- The experiment has data collection.
- The experiment has conduction of the experiment.
- Conducting the experiment has one or more environments. Also, it has a date.
- The experiment has one or more validations of the material.
- Material validation uses one or more experimental materials.
- The experiment has one or more experimental materials.
- The experimental material has one or more SPL artifacts and indicates the name of one or more SPLs.
- The SPL name has one or more SPLs sources.
- The experiment has one or more experimental designs.
- The experiment has one or more participants/experimental objects.
- The experiment has one or more variables.
- The experiment has one or more hypotheses.
- The experiment has one or more tasks.
- The experiment has a sample size.
- The experiment has one or more research topics.

19.5 An Ontology for SPL Experimentation

The literature covers some discussions about experimentation in SE, about its documentation, and quality. In particular the research topic on software product lines (SPL), we understand that there is a lack of formalization about the concepts of experimentation. Therefore, specific experiment elements are essential to plan, conduct, and disseminate the results. In this chapter, we propose an ontology for

SPL experiments, named OntoExper-SPL. We designed such an ontology based on guidelines found in the literature and an extensive systematic mapping study earlier. This ontology can contribute to better document the essential elements of an SPL experiment, helping to promote repeatability, replication, and reproducibility of experiments. To evaluate OntoExper-SPL, we used an ontology support tool and conducted an empirical study. Results showed OntoExper-SPL is feasible for formalizing experimental SPL concepts.

19.5.1 Software Engineering Ontologies

In a few words, an ontology is a set of entities that have relationships with each other or no. Entities have properties and constraints to represent their characteristics and attributes. Each entity has a population of individuals.

In the information science, the ontology is used as a form of representation of logical knowledge, allowing the inference of new facts based on the individuals stored in the ontology [12]. These definitions follow the representation pattern known as descriptive logic. The major reasons for building an ontology are (i) the definition of a common domain vocabulary, (ii) domain knowledge reuse, and (iii) information share.

The knowledge base has two main components: the concepts of a specific domain, called TBox (terminological box), and the individuals in that domain, called ABox (assertion box) [5]. The individuals in the ABox must comply with all the properties and restrictions defined in the TBox.

The work of [13] presents a *ontology-driven software engineering*, an SE based on ontologies. This theme is treated as a subarea of SE and aims to study how different ways in which ontologies, ontology engineering, and other procedural technologies can contribute to the software development process.

Ontologies ensure that the same language, methods, processes, and understanding about the SE area are used and shared formally [13].

19.5.2 Building the OntoExper-SPL

OntoExper-SPL went through a process of conception, construction of the project, application examples, and a preliminary assessment, in order to arrive at a final and usable ontology project. In this section, the ontology construction process will be presented following the steps of [27] and the typology of [1]; the elaboration of a graph as an initial model, which uses the clustered conceptual model as the basis for the experimental elements of SPL, also presents the project of OntoExper-SPL, where it was used as base technology OWL (Ontology Web Language, together with the Protégé tool; the final result of this step is an artifact of the OWL type containing the modeling of classes, subclasses, object properties, and data properties. In addition to the modeling, a program was created to populate the ontology using the metadata from previous works in an automated way. We provided a brief example of application of OntoExper-SPL at the end of the session.

19.5.2.1 Ontology Conception

For the construction of OntoExper-SPL, the method, **MFPFO**, described by Mendonca [27], was applied. The purpose of this method is to be multifaceted, annotated semantically for the modeling of a family of products. Such a method is capable of suggesting semantically related annotations, based on the project and the construction repository. The domain of application of this method is aimed at the family of products. The construction steps for this method are:

1. Construction of a product family taxonomy
2. Extraction of entities
3. Concept identification and generation of the faceted unit
4. Semantic annotation and facet modeling
5. Construction of a multifaceted and semantically annotated product family ontology
6. Ontology evaluation and validation

Using the typologies proposed by Almeida and Bax [1], we defined the type of ontology for OntoExper-SPL. It is characterized as follows: **as to function** is a domain ontology, **as to degree of formalism** is a semiformal ontology, **as to application** is a specification ontology, **as to structure** is a domain ontology, and **regarding content** is an ontology for knowledge modeling.

The OntoExper-SPL elaboration process followed the steps proposed by Monteiro [28]:

- Definition and structuring of terms by means of classes.
- Establishment of properties (attributes) inherent to the concept represented by a term.
- Population of the structure that satisfies a concept and its properties.
- Establishment of relationships between concepts.
- Elaboration of sentences to restrict inferences of knowledge based on the structure. This step was not carried out.

The ontology's initial modeling is based on an exploratory data analysis and the conceptual model presented in Fig. 19.4; this model contains information and metadata from experiments in SPL that are important for the elaboration of the OntoExper-SPL.

Figure 19.4 presents an initial graph that represents this model with the main definitions of the terms of an experiment proposed by Wohlin et al. [43]: SPL experiment, documentation, template, evaluation, discussion, analysis, execution, planning, and packaging. In this figure, the terms are the vertices of the graph and their relations are the edges. Undotted edges represent hierarchical relationships,

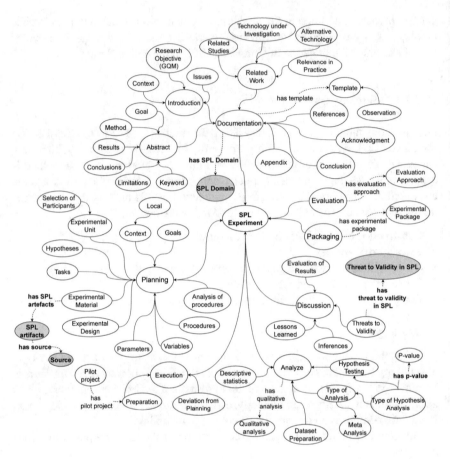

Fig. 19.4 Initial graph of the ontology proposal [42]

and dotted edges are composite relationships. The gray and bold vertices are the SPL-specific terms.

In Fig. 19.4, SPL terms are highlighted as an extension of the terms proposed by Wohlin et al. [43], for example, SPL Domain extends from Documentation by the relation has SPL domain, SPL Artifacts extends from Experimental Materials by the relation has SPL artifacts, and finally Validity Threat in SPL extends from Validity Threat by the relation has validity threat in SPL.

Figure 19.5 presents a modification of the original conceptual model represented in Fig. 19.3, applying a clustering separating a cluster for each phase of the experimental template, except the packaging. In this way, it is possible to have a more abstract understanding of the relationships between the domain terms identified in the original conceptual model and the phases of the [43] template.

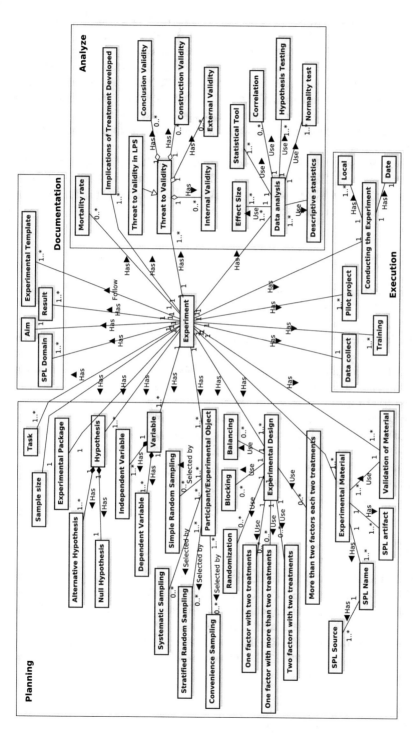

Fig. 19.5 Clustered conceptual model [42]

Through a class diagram, we can represent, in a more intuitive way, the modeling performed with graph. This representation aims to transform each term of the graph into a class of the object orientation concept. In this representation, the relationship between the terms (classes) and their properties (attributes) is perceptible to the ES user. The extension of the SPL terms becomes even clearer with this form of representation, which highlights the main relationship when defining the composition of the Experiment and ExperimentSPL class. In this representation, the types of properties are also explicit, facilitating the execution and insertion of *ABox* in the modeling.

Figure 19.6 presents the class diagram as a model of the ontology. This diagram represents all the class compositions that exist with Experiment and ExperimentSPL, as well as the hierarchical relationships, for example, ExperimentSPL is a subclass of Experiment.

19.5.2.2   Ontology Design

The OWL standard was used in OntoExper-SPL to define all elements, classes, and subclasses.

We used Protégé for the final design of the ontology. It can be used by both system developers and domain experts to create knowledge bases, allowing the representation of knowledge an area. We defined our entities based on the class diagram built in the concept phase, with the following order: (i) class definition, (ii) definition of object properties, and (iii) definition of data properties. Table 19.2 presents all elements defined in Protégé.

Protégé generates a file *.owl* containing the ontology definition. We use the WebVOWL[4] tool to generate an image of the final graph generated by Protégé. Figure 19.7 provides an overview in graph format of the project, containing all classes and subclasses and their relationships through object properties. It also presents some of these relationships in a ternary fashion with dotted circles, thus indicating a many-to-many relationship.

19.5.2.3   Populating Ontology

To insert the individuals in the ontology, we evaluated the Protégé tool. It has the ability to perform this operation, but the process of inserting individuals into the ontology is performed manually, individual by individual, through the Individuals by Class menu. In this menu, you must select property by property for each individual. Note that each individual has 86 data properties, plus 8 object properties, and a total of 94 relationships for each individual. In this way,

---

[4] http://www.visualdataweb.de/webvowl/.

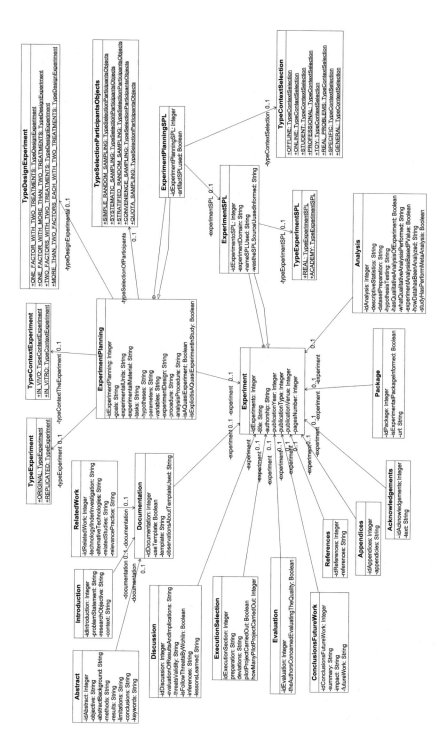

Fig. 19.6 Class diagram highlighting SPL subclasses for ontology modeling [42]

Table 19.2 Ontology design—classes and properties of modeling [42]

Element	Definition
Classes	Abstract, Acknowledgments, Analysis, Appendices, ConclusionsFutureWork, Discussion, DiscussionSPL, Documentation, Evaluation, ExecutionSection, Experiment, ExperimentSPL, ExperimentPlanning, ExperimentPlanningSPL, Introduction, Package, References, RelatatedWork, TypeContextExperiment, TypeContextSelection, TypeDesignExperiment, TypeEsperiment, TypeEsperimentSPL, TypeSelectioParticipantObjects
Object properties	documentation, experiment, typeContextxperiment, typeContextSelection, typeDesignExperiment, typeExperiment, typeExperimentSPL, typeSelectionOfParticipants
Data properties	idExperiment, title, authorship, publicationYear, publicationType, publicationVenue, pagesNumber, idExperimentSPL, nameSPLUsed, wasTheSPLSourceUsedInformed, idDocumentation, useTemplate, template, observationsAboutTemplateUsed, idAbstract, objective, abstractBackground, methods, results, limitations, conclusions, keywords, idIntroduction, problemStatement, researchObjective, context, idRelatedWork, technologyUnderInvestigation, alternativeTechnologies, relatedStudies, relevancePractice, idConclusionsFutureWork, summary, impact, futureWork, idExperimentPlanning, goals, experimentalUnits, experimentalMaterial, tasks, hypotheses, parameters, variables, experimentDesign, procedureProcedure, explicitQuesiExperimentInStudy, isAQuasiExperiment, idExperimentPlanningSPL, artifactSPLused, idExecutionSection, preparation, deviations, pilotProjectCarriedOut, howManyPilotProjectCarriedOut, idAnalysis, descriptiveStatistics, datasetPreparation, hyp othesisTesting, whatQualitativeAnalysisPerformed, howDatahasBeenAnalyzed, experimentAnalysisBasedPValue, hasQualitativeAnalysisOfExperiment, studyHasPerformMetaAnalysis, idDiscussion, evaluationOfResultsAndImplications, inferences, lessonsLearned, threatsValidity, isFollowThreatsByWohlin, idDiscussionSPL, threatsValiditySPL, idAcknowledgements, acknowledgments, idReferences, references, idAppendices, appendices, idEvaluation, theAuthorsConcernedEvaluatingTheQuality, idPackage, isExperimentalPackageInformed, url, isLinkAvailable

we understand that it would be a very time-consuming process for the insertion of individuals in mass, and we chose to use an automated script for this process.

The automation script for the insertion of mass individuals uses the Python programming language [41], together with the Pandas [26] and OwlReady2 [22] library, specialized in data manipulation and ontological models, respectively. Experiment articles are collected and stored in a spreadsheet with the following structure, each row represents an experiment study in SPL, and each column represents a characteristic extracted from these articles. The script to insert individuals into the OntoExper-SPL performs the following operations to manipulate the data in the worksheet:

First operation: separation *(split)* of data from a single column to two data properties of the ontology.

Second operation: transformation of Boolean data, empty strings, and numbers.

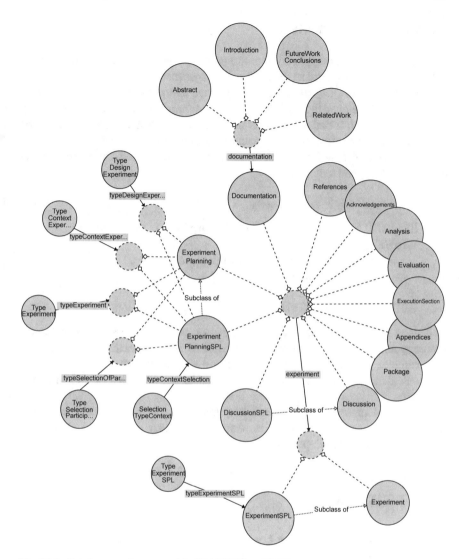

Fig. 19.7 Ontology graph generated by WebVOWL tool [42]

Third operation: dataset separation with explicit SPL information.

Fourth operation: standardization of constant and null data. In null cases, a default value is assigned.

Fifth operation: process of inserting data from the worksheet that processes row by row of the worksheet and creates the individuals one by one of each class modeled in the ontology with their respective attributes.

Sixth operation: simple validation step, where the number of rows in the spreadsheet is checked with the number of individuals inserted in the ontology.

19.5.2.4   Use Case Scenario

In order to illustrate an application to the proposed ontology, we present a simple use case scenario that extracts the most often experiment report template.

The query SPARQL [30] is a query language and protocol for accessing RDF modeled data developed by the *W3C RDF Data Access Working Group*.[5] As a query language, SPARQL is data-driven so it only queries as information presented in the models, there is no reference to this query language [15] on Listing 19.1 returns all experiments template and how many times each have been used. From that, we can extract the most used template.

Listing 19.1   Example of an SPARQL query

```
SELECT ?template (count(?template) as ?count)
WHERE {
     ?doc rdf:type :Documentation .
     ?doc :template ?template .
}
GROUP BY ?template
```

This example runs through 1 class (`Documentation`) of the 24 classes in the ontology and 1 data property (`template`) of 87 data properties. Based on it, in the example, we used 0.0004% of the response capacity that the model allows. This calculation checks the possibilities of paths between classes and ontology properties.

This initial query example shows how inference mechanisms can be created in this ontology model. Thus, it is possible to extract information about SPL experiments using OntoExper-SPL.

19.6   Final Remarks

In this chapter, we presented a brief introduction to software engineering (SE) experimentation and its main elements such as scope, planning, operation, analysis and interpretation, presentation, and packaging. An introduction about software product line and the relevance of this topic to the subject of experimentation in SE was presented.

In the sequence, the main approaches to quality of experiments in software engineering were presented, which are simple approaches, checklists, quality scales, and expert opinion. Besides these approaches in SE, statistical approaches such as statistical power, effect size, quasi-experimentation, and experiment report are also applied. As a result of a systematic study by the authors themselves, we

---

[5] https://www.w3.org/2003/12/swa/dawg-charter.

presented a guideline to report SPL experiments, containing 25 guidelines for conducting and measuring the quality of experiments in SE. These guidelines are a compilation of the studies by KI [20] and KA [17] and an extensive systematic mapping on the subject, plus three new guidelines proposed by the author: (G.9) Validate the materials used in experiment. (G.21) Discuss the results obtained from the point of view of researchers and practitioners. (G.24) Inform the source of experimental package. The guideline ends with a conceptual model about the quality of experiments in SE.

The chapter continued with an approach on a proposed ontology to represent knowledge in experiments in SE, presenting an initial vision on ontology in SE and then deepening the construction of the OntoExper-SPL, going through its conception using the MFPFO technique and characterizing the ontology as follows: as to function is a domain ontology, as to degree of formalism is a semiformal ontology, as to application is a specification ontology, as to structure is a domain ontology, and regarding content is an ontology for knowledge modeling. Then the ontology project was presented based on the main concepts of experimentation explored in the beginning of the chapter and in the sequence a script for populating the proposed ontology, closing the chapter with a use case scenario.

Acknowledgments Dr. Igor Steinmacher receives a CNPq PQ2 Research Productivity Fellowship (process #313067/2020-1). Viviane R. Furtado would like to thank CAPES/Brazil (code 001) for supporting this work. Edson Oliveira Jr. would like to thank CAPES (PROCAD) for supporting this work.

References

1. Almeida, M.B., Bax, M.P.: An overview about ontologies: research about definitions, types, applications, evaluation and construction methods. information science. Ciência da informação **32**(3), 7–20 (2003). In Portuguese
2. Arcuri, A., Briand, L.: A hitchhiker's guide to statistical tests for assessing randomized algorithms in software engineering. Software Testing, Verification and Reliability, **24**(3), 219–250 (2014)
3. Asadi, M., Soltani, S., Gašević, D., Hatala, M.: The effects of visualization and interaction techniques on feature model configuration. Empir. Softw. Eng., 1–38 (2016)
4. Basili, V.R., Rombach, H.D.: The TAME project: towards improvement-oriented software environments. IEEE Trans. Softw. Eng. **14**(6), 758–773 (1988)
5. Calvanese, D., De Giacomo, G., Lembo, D., Lenzerini, M., Rosati, R.: Dl-lite: tractable description logics for ontologies. In: Proceedings of the 20th National Conference on Artificial Intelligence (AAAI 2005), vol. 5, pp. 602–607 (2005)
6. Cohen, J.: Statistical power analysis. Curr. Dir. Psychol. Sci. **1**(3), 98–101 (1992)
7. Dieste, O., Juristo, N.: Challenges of evaluating the quality of software engineering experiments. In: Perspectives on the Future of Software Engineering, pp. 159–177. Springer, Berlin (2013)
8. Dieste, O., Grim, A., Juristo, N., Saxena, H.: Quantitative determination of the relationship between internal validity and bias in software engineering experiments: consequences for systematic literature reviews. In: 5th International Symposium on Empirical Software Engineering and Measurement (ESEM) pp. 285–294 (2011)

9. Eyal-Salman, H., Seriai, A.D., Dony, C.: Feature location in a collection of product variants: combining information retrieval and hierarchical clustering. In: SEKE: Software Engineering and Knowledge Engineering, pp. 426–430 (2014)
10. Furtado, V.R., Vignando, H., França, V., OliveiraJr, E.: Comparing approaches for quality evaluation of software engineering experiments: an empirical study on software product line experiments. J. Comput. Sci., 1396–1429 (2019)
11. Furtado, V., OliveiraJr, E., Kalinowski, M.: Guidelines for promoting software product line experiments. In: Brazilian Conference on Software Components, Architecture, and Reuse, pp. 31–40. ACM, New York (2021)
12. Gruber, T.R.: A translation approach to portable ontology specifications. Knowl. Acquis. **5**(2), 199–220 (1993)
13. Isotani, S., Bittencourt, I.I., Barbosa, E.F., Dermeval, D., Paiva, R.O.A.: Ontology driven software engineering: a review of challenges and opportunities. IEEE Lat. Am. Trans. **13**(3), 863–869 (2015)
14. Jedlitschka, A., Ciolkowski, M., Pfahl, D.: Reporting experiments in software engineering. In: Shull, F., Singer, J., Sjøberg, D.I.K. (eds.) Guide to Advanced Empirical Software Engineering, pp. 201–228. Springer, London (2008). https://doi.org/10.1007/978-1-84800-044-5_8
15. Jena, A.: Semantic web framework for Java (2007). https://jena.apache.org/
16. Jolliffe, I.: Principal component analysis. In: International Encyclopedia of Statistical Science, pp. 1094–1096. Springer, Berlin (2011)
17. Kampenes, V.: Quality of design, analysis and reporting of software engineering experiments: a systematic review. Ph.D. Thesis, Department of Informatics, Faculty of Mathematics and Natural Sciences, University of Oslo (2007)
18. Kitchenham, B.A., Pfleeger, S.L., Pickard, L.M., Jones, P.W., Hoaglin, D.C., El Emam, K., Rosenberg, J.: Preliminary guidelines for empirical research in software engineering. IEEE Trans. Softw. Eng. **28**(8), 721–734 (2002)
19. Kitchenham, B., Al-Khilidar, H., Babar, M.A., Berry, M., Cox, K., Keung, J., Kurniawati, F., Staples, M., Zhang, H., Zhu, L.: Evaluating guidelines for reporting empirical software engineering studies. Empir. Softw. Eng. **13**(1), 97–121 (2008)
20. Kitchenham, B., Sjøberg, D.I.K., Brereton, O.P., Budgen, D., Dybå, T., Höst, M., Pfahl, D., Runeson, P.: Can we evaluate the quality of software engineering experiments? In: International Symposium on Empirical Software Engineering and Measurement, pp. 1–8 (2010)
21. Kitchenham, B.A., Budgen, D., Brereton, P.: Evidence-Based Software Engineering and Systematic Reviews, vol. 4. CRC Press, Boca Raton (2016)
22. Lamy, J.B.: Owlready: ontology-oriented programming in python with automatic classification and high level constructs for biomedical ontologies. Artif. Intell. Med. **80**, 11–28 (2017)
23. LiZhang, X.L.: An evolutionary methodology for optimized feature selection in software product lines. In: International Conference on Software Engineering and Knowledge Engineering, SEKE (2014)
24. Lopez-Herrejon, R.E., Linsbauer, L., Galindo, J.A., Parejo, J.A., Benavides, D., Segura, S., Egyed, A.: An assessment of search-based techniques for reverse engineering feature models. J. Syst. Softw. **103**, 353–369 (2015)
25. Machado, I.d.C., Silveira Neto, P.A.d.M., Almeida, E.S.d., Meira, S.R.d.L.: Riple-te: a process for testing software product lines. In: SEKE, pp. 711–716 (2011)
26. McKinney, W.: Data structures for statistical computing in python. In: Proceedings of the 9th Python in Science Conference, pp. 51–56 (2010)
27. Mendonca, F.M.: OntoForInfoScience: methodology for building ontologies by information scientists – a practical application in the development of the ontology about components of human blood (Hemonto) (2015)
28. Monteiro, F.: Modelagem conceitual: a construção de uma ontologia sobre avaliação do ciclo de vida (acv) para fomentar a disseminação de seus conceitos (2007)
29. Petersen, K., Vakkalanka, S., Kuzniarz, L.: Guidelines for conducting systematic mapping studies in software engineering: an update. Inf. Softw. Technol. **64**, 1–18 (2015)

30. Prud'hommeaux, E., Seaborne, A.: SPARQL Query Language for RDF. W3C Recommendation (2008). http://www.w3.org/TR/rdf-sparql-query/
31. Pucci, J.N.: Supporting the execution of controlled experiments using an ontology for em packaging: the tool OntoExpTool. Master's Thesis, Paulista State University (UNESP), São José do Rio Preto (2015). 105 p. In Portuguese
32. Reinhartz-Berger, I., Figl, K., Haugen, Ø.: Comprehending feature models expressed in CVL. In: International Conference on Model Driven Engineering Languages and Systems, pp. 501–517 (2014)
33. Ribeiro, M., Borba, P., Kästner, C.: Feature maintenance with emergent interfaces. In: 36th International Conference on Software Engineering, pp. 989–1000 (2014)
34. Rodrigues, I.P., Bacelo, A.P.T., Silveira, M.S., Campos, M.d.B., Rodrigues, E.M.: Evaluating the representation of user interface elements in feature models: an empirical study. In: SEKE, pp. 628–633 (2016)
35. Santos, W.B., Almeida, E.S.d., Meira, S.R.d.L.: Tirt: A traceability information retrieval tool for software product lines projects. In: Euromicro Conference on Software Engineering and Advanced Applications, pp. 93–100 (2012)
36. Santos, A.R., Machado, I.d.C., Almeida, E.S.d.: Riple-hc: Javascript systems meets spl composition. In: International Systems and Software Product Line Conference, pp. 154–163 (2016)
37. Silveira Neto, P.A.d.M., Machado, I.d.C., Cavalcanti, Y.C., Almeida, E.S.d., Garcia, V.C., Meira, S.R.d.L.: A regression testing approach for software product lines architectures. In: Software Components, Architectures and Reuse (SBCARS), pp. 41–50 (2010)
38. Silveira Neto, P.A.d.M., Machado, I.d.C., Cavalcanti, Y.C., Almeida, E.S.d., Garcia, V.C., Meira, S.R.d.L.: An experimental study to evaluate a spl architecture regression testing approach. In: Information Reuse and Integration (IRI), pp. 608–615 (2012)
39. Sjøberg, D.I.K., Anda, B., Arisholm, E., Dyba, T., Jorgensen, M., Karahasanovic, A., Koren, E.F., Vokác, M.: Conducting realistic experiments in software engineering. Empir. Softw. Eng., 17–26 (2002)
40. Teixeira, E.O.: Quality analysis of controlled experiments in the context of empirical software engineering. Master's Thesis, Federal University of Pernambuco, Recife (2014). 109 p. In Portuguese
41. Van Rossum, G., Drake Jr, F.L.: Python tutorial. In: Centrum voor Wiskunde en Informatica Amsterdam (1995)
42. Vignando, H.: Ontoexper-spl: an ontology to support software product line experiments experiments. Master's Thesis, State University of Maringá, Maringá-PR (2020). In Portuguese
43. Wohlin, C., Runeson, P., Höst, M., Ohlsson, M.C., Regnell, B., Wesslén, A.: Experimentation in Software Engineering. Springer Science & Business Media, Berlin (2012)

Chapter 20
Experimentally Based Evaluations of the SMarty Approach

Anderson S. Marcolino, Thais S. Nepomuceno, Lilian P. Scatalon, and Edson OliveiraJr

Abstract The Stereotype-based Management of Variability (SMarty), presented in Chap. 4, allows the management of variabilities through a UML profile and a process that encompass a set of well-defined guidelines for the identification, representation, and traceability of variabilities in UML models. Thus, in this chapter, we present the experimental studies carried out with the SMarty approach compared to other variability management approaches, in addition to the guidelines created from such experiments for the evolution of SMarty. This chapter was structured according to the guidelines defined by Furtado et al., explaining the methodology applied in each experiment carried out, the objectives with the application of such an experiment, the instrumentation and the hypotheses raised, as well as the statistical tests carried out, with the data obtained through the experiments, to determine the effectiveness of the approaches, the correlation of the participant's level of knowledge with the effectiveness of the configured product, and the effectiveness in tracking elements between the diagrams.

20.1 Experiments on UML-Based Variability Management Approaches

Experimentation is a way to obtain discoveries about something that was not foreseen; it is at the center of the scientific process, making new directions taken in a given research, as it is a way to verify and validate formulated theories. Experimentation is mainly used where theory and deductive analysis do not reach [2, 9, 26, 27].

A. S. Marcolino (✉)
Engineering and Exact Science Department, Federal University of Paraná, Palotina, PR, Brazil
e-mail: anderson.marcolino@ufpr.br

T. S. Nepomuceno · L. P. Scatalon · E. OliveiraJr
Informatics Department, State University of Maringá, Maringá, PR, Brazil
e-mail: edson@din.uem.br

© Springer Nature Switzerland AG 2023
E. OliveiraJr (ed), *UML-Based Software Product Line Engineering with SMarty*,
https://doi.org/10.1007/978-3-031-18556-4_20

Knowing the importance of conducting experiments, in this chapter, it discusses several experiments performed to compare the SMarty approach effectiveness with other UML-based variability management approaches for the main UML diagrams (use case, class, sequence, and component diagrams).

The effectiveness was the main indicator chosen to evaluate the most significant processes for UML-based variability management approaches: the identification, representation, configuration, and support of traceability of variabilities in UML diagrams, regarding each elements of their respective approach.

It is known that UML is a widespread language to represent and support software projects and its phases, but being adopted in the context of software product lines, the complexity of variability, variants, and their constraints can cause difficulty to the application domain, resulting in products with low quality or even imply serious problems hampering the effective use of such software.

In this perspective, knowing the effectiveness of each UML-based variability management approaches, their weaknesses and strengths allow the conduct of more successful projects both in academic and industry areas. Additionally, considering its newer than other approaches, the SMarty approach, it is needed in the conduct of evaluations that go further in the identification of its effectiveness, enabling also to identify elements that need some improvements. Furthermore, the experimental evaluation presented also gives support for the conduction of new evaluations.

Based on such motivations and experimentation which are important for the area, seven experimental evaluations were conducted and are discussed in this chapter. Figure 20.1 summarizes the experimental design of each study.

# Experimental Study	Approach					SPL				Evaluation of Effectiveness related to...					UML Model			
	SMarty		PLUS	Ziadi et al.	Razavian	e-Commerce	Banking	Arcade Game Maker	Mobile Media	Identification of Variabilities	Representation of Variabilities	Configuration of Products	Support for Rastreability	Knowledge Correlation	Use Case	Class	Sequence	Components
	V 5.0	V 5.1																
#1	•		•			•				•	•			•	•			
#2	•		•			•		•		•	•		•			•		
#3		•	•			•		•		•	•		•			•		
#4		•		•			•	•		•	•		•				•	
#5	•	•							•		•	•	•		•	•		
#6		•	•		•				•		•	•	•			•		•
#7		•		•				•			•	•	•			•	•	

Fig. 20.1 Summary of experimental studies

Considering the specificities and similarities among the parts of each experimental study, this chapter is organized summarizing each phase conducted and their elements accordingly with the effectiveness evaluation. It is highlighted that there are two sets of experiments, considering their characteristics: the first set is composed of studies on the evaluation of effectiveness related to identification and representation of variabilities (Experiments from #1 to #4) and the second set of studies on the evaluation of effectiveness related to configuration of products and support of traceability (Experiments from #5 to #7). For both sets of experiments, the methodology and experimental design are presented chronologically, in order by the identification column "# Experimental Study" of Fig. 20.1 divided according with the Experimental Guidelines presented in Chap. 19. At the end, conclusions for each experiment and in general context are presented.

A total of seven experiments were conducted (Fig. 20.1):

- SMarty 5.0 Effectiveness for use case evaluated with PLUS (Product Line UML-based Software engineering) method [11]
- SMarty 5.0 Effectiveness for class evaluated with PLUS method [12]
- SMarty 5.1 Effectiveness for class evaluated with PLUS method [14]
- SMarty 5.1 Effectiveness for sequence evaluated with the Ziadi et al. approach [13]
- SMarty 5.1 Effectiveness for use case and class evaluated with PLUS method [16]
- SMarty 5.1 Effectiveness for class and component evaluated with the Razavian and Khosravi's method [18, 19]
- SMarty 5.1 Effectiveness for class and sequence evaluated with the Ziadi et al. approach [17]

The UML-based variability management approaches adopted in each experimental evaluation are briefly presented next.

20.1.1 The UML-Based Variability Management Approaches

The UML-Based Variability Management Approaches leverage provided by the UML and add the needed elements to represent software product lines through them. However, each of them use different methods and strategies to make such integration.

Based on the importance of such approaches and method for SPL community, results of systematic reviews in different primary studies bases and indexed repositories allowed the selection of several UML-Based Variability Management Approaches and methods to be compared with SMarty Approach in the experimental studies discussed in this chapter. The selected approaches and methods were: Product Line UML-based Software Engineering (PLUS) Method [7], The Ziadi et al. Approach [32, 33] and The Razavian and Khosravi Method [21].

20.1.1.1 Product Line UML-Based Software Engineering (PLUS) Method

The PLUS method, proposed by Gomaa [7], allows its integration with other software process models, such as the unified process (UP) development.

Gomaa proposes several SPL activities for requirement, analysis, and design. The requirement activity encompasses SPL scope definition, use case modeling, and feature modeling. The PLUS use case modeling activity aims to explicitly model commonalities and variabilities.

PLUS does not provide a definition of a UML profile; thus, there are no explicit meta-attributes and classes for the variability modeling activity and also do not offer support for tracking elements among UML diagram elements. The method uses stereotypes to provide identification of variation points and variants, in several of them being specific to certain UML models. The rationale with regard to the use of such stereotypes is twofold: forward evolutionary engineering and reverse evolutionary engineering. The set of stereotypes for identification of variant components to represent variability are described as follows:

- ≪kernel≫ represents use case and class diagrams of mandatory elements.
- ≪optional≫ represents use case and class diagrams of optional elements for a specific product.
- ≪alternative≫ represents use case and class diagrams of mutually exclusive elements. This stereotype is not used in class diagrams.

Figure 20.2a represents the Arcade Game Maker (AGM) SPL class diagram modeled according to PLUS, with respective stereotypes.

PLUS is a well-known method, investigated by several studies in the literature, such as Bragança and Machado [3], Gomaa [7], Korherr and List [10], Ziadi et al. [33], and Chen et al. [5].

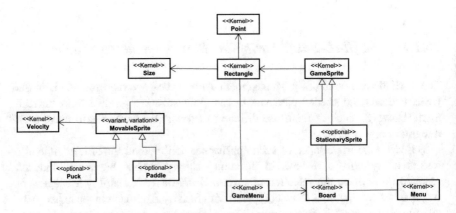

Fig. 20.2 AGM class diagram according to PLUS. Adapted from [20]

20.1.1.2 The Ziadi et al. Approach

The Ziadi et al. approach [32, 33] is supported by a UML profile, which allows its integration with UML tools to identify and represent variabilities for the following UML models: class and sequence. Such approach is one of the most representative approaches for managing variabilities in UML sequence models [5].

There is a set of explicit meta-attributes (tagged values) and meta-classes for performing variability modeling activity. The Ziadi et al. approach uses stereotypes to provide identification of variation points and variants, for class and sequence.

The stereotypes proposed by Ziadi et al. to sequence models are as follows:

- ≪optionalLifeline≫ is used to indicate optional and alternative *lifelines*.
- ≪optionalInteraction≫ is used to represent interactions that might or not might be present in SPL-specific products.
- ≪variation≫ is used to represent the variation point of alternative inclusive or exclusive variants.
- ≪variant≫ is used to represent the variants of a variation point.
- ≪virtual≫ is used to indicate that an interaction is a virtual part. It might be redefined by other sequence diagrams, and it might represent variabilities. It is used in specific cases, in which the SPL needs to model a behavior that can be modified.

Figure 20.3 represents the banking product line sequence diagram modeled according to Ziadi et al. approach, with respective stereotypes. Such SPL is described in Ziadi et al. work [32, 33], and the excerpt in Fig. 20.3 represents both main bank PL sequence and the specific withdraw from account sequence interactions and elements.

For extending the semantic for class models and sequence trough a UML profile, its stereotypes must be applied to the elements that were extended from meta-class from UML meta-model, and it represents a problem for the Ziadi proposal.

The Ziadi et al. approach uses elements such as UML frame. However, this element is not present in UML modeling tools, such as Poseidon 8.0,[1] MagicDraw 11,[2] and Astah 8.5.[3] Thus, the absence of such an element makes it difficult to process the identification of variabilities in SPL that needs such graphical representation.

20.1.1.3 The Razavian and Khosravi's Method

Razavian and Khosravi [21] propose modeling variability in components, connectors, and interfaces of components using the following stereotypes:

---

[1] http://www.gentleware.com/.

[2] http://www.nomagic.com/.

[3] http://astah.net/.

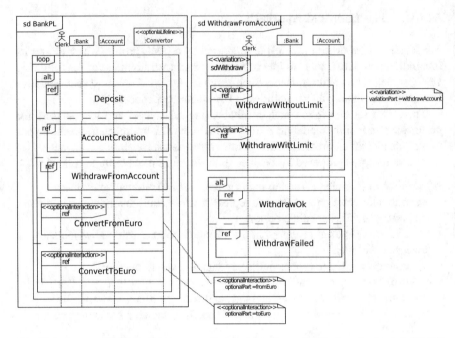

Fig. 20.3 Excerpt of banking PL sequence diagram according to the Ziadi et al. approach [32, 33]

- ≪alt_vp≫ represents an alternative variation point, in which variants are represented by ≪variant≫.
- ≪opt_vp≫ represents optional variation points, in which variants are represented by ≪variant≫.
- ≪variant≫ represents variants associated with a given variation point.
- ≪optional≫ represents elements which might be present in an SPL-specific product.
- ≪altv_vp≫ represents alternative variation points in a given ≪variant≫.
- ≪optv_vp≫ represents optional variation points in a given ≪variant≫.

Figure 20.4 depicts an example of the backgroundMgr component, which is an alternative variation point (≪alt_vp≫) and has two variant interfaces, namely, BackgroundColorMgt and BackgroundTypeMgt, annotated with the stereotype ≪variant≫.

The variant BackgroundColorMgt interface is also a variation point; thus, it is annotated with the ≪altv_vp≫ stereotype. This variation point has three variants, red, white, and black, annotated with ≪variant≫.

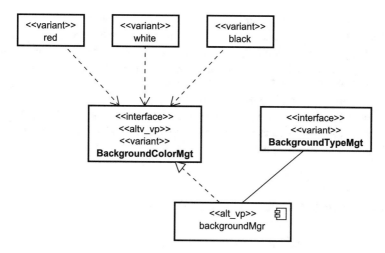

Fig. 20.4 Example of a component diagram according to Razavian and Khosravi's method

20.2 Experimental Evaluations of Effectiveness of Identification and Representation of Variabilities

The experimental evaluations are characterized as a quasi-experiment [29] that relaxes the conditions imposed by probability distributions and statistical inferences for the population. Therefore, we performed the nonequivalent grouping method, considering that the population distribution was not random.

20.2.1 Objectives (G.1)

The seven experiments divided into two sets of experiments aimed at the identification of effectiveness related to identification and representation of variabilities (Experiments from #1 to #4) and the identification of effectiveness related to configuration of products and support of traceability (Experiments from #5 to #7). Effectiveness considered the metric which considers how good a UML-based method or approach is in the tasks of identification, representation, configuration, and support of traceability.

In this perspective, the main research question investigated by means of the seven experiments conducted is *"Is SMarty a better UML-based variability management approach than PLUS, Ziadi et al. approach, and Razavian and Khosravi's method in the identification, representation, configuration, and support of traceability of SPL in UML use case, class, sequence, and component diagrams?"*

Below presents a GQM template:

The goal of the experiment [**#id**] was to **compare** the [**Approach/method Compared**] and the *SMarty* approach **for the purpose of** identifying the most effective, **with respect to** the [**Capability of**...] in software product line [**UML diagrams**], **from the point of view of** software product line architects, **in the context of** [**participants' profile and origin**].

Table 20.1 summarizes the main objectives of the experiments individually. Each line represents a specific set of items that must be considered in filling the GQM (goal, question, metric)[2] template.

20.2.2 Hypothesis Formulation (G.2)

The hypothesis template tested in the studies are:

- **Null hypothesis** (H_0): There is no significant difference in effectiveness between the approaches.

  H_0: $\mu(effectiveness(SMarty)) = \mu(effectiveness([$**Approach/method Compared**$]))$.
- **Alternative hypothesis** (H_1): There is a significant difference in effectiveness between the SMarty and [**Approach/method Compared**] in terms of [**Capability of**...] from [**UML Diagrams**].

  H_1: $\mu(effectiveness(SMarty)) \neq \mu(effectiveness([$**Approach/method Compared**$]))$.

Items presented on Table 20.1 may be used to fill in the information for each study hypothesis, as in GQM template.

For study #5, two additional sets of hypothesis regarding (1) the number of queries to instructional materials when the participants are generating specific products and (2) the significance of difference in effectiveness between the traceability of elements in UML diagrams were also defined.

For the number of queries:

- Null hypothesis ($H0_{cons}$): There is no significant difference between the SMarty and PLUS approaches in the number of queries to instructional materials when generating specific products.

  $H0_{cons}$: $\mu(\textbf{Query (SMarty)}) = \mu(\textbf{Query (PLUS)})$
- Alternative hypothesis ($H1_{cons}$): There is a significant difference between the SMarty and PLUS approaches in the number of queries to instructional materials when generating specific products.

  $H1_{cons}$: $\mu(\textbf{Query (SMarty)}) \neq \mu(\textbf{Query (PLUS)})$

For the effectiveness of tracking elements between diagrams with each approach:

- Null hypothesis ($H0_{efet}$): There is no significant difference in effectiveness between the traceability of elements between the use case and class diagrams using the SMarty and PLUS approaches.

Table 20.1 Experimental GQM and hypothesis information

#Id	Approach/method compared	Capability of...	UML diagrams	Participants' profile and origin
#1	PLUS	Identification and representation of variabilities	Use case	Undergraduate students and lecturers of the Software Engineering area from the State University of Maringá (UEM), Federal Technological University of Paraná (UTFPR), and Federal University of Amazonas (UFAM)
#2	PLUS	Identification and representation of variabilities	Class	Master and Ph.D. students of the Software Engineering area from the Computing Systems Department University of São Paulo—ICMC/USP and Federal University of São Carlos—UFSCar
#3	PLUS	Resolving and generating consistent products	Class	Master and Ph.D. students of the Software Engineering area from the University of São Paulo—ICMC/USP
#4	Ziadi et al.	Identification and representation of variabilities	Sequence	Master and Ph.D. students of the Software Engineering area from the Federal University of Paraná (UFPR) and State University of Maringá (UEM)
#5	PLUS	Configuration of specific products	Use case and class	Undergraduate academics who have some knowledge about software product line and variability in SPL from the State University of Maringá and the Federal Technological University of Paraná
#6	PLUS and Razavian and Khosravi's method	Configuration and traceability of specific products	Class and component	Students and practitioners from two Brazilian universities
#7	Ziadi et al.	Configuration of specific products	Sequence and class	Undergraduate and graduate students who have previous knowledge about UML, SPL, and variability

$H0_{Efet}$: μ(**Effectiveness(SMarty)**) = μ(**Effectiveness(PLUS)**)

- Alternative hypothesis ($H1_{efet}$): There is a significant difference in effectiveness between the traceability of elements between the use case and class diagrams using the SMarty and PLUS approaches.

$H1_{efet}$: μ(**Effectiveness(SMarty)**) $\neq$ μ(**Effectiveness(PLUS)**)

20.2.3   Variable Definitions (G.3)

For studies from #1 to #5, the effectiveness equation is defined as below:

$$effectiveness(z) = \begin{cases} nVarC, \text{ if } nVarI = 0 \\ nVarC - nVarI, \text{ if } nVarI > 0 \end{cases} \qquad (20.1)$$

where

- z is the variability management approach.
- $nVarC$ is the number of correct identified variabilities according to the z approach.
- $nVarI$ is the number of incorrect identified variabilities according to the z approach.

For study #5 to calculate the effectiveness, we consider the following equation:

$$\textbf{Effectiveness(z)} = \textbf{nVarC/Total} \qquad (20.2)$$

where

- **z** is the variability management approach.
- **nVarC** is the number of elements with correctly resolved variability.
- **Total** is the total number of elements in the diagram.

The number of consultations with instructional materials is a discrete value noted by the participant throughout the experiment. The influence of knowledge of each participant will be calculated using the correlation between the five knowledge levels of the characterization questionnaire and the obtained value of effectiveness for each participant.

For studies #6 and #7, the effectiveness equation is:

$$\textbf{Effectiveness(z, d)} = \textbf{nCorrElem/TotalElem} \qquad (20.3)$$

where

- **z** is PLUS, Razavian and Khosravi's method, or SMarty.
- **d** is class diagram or component diagram.
- **nCorrElem** is the number of correct resolved/traced variability elements of a given diagram d using the **z** approach.
- **TotalElem** is the total number of variability elements of a given diagram d using the **z** approach.

Table 20.2 presents the independent and dependent variables for each study.

Table 20.2 Independent and dependent variables

#Id	Independent variables	Dependent variables
#1	The variability management approach, which is a factor with two treatments (SMarty and PLUS), and the e-commerce SPL, which is a variable with a prefixed value. A variability element might be either a variation point or a variant	The effectiveness was calculated for each variability management approach (SMarty and PLUS) as follows
#2	The effectiveness calculated for each variability management approach (SMarty and PLUS)	The variability management approach, which is a factor with two treatments (SMarty and PLUS), and the SPL, which is a factor with two treatments: e-commerce and Arcade Game Maker
#3	Independent and dependent variables are the same from study #2. The same effectiveness equation was taken into account, but correct and incorrect variabilities were replaced with the number of errors and hits with relation to each selected element for the subject's specific product configuration	
#4	The effectiveness calculated for each variability management approach (SMarty and Ziadi et al.)	The variability management approach, which is a factor with two treatments (SMarty and Ziadi et al.), and the SPL, which is a factor with two treatments: banking and Arcade Game Maker
#5	The first variability management approach, which is a factor with two treatments: the SMarty approach and the PLUS method. The second variable is prefixed, being MM SPL	The output variables of the experiment are the effectiveness, the number of queries to the material of each approach, the influence of the participants' knowledge on the observed value of effectiveness, and the effectiveness of each approach in tracking elements between diagrams
#6	Approach being analyzed, which is a factor with two controls, the PLUS method and the Razavian and Khosravi's method, and one treatment, the SMarty approach; prefixed variable for SPL, the mobile media, which was chosen since it has several types of variabilities and possibilities for product configuration, yet with diagrams simple enough to be used for a study without tool support	Effectiveness of configuring products, number of consultations to instructional material, influence of participant's knowledge on UML and SPL/variability, and effectiveness at traceability
#7	The variability management approach, which is a factor with two treatments: SMarty and Ziadi et al. and a prefixed variable, the AGM SPL	The effectiveness on correctly configuring products, the influence of the participants' knowledge on the observed value of effectiveness, and the traceability capability of each approach

Table 20.3 Independent and dependent variables

#Id	Total of participants	Degree
#1	24	21 are graduate students and 3 are lecturers of the Software Engineering area
#2	20	Master and Ph.D. students of Software Engineering area were selected for this study
#3	24	12 masters and 12 Ph.D. students of Software Engineering area. None of them attended study #2
#4	14	Masters and Ph.D. students of Software Engineering area were selected for this study
#5	46	10 are masters and 3 Ph.D. students of Software Engineering area, and 33 are undergraduate and graduate students in Computer Science and Computer Engineering.
#6	51	11 are masters and 3 Ph.D. students of Software Engineering area and 37 are Undergraduate and graduate students in Computer Science and Computer Engineering
#7	30	Undergraduate and graduate students in Computer Science and Computer Engineering, some with expertise in the industry

20.2.4 Sample Size (G.4)

Table 20.3 presents the sample size of each experiment.

20.2.5 Participants' Definition and Selection (G.5)

For the seven experimental studies, participants were selected in a non-probabilistic manner. The subjects must be graduate students, lecturers, or practitioners of the software engineering area with at least minimal knowledge in modeling UML diagrams. In addition, after the training sessions, each subject must be familiar with the essential variability management concepts.

Tables 20.4 and 20.5 present knowledge description of all participants for each approach to **Experiment #5**.

For **Experiment #6**, Tables 20.6, 20.9, and 20.7 present knowledge description of all participants for each approach (Tables 20.8 and 20.9).

Finally, for **Experiment #7**, the description of each participant's knowledge is described in Table 20.10.

Table 20.4 Description of the knowledge level of the participants who used PLUS—Experiment #5

PLUS

Part. ID	Knowledge		Education	Industry/academia	Experience (months)
	UML	SPL and variab.			
1	Basic	Basic	Bachelor	Acad.	48
3	Basic	None	Bachelor	Acad.	36
5	Moderate	Read	Bachelor	Acad.	24
7	Basic	None	Bachelor	Acad.	36
9	Basic	Read	Bachelor	Acad.	36
11	Basic	None	Bachelor	Acad.	48
13	Basic	None	Bachelor	Acad.	24
15	Basic	None	Bachelor	Acad.	30
17	Advanced	Read	Bachelor	Acad.	38
19	Basic	None	Bachelor	Acad.	36
21	Basic	None	Bachelor	Acad.	40
23	Moderate	None	Bachelor	Acad.	36
25	Basic	None	Bachelor	Acad.	40
27	Moderate	Read	Bachelor	Acad.	48
29	Moderate	None	Bachelor	Acad.	24
31	Basic	None	Bachelor	Acad.	24
33	Advanced	None	Bachelor	Acad.	24
35	Moderate	None	Bachelor	Acad.	8
37	Moderate	None	Bachelor	Acad.	36
39	Advanced	Read	Bachelor	Acad.	36
41	Basic	Read	Bachelor	Acad.	36
43	Moderate	Read	Bachelor	Acad.	24
45	Moderate	None	Bachelor	Acad.	36

20.2.6   Research Experiment Topic Definition (G.6)

The seven experimental studies were conducted in the Software Engineering and SPL research topics.

20.2.7   Experimental Design Definition (G.7)

Table 20.3 present the experimental design definition, regarding the independent and dependent variables.

Table 20.5 Knowledge level of the participants who used SMarty—Experiment #5

SMarty					
	Knowledge				
Part. ID	UML	SPL and variability	Education level	Industry/academy	Time (months)
2	Moderate	None	Bachelor	Acad.	36
4	Basic	None	Bachelor	Acad.	36
6	Basic	None	Bachelor	Acad.	48
8	Basic	None	Bachelor	Acad.	48
10	Moderate	None	Bachelor	Acad.	25
12	Basic	None	Bachelor	Acad.	36
14	Basic	None	Bachelor	Acad.	30
16	Basic	None	Bachelor	Acad.	24
18	Basic	Only reading	Bachelor	Acad.	24
20	Basic	Only reading	Bachelor	Acad.	36
22	Moderate	None	Bachelor	Acad.	24
24	Advanced	Only reading	Bachelor	Acad.	36
26	Moderate	None	Bachelor	Acad.	30
28	Advanced	Only reading	Bachelor	Acad.	48
30	Moderate	None	Bachelor	Acad.	48
32	Moderate	None	Bachelor	Acad.	24
34	Advanced	Only reading	Bachelor	Acad.	36
36	Moderate	Only reading	Bachelor	Acad.	36
38	Moderate	None	Bachelor	Acad.	36
40	Basic	Only reading	Bachelor	Acad.	36
42	Basic	None	Bachelor	Acad.	24
44	Basic	None	Bachelor	Acad.	30
46	Moderate	None	Bachelor	Acad.	36

20.2.8 Experimental Material Definition and Selection (G.8)

For all participants in the experiments, the materials distributed were:

- Informed consent term (ICT): containing the main information about the experiment to be applied, such as confidentiality, procedures, and benefits. This document allowed the participant to make their decision about their participation in the research fairly.
- Characterization questionnaire: applied to participants to analyze the level of knowledge and experience about UML, SPL, and variability in SPL.
- Document with theoretical synthesis: contents seen during training on each approach. To facilitate the location of the information by the participant, the document was divided into three sections—the first with the main concepts of the software product line and on traceability (the latter only for Experiments #5, #6, and #7), the second with the general description of the SPL to be used, and, as the participants were divided into blocks (one block for each approach), the

Table 20.6 Participants' knowledge using PLUS—Experiment #6

PLUS					
	Knowledge				
Partic.	UML	SPL and variab.	Graduation level	Academia/industry	Experience (months)
1	Basic	Read	M.Sc.	Indus.	60
4	Basic	Basic	M.Sc.	Indus.	144
7	Basic	Read	M.Sc.	Acad.	24
10	Moderate	Read	M.Sc.	Acad.	12
13	Basic	Read	M.Sc.	Indus.	60
16	Basic	Read	M.Sc.	Acad.	36
19	None	Read	M.Sc.	Indus.	72
22	Basic	None	Bachelor	Indus.	84
25	Basic	None	Bachelor	Acad.	24
28	Basic	Read	Bachelor	Indus.	18
31	Basic	Read	Bachelor	Indus.	84
34	Moderate	Read	Bachelor	Acad.	24
37	Basic	Read	Bachelor	Acad.	24
40	Moderate	None	Bachelor	Indus.	14
43	Basic	None	Bachelor	Indus.	12
46	Moderate	None	Bachelor	Acad.	24
49	Basic	Read	Bachelor	Acad.	24

third with included information about the approaches, which was different for each group:

- Block with the PLUS approach: comprised a summary of the concepts of the PLUS approach, as well as its stereotypes and examples
- Block with the SMarty approach: concepts about the SMarty approach, its stereotypes, and examples
- Block with the Razavian and Khosravi's approach: concepts about the Razavian and Khosravi's approach, its stereotypes, and examples
- Block with the Ziadi et al. approach: concepts about the Ziadi et al. approach, its stereotypes, and examples

Only for Experiment #7, in addition to the previous documents, videos were made available in Portuguese with an explanation of SPL, approaches, and examples.

20.2.8.1 Description of the SPL Adopted (G.8.1)

Experiment #1 The electronic commerce (e-commerce) SPL, proposed by Gomaa [7], was taken into consideration to apply the PLUS method and the SMarty approach aiming the representation of variabilities in use case.

Table 20.7 Participants' knowledge using Razavian and Khosravi's method—Experiment #6

Razavian and Khosravi's method

Partic. ID	Knowledge				Academia/industry	Time of experience (months)
	UML	SPL and variab.	Graduation level			
3	Moderate	Read	Ph.D.		Acad.	60
6	Moderate	Read	Ph.D.		Acad.	72
9	Basic	Read	Ph.D.		Acad.	60
12	Basic	None	M.Sc.		Indus.	6
15	Moderate	Read	M.Sc.		Acad.	60
18	Advanced	Moderate	M.Sc.		Indus.	120
21	Basic	Read	M.Sc.		Indus.	17
24	Moderate	None	Bachelor		Acad.	36
27	Moderate	None	Bachelor		Acad.	36
30	Basic	None	Bachelor		Acad.	24
33	Moderate	Basic	Bachelor		Indus.	5
36	Basic	Read	Bachelor		Acad.	24
39	Moderate	Read	Bachelor		Acad.	24
42	Basic	Basic	Bachelor		Acad.	24
45	Moderate	None	Bachelor		Acad.	24
48	Moderate	Basic	Bachelor		Indus.	12
51	Moderate	None	Bachelor		Acad.	24

Table 20.8 Experimental design

#Id	Description
#1	The independent variables are PLUS, SMarty, and the SPL. PLUS and SMarty approaches are the compared factors and the SPL electronic commerce (e-commerce) is an independent factor proposed by Gomaa [7]. The treatment is the study execution, and the dependent variable is the effectiveness
#2 and #3	The independent variables are PLUS, SMarty, and two SPLs. PLUS and SMarty approaches are the compared factors, and the SPL electronic commerce (e-commerce) and pedagogical SPL for Arcade Game Maker, proposed by SEI [22], are the SPL independent factors. The treatment is the study execution, and the dependent variable is the effectiveness
#4	The independent variables are PLUS, SMarty, and two SPLs. PLUS and SMarty approaches are the compared factors and SPL for banking transactions, proposed by Ziadi et al. [32], and a pedagogical SPL for Arcade Game Maker, proposed by SEI [22], are the SPL independent factors. The treatment is the study execution and the dependent variable is the effectiveness
#5	The independent variables are the variability management approach, which is a factor with two treatments, the SMarty approach and the PLUS method, and a prefixed variable, being MM SPL. The dependent variables are the effectiveness, the number of queries to the material of each approach, the influence of the participants' knowledge on the observed value of effectiveness, and the effectiveness of each approach in tracking elements between diagrams
#6	The independent variables are the approach being analyzed, which is a factor with two controls, the PLUS method and the Razavian and Khosravi's method, and one treatment, the SMarty approach, and a prefixed variable for SPL, the mobile media. Dependent variables are the effectiveness of configuring products, number of consultations to instructional material, influence of participant's knowledge on UML and SPL/variability, and effectiveness at traceability
#7	Independent variables are the variability management approach, which is a factor with two treatments, SMarty and Ziadi et al., and a prefixed variable, the AGM SPL. Dependent variables are the effectiveness on correctly configuring products, the influence of the participants' knowledge on the observed value of effectiveness, and the traceability capability of each approach

Experiment #2 and Experiment #3 The electronic commerce (e-commerce) SPL, proposed by Gomaa [7], and pedagogical Arcade Game Maker SPL, proposed by SEI [22], are the SPL that were taken into consideration to apply the PLUS method and the SMarty approach aiming the representation of variabilities in class diagrams.

Experiment #4 The SPL for banking transactions, proposed by Ziadi et al. [32], and a pedagogical Arcade Game Maker SPL, proposed by SEI [22], were taken into consideration to apply the Ziadi et al. and the SMarty approaches aiming the representation of variabilities in sequence models.

Experiment #5 and Experiment #6 For experiments 5 and 6, MM (mobile media) SPL was used. MM [31] is an SPL composed of applications (products) that manipulate music, videos, and photos for mobile devices, such as cell phones and palm tops. It provides support to manage (create, delete, view, play, send) different

Table 20.9 Participants' knowledge using SMarty—Experiment #6

SMarty

Partic. ID	Knowledge		Graduation level	Academia/industry	Experience (months)
	UML	SPL and variab.			
2	Advanced	Moderate	M.Sc.	Indus.	240
5	Moderate	Read	M.Sc.	Indus.	204
8	Moderate	Read	M.Sc.	Acad.	12
11	Basic	None	M.Sc.	Indus.	156
14	Basic	None	M.Sc.	Indus.	36
17	None	Read	M.Sc.	–	–
20	None	None	Bachelor	Acad.	24
23	Basic	Read	Bachelor	Acad.	24
26	Basic	Read	Bachelor	Acad.	24
29	Basic	Basic	Bachelor	Acad.	24
32	Moderate	Basic	Bachelor	Acad.	24
35	Moderate	Read	Bachelor	Acad.	24
38	Basic	Read	Bachelor	Acad.	24
41	None	Read	Bachelor	Acad.	24
44	Basic	None	Bachelor	Indus.	34
47	Basic	None	Bachelor	Acad.	24
50	Basic	Read	Bachelor	Indus.	12

types of media. MM emerged from the extension of an existing SPL called mobile photo [31], through the insertion of new multimedia properties, such as video and music manipulation, which can only be performed on certain types of devices. In a way, it can be said that the insertion of optional and alternative features to certain devices characterized the emergence of mobile media.

Experiment #7 The Arcade Game Maker (AGM) SPL used as an experimental object is not a real case of the software industry, but a pedagogical one.

20.2.8.2   Source of the SPL (G.8.1.1)

Experiment #1 Gomaa [7]

Experiment #2 and Experiment #3 Gomaa [7] and Software Engineering Institute [22]

Experiment #4 Ziadi et al. [32] and Software Engineering Institute [22]

Experiment #5 and Experiment #6 Young[31]

Table 20.10 Knowledge level of participants—Experiment #7

Part. ID	Knowledge		Education	Industry/academia	Experience (months)
	UML	SPL/variab.			
1	Basic	Basic	Masters St.	Academia	36
2	Moderate	Have read	Masters St.	Industry	36
3	Moderate	Basic	Masters St.	Academia	50
4	Moderate	Basic	Masters St.	Academia	48
5	Basic	Have read	Bachelor	Industry	25
6	Basic	None	Bachelor	Industry	12
7	Basic	None	Bachelor	Industry	30
8	Moderate	Have read	Bachelor	Academia	10
9	Basic	Have read	Bachelor	Academia	60
10	Moderate	Have read	Bachelor	Academia	36
11	Basic	None	Bachelor	Academia	8
12	Basic	Have read	Bachelor	Industry	36
13	Basic	Have read	Bachelor	Industry	30
14	Basic	Have read	Bachelor	Industry	48
15	Moderate	None	Bachelor	Academia	48
16	Basic	None	Bachelor	Academia	24
17	Moderate	Have read	Bachelor	Industry	20
18	Moderate	Have read	Bachelor	Industry	15
19	Moderate	None	Bachelor	Industry	36
20	Moderate	Have read	Bachelor	Academia	36
21	Basic	None	Bachelor	Academia	24
22	Basic	None	Bachelor	Industry	34
23	Basic	None	Bachelor	Industry	40
24	Moderate	None	Bachelor	Academia	36
25	Moderate	None	Bachelor	Academia	36
26	Basic	None	Bachelor	Academia	36
27	Moderate	None	Masters St.	Academia	36
28	Basic	None	Bachelor	Industry	60
29	Basic	None	Bachelor	Academia	36
30	Basic	None	Bachelor	Industry	26

Experiment #7 https://resources.sei.cmu.edu/asset_files/WhitePaper/2009_019_001_485943.pdf

20.2.8.3 SPL Artifacts (G.8.2)

Experiment #1 Figure 20.5 presented the use case diagram of the e-commerce SPL.

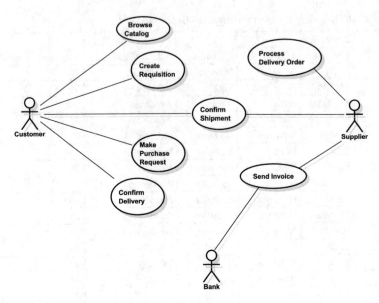

Fig. 20.5 E-commerce use case. Adapted from [7]

Experiment #2 and Experiment #3 Figure 20.5 depicts the use case diagram of e-commerce SPL, and Fig. 20.2 depicts AGM class diagram according to PLUS.

Experiment #4 Figure 20.3 presented the sequence diagram of banking SPL.

Experiment #5 and Experiment #6 Figure 20.6 shows part of a class diagram of the MM SPL.

Experiment #7 In Figs. 20.7 and 20.8, two diagrams of the SPL AGM are illustrated, one of use cases and the other of classes.

20.2.9 Experimental Material Validation (G.9)

For all the seven experimental studies, the experimental materials were reviewed by professors of Software Engineering with knowledge in variability management in SPL. From the application of this project, they gave suggestions of improvements that we applied in the material created, and errors in the material could be corrected.

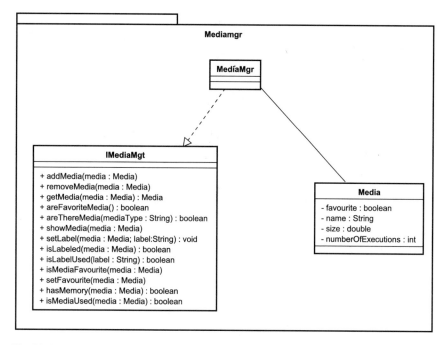

Fig. 20.6 MM artifacts—part of the class diagram adapted from Fig. 20.5

20.2.10   Experimental Task Description (G.10)

Each experiment has its specific experimental tasks.

In Experiment #1, subjects were divided into two groups: one group focused on PLUS method and one group focused on the SMarty approach. Each group had the task to identify and represent variabilities according with their respective approach. Each group was participated in training sections before the execution of their tasks.

In Experiment #2, subjects were separated into two groups, balanced by their knowledge: one group focused on the PLUS method and one group focused on the SMarty approach. One group was trained to identify and represent variabilities according to the SMarty approach, and the other group was trained to identify and represent variabilities according to the PLUS method.

In Experiment #3, the participation procedure differs from Study #2 mainly in the execution. Basically, a subject resolves and derives two specific products, one based on the e-commerce SPL and other based on the AGM SPL. Both products are represented in UML class diagrams modeled with SMarty or PLUS approaches, randomly distributed to subjects in an equal number.

In Experiment #4, subjects were divided into two groups, balanced by their knowledge: one group focused on the Ziadi et al. approach and one group focused on the SMarty approach. One group was trained to identify and represent variabilities

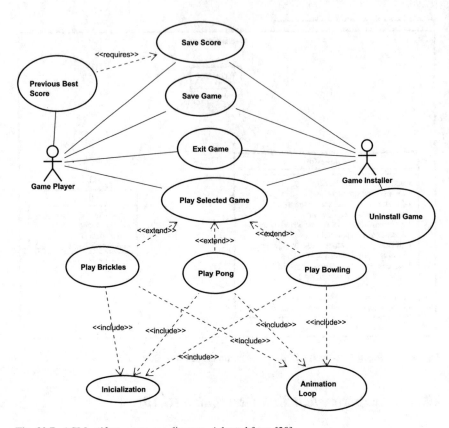

Fig. 20.7 AGM artifact—use case diagram. Adapted from [20]

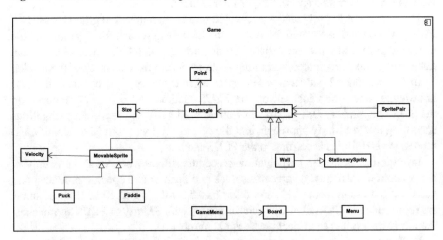

Fig. 20.8 AGM artifact—class diagram. Adapted from [20]

according to the SMarty approach, and the other group was trained to identify and represent variabilities according to the Ziadi et al. approach.

In Experiment #5, the group of students was divided according to the approach received by each participant; this division aimed to ensure that participants had similar levels of knowledge and that there was no influence on results. Participants with PLUS stayed in the room to receive the training, while others waited outside. At the end of the training with the PLUS method, the participants were sent to another room, supervised by a person, and started configuring the products. In sequence, participants of the SMarty approach were trained and also started to configure the products.

Each group received a form with the identification of the activity to be performed. Half of the group received the form to specify two product configurations using the MM SPL use case diagram with the SMarty approach, while the other half received the form to specify two products from the MM use case and class diagram modeled with the PLUS approach. At the same time as the participants were generating the respective configurations, they pointed out the number of consultations to the instructional material.

In Experiment #6, participants were divided into three groups balancing them according to their knowledge on UML and SPL/variability; experimenter informed participants they were allowed to use the instructional material during the experiment tasks; experimenter randomly distributed to participants a class diagram according to PLUS or SMarty, or a component diagram according to PLUS or SMarty according to Razavian and Khosravi's method or SMarty, and respective document with questions and tasks to be performed; experimenter asked participants to take notes on how many times they consult the instructional material during tasks; participants configured one specific instance (product) based on the diagrams from the mobile media SPL; participants answered questions on product configuration and traceability by analyzing whether the approach allows identifying variability from one level to another (class to component diagram traceability) and vice-versa; participants responded to couple open questions on improvements and difficulties faced in the experiment; participants gave instruments to experimenter and finished their tasks in the experiment.

Finally, in Experiment #7, the group of participants was divided according to the approach received by each participant. The division was done at random. Each group received a document identifying the tasks to perform. Half of the group configured products from an AGM SPL class diagram, while the other half did it from a sequence diagram.

20.2.11 Training Requirement Description (G.11)

For the seven experiments, subjects were divided into two groups. One group was trained to identify or represent variabilities or create configurations based on a set of variabilities according to one method/approach. The other group was trained also to identify or represent variabilities or create configurations based on a set of variabilities but in according to other methods/approaches.

20.2.12 Pilot Project Conduction (G.12)

The seven experiments passed through pilot projects. Each pilot was performed for evaluating the study instrumentation taking into account two lecturers of software engineering. Thus, adjustments on the instrumentation were made based on the pilot project results.

The pilot project leaded us to use only one approach for each subject. This is justified by avoiding the bias of subjects learning from the use of a previous approach. Note that the pilot data was not taken into consideration by the overall experimental study data analysis.

20.2.13 Experimental Environment Conduction (G.13)

For each of the seven studies, the experimental environment for the executions was in classrooms in educational institutions where the participants study.

20.2.14 Experimental Date of Execution (G.14)

Each of the seven experiments occurred in specific period of time. Experiment #1 was conducted among March and May of 2013. Experiment #2 was conducted among April and June of 2013. Experiment #3 was conducted among August and September of 2013. Experiment #4 was conducted among October and November of 2013. Experiment #5 was conducted between April and May 2019. Experiment #6 study was carried out in October and November 2019. And for Experiment #7, the date of execution of the experiment was between June and September 2020.

20.2.15 Experimental Execution (G.15)

The experimental execution was similar for the seven studies, changing the documents and adding some specific tasks, especially for #5; #6, regarding the register of queries to instructional materials when generating specific products and the traceability of elements; and #7, which also was executed online, where a link was made available on *Google Drive* containing all the documentation and training necessary for the execution of the experiment.

In this context, the standard procedures adopted for each subject participation are:

1. The subject attends the place where the study was conducted.
2. The experimenter gives the subject a set of documents:

   - The experimental study term of agreement
   - The characterization questionnaire
   - Essential concepts on variability management in SPL
   - The description of experiment study SPL model or models, when more than one was used

3. The subject reads each given document.
4. The experimenter explains the given documents.
5. The experimenter randomly associates each subject with SMarty and PLUS, Ziadi et al., or Razavian and Khosravi's method—it highlighted that adopted approaches received a nickname to avoid its identification by the participant.
6. The experimenter trains the subjects on the respective approach.
7. The subject reads and clarifies possible doubts about his/her assigned approach.
8. The subject identifies variabilities, represents variabilities, or makes configurations based on variability UML model representation considering both SPL model and UML diagram according to his/her approach received, respectively.

20.2.16 Data Collected Description (GD.16)

20.2.16.1 Experiment #1

The main assessment tool was the e-commerce use case model with variabilities represented according to the PLUS and SMarty approaches. The main task for each subject was reading and understanding the e-commerce SPL overview. Then, the subjects annotated variabilities in the e-commerce use case model.

Collected data is presented in Table 20.11 and analyzed using appropriate statistical methods. For each subject ("Subject #" column), it collected the following data for his/her given approach: the number of correct and incorrect identified and represented variabilities and the effectiveness calculation.

20.2.16.2 Experiment #2

The main assessment tools were the e-commerce and Arcade Game Maker class model with variabilities represented according to the PLUS and SMarty approaches. Both, the e-commerce and Arcade Game Maker class models, were distributed in an equal number. The e-commerce was the first and the Arcade Game Maker the second. The subjects were free to change the order of SPLs and their respective resolutions.

Table 20.11 Result summarization for Experiments #1, #2, #3, and #4

#Id	Item	Approach/method compared					SMarty				
		Correct identified variabilities	Incorrect identified variabilities	Effectiveness	Knowledge level	#Queries to SPL specification	Correct identified variabilities	Incorrect identified variabilities	Effectiveness	Knowledge level	#Queries to SPL specification
#1	Mean	6.33	4.66	1.66	–	–	7.66	3.33	4.33	–	–
	Std. Dev.	2.05	2.05	4.10	-	–	2.68	2.68	5.37	–	–
	Median	5.50	5.50	0	–	–	8.50	2.50	6.00	–	–
#2	Mean	26.5	3.5	23.0	–	–	21.7	8.1	13.6	–	–
	Std; Dev.	3.4	3.4	6.7	–	–	5.1	4.9	10.0	–	–
	Median	28.5	1.5	27.0	–	–	22.0	8.0	14.0	–	–
#3	Mean	12.29	1.71	10.58	2.21	4.25	12.33	1.58	10.75	2.21	1.71
	Std. Dev.	1.74	1.57	3.13	0.98	5.71	2.07	2.02	4.07	0.87	3.12
	Median	13.0	1.00	12.00	2.50	0.50	13.50	0.50	13.00	2.00	0
#4	Mean	20.0	11.4	8.6	–	–	28.4	3.6	24.9	–	–
	Std. Dev.	8.2	8.2	16.3	–	–	6.4	6.4	12.9	–	–
	Median	19.0	9.0	10.	–	–	32.0	0	32.0	–	–

The main task for each subject was reading and understanding the e-commerce and Arcade Game Maker SPLs overviews. Then, the subjects annotated variabilities in the e-commerce and Arcade Game Maker class model (Table 20.11).

20.2.16.3 Experiment #3

The participation procedure differs from Study #2 mainly in the execution. Basically, a subject resolves and derives two specific products, one based on the e-commerce SPL and other based on the AGM SPL. Both products are represented in UML class diagrams modeled with PLUS or SMarty approaches, randomly distributed to subjects in an equal number.

Collected results from deriving products are summarized in Table 20.11, which shows the calculated effectiveness, the knowledge level, and the number of consultations to SPL specification documents. As the same statistical tests of Study #2 were performed, they were omitted herein.

20.2.16.4 Experiment #4

The main assessment tools were the banking and Arcade Game Maker sequence models with variabilities represented according to Ziadi et al. and SMarty approaches. Both, the Banking and Arcade Game Maker sequence models, were distributed and ordered in equal numbers and randomly. The subjects were warned to not change the order of SPLs and their respective resolutions. Table 20.11 summarized data collected.

The main task for each subject was reading and understanding the banking and Arcade Game Maker SPL overviews. Then, the subjects annotated variabilities in the banking and Arcade Game Maker sequence models.

20.2.16.5 Experiment #5

After answering the characterization questionnaire, the group of students was divided according to the approach (SMarty or PLUS) received by each participant. This division was made so that in each group the level of knowledge of the participants was similar so that there was no influence on the results obtained. Participants with PLUS stayed in the room to receive the training, while others waited outside. At the end of the training with the PLUS method, the participants were sent to another room, supervised by a person, and already started the configuration of the products and the tracing of elements between the diagrams. In sequence, the participants of the SMarty approach were trained and also started the configuration of the products and the tracing of elements between the diagrams. Table 20.12 summarized data collected.

Table 20.12 Result summarization for Experiments #5, #6, and #7

			Approach/method compared						SMarty					
#Id	Diagram	Item	Correct identified variabili-ties	Total	Effectiveness	Rastreab. use cases to classes	Rastreab. classes to use cases	#Queries to SPL specif.	Correct identified variabili-ties	Total	Effectiveness	Rastreab. use cases to classes	Rastreab. classes to use cases	#Queries to SPL specif.
#5	PLUS		PLUS						SMarty					
	Use case	Mean	9.77	10	0.97	0.63	–	0.22	9.88	10	0.98	0.61	–	0.33
		Std. dev.	0.53	0	0.05	0.46	–	2.12	0.31	0	0.03	0.40	–	0.81
		Median	10	10	1	1	–	0	10	10	1	0.75	–	0
	Class	Mean	9.94	10	0.99	–	0.22	0.22	8.11	10	0.81	–	0.44	0.33
		Std. dev.	0.22	0	0.02	–	0.34	2.12	2.96	0	0.29	–	0.46	0.81
		Median	10	10	1	–	0	0	9.5	10	0.95	–	0.25	0
#6	PLUS		PLUS						SMarty					
	Class	Mean	8.70	10	0.87	–	–	–	9.29	10	0.93	–	–	–
		Std. dev.	1.99	0	0.19	–	–	–	1.79	0	0.18	–	–	–
		Median	10	10	1	–	–	–	1	10	1	–	–	–
	Razavian and Khosravi		Razavian and Khosravi						SMarty					
	Component	Mean	8.58	10	0.86	–	–	–	8.82	10	0.88	–	–	–
		Std. dev.	1.90	0	0.19	–	–	–	2.37	0	0.23	–	–	–
		Median	9	10	0.9	–	–	–	10	10	1	–	–	–
#7	Ziadi et al.		Ziadi et al.						SMarty					
	Class	Mean	8.22	10	0.82	–	–	–	9.6	10	0.96	–	–	–
		Std. dev.	1.66	0	0.16	–	–	–	0.63	0	0.06	–	–	–
		Median	8	10	0.80	–	–	–	10	10	1	–	–	–
	Sequence	Mean	7.66	10	0.76	–	–	–	9.2	10	0.92	–	–	–
		Std. dev.	1.29	0	0.12	–	–	–	0.77	0	0.07	–	–	–
		Median	7	10	0.7	–	–	–	9	10	0.9	–	–	–

Each group received a form with the identification of the activity to be performed. Half of the group received the form to specify two product configurations using the MM SPL use case diagram with the SMarty approach, while the other half received the form to specify two products from the MM use case diagram and classes modeled with the PLUS approach. At the same time that the participants were generating the respective configurations, they pointed out the number of consultations to the instructional material.

20.2.16.6 Experiment #6

The group of students was divided according to the approach received (SMarty, PLUS, or Razavian and Khosravi) by each participant; this division was made in a way that in each group the level of knowledge of the participants was similar so that there was no influence on the results obtained. This information was obtained with the application of a characterization questionnaire. Participants who received the PLUS method stayed in the room to receive the training, while others waited outside. At the end of the training with the PLUS method, the participants were sent to another room, supervised by a person, and they started configuring the products. In sequence, the participants of the SMarty approach were trained and also started configuring the products. Finally, students of the Razavian approach received training and performed the configuration in sequence. Table 20.12 summarized data collected.

Each group received a form with the identification of the activity to be performed. One third of the group received the form to specify two product configurations using the class diagram and another one of MM SPL components with the SMarty approach, while another part received the form to specify a product from the class diagram with the PLUS method and the third part from the component diagram with the Razavian and Khosravi's approach. Participants configured the products, and those using the SMarty approach also analyzed traceability between models using the response form.

20.2.16.7 Experiment #7

In the same way, the participants were divided according to the approach (SMarty or Ziadi et al.) received by each one. The experiment was carried out individually.

Each person received a form with the identification of the activity to be performed. Half of the group received the form to specify two product configurations using the SPL AGM class and sequence diagram and to trace elements between the models with the SMarty approach, while the other part received the form to specify a product from the diagram of classes and sequence with the approach Ziadi et al. Table 20.12 presented the data collected.

20.2.17   Data Analysis Procedures (GD.17)

20.2.17.1   Experiment #1

- **Collected Data Normality Tests:** The Shapiro-Wilk [23] normality test was applied to the e-commerce sample (Table 20.11) providing the following results:

  - For PLUS with sample size (N) 12, mean value (μ) 1.6667, and standard deviation value (σ) 4.1096, it was obtained $p = 0.0827$, which means that with $\alpha = 0.05$, the sample is normal.
  - For the SMarty approach with sample size (N) 12, mean value (μ) 4.500, and standard deviation value (σ) 5.5453, it was obtained $p = 0.1378$, which means that with $\alpha = 0.05$, the sample is normal.

- **T Test for PLUS Sample and SMarty Sample:** This kind of test can be applied for both independent and paired samples. In the case of this study, sample for PLUS and sample for SMarty are independent.

  First, we obtained the value of T, which allows the identification of the range entered in the statistical table t (*student*). This value is calculated using the average of SMarty sample ($\mu1 = 4.5000$) and PLUS sample ($\mu2 = 1.6667$), standard deviation value of both ($\sigma1 = 5.5453$ and $\sigma2 = 4.1096$), and the sample sizes ($N = 12$). It obtained the value $t = 3.9699$.

  By taking the sample size ($N = 12$), we obtained the degree of freedom (df), which combined to the t value indicates which value of p in the t table must be selected. The p value is used to accept or reject the T test null hypothesis (H_0).

  By searching the index df and defining the value t at the t table (*student*), we found a value which is greater than 0.001, with a significance level (α) of 0.05. The relation between α and p produces $p = 0.001$, which is less than $\alpha = 0.05$. Therefore, the null hypothesis H_0 must be rejected and (H_1) must be accepted. It means that there is evidence that SMarty approaches are more effective in identifying and representing variability in use case models than PLUS. This result also corroborates to reject the null hypothesis (H_0) of this experimental study and accept the alternative hypothesis (H_1).

- **Correlation Between the Approach Effectiveness and the Subject Variability Characterization**

  - **Subject Variability Characterization Normality Test:** Shapiro-Wilk was applied to the data extracted from the subject characterization questionnaire of each approach:

    · For PLUS approach with sample size (N) 12, mean value of (μ) 2.2500, and standard deviation value of (σ) 0.9242, the calculated variability knowledge level was $p = 0.0002$. This value with $\alpha = 0.05$ indicates that the characterization data is normal.

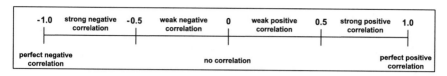

Fig. 20.9 Spearman's rank correlation scale. Adapted from [25]

· For the SMarty approach with sample size (N) 12, mean value of (μ) 2.9167, and standard deviation value of (σ) 1.1149, the calculated variability knowledge level was $p = 0.4333$. This value with $\alpha = 0.05$ indicates that the characterization data is non-normal.

- **Spearman's Correlation:** This technique was applied to verify whether there is a correlation between the effectiveness of each approach (PLUS and SMarty) and the level of knowledge of the subjects. Equation 20.4 shows the formula to calculate the Spearman ρ correlation, where n is the sample size:

$$\rho = \{1 - \frac{6}{n(n^2 - 1)} \sum_{i=1}^{n} d_i^2 \quad (20.4)$$

The analysis of Spearman's correlation takes into account the scale depicted in Fig. 20.9.

Table 20.13 presents the data needed to calculate the Spearman's correlation for PLUS and SMarty effectiveness and the subject level of variability knowledge.

Equations 20.5 and 20.6 present the calculation of the Spearman's correlation for PLUS (Corr.1) and SMarty (Corr.2) approaches, respectively:

$$\rho(Corr.1) = 1 - \frac{6}{12(12^2 - 1)} * 112 = 1 - 0.39 = 0.61 \} \quad (20.5)$$

$$\rho(Corr.2) = 1 - \frac{6}{12(12^2 - 1)} * 300 = 1 - 1.04 = -0.04 \} \quad (20.6)$$

Corr. 1 for PLUS showed that there was a positive strong correlation ($\rho = 0.61$). This means that the subjects' knowledge level on variability is important to correctly apply the PLUS method stereotypes for identifying and representing variability in use case models. On the other hand, Corr.2 showed that there was a negative weak correlation ($\rho = -0.04$). This means that the subjects' knowledge level on variability is not important to correctly apply the SMarty approach stereotypes for identifying and representing variability in use case models.

An important evidence of this analysis is that the PLUS method does not provide guidelines to identify and represent variabilities in use case

Table 20.13 Spearman's correlation between PLUS and SMarty effectiveness and the subjects' knowledge level

PLUS (X)							SMarty approach (Y)						
#	Effectiveness	r_{a1}	Knowledge level	r_{b3}	$r_{a1}-r_{b1}$	$d1^2$	#	Effectiveness	r_{a2}	Knowledge level	r_{b2}	$r_{a2}-r_{b2}$	$d2^2$
1	1.0	4	5	6	−2	4	1	−7.00	10	5	12	−2	4
2	9.0	6	3	1	5	25	2	7.0	7	4	5	2	4
3	7.00	3	2	2	1	1	3	5.00	3	4	7	−4	16
4	5.00	2	2	3	−1	1	4	5.0	11	4	8	3	9
5	5.00	5	2	4	1	1	5	11.00	5	3	1	4	16
6	5.00	10	2	5	5	25	6	7.00	6	3	4	2	4
7	−1.00	7	2	8	−1	1	7	−1.00	1	3	9	−8	64
8	−1.00	12	2	9	3	9	8	11.00	12	2	2	10	100
9	−3.00	8	2	10	−2	4	9	9.00	4	2	3	1	1
10	−3.00	9	2	11	−2	4	10	−1.00	2	2	10	−8	64
11	−3.00	11	2	12	−1	1	11	−1.00	8	2	11	−3	9
12	−1.00	1	1	7	−6	36	12	7.00	9	1	6	3	9

models. Thus, there is a need for previous variability knowledge to properly apply the PLUS stereotypes. In addition, the SMarty approach provides a set of guidelines, which may improve the activity of identification and representation of variabilities in use case models even for those subjects with lower variability knowledge level.

20.2.17.2 Experiment #2

Based on the results obtained by analyzing the application of the PLUS and SMarty approaches to the e-commerce and Arcade Game Maker SPLs, the following steps were taken for the identification of which methodology is more effective in identify and representing variabilities in SPL class models:

- Analyze and interpret the PLUS and SMarty collected data (sample) by means of the Shapiro-Wilk normality test and the Mann-Whitney-Wilcoxon to validate their statistical power.
- Analyze and interpret the correlation between the effectiveness of the approaches and the subjects' characterization questionnaire by means of Shapiro–Wilk normality tests and the Spearman's ranking correlation techniques.

- **Collected Data Normality Tests:** The Shapiro-Wilk [23] normality test was applied to the e-commerce and Arcade Game Maker samples providing the following results:

    PLUS approach(N=10)

    E-commerce SPL effectiveness: mean value (μ) 12.8, standard deviation value of (σ) 4.0855; the effectiveness for PLUS for the *e-commerce* SPL was $p = 0.0147$ for the *Shapiro-Wilk* normality test.

    In the *Shapiro-Wilk* test for a sample size *(N)* 10 with 95% of significance level ($\alpha = 0.05$), $p = 0.0147$ ($0.0147 < 0.05$), and calculated value of $W = 0.8005 < W = 0.8420$, the sample is considered non-normal.

    Arcade Game Maker SPL effectiveness: mean value (μ) 10.2, standard deviation value (σ) 2.9814; the effectiveness for PLUS for the *Arcade Game Maker* SPL was $p = 0.0002$ for the *Shapiro-Wilk* test.

    In the *Shapiro-Wilk* test, for ($\alpha = 0.05$), $p = 0.0002$ ($0.0147 < 0.05$), and calculated value $W = 0.6587 < W = 0.8420$, the sample is considered non-normal.

    Total effectiveness: mean value (μ) 23, standard deviation value of (σ) 6.8493; the total effectiveness for PLUS was $p = 0.0062$ for the *Shapiro-Wilk* test.

    Finally, for ($\alpha = 0.05$), $p = 0.0062$ ($0.0062 < 0.05$) and calculated value of $W = 0.7697 < W = 0.8420$, the sample is considered non-normal.

    SMarty Approach(N=10)

    E-commerce SPL effectiveness: mean (μ) 3.4, standard deviation of (σ) 8.4876; the effectiveness for the SMarty approach for the *e-commerce* SPL was $p = 0.3568$ for the *Shapiro-Wilk* test.

In the *Shapiro-Wilk* test, for a sample size of 10 with 95% of significance level ($\alpha = 0.05$), $p = 0.3568$ ($0.3568 > 0.05$), and calculated value $W = 0.9199 > W = 0.8420$, the sample is considered normal.

Arcade Game Maker SPL effectiveness: mean (μ) 10.2, standard deviation value of (σ) 3.1559; the effectiveness for the SMarty approach for *Arcade Game Maker* SPL was $p = 0.3254$ for the *Shapiro-Wilk* test.

In the *Shapiro-Wilk* test, for ($\alpha = 0.05$), $p = 0.3254$ ($0.3254 > 0.05$), and calculated value of $W = 0.9160 > W = 0.8420$, the sample is considered normal.

Total effectiveness: mean (μ) 10.2, standard deviation (σ) 3.1559; the total effectiveness for the SMarty approach was $p = 0.5286$ for the *Shapiro-Wilk* test.

Finally, for ($\alpha = 0.05$), $p = 0.5286$ ($0.5286 > 0.05$), and calculated value $W = 0.9777 > W = 0.8420$, the sample is considered normal.

- **Mann-Whitney-Wilcoxon for PLUS and SMarty Samples** This kind of test can be applied for both independent and paired samples. In the case of this study, PLUS and SMarty samples are independent, and both samples are non-normal.

  First, samples were unified into one; thus, that identifies the source of the same PLUS and SMarty approaches. Then, weights were assigned according to their position, such as if a PLUS sample value compared to a SMarty sample value are the same (draw), the weight is the same for both.

  Weights were summed up once they were distributed for each sample value.

  Table 20.14 presents the total value for each sample.

  For the values, it applied Eq. 20.7, shown as follows:

$$U(appch) = N_1 * N_2 + \frac{N_1 * (N_1 + 1)}{2} - \sum_{i=1}^{n} total_2 \tag{20.7}$$

where

- $U(appch)$ is the equation for each of the independent sample (appch).
- N_1 is the size of the sample for the X approach that will be calculated.
- N_2 is the size of the sample for the compared approach (Y).
- $total_2$ is the sum of the weight given for the compared approach.

Equations 20.8 and 20.9 present the values for X and Y approaches, respectively.

$$U(PLUS) = 10 * 10 + \frac{10 * (10 + 1)}{2} - 41 = 69.5 \tag{20.8}$$

$$U(SMarty) = 10 * 10 + \frac{10 * (10 + 1)}{2} - 85.5 = 114 \tag{20.9}$$

After calculating the equation for each approach, Eq. 20.10 is calculated:

$$U = min(U(PLUS), U(SMarty)) \tag{20.10}$$

Table 20.14 PLUS and SMarty samples for Mann-Whitney-Wilcoxon test

Mann-Whitney-Wilcoxon rank				
Sample				
PLUS (N1 = 10) SMarty (N2 = 10)				
#	Sample		PLUS approach	SMarty approach
1	28	PLUS	1.5	–
2	28	PLUS	1.5	–
3	28	PLUS	1.5	–
4	28	PLUS	1.5	–
5	28	PLUS	1.5	–
6	28	SMarty	–	1.5
7	28	SMarty	–	1.5
8	26	PLUS	3	–
9	22	PLUS	4.5	–
10	22	SMarty	–	4.5
11	20	PLUS	6	–
12	18	SMarty	–	7
13	16	SMarty	–	8
14	14	PLUS	9	–
15	12	SMarty	–	10
16	8	PLUS	11	–
17	6	SMarty	–	12
18	4	SMarty	–	13.5
19	4	SMarty	–	13.5
20	−2	SMarty	–	14
Total			41	85.5

where

- U is the value for the statistic test, which accepts or rejects the null hypothesis (H_0).
- $min(U(PLUS), U(SMarty))$ returns the smallest value between Eqs. 20.8 and 20.9, respectively.

Thus, applying the values obtained by Eqs. 20.8 and 20.9, we obtained:

$$U = min(U(X) = 69.5, U(Y) = 114) = 69.5 \qquad (20.11)$$

With the value of $U = 69.5$, which corresponds to PLUS, we conclude that there are significant differences which lead to reject the null hypothesis (H_0) and accepted the alternative hypothesis (H_1), where the PLUS approach is different from the Y approach.

The statistic test identifies if the two samples have the same distribution of their weights, in this study, the same effectiveness of their weights. There are evidences that both values are different (69.5 > 114), which lead to reject the null (H_0) hypothesis and accept the alternative hypothesis (H_1).

Therefore, with the statistical difference evidenced by Mann-Whitney-Wilcoxon test and the effectiveness value, we obtained evidences that PLUS is more effective than the SMarty approach, to represent variabilities in UML class model.

- **Correlation Between the Approach Effectiveness and the Subject Variability Characterization (Prior Subject SPL Knowledge Influence the Application of the Method/Approach to UML Class Models)**

  - *Knowledge level in SPL for subjects from X approach:* sample size of (N) 10, with mean (μ) 2.2, standard deviation value of (σ) 1.1967; the knowledge level of subjects was $p = 0.0450$ for the *Shapiro-Wilk* test.

    In the *Shapiro-Wilk*, for a sample size of 10 with 95% significance level ($\alpha = 0.05$), $p = 0.0450$ (0.0450 < 0.05), and calculated value $W = 0.8407$ less than $W = 0.8420$, the sample is considered non-normal.
  - *Knowledge level in SPL for subjects from Y approach:* sample size of (N) 10, with mean value (μ) 2.1, standard deviation of (σ) 0.8164, the knowledge level $p = 0.0166$ for the *Shapiro-Wilk* test.

    In this *Shapiro-Wilk* test, for a sample size of 10 with 95% significance level ($\alpha = 0.05$), for the Y approach, $p = 0.0166$ (0.0166 < 0.05) and calculated value $W = 0.8050$ greater than $W = 0.8420$, the sample is considered non-normal.
  - **Spearman's Correlation:** This technique was applied to identify whether there is a correlation between the effectiveness of each approach (PLUS and SMarty) and the level of knowledge of the subjects (Eq. 20.4). The calculation for each correlation, according to the approach and SPLs, is shown in Eqs. 20.12, 20.13, 20.14, and 20.15.

$$\rho(Corr.1) = 1 - \frac{6}{10(10^2 - 1)} * 100 = 1 - 0.60 = 0.39 \Big\} \qquad (20.12)$$

$$\rho(Corr.2) = 1 - \frac{6}{10(10^2 - 1)} * 126 = 1 - 0.76 = 0.23 \Big\} \qquad (20.13)$$

$$\rho(Corr.3) = 1 - \frac{6}{10(10^2 - 1)} * 92 = 1 - 0.55 = 0.44 \Big\} \qquad (20.14)$$

$$\rho(Corr.4) = 1 - \frac{6}{10(10^2 - 1)} * 104 = 1 - 0.63 = 0.37 \Big\} \qquad (20.15)$$

Thus, it obtained the following values for ρ as well as the classification scale by Spearman shown in Fig. 20.10:

| | Coefficient, r | |
Strength of Association	Positive	Negative
Weak	0.1 to 0.29	-0.1 to -0.29
Moderate	0.3 to 0.49	-0.3 to -0.49
Strong	0.5 to 1.0	-0.5 to -1.0

Fig. 20.10 Pearson's correlation scale

- *PLUS—e-commerce SPL:* $\rho = 0.39$, weak positive correlation
- *SMarty—e-commerce SPL:* $\rho = 0.23$, weak positive correlation
- *PLUS—Arcade Game Maker SPL:* $\rho = 0.44$, weak positive correlation
- *SMarty—Arcade Game Maker SPL:* $\rho = 0.37$, weak positive correlation

Analyzing the results obtained by means of Spearman's correlations, we can observe that all of them lie within the same range of classification scale. Note a difference between the value obtained for PLUS with relation to the SMarty approach.

For the *e-commerce* SPL, there is a difference of 0.16 more for PLUS, which indicates a higher correlation. Thus, the level of knowledge of participants who used the method may have outcome influence. For *Arcade Game Maker* SPL, there was a difference of 0.07 to PLUS, also leading to the same conclusion.

20.2.17.3   Experiment #3

- **Collected Data Normality Tests:** The Shapiro-Wilk normality test was applied to the e-commerce and AGM SPL samples. As the results for the normality test indicated for both samples a non-normal result, PLUS ($N = 24$) and the SMarty approach ($N = 24$), a nonparametric test was conducted for the sample to identify which approaches have a significant effectiveness in the interpretations leading to a correct instantiation of products.
- **Mann-Whitney-Wilcoxon Test:** The values identified in the test demonstrate that a significant difference between the samples does not exist. The p was calculated to be compared with the level of significance of 95% ($\alpha = 0.05$) to confirm the result. The calculated value for p was 0.533, and in comparison $p = 0.533 > \alpha = 0.05$ confirms that the null hypothesis (H_0) must be accepted. Therefore, there are no statistical difference between the median of the effectiveness in relation to the capacity of interpretation and generation of correct product configurations based on SPLs designed in UML class models with the PLUS method or with the SMarty 5.1 approach.

To evaluate the results of the calculated effectiveness, the number of checks in the SPL specification documents for the creation of the products was considered for analysis. These checks consequently influence the effectiveness for the approaches. Besides this, the Spearman's correlation test was calculated to analyze the possible influence of the subjects' previous knowledge, which may also influence the effectiveness.

20.2.17.4 Comparison of the Quantity of Checks in the SPL Description to Support the Understanding of Classes

The descriptive statistic of the quantity of classes in which additional information was checked by the subjects and induced to a correct selection, increasing the calculated effectiveness, is presented in Table 20.11.

These values correspond to each class assigned as "Yes" and led to the increase of the effectiveness. They were considered for analysis because, with consults to the description of the product to verify their meaning which, according to the interpretation of the subject, was not clear in the class model, it was possibly a correct selection of them. Thus, the consult resulted in a greater effectiveness for the approach, in which classes were consulted.

- **Normality Test:** The Shapiro-Wilk normality test [23] was also applied for the sample of the number of checks in the SPL description which led to a hit and, therefore, the increase of the effectiveness for their respective approach (Table 20.11). The results are presented as follows:

    Total of Checks for PLUS (N=24): The normality test indicated for a mean (N) of size 24 with 95% significance level ($\alpha = 0.05$), $p = 0.0001$ (0.0001 < 0.05), and a calculated value of $W = 0.7888 < W = 0.9160$, i.e., the sample was non-normal.

    Total of Checks for SMarty (N=24): The normality test indicated for a mean (N) of size 24 with 95% significance level ($\alpha = 0.05$), $p = 0.000001$ (0.000001 < 0.05), and a calculated value of $W = 0.6187 < W = 0.9160$, i.e., the sample was non-normal.

- **Test Mann-Whitney-Wilcoxon for the Sample of Checks in the Descriptions of the SPLs for PLUS and SMarty Approaches:** Since the set of hypotheses defined for the test was the same of Study #1, we can move forward to the analysis of the results. The values analyzed through the test presented a statistical difference. The value of p, to be compared with the significance level of 95% ($\alpha = 0.05$), was 0.048, that is, $p = 0.048 < \alpha = 0.05$. Therefore, the null hypothesis (H_0) was rejected, proving that the mean of checks for each approach influences the number of hits and, consequently, the calculated value for effectiveness.

    The lower the number of checks is, the greater is the support of the approach considered. PLUS presents a mean of 4.25 (total of 102) and SMarty presents a mean of 1.71 (total of 41). Thus, the number of checks indicates that, by the interpretation of the SPLs class models, there is support enough to guarantee a better understanding of the variabilities represented by SMarty.

Despite the reduced number of stereotypes to be applied, it is necessary to have additional checks to generate software product configurations with PLUS. On the other hand, the set of guidelines gives an additional support to interpret all the variabilities and elements graphically represented on the SPL class models, reducing the need of additional documents.

Besides the results obtained, the Spearman's correlation was calculated to verify if there is any influence in the effectiveness values with regard to the subject's previous knowledge that, summed up with the number of checks, may have influence in the effectiveness final value.

- **Correlation Among the Effectiveness of the Approaches and the Subject Variability Characterization**

  - **Spearman's Correlation:** The following values were calculated for ρ and applied in the Spearman's scale (Fig. 20.10):

    · *PLUS:* $\rho = 0.4956$—weak positive correlation
    · *SMarty approach:* $\rho = -0.1015$—weak negative correlation

    Analyzing the obtained results for the Spearman's correlation, we observed that PLUS had a weak positive correlation. In other words, it was more influenced by the knowledge level of the subjects in comparison with the results of the SMarty approach, which presented a weak negative correlation.

    An issue that may attenuate the influence of the knowledge of SMarty is the existence of *SMartProfile*. It supports both the approach application as the interpretation of the different elements of the UML models that it encompasses. This result is in agreement with a key approach for aspects such as time learning and applying new techniques.

    The need of training and the cost (in terms of time) for the adoption of new approaches in industry are issues that influence the adoption of new technologies. Thus, SMarty allows an easier adoption due to the supported elements and guidelines. The UML profile facilitates the use of modeling tools and the guidelines facilitate implementation and understanding of the represented elements, leading to more concise products.

20.2.17.5 Experiment #4

Based on the results obtained by analyzing the application of the Ziadi et al. and SMarty approaches to the banking and Arcade Game Maker SPLs, the following steps were taken to identify which methodology is more effective in identify and representing variabilities in SPL sequence models and if prior subject's SPL knowledge influence the application of the method/approach to UML sequence models:

- Analyze and interpret the Ziadi et al. and PLUS collected data (sample) by means of the Shapiro-Wilk normality test and the T test to validate their statistical power
- Analyze and interpret the correlation between the effectiveness of the approaches and the subjects' characterization questionnaire by means of Shapiro-Wilk normality tests and the Pearson's ranking correlation techniques.

- **Collected Data Normality Tests:** The Shapiro-Wilk [23] normality test was applied to the banking and Arcade Game Maker samples (Table 20.11) providing the following results:

    Ziadi et al. Approach (N=7)

    Banking SPL effectiveness: mean value (μ) 2.71, standard deviation value of (σ) 3.9175; the effectiveness for the Ziadi et al. approach for the *Banking* SPL was $p = 0.1333$ for the *Shapiro-Wilk* normality test.

    In the *Shapiro-Wilk* test for a sample size *(N)* 7 with 95% significance level ($\alpha = 0.05$), $p = 0.1333$ (0.1333 > 0.05), and calculated value of $W = 0.8538 > W = 0.8030$, the sample is considered normal.

    Arcade Game Maker SPL effectiveness: mean value (μ) 5.85, standard deviation value (σ) 14.4956; the effectiveness for the Ziadi et al. approach for the *Arcade Game Maker* SPL was $p = 0.4813$ for the *Shapiro-Wilk* test.

    In the *Shapiro-Wilk* test, for ($\alpha = 0.05$), $p = 0.4813$ (0.4813 > 0.05), and calculated value $W = 0.9215 > W = 0.8030$, the sample is considered non-normal.

    Total effectiveness: mean value (μ) 8.57, standard deviation value of (σ) 16.3432; the total effectiveness for X approach was $p = 0.9456$ for the *Shapiro-Wilk* test.

    Finally, for ($\alpha = 0.05$), $p = 0.9456$ (0.9456 > 0.05), and calculated value of $W = 0.9456 < W = 0.8030$, the sample is considered normal.

    The SMarty Approach (N=7)

    Banking SPL effectiveness: mean (μ) 4.71, standard deviation of (σ) 3.1036; the effectiveness for the SMarty approach for the *Banking* SPL was $p = 0.0111$ for the *Shapiro-Wilk* test.

    In the *Shapiro-Wilk* test, for a sample size of 7 with 95% significance level ($\alpha = 0.05$), $p = 0.0111$ (0.0111 < 0.05), and calculated value $W = 0.7444 > W = 0.8030$, the sample is considered non-normal.

    Arcade Game Maker SPL effectiveness: mean (μ) 20.14, standard deviation value of (σ) 10.3568; the effectiveness for the SMarty approach for *Arcade Game Maker* SPL was $p = 0.00003$ for the *Shapiro-Wilk* test.

    In the *Shapiro-Wilk* test, for ($\alpha = 0.05$), $p = 0.00003$ (0.00003 < 0.05), and calculated value of $W = 0.5276 > W = 0.8030$, the sample is considered normal.

Total effectiveness: mean (μ) 24.8, standard deviation (σ) 12.8666; the total effectiveness for the SMarty approach was $p = 0.0002$ for the *Shapiro-Wilk* test.

Finally, for ($\alpha = 0.05$), $p = 0.0002$ ($0.0002 > 0.05$), and calculated value $W = 0.5988 > W = 0.8030$, the sample is considered normal.

- **T Test:** This kind of test can be applied for both independent and paired samples [29]. In the case of this study, Ziadi et al. sample and SMarty sample are independent qs each sample size is less than 30 and both samples are normal.

   First, we obtained the value of T, which allows the identification of the range entered in the statistical table t (*student*). This value is calculated using the average of Ziadi et al. sample ($\mu 1 = 8.5714$) and sample X ($\mu 2 = 24.8571$), standard deviation value of both ($\sigma 1 = 16.3432$ and $\sigma 2 = 12.8666$), and the sample sizes ($N = 7$). It was obtained the value $t_{calculated} = 8.4014$.

   By taking the sample size ($N = 7$), we obtained the degree of freedom (df), which combined to the t value indicates which value of p in the t table must be selected. The p value is used to accept or reject the T test null hypothesis (H_0).

   By searching the index $df = 12$ and defining the value t at the t table (*student*), a value for critical t of 2.1790 ($t_{critial} = 2.1790$) was found, with a significance level (α) of 0.05. Thus, comparing the $t_{critial}$ with the $t_{calculated}$, the null hypothesis H_0 must be rejected, and (H_1) must be accepted ($t_{calculated}(8.4014) >= t_{critial}(2.1790)$).

   Therefore, based on the result from the T test, the null hypothesis (H_0) of this experimental study must be rejected, and the alternative hypothesis must be accepted. It means that the SMarty approach is more effective than the Ziadi et al. approach for representing variability at SPL sequence level for this experimental study.

- **Correlation Between the Approach Effectiveness and the Subjects' Variability Characterization**

   - **Knowledge Level in SPL for Subjects from Ziadi et al. Approach:** sample size of (N) 7, with mean (μ) 2.5, standard deviation value of (σ) 0.9574; the knowledge level of subjects was $p = 0.4817$ for the *Shapiro-Wilk* test.

     In the *Shapiro-Wilk*, for a sample size of 7 with 95% of significance level ($\alpha = 0.05$), $p = 0.4817$ ($0.4817 > 0.05$), and calculated value $W = 0.9215$ less than $W = 0.8030$, the sample is considered normal.

   - **Knowledge Level in SPL for Subjects from SMarty Approach:** sample size of (N) 7, with mean value (μ) 4.5, standard deviation of (σ) 0.5000; the knowledge level $p = 0.4817$ for the *Shapiro-Wilk* test.

     In this *Shapiro-Wilk* test, for a sample size of 7 with 95% significance level ($\alpha = 0.05$), for the SMarty approach, $p = 0.4817$ ($0.4817 < 0.05$), and calculated value $W = 0.9215$ greater than $W = 0.8030$, the sample is considered normal.

- **Pearson's Correlation:** This technique was applied to identify whether there is a correlation between the effectiveness of each approach (Ziadi et al. and SMarty) and the level of knowledge of the subjects for parametric values. The values from Table 20.16 were applied on Eq. 20.16 that shows the formula to calculate the Pearson's ρ correlation:

$$r = \frac{n(\Sigma ab) - (\Sigma a)(\Sigma b)}{\sqrt{[n(\Sigma a^2) - (\Sigma a)^2][n(\Sigma b^2) - (\Sigma b)^2]}} \tag{20.16}$$

The calculation for each correlation, according to the approach and SPLs, is shown in Eqs. 20.17 and 20.18:

$$r(Corr.1) = \frac{994 - 60 * 16}{\sqrt{13088 * 52}} = 0.0412 \Big\} \tag{20.17}$$

$$r(Corr.2) = \frac{4774 - 174 * 26}{\sqrt{8112 * 52}} = 0.3849 \Big\} \tag{20.18}$$

Thus, the following values for r as well as the classification scale by Pearson [24] and [8] shown in Fig. 20.10 were obtained:

· *Result correlation for Ziadi et al. and knowledge level in SPL: r = 0.0412*—weak positive relationship
· *Result correlation for SMarty and knowledge level in SPL: r = 0.3849*—moderate positive relationship

Analyzing the results obtained by means of Pearson's correlation, it was observed that for the X approach the knowledge level in SPL of each subject, there is a weak positive relationship and for the Y approach, there is a moderate positive relationship. Thus, the knowledge level in SPL may have weakly influenced the process of representation of variability in UML sequence models (Table 20.15).

Table 20.15 Pearson's correlation for knowledge level of subjects for the X and Y approaches

Ziadi et al. (X)			SMarty approach (Y)		
#	Effectiveness	Knowledge level	#	Effectiveness	Knowledge level
1	6	51	1	26	4
2	10	1	2	32	5
3	−24	2	3	32	4
4	30	2	4	32	5
5	14	3	5	26	2
6	24	3	6	32	3
7	0	4	7	−6	3

20.2.17.6   Experiment #5

Effectiveness of Approaches

- **Collected Data Normality Tests:** For the normality test of the effectiveness samples, the Shapiro-Wilk test was applied, both for the effectiveness samples with use case and class diagrams of the two approaches. The samples obtained $p >$ (= 0.05), therefore not being normally distributed. Thus, the nonparametric Mann-Whitney-Wilcoxon test was conducted for the samples to indicate which approach had the best effectiveness in the configuration of products.

- **Mann-Whitney-Wilcoxon Test**
  Use Case Diagram: The calculated value for p was 0.1898, and in comparison $p = 0.1898 > \alpha = 0.05$ confirming that the null hypothesis ($H0_{efet}$) cannot be refuted. Thus, there is no statistically significant difference between the effectiveness samples in configuring products from use case diagrams. The Cohen's test was applied to the product effectiveness samples configured with the PLUS method and the SMarty approach from a use case diagram, in order to know the significance and difference of the samples. The value obtained for d was -0.4844 and indicates that the difference in values is small.
  Class Diagram: The value identified in the test was $p = 0.02797$ and in comparison $p = 0.02797 < \alpha = 0.05$ confirming that there is no evidence that the null hypothesis ($H0_{efet}$) should be accepted and thus PLUS method provides better support in setting up effective products from class diagrams. For the class diagram, the Cohen's test was also applied, and the value obtained for d was 0.5168, indicating an average difference between the effectiveness samples in the configuration of products.

Number of Queries to Materials
The number of consultations in the material available on the MM SPL, the PLUS method, and the SMarty approach was accounted for in order to understand which of the two approaches offers a clearer and easier understanding for interpreting the variability modeling in use cases. Thus, the smaller the number of consultations, the more it is understood that the approach offers greater comprehensibility.

- **Collected Data Normality Test:** The Shapiro-Wilk test was applied to samples of the number of consultations with the materials.
  PLUS method queries (N = 23):
  The normality test indicated for a sample size of 23 with 95% significance ($\alpha = 0.05$), $p = 3.296e{-}8 (< 0.05)$. The sample is therefore not normally distributed.
  SMarty approach queries (N = 18)
  The normality test indicated, as for the PLUS sample, for a sample of size 18 with 95% significance ($\alpha = 0.05$), $p = 4.344e{-}7 (< 0.05)$. The sample is therefore not normally distributed.

As both tests resulted in samples not normally distributed, the nonparametric Mann-Whitney-Wilcoxon test was conducted for the samples to indicate whether there is a significant difference in the number of queries to the materials.

- **Mann-Whitney-Wilcoxon Test:** The values analyzed through the test did not show a statistical difference. The p value, to be compared with a significance level of 95% ($\alpha = 0.05$), was 0.6349.

  Thus, $p = 0.6349 > \alpha = 0.05$; the null hypothesis ($H0_{cons}$) could not be refuted, providing evidence that an understandability relationship could not be established based on the number of consultations to the materials of each approach.

- **Correlation Between Effectiveness and Knowledge Level of UML Participants**

  To establish whether there is a correlation between the effectiveness obtained by each participant and their level of knowledge in UML, Spearman's correlation was used, since there was a conversion from ordinal nominal scales to discrete values.

  The following values were calculated separately for each diagram using the Spearman's scale (Fig. 20.10):

  – **Use Case Diagram:**

    · PLUS approach: $p = 0.32$ weak positive correlation
    · SMarty approach: $p = 0.16$ weak positive correlation

  – **Class Diagram:**

    · PLUS approach: $p = 0.24$ weak positive correlation
    · SMarty approach: $p = 0.41$ weak positive correlation

  We want the correlation value to be as small as possible so that the approach is easier to understand. Regarding the use case diagram, in the case of the PLUS method, the participant's knowledge level has greater influence than SMarty's knowledge level. As for the class case diagram, for the SMarty approach, the participant's knowledge level has greater influence than the PLUS knowledge level.

- **Effectiveness in Tracking Elements Between Diagrams**

  – **Normality Test:** The Shapiro-Wilk test was applied to test the normality of the samples of hits of traced elements, both for the samples tracing elements from the use case diagram to the class diagram and from the class-to-use-case diagram. Samples obtained $p < (\alpha = 0.05)$, therefore not being normally distributed. Thus, the nonparametric Mann-Whitney-Wilcoxon test was conducted for the samples to indicate which approach had the best effectiveness in the traceability of elements between the diagrams.

- **Mann-Whitney-Wilcoxon Test:**
- $UseCases \rightarrow Classes$

    The calculated value for p was 0.6442, and in comparison, p = 0.6442 > α = 0.05 confirming that the null hypothesis ($H0_{efet}$) cannot be refuted. Thus, there is no statistically significant difference between the effectiveness of tracing elements from the use case diagram to the class one, using the SMarty approach or the PLUS method.
- $Classes \rightarrow UseCases$

    The value identified in the test was p = 0.176 and in comparison p = 0.176 < α = 0.05, confirming that there is no evidence that the null hypothesis ($H0_{efet}$) should be accepted. This means that the SMarty approach provides better support in tracing elements from the class diagram to the use case diagram.

20.2.17.7 Experiment #6

20.2.17.8 Effectiveness at Configuring Products

- **Shapiro-Wilk Normality Test:** This test revealed our three samples are non-normally distributed as all p-values had values greater than 0.05. Therefore, we chose the nonparametric Mann-Whitney-Wilcoxon hypothesis test for the effectiveness of approaches at configuring products according to the design type of the experiment.

- **Mann-Whitney-Wilcoxon Hypothesis Test:** We tested two groups of samples, one for class diagrams with SMarty and PLUS and one for component diagrams with SMarty and Razavian and Khosravi's method.

    For **class diagrams**, we obtained p = 0.2539, which is greater than α = 0.05. This means we could not reject the null hypothesis (H0). Then, we applied the Cohen's test for effect size analysis. We obtained d = −0.310, which indicates a small difference among obtained values.

    For **component diagrams**, we obtained p = 0.3884, which is greater than α = 0.05. This means we could not reject the null hypothesis (H0). Then, we applied the Cohen's test for effect size analysis. We obtained d = 0.109, which indicates a small difference among obtained values.

    By analyzing the case of class diagrams, SMarty had effectiveness mean of 0.93 and standard deviation of 0.18, whereas PLUS had effectiveness mean of 0.87 and standard deviation of 0.20—both with median 1 for effectiveness. However, SMarty had 13 configured products with effectiveness of 1.0, whereas PLUS had 10, which justifies their means and standard deviations. Therefore, although H0 for class diagrams could not be rejected, SMarty had a slight advantage at configuring products than PLUS, mostly because we suppose (i) SMarty provides a process for guiding users on identifying, representing, and configuring products, which makes it easier to configure products; (ii) SMarty provides several different stereotypes for class diagrams, which might lead to a more precise configuration; and (iii) PLUS has only three stereotypes possible to be applied to class diagrams, which makes it easier to configure products.

For component diagrams, SMarty had effectiveness mean of 0.88, standard deviation of 0.24, and median of 1. Razavian and Khosravi's method had mean of 0.86, standard deviation of 0.19, and median of 0.9. However, SMarty had ten configured products with effectiveness of 1.0, whereas Razavian and Khosravi's method had 08, which means SMarty has at least 50% configured products with effectiveness of 1.0. Therefore, although H0 for component diagrams could not be rejected, SMarty had a slight advantage at configuring products than Razavian and Khosravi's method. We have the same assumptions of class diagrams, except the higher number and less simplicity of stereotypes of Razavian and Khosravi's method compared to PLUS.

20.2.17.9 Effectiveness vs. Participants' Knowledge

We wanted to measure the influence of UML's previous knowledge on the effectiveness of each approach. To do so, we correlated the effectiveness and the participants' knowledge level using the Spearman's ranking correlation (ρ) technique, as follows:

- For **class diagrams**, PLUS obtained $\rho = 0.32$ (weak positive), and SMarty obtained $\rho = 0.41$ (weak positive).
- For **component diagrams**, SMarty obtained $\rho = 0.26$ (weak positive), and Razavian and Khosravi's method obtained $\rho = 0.0$ (no correlation).

Analyzing such correlations we identified, Razavian and Khosravi's method effectiveness has no correlation to the participants' knowledge on UML, which is a desired result; the lesser the knowledge required, the higher the comprehensibility. All other correlations are positive weak, which means there is a minimal correlation between approaches and the level of participants' knowledge on UML, an undesired result.

In this research question, we analyzed which approach had less influence by the previous knowledge of their participants on UML. To do so, we correlated obtained effectiveness to the level of knowledge. Therefore, we assume the lower the correlation, the lower is the level of knowledge required for users of a given approach.

By analyzing class diagram correlation, SMarty had correlation value (ρ) 0.41 and PLUS 0.32. This means, SMarty required more knowledge on UML than PLUS. This might be justified as SMarty provides stereotypes for representing variability in all kinds of class relationships, such as aggregation and composition. This might require more knowledge on UML at configuring which variants to select.

With regard to component diagrams, SMarty had correlation value (ρ) of 0.26 and Razavian and Khosravi's method of 0.0. This means, Razavian and Khosravi's method requires practically no knowledge on UML at configuring products. On the other hand, SMarty requires some level of knowledge, especially because we believe it has a large set of stereotypes for representing variability in component diagram elements, such as components, interfaces, ports, and connectors.

20.2.17.10   Traceability in Diagram Elements

At the beginning of this study, our idea was to analyze traceability capabilities among these three approaches. However, PLUS and Razavian and Khosravi's method do not provide any mechanism for tracing elements in respective diagram elements. Therefore, in this section, we analyze only the SMarty traceability mechanism.

We provided SMarty participants two questions on traceability both of them with a Likert scale:

- Question 1: "**Assuming that in a product configuration the functionality related to media sharing is excluded from the class diagram, are changes/impacts in the component diagram identifiable with support of the SMarty approach?**"
- Question 2: "**If the MediaMgr component is excluded from the component diagram in a possible product configuration, is it possible for SMarty to identify the impacts that this change would have on the class diagram?**"

To answer question 1, participants should analyze whether and how is it possible to trace variabilities from class diagram elements (lower level of abstraction) to component diagram elements (higher level of abstraction). Then, to answer question 2, participants should do the opposite, from component diagram elements to class diagram elements.

Traceability was analyzed for SMarty, as it provides a means to it. We analyzed it in both directions: from class diagram elements (lower level of abstraction) to component diagram elements (higher level of abstraction) and vice-versa.

From **class to component**, 88.2% of participants agree with SMarty supports identifying and understanding impacts at component diagram level when changes are made at the class level. Only 11.8% partially disagrees with it. None of them totally disagrees with it. It means most of participants had the perception that using the realizes+ tagged value of the <<variability>> stereotype provides a means to trace variabilities in higher level of abstraction elements.

From **component to class**, 100% of participants agrees with SMarty supports identifying and understanding impacts at class diagram level when changes are made at the component level. It means all participants had the perception that using the realizes- tagged value of the <<variability>> stereotype provides a means to trace variabilities in lower level of abstraction elements.

20.2.17.11 Experiment #7

20.2.17.12 Effectiveness at Configuring Products

The results collected from the configuration of the products by each participant are shown in Table 20.12, which refers to Ziadi et al. and SMarty. Such table lists information on the correct resolved variabilities (Corr), the total number of variability for a given diagram (total), and the effectiveness (Eff) of each approach.

- **Collected Data Normality Test:** We applied the Shapiro-Wilk test to the SMarty and Ziadi et al. effectiveness samples for class and sequence diagrams. We can observe all samples obtained $p < (\alpha = 0.05)$; therefore, they do not follow a normal distribution:
  - Ziadi et al. for class diagram (N = 15): $p = 0.0071$
  - Ziadi et al. for sequence diagram (N = 15): $p = 0.02453$
  - SMarty for class diagram (N = 15): $p = 0.00011$
  - SMarty for sequence diagram (N = 15): $p = 0.0043$

  Based on the non-normality of samples, we decided to apply the Mann-Whitney-Wilcoxon hypothesis test for the samples to indicate whether there is a significant difference between them according to the hypotheses established, as follows:
  For class diagram effectiveness samples:
  The calculated value for p was 0.0299 ($<\alpha = 0.05$). Therefore, we could reject $H0_{eff\_cls}$. It means there is a significant difference between the effectiveness of Ziadi et al. and SMarty samples for effectiveness in configuring products from class diagrams.
  For sequence diagram effectiveness samples:
  The value of p calculated in the test was 0.001846 ($<\alpha = 0.05$). Thus, we could reject $H0_{eff\_seq}$. It means there is a significant difference between the effectiveness of Ziadi et al. and SMarty samples for effectiveness in configuring products from sequence diagrams.

- **Effect Size**
  We calculated the effect size of each hypothesis test to confirm the strength of respective samples, as follows:
  For class diagram effectiveness:
  The Cohen d test was applied, and we obtained -1.05, which indicates a large difference between the samples for class diagrams.
  For sequence diagram effectiveness: For the sequence diagram, the Cohen's test returned the value -1.44, which indicates a large difference between the samples of effectiveness in the configuration of products from sequence diagrams.
  Observing the results of this study, we note a great difference between samples in terms of effectiveness.

Analyzing the **results on class diagrams**, SMarty had a mean of effectiveness of 0.96, a standard deviation of 0.06, and a median of 1.0, while Ziadi et al. obtained a mean of 0.82, a standard deviation of 0.16, and a median of 0.8. SMarty participants configured ten products with 100% effectiveness, which represents more than half of the sample (median $= 1.0$). On the other hand, Ziadi et al. obtained only six products totally correctly configured, which means less than 50% of the sample (median $= 0.8$).

Although SMarty had better results than Ziadi et al. for class diagrams effectiveness, SMarty participants experienced partially wrong configuration of certain products, which indicates a lack of total comprehensibility of the configuration process of the approach. Therefore, we provide and discuss new guidelines to aid in this process.

In relation to the **sequence diagram**, SMarty obtained an effectiveness mean of 0.92, a standard deviation of 0.07, and a median of 0.9, whereas Ziadi et al. obtained a mean of 0.76, a standard deviation of 0.12, and a median of 0.7. SMarty participants configured six products with 100% effectiveness, which represents less than half of the sample (median $= 0.9$). Ziadi et al. obtained only two products totally correctly configured, which means much less than 50% of the sample (median $= 0.7$).

We understand sequence diagrams are more difficult to understand and to configure products with both approaches. Comparing both approaches, SMarty obtained way better results than Ziadi et al. However, especially for SMarty, this result corroborates the conclusion on the class diagrams about the lack of guidelines to support its configuration process.

All of these results provide evidence on the advantage of SMarty over Ziadi et al. We assume participants who used SMarty had better results because:

- **SMarty provides a process to guide the user on representation and identification of variability.**
- **SMarty provides several stereotypes for class and sequence diagrams, not available in Ziadi et al., which may make product configuration easier.**

- **Correlation Between Effectiveness and Participants' Knowledge Level (RQ2)**

  In this section, we want to check whether there is a correlation between the effectiveness and the participant level of knowledge. To do so, we used the Spearman's correlation technique (Eq. 20.4) as we performed a conversion of nominal scales to discrete values regarding the participant knowledge.

  We then found the following values for each diagram:

  - **For class diagrams:**

    - Ziadi et al.: $\rho = 0.77$ a strong positive correlation
    - SMarty: $\rho = 0.27$ a weak positive correlation

- **For sequence diagrams:**

  · Ziadi et al.: $\rho = 0.66$ a strong positive correlation
  · SMarty: $\rho 0.05$ a weak positive correlation

We understand the lower the correlation ρ value, the lesser the influence of the participant knowledge on the obtained effectiveness. Therefore, SMarty obtained better results than Ziadi et al. as the former demands less previous knowledge to configure products and to trace variabilities in both class and sequence diagrams. This is particularly important to SMarty newcomers to comprehend its syntax and semantics for modeling variability in UML-based SPLs.

In this research question, we analyzed which approach had the least influence of the participants' prior knowledge. Therefore, we correlated the effectiveness obtained to the level of knowledge.

When analyzing the correlation of the **class diagrams**, SMarty had ρ value 0.27 and Ziadi et al. 0.77. With regard to Ziadi et al., the same knowledge tends to lead to a specific effectiveness value at configuring products. It means the participant's knowledge highly determines his/her effectiveness. On the other hand, in the SMarty approach, there is no tendency of the same knowledge to determine the effectiveness. For SMarty, it is important as it provides numerous stereotypes Ziadi et al. does not provide, and SMarty provides a process to identify and represent variabilities, which may influence the effectiveness at configuring products.

With relation to **sequence diagrams**, SMarty had ρ value 0.05 and Ziadi et al. 0.66. As SMarty had a way less correlation ρ value than Ziadi et al., the same rationale can be used to interpret their results.

Therefore, we can summarize the results as follows: **the participant's knowledge seems to be irrelevant to SMarty at configuring product from both class and sequence diagrams**.

- **Traceability**

  As the Ziadi et al. approach has no traceability mechanisms, we analyzed such mechanisms in SMarty.

  To do so, we defined two Likert-scaled questions to the experiment participants who used the SMarty approach:

  - **Question #1:** Assuming that in a product configuration the features related to the Game Sprite are excluded from the class diagram, can you observe/identify the respective changes/impacts in the sequence diagram?
  - **Question #2:** If **play game** does not exist in the sequence diagram, can you observe/identify the respective changes/impacts in the class diagram?

  We summarize the answers in Table 20.16.

  As observed in Table 20.16, 13 (86.66%) participants agree changes can be traced to sequence diagrams when a related variability element is modified in a

Table 20.16 SMarty round-trip traceability to/from class and sequence diagrams

Likert labels	Count	Percentage (%)
Question #1: class to sequence		
I totally agree	8	53.33
I partially agree	5	33.33
I partially disagree	2	13.33
I totally disagree	0	0.00
Total	15	100.0
Question #2: sequence to class		
I totally agree	6	40.00
I partially agree	5	33.30
I partially disagree	3	20.00
I totally disagree	1	6.70
Total	15	100.0

class diagram by using the <<variability>> attribute `realizes-`. We assume sequence diagrams have lower abstraction level than class diagrams.

The same conclusion is valid for tracing elements from sequence to class diagrams as 11 (73.33%) participants could observe/identify such changes by means of the attribute `realizes+`.

Based on these results, we understand traceability in SMarty is promising; thus, we need to reach 100% satisfaction of its users.

We analyzed traceability for SMarty in a round-trip flavor, from class to sequence diagrams and from sequence to class diagrams.

From **class to sequence diagrams**, 86.66% of participants agree with SMarty support at identifying and tracing the impacts at the sequence diagram level when changes are made at the class level. This means the majority of participants really comprehend the SMarty mechanism to trace variabilities from a higher abstraction level diagram (class) to a lower level diagram (sequence) by means of the <<variability>> attribute `realizes-`. However, it seems there were certain issues making it difficult to a small portion (13.33%) of the participants to trace variabilities.

With regard to **sequence to class diagrams**, 73.3% of participants agree with SMarty support at identifying and tracing the impacts at the class diagram level when changes are made at the sequence level. Again, the majority of participants really comprehend the SMarty mechanism to trace variabilities from a lower abstraction level diagram (sequence) to a higher level diagram (class) by means of the <<variability>> attribute `realizes+`.

Unfortunately, for the traceability analysis, we did not ask any open questions to participants to express their thoughts on it, because we did not want to extend the time for the participation in the experiment, thus causing more fatigue threats.

20.2.18 Mortality Rate (GD.18)

No participant's result was excluded for the experiments, except for Experiment #5. Three participant's results were excluded for the Experiment #5 by two reasons: the participant handed in the blank answer form or the number of effectiveness obtained was far below the average effectiveness.

20.2.19 Statistical Data Analysis Tools (GD.19)

The Spearman's correlation was calculated in PSPP tool, while other statistic tests were calculated with R.

20.2.20 Effect Size (GD.20)

20.2.20.1 Experiment #1

T test applied for the sample of effectiveness in identification and representation of variabilities collected a value of $p = 0.001$, which is less than $\alpha = 0.05$. Therefore, there is evidence that SMarty is more effective in identifying and representing variability in use case diagrams than the PLUS method.

20.2.20.2 Experiment #2

We applied the Mann-Whitney-Wilcoxon test, which identifies if the two samples have the same distribution of their weights. There are evidences that both values are different ($69.5 > 114$), which leads to reject the null (H_0) hypothesis and accepted the alternative hypothesis (H_1). It means that the PLUS method is more effective than the SMarty approach for representing variability at SPL class level for this experimental study.

20.2.20.3 Experiment #3

The Mann-Whitney-Wilcoxon was applied. The lower the number of checks is, the greater is the support of the approach considered. PLUS method presents a mean of 4.25 (total of 102), and the SMarty approach presents a mean of 1.71 (total of 41). Thus, the number of checks indicates that by the interpretation of the SPL class models, there is support enough to guarantee a better understanding of the variabilities represented by SMarty.

Despite the reduced number of stereotypes to be applied, it is necessary to have additional checks to generate software product configurations with PLUS. On the other hand, the set of guidelines gives an additional support to interpret all the variabilities and elements graphically represented on the SPL class models, reducing the need of additional documents.

20.2.20.4 Experiment #4

The T test was applied, and based on critical value found (t of 2.1790), SMarty approach is more effective than Ziadi et al. approach for representing variability at SPL sequence level for this experimental study.

20.2.20.5 Experiment #5

Use Case Diagram
Cohen's test was applied to the effectiveness samples of the products configured with the PLUS method and the SMarty approach from a use case diagram, in order to know the significance and difference of the samples. The value obtained for d was −0.4844 and indicates that the difference in values is small.

Class Diagram
For the class diagram, the Cohen's test was also applied, and the value obtained for d was 0.5168, indicating an average difference between the samples of effectiveness in the configuration of products.

20.2.20.6 Experiment #6

Class Diagram
Cohen's test was applied to the effectiveness samples of the products configured with the PLUS method and the SMarty approach from a class diagram, in order to know the significance and difference of the samples. The value obtained for d was −0.310 and indicates that the difference in values is small.

Component Diagram
For the component diagram, the Cohen's test was also applied, and the value obtained for d was 0.109, indicating an insignificant difference between the samples of effectiveness in the configuration of products.

20.2.20.7   Experiment #7

Class Diagram
Cohen's test was applied to the effectiveness samples of the products configured with the Ziadi et al. method and the SMarty approach using a class diagram, in order to know the significance and difference of the samples. The value obtained for d was −1.05 and indicates that the difference in values is large.

Sequence Diagram
For the sequence diagram, the Cohen's test was also applied, and the value obtained for d was −1.44, indicating a large difference between the samples of effectiveness in the configuration of products.

Considering all values, the biggest difference found by the Cohen's test was −1.05 in Experiment #5 with class diagrams, which indicated a large difference between the effectiveness samples compared, whereas the value 0.109 was the lowest value, indicating an insignificant difference in the effectiveness values in Experiment #6 with component diagrams.

20.2.21   Results in the Point of View of Researchers and Practitioners (GD.21)

From the professionals point of view, the implementation of the tool based on the improvement of SMarty, by this study, brings an essential *feature* and that rare case tools of the most varied purposes provide traceability [1, 4, 28] of the artifacts produced during the software development process. This *feature* has an important impact differential on software projects as it allows, for example, to identify inconsistencies between diagram elements and requirements, in addition to allowing the possibility of understanding *round-trip* design decisions.

20.2.22   Implications of Developed Treatments (GD.22)

The evaluated and improved treatment was the SMarty approach with regard to product configuration and traceability and UML class diagram guidelines. For that, SMarty users can now count on these two new *features* of the approach, which makes it particularly more attractive other similar approaches.

20.2.23 Threats to Validity Identified in the Experiment (GD.23)

Below we present a summary of the identified threats to validity for the seven experimental studies:

1. **Threats to Conclusion Validity:** The major concern is the sample size, which must be increased in prospective studies and the academic level of the participants, with no professional experience.

2. **Threats to Construct Validity:** Study instrumentation and its validity are major potential construct threats to this experiment. To mitigate it, we performed a pilot project with several students and a lecturer of Software Engineering from the State University of Maringá (UEM) with grounded knowledge in SPL/variability aiming at evaluation of such instrumentation and potential improvements.

3. **Threats to Internal Validity:** We dealt with the following issues:

   - **Differences Among Subjects:** As we took into consideration a small sample, variations in the subject skills were reduced by performing the tasks in the same order. The subjects' experience had approximately the same level for UML modeling and variability concepts.
   - **Fatigue Effects:** On average, the experiment lasted at least 100 minutes; thus, fatigue was considered not relevant.
   - **Influence Among Subjects:** It could not be really controlled. Subjects took the experiment under supervision of a human observer. We believe that this issue did not affect the internal validity.

4. **Threats to External Validity:** Two threats were detected.

   - **Instrumentation:** Failing to use real use case models, all the used SPL is not commercial. More experimental studies must be conducted using real PLs, developed by industry.
   - **Subjects:** Lecturers and graduate students of Software Engineering were selected. However, more experiments taking into account industry practitioners must be conducted, allowing to generalizing the study results. The level of knowledge of the participants can also be a threat, since some have more knowledge than others about related topics (SPL and variability in SPL); however, authors such as Falessi et al. [6] discuss the importance of using students in experimental studies and emphasize that no one population should be considered better than another.

20.2.24 Experimental Package Source (GD.24)

For Experiments from #1 to #4, experimental package sources are available at http://ws2.din.uem.br/~smarty/trab1.html. The experimental package for Experiment #5 is available at https://doi.org/10.5281/zenodo.4308863, for Experiment #6 at https://doi.org/10.5281/zenodo.4304279, and for Experiment #7 at https://doi.org/10.5281/zenodo.3569423.

20.2.25 Experimental Template Used to Conduct, Plan, or Document the Experiment (GD.25)

The seven experimental studies were based on the template proposed by Wohlin [30].

20.3 SMarty Improvements Based on the Experimental Evaluations

The experimental set of studies, besides from possible investigation about the effectiveness of SMarty in UML diagrams, also allowed the conduction of improvements in the approach. This section presents the evolution of the SMarty approach performed based on the results of Experiment #2 and Experiment #7 mainly.

20.3.1 Evolution of the SMarty Approach for Identification and Representation of Variabilities

Experiment #2, in the context of identification and representation of variabilities, provided results to make possible a set of improvements for SMarty. The participants' feedbacks that allowed the conduction of such improvements are described below:

- **E-Commerce SPL**: Subjects who applied the SMarty approach reported difficulties in identifying variabilities for the *e-commerce* SPL class model as there is no elements of class modeling, such as inheritance, aggregation, and generalization. Thus, there is a need to analyze the *e-commerce* SPL toward incorporating new guidelines to SMartyProcess to deal with models, such as in the *e-commerce*SPL, developed by Gomaa [7].
- Training on the Application of the Approaches: Subjects indicated that they need more time for training and application of exercises to gather more knowledge on the approaches.
- Amount of Stereotypes of Each Approach: Subjects questioned the difference between the approaches, since SMarty has several more stereotypes than the PLUS method.
- Arrangement of PL Models for Identifying Variabilities: The *e-commerce* model was more complex than the AGM model, and it was the first model to be solved.

Subjects indicated to change the order, setting the AGM SPL model class to be taken before the *e-commerce* model.

By taking these considerations, some actions were established to improve SMarty:

- New guidelines were added to the SMartyProcess, encompassing the level of abstraction and elements of the *e-commerce* and facilitating the use of SMarty templates for UML class elements.
- It was realized that with a few stereotypes, PLUS tends to be more effective in their application. However, when trying to resolve the variabilities to generate specific products, PLUS is more error-prone than SMarty, as PLUS represents coarse grain variabilities, whereas SMarty represents fine-grained variabilities.

Based on the feedback of the subjects and conclusions about the results, new guidelines for class models were proposed for SMarty.

- **CL2.** Class model elements with associations were their attributes have aggrerationKind as none or do not represent aggregation or composition, suggest mandatory or optional variants.
- **CL2.1.** Class model elements with the value of associations multiplicity in the opposite side equals to $*$ (zero or more) or $0..n$, where n is any integer different from zero, suggest optionals variants classes or an optional classes.

The remaining guidelines for class models (CL3 and CL4) have not changed.

For guideline CL1, it was inserted to indicate suggestion, since they should not overlap the indications present in the description of the SPL, and some participants used the same as a final statement for the classification of variants in the class model.

Guideline CL2 received a guideline supplement, the CL2.1, that supports the process of identifying the classes that represent optional variants. CL2.1 was created based on the model of *e-commerce* SPL, in which there is a near absence of relationships presented in CL1, which hampered the identification of such variants.

20.3.2 Evolution of the SMarty Approach for Configuration and Support for Traceability

With the results of Experiment #7, we understand SMarty has much to evolve.

An improvement idea is to use icons instead of stereotypes to represent variability, which can graphically facilitate the understanding of modeled variability elements. Icons are supported for most general-purpose UML tools; thus, it does not jeopardize such graphical mechanism.

Another point is the obtained results provide subsidies for a tool, which is current under development to support UML-based SPLs, taking into account any UML metamodel-based profile for representing variabilities, such as Ziadi et al. and Gomaa [7].

Configuring a valid product is not a trivial task, even using a simple SPL. Although we provided training for the participants, as well as documentation for consultation, they still faced difficulties in correctly configuring the products in both approaches. Thus, we understand that an automated tool will mitigate such a problem. To start supporting this, we provide guidelines for product configuration as follows ("C" stands for configuration):

- C.1—Select the product to configure all mandatory UML elements, marked with the stereotype <<mandatory>>.
- C.2—Resolve the variation points tagged with <<variationPoint>> according to the variability notation, observing the minimum and the maximum number of variants that must be chosen. With relation to the choice of variants, the following may happen:
  - C.2.1—If variants are tagged with <<alternative_OR>>, at least one of them must be selected to resolve its variation point. In case variants are tagged with <<alternative_XOR>>, only one of them must be selected.
- C.3—A given variant (V1) with a <<requires>> relationship with another variant (V2) when V1 is selected to be part of a given product; V2 must also be selected for such product.
- C.4—A given variant (V1) with a <<mutex>> relationship with another variant (V2) when V1 is selected to be part of a given product; V2 must not be selected for such product.

Although SMarty has support for traceability, participants informally complained about the lack of a guide to do this. Therefore, we created a set of guidelines to assist such an activity. The guidelines are as follows ("T" stands for traceability):

- T.1—Identify the respective variability tagged with <<variability>> to which one wants to trace and its attributes `realizes-` and `realizes+`.
- T.2—To trace variabilities in higher abstract-level diagrams, one should identify all variability names in the `realizes+`.
- T.3—To trace variabilities in lower abstract-level diagrams, one should identify all variability names in the `realizes-`.
- T.4—Once variabilities are identified, go to each higher/lower level diagram and locate them. In case more variabilities should be traced from those located, start applying these guidelines again from T1.

20.4   Lessons Learned and SMarty Improvements

In this section, we briefly discuss main lessons learned during this experiment with relation to the SMarty approach. In addition, we present improvements the SMarty approach should address to evolve as a UML-based variability management approach for SPLs.

With the conduction of this experiment, we obtained evidence, and, consequently, we learned some lessons that could be applied to prospective experiments. This learning contributes to empirically make SMarty more effective.

The first point that differentiated this experiment from others already carried out was the form of conducting the training sessions. Training was performed throughout a video, which was part of the experimental instrumentation received by each participant. Therefore, the training could be attended as many times as the participants' convenience.

Although we were forced to adopt this method of training because of the COVID-19 pandemic, we learned it may have positively influenced the effectiveness of the products configured by the participants. Therefore, we plan to keep adopting this kind of training for prospective experiments.

Another aspect which contributed to good results of this experiment is several participants carried out the experiment remotely. In previous experiments, in the process stages, the participants were physically present, which may negatively affect the readability of diagrams and the amount of material received. This issue was solved with a remote process in this experiment, since the diagrams could be easily enlarged, for better visualization.

We also learned that even selecting non-widely experienced participants, they obtained very good results for both approaches. We understand this might be a result of the remote experiment process adopted for the majority of participants, thus again positively impacting this study.

Another learning experience was about time. Previously, the experiments had a time frame predefined for an 1 and 40 minutes, which is the period of a class in most universities in (omitted). In the remote format process, we defined no time frame for participants to participate. Therefore, we drastically reduced fatigue effects, thus making participants more motivated to provide accurate responses in the experiment.

We plan to adopt all these lessons for prospective experiments in our research group.

20.5 Final Remarks

For **Experiment #1**, we show how the effectiveness of a variability management approach (SMarty) can be analyzed to facilitate and improve variability activities in an SPL perspective. This experimental study provides evidence that SMarty is more effective than PLUS. As a last step of this study, it performed a correlation between the variability knowledge level of the subjects and the effectiveness of each approach. The PLUS method does not provide guidelines for the identification and representation of variability in use case diagrams. This indicates that the participant needs prior knowledge of variability to use the PLUS method. Meanwhile, the SMarty approach provides a set of guidelines, for representation/identification of variabilities, with evidence such guidelines help in the tasks mentioned in SMarty use case diagrams without prior knowledge of the participants' variabilities.

In **Experiment #2**, we demonstrated the ability to use variability management approaches. Their effectiveness was analyzed by modeling variability in class models of two SPLs. There are indications that the PLUS method is more effective than the SMarty approach in representing variability in UML class models with e-commerce and the AGM SPLs. Such evidence may be related to the fact that PLUS has only two stereotypes to identify variability ($<<$ *kernel* $>>$ and $<<$ *optional* $>>$). Although SMarty has more stereotypes, it thus allows one to accurately represent variabilities in a nonambiguous way. SMarty is supported by a proper UML extension encompassing better implementation and understanding. After analyzing the results and feedback of the subjects, it was able to identify points for the evolution of the experiment and the SMarty approach, which were made and discussed in Sect. 20.3. Experiment #2 contributed to the SMarty evolution as we took advantage of the results of the experiment carried out and the subject's feedback. New guidelines for class models were added to SMarty encompassing different class modeling elements, supporting a better training of the software engineers on the SMartyProcess and the improvement on the set of its guidelines.

Experiment (#3) provided data about the SMarty capability to be understood, generating software product configurations, in a concise way, as compared to the PLUS method. The latter is easier to apply but generates ambiguous interpretation of its elements. If the configurations are inconsistent, the derivation of specific products will present lower quality of the products and consequently will decrease the benefits in adoption of SPL methodology. In the second study, there is no statistical significance of the values of effectiveness. However, in relation to the number of additional consults to SPL descriptions, it was identified statistically that PLUS needs more consults than SMarty, influencing the calculated effectiveness.

Experiment #4 analyzed the effectiveness by modeling variability in sequence models of two SPLs. The results obtained provide evidence that the SMarty approach is effective for modeling variability in UML sequence models, taking into account the banking and the AGM SPLs for this study. In addition, by statistical tests, there were indications that previous knowledge in SPL did not influence the process of representing variability in UML sequence models.

For **Experiment #5**, we presented a controlled experiment carried out to compare the effectiveness of the PLUS and SMarty variability management approaches, when used to configure products from use case and class diagrams. The study was developed around four research questions. Regarding the effectiveness of the two approaches, the results showed an advantage of the PLUS method in relation to the SMarty approach in the configuration of products from the class diagram. For the use case diagram, there was no significant difference in configuring products with PLUS or SMarty for this study. Additionally, it was possible to provide evidence that the number of consultations to the instructional material of each approach did not influence the calculated value of effectiveness of each approach. There are indications that the participant's previous level of knowledge in SPL, variability, and UML may be related to the improvement in the effectiveness of use in product configuration approaches, especially with regard to the SMarty approach. Thus, less experienced participants were able to configure products more effectively with

SMarty. Furthermore, it is understood that the SMarty approach provides more support for element tracking between diagrams; however, this aspect still needs to be improved.

In **Experiment #6**, we compared the effectiveness of the Ziadi et al. and the SMarty variability management approaches. The results on the effectiveness at configuring products showed an advantage of SMarty in relation to Ziadi et al. for both class and sequence diagrams. We provide evidence the previous knowledge of the participants in SPL, variability, and UML may be related to the effectiveness of Ziadi et al. to product configuration. Especially for SMarty, the knowledge seems not to determine such effectiveness, thus demanding less experienced participants. We understand SMarty provides subsidies for traceability of variability-related elements in both class and sequence diagrams. However, this aspect still needs to be improved. Ziadi, on the other hand, cannot be evaluated for not providing support for traceability of elements. **Experiment #7** was conducted to compare SMarty to two other approaches: PLUS for class diagrams and Razavian and Khosravi's method for component diagrams. We performed such comparison to answer three main points: more effective regarding the configuration of specific products in sequence and class diagrams, the relevance of the knowledge of each participant, and the traceability capacity of each approach. With regard to more effective, results showed SMarty is slightly more effective in configuring products compared to other two approaches. Despite a very small difference between the calculated values, there is evidence that the participants' previous level of knowledge in UML may be related to the improvement of the effectiveness of the use of approaches in product configuration. With class diagrams, less experienced participants were able to configure products more effectively with PLUS. With component diagrams, less experienced participants were able to configure products more effectively with the Razavian and Khosravi's method. Regarding SMarty variability traceability in class and component diagrams, we understand it offers support to aid understanding of such mechanism by users; however, this aspect should still be improved.

The results of the experiments showed that SMarty is more effective for use case, sequence, and component diagrams, in identification, representation, configuration, and traceability. Only class diagram evaluations showed positive efficacy for PLUS. In Experiment #2 PLUS, it had the greatest efficiency in the representation and identification of variabilities. In Experiment #3, after improvements in SMarty's guidelines, PLUS and SMarty did not show a statistically significant difference in the effectiveness of identifying and representing variabilities. The same result was identified for use case and class in Experiment #5.

Therefore, answering the general question of the chapter, *"Is SMarty a better UML-based variability management approach than PLUS, Ziadi et al. approach, and the Razavian and Khosravi's method in the identification, representation, configuration, and support of traceability of SPL in UML use case, class, sequence, and component diagrams?"* We cannot generalize and assume that SMarty is the best approach for identifying and representing variability and configuring products; however, the statistical tests proved to be superior in most cases for SMarty as shown in Table 20.17.

Table 20.17 Result summary for all experiments

Id	Diagram	Approach/method	Effectiveness (mean)	Effectiveness result	Knowledge correlation	Correlation result	Queries to inst. materials	Queries to inst. material result	Traceability	Traceability result
#1	Use case	PLUS	1.66	SMarty more effective	0.61	Strong positive	–	–	–	–
		SMarty	4.33		–0.04	Weak negative	–	–	–	–
#2	Class	PLUS	23.0	PLUS more effective	0.39 (e-commerce) 0.44 (AGM)	Weak positive	–	–	–	–
		SMarty	13.6		0.39 (e-commerce) 0.37 (AGM)	Weak positive				
#3	Class	PLUS	10.58	No statistical difference	0.49	Weak positive	–	–	–	–
		SMarty	10.75		–0.10	Weak negative	–	–	–	–
#4	Sequence	PLUS	8.6	SMarty more effective	–0.07	Weak positive	–	–	–	–
		SMarty	24.9		0.61	Strong positive	–	–	–	–
#5	Use case	PLUS	0.97	No stat. difference	0.32	Weak positive	0.22	No stat. difference	0.63	No stat. difference
		SMarty	0.98		0.16	Weak positive	0.33		0.61	
	Class	PLUS	0.99	PLUS more effective	0.24	Weak positive	0.22		0.22	SMarty more effective
		SMarty	0.81		0.41	Weak positive	0.33		0.44	
#6	Class	PLUS	0.87	SMarty more effective	0.32	Weak positive	–	–	–	–
		SMarty	0.93		0.41	Weak positive	–	–	–	–
	Component	Razavian and Khosravi's	0.86	No statistical difference	0	No correlation	–	–	–	–
		SMarty	0.83		0.26	Weak positive				
#7	Sequence	Ziadi et al.	0.76	SMarty more effective	0.66	Strong positive	–	–	–	–
		SMarty	0.92		0.05	Weak positive	–	–	–	–
	Class	Ziadi et al.	0.82	SMarty more effective	0.77	Strong positive	–	–	–	–
		SMarty	0.96		0.27	Weak positive	–	–	–	–

In most experiments, for participants who used the Razavian and Khosravi's, Ziadi et al., or PLUS method, previous knowledge about variability was important to guide the subjects in the correct identification of variability in models of use cases, classes, sequence, and components. On the other hand, for SMarty, such prior knowledge was not important to identify and represent variability in such models. One of the main reasons could be that SMarty provides a set of guidelines to identify and represent variabilities, facilitating this activity.

Despite the results, as discussed in each experiment, PLUS has the advantage in terms of quantity of stereotypes, having only tree stereotypes to represent variabilities. Such reduced group allows a faster identification and representation. However, in terms of creation of configurations, the reduced number of stereotypes is error-prone, while SMarty has, besides more stereotypes to support the creation of configurations, also a set of guidelines.

Several industry sectors use UML successfully and lack tools to support the identification and representation of variability, as well as product configuration in the SPL molds, seeking to increase software reuse and, consequently, improve the quality of their products and processes.

With that in mind, the results of the experiments reported with diagrams of classes, use cases, sequence, and components provided subsidies for the development of a tool—SMarty modeling: an environment that adopts the SMarty profile approach to engineering UML-based SPLs where variabilities are modeled as stereotypes using any supported UML profile.

Acknowledgement The work is supported by the Brazilian funding agency CAPES—Finance Code 001.

References

1. Anquetil, N., Kulesza, U., Mitschke, R., Moreira, A., Royer, J.C., Rummler, A., Sousa, A.: A model-driven traceability framework for software product lines. Softw. Syst. Model. **9**, 427–451 (2010). https://doi.org/10.1007/s10270-009-0120-9
2. Basili, V.R., Selby, R.W., Hutchens, D.H.: Experimentation in software engineering. IEEE Trans. Softw. Eng. **12**(7), 733–743 (1986)
3. Bragança, A., Machado, R.J.: Extending UML 2.0 metamodel for complementary usages of the ≪extend≫ relationship within use case variability specification. In: Proceedings of the International Software Product Line Conference, pp. 123–130. IEEE Computer Society, Washington, DC (2006)
4. Cavalcanti, Y., Machado, I., Neto, P., Lobato, L.: Handling Variability and Traceability over SPL Disciplines (2012). https://doi.org/10.5772/38352
5. Chen, L., Ali Babar, M., Ali, N.: Variability Management in Software Product Lines: a Systematic Review. In: Proceedings of the International Software Product Line Conference, pp. 81–90. Carnegie Mellon University, Pittsburgh, PA, USA (2009)
6. Falessi, D., Juristo, N., Wohlin, C., Turhan, B., Münch, J., Jedlitschka, A., Oivo, M.: Empirical software engineering experts on the use of students and professionals in experiments. Empir. Softw. Eng. **23**(1), 452–489 (2018). https://doi.org/10.1007/s10664-017-9523-3

7. Gomaa, H.: Designing Software Product Lines with UML: From Use Cases to Pattern-Based Software Architectures. Addison Wesley Longman, Redwood City (2004)
8. Higgins, J., Ed.D.: The Radical Statistician. The Management Advantage, Lafayette (2005)
9. Juristo, N., Moreno, A.: Basics of Software Engineering Experimentation. Springer, Berlin (2001)
10. Korherr, B., List, B.: A UML 2 profile for variability models and their dependency to business processes. In: Proceedings of the International Conference on Database and Expert Systems Applications, pp. 829–834. IEEE, Washington, DC (2007)
11. Marcolino, A.S., OliveiraJr, E., Gimenes, I., Maldonado J.C.:Towards the effectiveness of a variability management approach at use case level. In: International Conference on Software Engineering and Knowledge Engineering. pp. 214–219. Boston, MA (2013)
12. Marcolino, A.S., OliveiraJr, E., Gimenes, I., Barbosa, E.F.: Empirically based evolution of a variability management approach at UML class level. In: IEEE 38th Annual Computer Software and Applications Conference, pp. 354–363, IEEE, Vasteras (2014)
13. Marcolino, A.S., OliveiraJr, E., Gimenes, I.: Towards the effectiveness of the SMarty approach for variability management at sequence diagram level. In: 16th International Conference on Enterprise Information Systems, pp. 249–256. Lisbon (2014)
14. Marcolino, A.S., OliveiraJr, E., Gimenes, I., Barbosa, E.F.: Variability resolution and product configuration with SMarty: an experimental study on uml class diagrams J. Comput. Sci. 13, 307–319 (2017)
15. McGregor, J.: Arcade game maker pedagogical product line: concept of operations. Version 2, 2005 (2005)
16. Nepomuceno, T.S., OliveiraJr, E.: Configuring software product line specific products with SMarty and PLUS: An experimental study on use case diagrams In: Proceedings of the 17th Brazilian Symposium on Software Quality - SBQS, pp. 81–90. ACM Press, New York (2018)
17. Nepomuceno, T.S., OliveiraJr, E.: Software product line traceability and product configuration in class and sequence diagrams: An empirical study. In: International Conference on Enterprise Information Systems, pp. 195–202. Lisbon (2021)
18. Nepomuceno, T., OliveiraJr, E., Geraldi, R., Malucelli, A., Reinehr, S., Silva, M.A.G.:Software product line configuration and traceability: An empirical study on SMarty class and component diagrams In: 2020 IEEE 44th Annual Computers, Software, and Applications Conference (COMPSAC), pp. 979–984. Madrid (2020)
19. Nepomuceno, T., OliveiraJr, E., Geraldi, R., Penteado, R.M., Silva, M.A.G., Zorzo, A.F.:Empirical study on product configuration and traceability in UML-based product-lines In: Ibero-American Conference on Software Engineering, pp. 1–14. Curitiba, PR (2020)
20. OliveiraJr, E., Gimenes, I.M.S., Maldonado, J.C.: Systematic management of variability in UML-based software product lines J. Univer. Comput. Sci. 16, 2374–2393 (2010)
21. Razavian, M., Khosravi, R.: Modeling variability in the component and connector view of architecture using UML. In: International Conference on Computer Systems and Applications, pp. 801–809 (2008). https://doi.org/10.1109/AICCSA.2008.4493618
22. SEI: A framework for software product line practice (Acessado em 10/11/2012). http://www.sei.cmu.edu/productlines/framereport/index.html
23. Shapiro, S.S., Wilk, M.B.: An analysis of variance test for normality (complete samples). Biometrika 52(3/4), 591–611 (1965)
24. Soper, H., Young, A., Cave, B., Lee, A., Pearson, K.: On the distribution of the correlation coefficient in small samples. Appendix II to the papers of "Student" and R.A. fisher. Biometrika 11, 328–413 (1917)
25. Spearman, C.: The proof and measurement of association between two things. By C. Spearman, 1904. Amer. J. Psychol. 100(3-4), 441–471 (1987). http://view.ncbi.nlm.nih.gov/pubmed/3322052
26. Tichy, W.F.: Should computer scientists experiment more? Computer 31(5), 32–40 (1998). https://doi.org/10.1109/2.675631
27. Travassos, G.: Introdução à engenharia de software experimental (2002). https://books.google.com.br/books?id=4SnKZwEACAAJ

28. Vale, T., de Almeida, E.S., Alves, V., Kulesza, U., Niu, N., de Lima, R.: Software product lines traceability: A systematic mapping study. Inf. Softw. Technol. **84**, 1–18 (2017). https://doi. org/10.1016/j.infsof.2016.12.004
29. Wohlin, C., Runeson, P., Höst, M., Ohlsson, M.C., Regnell, B., Wesslén, A.: Experimentation in Software Engineering: An Introduction. Kluwer Academic Publishers, Norwell (2000)
30. Wohlin, C., Runeson, P., Höst, M., Ohlsson, M.C., Regnell, B., Wesslén, A.: Experimentation in Software Engineering. Springer Science & Business Media, Berlin (2012)
31. Young, T.J.: Using aspect to build a software product line for mobile devices. Ph.D. Thesis, University of British Columbia (2005). http://dx.doi.org/10.14288/1.0051632. https://open. library.ubc.ca/collections/ubctheses/831/items/1.0051632
32. Ziadi, T., Jezequel, J.M.: Software product line engineering with the UML: Deriving products. In: Käköla, T., Duenas, J. (eds.) Software Product Lines, pp. 557–588. Springer, Berlin (2006). https://doi.org/10.1007/978-3-540-33253-4_15. http://dx.doi.org/10.1007/978-3-540-33253-4_15
33. Ziadi, T., Helouet, L., marc Jezequel, J.: Towards a UML profile for software product lines. In: Product Family Engineering Conference, pp. 129–139. Springer, Berlin (2003)

Printed in the United States
by Baker & Taylor Publisher Services